IRREPARABLE EVIL

IRREPARABLE EVIL

IRREPARABLE EVIL

An Essay in Moral and Reparatory History

DAVID SCOTT

Columbia University Press
New York

Columbia University Press
Publishers Since 1893
New York   Chichester, West Sussex
cup.columbia.edu

Copyright © 2024 David Scott
All rights reserved

Library of Congress Cataloging-in-Publication Data
Names: Scott, David, 1958–. author.
Title: Irreparable evil : an essay in moral and reparatory history /
   David Scott.
Description: New York : Columbia University Press, [2024] |
   Includes bibliographical references and index.
Identifiers: LCCN 2023031376 | ISBN 9780231213042 (hardback) |
   ISBN 9780231213059 (trade paperback) | ISBN 9780231559690 (ebook)
Subjects: LCSH: Slavery—Moral and ethical aspects—America. |
   Slavery—Moral and ethical aspects—Caribbean Area. | Reparations for
   historical injustices—America. | Reparations for historical
   injustices—Caribbean Area. | Enslaved persons—America—History. |
   Enslaved persons—Caribbean Area—History.
Classification: LCC HT1048 .S36 2024 | DDC 305.896/0729—dc23/eng/20231115
LC record available at https://lccn.loc.gov/2023031376

Printed and bound by CPI Group (UK) Ltd, Croydon, CR0 4YY

Cover design: Astryd Design, Inc.
Cover image: Charles Campbell

For Talal . . . and all the years of friendship

CONTENTS

Prologue: On the Devastation of Lifeworlds and Forms of Life   1

PART I

1   The Idea of a Moral and Reparatory History   35

PART II

2   Incomparable Evil   81

3   Incommensurable Evils   136

PART III

4   Slavery's Evil Lifeworld   191

5   Evil Enrichment   251

Epilogue: On Irreparability   311

Acknowledgments   319

Notes   323

Index   379

IRREPARABLE EVIL

PROLOGUE

On the Devastation of Lifeworlds and Forms of Life

What might it mean to describe an atrocity as the devastation of a *lifeworld* and of a *form of life*? What is devastated about the lives of people when it is their lifeworlds and their forms of life that are destroyed rather than, or at least more so than, their physical lives? It seems obvious to many that the deliberate, unprovoked destruction of human lives is an atrocity inasmuch as such destruction, apart from everything else it does, wrongfully forecloses human possibility, human *futurity*. This futurity is a prospect we naturally take to be an ultimate good. But in a different yet equally relevant sense, is it not the case that the deliberate destruction of human lifeworlds and forms of life also wrongfully forecloses certain *kinds* of human possibility, certain kinds of human futurity—the vitality, for example, over generations, of the conditions of collective human flourishing, human well-being? Might this too—the vitality of lifeworlds and forms of life—be perceived as an ultimate good? Why are we more attuned morally to the violent destruction of the *zoe* of human lives than we are to the violent destruction of the *bios* of human lifeworlds and forms of life? If the deliberate mass destruction of human lives is a manifest evil, why should we not also think of the deliberate mass destruction of human lifeworlds and forms of life as evil? These are some of my broad questions.

In this book, I consider the historic atrocity of New World slavery perpetrated against Africans kidnapped and transported to the Americas, and against their Creole descendants, over more than three hundred years. New World slavery was an evil. But under which description should it appear to us in this light? Is there a specificity to the evil of New World slavery? Certainly, from the moment of their capture through their forced march to the coastal slave forts while shackled in coffles, from their deportation across the Middle Passage in slave ships and

2 PROLOGUE

their sale in slave markets, to their permanent enslavement on large-scale agricultural plantations, enslaved men, women, and children were subjected to horrific physical and psychological brutality. New World slavery was an institutionalized system of domination characterized by unmitigated violence. Killing maiming, raping, and dismembering were routine practices, not exceptional ones. Unwarranted physical death was commonplace. Under this description alone, New World slavery was an undisputable moral evil. Still, part of what makes New World slavery distinctive is that—as central as killing and maiming were to its machinery of ordinary and spectacular brutality—its avowed objective was not the death of its victims. Again, to underline, death by killing was not incidental; it occurred too often and too indifferently for that to have been the case. But it was not the raison d'être of the institutional practice, the motivation or justification for its existence as an institution. New World slavery was a structure of extreme domination that depended as much (or more) on life as it did on its capacity to inflict or threaten death. Indeed, arguably, the *threat* of brutal death was precisely one perverse dimension of its investment in life. To be sure, New World slavery coercively imposed a certain kind of life: a traumatized, terrorized life; a foreshortened, distorted, and eminently disposable life; a life, in other words, devoid of vitality. The evil of New World slavery, therefore, does not inhere only in its overt physical violence against its subjugated victims; it inheres also—perhaps more profoundly—in the social-cultural-psychological devastation it inflicted upon the lives of the enslaved. This pervasive devastation was itself a dimension of the systematic process of *transforming* African men, women, and children from a range of cultural and linguistic backgrounds and social and political statuses into ciphers of enslaved people—into chattel. This process ruptured and disorganized inherited modes of living and replaced them with a new rigid and constraining racial regime of bondage. How should we understand this process of devastation? What, exactly, is devastated when people are violently uprooted and permanently alienated from the sources of their age-old traditions?

In a measure, this is an old story in Caribbean cultural theory, which forms one background to my considerations in this book. Caribbean cultural theory has been concerned precisely with the social and cultural processes by which African captives were transformed into slaves, and by which the lives of their Caribbean-born descendants remained enslaved. Two interconnected debates are worth briefly mentioning in this respect. The first debate concerns the extent to which these processes were either purely accommodative or at least partially interactive. Famously, *acculturation* names the former and *creolization* the latter. Acculturation suggests a framework in which the enslaved could do little more than conform to the dominant (White/European) values and world-view introduced by the slave plantation regime, whereas creolization imagines a more creative and syncretistic process in which the enslaved were active participants in the making of new cultural worlds.[1] In a certain sense, one framework emphasizes dominant powers, whereas the other emphasizes cultural process; one sees the enslaved as a victim, the other as an agent. The second related debate concerns, on the one hand, those who see slavery largely as a destructive system of brutalizing domination and, on the other hand, those who focus on the opportunities, however narrow, that the system offered for cultural transformation, or that the enslaved were able to appropriate for transformative self-remaking.[2]

Now, it is important to recognize that the contrastive pictures sketched in these debates (however polemically they may be articulated) are best understood as indicating tendencies along a spectrum rather than static positions in a binary field of mutually exclusive oppositions. I believe that these debates cannot be decided completely in favor of either side because each one is grappling with a different end or a different aspect of the same overall cultural-historical process of enslavement and deracination. Both sides are vital to the productive contentiousness that animates Caribbean intellectual traditions. Naturally I have my quibbles about various positions in these debates, but I do not wish to enter here into a dispute about them—my views will be easy enough to discern as and when they become relevant. Here I wish only to render the insights from this interminable Caribbean debate into the slightly different conceptual idiom of lifeworld and form of life in the hope of teasing out of a recognizable historical experience the moral-political implications that concern me most in this book.

The ideas of *lifeworld* and *form of life* do not belong to the same conceptual vocabulary. The former draws its inspiration from the social phenomenology of Alfred Schutz, whereas the latter is informed by the language philosophy of Ludwig Wittgenstein.[3] However, both are in search of a register of inquiry and intelligibility that exceeds what is transparently given on the visible surface of social behavior. Without, I hope, doing too much damage to the integrity of either, I want to think with them together as slightly different yet linked

4   PROLOGUE

dimensions of social-cultural-historical life. As I understand it—and I am perhaps being recklessly brief and condensed here—the phenomenological idea of a lifeworld comprehends the field of social relations that constitute the lived reality of symbolic action and interaction, of subjectivity and inter-subjectivity. It seeks to grasp not so much *what* people do in their overt social intercourse as the *orientation* in space and time that informs and shapes their conduct during the face-to-face occasions or situations that make up social intercourse. A lifeworld, then, concerns the elementary structures of everyday life that can be thought of as constituting the *foundations* (as opposed to the surfaces) of social experience. Notably, therefore, what a lifeworld encompasses is essentially the taken-for-granted dimension of the experience of the social world. The experience of a lifeworld involves, famously, what Schutz called (after Edmund Husserl) a kind of *epochē*, a bracketing or suspension of any critical attitude toward the world.

By comparison, the Wittgensteinian notion of a form of life encompasses the idea of the background schema or paradigm that shapes our social practices, conditioning and animating our modes of intelligibility, our routes toward meaning, our elementary structures of reason, and our styles of characteristic response. Forms of life are not private rules but parts of a common world; they are shared conventions that rest on unformulated and tacit agreement. Forms of life are less the empirically observable actions and utterances and feelings, than the generative patterns of activity and regularities of expectation and interest that are, in some relevant sense, constitutive of them. As such, forms of life are not given to us in a readily and self-evidently describable way. This is because a form of life has a totalizing and implicit quality to it. We cannot stand away from our forms of life in order to appraise them in comparative perspective. And other forms of life are available to us only within the context of our own. Later I return to the internal argument of whether forms of life are to be understood as "transcendental" or "anthropological." But setting that dispute aside for the moment, notably, each of these arguably cognate terms—lifeworld and form of life—is embedded in its own vocabulary of social action and social thought that in turn derives from its own distinct intellectual tradition. The terms are not identical, therefore, in their range of reference. But they both, nevertheless, seem to me to map and help us explore an arena of human life that has less to do with immediately discoverable actions and utterances and more to do with the common and implicit and organizing conditions of potentiality and possibility underlying these actions and utterances. It is in this sense that they suggest themselves to me in this book.

⚬

To reiterate the question with which I began: What might it mean to describe an atrocity as the devastation of a lifeworld and a form of life? One way to begin to explore this seemingly enigmatic question is by reflecting on an attempt to answer an allied version of it—namely, Jonathan Lear's provocative book *Radical Hope: Ethics in the Face of Cultural Devastation*, published in 2006.[4] Lear's explicit invitation is to think about the nature of extreme cultural *catastrophe* rather than extreme moral *atrocity* (an important distinction in thinking about evil, as we will see), but his concerns are too close to mine to ignore. Moreover, Lear is a much admired philosopher with illuminating routes into and out of Aristotle, Wittgenstein, Kierkegaard, and Freud, among others, that seem to me richly suggestive and congenial for some of what I am after in this book.[5] Furthermore, Lear also contributes to a mode of thinking about philosophy, and a *style* of thinking philosophically, not only as a form of investigation into dimensions of forms of life but also as an intellectual form of life in itself.[6]

Perhaps it is not surprising that *Radical Hope* is shaped by an awareness of a historical present that seems to call for precisely the direction of intervention Lear undertakes. Lear aims, he says, for a critical reflection on the time and the world in which we live. But what time and world is that? And who are *we* who inhabit them? For my concerns, how we name these is not irrelevant. Curiously, Lear's reflections on the temporal and geopolitical *locations* of his intervention, and the identity of the plural pronoun *we*, are not nearly as integrated into the structure of his argument as one would have expected or hoped for in a book as otherwise reflexive as this one is. These reflections, in fact, form but one paragraph. Ours is a time, Lear writes early on, of a "heightened sense that civilizations are themselves vulnerable." What does Lear mean here by "*themselves* vulnerable"? Vulnerable *as* civilizations? As opposed to what *other* sense of vulnerable? What, to Lear's way of thinking, are *civilizations*? Whether or not the allusiveness in Lear's formulations of the present is deliberate, it bears underlining for the kinds of silences and omissions we encounter throughout his suggestive book. Our heightened awareness, moreover, Lear says, is that such civilizations are vulnerable in a way or to a "menace" that we "cannot quite name." The enigmatic or inscrutable

6 PROLOGUE

quality of the jeopardy we face is crucial to Lear's theoretical work in terms of forms of life. "Perhaps," he goes on, "if we could give a name to our shared sense of vulnerability, we could find better ways to live with it."[7] But again, what does Lear mean by learning to better live with our vulnerability? What critical *attitude* should this learning take? What does his idea imply about the challenges and tasks of criticism, including such moral criticism as he himself is engaged with in *Radical Hope*? Can we live with our general vulnerability to devastation and yet live against the normalization of *specific* historical devastations?

Unfortunately, we are not given any more guidance or instruction from Lear than these perfunctory remarks regarding how he thinks the relation between the past and the present, and between these and the reflective commitments his moral philosophy commends, should be understood. And yet it seems to me that, indeed, something *more* needs to be said, for it is not clear why a shared sense of vulnerability should give rise to the "widespread intolerance we see around us today—from all points on the political spectrum."[8] There may well be a common sense of unease or anguish that contemporary forms of life are pervasively threatened, but this is hardly likely to be a peril *equally* shared by everyone within or across civilizations (whatever understanding we attach to the idea of a civilization). Something is missing here, I believe, from Lear's mode of philosophical attention to the present, or idea of the present. Perhaps this has to do with his treatment (or his lack of treatment) of historical institutions of *power*. I shall return to this in a moment.

From my perspective, however, part of what makes *Radical Hope* so provocative a book to think with (as Claude Lévi-Strauss might have said) is its *approach* to its subject matter and the *register* at which it locates the problem of devastation—and it is these that I want to consider briefly, at least enough to orient us to my own preoccupations. Specifically, *Radical Hope* is about the cultural breakdown and cultural loss suffered by the Crow Nation, a Native American Plains people, toward the end of the nineteenth century. Faced with deepening violent conflict with their traditional enemies (the Sioux principal among them) and dwindling herds of buffalo, their traditional hunt, the Crow entered into successive agreements with the aggressively expanding post–Civil War U.S. state that eventually, between 1882 and 1884, confined them to a reservation. The Crow might not have perceived the implications in advance, but this arrangement effectively marked a decisive end to their traditional nomadic, hunting, and warring way of life. What provokes Lear, specifically, is something almost unfathomable about the way this history is recounted by the last great Crow chief, Plenty Coups, to his White biographer Frank Linderman. According to Linderman, Lear says, he was not able to get the otherwise agreeably forthcoming Plenty Coups to talk about what happened after the Crow were confined to the reservation. In part, Linderman recalls Plenty Coups saying to him, "I can think back and tell you much more of war and horse-stealing. But when the buffalo went away the hearts of my people fell to the ground, and they could not lift them up again. After this nothing happened."[9] It is this remark—"after this nothing happened"—that haunts and compels Lear and drives the interpretive work of his book.

Lear rightly thinks this is a curiously paradoxical remark to make: from a certain perspective at least, after their enforced confinement to the reservation a great deal clearly did continue to happen both in the life of the Crow Nation generally and in Plenty Coups's life specifically. So, then, how should we understand Plenty Coups's remark? Responding to this question is the hermeneutic project in *Radical Hope*. Notably, Lear's approach is expressly described by way of contrast to that of a historical-cultural anthropology of the Crow, even though it depends, to a not insignificant degree, on Crow historical and anthropological materials (Robert Lowie's, for example), and more generally on assumptions about cultural formations and processes.[10] It is less the cultural-historical specificity of the Crow calamity that interests Lear than what he calls the larger "ontological vulnerability" to devastation that we are *all* potentially exposed to as human beings and that is *exemplified* in the historical instance of the Crow.[11] Put another way, Lear's aim is to understand the cultural calamity that befell the Crow as an expression of a deeper ontological dimension of vulnerability: it is the human universality *immanent* in the cultural particularity that interests him most. This is why Lear describes his approach as a "philosophical anthropology"—the philosophical anthropology of an "ontological fact"—and distinguishes it sharply from cultural or historical anthropology and the specific facts he takes that discipline to illuminate. On his (I would say) tendentious account, an anthropological approach is concerned with "actuality" (that is, with what really happened culturally and historically to the Crow), whereas, by contrast, his philosophical approach is concerned with "possibility" (that is, with a plausible way of describing the ethical contours of the *kind* of cultural destruction, or the *register* of cultural destruction) that the Crow *must* have endured for Plenty Coups's remark—"after this nothing happened"—to be ontologically true.[12] Not cultural truth but *human* truth is what Lear is after.

8   PROLOGUE

Radical Hope is one long speculative "what if" inquiry—*What if* Plenty Coups's remark gave some insight not so much into the empirical reality of the Crow experience as into the ontological structure of a mode of human experience of temporal rupture that was such that it could effectively bring the temporal "happening" of things to an end?

Whichever way we judge the coherence of the distinction between anthropology and philosophy Lear makes, it is heuristically crucial to his whole enterprise. In a certain all too familiar sense, the anthropological Crow serve largely as the *occasion* for philosophical reflection.[13] My doubts about this disciplinary division of labor will be apparent, but what principally interests me is how by means of the contrast Lear seeks to identify a particular register of investigation. I might call it an *archaeological* register (even if Michel Foucault doesn't figure among Lear's philosophical interlocutors) because what it aims to locate is not plainly or superficially self-evident but inheres rather at the deep-structural level of a discursive formation—what Foucault might have spoken of in terms of the conceptual conditions of possibility-and-impossibility of certain kinds of utterance or discourse, of what can or cannot (or, as in the case at hand, cannot *any longer*) be said.[14] That is to say, what is centrally important to Lear's direction of inquiry is the description of a breakdown or loss that is not the breakdown or loss of explicitly held positions or perspectives within the self-conscious language of a cultural paradigm or cultural schema but a breakdown or loss of the underlying *conditions* of possibility of the cultural paradigm or cultural schema itself. On Lear's account, Plenty Coups was "a witness to a peculiar form of human vulnerability." The word *witness* here is significant. For Lear, Plenty Coups was not a "victim." In any case, the vulnerability to which he bore witness is not the mundane vulnerability to such common facts of everyday human life as old age or sickness or death. Rather, it is, he says, a vulnerability that "we acquire as a result of the fact that we essentially inhabit a way of life." What does Lear mean by this? "Humans," he goes on to say, "are by nature cultural animals: we necessarily inhabit a way of life expressed in a culture."[15] Thus, strikingly, a "way of life" and a "culture," though evidently related, are not exactly one and the same; or at least, they do not belong to the same analytical register. A way of life appears to stand in relation to a culture as (to mix my theoretical idioms here) the archaeological "base" stands in relation to the anthropological "superstructure": that is, a visible culture *expresses* an underlying way of life; a way of life is conveyed or articulated or represented *in* a culture.[16] But curiously, in the subtitle of *Radical Hope* it is not devastation of a way or form of life that is announced as the analytical concern but "cultural" devastation.

It is instructive, moreover, that Lear will go on to use the phrase "way of life" more or less interchangeably with "form of life," without further explanatory or clarifying comment. For arguably (to pursue the disciplinary tension and what it illuminates) the former might well be thought of as having latent *anthropological* resonances, whereas the latter clearly has *philosophical* ones connected to a family of Wittgensteinian ideas concerning the role of concepts embedded in the language-games that organize the lives we live. Might there be some slippage here? Is Lear blurring—if not diminishing—the contrast he himself has set in motion? There is, in fact, a whole unmentioned debate surrounding Wittgenstein's idea of forms of life to which Lear himself has been an important contributor.[17] And in this debate, he has typically been read as defending a "transcendental" (read *philosophical*) interpretation of Wittgenstein, against an "anthropological" one.[18] And yet, in *Radical Hope* there is a suggestive *existential* current at play, one manifestation of which is Lear's admiring invocation (albeit in a footnote) of John Haugeland's reinterpretation of Heidegger's Dasein *away* from the idea of individual "Being" and toward that of a "living way of life."[19] So, altogether, it seems as though the disciplinary stakes or the disciplinary distinctions might be more complicated than Lear proposes—the anthropological and the philosophical go on bleeding into each other more than he can easily anticipate, or quite control. My point, though, is not to merely impugn Lear's heuristic schema, to find fault with it, only to observe its perhaps chronic instability. For what remains essential is his attempt to locate a register of ineliminable vulnerability that exceeds particular experience.

In this sense, the significance of *Radical Hope* is that Lear is concerned with the possibility of an extremity in which this background condition of a form of life could, catastrophically, *break down*. According to Lear, human ways of life are inherently vulnerable, and we as participants in them "thereby inherit [that] vulnerability."[20] When a way of life as a way of life collapses, he suggests, things as they have hitherto been known to occur "cease to happen." What takes place here is a loss of the old conceptual way of life; that is, the loss of the conceptual frame in which the intelligibility of an old way of life was activated, understood, and argued over. And this is what cultural devastation is on Lear's account—the breakdown and loss of the intelligible world, the world people have hitherto taken for granted.

10 PROLOGUE

For Lear, then, the idea of a form of life or a way of life is meant to point to more than the empirical evidence of those sociocultural arrangements that are readily apprehensible or observable. For him, a form of life references the background *paradigm* among a specific group of people that organizes and structures the field of meaningful conceptual options, the language-game played out through their practices. Lear's question is this: "What is it about a form of life's coming to an end that makes it such that for the inhabitants of that life things cease to happen? Not just that it would *seem* to them that things ceased to happen but what it would *be* for things to cease happening."[21] Note the emphasis. The Crow, Lear argues, could have had no conscious understanding of this ontological dimension of their vulnerability. Perhaps it is in the nature of forms of life that no one can have a reflective understanding of their ontological vulnerability, insofar as one cannot stand back far enough to see the paradigm itself by which one lives. So when the calamity of the transfer to the reservation hit them, the Crow had no idea of what they were going to have to endure. In the context of their hitherto ongoing form of life, centrally organized as it had been, time out of mind, around nomadism, buffalo hunting, and war (including preparation for war) with rival tribes such as the Sioux, the Blackfeet, and the Cheyenne, the Crow people had lived within a range of comprehensible possibility-and-impossibility, a range of the plausible consequences of the success or failure of their various endeavors and campaigns and commitments. They knew, for example, and reckoned in their calculative rationalities, that in their age-old conflict with the Sioux they could succeed or they could fail, and if they failed they could very well be violently wiped out completely as a viable people. This would have been a disaster, to be sure, but a *conceivable* one that could even be anticipated and warded off, given their sense of the overall balance of forces within the field of rivals. (Anticipating somewhat, it is not hard to see why this form of conceptualization would interest me. When those African captives were rounded up and driven aboard those slave ships, they could have had no foresight about what to expect. The disaster toward which they were headed across the Middle Passage was in no way a conceivable one within their forms of life. They might have come to realize that they would not be eaten or gather that what was wanted was their labor, but this would not have helped them prepare for the coming disaster.)

Indeed, it was in the context of the conscious possibility of perishing as the people they knew themselves to be that the Crow took the unprecedented step of striking an alliance with the U.S. state in a "common" battle to subdue the Sioux.[22]

But what breaks down, as the Crow relation with the U.S. state deepens and they accept or are obliged to move onto the reservation, is not anything within their customary range of possibility and intelligibility but rather the very paradigm itself of possibility-and-impossibility and intelligibility-and-nonintelligibility.[23] It is this breakdown that marks the beginning of an absolute cultural devastation, not the collapse or loss of any specific perspective but the beginning of the collapse of a *whole* Crow form of life. Notably, Lear writes, "We do not grasp the devastation that the Crow endured so long as we think that the issue is who gets to tell the story." That is, the problem is not exactly one of narrative perspective. As he goes on, "For the problem goes deeper than competing narratives. The issue is that the Crow have lost the concepts with which they would construct a narrative"—meaning a common narrative, one that collectively expresses and articulates a common lifeworld. What is at stake is "a *real loss*, not just one that is described from a certain point of view. It is the *real loss of a point of view*."[24] It is this kind of breakdown that is a breakdown not just of occurrences—good or bad, sad or happy, fortuitous or predictable, convenient or inconvenient—but "a breakdown of the field in which occurrences occur."[25] What is lost is not simply the narratives people might compose about themselves in their inherited cultural languages but also the concepts out of which those narratives are constructed in the first place, or the conceptual field in which they are anchored. The devastation the Crow suffered, then, was a *loss of concepts*. It is with such a loss of concepts that one can say, henceforth, nothing *happens*, or nothing can *count* as happening—as the concept of a "happening." Here is the generative archaeological center of Lear's argument—the interconnection between the idea of a breakdown of a form of life and the idea of a loss of concepts. The breakdown of a form of life consists of a loss of concepts, and by extension (though Lear does not name it so) a loss of the *language-game* in which these concepts gain their conceptual uptake. As though conjugating Wittgenstein with Heidegger, intelligibility and possibility, language and being, this is the arena of Lear's idea of *ontological* vulnerability.

It is curious that although it is central to Lear's argument about what the Crow suffer in the collapse of their form of life, the connected idea of a "loss of concepts" receives only passing attention in *Radical Hope*. Lear merely points us to a footnote citation (that includes no substantive comment) to the work

12 PROLOGUE

of Cora Diamond, Alasdair MacIntyre, and Elizabeth Anscombe.[26] But perhaps something should be said, however briefly, about this idea as a way of further clarifying the parameters of what Lear is (or is not) getting at with respect to the idea of cultural devastation, and these authors are certainly one place to begin. In Diamond's illuminating essay "Losing Your Concepts," published almost two decades before the appearance of Lear's book, she offers a sensitive discussion of some of the diverging and converging approaches to the idea of losing concepts among a number of philosophers especially attuned to language, including MacIntyre, Anscombe, Stanley Cavell, and Iris Murdoch.[27] Indeed, Diamond's essay is especially helpful not only for what it illuminates about Lear's directions but also partly because of the exemplary subtlety and self-conscious provisionality of her approach to language and thinking (one that sometimes involves less an attempt to answer questions than to show, as she puts it, the "difficulties in any attempt to do so") and partly for how it enables my own broader concerns in this book with both the loss and the *displacement* of concepts, including interpretive ones.[28] Even though Diamond is clearly involved in something of a polemic against certain assumptions within analytical philosophy (empiricist assumptions about language use, for example) such that her claims are sometimes closely tied to specific and not always fully spelled out instances that would scarcely concern me here, her essay offers an insightful entry into a variety of formulations of the idea of concept loss. However, at least for my purposes, it is the related perspectives represented by MacIntyre, Anscombe, and Murdoch that are of special interest because they come closest to what I take Lear to be arguing for in his idea of concept loss, and to the uses of it that form one part of the background to my thinking in this book.

Readers of *After Virtue* will doubtlessly recall the opening chapter, "A Disquieting Suggestion," in which MacIntyre commends a picture of the "disordered state" of the modern language of morality. Moderns, he argues, have lost an older and coherent conceptual language of moral comprehension. What we now possess, he says, are "fragments of a conceptual scheme, parts of which now lack those contexts from which their significance derived." So though we continue to use some of the old moral expressions, sometimes even with a sense of conviction, the background forms of life that gave them their substantive and integrated intelligibility have collapsed or disappeared, and left behind mere "simulacra" of what had once been alive and robust.[29] Diamond shows that MacIntyre (though with a much larger and more sweeping agenda) is influenced in this view by Anscombe's famous 1958 essay, "Modern Moral Philosophy."[30] As Diamond suggests, some of Anscombe's conclusions are at variance with MacIntyre's. Anscombe argues that the notion of "ought" in the moral language of obligation requires a background framework that now no longer historically exists—namely, a divine law conception of ethics.[31] We continue to use the idea of "ought" but without its old context and consequently do so in a much enfeebled and less convincing way.[32] On the whole, however, moral thinking need not entirely depend on this background and is therefore able to carry on more or less undisturbed, at least in the course of "ordinary" moral reasoning. Therefore, unlike MacIntyre, Anscombe does not see modern moral thought *in general* as being in disarray. Moreover, Diamond suggests that it isn't clear that for Anscombe those who still accept a law conception of ethics couldn't continue to use the notion that required it as a background. In other words, Anscombe does not necessarily share MacIntyre's broader story of a corrupting and destructive modernity. Again, unlike MacIntyre, Anscombe does not take it that the current state of affairs makes it difficult if not impossible for philosophers to even recognize the incoherence of their conceptual languages. For MacIntyre, concept loss is both radical and radically *obscuring*. Whereas what is lost for Anscombe are specific concepts attached to specific features of the social world, what is lost for MacIntyre is an interconnected paradigm of concepts related to an interconnected social-historical lifeworld. At the same time, Diamond suggests, Anscombe *does* share with MacIntyre the overall structure of an argument—namely, that it is not directly (or not importantly) the concepts themselves that have been lost but the *background* that organizes the context of intelligibility for those concepts. For both Anscombe and MacIntyre, on this view, we might very well go on using the old words and notions, but in the absence of the *old form of life* that hitherto gave them point these words and notions can no longer carry the old conceptual sense and significance.[33] They are merely fragments of a conceptual scheme that has effectively decayed if not vanished—the survival, as Anscombe said, "of a concept outside the framework of thought that made it really intelligible."[34]

A central dimension of Diamond's critical concern with a certain kind of "linguistic philosophy" turns on the importance of the idea that concepts are not mere abstractions but integral parts of forms of life; concepts don't exist apart from those forms of life. Concepts cannot be cleanly divorced from their lifeworlds. As Diamond writes, "grasping a concept (even one like that of a human being, which is a descriptive concept if any are) is not a matter just of knowing how to group things under that concept; it is being able to participate in life-with-the-concept."[35] It seems to me that this is a view of language and conceptual life shared by Lear—at least to some extent. He writes, "Concepts get their lives through the lives we are able to live with them."[36] It is true that Lear, as I understand him, is making an argument nowhere near as extensive as MacIntyre's; he does not likely share MacIntyre's deep distrust of modernity. Indeed, Lear is not concerned, for example, as one could imagine MacIntyre being, with whether the reservation was precisely an instance of *modern* power that inflicted precisely the devastation the Crow experienced.[37] But Lear is certainly keenly attuned to the idea that the meaning of concepts is their meaning-in-social-use, and so perhaps closer to Anscombe in the restricted sense he makes of the idea of concept loss and its historical context. Therefore, what the Crow lost as they were moved onto the reservation in their deal with the U.S. state wasn't something abstract or isolable. It wasn't, for example, that the words or notions themselves that they had previously used—such as "counting coups"—were forgotten. It wasn't merely a question of the breakdown of memory such that with the remembrance, say, of the appropriate words or notions for the appropriate occasions there could be a return to their former selves and former lives. Rather, what the Crow lost was the living context that rendered their words and notions intelligible, possible, and relevant to a form of life. For the Crow, there was a general breakdown or loss of the background required for the concepts in terms of which people understood things to be happening, to be occurring. Such loss, Lear cogently argues, has implications for how the Crow understood themselves as distinctive subjects located in time and space. What they hitherto took for granted about the parameters of who they are is now rendered *problematic*.[38] Such loss, I might say (in the context of my project), is *irreparable*, for what has been lost cannot be regained. All that can be reconstructed are simulacra, mimeses—as happened, for example, with the Sun Dance that was reintroduced to Crow life after the death of Plenty Coups: "One might teach people the relevant steps; people might learn how to go through the motions; and they can even call it the 'Sun Dance'; but the Sun Dance itself has gone out of existence."[39]

It seems to me that there is crucial insight here about the character of cultural catastrophe. There are kinds of experiences of loss or potential loss or collapse or potential collapse that people are able to imagine or assimilate or account for within the existing terms and standards and values of their background paradigm or underlying language-game. In this case, people are able to hold onto their basic bearings, the cognitive threads that have implicitly and explicitly oriented them. The world as they know it remains intelligible, even if adversely or painfully so, even if they have suffered terribly as a consequence of their actions or the actions of others. Here the subjects are still able, in however qualified a way, to identify or represent to themselves the loss or damage or collapse they experience. They remain *within* a recognizable form of life, even if many individual lives have been ruthlessly maimed and destroyed. But there are also kinds of loss or damage or collapse that are not exactly or only of this kind but are precisely loss or collapse of, or damage to, the *whole* way of life itself, the cognitive-moral paradigm that informs it and that gives orientation or *telos* to the concepts that animate it. With this kind of devastation, the loss involved is likely to be irreversible and irrecoverable. Individuals may retain fragmentary memories of the old way of life—there may, for example, be rituals and words and stories and names and places and such that some people remember, and this may even persist across a number of generations—but one implication of this kind of loss (that both Lear and MacIntyre point to) is that the ground on which these memories now subsist has been coercively, irrevocably redrawn. However vibrant and compelling these memories are, what is centrally important is that they can no longer be *integrated* into a conceptual and practical background that structures what once was a whole way of life. That background is now gone forever.

Arguably, however, even as Lear brings this archaeological level of concept loss into view, he perhaps overlooks or occludes or anyway *underplays* something else—namely, *power*, or at least (since he is, necessarily, talking about power) a particular aspect of power, *settler colonial* power. It is an overall feature of Lear's discussion, as I have pointed out, that it is less the collective moral *agency* (of the expansionist U.S. state apparatuses, for example) involved in the disaster inflicted on the Crow that interests him than the *effect* of cultural breakdown, less the *atrocity* committed than the catastrophic devastation suffered. To return for a moment to the strained distinction between cultural anthropology and philosophical anthropology, what is perhaps less than adequately considered in Lear's analysis is the relevant *context* of description for conceptual or moral discourse, and thereby the relevant conception of the varied powers that animate context with shaping or transforming force. For Lear, the breakdown and loss suffered in cultural devastation is a universal human possibility derived from an

16 PROLOGUE

ontological vulnerability. Quite so. But surely, as Lear knows very well, cultural devastation did not randomly *befall* the Crow, in the form of abstract universality or bad luck. Nor was that disaster an effect of a benign or neutral *inadvertence* on the part of the powers involved (as British colonial officials famously understood the destructive expansion of their colonial project). Cultural devastation *overcame* the Crow in the specific historical and motivated form of the rapidly and rapaciously expanding racializing and civilizing settler colonial power of the U.S. state, or more precisely, in the form of one of the governing or governmentalizing institutions of settler colonial power—namely, the *reservation*. The Native reservation, like the slave plantation, is a modern institution and a technology of transforming power—specifically of powers that do not necessarily have as their telos the destruction of physical life (however much life may be lost), but more importantly the *creation of inescapably dominant conditions* in which old paradigms and conceptions of life and lifeworlds are undermined, rendered unusable and redundant, and new conceptions and paradigms of life and lifeworlds, hitherto barely conceivable to its victims and often incoherent to them, are imposed and rendered unavoidable or inexorable. This is a process set in motion by modern power—modern colonial power specifically. And it is one that Lear neatly evades.

In rationally seeking to navigate their precarity as they understood it in their rapidly changing landscape, in the recognizable form of the potential damage that could be inflicted on them by the Sioux, the Crow gambled with as much foresight as they could, and that gamble brought them into the unknown world of a more profound and ultimately more fundamentally transforming power than they could have had any conception of: the power of the modern U.S. state. Within their context of intelligibility, the Crow perfectly grasped that in their common rivalry the Sioux had the capacity and the will to destroy them (by physical death or incorporation), to bring about the end of the Crow as a distinctive people, and they sought to shield themselves against this knowable eventuality by allying themselves with an unknown and unknowably modern power that seemed at least willing (however self-interestedly) to guarantee their *physical* survival. The U.S. state presented itself as just such a power. But what the Crow could not foresee from within their cultural paradigm was that this physical survival would be secured at the price of a reorganization of the very conditions of cultural intelligibility. Perhaps in some relevant sense they had some semblance of "agency" in their dealings with the U.S. state—in

Lear's account, Plenty Coups is a thoughtful, rational, and moral agent. But just as certainly, as the anthropologist Stanley Diamond would have said, the Crow were not *volunteers* in the modern civilizational process that overtook them—they were *conscripts* drawn into a process larger and more destructive than they could possibly have fathomed.[40] The story Lear tells is that of a modern *tragedy*, not because it is dire or inconsolably sad (which it is, without question) but because the Crow were faced with a tragic choice between undesirable alternatives. In avoiding formal conquest, the Crow found themselves conscripts of a modern power of which they did not have (and could not have had) a clear conception and whose subjugating effects, though it preserved their physical lives, destroyed forever their traditional idea of the meaning of the historical traditions of that life. Instructively, then, we are dealing here with a register of destructive power that is not necessarily driven by physical violence and death. Or anyway, it is not external physical violence unleashed against the Crow that eventually destroyed them as the people they once were. Rather, they were destroyed by being inserted into an insidious structure by a modern power that systematically disabled from within their ability to reproduce their traditional ways of life. In this book, albeit in a discussion of a different historical context, that of New World slavery, I want to describe the modern powers directed at this kind of cultural destruction—the destruction of a form of life—as *evil*.

Lear's book is about ethics—it announces itself as such—but it is not about evil or any sort of wrongdoing. This is not part of Lear's conceptual vocabulary. Notably, nowhere in *Radical Hope* is Lear concerned with *moral wrong* per se and the *moral obligations* that might follow from it, with whether—as a consequence of the profound wrong suffered by the Crow at the hands of the U.S. state— there is a debt of repair owed to them. As it appears in Lear's philosophical anthropology, the U.S. state is not a *blameworthy* actor, morally responsible for *wrongful* action perpetrated against the Crow. Indeed, though ethical concern is at the heart of his book (specifically the kind of moral hope—*radical* hope—that characterized the actions of Plenty Coups in attempting to ensure the survival of his people), it isn't clear that moral *wrong* is what he thinks the Crow suffered. Again, notably, it is the *effect* and not the agency of the destructive action that most concerns Lear. The conceptual collapse he so vividly describes all too often appears as almost an innocent consequence of actions for which *no one* bears moral responsibility. The loss of concepts appears to have a moral impact in terms of the collapse of a whole way of life but not in terms of whether what

18 PROLOGUE

was suffered by the Crow was wrongfully caused by responsible human agency, collective or individual, motivated or not: it is a catastrophe, not an *atrocity* (to use a distinction Claudia Card makes and to which I return in a later chapter). In a certain perhaps obvious respect, Lear's insightful work evades and obscures any way of connecting the palpable and constraining moral and social powers shaping the contexts of the Crow to the disaster of their historical experience.

In my view, the loss of concepts and the moral wrong that perpetuated it are indivisible halves of a single whole. Arguably, not all moral wrong produces a loss of concepts, and perhaps not all concept loss is a consequence of moral wrongdoing. But in the case of the Crow as described by Lear, and in the case that interests me in this book, the African victims of the transatlantic slave trade and New World slavery, and their descendants, the two are not separable—they are parts of a single process of destruction. In each case, the wrong is the wrong of an atrocity precisely *because* what the wrongdoing powers perpetrate (quite apart from the routine commission of violence and violent death against members of the group in question) is the disorganization and effective destruction of the old and constitutive background conditions of a long-standing way of human life and human flourishing (whatever their internal modes of dissent and conflict might have been), together with the coercive construction of new and modern conditions of domination in the totalizing forms, respectively, of the reservation and the plantation. These modern powers, and the rationalities and technologies through which they exercised their sovereignty over the people they brought within their purview of rule, were undoubtedly powers of coercion and force. But beyond the physical suffering occasioned by this coercion and force, the wanton maiming and death, what these conscripts of modernity are made to suffer is the irretrievable loss of the integrated concepts—the conceptual paradigms—that informed their former inherited ways of life. In my view this is not only wrong but is wrong that is evil—the systematic destruction of a people's ability to reproduce their way of life.

A PARTIAL PORTRAIT OF SLAVERY AS A HISTORICAL ATROCITY

In this book I am principally concerned with thinking specifically about the moral and political implications of the atrocity of New World slavery. How should we describe the devastation brought about by plantation slavery in the lives of the enslaved? How should we describe plantation slavery as an institutionalized and transgenerational structure of domination? As I have said, New World slavery involved scarcely imaginable practices of barbaric violence that were carried out on a routine basis. But can the destructive powers of slavery also be described in terms of the devastation of inherited lifeworlds and forms of life? Can these powers be described, on the one hand, as the devastation of the relations of inheritance of old lifeworlds and forms of life and, on the other, as the institution of new, coercively distorting enslaved lifeworlds and forms of life? These are the questions that interest me. In this book, though I am in no way writing a history, there *is* history that matters—history that informs the picture of slavery I depict (and sometimes take for granted). In the construction of this picture, I take the anglophone Caribbean as my explicit and implicit geopolitical frame of reference, and within this wider frame, Jamaica most particularly. Even so, mindful as I am of the fact that the historiographical field of slavery studies is a contentious one (and rightly so), it may be useful to sketch—through largely Jamaican materials—a partial and rough-and-ready portrait of those aspects of the system of slavery that seem most pertinent to my project.

In the mid-eighteenth century, at the high point of British Caribbean slavery, Jamaica was unquestionably the most profitable and valued colony in the British American Empire, a prized "sugar island" of staggering wealth, not only enriching individual slaveowners and the British treasury but also stimulating the development of mercantilist capitalism and in doing so nourishing the making of the modern world.[41] That immense and perhaps incalculable prosperity and spectacular luxury and enrichment were generated out of one of the most remorselessly brutal systems of human bondage ever invented—namely, plantation slavery, which in Jamaica would extend from the late seventeenth until the early nineteenth century. In the course of a short and intensely volatile period, Jamaica had become the "jewel" in what a recent historian has appropriately called a *slave empire*.[42] In 1655, to tell it in brief, during the Anglo-Spanish war and following the failure of the Siege of Santo Domingo, the island had been captured for the English by that squabbling (and soon to be disgraced and imprisoned) pair, Admiral William Penn and General Robert Venables, as part of Oliver Cromwell's ambitious Western Design aimed at staking a definitive imperial claim on the Americas. Its future uncertain, Jamaica would remain a lucrative haven for buccaneers, harassing Spanish galleons in Caribbean waters and sacking Spanish possessions, until

20 PROLOGUE

the earthquake of 1692 destroyed the notorious Port Royal and forced a change in colonial policy toward the island.[43] In fact, already in 1664, when Thomas Modyford arrived in Jamaica as governor from Barbados, where experiments with large-scale sugar production had previously proved successful (and where he himself had become a successful planter), he immediately set about introducing the necessary state and commercial apparatuses for stimulating and supporting plantation agriculture. And after the earthquake, this would be Jamaica's future (and to some significant extent remains its present).

With meteoric strides, by the end of the seventeenth century Jamaica was developing into a powerhouse of a plantation economy, the epicenter of British Atlantic commercial capitalism.[44] The productivity of this economy very quickly came to depend almost exclusively on the availability of the comparatively cheap and relatively controllable labor of enslaved Africans shipped in ever-increasing numbers from the west coast of Africa across the Middle Passage of the Atlantic Ocean. As is well known, the incursion of European slave traders—organized in the English case by the Royal African Company and operating through a phalanx of such fortifications as the infamous Elimina and Cape Coast castles—led to an expansion and intensification of conflict and war among regional African polities that in turn fed captives into the insatiable maw of the transatlantic trade. Coffles of men, women, and children were force-marched from their destroyed interior villages to the coastal slave emporiums where a new form of violence and dehumanization lay in store for them as they waited to be transported into the complete unknown aboard that innovative oceanic technology of mortification and deprivation: the slave ship.[45] For Africans, it was the start of a novel experience of historical atrocity.

Eighteenth-century Jamaica was not merely a society in which significant numbers of enslaved people contributed to an otherwise varied economic system. By the early decades of that century of British cultural enlightenment, Jamaica had become a "genuine slave society," inasmuch as slaves were the vast majority of the population and the institution of slavery produced the internal generative dynamic of the social formation as a whole.[46] Like a palimpsest, the genocidal destruction of the Indigenous population cleared the physical and imaginative landscape of human habitation for the construction—the inscription—of a new order of life, labor, and legibility dominated by large-scale agricultural production centered on the early modern proto-capitalist complex of the sugar plantation.[47] Formally, of course, political rule was exerted through the emerging structures of the colonial state, through the office and presence of the governor, the planter-dominated House of Assembly, and the organs of coercion, including, crucially, the militia and garrisoned troops.[48] However, it was the plantation, an integrated quasi-autonomous social, economic, and jurisdictional domain, that effectively exerted rule as a totalizing institution in which slaveowners (or their various surrogates) were virtually sovereigns who not only set the agenda of production and authoritatively mediated social and personal relations but also adjudicated conduct and administered punishment for what they deemed infractions and transgressions.[49] The plantation became a ubiquitous form, the central, almost unmovable domain of institutional power in the island, in relation to which life and labor and death were organized. In fact, arguably, and despite the significance of Kingston as a commercial center in the British Americas, eighteenth-century Jamaica was little more than a network of large-scale slave plantations established for the express purpose of creating rapid wealth and nominally held together by the apparatuses of the colonial state.[50]

Unlike the pattern in mainland British America, eighteenth-century plantation Jamaica never became a "settler" colonial society, properly speaking. Despite the requirement of the "deficiency laws" (which established a legal minimum ratio of Whites to Blacks on plantations) and the active encouragement given to permanent planter residency, the White population scarcely grew by natural increase, and there remained about Jamaica a largely immigrant character without deep or generationally enduring stakes in the continuous well-being and identity of their adopted country. Absentee proprietorship was more norm than exception.[51] Nor, of course, did the Black population of traumatized enslaved people experience natural positive growth. Still, the prodigious and galloping need for enslaved labor meant that even between the mid-eighteenth century and the first years of the nineteenth the enslaved population grew by leaps and bounds on the basis of fresh imports of African captives.[52] It was a fractious, artificial structure narrowly kept in order by an openly vicious form of coercive power. Astute contemporary White observers with some years of residence in the island, such as James Knight (d. 1745 or 1746), Edward Long (1734–1813), and Bryan Edwards (1743–1800), all recognized the obvious danger to slave-owning lives and livelihoods of this demographic imbalance and instrumental social formation. The long continuous Maroon War of the early eighteenth century (settled in 1739) and the prolonged rebellion of 1760–61, the so-called Tacky Revolt, made clear that Blacks would not easily submit to the brutality meted out to

22 PROLOGUE

them. And yet, on the whole, led on by the prospect of quick, fabulous wealth Whites were determined to gamble on Jamaica.[53]

From its beginnings, Jamaican slave plantation society was, in formal and informal ways, a *racialized* order of White domination in which a principle and practice of absolute White superiority and privilege and liberty, on the one hand, and absolute Black subordination and inferiority and dependence, on the other, shaped every facet of social attitude and social action. The infinitesimally small White population exerted rule over the vast population of enslaved Blacks through instrumentalities of racial despotism and tyranny. Understandably Whites lived in perpetual fear of the Blacks they kept in bondage.[54] In a straightforward sense, they produced among themselves an internal rationality and makeshift ethos of racial solidarity, liberality, and hospitality in order to secure and demonstrate the unqualified unity of racial power against the hostile and threatening but altogether necessary presence of the Blacks they subjugated. This White domination, saturated as it was by a constant uneasiness and foreboding and dread, was held in place by a pervasive structure of continuous violence.[55] Naturally, the general aim of this often-arbitrary brutality was to induce in the enslaved a cowering apprehension, an anxious state of ceaseless expectation of assault and violation. The objective was to break the will of the African captives, to force and enforce acquiescence in their enslavement. Thus, from their sale on the auction block to the process of "seasoning"—by which the Africans were introduced to their new status and function and urged to accept submission, to at least accommodate to their subjugation—the enslaved were recruited into an institutionalized structure of regimented coercion and the continuous infliction of bodily and psychological harm.

There was brutality that was wholly routine, embodied in the ordinary round of slave plantation life: coerced labor in the cane fields was unsparingly back-breaking, and the enslaved suffered chronic exhaustion, not to speak of continuous hunger, sickness, injury, and early death. Slave life was unforgivingly hard and short. Brutality was systemic. As was the practice of humiliation. Beyond the infliction of bodily harm, management of enslaved people also appeared to require the degradation of their personhood. Slavery was at once an institutional relation of coercion and an *interpersonal* relation of enforced servility. The enslaved lived in a demeaning subjection in which they were continuously available to fulfill the needs and desires of their masters. Sexual predation and institutionally sanctioned rape were an unexceptional part of the gendered landscape of the structure of power embodied by White men.[56]

But there was also violence that was meant to be demonstrative, spectacular. The rule of White domination was a rule of sheer unmitigated dehumanizing *terror*. The sovereignty of White tyranny was exercised on the enslaved with unrelieved viciousness. The whip was the basic instrument of spectacular violence, and slaves were flogged as a matter of course. It vividly demonstrated the tyrannical power of the master. Whites carried out—and prided themselves in being able to carry out—their outrages with regularity and virtual impunity. Indeed, they cultivated a customary attitude toward Blacks being treated not only as inferior but also as dangerous and unpredictable, requiring not simply force to maintain submission and control but also periodic demonstrations of excessive violence. Newly landed Whites, whatever their sense of taste and civility and enlightenment upon arrival might have been, quickly learned to assert their control and command and superiority by whipping and maiming and demeaning Blacks at will. Needless to say, those Blacks who dared to attack the plantation system or injure Whites or destroy their property were made an example of in hideous acts of public reprisal—hanging, gibbeting, and more.

Beyond even this was a register of violence and violation that was not simply punishment for miscreant behavior or reprisals for harms to Whites or damages to their property, but was something more like sadistic pleasure. The abject dependence of the enslaved left them vulnerable to perversions such as those invented by Thomas Thistlewood, who arrived in Jamaica in 1750. Infamously, Thistlewood occasionally subjected slaves to what he called "Derby's dose," which involved having a slave defecate into the mouth of the offending slave. He would also occasionally have one slave urinate into the eyes and mouth of some transgressing Black.[57] It is difficult to imagine what purpose was served by these practices other than being an experiment in extreme debasement. These were perversely ingenious ways of assaulting Blacks with techniques of barbarism clearly directed not simply at the infliction of physical pain alone but perhaps more especially at irrevocably wounding the very humanity—the very *sense* of dignity—of the enslaved.

To be sure, this is an incomplete social portrait of the regime of violating racist power that characterized eighteenth-century slave plantation Jamaica. Undoubtedly, much more could be said about its routine as well as its spectacular orders of brutality, its vicious sadism, but this seems to me enough to sustain

24 PROLOGUE

the view that New World slavery was an institutionalized and transgenerational atrocity. Still, this is perhaps not the *only* way to describe the devastation to which the African captives transported to Jamaica (and elsewhere in the Americas) across the Middle Passage were subjected. (And remember that well into the late eighteenth century Jamaica was populated largely by African—as opposed to Creole—slaves.) Arguably, these African captives were not only killed and maimed and humiliated and debased but also subjected to a process much like the one described for the Crow by Jonathan Lear—namely, a process by which their tacit connections to assumed forms of life, and the conceptual fields that constituted them, were forever severed. In Lear's vocabulary, this is the *ontological* dimension of that subjection. Not only were the men, women, and children who were forced into slavery in the Americas physically brutalized and spiritually humiliated; they were also willfully uprooted and displaced from their ancestral forms of life and initiated into a process, "seasoning," by which they were *transformed* from people embedded in dense, implicit networks of cultural tradition (ways of life, of course, with their own idioms and practices of subjection and exclusion) into enslaved subpersons cut off from their accustomed structures and patterns of social interaction, social reproduction, and social recognition. These men, women, and children must have suffered the kind of breakdown and loss Lear describes—that is, the breakdown and loss not of specific perspectives but of the implicit paradigms or schemas that necessarily shape the intelligibility and point of any perspective they could have had. These individual men, women, and children may well have carried much with them to Jamaica—songs, rituals, cuisines, stories, names, habits, and techniques that made up the rich texture of their cultural lifeworlds (and that, indeed, still texture the "African" character of Caribbean life)—but what they could not have carried across the Middle Passage was the *background* context in which these cultural elements were imbedded and from which they derived their coherence and their salience.

One can very easily imagine, I believe, an African equivalent to the Crow leader Plenty Coups, an African captive in eighteenth-century colonial Jamaica, now old and reflective, recounting her or his life experiences to a sympathetic European—an inquisitive Enlightenment traveler, perhaps—and telling them, to their consternation, that after the captives were forced aboard the slave ships bound for the New World "nothing happened." Not that, if you like, phenomenologically or historically or psychologically nothing happened, but that *ontologically*, in terms of their structure of temporal experience, nothing occurred that could be fitted into the intelligibility of their old forms of life. To go on living as best they could, in the unpropitious circumstances into which they had been forced, they would have had to invent new ways of living individually and collectively, new modes of interaction, new language forms, new familial arrangements, none of which would have the slightest legitimacy or authority in the context of the powers of the plantation regime. Part of the disaster (I want to say, part of the tragedy) of this kind of breakdown (or rather, this *level* of the larger breakdown) is that it is not, strictly speaking, foreseeable; it cannot be clearly identified or even described. As Lear suggests, no one lives with an explicit sense of their own form of life, its contours and parameters, with a self-conscious understanding of the ontological vulnerability to which they are exposed. You cannot ever reflectively stand back far enough to see—let alone fully describe—the organizational structure of the paradigm that animates one's form of life and that is now subject to devastating destruction. So when those African men, women, and children were imprisoned in the holds of slave ships to cross the Atlantic, they could have had no idea of what awaited them, no idea of what they would have to change in themselves to meet the new challenge. In these terms, what the breakdown that takes place at the level of forms of life suggests is less about how cultural ideas can come to be forgotten than about how they can come to be *disabled*. It is not so much a matter of memory or narrative. It is that the old pathways organizing and animating the uses of these memorial narrative ideas now effectively can go *nowhere*—they cannot lead to their former destinations. I believe that the destruction of the conditions of the forms of life of the enslaved is an incalculable and irreparable enormity—and therefore part of the evil to which they were subjected.

ITINERARY

The path of my itinerary in *Irreparable Evil* is a circumscribed one, tentative and exploratory. Each of the chapters can be read separately, apart from the others, and more or less in any order. Nevertheless, if not exactly one seamlessly unfolding monograph, I think of the whole at least as an interconnected chain of arguments to do with moral-historical criticism concerned with the unreconciled and unreconcilable past of New World slavery in contemporary Black life.

26 PROLOGUE

Part 1 consists of a single chapter, "The Idea of a Moral and Reparatory History," the purpose of which is to sketch the general problem-space of the intervention that concerns me. The chapter outlines central dimensions of the contemporary *problem* of New World slavery as a problem for moral-political criticism. It poses what seems to me an unavoidable question: What is the conceptual *story-form* in which the past of New World slavery ought to appear as a problem for contemporary critical intervention—and why *this* story-form and not some other? As a provisional answer, I offer the view that in the current conjuncture (the contours of which I try to spell out, at least sufficient to my task) the story-form of New World slavery ought to be oriented—or *reoriented*—in the direction of a moral and, specifically, *reparatory* history of the present. I suggest that this problem-space of moral history should be understood, in part anyway, as a response to a displacement of an age of emancipation by one reorganized by the regime of human rights and humanitarianism and the cognate concepts (among them, trauma, sentiment, wrong, memory, social suffering, repair) through which its ideological self-image and its governing powers are articulated. I take this historical shift to be the sign of a *moral turn* in our wider comprehension of how to think about the world we live in—a turn neither to be simply lamented nor celebrated but interrogated as one of the conditions for beginning to imagine alternative political paths beyond our present impasse. It will become evident, I hope, that this is also the problem-space of the tragic; part of my project here is to deepen and widen the argument about the present of the past of New World slavery that I set out in *Conscripts of Modernity* many years ago.[58] The efficacy of the tragic owes, in some measure, to the efficacy of the moral turn. In this context, I suggest that an idea of evil is especially germane to contemporary moral-political reason. In concert with a number of thinkers, I believe that evil can help to concentrate our attention on especially egregious kinds of moral wrong and moral harm, of which New World slavery is one pronounced, if insufficiently regarded, historical instance. Against this background, I think of a reparatory history as that dimension of moral history concerned specifically with historical wrongs that remain unrepaired in the present. Together with other critics, I hold that unrepaired wrong *remains* wrong and, moreover, that the unrepair of such wrong is itself a grievous wrong requiring redress in conjunction with the repair of the original wrong. Wrong is not static; it *compounds*. Note, however, that I do not assume that *all* past wrong can be repaired. Reparatory history, as I think of it, is neither progressivist nor redemptive; it does not unfold from evil toward good. To the contrary. With Hannah Arendt, a very complex figure for me, as you will see, I believe that some past evils are *irreconcilable* and *irreparable*. In my view, New World slavery was an evil of this sort, so egregious in its injury, so extended in its unmitigated duration, and so long in the disrespectful and shameful neglect of its repair as to now stand as a permanent, immovable wrong. And yet I nevertheless insist that the evil of New World slavery demands a thoroughgoing and immediate redress. Unlike other historical atrocities, one of the distinctive features of New World slavery is that it was not, properly speaking, an *event*—an aberrant interruption of history that came and went in a concentrated perpetration of genocidal violence. Rather, it was an intergenerational institution structurally integrated as an indispensable dimension of the evolution of the modern capitalist world. Therefore, even beyond its formal disappearance, its effects live on: the descendants of its victims continue to live in a global world of White supremacy and within nation-states that are structured by the racialized subjugation, poverty, and terror that slavery brought into being. New World slavery is paradoxical inasmuch as it is at once irreparable and yet demands repair. I close the chapter with some reflections on the liberal character of certain arguments for reparations and the need for an incisive interrogation of the complicities between liberalism and White supremacy that have structured the modern world and disagreements about it.

Part 2 consists of two chapters, both concerned with an interconnected issue—namely, the relative invisibility of New World slavery as a historical evil. Chapter 2, "Incomparable Evil," considers aspects of the way in which the idea of evil has been put to work in recent critical and moral-political work. In a certain respect, my concern is with the seeming difficulty in much scholarship on evil to squarely think New World slavery as an instance of evil. In a very substantial way, the contemporary contours of the problem of evil are established through a discernible and intertwined complex, which includes the valorization of the twentieth century as *the* century of evil; the almost metaphysical place accorded to the Holocaust in the contemporary imaginary of evil; the unshakable presumption of the primacy of mass killing or genocide as the chief marker of the presence of evil; and the defining place occupied by Arendt as the exemplary theorist of evil. In this chapter, I seek to trouble the stability of this authorizing chain of assumptions. I begin with the simple reminder of some pertinent aspects of the *historicity* through which the present hegemonic image of the Nazi genocide of European Jews was established, the rise of the Holocaust as the *paradigm* of evil.

28 PROLOGUE

What is notable is that the Holocaust is not one among historical evils, not ever the first among historical evils. Indeed, it is scarcely *historical* at all. Rather, the Holocaust is the *meta*-evil, the evil that *defines* what evil is. Against this background, I turn my attention to a consideration of Hannah Arendt, a thinker with whom, as I have suggested, I have a complex relationship. She informed my past reflections on revolution and the tragic in *Conscripts of Modernity* and *Omens of Adversity*, and on thinking and friendship in *Stuart Hall's Voice*.[59] In this chapter, what interests me is the spectacular rise of Arendt as *the* exemplary thinker of our time, the assumed embodiment of the contemporary moral turn, and how this rise serves to shape—or perhaps misshape—the way her thinking about evil is *read* by even her most astute interpreters and commentators. In this respect, I focus on the work of Richard Bernstein. Certainly, Arendt is one of the thinkers through whom the idea of the Holocaust-as-exceptional-evil is authorized. But to a surprising degree, there is among some of her most recent interpreters (participants, I believe, in the ideological self-image of the moral turn) the assumption that her work can be read *through* her thinking on evil, as though evil was, or had somehow become, the *master concept* of her thought. I want to dispute this strangely ahistorical practice of reading Arendt. But one consequence of this unquestioning and insular reading of her (sophisticated as it is on many dimensions I am sure I have no access to) is that these interpreters are entirely consumed with the problem of the *meaning* of her ideas about evil and the extent to which the earlier idea of "radical evil" in *The Origins of Totalitarianism* was displaced by or absorbed into the later one of the "banality of evil" in *Eichmann in Jerusalem*.[60] As a result, these interpreters are unable to explore, let alone appreciate, the rhetorical *work of exception* through which the death camps are constructed by her as the exemplary site of incomparable evil, and how this exemplarity is explicitly rendered in part by *diminishing* the evil of other atrocities, New World slavery central among them.

Chapter 3, "Incommensurable Evils," is concerned with the discussion of a number of accounts of evil—those of John Kekes, Claudia Card, and most especially Laurence Mordekhai Thomas—that seem to me to be of profound importance. Thomas is the author of a remarkable book, *Vessels of Evil: American Slavery and the Holocaust*, first published in 1993.[61] Not as widely read as I think it should be, *Vessels of Evil* is a modestly composed but subtle and insightful intervention into the land-mined arena of the comparison of New World slavery and the Holocaust. Notably, Arendt is scarcely mentioned, but Thomas's chief concern is

PROLOGUE 29

to dislodge the invidious but all-too-pervasive approach to considerations (both popular and scholarly) of these wrongs that turn on assumptions or claims about which of the two was the *worse* wrong. Thomas suggests a mode of comparison that enables us to redescribe both as *maximum* evils, if nevertheless evils organized around contrasting practices of moral wrongdoing. Whereas the subjugation of the Jews by the Nazis was organized around a systematic practice of mass murder, the subjugation of Blacks in the Americas was organized around the mass destruction of the conditions of autonomy within cultural life. Certainly, there was mass death under slavery, whether during the Middle Passage or on the slave plantations, just as there was destruction of the conditions of the cultural life of Jews under the Nazis. But death was not the raison d'être of New World slavery, just as the destruction of culture was not the principal aim of Nazi policy toward the Jews. This redescription of the grounds of comparison also entails a reconceptualization of how we understand extremities of wrong, how we think about which kinds of wrong *count* and which do not count in the scales of evil. Thomas's book raises hard questions about the fetishization of physical *death* in considerations of the moral evil of atrocity, and the relegation to comparative irrelevance of kinds of wrong that aim not so much at death as at the production and reproduction of *distorted life*. In Thomas's view, what New World slavery destroyed, above all, was the *narrative* that bound together the traditions of people kidnapped and transported from their communities in Africa, and thus devastated the cultural capacity of the enslaved to produce and reproduce a coherent identity for themselves. I suggest that this is a very compelling argument, but I want to take issue with some of the assumptions about narrative and social life upon which it depends. Not surprising, perhaps, Thomas's picture of slavery is indebted to the work of Orlando Patterson, in particular to Patterson's idea of "natal alienation," the dynamic of cultural destruction to which the enslaved were subjected, first described in his 1982 *Slavery and Social Death*.[62] Although clearly attuned to Patterson's wider sense of the fundamental *catastrophe* of New World slavery, I suggest that Thomas misreads and thus misconstrues Patterson's conception of the effects of slavery's subjugating powers on the enslaved. True, I argue, Patterson holds that the enslaved suffer the loss of a coherent, continuous narrative of identity; but more crucial to him, I believe, than the loss of narrative per se is the loss of the social and familial context of a *lifeworld* and the background *form of life* that shapes its narrative and other potentialities. Furthermore, as we will see, Thomas is a thinker of profound humanity who has

30 PROLOGUE

written (in the wake of *Vessels of Evil*) acutely about the role of forgiveness for evil. I close this chapter with a brief discussion of what is less than satisfactory about this dimension of his otherwise generous and insightful argument.

Part 3 of *Irreparable Evil* also consists of two chapters. The first of them, chapter 4, "Slavery's Evil Lifeworld," continues the discussion of Patterson's work on slavery in an attempt to better characterize the sense or senses in which New World slavery constituted a moral evil—an evil lifeworld. In spite of, if not because of, its recent rise to prominence in at least certain accounts of Black life (largely with tacit generalizing reference to continental African America), Patterson's work has been less engaged than *invoked*, and in the process it is often enough reduced to a single resonant but often misunderstood phrase, *social death*. Patterson is a complicated intellectual figure, a moral and historical sociologist who is not easily or compactly slotted into the readily available pigeonholes of scholarly classification.[63] Certainly, he has largely stood against the fashion-setting trends in the now sprawling historiography of New World slavery, and he has remained consistently committed to what one might call a *catastrophic* vision of the atrocity of slavery—the unremitting sense that for the enslaved the institution of slavery amounted to social and cultural devastation. Of course, it is Patterson's later work that has drawn attention, or rather one single work—*Slavery and Social Death*. I suggest, however, that there is a continuous thread connecting the later work (including the much-neglected *Freedom in the Making of Western Culture*, published in 1991) to his earlier work on Jamaican slavery, especially *The Sociology of Slavery*, published in 1967.[64] That thread turns around Patterson's dogged concern to conceptualize an answer to a *single* if multifaceted question to do with the *powers* of slavery: How should the internal dynamic of slavery's powers of domination be described, and what did these powers *do* to the enslaved? In this respect, it is too often forgotten that in addition to being a consummate sociologist Patterson has also been a practicing novelist. It is the novel, in its realist and existentialist form, that has offered him a fictive phenomenological terrain on which to explore some of the more nuanced features of personality and society that his social science, however subtle, largely precludes. Indeed, the center of chapter 4 consists of an extended reading of Patterson's third novel, *Die the Long Day*, published in 1972, a historical novel about eighteenth-century slavery in British colonial Jamaica.[65] Not only does the novel draw on and reanimate the conceptual landscape of the earlier historical sociology of Jamaican slavery (especially around such questions as "accommodation" and "resistance") but it anticipates the later ideas about natal alienation and social death. *Die the Long Day* is a novel about the distinctive moral evil of plantation slavery. Patterson invites us to see slavery in and through the socialized personalities of his fictive characters, the remarkable Quasheba most outstandingly, and in the organization of the plot that centers on her actions to see it as, in effect, a systemic form of evil, an evil lifeworld. By this I mean that New World slavery produced and reproduced a structure of systematic brutality and an almost continuous exposure to wanton and gratuitous violence and violation, but it also depended on the systematic destruction of vital and nourishing connections to the former lifeworlds of the enslaved together with the establishment of a social order that systematically precluded, for generations of enslaved peoples, the construction of coherent and long-lasting forms of alternative social organization. It will be evident then, I hope, that what is evil about New World slavery is not just the concept-loss associated with former narrative traditions but also the coercive narrowing and distortion of the new social conditions in which moral life was obliged to subsist.

Chapter 5, "Evil Enrichment," is concerned with colonial debt, with the coercively asymmetrical relationship between colonial extraction and metropolitan accumulation. Caribbean anticolonial intellectuals were acutely aware of the incalculable contribution of enslaved labor to the fabulous wealth of the colonial metropoles, not just to individual fortunes but also to the vast civic, infrastructural, and institutional prosperity of the societies and polities themselves. In a certain sense, the anticolonial anglophone Caribbean intellectual tradition was inaugurated around this theme of evil enrichment and its moral-political implications. It is not often remembered that C. L. R. James opened *The Black Jacobins*, published in 1938, with this pointed and poignant recognition.[66] And it was Eric Williams who, in his 1944 masterpiece *Capitalism and Slavery*, relentlessly pursued and amplified the theme.[67] There is now an extensive literature on Williams and *Capitalism and Slavery*—and a telling (and largely ignored) contrast between Caribbean scholars focused on Williams the anticolonial intellectual and North Atlantic scholars preoccupied with the historical truth of the so-called Williams theses. What interests me in this chapter is the moral-political labor of *Capitalism and Slavery* (in contrast with that of the 1938 doctoral dissertation on which it is partially based) as a mode of intervention into a specific conjuncture of British colonial historiography on slavery and abolition—a rhetorical labor, I argue, carried out with the help of the trope of *irony*. With merciless parody, caricature, and mockery, Williams rips away the racist colonial mask of benevolent disavowal to reveal the venal material interests at work. Reginald Coupland is his principal target. For Williams, the colonial slave relation incurred a *debt*. He believed that something was *owed* for the centuries of brutal exploitation of enslaved men and women and the staggering metropolitan enrichment it enabled. Notably, though, as may seem perfectly understandable in retrospect, Williams mobilizes this strategy of critique within the language-game of nation-state *sovereignty*. For Williams, what is owed to the descendants of the enslaved is *political freedom*. In the anticolonial politics from the 1940s until very near the present, however, this has amounted to a claim on the part of the Creole Brown and Black middle-class elites to a right to inherit rule over the descendants of the enslaved. But perhaps this conjuncture, in which the past in the present is articulated in an anticolonial key, has now been superseded. The chapter closes with a brief discussion of Hilary Beckles's *Britain's Black Debt*, the first explicitly reparatory history of the Caribbean past.[68] Beckles sees his 2013 book as a direct descendant of *Capitalism and Slavery*. But in a postcolonial conjuncture marked by the exhaustion of the anticolonial sovereignty paradigm, he links Britain's debt for slavery not to the seemingly settled demand for political freedom but to a demand for *economic* compensation. While noting the virtues of *Britain's Black Debt*, I raise a number of doubts about its central argument concerning the alleged acknowledged *illegality* of slavery to British contemporaries. The historical argument is unconvincing at best, but what is more important to recognize is that Beckles is motivated by the desire to ground his claim for reparation in the international law doctrine that past crime incurs a contemporary legal obligation. It is this motivation that reveals the liberal legalism (including humanitarian legalism) in which his moral-political project is embedded, a project that leaves outside the frame of critique the basic contours of the abiding neocolonial structure of Caribbean polities.

Finally, in a brief epilogue, I consider the problem of the irreparability of certain kinds of evil—absolute evils such as New World slavery. In doing so I return to Hannah Arendt and her discussion in *The Human Condition* of kinds of evil that one can neither punish nor forgive.[69] I close on this note not because it is the end of the story—it is not. There is much more to say (just not here) about folding the implications of the persistence of irreparable past evils into a differently durable sense of future possibility.

PART I

PART I

CHAPTER 1

THE IDEA OF A MORAL AND REPARATORY HISTORY

HISTORICIZING THE PROBLEM ABOUT NEW WORLD SLAVERY

In this chapter, my central concern is a broad outline of what I take to be the contemporary critical-conceptual *problem* about New World slavery. The question that animates and guides this concern is the following: What is the conceptual *story* of the past of New World slavery that ought to command our critical attention in the present conjuncture, and why *this* story and not some other? Or in a slightly different phrasing, under what *description* of the past should we approach and formulate the problem about New World slavery? The provisional answer I offer is this: In the current conjuncture (relevant elements of which I will describe in a moment), the story of New World slavery ought to be oriented, or *reoriented*, by a *moral* and *reparatory* history of the past in the present. Such a moral and reparatory history, I suggest, would embrace the idea that, whatever else it was, New World slavery was also a historical *atrocity*—that is, a moral *evil*—that was perpetrated over generations on the humanity of Africans and peoples of African descent enslaved in the New World, and as such it *demands* a moral and reparatory response. Again, within this frame, New World slavery should be pictured, alongside however else it is pictured, as a historical structure of racialized powers that aimed both at the physical being and physical capacities of the enslaved and, perhaps more enduringly, also at their *moral* being and *moral* capacities. On this view, New World slavery not only exploited the enslaved (in the sense of brutally extracting a stupendous surplus value from their unfree labor for accumulation largely elsewhere) and subjected their bodies to ongoing physical violence (violent death, often enough) but also *wronged* them in the

36 PART I

sense of continuously subjecting them to a relentless dehumanization by systematically distorting and undermining their capacity for individual and collective self-possession, personhood, and self-determination. Thinking about New World slavery as a moral and reparatory problem is meant to capture the grammar and character of this wrong and its harms and point in the direction of its corrective political-economic implications.[1]

Notice, then, that my overall question, regarding the *kind* of story the present should demand about the past of New World slavery and my provisional answer to it concerning the idea of a specifically moral and reparatory history, imply a certain *historicity* to the *conceptual* problem about histories of New World slavery (indeed, of any history). They imply, that is, that there can be no *single* story-form that is always and forever the *only*, or the *best* story-form for capturing or expressing the *point* in the present of reconstructing an adequate past of New World slavery. The problem about the past of New World slavery is always *also* a problem about *some* present. Perhaps this is by now an obvious historiographical principle. In any case, my question and my provisional answer imply that not only the historical facts concerning the institution of slavery but also the intellectual inquiry into these facts has a history, and one that is simultaneously *social* and *conceptual*. The historiography of New World slavery, now a vast domain of academic scholarship (namely, "slavery studies"), is genealogically subject to what Michel Foucault in his late work (part and parcel of his own moral turn) called historical "modes of problematization"—that is, discursive networks that shape the conceptual field of problems in which an *object* of knowledge is constituted as an object of knowledge *as such* and argued over by *subjects* of knowledge (including self-knowledge) constituted as variously situated subjects of knowledge as such.[2] Thus the mode of problematization of a knowledge-object (New World slavery, in this case) is less the study of its seemingly autonomous and unmediated constituent relations—its fixed and transparent semantic reference, its *meaning*—than the genealogy of the conditions that gave rise to it in the first place as an authoritative knowledge-object and the rival discursive positions taken up in the relevant present by those implicated in its modes of appearance and subjectivity. In just this sense, the history of the historical study of New World slavery, say, from the early twentieth century onward, as a whole as well as in the relevant geopolitical regions of the New World, can be written as a history of the varied problematizations or (supplementing Foucault here with R. G. Collingwood and others inspired by him) the varied "question-answer"

THE IDEA OF A MORAL AND REPARATORY HISTORY   37

complexes in relation to which the past of slavery has been rendered relevant to varied historical presents—and in particular the varied historical presents of New World peoples of African descent themselves, whose lives have been foundationally and forever entangled in the history of that institution and its aftermaths.[3] Consequently, I want to think of this historicity as partly but nevertheless significantly internal to Black New World *intellectual traditions* in which a past of the present of New World slavery is always—if variously—morally and politically *at stake*. In this book, as I have indicated, I am primarily (though not exclusively) concerned with Caribbean intellectual traditions of thinking about the past of New World slavery.[4]

The chief virtue of thinking through conjunctures or problem-spaces, as Stuart Hall reminded us endlessly, is less what they teach us about past presents than how they orient us to present ones. The idea of conjunctures or problem-spaces, in other words, is meant to attune us not only to the historicity of presents that now belong to a past but also to the historicity of our own more immediate presents, to the shifting complex of questions that make up our own living contexts of intervention and investigation. In the same way that in any inquiry into past histories (of a practice, say, or an event or an institution) we are obliged to ask about the *governing* story-forms that constituted them, as a corollary, we ought also to ask whether or to what extent those inherited story-forms should be thought of as *continuing* to have the same critical yield as they once did in the conjunctures that brought them into being in the first place. And if they do not, we need to ask how we should rethink what the conceptual point is of the story we ourselves are now seeking to tell about that past (practice, event, institution) in the present—in other words, what the question is that we believe the conceptual intervention should *now* aim to answer. How, if necessary, should we *change* the question? Such an exploration is, of course, always partly speculative precisely because historical relations are never entirely stable, never neatly, cleanly available for conclusive representation and elucidation. But part of what the speculative sensing of an *emerging* conjuncture or problem-space entails (as, again, Hall helps us to recognize) is the apprehension, however inchoate or embryonic, of the ways in which the point of an old domain of questions has become less tenable or less salient than it once appeared to be; the apprehension that, consequently, it may be necessary, as a matter of gaining a new ground of critical traction, to alter the questions we are asking—to "bend the twig" in new directions, as Hall liked to say (borrowing from Althusser)—so as to revise or

38 PART I

expand or otherwise transform the conceptual or cognitive space of inquiry and thus perhaps revise or expand or otherwise transform the moral-political horizon of intervention.[5]

My suggestion here of a reorientation of the story of New World slavery in the direction of a moral and reparatory history is motivated by this general approach to pasts in the present, and by the suspicion, specifically, that an old domain of questions about the past in the present of New World slavery is no longer as compelling and consequential as it once was. What is that old domain of questions? And what is the new conjuncture or problem-space in which those old questions about the slave past now appear conceptually depleted, or enervated, and in which new questions are gradually assuming relevance, or arguably *should* assume relevance? Is there something about the present (in particular, the present of postslavery Black life) that strongly urges the direction of a specifically moral and reparatory history as opposed to some other historical orientation?

In New World, including Caribbean, Black intellectual traditions, New World slavery is undoubtedly the *immovable* social fact that animates—one is tempted to say, that ontologically *grounds*—the founding narrative of Black life, the founding rupture, at once atrocity and catastrophe, that inaugurates the story of modern Black experience.[6] As is well-enough known, one powerful twentieth-century story-form in terms of which the past-in-the-present of New World slavery has historically been narrated is that of *emancipationism*. By this I mean a story-form that organizes the relation between narrative, time, and social identity in such a way that in the temporal relations among pasts, presents, and futures the future always appears as *overcoming* the past—typically a future of Black *freedom* that overcomes and thus releases us from an odious and unwanted past of racial domination rooted in slavery. Thus the narrative *rhythm* of emancipationism is one of progressive change, sometimes radical or revolutionary change. And the *direction* of that change, moreover, is teleological, tilted toward a horizon given, however dimly, in advance. The narrative of emancipationism is therefore always a *utopian* one in the sense that it sets in motion an ameliorating or improving story of which the surpassing culmination is the *realization* of a new and unprecedented age. Emancipationism, then, is unfailingly a great dramatic narrative, heroic in spirit, epic in arc, and Romantic in temper and tone—and almost invariably *vindicationist*. What vindicationism infuses emancipationism with is *moral gravity* and an aggrieved sense of *justification*—it offers a profound confirmation of the *righteousness* of the cause in which the unbearable past is overcome in the determined struggle for the desired and hoped-for future. Vindicationism offers an absolving exoneration of the identities and demands of the protagonists who are seeking to bring the future into the present. It bears out the rightness of their cause, it redeems their suffering, and it gives purpose to their sacrifice and their search for salvation. Importantly, too, emancipationism and vindicationism are not merely abstract, cerebral, or intellectual story-forms—they are story-forms deeply embedded in the social forms and relations and embodied traditions of Black life. Certainly, what emancipationism and vindicationism have inspired in African-descended peoples in the Caribbean and the wider New World are not only the self-conscious terms of an intellectual argument but also the affective dispositions of a *habitus*, or a form of life.

It is well known that for a very long time and for wholly intelligible reasons peoples of African descent in the New World have willfully and poetically constructed their stories of the relation between their slave pasts, their unfree and unjust presents, and their possible free futures as a great dramatic narrative of emancipation and vindication, an empowering progressive story of redemptive overcoming. The varied styles and idioms and forms of this heroic narrative are as familiar in the African Americas of the continental United States as of the archipelagic Caribbean. In this narrative, African-descended peoples have mobilized a picture of the slave past—of the wanton brutalities of the Middle Passage, the cruel indignities of the auction block, the inconsolable loss of family and kin, the irretrievable rupture of cultural memory, the coercive resocialization as racialized and enslaved subjects, and the unspeakable violations to body and mind and spirit of plantation life—in order to incite their indignation at the wrongs inflicted upon them, to nourish their affective longing for cultural coherence, and to feed their rational will to political self-determination. In short, in order to vindicate their transgressed humanity and to restore a basic semblance of dignity, African-descended peoples developed a radical tradition of cultivating the promise of social and spiritual redemption, from Negritude and Rastafari to Fanonian liberationism and Black nationalism and Black Marxism, varieties of what Robin D. G. Kelley has eloquently called Black freedom dreams and Anthony Bogues refers to as Black heretical and prophetic visions.[7]

40 PART I

Of course, I too (a child of the Jamaican 1970s) have been interpellated by this cultural-intellectual tradition. I believe, however, and have been saying so for a while (since *Refashioning Futures*, anyway), that we live today across the global Black world in the middle of the unprecedented unraveling of the self-evident purchase of this whole cultural-political narrative of revolutionary Black redemption told as a slavery-to-freedom story.[8] To be sure, there is a fundamental sense in which the transformation to which I am pointing here—the collapse of the narrative of emancipation—has a wider reference than the distinctive historical forms of Black life.[9] Indeed, the transformation concerns the structures of the *modern* experience of time as such. In an immutable, irreversible way, I believe, the very center of gravity of our temporal lives—as moderns, including as Black moderns—has profoundly shifted such that the old progressivist rhythm in which time was experienced as a continuous, linear flow, and in which past, present, and future were *experienced* as following (and *argued* over as if they followed) one another in regular, predictable succession, has been interrupted, the familiar articulations among them has come *unhinged*. The coherence of the old expectation of how futures emerge out of the experience of pasts in the present has been irrevocably, irretrievably, broken. It is not, obviously, that past expectations have simply vanished from our imaginations. Fragments of the temporality of "futures past" still persist—in haphazard form, perhaps, with more or less generational attachment, nostalgic fixation—but they no longer add up to a coherent frame of anticipatory time linking temporal experience with plausible temporal expectations.[10] A strange and disorienting conceptual vacancy has opened up and rendered us more or less bereft of a common affirmative language of progressive political futurity. Or, anyway, so I have been arguing.

Certainly, one of the exemplary casualties of the collapse of the structures of modern, progressivist time has been precisely the experience and expectation of postslavery Black futurity as a time of freedom-making. Surely Black experience has been one of the paradigmatic sites for the elaboration of modern temporality, including the temporality of modern emancipationism. Thus the interconnected stories of enslavement, slave emancipation, and postslavery Black liberation have provided vivid instances of the construction of modernist or dialectical futurities. However, I do not believe that this story is quite so seamlessly available in the present as it has been in the past. The conceptual account of the story-form of Black emancipationism has not only diminished in compelling force but also has become more or less incoherent inasmuch as the anticipated futures that organized its salience (whether in the name of decolonization, socialism, or Black power) have collapsed or evaporated or vanished. And it is no longer clear how and with which concepts we can reimagine the horizon of Black freedom, let alone how to activate the organized social and political momentum for change by which to translate the present into a new future.

In a certain sense, what I'm saying here is that we (Blacks, moderns) have come to suffer from what I described in the prologue as a *loss of concepts*. I am suggesting that we have lost the old concept of revolution and the emancipationist narrative that organized the temporality that gave it structure because the background conditions that enlivened and secured the intelligibility of these concepts and narratives have by and large been lost. In my view, it is partly this radical discordance that has lent the idea of the *tragic* an aptness for describing our general predicament. For what the tragic inspires is responsiveness to the experience of a collision of incommensurable intelligibilities, perhaps the collision between the fading old concepts and the incipiently emergent new ones. Indeed, as I have noted, Cora Diamond invites us to consider whether or to what extent the loss of some concepts might be connected to the *gain* of others.[11] In this respect, one way of putting what interests me is whether we can say that, in the space vacated by the loss of the old concept of revolution and the idea of the political associated with it, there has emerged a new and contested moral-political concept of *reparations*.

This experience of the loss of concepts—specifically, the loss of the concepts of Black and socialist revolutions—was precisely what inspired my exploration in *Conscripts of Modernity* of C. L. R. James's great history of the Haitian Revolution, *The Black Jacobins*.[12] In many respects, certainly in a radical Caribbean intellectual tradition, *The Black Jacobins* is a paradigmatic instance of a revolutionary emancipationist and vindicationist narrative.[13] James, as he himself often repeated, was aiming to do for the Haitian Revolution what Jules Michelet did for the French Revolution in the middle of the nineteenth century and what Leon Trotsky did for the Russian Revolution in the early twentieth century: namely, to write a revolutionary history of an epochal revolution. Thus *The Black Jacobins* is not only a history but a *revolutionary* history of the only successful slave revolution in the New World. It is this that makes it such an enduring classic. Obviously, I won't need to repeat in detail here James's famous account of the rise and fall of his beloved hero Toussaint Louverture (for James, the first West Indian political intellectual), but part of what makes it so compelling a dramatic narrative is the way in which its story of the misery and vicious cruelty and humiliation of the slave past is anchored to the progressive—indeed, *epic*—rhythm of the liberationist expectation of a Black, anticolonial, and socialist future *to come*. In fact, the two are conceptually inseparable: the intelligibility of its imagined future *derives* from the emancipationist construction of the past in the present; and the progressivist construction of the slave past is the *guarantee* of the teleological rhythm that brings the revolutionary future into the present. In a formal way, therefore, emancipationist historical narratives like James's in *The Black Jacobins* can make hermeneutic sense only when they are harnessed to a progression of social change and a horizon of futurity in which the suffering of the past (or better, the past as a state of suffering) is redeemed and overcome in the making of the new future. But, alas, one would be hard-pressed now, I am sure, to argue that this self-evidently remains the case in the present—after decolonization, after civil rights, after Black Power, after socialism. We live, in short, among the ruins of these revolutionary "futures past."

And yet, memorably, the seminal genius of *The Black Jacobins* is the way James embedded in its recursive narrative, in the new conjunctures of uncertainty and defeat in which he sought to rethink and revise it, a pronounced if speculative intuition that there may well be something not entirely adequate about the terms of its earlier vindicationist poetics. This is the conceptual space in which he mobilized—and indeed became preoccupied with—the idea of the tragic. Like a number of other sensitive thinkers reorienting and reattuning themselves in the postwar, postrevolutionary, and end-of-empire 1950s and early 1960s—think, variously, across different intellectual-political traditions, of Albert Camus, Sidney Hook, Hannah Arendt, George Steiner, and Raymond Williams—James *turned* to the tragic in search of conceptual resources with which to unsettle dominant teleological forms of history-telling (liberal as well as Marxist) and to complicate the understanding of the relationship between time (historical time, civilizational time), contingency, and human action.[14] Not only in his work on Herman Melville, or the wider work published as *American Civilization*, or *Beyond a Boundary*, but also in the abandoned notes he was assembling for the largely unpublished "Preface to Criticism," it is clear that James was developing a moral-literary-political theorization (if not exactly a *theory*) of tragic sensibility.[15] The value of the idea of the tragic I have been arguing (learning from, if not always directly following, James) is that it offers a strong doubt about teleologies of history in which heroic subjects of radical rational self-determination and committed resolve realize their moral and political destinies, and it does so in part by urging an attunement to the contingencies that can afflict human action in time, and therefore a sensitivity to the constraints of human finitude, the pervasive, ineliminable proximity of conflict and collision and failure, of irreversible catastrophe and death.

In the tragic we are given a picture of human undertakings that almost invariably ends in human misery and human suffering. This is not because misery and suffering are all that human life amounts to but because there is a sobering moral *insight* concerning our limits as well as our excellences to be had from starting off with the recognition that well-intentioned human purposes often have unintended negative consequences, are never invulnerable to chance, and are sometimes undermined by forces (from within or without) over which we have at best limited control.[16] What I did not know to say in *Conscripts of Modernity*, in the conjuncture in which I was seeking to formulate a usable conception of the tragic in reference to James's *The Black Jacobins* (and why this should have been the case is a conceptual-historiographical question in its own right), I can now say: namely, that the idea of the tragic belongs precisely to the wider lexicon and idiom of a *moral* historical sensibility. Admittedly, not all moral histories need, necessarily, to be tragic in narrative or poetic structure, but I suggest that tragic histories are always moral in orientation and implication because a tragic history is concerned with the contingency to which human conduct and human action in time is inescapably vulnerable.[17] Note, however, that my point here is *not* that *The Black Jacobins* can now at last be recognized for what it somehow *really* was all along—namely, moral (as opposed to revolutionary) history. My point, rather, is that in a different conjuncture than the one in which James wrote it (one such as ours, for example) *The Black Jacobins* can be read in a way that underlines a *dimension* of it—its tragic dimension and, more broadly, its *moral* concern with the contingency of human action at its limits, for example—that might hitherto have been obscured or ignored. Indeed, James himself prepares us for this way of reading him. In a wonderfully insightful passage in *Mariners, Renegades, and Castaways: Herman Melville and the World We Live in* (a passage to which I will have reason to return in the next chapter), James writes, "There is always, when reading great masterpieces of the past, a difference in the emphasis of the author and the reader."[18] Here, in a sentence, is the point I am making.

THE PROBLEM-SPACE OF MORAL HISTORY

By moral history I do not mean a history of morality or ethics, though such histories of moral philosophy are not irrelevant to my thinking.[19] Nor do I mean a *moralizing* history, though, again, normative expectations and normative judgments regarding the historical past are not entirely external to my purposes. What I mean by moral history is something more akin to a *genealogy* of the conceptual *location* of moral concern or moral awareness—a history that thinks the past through a conceptual window by means of which a moral domain or dimension is foregrounded. The idea of an intellectual *turn* to the moral might be helpful to consider here. I think it is fair to speak of a contemporary moral turn in the humanities and social sciences, that is, a notable shift or reorientation in *conceptual attention* over the last couple of decades that has brought hitherto muted dimensions of human *being* and *action* and *discourse* into view—not in a passive way but in a *generative* and theoretically consequential one. Where, for example, what was called (almost yesterday, historically) the *linguistic* turn initiated a paradigm revision bringing formerly unaccentuated epistemological questions about the language of representation into view (the whole now familiar problem about "essence," and so on), the moral turn initiates one that, without necessarily cancelling or crossing out the earlier paradigm revision, gives particular focus and concentration to dimensions of human being and action and discourse concerned broadly with what we might call the *ethos of human conduct*.[20] These dimensions encompass such issues as the goods and ends agents pursue; the social imaginary by which these goods and ends are conceived and the standards by which they are ranked; how these goods and ends are defended against rivals; the means by which their realization is sought; and the relation between these means and their varying internal and external conditions. Within this frame, a number of recognizably moral concepts, none of them recently invented, have acquired a new salience and resonance. Among them are responsibility, justice, will, right, wrong, chance, determination, judgment, memory, and pain.

Obviously, I do not mean to suggest that these are features of human affairs that have hitherto been completely ignored—hardly so, and certainly not by moral philosophers, moral psychologists, and anthropologists. I only mean to propose that these moral ideas have acquired a new, urgent, and more widespread prominence, a new conceptual way of organizing knowledge-domains, a new

THE IDEA OF A MORAL AND REPARATORY HISTORY   45

set of prerogatives for setting in motion the very point of any inquiry across a number of disciplines beyond philosophy, including history, political theory, anthropology, and literature.[21] There is a notable sense in which some shaping consideration of the moral—an almost pandemic sense of inexorable moral predicaments—has now become virtually *unavoidable* in contemporary critical thinking.

It is sometimes suggested (sometimes tacitly, sometimes not) that moral history is—or should be—concerned above all with the twentieth century, as though that century was somehow more, or more distinctly, reprehensible than other centuries past.[22] This not so much a historically mistaken view as an *ideological* perspective that is scarcely worth responding to on its own terms—it depends so patently for its attraction and persuasiveness on the unacknowledged privileging of *certain* pasts, or certain ideas about certain pasts, and the disregard or disavowal of others (I return to this privileging in the next chapter).[23] I do think, however, that there is a profound sense in which the genealogical *intelligibility* of the moral as an object-domain of distinct preoccupation *is* a significantly widespread twentieth-century (and, more specifically, a late twentieth-century, post–Cold War) experience. In this regard, we might well ask: What is the *problem-space* of moral history? What is the question to which a moral history purports to offer an answer? What are the distinctive concepts of a moral history? One admittedly shorthand way of trying to characterize the problem-space of moral history (using the temporal-conceptual language I used earlier) is to say that the modern age of universal revolutions (of socialist or Black or national or women's liberations), and even, alas, of good old-fashioned progressive social democracy, has been effectively *displaced* by a new age—namely, an age of global humanitarianism and human rights.[24] In a fundamental sense, humanitarianism and human rights have emerged in the post–Cold War era, in the wake of the seeming resolution of the great antagonism between capitalism and communism, as a new zeitgeist, a new "self-image" for our age (as Alasdair MacIntyre might say), or a "last utopia" (in Samuel Moyn's suggestive phrase).[25] Again, I do not mean to imply that this is a false or false-conscious image, though it is certainly a *motivated* one embodying a certain distribution of empowering, concept-organizing knowledge. I *do* mean to imply, however, that this new social imaginary and rationality is not only pervasive in extent, it is also *generative* in force and impact inasmuch as it positively constitutes the new normative background as well as the new normative horizon in relation to which we are obliged to problematize our dissatisfactions with our world, what we consider wrong with it, and what we might do to address these dissatisfactions to change it for the better.[26]

It is true that there is much that might be doubtful about the discourse and practice of international humanitarianism and human rights, about, say, its inseparable entanglement with liberal individualism and neoliberal globalization, with new doctrines about the responsibility to intervene in the name of protection, with U.S. imperial power, with continued Western cultural hegemony, and so on. But there may well be as much about what this age illuminates as about what it occludes (effective sides of the same conceptual coin, in any case), as much about what it brings into being or makes visible, or anyway *conceivable*, as about what it leaves out or ignores or flattens, that is critically worth attending to—at least on the genealogical principle that we are where we are, and however we got here, within the discursive field of this conjuncture, we shall have to find our way *from* here. To put this another way: escaping or exiting the hegemony of the liberal humanitarian present is not really an option—there is no way out but *through*.

In this respect, moral history need not be simply a mode of conformism to the normative humanitarian self-image of the age; it can be a mode of (immanent) critique. Or so, anyway, Didier Fassin believes and argues with some amount of persuasiveness. Fassin is a protagonist of the moral turn in anthropology and has written an important book, *Humanitarian Reason*, which offers itself precisely as a "moral history of the present" framed in terms of a critical engagement with the social imaginary and language-games of humanitarianism.[27] As Fassin understands it, moral history is the history of humanitarian *reason*—that distinctive form of reason driven by a concern with moral sentiment, especially the sentiments of compassion and sympathy, that draws our attention toward the sufferings and misfortunes of others. Arguably, Fassin has a much more capacious view of the range of moral-historical preoccupation than I have, urging as he does that humanitarianism takes as its object a wide variety of concerns, from quotidian matters such as poverty and homelessness and unemployment to extreme ones such as wars and epidemics and other disasters. Linking values and affect, and hearts and minds, and reasons and feelings, Fassin says that humanitarianism is concerned with situations of grave as well as everyday precariousness. Indeed, *precarity*—the extreme condition of parlous, dire, exigency—is a central term in his moral-historical identification of what is wrong with the present. Notably, unlike many contemporary commentators on the subject, Fassin does not treat humanitarianism as though it were a triumphant point of arrival in a great progressivist history of the modern West.[28] Nor, just as notably, does he take it to be a negative reality to be lamented or condemned or overcome. To Fassin, the rise of humanitarianism is a *social fact*, and whether we like it or not, and however unevenly and unequally it is socially and globally experienced, we all inhabit a conjuncture not merely shaped by the rhetoric and techniques of its rationality but *governed* by them as well. That is, humanitarianism should be thought of as a structure of powers that organize and drive a *governmental* reason.

In an obvious way, Fassin is much influenced by Foucault's genealogical critique, a mode of paradoxical critical thinking—both/and rather than either/or—that, as he puts it, "sits at the crossroads between . . . curiosity and indignation, between the desire to understand and the will to transform."[29] If, as he argues, humanitarian reason is one of the authoritative rationalities shaping the present, the challenge of critique is to fashion a posture that is less prescriptive than descriptive (or perhaps better, *redescriptive*), less an approach to an "object of judgment" than one to an "object of investigation," the objective being to unsettle or dislodge the normative "consensus" that secures its hegemony. And to accomplish the right critical distance necessary for this mode of critique, Fassin argues, the critic should take up a stance on what he calls the "frontiers" between the "inside" and the "outside" of a sphere of inquiry—on the "threshold . . . where one step to either side takes us out into the light or plunges us into the darkness."[30] It is not hard to see why Fassin believes that ethnography has a certain privileged relation to the practice of critique. Working with the balancing act of this stance, he says, he has sought to grasp what humanitarian reason "means and what it hides, to take it neither as the best of all possible governments, nor as an illusion that misleads us."[31]

What has driven the current attention to compassion and sympathy? Curiously, given his Foucauldian proclivity, Fassin does not offer us a deep genealogy of the contemporary turn to moral history. He sketches in quick strokes two "temporalities," as he calls them, that form the historical background to the rise of humanitarian reason. The first temporality tracks the more long-range story of the emergence of the language of moral sentiments in the eighteenth-century Scottish Enlightenment. This is the story of the moral philosophy of such thinkers as Adam Smith, David Hume, and Francis Hutcheson.[32]

Against the disembodied calculative reason of their day, these thinkers sought to give us an idiom of sympathy and passion and virtue that has been a rich source of humanitarian reason. The second temporality tracks the more recent story of the articulation of these moral sentiments with public and international political action at the end of the twentieth century.[33] But what the relationship is between these discontinuous historical conjunctures of concern with moral sentiment remains unclear. To what extent are these the same or different concepts of moral sentiment? How are we to determine this? Is there a *conceptual* history of the present here waiting to be written in more exacting detail?[34] Still, although Fassin seems keen to evade any suggestion of a reductive, *causal* historical narrative, he does want us to recognize a fundamental conceptual *reorganization* of our apprehensible or *describable* world such that an older social-political language-game has been displaced by the rise of a humanitarian order structured around a different set of provocations and preoccupations. Within the new normative regime, he succinctly says: "Inequality is replaced by exclusion, domination is transformed into misfortune, injustice is articulated as suffering, violence is expressed in terms of trauma. While the old vocabulary of social critique has certainly not entirely disappeared, the new lexicon of moral sentiments tends to mask it in a process of semantic sedimentation that has perceptible effects both in public action and in individual practices."[35]

Of course, Fassin does not simply accept this consensual view. Although humanitarian reason responds to what is "intolerable about the state of the contemporary world," and this is to be applauded, the critique he practices aims to pay close attention not only to individual and social suffering but to their material contexts as well. As he says, in an important qualifying passage, "In the face of violence, disaster, and epidemics, and also poverty, insecurity, and misfortune, what is intolerable is not only the presence of the tragic but the inequality in which it is embedded." And inequality obviously is a *moral-political* matter. Therefore, the critique of humanitarian reason ultimately has to encompass not only the suffering and its circumstances but also, however obliquely, the problem of justice. "The suffering of the unemployed man, the refugee, and the disaster victim," Fassin writes, "is not simply the product of misfortune, it is also a manifestation of injustice."[36] And so, intriguingly, despite the hesitations and reservations concerning normative judgment, the critique of humanitarian reason is led, genealogically, precisely in the direction of a counternormative judgment.

And yet I have some doubts about the formulation of the critique Fassin offers, in particular the familiar asymmetrical structure of metropolitan benevolence—the stance of the good Samaritan (pictured on the evocative cover of the book)—that organizes its practice and its self-consciousness. As though the compulsion were unavoidable, humanitarian reason, we are told, is a mode of rendering "them" intelligible to "us," a way of making visible to the West the suffering of others. As Fassin writes, in a somewhat startling phrase, by the "grace of humanitarian reason" these (largely non-European) others become "simply a little more human to us."[37] The disturbing implications of the White sentimental conceit embodied in this conceptual formulation—the benediction of humanitarian reason—becomes more evident in the dramatic account that closes his book, of the terrible discovery in April 1999 of the bodies of two boys in the undercarriage of a Sabina flight from Conakry to Brussels. The boys had evidently died from hyperthermia or suffocation. In his account, Fassin focuses his attention on the poignant letter found in the hand of one of the dead boys, a letter addressed, in the rhetoric of entreaty and supplication, to the magnanimity and generosity of Europe. The letter's language, Fassin says, cannot be reduced simply to its seeming posture of colonial mimicry, the exultant desire for Europe. This is entirely right. But then, how should it be understood? In Fassin's somewhat self-congratulatory view, the letter "touched the heart of Western Europe" precisely because it was framed in the "language of humanitarian reason." And he goes on: "The reason the boys' words affect us so powerfully is . . . because they turn back toward us the image we want to present to the world, and because their death puts our powerlessness to the test."[38] Surely, though, something is profoundly ill-considered about this account (again, with its needy "they" and interpretive "us"), its undoubtedly genuine pathos notwithstanding. Certainly, this is not why the letter affects *me* so deeply. To call these deaths a "tragic event" is (at least on the description offered) to misspeak, not only theoretically but also morally and politically. Note that very little—almost nothing—in Fassin's generous and sophisticated critique of humanitarian reason has much to say about the catastrophic structural history of the colonial past and its long aftermath of which these terrible and inexcusable deaths are but one appalling episode. To his credit, as we have just seen, Fassin recognizes that incidents of human suffering such as these deaths are not merely misfortunes but also injustices. Yet he seems to resolutely release humanitarian reason from the obligation to think critically about what, in the case of these desperate postcolonial boys, corrective justice

50 PART I

might *demand*. It would seem to me that there is a historical structure of domination that shaped the course of action taken by these boys that has to be part of what critique, however immanent, seeks to grasp. But here, perhaps, lies the limit to Fassin's critique of humanitarian reason.

I agree that the challenge of a morally attuned critical inquiry should take the form of a both/and rather than an either/or investigation. This is a form of inquiry that reflexively recognizes (rather than normatively assumes and therefore complacently approves) the historic cognitive rupture and displacement that simultaneously emptied an older language-game of its critical powers and (socialist) political project and installed in its place a language-game with different critical powers and (neoliberal) political project. This is where we are: the conjuncture of the present. However, if these new critical powers of humanitarian moral inquiry allow us to identify, appreciate, and explore dimensions of social suffering and the uncanny endurance of the past in the present, it often appears to do so at the high price of shielding the neoliberal and postcolonial political-economic order from scrutiny and critique. It occludes the persistence of a global disorder of precarity inherited from the old colonial formations. The moral-reparatory challenge, as I will urge in a moment, embodies a critical redescription of the relationship between the moral and the political. As I imagine it, this entails folding a responsiveness to multiple dimensions of social suffering and moral wrong into a radical critique of the broader structures of political and economic order that are at least contributing conditions to the reproduction of domination and injustice.

EVIL AS A PROBLEM OF MORAL HISTORY

In attending to the ethos of human being and human action as part of a moral history, it may not be surprising that there has also been a marked focus on certain *kinds* of human being and human action more than on others—namely, those modes of being and action implicated in the perpetration of *wrongdoing* and the injury and suffering that result from such wrongdoing. Especially notable in this respect, to my mind, is the turn to considerations of *evil* as a distinctive problem that demands close and, indeed, *urgent* attention. Evil has emerged in moral theorizing as a potentially critical concept meant to capture the depth of moral significance of certain kinds of wrongful action and injury in the past and the present. In the contemporary discussions that I am concerned with, and irrespective of the theoretical orientations involved, the concept of evil at stake is imagined as an expressly *secular*—or rather, *post*secular—one. These discussions are secular inasmuch as they are not concerned with the older theological theme focused on whether God can coexist with evil, or how a presumably omniscient, omnipotent, and omnibenevolent God could allow or abide the suffering of innocent people. But they are also postsecular in that they express a certain unease about the calculative reasons of secularity as well. In these discussions, evil concerns the all too human actions of moral agents perpetrated against other moral agents within dimensions of historical time.

In particular, I have in mind here the work of such thinkers (listed more or less at random) as John Kekes, Claudia Card, Laurence Mordekhai Thomas, Todd Calder, Paul Formosa, Raimond Gaita, Luke Russell, Marcus Singer, and Mary Midgely, among those variously concerned to *characterize* the distinctiveness of evil as a wrong; and Richard Bernstein, Susan Neiman, and Peter Dews, among those variously seeking to offer a *philosophic* history of the modern concept of evil.[39] These are by and large thinkers who are very much aware of the potential political abuse of the idea of evil in the sloganeering demonization of enemies, and the consequent arguments offered against its conceptual relevance by "evil-skeptics," such as Phillip Cole, for example. Nevertheless they persist in urging that there is something potentially discerning and clarifying rather than obscuring and mystifying to be made of the idea of evil.[40] In the next chapter I discuss some of what the contemporary discussion owes to Immanuel Kant's late and elusive ideas about evil (his supposed break with the earlier "privation" theory and articulation of a positive "radical evil" as a natural and ineradicable propensity of the human will), and especially what it owes to Hannah Arendt's equally elusive appropriation and translation of these ideas in relation to a specific twentieth-century historical event that has come to stand for moral evil as such. Here, though, I only want to sketch broadly some of the justification for my drafting the concept of evil into a moral history—and into a moral history of New World slavery in particular.

The discerning and clarifying value of the concept of evil, it seems to me, is that it allows us to discriminate among kinds of wrongful action and kinds of wrongful harm. As several thinkers urge, evil is more than ordinary wrongdoing, it is not mere misconduct, or mistreatment, or vice—it is not just action that is very, very bad.[41] Not all wrongs are evils. Rather, the concept of evil is meant to pick out qualitatively extreme conduct—that is, conduct that is especially damaging and lethal and violating and pernicious inasmuch as it strikes at some core of our basic sense of human well-being and human flourishing. As Marcus Singer says of evil, in an often-quoted remark, it is the worst term of moral opprobrium or condemnation that can be applied to a human being.[42] Thus evil crosses a moral line, if not an always stable or self-evident one. Evil, moreover, presupposes knowledge on the part of the evildoer. It is action that is known to grievously and gratuitously harm the victim, whether in physical or nonphysical ways, or in material or spiritual ways. And so, whether or not it is specifically motivated to cause the detrimental injury it causes, whether or not there is a discernible intention to violate, whether or not pleasure is derived from the suffering caused, whether or not the action is performed because it causes the harm it causes, it is never action performed innocently or in ignorance. Evil, therefore, is always action that results in foreseeable and, consequently, preventable harm. For theorists of evil, then, evil action is morally *inexcusable* action. It is unwarrantable, unjustifiable on any claim to any reason. Most important in this respect, not only does evil action encompass what is directly inflicted by evildoers, but it also encompasses those actions (whether of commission or omission) that sustain or perpetuate or otherwise *tolerate* evil.

Of course, the concept of evil is not meant only to pick out what is done to others by perpetrators. For many theorists, evil also refers to the quality of the harm *suffered* by the victims of evil actions. For theorists such as Claudia Card, John Kekes, and Paul Formosa, evil does more than simply harm, callously and cruelly. Evil produces *unbearable* or *intolerable* harm to those upon whom it is inflicted—sometimes in the sense that it destroys *physical* life itself (in various kinds of killing), or *physical capacity* (in various kinds of maiming or mutilation), and sometimes in the sense that it destroys *moral* life (in humiliations and affronts and other such moral injuries, or in the distortion of the fabric of those moral *relations* that make individual and social life in a community of norms viable, valuable, in short, valid).[43] For victims, evil can be "life-ending" or "life-wrecking," in Formosa's terms—and, as we know, these are not necessarily cleanly separable.[44] The point about the quality of the harms of evil, then, is that they are, by definition, *devastating* inasmuch as they lay waste to central features of what it means to be a human being or to live a fully functioning human life.

Perhaps understandably, much of the recent discussion of evil has focused on the deeds and experiences of individuals. This certainly interests me as well, as will be seen in a later chapter. However, I am especially concerned here with large-scale, systematic wrongs—*large-scale* in the sense that they involve significant numbers of people, and in particular, significant numbers of victims; and *systematic* in the sense that these wrongs are deliberately organized into a program or a regime or an institution. These kinds of wrongs are *atrocities*. With Card, I take atrocities to be especially illuminating of evils. Clearly, although not all evils take place at the scale of atrocities, indubitably all atrocities should be understood as evils. They knowingly involve the organized perpetration of inexcusable and unbearable harms on numbers of relatively indefensible people. As I suggest in more detail later in this book, not all atrocities are of the same sort, materially or ideologically. They don't all involve the same practice of systematic wrong, the same harms, the same evil—which emphatically, however, is *not* to say that there is something to be gained by thinking of some atrocities as worse than others, or that atrocities can or should be compared on a scale of relative harm. Yet the differences matter for how we think about the varied *powers* and *effects* of evil. Some atrocities, evidently, are more *event*-like, such as the Holocaust, for example, involving the administration of a heinous political policy of mass murder over a concentrated period of time. Other atrocities are *institutionalized*, in the sense that they become historically and structurally integrated into the transgenerational reproduction of a social and economic form with long-term local as well as global implications—New World slavery, for example. The goal of such institutionalized evils may not be physical death per se, the deliberate, systematic elimination of people or some whole category of people. These evils may be motivated instead by the creation of such constrained or distorted conditions of subjugated social life as might facilitate the production of rapid wealth and splendor for the perpetrators and their beneficiaries. New World slavery was an institutionalized evil of this sort. In the relentless pursuit of economic gain, this institutionalized evil involved not only the systematic exercise of the organized means of inflicting ruinous harm on the individual lives of the enslaved, each in the unrepeatable singularity of their particular biographical lifetime, but also—and perhaps more devastating still, from the perspective of the successive and overlapping generations that suffered the evil—the distortion of the social, familial, political, economic, and cultural conditions of their individual and collective lives as a whole.

To be sure, recent writers on evil, such as those to whom I have referred, are not necessarily all in a conversation with each other, nor do their views necessarily add up to a concerted vision, even less a comprehensive *theory*, of the causes or

54 PART I

character of evil. However, they do, I think, together *point* in the direction of a broad conjuncture of intersecting preoccupations, enough, perhaps, to signal at least the outline of the contemporary problem-space of evil. How should we think of this problem-space? How should we relate the emergence of this conceptual discussion of evil to the wider moral turn in the humanities and social sciences? What is the question (or more likely, the inchoate anxiety or incipient worry) in the present to which the problem of evil appears to be at least the domain of an answer? I have already indicated the exhaustion of the great secular-modernist narratives of social and economic and political progress, principally Marxism and liberalism, those world-historical nineteenth- and twentieth-century political antagonists. Whatever their considerable ideological differences, what these rival enlightenment accounts had in common was of course their optimistic self-confidence in the powers of reason (the powers, above all, of reasons of state) to identify the sources of our social discontent and to offer the rational basis of a path beyond it. They shared a common *humanism*, in the suggestive sense of that term used by David Cooper in *The Measure of Things*: that is, they assumed (and indeed, valorized) a largely socially constructed world, a world that, insofar as it was assembled by the conscious activity of human agency was rationally accessible and describable and calculable, and therefore rationally revisable through fresh interventions of conscious redescription and reforming mastery.[45] To this extent, both Marxism and liberalism disputed the possibility of *mystery*, of what might resist—or else exceed—transparently available description or moral-political control. In these discourses, the future was a luminous, assured, and eminently achievable prospect; the past a time of backwardness to be gladly and rapidly left behind. In contrast to the improving ethos of this orientation, whatever it is that is wrong with our present world (not least our political and economic and environmental worlds) it is a world that seems to confound, or at least not conform to, the rational intelligibilities embodied in liberalism and Marxism. An intractable element of recalcitrance and opacity and unpredictability attaches to our world. So it is not surprising that in our postprogressive world we are haunted by catastrophe and by enigma and by an anticipation not of possibility but of *doom*. The evident exhaustion of these optimistic narratives of rational progress has left us with a less transparent world, a contracting, nervous, and less readily comprehensible world.

In a profound sense, our confidence in our human rational capacity to understand, much less fix, our world has substantially diminished, more or less vanished. With this moral and conceptual *darkening* of our lifeworld, a kind of *void* has opened, a generalized and barely nameable precarity (at once material and spiritual) that has brought into sharp relief the human capacity for perversion and cruelty, barbarism and degradation, and that throws into question all our moral assumptions about judgment, responsibility, culpability, and compassion—indeed, all our moral assumptions about human life itself.[46] It is in this yawning void, I believe, that an idea of evil has acquired dense and critical force, as a way of evoking a sense of the entrenched, maybe ineradicable nontransparency of human action, and an intuition about our human capacity to inflict unbearable suffering and perpetrate seemingly gratuitous violent harms on each other.[47]

One important story that has reemerged in the context of the new moral age of human rights is that of antislavery abolitionism as an inaugural episode in the development of humanitarianism, or at least of humanitarian sensibility. In a fascinating way, from their embattled role in the historiography of slave emancipation, the late eighteenth- and nineteenth-century social movements organized against the slave trade and slavery itself, in Britain, France, and the United States principally, are now widely seen as among the pivotal original sources of the development of the new empathetic receptivity to the idea of a universal humanity.[48] The antislavery movement, says Michael Barnett, in his influential history of humanitarianism, was "an historic breaching of the established categories of humanity" and an eloquent anticipation of the coming age of human rights.[49] The so-called great moral awakening that was animated by Romantic and evangelical Christian ideas about suffering and compassion helped, it is argued, to stimulate the growth of an enlarged capacity to see all human beings—including Africans and their New World enslaved descendants—as worthy children of God, as endowed with reason (however limited), and as bearers of natural rights. Paternalism has not been a stranger to humanitarian interest in the welfare of the enslaved. Even savages, it turned out, could be saved—sometimes from themselves. The problem about slavery, for these "pioneers of humanitarian action," however, was not always about the enslavement of Africans as such, the concrete reality of their experience of moral and physical harms, but about the violating (often sexual, sometimes murderous, always odious) brutishness to

56   PART I

which the slaveholders themselves were inclined.[50] Abolitionism proved to be
as much about the moral progress of the enslavers as about the salvation of
the enslaved.

In this uplifting narrative of the prehistory of contemporary humanitarianism, the familiar names are typically White men such as James Ramsey, Thomas
Clarkson, and Granville Sharp, all of them noteworthy critics of the slave trade
and to a degree of slavery itself. Sometimes, of course, for good measure, also
included in the familiar story is Olaudah Equiano, author of *The Interesting
Narrative of the Life of Olaudah Equiano, or Gustavus Vassa, the African*, first published in 1789. Undoubtedly, Equiano was one of the most singular Black cosmopolitans in eighteenth-century England.[51] But one of the often-neglected
Black protagonists in the rising tide of late eighteenth-century abolitionism was
another, more obscure, figure, the African Quobna Ottobah Cugoano, otherwise
known as James Stewart. Perhaps fortuitously, Cugoano had arrived in England
in late 1772, in the wake of the *James Somerset* case decided in June that year,
and which, though notoriously ambiguous in the wording (and perhaps spirit) of
the ruling by Lord Chief Justice Mansfield, was widely taken to authoritatively
refuse legal sanction to slavery in England (I return to this theme in chapter 5).[52]
By contrast with his notable friend Equiano, Cugoano appears to have been less
committed to the assimilative ethos of the Black British gentleman and more
openly critical of the prevailing racial and commercial status quo. His remarkable book, *Thoughts and Sentiments on the Evil and Wicked Traffic of the Slavery and
Commerce of the Human Species*, first published in 1787, seems to have barely circulated and been largely ignored by contemporary reviewers.[53] But this is perhaps
understandable because, by contrast with Equiano, Cugoano is scarcely concerned
with the solicitous and humanizing abolitionist device of autobiography. In fact,
Cugoano offers but the briefest account of his capture in Africa, trans-shipment
across the Middle Passage, enslavement in Grenada, and conversion and freedom in England. *Thoughts and Sentiments*, rather, is a moral-political treatise,
framed in the familiar tropes and strategies of eighteenth-century abolitionism—
characterized by a Christian theory of natural rights, a marked comparative historical sensibility, a commitment to reason and moral sentiment, and a respect
for property—but more uncompromisingly radical inasmuch as it was aimed at
the *systemic* features of slavery's evil, embodying seamlessly the traffic in Africans,
their enslavement in the colonies, and the unjust commercial enrichment of the
imperial metropole.[54] This comprehensive critique set Cugoano apart from all

THE IDEA OF A MORAL AND REPARATORY H STORY   57

other abolitionists. Where the abolitionist norm in the 1780s and 1790s was to attack the slave trade but not colonial enslavement, Cugoano condemned the hypocrisy of a supposed rational, Christian, and liberal society engaging in, and profiting from, the kidnapping, sale, and enslavement of Africans.[55] It would be needless, he says cogently and polemically, "to arrange an history of all the base treatment which the African Slaves are subjected to, in order to shew the exceeding wickedness and evil of that insidious traffic, as the whole may easily appear in every part, and at every view, to be wholly and totally inimical to every idea of justice, equity, reason and humanity."[56] But, of course, this is precisely the moral critique he offers, folded into the affirmation of the humanity of his African brethren. Does Cugoano have an insight here into the late eighteenth-century philosophical debate about the human propensity to evil, into the transgression of the moral law that White enlightened Europeans were willing to perpetrate against fellow human beings for the sake of commercial self-interest and self-love? Kant might well have benefited from reading Cugoano's *Thoughts and Sentiments*.

So, in an intriguing and still inchoate sense, the problem about New World slavery can be thought of as part of the *unconscious*, so to speak, of the contemporary moral turn. At any rate, this is what is suggested by Steven Mintz in the introduction to his coedited volume, significantly titled *The Problem of Evil*, whose essays deal largely with aspects of slavery and race in the United States. In this highly unusual and welcome collection, Mintz rightly insists on seeing slavery as at the "core," as he put it, "of any thorough understanding of modernity." What he means by this is that slavery was central not only to the making of modern capitalism (a familiar if controversial story linked to Eric Williams's great book, *Capitalism and Slavery*, to which I return in chapter 5) but also to the making of distinctly modern moral conceptions and attitudes and sensibilities, not least conceptions and attitudes and sensibilities concerned with (racial) identity and liberty and equality. Mintz is committed to the idea of a *moral* history (to him, part of a larger history of ideas or intellectual history), and for him moral history is intimately tied to the idea of a postsecular conception of historical *evil*. He is aware of the new, post-9/11 "pervasiveness of a language of evil in contemporary culture" and obviously believes that this is to be not merely lamented or dismissed but learned from and put to use in some engaged conceptual-historical fashion.[57] One key ambition of a moral history oriented around evil, Mintz argues, must be to understand the varied material and discursive conditions that serve to "misshape societies and allow collective evils to

58 PART I

develop, take root, and flourish." And in the context of the United States, he maintains, it is, above all, slavery that makes a demand on an evil-centered moral history. For slavery, Mintz says, "is a historical evil that the United States has never properly acknowledged or atoned for."[58] Clearly enormously influenced by the example of David Brion Davis's early preoccupation with what he called the problem of the changing "moral perception" of the "social evil" of slavery, Mintz urges a direction of moral-historical inquiry that explores "the evolution of moral sensibilities and the development of ideals of freedom and equality; questions of complicity and moral responsibility; slavery's legacies and societies' historical debts; and issues of meaning, including African Americans' shifting and contested memory of enslavement."[59] Moral history incites us to rehistoricize New World slavery as a problem of evil in precisely this way.

REPARATORY HISTORY AS GENEALOGICAL CRITIQUE

The form of moral history that especially concerns me in this book is *reparatory* history. In my view, reparatory history is, necessarily, moral (or moral-political) history, though arguably not all moral history is reparatory in orientation. Specifically, I take reparatory history to be that *dimension* of moral history concerned with past evils—in particular, past atrocities like New World slavery—that remain unrepaired in the present. On this view, a reparatory history is a critical history of the present of such evil pasts, constructed in such a way as to problematize and illuminate what the present *owes* morally and politically to that unrepaired past. A reparatory history, therefore, is concerned with the political repair of moral *debt*.[60]

In this book, I mobilize reparatory history as a mode of genealogical critique that aims to rethink the language-game of Black critical intervention. As such, reparatory history seeks to rehistoricize the problem of slavery for a Black present that can no longer straightforwardly draw its inspiration from the old narrative of emancipation. Reparatory history reflectively affirms the effective displacement of earlier modes of Black critique, even as it recognizes the ways in which fragments of the language-games of these older critical-historical strategies more or less persist. In a sense, reparatory history inhabits a conjuncture of failure of the earlier liberationist ideals and of the rhythms of temporality they have depended upon. But a reparatory history, as I commend it, does not seek merely to reoccupy the old conjuncture and reactivate the great modernist narrative of Black liberation. Nor, however, does a reparatory history as genealogical critique simply adapt itself to the normative self-image of neoliberal human rights and racial reconciliation. The reparatory historical reason that seems to me worth thinking *with* and thinking *through* is one that aims to rebuild a practice of Black critique capacious enough to hold onto the recognition that the repair of Black pasts will in part depend on the reorganization of the political-economic-moral conditions of Black futurity.

As I think of them, reparatory histories are distinct inasmuch as they register the generative trace of past atrocity that is not, in fact, past, but that *haunts* the present. I obviously do not mean to suggest that there are some histories in respect of which the past is safely and securely in the past, over and done with, severed from all connection to the present. There are likely no such pasts. I mean, rather, to point to what are evil or *egregious* histories in which the material and moral psychological legacies of past atrocity are especially, because rancorously, *palpable*. These are pasts that are collectively and individually, publicly and personally, unresolved and unreconciled—perhaps, stubbornly unresolvable and irreconcilable—in the present. And here, again, I am referring not merely to histories shaped (as all histories in some sense presumably are) by disagreement, conflict, and struggle but also to histories of the present pervasively, perhaps permanently, unsettled by a dark and ceaselessly troubled past that lingers, that lives on, in an encumbering and burdensomely revenant-like way, in the present. These are pasts, as we might say, with *afterlives* (often repressed and therefore unconscious ones), pasts that continue to weigh, like Marx's dead generations of the unappeased, on the collective and individual psyches of the living.[61] The pasts of New World slavery, I argue, are pasts like this. In my view, the special value of the now much-over-used idea of "haunting" pasts is that it helps to attune us to the poignant, sometimes intangible senses in which an appalling or unspeakable or indescribable wrong has been committed in the past and left, in its wake, a wound that will not heal, a suppurating and insupportable injury to spirit as much as body that continues to rankle—with anguished indignation, with humiliated resentment—and that, inchoately perhaps, but relentlessly even so, afflicts and torments the present.[62] The pasts of New World slavery are pasts like this.

Further, and perhaps crucially, reparatory history points not only to pasts that have not been resolved or reconciled but also to pasts that are positively *disavowed*

60 PART I

as pasts requiring resolution or reconciliation by those who either perpetrated the historical wrong or who are its contemporary heirs and beneficiaries.[63] These disowned pasts are pasts for which no *responsibility* is acknowledged or accepted, in which innocence is claimed or assumed, and for which, therefore, there has been no public (indeed, sometimes no private) accounting or *reckoning*. The history of New World slavery, I believe, presents us with one such unresolved and unrepaired and disavowed past whose disturbed and disconsolate afterlives constitute our racial present.

Consequently, a reparatory historical rationality depends on a sense of temporality that is neither simply linear nor strictly successive—that is, not descriptively progressive or prescriptively progressivist. It does not presuppose the normative narrative of a steadily rising curve from wrong to right; it does not presuppose the internal teleologic of a story of moral improvement. Therefore, a reparatory historical reason does not take it for granted that all historical wrongs are such as can be repaired. In my view, a reparatory historical reason is not *compensatory*; it need offer no balm of *restitution*. It does not aim to constitute for itself a consoling rhythm of futurity that redeems the past. To the contrary what such a sense of reparatory history tries to do is to attune itself to the discomfiting thought that some loss or damage or injury or failure can, alas, be permanent—that is, irreparable—in the appalling sense meant by George Steiner when he observed, acutely, that "Oedipus does not get his eyes back."[64] I believe that it is simply realism to recognize that not all evil pasts can give rise to happy futures, that not all ruptured pasts can be put back together again.[65] To my mind, therefore, the sensibility of a moral and reparatory history of the sort that I commend is both catastrophic and tragic. It is catastrophic in the sense that it registers a founding social rupture and devastation that precludes the return to a former way of life. In the historiography of New World slavery the Middle Passage is the name of that founding rupture that would precipitate in turn a successive avalanche of catastrophes that constitute the ground of what is called the Black diaspora. And moral and reparatory history is tragic inasmuch as it aims to be responsive to the fact that, once set in motion, some human actions are, quite simply, irreversible, the consequences unstoppable by remedial intervention. As I have already suggested, part of what is distinctive about New World slavery as a historical atrocity is that it was *not* an aberrant event in the course of a seeming historical norm but a *structure* of brutally coercive social relations embedded (constitutively, some would say, inaugurally) in the engine of a globalizing and modernizing social and economic force, namely, historical capitalism. Consequently, the harms of New World slavery are incalculable, they do not amount to a discrete assortment of bad things (stolen property and so forth) for which compensation or restitution can be rationally calculated or represented. The debt to Africans and African-descended peoples is a generalized debt in the ledger of the modern world itself.

As I think of it, reparatory history embodies this paradox: it is a history of unrepaired injustice that calls out for just repair (material as much as spiritual); but it includes the idea that some pasts are in fact irreparable, the idea that the evil wrong that produced them in the first place was such that not only can it *not* be undone (because the tape of time cannot be unwound or rewound) but also it cannot—or cannot any longer—be repaired. It includes the idea that where some evils are concerned, we may not even be able to articulate fully what such repair might or should look like or entail. Which is not to say, I wish to underline, that we ought not to commit ourselves to rethinking, reparatively, the moral history of what is irreparable. To the contrary: paradoxically, moral wrongs demand moral and political response *even when they cannot be repaired*. In my view, New World slavery is one such wrong that, while irreparable, demands a moral and reparatory response.

———◆———

There is now a good deal written in favor (in principle, anyway) of an idea of reparation for past atrocities such as the settler colonial appropriation of Native lands or the enslavement of transplanted Africans on New World plantations, and not least by White liberal or mainstream political, legal, and philosophical thinkers. I am not going to rehearse the full scope of this work here. Suffice it to say that most of this work quickly enough arrives at a tacit, largely unexamined, and seemingly immovable limit—a limit defined, in effect, by liberalism and capitalism, by the power structures of the historically given world. Rarely framed in this way explicitly—that is, as a forthright ideological embrace of liberalism and capitalism (the global triumph of liberal capitalism makes this unnecessary)—this reparatory thinking is nevertheless typically offered as a progressive, forward-looking, and reconciliationist orientation. Change is necessary, undoubtedly, even serious change, but it will have to be change within suitably constrained boundaries. In this work, then, the description of the now

62   PART I

acknowledged wrong of the past atrocity and of the recognized obligation to repair that wrong are offered within a framework that aims above all to preserve the regimes of property and privilege that sustain a status quo brought into being in the first place by the historical atrocity. Let us briefly look at two contrasting-yet-converging examples of White philosophers who have thought conscientiously about reparation: Jeremy Waldron and Janna Thompson.

Jeremy Waldron is a liberal philosopher well known for his work on law and property and who, perhaps not irrelevantly, has a personal connection to the former British colony of New Zealand. In this geopolitical context, some of these questions about repair of historical wrongs have taken on an especially contested political character in relation to Maori claims for reparation in respect of the settler-colonial expropriation of their ancestral lands. Against this background, Waldron has written at least two major interconnected essays on the topic of reparation, arguing in both instances that whereas in principle the commission of wrong should oblige acceptance of the responsibility to repair, some historical injustices *can* and *should* be understood to have *faded* in terms of their significance for—and claims on—the present. I want to take up the formulation of this idea in the second of these essays—namely, "Redressing Historic Injustice," published in 2002. This essay is especially interesting for my purposes here because although its theme is roughly the same as his earlier essay, "Superseding Historic Injustice," published a decade before, "Redressing Historic Injustice" has the added dimension of being explicitly framed by a Kantian commitment to Enlightenment cosmopolitan rights.[66] This is its presumed horizon, the vector of Waldron's overall futural concerns. The position he takes is that demands for rectification should always be balanced against the normative privilege of the ideal of a cosmopolitan futurity to which we should all be morally bound.

Waldron takes aim specifically at historical injustice in the colonial past. On his view, whatever histories of violence and expropriation led in the first place to those unjust pasts, they are now over and done with. For better or for worse, he says, having been thrown together in that unfortunate historical way, this is who "we" are now: interdependent neighbors in a global community. It is not surprising then that "Redressing Historic Injustice" is driven by a barely concealed irritation with those—the "reparationists," as he somewhat dismissively calls them—who feel that the past is not, in fact, in the past, that its wounding wrongs continue to psychologically haunt and structurally disfigure the present, and who reiterate that indeed something continues to be owed in respect of the

THE IDEA OF A MORAL AND REPARATORY HISTORY   63

redress of the original and persisting wrongs. Waldron's writings on the challenge of reparatory justice illuminate one way in which an informed and prominently enlightened liberalism seeks to both affirm the legitimacy of claims to repair *and* simultaneously evade owning up to past injustice, to appear tough-mindedly fair and at the same time to actively sidestep the responsibility to rectify past wrong. And in so doing, it fastidiously shields itself from the taint of implication and therefore from any moral and political obligation to alter the basic outline of the inherited status quo. Waldron does so by way of an appeal to a *reconciliatory* future. "The reparationist enterprise fails," he says, "to take proper account of the fact that the people, entities, and circumstances in relation to which justice must be done have changed radically" from what they were when the injustice was perpetrated and instituted. We cannot dwell on this past, Waldron insists. Circumstances change after all, and present people are not who past people were. "We must come to terms with each other here and now, irrespective of how we all got here"—for "here we all are."[67] This is why, he maintains, if there is to be any reparatory justice at all, what is required is a future-oriented and not a past-oriented formulation of the problem.

But doesn't Waldron's account merely overlook deeper issues? Suppose how you got here is part of the same historical structure that keeps others in their subordinate and exploited position; suppose, in other words, your advantages are systemically and not contingently or randomly connected to the historically created disadvantages of others. What then? Is the history of the colonial past unconnected to the powers that organize the relative destitution of the former colonies and the relative prosperity of the former colonial states, or the relative dispossession and impoverishment of the descendants of the original inhabitants and the relative enrichment of the settlers and their descendants? Moreover, shouldn't we be asking *who* should feel obliged to come to terms with *whom?* Who is indebted to whom? What should compel the disadvantaged to come to terms with the advantaged, especially if there is a perceived connection between the unjust gains of the one and the wrongful losses of the other? And who in any case decides the conditions of such "coming to terms"? Is it the beneficiaries, as the drift of Waldron's account implies?

Part of what is deeply troubling about such forward-looking cosmopolitan arguments as Waldron's is that they appear to depend on the assumption, sometimes (as here) aggressively and defensively articulated, that the "settled expectations" of the beneficiaries of historical injustice ought not to be tampered

64 PART I

with or encroached upon, or in any way diminished, in the interest of a conception of justice that embodies addressing the unjust sources of this enrichment and imagining a mode of redistribution that goes some way to rectifying the historical outrage. To the contrary, for Waldron justice is about ensuring that the beneficiaries get to keep what they have, and more than this (as though to add insult to the injury), depends on the requirement that it is the responsibility of the descendants of the dispossessed to give up their resentments and demands and accept that the time for their reparation has passed. For Waldron, what really counts is not the scope of the injury of the violated or the expropriated or the subjugated, or the justification of their demands, but the extent to which the status quo of the propertied should remain undisturbed, unimpeded. The settled present, in short, ought at all costs to be safeguarded against the grievances from the past, even by means of doubtful arguments. Indeed, it is especially notable that toward the end of Waldron's essay we sense his mild (though unapologetic) discomfort as he becomes only too aware that his defense of the status quo may seem an outright compromise with injustice enacted by sophistical means, the exercise, as he tellingly puts it himself, of "an arcane and calculative casuistry."[68]

In contrast to Jeremy Waldron's Kantian cosmopolitanism, Janna Thompson is a philosopher with connections to settler Australia who offers an approach to reparations informed by more reflective and more communitarian ideals. Importantly, and again in contrast to Waldron's liberal solipsism, Thompson demonstrates a willingness to dialogue (however narrowly) with the work of Black critics on reparatory justice, such as Randall Robinson and Bernard Boxill.[69] Notably, Thompson's orientation is less defensively conservative than Waldron's. Indeed, she is concerned to give a robust philosophical shape to reparative claims against historical injustice, not least to African American claims to redress for slavery. I have considered Thompson's principal work on reparations, *Taking Responsibility for the Past*, in some detail elsewhere and do not intend to reprise that argument here.[70] What especially interests me now is Thompson's commitment to a strong conception of historical obligations. The fact of historical injustice, she holds, gives rise to rights of repair, on the one hand, and an obligation to make amends, on the other. Where wrong has been committed, redress is due—redress that includes the acknowledgment of the wrongdoing and an apology for its commission. In line with Boxill, for example, Thompson takes seriously the idea that acknowledgment is necessary to address the *disrespect* the commission of the wrong implies.[71] And in line with Rodney Roberts, she affirms that there

THE IDEA OF A MORAL AND REPARATORY HISTORY   65

is no legitimate statute of limitations on historical injustice.[72] Past wrongdoing does not fade; it cannot be superseded by present circumstances, as Waldron insists it can be. With Margaret Walker and J. Angelo Corlett, Thompson argues cogently that unrectified wrong remains wrong still. Moreover, such wrong does not simply remain latent when unrepaired; the unrepair of a wrong is itself a wrong for which repair is due.[73]

And yet, for Thompson too, repair, though due, is not immune to the contingency of circumstances. The obligation to repair past wrong is historical in a distinctive sense, she argues, because those who are responsible for making good in the present (keeping the promise, paying the debt, honoring the contract, repairing the harm) are not necessarily the same as those who committed the wrong in the past, but rather are their descendants or successors. Indeed, she points out, it is this gap between the identity of the victims of the wrong and the claimants of the redress that often renders reparation for historical injustice especially fraught. In a sense, Thompson's work on obligation is directed at bridging this gap. Philosophical arguments about historical obligation, she maintains, typically work through assumptions about "historical title" (assumptions about the privilege of historically acquired rights of property or possession that can be passed on to people of succeeding generations) and consequently have nothing helpful to say about reparative responsibilities that stem also from injustices such as murder or torture or enslavement or denigration—violations, as Thompson says, while less tangible or computational, may in fact loom larger in the minds and memories of victims and their descendants.[74] Clearly, Thompson has in mind wrongs committed as a consequence of atrocities such as slavery. In any case, for her, arguments from historical title tend to look only toward the restitution of what is owed; they are "past-oriented" inasmuch as they seek the restoration of the status quo ante. As opposed to this, Thompson is committed to a model of historical obligation that looks to the future; although not unconcerned with the rightful return of ill-gotten possessions, this model is more interested in bringing about reconciliation of the conflict-riven communities.[75]

Thompson's idea of the historicity of historical obligation rests on an intriguing moral-sociological argument about societies or nations—namely, that they constitute what she calls "intergenerational communities." For her, an intergenerational community is one whose institutions and moral relationships persist over time and through a succession of generations, and that depends for its moral and political integrity on its members accepting transgenerational obligations and honoring transgenerational entitlements.[76] On this account, members of intergenerational communities make moral demands on their successors and think that such successors ought to honor these commitments. The guiding meta-ethical principle here is that "like cases should be treated alike"—in other words, those who impose duties on others must be prepared to accept relevantly similar duties.[77] Consequently, by imposing obligations on their successors, members of intergenerational communities acquire obligations of their own to fulfill similar responsibilities with respect to the commitments and relationships of their predecessors. The idea of obligations connected to intergenerational communities, Thompson argues, although "backward-looking" in its insistence that reparation is owed for past injustice, is more importantly "forward-looking" inasmuch as it is predicated on our moral relations with our successors, our moral implication in their future. And this gives her further reason for accepting a "reconciliatory" model of reparation, one that seeks less to repair the past than to secure an agreeable future.[78]

This restorative path is the real push of Thompson's argument. And on the forward-looking account she commends, reparatory entitlements are only contingent ones, that is, entitlements "all things being equal." This is not because they fade in significance but because rival obligations can come into conflict with each other, and this is especially difficult to avoid when obligations are historical. She writes, "Accepting an obligation to return land stolen by our predecessors forces us to make a decision about how we treat the entitlements of those who are now in possession (if these entitlements exist). Fulfilling reparative obligations may clash with a duty to make our society more equitable for all citizens."[79] This dilemma is in part why Thompson thinks that reparations should, in the end, be embedded in a future-oriented reconciliatory approach to historical injustice: "By insisting that reparation is owed for past injustices, this defense of historical obligation is backward-looking. But the justification contains forward-looking considerations. The existence of historical obligations is predicated on our moral relations to our successors. This way of thinking about historical obligations . . . affects how we judge particular demands for reparations, and it provides a reason for accepting the 'reconciliatory' approach to reparative justice."[80] But, again, as in the case of Waldron, the troubling questions remain: Who decides how to rank or balance the inevitably competing social claims? What powers of property and privilege, for example, shape which obligations are taken to be paramount or to have precedence over others? Thompson's sociology lacks a realistic conception of structures of power such as might give us insight into the systemic ways in which advantage and disadvantage, and inclusion and exclusion, are established, secured, and reproduced.

So if it is true that Waldron is more complacently or explicitly complicit with the status quo than Thompson, it is also true that neither offers any real challenge to the basic historical structures of property and privilege and power that underlie the liberal capitalist polity built on injustice and wrong. They have at best mild internal disagreements within the mainstream framework of liberalism. For Waldron, expropriated and violently displaced Indigenous peoples have no compelling rights of reparation that a Kantian cosmopolitan like himself need (any longer) answer to; and for Thompson, though in a measure more receptive to reparatory demands, such rights of repair as those Blacks may have in principle are entirely contingent (or at least, in the last saving instance, contingent) on the countermanding qualifying principle of "all things being equal." Both leave untroubled the historically entrenched arrangements of ill-gotten advantage and unjust enrichment produced by the historical atrocity in the first place. In both instances, the liberal project aims to leave intact the basic structures of the past in the present.

***

Arguably, however, whereas this response might well suit, or at least not unduly inconvenience, the principal beneficiaries of such advantage and enrichment, for those who have been historically victimized by the violating and expropriating powers of the liberal capitalist polity, it is woefully, even insultingly, denigratingly inadequate. Perhaps a more promising direction is staked out by the intervention activated by the Jamaican philosopher Charles Mills. To my mind, what Mills offered, at least from the publication of *The Racial Contract* in 1997, was a more searching reflective account of liberalism's fundamental (as opposed to merely random, accidental, or superficial) implication in the commission of profound and lasting historical atrocities—evils, I would call them (genocide, colonial land appropriation, enslavement, and so on)—and a richer more consequential account of what may be required to conceptualize a robust and morally appropriate direction of repair.[81] At least as I understand it, Mills's overall (and alas unfinished) project was to sketch a genealogical critique of liberalism in Marxism's wake that could have the potential of yielding a forceful critical

68 PART I

moral-political theorization of race, personhood, knowledge, and power.[82] If what he was after was not exactly a postliberalism in the manner of John Gray or a post-Marxism such as Ernesto Laclau and Chantal Mouffe pursued, it was perhaps a kind of post-Marxist liberalism that aimed to capture what he saw as the durable virtues of each.[83] A former (and by his own admission, a quite orthodox) Marxist himself, Mills later readily acknowledged Marxism's generally impoverished appreciation of political moralities and, more specifically, its seemingly chronic inability to recognize (much less adequately conceptualize) the political moralities of race—racial formations, both subjective and material—as anything more than epiphenomenal and derivative. But unlike many, Mills's work does not thereby consider Marxism as rendered wholly irrelevant to contemporary critical thinking. What it principally aims to retain from Marxism is the centrality of power in the form of systems and structures and regimes, as well as the *social* ontologies (of historically constituted second nature) that such social forms of power construct and shelter. Consequently, what we see in Mills's intervention is both a strong interdisciplinary social theory at the center of his philosophic critique of race *and* a raced self-consciousness at the center of his critique of liberal philosophy.

At the same time, Mills acknowledges the reality of a historical conjuncture—the moral-political present—in which liberalism's hegemony cannot be dismissed as a minor setback in an otherwise ongoing revolutionary story.[84] The "triumph of liberalism" is one that has to be taken seriously as an occasion for critical philosophical and political rethinking. In particular, on Mills's view, it may be necessary to immanently rethink the terms of liberalism itself, its founding concepts and normative commitments, and the narrative histories within which these are embedded. In this respect, he believes that the revival, after a long hiatus, of contractarian liberalism with the 1971 publication of John Rawls's *A Theory of Justice* (and all the ensuing arguments about it, pro and con) was a significant event—as much for what it enables us to better see as for what it obscures from our conceptual view.[85] The social contract idea, Mills holds—in the classical liberal formulations of Locke, Rousseau, and Kant—is a productive metaphor for thinking about the modern polity because it provides a model for understanding political community as constructed, and therefore open to criticism and the possibility (in principle) of *reconstruction*.[86] The contract idea obliges us to focus our attention on the idea of the basic agreement that assembles and structures the polity and that establishes the principles of fairness, equity, rights, and justice as

THE IDEA OF A MORAL AND REPARATORY HISTORY   69

the animating normative values upon which it functions. However, in line with its Kantian promise and the "ideal theory" that rationalizes its idea of a basic structure determined behind a "veil of ignorance," Rawls's story of the social contract famously purports to be a rational, neutral, and universal one, capable of providing the foundational moral-political grounds for a just polity.

Here is where Mills's genealogical intervention and critical revaluation are activated. For Mills the story of liberalism embodied in the contractarian auto-biographies that saturate our understanding is a motivated—and a mistaken—one. Far from being the neutral, universal, or color-blind doctrine or political practice that it purports to be in the stories it tells about itself, liberalism has historically been (sometimes explicitly, sometimes tacitly) an exclusive, discriminating, dominating liberalism, and in particular for Mills, given its relation to colonial slavery, a *racial* liberalism.[87] Mills's project, especially as articulated in *Black Rights/White Wrongs*, is to *deracialize* liberalism, and this entails at least two kinds of indispensable and interconnected critical revision: one *historical*, the other *conceptual*. Notably, then, in light of what I said a moment ago about Mills and Marxism, for Mills the critical project is not so much to jettison liberalism tout court as to subject it to a specific deracializing reconsideration.

For Mills, liberalism's autobiographies depend on an *ideological* history that subtracts or abstracts it from the real histories—in particular, the real histories of atrocity—in which it is culpably embedded. One revisionary history that seeks to embed liberalism in its proper context is Domenico Losurdo's much-debated *Liberalism: A Counter-History*, a work that Mills draws on, not surprisingly since its starting point is specifically to implicate liberalism in the atrocity of Native genocide and racial slavery.[88] The story of liberalism, Losurdo argues, cannot—except by sleight of hand—be told as though it were merely an abstract system of normative commitments to individual liberty, egalitarian fairness, and Enlightenment reason, progress, and universalism. Writing against what he felicitously calls the "habitual hagiography" of liberalism's accounts of itself, Losurdo argues that the story of liberalism has to be told as the history of real political struggles and movements, and therefore as the history of the social and political relations through which political orders and regimes have been established in its name—especially in the seventeenth- and eighteenth-century colonial political formations of Holland, Britain, and America.[89] Told in this way, the history of liberalism will be not the straightforward history of an unfettered and progressive commitment to liberty but the history of conquest, expropriation, mass murder, enslavement, systematic exploitation, and unjust enrichment. The making of the modern social-political world, Losurdo suggests, stands on an inescapable and constitutive paradox—namely, the "twin birth" of liberalism and colonial slavery: the proclamation of liberty for some (Whites) and slavery for others (Blacks), the capacity of some to be both committed opponents of tyranny ("political slavery") and steadfast champions of slave-owning (actual slavery).[90] The point is not that slavery merely persisted into the modern age in spite of (and alongside) the great doctrine of individual liberty. Slavery in the Americas was not simply a holdover from a premodern age. Rather, modern liberalism was a participant in the establishment, consolidation, and expansion of slavery as an institutionalized practice central to its emergent forms of economy and state. The modern liberal state was one of the moral and political conditions of the legitimation of slavery as a permanent and hereditary condition for Blacks, and of its justification, specifically, in a political morality of racial denigration, dispossession, exploitation, and exclusion. Therefore, the rise of liberalism as a moral and political formation and the establishment and reproduction of racial chattel slavery were part and parcel of a *single* intertwined history. Arguably, therefore, historical liberalism is inextricably tied to moral evil, not merely in the negative sense envisaged by John Kekes, that it lacks the moral resources to respond adequately to evil or combat evil when it appears, but in the positive sense that liberalism breeds—and breeds on—evil.[91]

Losurdo has certainly thrown down a gauntlet to those who believe in the self-evidence of liberalism's virtues. Of course, not everyone is completely persuaded by his argument. But agree or not with all the details of Losurdo's counterhistory of liberalism, the crucial point for Mills is that, as a practice, liberalism has always delimited an exclusive "community of the free," to whom its benefits and privileges accrue, and communities of the unfree, who could be legitimately and often violently excluded from these rights and advantages.

It has often been missed by Losurdo's critics that he is not simply issuing an edict of damnation for liberalism's evident historical crimes. The book is more complex—more ambitious—than that. Surely, as Losurdo affirms in the final pages, "being dissatisfied with the edifying picture of the habitual hagiography and situating oneself on the firm ground of reality, with its contradictions and conflicts, does not in any way mean denying the merits and strong points of the intellectual tradition under examination."[92] This should, of course, go without saying, but it doesn't. Losurdo's point is that only by means of a critical redescription of liberalism's history can one effectively "bid farewell" to the mythical story of a progressive evolution generated by "purely internal motivations and impulses," and thus be able to discern a more productive picture of liberalism's merits. First among these merits, Losurdo argues, is its *flexibility*. Liberalism has certainly changed from the seventeenth to the twentieth century, from Locke to Rawls, but this change has been a consequence of external challenges from radical political movements that have confronted the status quo, attacked its "exclusion clauses," and forced the extension of the range of communities to which its liberties apply. This capacity to respond to external challenges, Losurdo believes, distinguishes liberalism from its rivals: "Liberalism has proved capable of learning from its antagonist (the tradition that, starting with 'radicalism' and passing through Marx, issued in the revolutions which variously invoked him) to a far greater extent than its antagonist has proved capable of learning from it."[93] This way of historicizing liberalism is crucial to Mills's intervention because, like Losurdo, he too will want to imagine a radical transformation and extension of its political rationalities—specifically a deracializing transformation and extension—rather than a simple abandonment of the liberal social contract.

If this is its real (and realist) history, Mills ponders, what has enabled liberal contractarianism to pass itself off *conceptually* as an unencumbered, neutral, rational, and universal doctrine? Mills replies that this effect of neutrality, rationality, and universality is achieved by the theoretical device of "ideal theory." Now, in Western political philosophy, ideal theory is a normative abstraction concerned with specifying the conditions of justice in a perfectly just society; it asks what principles of fairness are needed to achieve that ideal.[34] Famously, for Rawls in *A Theory of Justice* this device was meant to stipulate a foundational baseline of agreement in relation to which a nonideal theory of justice in real-world social conditions could be constructed. This, of course, was the rationale for his controversial idea that the contractarian principles of justice should be formulated behind a socially blind "veil of ignorance."[95] Mills argues that it is precisely by this maneuver (in effect, a tacit maneuver of exclusion), offered on the pretext not of ideology but of theory or method, that liberal philosophy is able to permanently displace the implications of the actual history of domination with which liberalism is entangled—and thereby to tacitly generalize and normalize historical White (male) experience as universality. For Mills, the abstract ontology that liberalism has authoritatively depended upon is not really the neutral individualist ontology of equal personhood—of color-blind rights-bearing

72 PART I

subjects—that it appears to be in ideal theory but rather a racialized social ontology differentiating personhood from subpersonhood and inscribing in a systemic and structural way (and with binding legal force) a formal (and subsequently an informal) hierarchy in the distribution of rights and entitlements and privileges. As Mills puts it, historical liberalism is really a racial liberalism, a liberalism in which "conceptions of personhood and resulting schedules of rights, duties, and government responsibilities have all been racialized." Therefore, in point of fact, the contract is really a contract of racial domination, "an agreement among white contractors to subordinate and exploit nonwhite noncontractors for white benefit."[96] And on his account, so long as this deep, conceptually generative dimension of liberalism remains ignored—and therefore theoretically unreconstructed—liberalism will remain (irrespective of its moralizing proclamations to the contrary) a racial liberalism, unable to take seriously its embeddedness in a history of domination and the unjust enrichment that has accrued from this domination. By contrast, nonideal theory practices no such sleight-of-hand and so embodies at least the prospect of redress. As Mills writes, racial justice is "preeminently a matter of nonideal theory, of what corrective measures are called for to rectify a history of discrimination."[97]

Mills has been explicit that he takes his inspiration for the idea of a domination contract from, on the one hand, Rousseau's *Discourse on the Origins of Inequality*, and, on the other, Carole Pateman's *The Sexual Contract*. Note, then, that for Mills the problem about anti-Black racism is not primarily one of individual "attitudes" and "beliefs" (however noxious these might be) so much as a problem of the structures of systemic relations of domination (global as well as local or national) that historically have constituted the modern world. Such relations have organized not only the moral-psychological landscape of individual prejudice but also the moral economies of possession and dispossession, advantage and disadvantage, enrichment and impoverishment, that inhere at systemic levels. As Mills writes: "Whites contract to regard one another as moral equals who are superior to nonwhites and who create, accordingly, governments, legal systems, and economic structures that privilege them at the expense of people of color."[98] This idea of a domination contract, he holds, better captures the historical reality of sociopolitical exclusion that characterizes the actual modern world, and better enables us to consider what justice demands by the way of repair.

One of the conceptual resources for remapping the idea of a domination contract of racial injustice, Mills suggests, is "White supremacy." On the model of feminists deploying the idea of "patriarchy" as a conceptual way of capturing the systemic structures of gender inequality and injustice, and of Marxists deploying the idea of "class society" to shed light on the historical reality of economic exploitation, so Mills offers the idea of White supremacy to help grasp conceptually the architecture and dynamic of systemic racial domination. In tune with critical race theorists, Mills sees White supremacy as offering a framework in which to recognize race as more than a congeries of beliefs and attitudes, however important these are. White supremacy names a central dimension (note, not the only dimension) of the global historical structure of racial domination that the colonial project of conquest and enslavement brought into being, and that, in altered form, remains hegemonic. What the idea aims to illuminate is that racial structuring is not anomalous but typical, not superficial but thoroughgoing. The idea of White supremacy aims to map the historically interconnected ways in which, systematically rather than randomly, not only domestically but also globally, racial difference is inscribed in the normative asymmetrical order of privilege and subordination, entitlement and exclusion.[99] Mills, of course, fully recognizes that eighteenth-century liberalism is not the same as twentieth-century liberalism. If for the former the rationality of subordination was violently explicit in the contract—think of the racial contract of eighteenth-century Jamaica—this can no longer be admitted in its recent incarnation. Now, he says, liberalism is "race-evading" and "amnesiac": "The atrocities of the past now being an embarrassment, they must be denied, minimized, or conceptually bypassed. The cultivated amnesia, a set of constructed deafnesses and blindnesses, characterizes racial liberalism: subjects one cannot raise, issues one cannot broach, topics one cannot explore."[100] The idea of White supremacy helps point to the reality and centrality of racial exploitation, helps us discern that the modern political economy is simultaneously a racialized moral economy. Again, eighteenth-century colonial Jamaica is not the politically sovereign Jamaica of the twenty-first century, formally presided over by the new Black middle-class elites. No one would seriously doubt the significant transformations—at the level of the social ontology of Black personhood, for example—that characterize the last six decades of volatile independence. Still, the idea of White supremacy points us toward the ways in which external White imperial power structures of subordination continue to qualify and constrain Black sovereignty, and complicit internal structures of neoliberal domination continue to marginalize, impoverish, and disrespect the Black poor descendants of the enslaved.

74   PART I

Mills's genealogical critique (as I have called it) of White liberalism was not explicitly offered as a theory of Black reparation for New World slavery. Or to put it another way, it was less the moral-politics of repair as such that claimed his attention and animated his critique than the wider conceptual and moral-political conditions that would have to be present for any such theorization of repair to be a serious one—that is, to begin to meet the widespread Black experience of White harm and White disavowal of harm. Nevertheless, the reparatory implications are not hard to discern. Clearly, for example, given the social ontology of White supremacy that supports the racial domination contract, the direction of Mills's argument is away from the familiar (and complacently anemic) liberal idea (offered by Margaret Walker, among others) that repair consists of the restitution of ruptured moral relations between aggrieved and conflicting individuals. What would be required, rather, is a wider social and political transformation (at once global and local) in which the moral economy of White supremacy and the racial liberal polity that sustains it are dismantled. For Mills, the liberal political order is not effectively deracialized without the rectification of the past upon which the present imperial structure of racial privilege, advantage, and injustice are established. A corrective past-oriented posture is a *precondition* for any future-oriented moral political imagination. And this analytical framework seems to me to open a door by which to reintegrate a wider sense of what racial justice entails—including the redress of unjust accumulated enrichment by former European slaving powers; the unencumbered return to Indigenous peoples of their ancestral lands and possessions; an internal/national politics of participation, self-determination, and economic redistribution; and the emergence of an international society of meaningful sovereignty in the former colonized world.

To be sure, even if we grant the analytical justification of Mills's conceptual move (based on the idea that the contract, being essentially constructed, is therefore, in principle, reconstructable), it is not entirely clear, or necessarily persuasive, that what remains in the wake of his genealogical critique of racial liberalism is, recognizably, *liberalism*. The extent to which there is political or philosophical (as opposed to strategic) value in articulating these moral-political commitments in its name is not as clear as Mills thinks it is. There may be a sense in which Mills's critical gesture is in part *ironic*, as any immanent critique must be. What is lost and what is gained in brokering the deal to sit at the liberal table?

Like Losurdo's, Mills's wager is that he can rescue liberalism from itself, from its historical entanglements and contractual commitments. I am not so sure.

To sum up: In this chapter I have been concerned with the contemporary critical-conceptual problem about New World slavery. What, I asked, is the story of the past of New World slavery that ought to command our critical attention in the present? To put it slightly differently: What demand does the current conjuncture make on the past of New World slavery? The provisional answer I have been trying to work out, and work with, is that in—and for—the present the story of New World slavery ought to be reoriented by a moral and reparatory history of the past. My assumption has been that descriptions under which pasts are made to appear depend, at least in some measure, on the nature of the demand made on them by the present in which they are called upon. In a prior conjuncture, Black radical protagonists of Black and Third World social, economic, and political change told and enacted a redemptive story of overcoming the past-in-the-present of racial domination. The formal features of that story-form (an embodied hermeneutic sense of futural longing, a progressive temporal rhythm of forward-projected social movement, and a teleological destination) are well-enough known. But with the cognitive-historical breakdown or loss of the anticipated horizon of that political narrative (in the varied names of national liberation, socialism, and so forth), a critical urgency has emerged to think again about the future-in-the-present *from where we are*. And where we are now is a present not only characterized by this closure of the revolutionary path but also animated by the overdetermined ascendancy of the ethos and idiom of liberalism and, specifically, liberal human rights.

It is perhaps a truism to say that where one door is closed another one opens: where something valuable is lost with the vanishing of the old, something novel is gained with the emergence of the new; where something recedes that for so long has appeared self-evident, something else worthwhile comes prominently and generatively into view. The collapse of the transparent intelligibility of the Romantic revolutionary narrative has induced a retemporalization of the relations among pasts, presents, and futures. But paradoxically, if this retemporalization has now foreclosed the old options for new futures, it has also opened (however ambiguously) a remarkable recovery-discovery of the fullness of pasts, an almost obsessive sensibility for the very pastness of pasts—in the form of reorientations toward ruins, legacies, aftermaths, memories, traumas, all of which are concerned precisely with the stubborn, enduring, unsettling presence of irrepressible pasts. There has been a veritable reenchantment of pasts that in progressivist narratives had functioned principally as a diminished ground for the rhetorical work of overcoming. The idea of the tragic, I have argued, is one way of revising the conceptual labor of a historicity drained of assurances.

The falling away of the old contestations around political futurity—indeed, the seeming disgrace to which radical politics has been consigned—has nevertheless opened a discursive space for a reinvigoration of explicitly moral considerations or at least for a refiguration of the question of the moral in political consider-ations (the tragic as a refiguration of the relation between contingency, action and conduct is an instance of moral reframing). In this space (partly, of course the epistemic space of humanitarianism), we have become acutely aware of persisting problems of historical wrongdoing and demands for corrective justice to redress or repair these wrongs. In particular, we have become more acutely aware of the salience of the idea of evil as the name for especially dehumanizing or heinous historical wrongs—that is, historical atrocities—whose effects con-tinue to disfigure and haunt the present. Unrepaired wrong remains wrong—and, moreover, a wrong compounded by its persisting disavowal and nonrepair. This is the purview of reparatory history and reparatory critique. And New World slavery is a paradigm of an unrepaired evil.

The moral-political language of reparations has gained the contemporary prominence it has in a conjuncture shaped by the collapse of the paradigm of revolution and the triumph of liberalism, in particular liberal human rights. This is why, for example, the political morality of reparations is framed in terms of Black rights and justice rather than in terms of Black freedom, as in the paradigm of Black liberation. It is not surprising that liberal reparatory gestures are articu-lated in such a way as to foreclose (Waldron) or at least to forestall (Thompson) any serious critique of the basic structure—the liberal-capitalist polity—that is historically implicated in the atrocity of New World slavery. Reparations is seen as a palliative gesture for forging reconciliation, for mending the torn racial relations between Blacks and Whites, for extending tokens of compensation (in the familiar way of scholarships, monuments, museums, holidays). It is now a commonplace—and insulting—story. Against this backdrop, I have argued, the value of Charles Mills's intervention is to bring into genealogical focus a deeper, more complicated, more culpable story about the liberalism that is in fact our collective starting point—its internal, integral historical relation to the atrocity of New World slavery (and indeed the Native genocide that preceded and accompanied it) and the prevailing structures of White supremacy that remain its contemporary moral-political legacy. Mills may or may not agree with me that, in some sense at least, the evil of New World slavery is irreparable. The whole orientation of his work is to affirm the possibility of the work of rectification. In any case, the "dark ontology" (his phrase) of Black personhood, or Black subpersonhood, shaped by hundreds of years of racial abjection, exclusion, and disadvantage; and the neocolonial life-forms, structured by hundreds of years of extractive flows supporting unjust metropolitan enrichment, on one side, and chronic impoverishment and disadvantage, on the other—these require, Mills argues, more urgent and more fundamental corrective moral-political responses than are embodied in racial (but race-evading) liberalism and liberal reparatory philosophy.

PART II

CHAPTER 2

INCOMPARABLE EVIL

THE EXEMPLIFICATION OF EVIL

Evil, especially evil that is obdurate, unyielding, is worth critically thinking through as a matter of moral-political urgency. However, there is something profoundly troubling about some of the interconnected assumptions that serve to undergird at least a prominent dimension of contemporary discussion about evil—namely, that it operates through a series of unexamined *exceptionalizations* that render some historical experiences or practices or events not simply extraordinary or even unprecedented but unrivalled and unsurpassable, and, by contrast, make others marginal, mere empirical instances in the uneven scales of what *counts* as evil. Some evils are *exemplifications* of what evils are; some evils are not. This rhetorical technique of exception-making—now so fully naturalized as to scarcely appear problematic and so fully normalized as to seem beyond dispute— shapes this influential way of engaging the problem about evil by locating it authoritatively in a specific geopolitical space and historical time, providing it with its paradigmatic object, and conceptualizing it (or at least evoking it) through its exemplary thinker.

One provisional way of orienting ourselves around the conventional way of thinking about evil I am referring to, and thus around the themes that concern me in this chapter, is to take a careful look at the introduction to one recent and notable volume of essays, edited by María Pía Lara, that boldly purports to offer a variety of contemporary perspectives on, precisely, *rethinking* evil.[1] Lara's is but one of a number of collections published within the last two decades or so, each with its specificities but all covering an overlapping terrain of concern with evil as a contemporary issue.[2] The value of thinking about the introductions to such

82   PART II

volumes is not that they tell us everything there is to know but that in them we
have reason to expect a certain self-consciousness about the strategies by which
evil is hermeneutically made to appear as a relevant concern. Thus, as introductions do, Lara's also sets the stage and lays out the rationale—in this instance, in a
determinedly militant tone—for the essays that follow (that are, of course, not all
identical in thematic or conceptual character), allowing us to glean something
of what the editor thinks are not only the meanings of the relevant terms but the
point of the intervention as a whole being undertaken and the symbolic field in
which it is being played out. Lara opens her introduction by asserting that the
"past hundred years have been a long succession of genocides, mass killings, systematic rapes, ethnic cleansings, and tortures, in many places, including Europe."
Such episodes and events, she goes on, have severely undermined our trust in
the fundamental institutions of modern democratic society. There is thus an
urgency, she says, for a "postmetaphysical theory" of evil that can "support the
moral and political claims of human rights around the world."[3] Now, in these
preliminary remarks alone, a good deal is already evident about some of the basic
assumptions at work in the contemporary *theory-space* of evil—by which I mean
the contemporary discursive arena in which evil is rendered as a question that
demands an answer.

Note, to begin with, the *unexamined* way in which specifying "the past
hundred years" (principally, the twentieth century) explicitly marks out the
temporal boundaries of what is to *count* as a relevant historical atrocity. This is
a pervasive assumption among many writing about evil today—the notion that
the twentieth century was peculiarly vicious or especially cruel and is, therefore,
of all the eras of human history, the very definition of baseness and inhumanity.
Its spurious *presentism*, not to say patent absurdity, as a grounding historical
claim is rarely ever reflected upon let alone justified—much less deplored or
criticized.[4] The twentieth century is apparently, self-evidently, a great *exception*.
And not surprisingly, within the authoritative frame of this exception, certain
historical atrocities are effectively ruled out as candidates for consideration by
definition: New World slavery being the one that most interests me here. Evidently,
New World slavery—in which, of course, mass murder, rape, torture, and other
unspeakable atrocities were pervasive, endemic, routine occurrences—happened
too long ago to continue to haunt the contemporary memories of philosophers
like Lara. What constitution of *relevant* time, or *whose* experience of the relevant
past in the present, makes the enslavement of Black people in the New World

in the seventeenth, eighteenth, and nineteenth centuries appear forgettable, ignorable, not merely in everyday discourse but also in the basic understanding of the world we live in? That is, what philosophy of history does this reification of the twentieth century depend upon? What motivates its historiographical conceit, the guarantee of the exclusive privilege of its experience of time? What does this conceit conceal or disavow? How might we effectively grapple with its exclusionary conceptual-ideological effects? These are questions that concern me, I hope for obvious reasons.

Note also, in Lara's opening remarks, the *picture* evoked of the kinds of action that are to count as evils and the hierarchy that shapes the list of evil actions. First and foremost, it is genocides and mass killings that are evils. The rest—rapes, tortures—important though they are, come after, in the linear seriality of the list. It is simply self-evident to Lara and many others that it is the infliction of systematic and violent mass death that *defines* evil, or anyway defines the first or most horrific or most shocking of evils. But why should this be so? What are the metaphysical assumptions—about the sanctity of human life, say, or the ontological significance of the radical closure that human death marks—that form the basis of this view? What histories guarantee these assumptions their normative force? Evil is, above all, action that *negates* life, but can it also be action that *produces* kinds of life? This is less clear. Is it possible to imagine an institutionalized form of domination in which it is less the practice of extermination that defines the evil than the systematic coercive *formation* of subjugated lives?

Again, note that in Lara's formulation what we should be aiming for is a "theory" of evil, albeit a *postmetaphysical* one. Past theories of evil—whether to do with natural disasters or human failures—have been hopelessly inadequate. As she says later, this "lack of conceptual clarity has led to various attempts to conceptualize evil in religious, naturalistic, and psychological terms, but these have failed to bring us closer to the concept of evil and to answering the question of whether it is possible to argue that such a concept has any relevance for philosophy, and more concretely, for moral and political philosophy."[75] There is a curious progressivist historicity at work here (we will come across more of it later) in the view that past conceptions of evil were marked by a *lack* of something, in this instance "conceptual clarity," that precluded access to what we should be looking for—namely, the truth of evil ("the concept of evil")—and that, consequently, the problem at hand is to construct a postmetaphysical *theory* of evil that will correct these old and inadequate conceptions by overcoming that prevailing lack

84   PART II

of clarity. Now, not all contemporary philosophers thinking about evil subscribe to exactly Lara's view about theory, it is true—Richard Bernstein, for example, does not—but even when they do not, they almost invariably share the progressivist assumption that renders earlier ideas of evil as being deficient in relation to later ones.[6]

Finally, note that Lara's postmetaphysical project on evil is meant (again without further discussion, much less explication) specifically to support a "human rights" agenda. Why? What is this agenda? Is there something to be said about the *liberal* (or liberalizing) context and character of human rights regimes that might be relevant to a postmetaphysical idea of evil? Does the idea of human rights normalize a distinctive ethical perspective on, or political regime of wrong and repair? Might there be a (not merely contingent) relation between liberalism and the prevalence of evil in modern society that is being overlooked in this hasty conceptualization? Lara shows no interest in questions of this sort. Human rights are merely the self-evident and self-justifying ground of her perspective on evil. But doesn't this assumption of self-evidence impoverish her analysis in significant ways? As discussed in the previous chapter, the historical institution (or institutionalization) of human rights is itself a central part of the historical-ideological context for the moral turn in the humanities and social sciences, and therefore also for the rise of evil-talk specifically—evil-talk and human rights–talk are not unconnected, however much we may be obliged to acknowledge some conception of each or both together as inescapable in a contemporary consideration of atrocity.

The aim of *Rethinking Evil*, Lara tells us, is to offer a range of perspectives on a philosophical conception of evil that avoids the dead-ends of religious metaphysics—that is, theodicies that rely on the problem of suffering allowed by a transcendentally benevolent, omniscient, and omnipotent Creator-God. Lara does not name or engage any specific representative figure, but one can assume, I suppose, that she has in mind, among others, someone like Augustine of Hippo, perhaps the most significant early Christian theorist of evil.[7] This is a curious omission, not least because there are some, John Milbank, for example, who would question whether or to what extent Augustine's "privation" theory of evil (that is, evil not as the positive presence of malignity but as the lack or privation of the good) is as irrelevant to contemporary thinking as Lara seems to imagine.[8] In any case, the story of evil Lara frames is one that begins with Immanuel Kant, whose *Religion Within the Boundaries of Mere Reason*, published in 1793, is taken to be the inaugural work of a modern, secular theory of evil.[9] Here as elsewhere in the story of modern Western philosophy, Kant is a transitional figure in a secularizing Europe where moral and cosmological orientations haven't yet been completely cleaved from each other, where the boundaries of philosophy and theology are still relatively fluid, but where Christian Enlightenment thinkers (like Kant, a pious Lutheran, remember) are in search of a rational faith or a rational basis for faith.[10] *Religion* was published eight years after the foundational *Groundwork for a Metaphysics of Morals*. If in the earlier work Kant had confidently maintained that the universal moral law depends not upon the demonstration of God's existence but upon the claims of reason alone, in the later work he suggests a more complicated, more ambiguous relation of the moral law to moral depravity and wrongdoing. There is in *Religion* a more pronounced sense of the frailty and vulnerability of human nature, the ever-present potential of fallen moral agents, human beings failing to live up to the maxims or principles of the moral law. This failure, for Kant, is the province of evil.

At the center of Kant's conception of evil (and I am simplifying a great deal here for the sake of brevity) is the relation between our autonomy and responsibility (that is, our freedom and its moral implications) and the competing inclinations toward goodness and wrongdoing. We all have, as our basic background condition, a morally good will, but this will can be corrupted and perverted by the extent to which we choose the right maxims for the right reasons. The corrupting force for Kant is self-love. To prioritize self-love over the moral law (even if the actions that derive from it have the appearance of good) is evil. On Kant's account, this inclination to prioritize self-love is *ineradicable*. Evil, therefore, though no longer simply what is suffered but what is *chosen*, is nevertheless chosen in relation to what is universally given—namely, a "propensity to evil." Consequently, such evil as we are inclined toward is "radical" for Kant not because it is diabolical in character or effect but because it is deeply rooted in who we are, innately, as human beings.

Not surprisingly, perhaps, a number of contemporary philosophers believe that there is something disappointing or even incoherent in Kant's conception of evil. For example, it is argued that Kant *fails* to distinguish among levels of seriousness of harm. As Todd Calder remarks, it would seem intuitively "far worse to torture someone for sadistic pleasure than to tell the truth to gain a good reputation," but Kant's conception simply disregards this sort of distinction. Where the former would surely indicate the malign presence of an evil will, Calder says, the latter merely suggests a *lack* of the virtue of moral goodness.[1] More than this, however, it has been suggested that there is a fundamental contradiction between Kant's commitment to a naturally good will and moral freedom, on the one hand, and the insistence on an equally natural propensity to evil, on the other.[12] Now, I am not interested in determining the validity or limits of Kant's theory of evil, but it is worth noting (and recalling, perhaps, the discussion of Anscombe and MacIntyre from the previous chapter) that in chastising him for the improbableness or otherwise of his views, his critics often show precious little concern with trying to grasp which historical-conceptual *question* it might have been that he was trying to answer in following out his line of argument. They simply assert that Kant's conception does not meet their own (in effect, *contemporary*) sense of what a theory of evil is supposed to pick out as the worst kind of moral wrong. Suppose Kant was propelled by questions other than theirs? Part of the issue may be that these philosophers are often motivated by an arc of philosophic history that overcomes Kant *on the way* elsewhere—typically, toward Hannah Arendt. Indeed, Arendt is almost invariably the telos of the progressivist story of evil that begins with Kant.

Above all, it seems that Kant had no proper sense of evil as a historical *event*. Here is a significant passage from Lara making the argument for moving away from Kant, and in which the direction of a more adequate (that is, postmetaphysical) conception of evil is signaled by its concern with a specific historical event:

> From a postmetaphysical understanding, we develop a perspective on evil that relates it to the historical catastrophes of the twentieth century. We establish a space where our consciousness of evil can—indeed, must—be drawn from such tragedies as the Holocaust, and we delineate the ways in which such tragedies have allowed us to learn about and reconsider the concrete meanings of evil deeds. As [Susan] Neiman argues, " 'Auschwitz' . . . stands for all we mean when we use the word 'evil' today: absolute wrongdoing which leaves room for no account and no expiation."[13]

These are remarkable claims, offered as though they merely *confirmed* what some supposed *we* already believe. They are stated as though they ought to pass without need of critical notice, much less comment or analysis, and with the confidence of being self-evident and therefore being received unquestioningly by those who already tacitly agree. But *who* is their presumed audience? Who are *we*? Note, again, the privileged place of the twentieth century; but note in particular the historicity implied in the idea that where a postmetaphysical perspective on evil is definitionally connected to a historical context, one of catastrophe, a metaphysical perspective (presumably Kant's) evidently has *no* event-like historical location. What is the working assumption here about the relation between concepts and histories? Which concepts are presumed to have histories (that is, need to be *located* in their historical contexts) and which not? In particular, note how the Holocaust is made the *exceptional* instance of (twentieth-century) atrocity, the foundational context-event of a postmetaphysical theory of evil. But what of Kant's contexts? (I leave aside Lara's uses here of the idea of tragedy to merely reference a frighteningly bad occurrence; evil and the tragic may yet have a deeper, more complex connection than her passing reference allows.) Finally, note how this positioning of the Holocaust as an exception quickly turns into something more like a hyperbolic *reification* in Lara's citation of Susan Neiman (a contributor to her volume and the author of an authoritative book on evil in the Western philosophical tradition) for whom Auschwitz stands not for simply *much* of what we might mean by evil but for *everything* that we could ever mean by it.[14] What is there to charitably say in the face of such manifestly incoherent statements from such putatively authoritative thinkers except that they seem to speak to an already *chosen* interpretive community of like-minded participants whose identities are presumably affirmed by these exaggerated claims. Their point, quite evidently, is not so much rational as rhetorical—that is, they aim to *foreclose* rather than open up room for considered, let alone critical, discussion. I return to this exorbitance of the Holocaust as the very definition of evil in a moment because it is of central importance to my larger concerns with the displacement and invisibility of New World slavery's evil.

Perhaps predictably, for Lara (as for others) it is Hannah Arendt who is made to play the generative role in the argument about a postmetaphysical conception of evil. On Lara's account, Arendt is the first thinker to seriously push beyond Kant's early ideas of radical evil and is the more important for the fact that she mobilized her conceptions of evil precisely in order to illuminate a specific historical atrocity. Lara focuses on the well-known fact that over the course of her life Arendt developed at least two seemingly very different conceptions of evil, an early "political" one indebted to Kant's idea of "radical evil" and a later "moral" one (mediated by the influence of her great mentor, Karl Jaspers) that

88   PART II

she called the "banality of evil." The contrast between these ideas in fact forms the central tension framing discussions about Arendt and evil. I return to this later, but what I want to notice here is how, in respect of these contrasting ideas, Lara situates Arendt in relation to an *aspiration* to theory that she is then understood to fall short of realizing. Lara expresses a concern that there are "gaps" in Arendt's "conceptual path to evil."[15] Like many, Lara thinks the later conception (the "banality of evil") is an *advance* on the earlier one ("radical evil")—it seems, she says, "to lead to a more complex interpretation of human nature." But how so, precisely? She does not say. But that advance notwithstanding, Lara's overall judgment is that, in the end, "Arendt failed to offer a consistent perspective" on evil.[16] And this "final failure" on Arendt's part to develop a properly coherent and systematic "postmetaphysical theory of evil" has "impeded the effort to come to an agreement about her political and philosophical legacies."[17] More careful readers of Arendt may remember that she herself cast some doubt on this very way of reading her ideas; in a well-known essay she found it presciently necessary to caution that by "banality of evil" she did not mean to suggest a "theory or doctrine but something quite factual."[18] To be sure, it may not be entirely clear what Arendt meant by this characteristically allusive remark, but nevertheless, might this self-understanding have been worth pursing, engaging—at least questioning?

As I have suggested, embodied in Lara's formulations are progressivist assumptions about theory-making—that is, about how what are presumed to be "theories" emerge, in relation to which questions, in reference to which objects and truth-values, and so on—that seem to me doubtful. However widespread or commonly accepted, I am not sure that this is the most productive way to read Arendt's reflections and formulations on evil; indeed, I am not very certain that it is a helpful way to read *any* past theorist on any topic in any present. Certainly, it is not at all clear what is to be gained by reading Arendt as though she had been searching all along for, and at length failed to find, a consistent theory of evil. I am not persuaded that it is helpful to think of Arendt as being *in search* of a theory at all so much as trying to find a moral and political language with which to account conceptually for a shocking, seemingly unprecedented *experience*.

This authoritative structure of exception—the constituent themes of the unexamined privilege of the twentieth century in moral discourse about atrocities;

the assumption that genocide or mass killing is the principal index of evil's presence; the exceptionalization of the Holocaust as a meta-evil; the authorizing role of Hannah Arendt in contemporary discourse on evil—is crucial to my concern here with marking out the elements of the problem-space of evil and, therefore, to my larger concern with the problem of the evil of New World slavery and its relative invisibility to the relevant literature on moral evil and atrocity. In what follows, I have an admittedly restricted but interconnected itinerary. As a preliminary exercise and through a well-known essay by the cultural sociologist Jeffrey Alexander, I begin by exploring some aspects of the way in which what has come to be called "the Holocaust" was discursively constructed as an event of a certain kind. My aim here is not to revisit the historical circumstances themselves that now come under this authoritative description but to understand something of the discursive *process* by which the mass killing of Jews in the Second World War emerged as what Alexander calls a "moral universal"—that is, a meta-evil. What interests me is how this construction works to authoritatively shape the discursive space of visibility and intelligibility of all other atrocities, indeed of atrocity *as such*. What is it about the conditions of possibility of the story of New World slavery, for example, that seems to preclude its acquiring the general status of a moral universal, a meta-evil?

Against this background, the remainder of the chapter is taken up with thinking about the inexhaustibly complex figure of Hannah Arendt. I am interested not only in what she has written about evil but also and especially in the way she is *taken up* in relation to evil by her interpreters and commentators. This is because it is the contemporary question—the *present*—that interests me above all. Undoubtedly, Arendt is the most prominent figure both in contemporary discussions about evil and in the wider moral-political discourses of which these discussions are a dynamic part. My worry here, as should be evident from my remarks on María Pía Lara's invocation of Arendt, is that there is a peculiar, and peculiarly *unexamined*, way in which Arendt's moral-political views—including her views on evil—are read by her commentators and interpreters. Arendt scholarship (in the North Atlantic, anyway) can often feel like an exclusive club in which the initiated and the cognoscenti have it out among themselves in the endless round of a private conversation about a beloved and suddenly indispensable mentor. In the predictable and justifiable appreciation of her penetrating and often subtle moral-political insights, it seems to me there has been curiously little attempt on the part of these commentators and interpreters to *historicize*

90 PART II

Arendt's interventions in precisely the sense of *interventions*—that is, to *locate* them,
on the one hand, in respect of the varying conceptual-historical conjunctures or
moral-political problem-spaces in which they emerged and took shape and, on
the other, in respect of the *contrast* between these conjunctures or problem-spaces
and their own, however these might be understood and specified.[19] In respect of
evil, the principal question her interpreters pose has to do with the *meaning* of
her ideas about "radical evil" and the "banality of evil," articulated in *The Origins
of Totalitarianism* and *Eichmann in Jerusalem*, respectively, and how they stand in
relation to their conceptual complexity (measured, say, in terms of the problem
about intentions). But might we also reasonably ask: What were the questions
that Arendt was trying to answer with the ideas about evil she constructed in
any given historical moment? What *kind* of idea was evil to her in these historical
conjunctures? What role did it play in the organization of the arguments she was
seeking to advance? What was she seeking to *do* in drawing on an idea of evil
on these occasions? Moreover, can we discern points of convergence as well as
divergence, on the one hand, between the two defining problem-spaces in which
Arendt appears to construct a distinctive idea of evil (represented, respectively,
by *The Origins of Totalitarianism* and *Eichmann in Jerusalem*) and, on the other,
between these problem-spaces and our own, however that is described? Should
questions of this sort have some bearing on how we read her from her various
conjunctures into ours? Such perhaps are not so much matters of intellectual as
of *conceptual* history.[20]

These and other similarly oriented questions about *reading* Arendt shape the
direction of my overall concern in the rest of this chapter. In exploring them,
I take the philosopher Richard Bernstein as my principal guide and interlocutor.
This is because Bernstein is easily one of Arendt's most illuminating and insightful interpreters, not least where her thinking about evil is concerned or where
that thinking might profitably lead us. More broadly, however, as a philosopher
of pragmatist and hermeneutic inheritances (indeed, as a philosopher who has
urged an ongoing, robust, and open-ended dialogue among diverse intellectual
traditions), Bernstein has always demonstrated a commitment to a reflexive,
situated, and self-correcting orientation to intellectual inquiry—what he has
called "critical fallibilism"—and an admirable attunement, therefore, to the relations between philosophical inquiry and the historical and political contexts of
individual and social experience. These contexts, he urges (and I concur), render
philosophic concerns worldly, urgent, timely. Significantly, therefore, Bernstein

comes to Arendt's work from this background of considerable thinking about the reconstruction of the discursive contexts of critical theory, and presumably, also, a mindful orientation to the *labor* of critique.[21] And yet, however, Bernstein also seeks, more often than might have been hoped, to merely *affirm* a canonical picture of Arendt, one in which she is shielded from more than superficial scrutiny. As careful and discerning a commentator as Bernstein is he too often reads Arendt in a surprisingly unexamined way. In particular, as I will argue, in the mode of a history of ideas, he reads her as though the problem-space from which he takes up the question of evil was also hers, and therefore the only issue at stake is getting right the complex *meaning* of her ideas to better apply them in his present.

Now, admittedly, it is scarcely my intention to recover and reconstruct the historical conjunctures of either of Arendt's great books, *The Origins of Totalitarianism* or *Eichmann in Jerusalem*, let alone the historical contexts of Arendt's work as a whole I have a rather more limited and modest endeavor, which is a *clarificatory* one aimed at raising some questions about the way in which Arendt is read uncritically in order to authorize a certain (narrow) contemporary preoccupation with evil, one that reinscribes the exception of the Holocaust. My concern is less to join the fight over the relative significance of radical evil as opposed to the banality of evil than to underscore one dimension of what this preoccupation obscures—namely, the way Arendt's idea of the evil of the Holocaust, or more precisely the evil of the death camps (the principal site of Nazi evil according to her), is rhetorically established in part by *diminishing* the significance of other atrocities, not least among them New World slavery.

THE HOLOCAUST AS META-EVIL

I have cited María Pía Lara uncritically invoking the Holocaust as exception and mobilizing Susan Neiman to her aid. Neiman is of course a prominent scholar of Enlightenment philosophy. She is a well-known scholar of Kant—and herself a scholar of broadly Kantian persuasion—who has also written an elegant and perceptive book-length genealogy of the problem of evil from the eighteenth century to (roughly) the twenty-first century present, *Evil in Modern Thought*.[22] I do not intend to engage the substance of this book at any length; it has been much and (largely) favorably reviewed. I am interested in only some of the framing

92   PART II

assumptions that shape the overall story she tells about the modern career of evil, specifically the way it exceptionalizes the Holocaust and helps to render New World slavery all but invisible. An undoubtedly admirable aspect of Neiman's project, as suggested by her title, is to show how evil has in fact not been as irrelevant to the history of modern moral philosophy as is often believed; rather, modern philosophy can be written as a response, sometimes more implicit than not, to the *problem* of the problem of evil.[23] The animating center of Neiman's story hinges on what she sees as a poignant homology between the place-names *Lisbon* and *Auschwitz* as signifiers of evil in the eighteenth and twentieth centuries respectively. Thus she opens her book in the following rather arresting, perhaps even astonishing, way: "The eighteenth century used the word *Lisbon* much as we use the word *Auschwitz* today."[24] Might one wonder *who* the "eighteenth century" was that supposedly used Lisbon in this way, and more important, who the "we" are that Neiman invokes to secure the authority of this statement about the uses of Auschwitz as the twentieth-century signifier of evil. Again, what normative conceit or complacent ignorance does it conceal—or else *perform*? There is a presumption here, of course, that her assumed readers implicitly share a certain perspective or cultural-intellectual tradition concerning the Holocaust—or perhaps that the Holocaust *transcends* perspective or cultural-intellectual tradition (that it belongs, or has come to belong, or belongs in the *same* way, to everyone). Neiman's book neatly covers a necessarily expansive terrain, but it is clear that the axis around which its argument rotates, the point to which we are being led from the very beginning, is the Holocaust. The Holocaust is the assumed *telos*, in other words, of the normative history of evil in modern thought.[25]

It is an interesting fact that in the arc of Neiman's historical account there is no event—much less institution—that does for the nineteenth century what the Lisbon earthquake does for the eighteenth and the Holocaust for the twentieth (or for that matter, what 9/11 does for the twenty-first).[26] Why is that? New World slavery, for example, which by the early nineteenth century was certainly identified as an evil by abolitionist thinkers on both sides of the Atlantic, is virtually invisible to Neiman.[27] She certainly mentions slavery here and there a number of times, but it forms no *generative* or *integral* part of her story of evil in modern thought. Slavery's presence has an incidental, episodic quality. How is this possible? How should we understand the absence of New World slavery—and therefore the distinctive character of Black suffering—from the modern story of evil when New World slavery and the violations upon which it depended were constitutive dimensions of the making of the modern world itself in the eighteenth and nineteenth centuries? What motivates this omission? What sustains it? What is required to challenge it? Retrospectively reflecting on the book and its reception in a corrective afterword to the second edition, Neiman acknowledges a certain limitation of its argument but does so in a peculiar way that serves only to underline the civilizational conceit that shapes and saturates it. One of her critics, a scholar of Chinese history, rightly chastises her for her Eurocentrism, for passing off a "study of European philosophy" as an account of "the human condition" vaguely secured by her encompassing collective pronoun "we" (to which I have also referred). He wonders whether that "we" for whom only Europe is relevant continues to exist. Neiman stands appropriately "chastened" by the criticism and offers apologetically that she should indeed have been more scrupulous about delimiting the Western frame within which her story should be understood.[28] But would this provincialization really resolve the problem? Is there a history to be considered of the powers by which the modern West has not merely presumed to *represent* the human (philosophically or otherwise) but, more than this, *remade* the conditions for any possible ways of *being* human—such that these ways of life are now inescapably conscripted to the structures and imaginaries of the modern West? Is it so obvious, for example, what the modern West is in the creolized worlds transformed by the project of colonial Atlantic slavery? In other words, what is the relevant relation between the West and the modern? In any case, Neiman closes her reflections by asking whether her critic's suggestion that "those for whom only Europe is relevant no longer exist" might not be taken "as a mark of a more robust universalism that is one of the positive consequences of globalization—perhaps even a sign of moral progress."[29] *Here* is where she stands, within the moral shelter exemplified by her progressive cosmopolitan story. But is this any answer to the profound problem about her account that her critic throws into relief—namely, the assumption precisely of the moral universality of her examples, the Holocaust in particular, as signifiers of evil? Isn't the issue precisely that *we* are all presumed now to be part of (or to have been normatively *conscripted* into) the moral community that tacitly recognizes the universal authority of her instances—again, in particular the Holocaust?

Thus, in the portentous archive of the new literature on evil, it is the Holocaust that is the *paradigmatic* instance of historical moral wrong. The Holocaust stands apart as a unique and unparalleled event, an order of evil that not only supersedes

94   PART II

all other evils in its sheer enormity and horror but conceptually frames their intelligibility as well—they can be understood only in relation to this first of evils. The Holocaust, in other words, is a kind of meta-evil. Whatever it was in its own concrete *facticity* and *historicity*, what has come to be called *the* Holocaust is no longer just the proper name for a horrific empirical event—that is, the mass murder of European Jews carried out by the Nazis during the Second World War. It is now something larger—a form of *universality*, an order of truth. By contrast, for example, New World slavery scarcely appears in the growing archive of evil (it has no conceptual presence in Lara's edited volume nor in Neiman's monograph), and when it does appear, it can barely sustain that appearance beyond the odd sentence or two. Or rather, it typically appears, when it does appear, merely *en passant*, duly acknowledged but only as a particular item on the list of other historical evils. In consequence, New World slavery is always merely *empirical*. It has no *theoretical* value as such, as an exemplifying or paradigmatic order of truth about evil. It does not—cannot—rise to the status of universality. On the contrary, it remains a mere historical and therefore contingent instance of a larger class of reprehensible moral actions. What, conceptually and ideologically, are we to make of this?

In a now well-known and much-discussed essay, "On the Social Construction of Moral Universals," Jeffrey Alexander suggests an instructive way into this question.[30] First published in 2002, and widely anthologized since then, Alexander's essay offers an account of the discursive and symbolic transformation of the narrative frameworks by which, as he puts it, a "specific and situated historical event . . . marked by ethnic racial hatred, violence, and war" was turned into a "generalized symbol of human suffering and moral evil."[31] Notably, the essay forms a crucial chapter in the development and exemplification of the kind of interpretive social science of which Alexander has long been a protagonist and specifically of a historical sociology attentive to the "cultural" idioms—the "social unconscious," as he calls it at one point—that shape and drive collective understandings and social actions. His remark that "no trauma interprets itself" succinctly captures his hermeneutic orientation.[32] Thus, the essay is meant less as a fully fleshed out historical narrative account of the atrocity committed against European Jews than as a *conceptual* intervention in the theorization of the history of a fundamental social event.[33] Needless to say, I do not intend to rehearse Alexander's argument here in all its rich detail. But part of the "cultural" shift he is seeking to illuminate—one that resonates with my own sense of the contours of "our time" as sketched in the previous chapter—is a shift from a postwar "progressive" narrative that codes and frames a story about war and liberation and democracy to a post-1960s "tragic" narrative in which the mass killing of Jews, now renamed a Holocaust, moves into the center of the frame as the generative moral dynamic of a "trauma-drama." And in this process, as he says, there is a significant alteration of the sense and status of the problem of evil.

As Alexander reminds us, in the early years following the April 1945 discovery of the death camps by the Allied army and the end of the Second World War itself some months later, the idea of the Holocaust as we know it now did not exist—it had not yet been invented.[34] The mass murder of Jews by the Nazis, as a more and more comprehensive and ghastly picture of it gradually emerged, was initially imagined essentially as a specific *atrocity* of war. It was a war crime situated in the context of other brutalities associated with the war and involving victims who were not all necessarily Jewish—or whose Jewishness was not the only salient factor. To be sure, already before the outbreak of the war, certainly with the racially discriminatory Nuremberg Laws of September 1935 and the shocking Kristallnacht destruction and killings of November 1938, there was a growing sense that the Nazis represented a virulent form of political evil. But the quite evident anti-Semitic register of this evil was still folded into the broader narrative of the Nazis' hyperbolic ideology and murderous practices that were directed not only against Jews. And in the aftermath of the war, even as the evidence of the "Final Solution" became better known, the mass killings continued to be situated within a *progressive* story of American triumphalism, with its rhetoric of a militantly forward-looking and global-democratic worldview. The progressive character of this narrative, Alexander maintains, depended on "keeping Nazism situated and historical," and this militated against the "representation of absolute evil being universalized."[35] However, from the 1960s onward, and at a gathering pace, the conditions for this progressivist narrative were eroded, and in its place there emerged a "tragic" narrative that gave a different point to the public representation of the Nazi killing of European Jews.

In the new "culture structure," Alexander writes, whereas the Jewish mass murders are still of course "coded" as evil, the "weighting" of this representation undergoes significant change—it becomes, he says, "burdened with extraordinary gravitas."[36] Displacing the Kantian figure of "radical evil" with an explicitly Durkheimian one, Alexander says that the representation of the Nazi atrocity against the Jews is now charged with the sense of a "sacred-evil"—that is, "an evil

96 PART II

that recalled a trauma of such enormity and horror that it had to be radically set apart from the world and all of its other traumatizing events." Thus what comes to be called, in a new abstract and decontextualized identity, "the Holocaust" is now imagined not only as distinctive but as unique and unprecedented, and not only as unique and unprecedented, but also as the kind of event that is "inexplicable in ordinary rational terms."[37] Henceforth, Alexander maintains, in the tragic and "postprogressive" narrative, the Holocaust is almost never referred to without some evocation of a sense of its fundamental *enigma* and its *impenetrability*. (In a moment, I am going to suggest that it is, in large part, this postprogressive representation that Hannah Arendt contributed to and that in turn has helped to propel her into being thought of as the preeminent theorist of evil she is now taken to be. It is not, simply, that Arendt's views on evil were ahead of their time, as is sometimes suggested; rather, it is that a postprogressive frame has reorganized the place for a positive reception of these views and imposed on them, as we have seen with Lara, both a contemporary demand and a contemporary *aura*.) With these changes, a universalizing process of "symbolic extension" and "psychological identification" was put into motion such that what was once a specific atrocity afflicting one specific group of people now widened to become the "trauma of all mankind."[38]

One very important episode in the story of the universalization of the Holocaust is the rise and transformation of the idea of *genocide*. As is well known, the term was coined in 1944 by the Polish-Jewish jurist Raphaël Lemkin in his book *Axis Rule in Occupied Europe*, at a time when knowledge of the death camps and the scale of the Nazi extermination campaign was fragmentary at best. The term would go on to play an important role in the Nuremberg trials the following year, and in 1948 it was enshrined in international law as the Convention on the Prevention and Punishment of the Crime of Genocide.[39] As Alexander suggests, the invention of this generalized term was in effect an early moment in the universalization of the Jewish experience under the Nazis. When the term was first introduced, he reminds us, it was "intended to cover all the antinational activities carried out by the Nazis against the occupied nations inside Hitler's Reich." It is in the wake of the discovery of the camps that "the element of mass murder" came to be the main "focus" of the idea.[40] So, no longer structured in the form of a forward-oriented story, what we now have is a tragic trauma-drama rhetorically structured so as to compel a compulsively repetitive return to the scene of a special kind of mass killing—namely, genocide. And this structure of repetition helped to give the Holocaust a "mythical status that transformed it into the archetypal sacred-evil of our time" and the "most emotionally compelling trauma of the twentieth century."[41] Indeed, one can see here a connection between the reification of the Holocaust, on the one hand, and the reification of the twentieth century, on the other. It is the former, notably, that enables the latter, not the other way around. It is the rhetorical construction of the Holocaust as the defining atrocity of our age that invests the twentieth century with its seeming prerogative in the auratic discourse of evil.

There is much in Alexander's essay that I have not touched upon. And there are aspects of its argument that seem to me less persuasive than others, or indeed, sometimes to even run counter to the project of historical-conceptual redescription that explicitly shapes its overall purposes. For example, when Alexander offers in the opening gesture of the essay that the social construction of the Holocaust as a "generalized symbol of human suffering and moral evil" has "created unprecedented opportunities for ethnic, racial, and religious justice, for mutual recognition, and global conflicts becoming regulated in a more civil way," the stage seems to be set less for a conceptual redescription than for a *normative* progressivist one—one moreover, inscribed in a liberal humanitarianism.[42] This suspicion is further underlined when, later on, Alexander tells us that the "dramatic universalization" of the Holocaust story has "deepened contemporary sensitivity to social evil."[43] It's a puzzling formulation, given the interpretive framework and the accent on the social *construction* of evil elsewhere in the essay (and in other essays of his), and it gives the impression that in the end Alexander has himself fallen victim to the seduction of moral universalism he has so superbly outlined.[44] For my purposes here, though, it is enough to emphasize the central thread in Alexander's admirable account—namely, the conceptual history of the moral universalization of the Holocaust as a trauma-drama of "engorged evil" whose principal image is that of systematic mass killing or genocide in the twentieth century.[45]

So far I have aimed to show that at least one influential dimension of contemporary thinking about evil operates in a remarkably unexamined way through a series of interconnected exceptionalizations—that of the twentieth century as the century of evil and that of the Holocaust as the preeminent paradigm of evil. It is not just that the Holocaust is the most referenced example of evil, it is that the atrocity committed against European Jews summarized by that term has been turned into a meta-evil, the evil that defines evil as such. And in this

98   PART II

process, needless to say, other atrocities do not simply pale in significance but also can assume only a certain kind of significance—namely, as merely specific empirical instances in the overall hierarchy of evils. No other figure is as important to this story as Hannah Arendt, and it is to her that I now turn.

THE PROBLEM ABOUT HANNAH ARENDT

There is a *problem* about Hannah Arendt to be reflected upon. As I have already suggested, she is a (perhaps *the*) central figure in contemporary discussions of evil.[46] In many ways, it is she who is taken to have *established* the discursive contours, the impetus and direction and tone, of the whole philosophical debate about evil—or at least a large swath of it. It is she who *grounds* the idea of the Holocaust as the exemplification of evil and thus helps to exceptionalize the twentieth century as the century of evil. As such, Arendt has become a canonical figure in her own right. Therefore, it may not be surprising that, as often happens with canonical figures, she is regularly read as though from within the exclusive circle of a club of knowing participants who tend to merely affirm and reaffirm her prescience and reiterate, in the case of evil, a familiar preoccupation with the recurrent question concerning what Arendt really *meant* by "radical evil" and "banality of evil," and whether or to what extent the latter superseded the former in her later thinking. I have no doubt that, in their own way, these are important questions. But from a certain perspective outside this canonical discussion, it is striking what—both about Arendt and about evil—is often taken for granted by those embedded in this relatively insular conversation. In a modest way, I want to suggest that perhaps reading Arendt on evil may be less straightforward than it at first appears in the work of many of her commentators and interpreters, and that there may be an unexamined problem concerning *how* one reads her and *for what* that is worth deeper reflection. To put this in a slightly different and more direct way, I want to suggest that whatever Arendt *meant* by evil, it is not entirely clear what *kind* of idea it was meant to be and what *role* it was meant to play in the organization of her thinking—that is, in the organization of the *arguments* that constitute the texts in which an idea of evil features.[47]

In raising in this way the issue about how we *read* Arendt and for what, I take my direction from that insightful and far-reaching remark I earlier extracted from C. L. R. James concerning the temporal gap between writers and readers, for it pertains as much to considerations of Arendt. Recall that in his inimitable discussion of Herman Melville, one of Arendt's favorite American authors as is well known (the novella *Billy Budd* was the work she most admired), James writes, "There is always, when reading great masterpieces of the past, a difference in the emphasis of the author and the reader."[48] This is perhaps to say much the obvious—namely, that *past* authors and *present* readers do not self-evidently occupy the same problem-space of questions and answers; they are not necessarily *contemporaries*, properly speaking, and therefore one cannot simply transfer the conceptual insights past authors had of *their* presents into the conundrums of present readers such as ourselves. Memorably, James is trying to think about how to read Melville's writing from the 1850s (the imaginary of a protoindustrial America) into the world of the (authoritarian and protofascist) 1950s in which he is living. I take James (perspicuous as ever) to be offering a caution about the temporal and contextual instability of meaning, a caution that resonates well with Wittgenstein's well-known suggestion in *Philosophical Investigations* regarding meaning-in-use—because use, after all, is always (and multiply) located. Or as Ian Hacking put it, a little polemically, with a Wittgensteinian flourish: "Don't ask for the meaning; ask for the point."[49] In other words (to return to Arendt), is there a relevant difference between the contexts of Arendt's writing and reading about evil and those of *our* reading and writing of which we should be at least mindful? Should reading Arendt today entail some reflection on whether or to what extent her questions (the conundrums that shaped the problem-space into which she intervened) remain exactly ours—whether or how *our* questions can be read through *her* ideas?

Arendt has emerged as more than simply the most prominent theorist of evil. She is sometimes read these days by her best interpreters as though evil was not merely *one* among her generative ideas but in fact a central or basic or "fundamental" idea for her. Take Richard Bernstein, for example, an indisputably rich and distinguished interpreter of Arendt's views, as I've said, and someone to whose work I return again and again throughout this chapter. Here is how he opens the first of his two chapters on evil in his instructive book *Hannah Arendt and the Jewish Question*: "In 1945, Arendt declared: 'The problem of evil will be the most fundamental question of postwar intellectual life in Europe.' . . . She was wrong. Most postwar intellectuals avoided any direct confrontation with the problem of evil. But it did become fundamental for Arendt. She returned to it over and over again, and she was still struggling with it at the time of her

100   PART II

death."[50] How, though, are we meant to understand "fundamental" here? I have a doubt about Bernstein's axiomatic formulation in this passage because, as I have suggested, I take the discursive *location* of evil in Arendt's work to be more perplexed and uncertain than it is typically assumed to be—certainly more than it is assumed in Bernstein's authoritative pronouncement. Indeed, I think there is something simultaneously perceptive and misleading, at once illuminating and obscuring, in Bernstein's remark about Arendt and evil that is worth reflecting on, something specifically to do with the presumed *organizational* role of her ideas about evil within the relevant texts and by extension within the ethos of her work as a whole (which, I take it, is what "fundamental" suggests). What is perceptive and illuminating is the explicit recognition that whereas Arendt sought to introduce a problem about evil into political-philosophical criticism a early as the 1940s, this was evidently *not* a concern shared by her contemporaries in the United States and Europe. For Bernstein, the implication seems to be that Arendt had an insight or intuition that these contemporaries did not share and did not even notice in her work. I believe this is important. Evil did not *stick* as a postwar moral-political term of art.[51] What is obscuring and misleading, however, is the way Bernstein then proceeds as though this insight was not itself part of the very *problem* calling for exploration. It merely signals to him the transparent origin of the soon-to-be fundamental insight that can be tracked throughout her later work. However, is it so self-evident that for Arendt evil was ever *fundamental* in the way, say, that others of her recurrent terms more unambiguously were—plurality, natality, action, freedom, authority, thinking, and so on? Indeed, did evil ever really become a *concept* for her as these arguably did—that is, an idea that motivated and organized and drove analysis or argument rather than an idea that, say, retrospectively summarized a discussion? Bernstein does not take the contrast he discerns between Arendt and her contemporaries, and by extension, Arendt and *his* contemporaries, as the *starting point* of an interpretive problematization of the contrasting conjunctures in which Arendt wrote and in which she has been read. What was it that precluded Arendt's contemporaries and later commentators and interpreters from noticing this fundamental insight regarding evil in her work and responding to it critically? Bernstein does not say, much less probe. And what is it, by contrast, that enables *him* and his contemporaries to notice her insight, and notice it in such a way as to secure the plausibility of his axiomatic claim about its fundamental relation to the arc of her work? I wonder whether, to a significant degree, the conditions of reading Arendt *as though* evil was her "fundamental" question are shaped in important ways less by *her* conjuncture than by Bernstein's. Is it that evil was Arendt's fundamental question all along but was somehow mistakenly overlooked by her negligent earlier readers? Or might there be something about our own present—Bernstein's—that prompts *this* reading of her rather than some other?

Noticeably, beyond the bare reference to the sentence I have quoted from *Hannah Arendt and the Jewish Question*, Bernstein does not engage the 1945 essay "Nightmare and Flight" from which he extracts Arendt's remark expressing her expectation that evil would have a "fundamental" place in the intellectual life of postwar Europe. Evidently, in his view, it has no bearing on how we should understand what Arendt might have been getting at, the conundrum she is trying to illuminate, by way of this early invocation of evil. But such an engagement might well have set her remark within the wider context of her intervention and the question she was puzzling over that seemed to yield the idea of evil as the best response. I cannot offer a complete reconstruction of that conjuncture here, but some orienting remarks are in order.

It is perhaps not entirely surprising that Arendt should have had evil on her mind in the 1930s and 1940s, and not only because of the rise of the Third Reich. Recall that her doctoral dissertation, *Love and Saint Augustine*, was completed in 1929, that she took a copy with her when she fled Berlin in 1933, and that she periodically planned for its publication. Against canonical readings of Arendt that see her largely in relation to Kant, as overcoming Kant, it is increasingly being recognized that the dissertation's Augustinian themes and concepts had a lasting impact on her thinking, including specifically her thinking about evil.[52] Although Augustine's obsessive reflections on evil (it was a topic he returned to endlessly) were certainly not the dissertation's central focus, Arendt's concern with his idea of neighborly love (*caritas*) could not but set its contrasting terms— for example, wrong love (*cupiditas*)—into relief.[53] Wrong love, Arendt observes of the Christian tradition of which she was (and remained) a keen student, is the root of all evils.[54] (Kant had this Augustinian idea too.) In a sense, Arendt was already inside of a discursive field shaped by a problem about evil.

"Nightmare and Flight" is ostensibly a review of Denis de Rougemont's *The Devil's Share*, published in 1944, but it is really more a brief thought-exercise in which Arendt is working out, among other matters, her relation to her philosophic past, and to Martin Heidegger in particular, in the context of the Jewish catastrophe.[55] It is not irrelevant that it is Rougemont that she takes as the subject

102   PART II

for a review. Rougemont was a Swiss nonconformist Christian and a colleague of the philosopher Emmanuel Mounier and was perhaps better known for his earlier book, *Love in the Western World*, published in 1940.[56] Given its topic, Arendt would certainly have been familiar with this book. By contrast, *The Devil's Share* is, as Rougemont put it, a "little treatise" on the "Devil's activity in our time," part two of which was (hardly surprisingly, given the historical moment) devoted to reflections on Hitler's diabolical wickedness.[57] Arendt's remarks on the book are, by turns, condensed and measured, and characteristically searching and allusive. She is simultaneously sympathetic to, and critical of, Rougemont's attempt to capture the "nightmare of reality" that was the unfolding experience of Nazi totalitarianism. She recognizes the paradoxical senses in which he is courageous and yet timidly *constrained* within conventions of thinking that no longer have any basis in the reality of the time. Arendt suggests that Rougemont writes with evident "confusion," but a confusion, notably, that is perfectly understandable, inasmuch as it is "the direct result of experiences to which the author bears witness and from which he does not try to escape."[58] And yet, ultimately, the (tragic) paradox is that, almost in spite of himself, he *does* take "flight" in a useless, outmoded, and misguided conceptual language. For if Rougemont is confused, it is not simply because he is ignorant but because "in a desperate attempt not to be confronted with this nightmare in spiritual nakedness, he picks up from the great and beautiful arsenal of time-honored figures and images anything that seems to correspond to or interpret the new shocks that rock the old foundation," especially the figure of the Devil and the potent image of a monstrous evil.[59] Arendt painfully recognizes Rougemont's intellectual and existential dilemma. After all, in part it is hers too. The nightmare with which Rougemont is wrestling turns on the suspicion that what he is up against is a *limit* experience, the experience of a nihilism in which anything and everything is possible—or as Arendt puts it, in a phrase that recurs in other essays from the 1940s as well as in *The Origins of Totalitarianism*, though the Nazis are "men like ourselves" they have "proven what man is capable of."[60]

It is precisely at this point in the essay's rhetorical economy, with reference to the predicament that Rougemont is attempting to render, that Arendt offers the sentence partially quoted by Bernstein. The sentence reads: "In other words, the problem of evil will be the fundamental question of postwar intellectual life in Europe—as death became the fundamental problem after the last war."[61] To my mind, this remark is as revealing as it is obscure, and it bears reflection (however brief) rather than a mere passing evocation. Arendt's opening "in other words" suggests that her remark, drawing a significant contrast between the interpretive standpoints of the two world wars, is meant to function as a gloss on, or an upshot of, what Rougemont is inviting her—and us—to think about (even if he cannot adequately articulate it)—namely, the *limit* of our conceptual vocabulary. If the terrible image of death offered a poignant limit as the overwhelming experience of the First World War, in the Second World War, an inexpressible image of evil marks the absolute border of what man has proven himself capable. The difficulty, however, that Arendt has with Rougemont's account is that, in the end, instead of facing up to the manifest reality of "man's capacity for evil" he compromises his own insight by taking conceptual "flight" in metaphysical language and "writes on the nature of the Devil, thereby, despite all dialectics, evading the responsibility of man for his deeds." Christian metaphysical reference to the Devil, she seems to suggest, precludes human blameworthiness and therefore accountability and answerability. More broadly, her worry is that in Rougemont's hands this figure of evil turns out to be little more than a "personification of Heidegger's Nothingness" and thus ends up attempting to "explain the new experiences with the categories of the nineteen-twenties."[62] The allusion here, of course, is to Heidegger's 1927 masterwork, *Being and Time*, which was an acknowledged intellectual revolution when it appeared but whose conceptual terms Arendt was then (two decades later) in the process of reexamining and, to some degree, turning away from.[63] Rougemont's "flight from reality" takes him down the slippery slope of a Heideggerian-like "gnostic speculation."[64] His "ultimate consolation," Arendt writes, the redemptive appeal of Gnosticism, is the certainty that in the great struggle between the esoteric forces of good and evil victory will finally go to the good. For Arendt in 1945, there was simply no such moral-political refuge of certainty. For her—then, as later—attractive as this sort of "metaphysical opportunism" (as she called it) was, it was a dangerous abdication of the moral and political responsibility to press beyond the conventional vocabulary and face up to the new and frightening reality with which she and her contemporaries were confronted.[65]

Minimally, it seems to me, "Nightmare and Flight" is an important essay in Arendt's oeuvre not merely because in it she forecasts (mistakenly or not) the significance of the problem of evil to the postwar European world but also because in its compact beauty and pathos we find a brief and troubled conceptual-political intervention in which she is literally feeling her way, uncertainly, provisionally,

104   PART II

by turns empathetic and impatient, in an emerging conjuncture breaking open around her. And this conjuncture is shaped, on the one hand, by the pronounced and shocking novelty of the immediate reality of a political regime seemingly devoted to the destruction of the Jewish people and, on the other, by the limp ineffectiveness of her inherited moral-political language, in which even the great monstrous figure of the Devil and the idea of evil in Christian political theology, while temptingly attractive, nevertheless falls short of what is urgently needed— namely, a concept of moral *enormity* that could lay claim to a strong sense of moral-political *responsibility*.[66] There was nothing trivially unambiguous about this moral-intellectual-political struggle for her. As Philip Rieff helps us to see in his illuminating early discussion of *The Origins of Totalitarianism*, Arendt was herself given to a "covert" theology of spiritualized history.[67] Not so surprising, then, in the 1945 "Nightmare and Flight" one has the distinct sense of her wrestling with the dark angel in the path seeking to release herself from the broken heritage by which she has been formed in order to imagine a new descriptive-conceptual language in which to capture what she perceived to be a novel quality of violence and violation associated with the Nazi death camps, horrific accounts of which were literally emerging as she wrote. In the essay, noticeably, evil is not invested with a definitive *positive* content; it is characterized only by its extremity and potentiality, by what human beings are *capable* of once traditional *limits* are destroyed. Evil is a covering term that helps Arendt look directly into the face of her political reality without what she would later call "banisters," without taking flight in the consolations of gnostic speculation and the abdication of moral responsibility for human action to which its metaphysics leads.[68]

Evil in Arendt, then, is less self-evident than is often imagined. It seems to me an interesting fact, one not to my knowledge raised (let alone reflected on) by Bernstein or any other of Arendt's major commentators and interpreters, that the term *evil* does not appear in the index of either of the two principal books in which she is thought to have mobilized the idea—*The Origins of Totalitarianism* and *Eichmann in Jerusalem*—nor, indeed, does it appear in the indexes of the more formally philosophical works, *The Human Condition* and *The Life of the Mind*, in both of which evil plays a not insignificant role. The term does appear, curiously enough, in the index of *On Revolution*, published in the same year as *Eichmann in*

Jerusalem. Now, of course, this by itself need not necessarily be definitive or conclusive proof of anything—indexes, after all, have been known to be notoriously unreliable guides to a thinker's basic terms. Still, you might well have thought that if evil was indeed fundamental to Arendt's thinking it would be one of those terms she (or her publishers) would be concerned that a reader not miss, could easily find among the welter of words out of which any book is constructed. Again, this is not to diminish the significance of evil in Arendt's work, only to highlight precisely that there is a problem about reading Arendt on evil that, though it has been, should not be ignored.

Similarly, but arguably more important than indexes, it is often overlooked that evil does not appear in either *The Origins of Totalitarianism* or *Eichmann in Jerusalem* in anything resembling studied frequency, let alone in a robust or elaborated *conceptual* form. Indeed, given the outsized interpretive claims made on its behalf, one might have imagined that its presence in these texts would be more substantial and more generative—but evil seems scarcely to appear in any formal, structuring way in either book. Moreover, when it does appear, evil seems less like a dynamic organizing frame of analysis than a means of summarizing or glossing a train of thought. Take, for example, *The Origins of Totalitarianism*, the book with which I am most concerned. As every reader of it knows, this is an enormously complicated book, not only for its vast canvas and unwieldy structure but also for the revisions introduced into it over subsequent editions—not least where the notion of evil is concerned.[69] In the 1951 first edition (memorably published as *The Burden of Our Time* in Britain and as *The Origins of Totalitarianism* in the United States), evil in anything more than a passing reference appears on only two occasions—once in the preface and again in the briefly sketched "Concluding Remarks."

The preface to the 1951 edition (dated "summer 1950") offers a short and deftly poetic framing that displays an intriguing and somewhat disconcerting historiographic sensibility. It opens with an evocation of the catastrophe of the recently ended war, the overwhelming apprehension of ruin, the indigestible shock of the end of an old, familiar world of dependable values and secure traditions. Her book, she says, was written against the background of "reckless optimism and reckless despair" and with the conviction of a necessary realism.[70] Arendt sees the rise of totalitarianism not only as the cause of the disaster but also as one response to the preexisting state of political, economic, and moral crisis produced by the imperialism she then describes in part 2. The difficulty she sees in adequately coming to grips with totalitarianism is that in it we are witness to the ways in which the negative and positive effects of historical forces are "strangely intertwined" such that, for example, "without the fictitious world of totalitarian movements, in which with unparalleled clarity the essential uncertainties of our time have been spelled out, we might have been driven to our doom without ever becoming aware of what has been happening."[71] And it is with this irreconcilable sense of the historical *paradox* of what can be learned from the past that Arendt first explicitly poses the question of evil—in a remarkable single-sentence paragraph: "And if it is true that in the final stages an absolute evil appears (absolute because it can no longer be deduced from humanly comprehensible motives), it is also true that without it we might never have known the truly radical nature of Evil."[72]

Now, to my mind anyway, this passage is not easy to confidently situate or elucidate. Grammatically, to begin with, both the opening conjunction ("and") and the conditional ("if") are odd here, as though the theme of evil had already and more formally been introduced and these fleeting remarks were merely supplementary, a kind of confirmation of what had already been established. They give the feeling of a conclusion, even a coda, rather than the initial conceptual orientation a preface might be expected to provide. Substantively, Arendt speaks of a temporal moment, the "final stages," when an "absolute evil" appears. Here one can reasonably assume that the reference is to the death camps that were part of the "Final Solution" that became systematic Nazi policy after the Wannsee Conference in January 1942. Thus it is signaled that the death camps are to be at the center of Arendt's idea of absolute evil. But note the conceptual *instability* here. Arendt speaks in the same breath of *both* an "absolute" evil and the "radical nature" of Evil, in the latter case capped to suggest the almost allegorical or metaphysical standing of the proper noun. What the contrast and similarity between these expressions of an idea of evil exactly are is not specified—as though it were undecidable or self-evident or, again, irrelevant to the figuration of the problem at hand.

In "Concluding Remarks" at the close of the first edition, Arendt continues the theme of the previous chapter (chapter 12, "Totalitarianism in Power"), reflecting at an only slightly further critical and generalizing distance on its central motif—namely, the totalitarian belief that "everything is possible." Then, somewhat unexpectedly, she reintroduces the idea of absolute evil: "Difficult as it is to conceive of an absolute evil even in the face of its factual existence, it seems to be closely connected with the invention of a system in which all men are equally superfluous. The manipulators of this system believe in their own superfluousness as much as in that of all the others, and the totalitarian murderers are all the more dangerous because they do not care if they themselves are alive or dead, if they ever lived or never were born."[73] This theme of superfluousness is in fact developed with poignant effect in connection to the death camps in "Total Domination," the last section of "Totalitarianism in Power." One might have thought that it would have been there that Arendt would have elaborated in more detail the specific conceptual relevance of evil. But she does not, and note again the thoughtful hesitation in her description, and the consequent instability and undecidability in the characterization of evil. Absolute evil is difficult to conceive—even as it blankly stares one in the face—and it is only "closely connected" to (not definitionally specified in) a system in which human beings are made superfluous.

In the second edition of *The Origins of Totalitarianism*, published in 1958 (significantly, the same year as *The Human Condition*), Arendt introduced a number of revisions, or what she called "additions and enlargements," to the text: most importantly, of course, was the replacement of the 1951 "Concluding Remarks" with the more substantial chapter 13, "Ideology and Terror: A Novel form of Government"; and the addition of chapter 14, "Epilogue: Reflections on the Hungarian Revolution," marking the enormous importance of this event for her thinking about politics (chapter 14 was removed in subsequent editions).[74] Notably, neither of the new chapters concerns itself with evil. However, elements from the 1951 "Concluding Remarks" were moved to chapter 12, "Totalitarianism in Power," and these remarks were significantly expanded in terms of the question of evil. It is in these transplanted and transfigured remarks that Arendt introduces her famous reference to Kant's idea of evil and will from his *Religion Within the Boundaries of Mere Reason*. The paragraph on evil, no less unexpected than in the earlier edition, now begins this way:

> It is inherent in our entire philosophical tradition that we cannot conceive of a "radical evil," and this is true both for Christian theology, which conceded even to the Devil himself a celestial origin, as well as for Kant, the only philosopher who, in the word he coined for it, at least must have suspected the existence of this evil even though he immediately rationalized it in the concept of a "perverted ill will" that could be explained by comprehensive

108 PART II

motives. Therefore, we actually have nothing to fall back on in order to understand a phenomenon that nevertheless confronts us with its overpowering reality.[75]

Arendt then resumes the theme of what "seems discernible"—namely, the relationship between evil and the "system in which all men have become equally superfluous."[76] Again, as with the earlier cited passage on evil from the preface and the 1951 conclusion, this one too has a somewhat enigmatic quality about it. Although radical evil seems to lie beyond the conceptual resources of the Western philosophical tradition, in either its Christian or Kantian iterations, whether in relation to the Devil or the will, it still has to be characterized in some form given its overwhelming facticity. This, of course, is the conceptual labor of the idea of "superfluousness."

It is curious that Arendt speaks in these passages with such notable looseness just when *we* (contemporary readers) might think we are most in need of more elaborated conceptual precision, a more precise handle by which to get hold of evil's conceptual reference. But my point is not to condemn Arendt for conceptual inadequacy (as María Pía Lara might). The absence of a pronounced conceptual architecture of evil need not necessarily negate its significance for Arendt. But it might place a certain burden on her interpreters and commentators to be more circumspect in their discussions of her ideas than they have seemed inclined to be. And this might help to illuminate some crucial differences between a conjuncture in which Arendt is perhaps searching for a language in which to capture and name a novel experience, and our own, when an idea of evil, emerging out of this background (and with Arendt's help), is becoming a more dynamic and formally organizing *concept*.

In light of these unsettling blind spots, it may be instructive to briefly reflect on Arendt's recent rise to prominence as a theorist of "our time" because this may help to situate her contribution—that is, what it might be about her work, including her work on evil, that seems to so resonate with the present. In some sense, Arendt is the paradigmatic theorist of the ethical turn, certainly within political studies. At the same time, as I have repeatedly noted, this seeming resonance may have as much to do with features of her thought as with features of our own conjuncture—or with the way these are connected or conjugated—and this I argue should have implications for how we read Arendt out of her present into ours.

In this endeavor, I again turn to the work of Richard Bernstein. Certainly, one of Bernstein's abiding concerns in recent years has been to focus our attention on the reasons for Arendt's contemporary relevance. This is what his short book *Why Read Hannah Arendt Now*, published in 2018, is concerned with.[77] Let us note to begin with that *Why Read Hannah Arendt Now* is not posing a question so much as offering an authoritative, almost imperative statement about why we ought to read her work in the present (the title bears no question mark). Still, part of what is attractive about this little book is the sense of intimacy with which Bernstein talks about Arendt, the sense of his easy familiarity not only with the substance of her work but also with the style of her thinking, the *mentality* or cast of mind that informed it.[78] Even in its brief compass, therefore, *Why Read Hannah Arendt Now* offers an uncommonly perceptive portrait of Arendt's approach to the matters that concerned her. Explicitly evoking his own conjuncture (the *now* of the title), Bernstein is intrigued by the somewhat unexpected renown that has gathered around Arendt in the last two or three decades. At the time of her sudden death in December 1975, Bernstein notes that Arendt was not by any means unknown but neither was she a very prominent figure in either Europe or the United States. She was certainly not widely considered to be a major political theorist and was known primarily for the bitter controversy that took shape around her 1963 *Eichmann in Jerusalem* and especially for the phrase—"the banality of evil"—it formulates.[79] By contrast, in recent decades Hannah Arendt has emerged not only as one of the most significant theorists across a wide swath of moral and political concerns but also as a theorist who appears as almost the all-purpose embodiment of a contemporary moral-political demand. How should we understand this?

Why, Bernstein asks, has there been a "recent spike of interest" in Arendt's work? What accounts for this? The answer Bernstein gives is the by-now familiar one—namely, that Arendt "was remarkably perceptive about some of the deepest problems, perplexities, and dangerous tendencies in modern political life," many of which, far from waning much less disappearing, have only "become more intense and more dangerous."[80] In tune with Elisabeth Young-Bruehl in her earlier book on Arendt's timeliness, *Why Arendt Matters*, Bernstein links this relevance to Arendt's conceptualization of "dark times."[81] Bernstein too picks up on the idea that, for Arendt, "dark times" did not have exclusively to do with the "horrors" of totalitarian violence, but also, perhaps more, with the extinguishing of the light that sustains the public spaces of appearance, discussion, and renewal. His sense is that we, today, are also "living in dark times that are engulfing the entire world," and such darkness calls for someone who can provide us with illumination—that is, someone like Hannah Arendt. Bernstein writes: "I want to show that Arendt provides such illumination, that she helps us to gain critical perspective on our current political problems and perplexities. She is an astute critic of dangerous tendencies in modern life and she illuminates the potentialities for restoring the dignity of politics." And this, he says, is why Arendt is "worth reading and rereading today."[82] Bernstein's book then ranges across a number of vital topics that are meant to demonstrate why her work is indispensable to our time. Among them are statelessness and refugees; the right to have rights; Zionism; racism and segregation; truth, politics and lying; plurality; and personal and political responsibility. In each of these areas, Arendt is shown to have had insights that are worth holding onto and deepening. "Arendt should be read today because she was so perceptive in comprehending the dangers that still confront us and warned us about becoming indifferent or cynical," Bernstein concludes. "She urged us to take responsibility for our political destinies. She taught us that we have the capacity to act in concert, to initiate, to begin, to strive to make freedom a worldly reality."[83]

To be sure, I could hardly disagree with Bernstein's eloquent and perceptive remarks that draw our attention into the hinterland of Arendt's sensibilities. But I wonder whether in his understandable desire to illuminate Arendt's contemporary relevance he doesn't overlook something or take something for granted about the conceptual relation between pasts and presents, about the difference in emphasis, as C. L. R. James would say, between past authors and present readers. We are, of course, obliged to note that Bernstein's book is deliberately written in a non-academic style, for a more general audience, and thus has, perhaps, a restricted critical ambition. In any case, his inquiries certainly prompt us to press further the question of *how* and *to what end* to historicize Arendt. As others have also done, Bernstein underlines the fact that Arendt was a reflective and conceptual thinker who thought out of, or in relation to, her own *experience*—that is, she was an adept at rendering the particularity of her experience as the ground for wider reflection.[84] This is something both distinctive and admirable about her intellectual cast of mind. This quality of her intelligence is in part why she could be so alert to the sense of rupture between past and present conceptions and conventions of moral-political rule inaugurated by the Nazi regime—the significance of "totalitarianism," for example, as an unprecedented political form, and evil as a resonant moral category. All of Arendt's work, it has been said, can be described as a reflective elaboration of the experience of this moral-historical-conceptual break. But, still, even if we are to accept her account of this radical epistemic discontinuity in the moral-political story of the modern world (and there are good reasons, I think, to challenge it as a specifically European, not to say, Eurocentric, story), can Arendt's experience of it simply be read into the conceptual *topos* of our conjuncture in an unexamined way? Are dark times only more or less dark, or are they also sometimes, and more importantly, *differently* dark? Surely the relation between experience and conceptual thinking is not as innocent or transparent as this assumption suggests. If part of the productive point about Arendt's thinking is that her concepts were to a large degree anchored in—or at least, generated out of—the vantage point of her experience, shouldn't the principle of this relationality also be brought to bear on how we, her contemporary readers, think with and through her? It is this relation that I think goes unexamined in Bernstein's account.

In just this connection, let me return to the pertinent question of Arendt on race, because it also illustrates a distinctive way of handling, as a matter of reading Arendt *now*, some awkward issues concerning her approach to the questions that preoccupied her and that have a direct bearing on my concern here with New World slavery. Notably, this is not a topic that Young-Bruehl takes up in her authoritative assessment of Arendt's contemporary relevance, so it is to Bernstein's credit that he does not evade Arendt's problematic attitudes and positions regarding Black experience, and Black people.[85] Arendt, he says, "was often insightful, but at times she could also be obtuse and guilty of what she took to be the worst sin of intellectuals—imposing her categories on the world instead of being sensitive to the complexities of reality."[86] Indeed, Arendt was well known to often speak with unhindered, even arrogant, sometimes ill-informed authority about the world around her.[87] This was undoubtedly the case where Black experience and Black people are concerned. However, Bernstein feels that nothing more than an overreaching insensitivity was the real trouble with her infamous essay "Reflections on Little Rock," ostensibly a discussion of desegregation in the U.S. South, written in 1957 but published (after some complications) in *Dissent* in 1959.[88] Bernstein rehearses in brief the broad context of the essay and sets out some of Arendt's chief points, including her well-known opposition to federally imposed integration of public schools, and also her startling suggestion

112   PART II

that Black parents were using their children to fight what really should be adult political battles.[89]

Bernstein readily agrees that some of Arendt's views in this essay are egregious. But his principal concern seems to be to shield her from the charge of outright anti-Black racism. Arendt's failure, he suggests, was a failure of "understanding," one that, uncharacteristically in this case, she was willing to admit in her (private) response to Ralph Ellison's (public) criticism.[90] In this respect, Bernstein cites Danielle Allen and Kathryn Gines as (Black) critics who have written "detailed critiques, pointing out Arendt's factual errors and misguided opinions."[91] But how, I want to inquire, is he reading these criticisms? What is he reading them to *say*? Certainly, it is true that neither Allen in *Talking to Strangers* nor Gines in *Hannah Arendt and the Negro Question* is so unsubtle as to suggest that Arendt was a "white supremacist" (whatever Bernstein might take that term to mean in this context). But the evident relief he feels that Arendt is not dismissively and irredeemably cast within the shadow of this ascription perhaps only deflects our attention from the deeper complexity surrounding her perspective not only on "race" as a descriptive category but also on Blackness as historically embodied social experience. Contrary to Bernstein, for example, Gines's book-length doubts seem to me less about mere "facts" and "opinions" (relatively superficial matters, after all) than about whether or to what extent, when it came to Black lives and Black experience, Arendt's *subject-position* and *voice*, the assumed social *location* from which she saw and spoke in reference to Black people, were shaped and inflected by a mentality of *normative Whiteness*—that is, the unexamined and unacknowledged moral and epistemological privilege of tacit White identity—such that, as Gines suggests, whether or not one calls Arendt an anti-Black racist, one can discern "elements of racism in her analysis and in her descriptions of persons of African descent."[92] What Gines explores is, in fact, the not so unfamiliar (if nevertheless very often unspoken or obscured or disavowed) paradox of a White thinker (or a European immigrant who has *become* White in the binary racialized context of the United States) who holds views on any number of putatively raceless topics that seem entirely worthy and blameless, unmarked by a raced subjectivity, but who, when it comes to matters directly concerning Black lives, not only ventures to pronounce on these lives with uninhibited authority but, in doing so, and in a quite natural and naturalizing way, also adopts the voice and tone and subject-position expressive of a hegemonic and authoritative norm of Whiteness—one in which the otherness of a speechless Blackness is merely a discursive effect.[93] Bernstein is not entirely unaware that there is a discordant form of disavowal at work in Arendt's treatment of Black experience. He notes, for example, the well-known fact that the very conceptual idiom with which she defends Jews against anti-Semitic persecution and discrimination and prejudice (namely, the ground of individual experience and identity) is somehow made unavailable to, or withheld from, Blacks.[94] But for Bernstein, oddly, this inconsistency is nothing more than a matter of Arendt's idiosyncratic "obtuseness" or "insensitivity" and therefore quite beneath the dignity of formal let alone systematic inquiry.[95]

Bernstein believes that more important than dwelling too much on Arendt's misguided views about Black life is to use "Arendt against Arendt" in order to recover her critical relevance—that is, to read for the *best* Arendt, not the worst.[96] I agree that we should stand ready to do just this, with Arendt as with any thinker of her intellectual complexity. Thus, notably, Bernstein turns to *The Origins of Totalitarianism* for the resources with which to read Arendt against the grain of her own ill-judged assertions. For here, in his view, we have an Arendt who demonstrated the devastating ferocity of the scientific racism that accompanied late nineteenth-century imperialism and the "scramble for Africa." But, once again, evidently Bernstein has not really read Gines. who offers a detailed discussion of the dubious constructions that shape the idea of imperialism in Arendt's book.[97] Had Bernstein done so he might have been open to raising questions about some of the cardinal distinctions—between "colonialism" and "imperialism," for example, or between "race thinking" and "racism"— through which this section of Arendt's book works, not to mention her racialized self-positioning with respect to Africans.[98] Bernstein flatly accepts at face value Arendt's quasi-historical account according to which the colonizing project that involved the extermination of Native people in the Americas, a project whose flipside of course was the enslavement of Africans kidnapped and transported across the Atlantic, was somehow surpassed by "something different and much more vicious" with the rise of late nineteenth-century imperialism. Now, no student of the seventeenth- and eighteenth-century colonizing project in the Caribbean and mainland North America would fail to recognize the discursive and structural historical shifts in the late nineteenth century, in particular given the impact of social Darwinism and the rise of scientific racism, but none of these, surely, would diminish in the process the founding problem of Native genocide and African slavery. "While imperialism may differ from colonialism in its timing, some of its motivations, and its role as a precursor to totalitarianism," Gines writes, "it is also the case that, like imperialism, colonialism in the Americas and

114   PART II

Australia employed violent, religious, and racist tactics for the purpose of economic expansion."[99] Indeed, it is a central part of this story of the Americas, that the primitive accumulation made possible by the exterminating, enslaving, and expansionist colonizing project was itself a fundamental *condition* for the later imperial developments. It is puzzling that Bernstein does not wonder whether Arendt's *way* of telling the story she tells about imperialism and the transformation of capitalism it depended upon isn't in part motivated by her need to establish a particular link between the supposed features of imperialism and those she ascribes to political anti-Semitism, on the one hand, and totalitarianism, on the other. Isn't this, after all, not the telos of her book?

It may be that Bernstein's aim is nothing so unsophisticated as to specifically exonerate Arendt, but he certainly does not inquire into her thinking (the explicit task of his book) in such a way as to risk exposing her to any criticism more significant than passing, incidental obliviousness or hasty judgment—certainly he offers nothing that might help us to really begin to understand, for example the nature of her experience of *learning* to come to terms, as a German-Jewish woman, with the specific features of racial and racist America and the political ontology of Black America. He seems reluctant to appreciate, perhaps, that it may well be a familiar paradox of racial formations that Arendt *could* have explicitly and formally "condemned racist ideology" all her life as he and others say she did (concerning the Jewish experience most pronouncedly and persistently, but not only), while still adopting tacit or even not-so-tacit subject-positions with respect to Black lives that in effect reproduced normative White racialized and racist assumptions about them. Such an appreciation, needless to say, would entail not necessarily a simple or simple-minded rejection of Arendt ("canceling" her, in contemporary jargon) but a riskier exploration of the irreducible complexity of a thinker worthy of engaged inquiry. By the same token, my point is not to criticize Bernstein for being an apologist for Arendt so much as to signal the importance of a more unflinching account of her work in tune with precisely the fallibilistic interpretive approach his pragmatism encourages.

I have already said that to me Hannah Arendt is one of the paradigmatic thinkers of the ethical turn in the humanities and social sciences. Or to put it slightly differently, I might suggest that it is in the context of the post–Cold War epistemic shift (see chapter 1) that brought moral considerations into the generative foreground that her work has assumed the pronounced significance that it has, and come to seem especially insightful, even indispensable. It is not, of course, that Arendt thought of herself as a *moral* philosopher or indeed as a philosopher of any kind. To the contrary, it is well known that she rejected the title 'philosopher" and expressly understood the domain of her thinking to be that of the political realm.[100] Rather, what is interesting about Arendt's work and what stands out from our retrospect and from the vantage of the present conjuncture is that the main categories of her political thinking—among them, plurality, action, forgiveness, promising, friendship, responsibility, judgment, and willingness, not to mention evil—lend themselves to precisely the kinds of moral inquiry the present appears to demand. In a certain sense, it is not so surprising that during the Cold War years of her productive life (from the late 1940s through the early 1970s), when the principal axis of antagonism turned around the political-ideological rivalry between liberalism and Marxism, Arendt was if not ignored then at least not treated with the reverence she now commands, that her work did not touch so resonant a chord as it now so palpably does. Her conceptual orientations were connected to *both* liberalism and Marxism and yet reducible to *neither* of them.[101] It is in the aftermath of the exhaustion of the world-historical drama of contestation between liberalism and Marxism that the question of the ethical has come to appear vitally important, and it seems to me that it is in precisely this context that Arendt's work has assumed pronounced value. Read, as it now is, outside the nexus shaped by the old antagonisms between liberalism and Marxism, her categories suddenly seem to offer an idiom in which to talk about the predicament of the current conjuncture; they seem to be, uncannily, meant for us.[102]

ARENDT AND THE *WORK* OF EVIL

What is the work of evil in Hannah Arendt's texts? Contrary to canonical assumptions about Arendt and evil among her commentators and interpreters (caught up as they often are in the endless in-house debate about the relative superiority of the idea of "radical evil" as opposed to "banality of evil"), I think this is a not uncomplicated question. Arendt has to be *read*. Evil, I have suggested at the outset, has been principally associated with genocide—that is, with the commission of systematic mass killing aimed at ethnic extermination, especially in

116 PART II

the twentieth century. The Holocaust provides the paradigmatic image of this dominant conception of evil and thus, in effect, the paradigmatic image of evil as such. Arendt, of course, is profoundly implicated in the production and authorization of this powerful and now commonplace image. For her, memorably, the Nazi death camps were the principal instruments for carrying out the policy of extermination. It is notable, however, and not sufficiently recognized, that Arendt's picture of evil was not simply reducible to the *event* of extermination. For her, the evil suffered by European Jews under the Nazis was far more complicated and pernicious than that of sheer mass killing (as evil as such killing was and is). More than the final event of physical extermination, what especially interested her was the *process* by which Jews were systematically rendered *killable*—and she named this process "making human beings as human beings superfluous." Extermination was only the endpoint in this evil process of making people superfluous. Still, for Arendt the evil perpetrated in the death camps was exceptional, incomparable to anything else in known history. Furthermore, and notably, the exceptional character of the death camps is partly established (rhetorically, perhaps *polemically*) by explicitly *diminishing* the evil of other atrocities, including New World slavery.

In this section, I explore the *work* of evil in Arendt's thinking. I am concerned primarily with *The Origins of Totalitarianism*, not only because this is her first major formulation of an idea of evil but because it is here that the idea of evil as making people superfluous is articulated, and, moreover, it is here too that the idea of slavery emerges in a subordinate place in her hierarchy of evils. Again, I shall take Richard Bernstein as my guide. Not only has he thus far offered the richest and most searching discussion of Arendt's ideas about evil, but he has drawn our attention most instructively to the centrality for her of the distinctive evil of making people superfluous. In this way, I believe, he offers some suggestive insights for questioning or *dissolving* the death-centered picture of the evil of the Holocaust, or at least for making it less easy to mobilize Arendt as the figure authorizing this conception. In a certain sense, this opens the possibility of also connecting her thinking about evil to the one advanced by Claudia Card (briefly explored in chapter 3) in which she uses Orlando Patterson's idea of "social death"—an idea quite close to that of human superfluousness—to rethink the idea of genocide, including the Nazi genocide of the Jews. At the same time, however, as before, it will be notable that Bernstein both illuminates and obscures, and he does so partly in virtue of the fact that he focuses solely on the *meaning* of evil in Arendt's books rather than the *work* these ideas perform in the economy of her texts. And one upshot of this is that he overlooks aspects of what Arendt is doing rhetorically with radical evil in establishing the singularity of the death camps and specifically the way in which she explicitly exceptionalizes this evil in relation to such other atrocities as New World slavery. I come to this in the final section.

Richard Bernstein's two books—his 1996 *Hannah Arendt and the Jewish Question* (to which I have already referred) and the later *Radical Evil: A Philosophical Interrogation*, published in 2002—are exemplary instances of the pragmatic fallibilism he practices. These two books diverge and converge in the way they treat the theme of Arendt and evil. Whereas *Hannah Arendt and the Jewish Question* is a reinterpretation of her ideas of evil in the context of her larger work (Arendt in relation to evil), *Radical Evil* is an interpretation of the significance of Arendt's ideas as the gateway into the problematic of evil (evil in relation to Arendt). Indeed, it is tempting to speculate on the temporal distance that separates the *conjunctures* in which these books appeared, the temporal distance that separates and connects the immediate post–Cold War 1990s, when Arendt had begun to emerge as a serious subject of political-philosophical discussion (at least in the North Atlantic), and the post–post–Cold War (or post-9/11) 2000s, when the emergence of a wider perhaps urgent concern with the question of evil brought into particular focus this dimension of her thinking and made her the preeminent thinker on evil.

In *Hannah Arendt and the Jewish Question*, Bernstein's principal interest is with Arendt's overall intellectual project, at least as this can be refracted through the Jewish question, including her own Jewish experience—both, certainly, important and recurrent themes in her earlier and later work. In this book, Bernstein devotes two substantive chapters to a consideration of her ideas about evil, one focused on the relation between "radical evil" and the "banality of evil" in *The Origins of Totalitarianism* and *Eichmann in Jerusalem*, respectively, and the other concerned with the relation between evil and "thinking" and "judging" in the context of Arendt's great unfinished work, *The Life of the Mind*. In the first of the book's chapters on evil (the one that concerns me), Bernstein initiates an intervention into what he takes to be the most salient debate concerning

118   PART II

Arendt and evil—namely, whether, or to what extent, her two main ideas about evil (radical evil and the banality of evil) are consistent or *compatible* with each other. This is the *paradigm-shaping* debate that emerged in the wake of the publication of *Eichmann in Jerusalem*, and has apparently remained unresolved. Against the canonical reading, Bernstein believes that, properly understood, these contrasting ideas, or at least the "thought-trains" that constituted them, are indeed compatible with each other and are in fact not even as temporally unrelated as has often been assumed. As so often with Bernstein's work on Arendt, the hermeneutic endeavor he initiates is meant to clarify an area of obscurity where our understanding of her sometimes-dense thinking is concerned. The aim of this chapter, he says, is to combat the "enormous confusion over what she might have meant by these expressions," radical evil and the banality of evil. Notably, then, *meaning*—not doing—is the principal dimension of Bernstein's interpretive strategy. Arendt's "struggle to probe the problem of evil in the twentieth century is far more complex and subtle than it might seem," he holds, and thus the task he assigns himself is to follow the labyrinthine and sometimes misleading clues left by Arendt herself much like one would do with a detective story—only here, Bernstein argues, it is a detective story that does not arrive at a neatly wrapped-up conclusion. The two questions that need to be addressed, he maintains, are the following: "What does Arendt mean by radical evil? And did she change her mind about the meaning of evil?"[103] In the style of a philosophic sleuth, Bernstein sets off to uncover or reconstruct Arendt's meaning of evil, or to render that meaning clearer and more consistent than she might have done herself.

In contrast to the earlier book, in *Radical Evil* the entire problem, as such, is evil, the aim being to construct a sort of intellectual history of evil in the modern Western philosophical tradition. In this it bears a strong resemblance to Susan Neiman's *Evil in Modern Thought*, also published, perhaps coincidentally, in 2002. And much like in Neiman's book, the animating figure at the center of *Radical Evil* is none other than Hannah Arendt. It is Arendt's allusive reference to Kant's idea of radical evil toward the end of the 1958 edition of *The Origins of Totalitarianism* that sets in motion the problem Bernstein aims to grapple with; and through the long arc of dialogical "interrogations" he initiates with the various philosophers he takes as the crucial nodal points in the tradition's thinking about evil, we already know that it is Arendt toward whom we have been heading all along.[104] Each of Bernstein's preceding chapters—those on Kant, Hegel, and Schelling through those on Nietzsche and Freud, to those on Levinas and Jonas— is a learned exploration of a formative moment in an overall story of Western philosophy and evil. Ultimately, however, it is really Arendt who commands our attention, who demands illumination and clarification. In fact, it is the discussion of the relation between radical evil and the banality of evil (drawn largely, it appears, from *Hannah Arendt and the Jewish Question*) that closes the book's substantive argument and that animates the wider, concluding reflections.[105]

Bernstein is motivated in *Radical Evil* by the "disparity" he discerns between, on the one hand, our contemporary apprehension of evil, the "moral passion" with which we respond to the atrocities and outrages of our time (events that, as Arendt would have said, we simply cannot *reconcile* ourselves to), and, on the other, the prevailing "poverty" of our conceptual languages of description and analysis of evil.[106] Bernstein is sensitive to the relative absence of evil in the vocabulary of moral thinking. He notes, rightly, that even though an idiom of "injustice" (often thought of these days in terms of the "violation of human rights") is widespread, there is a reluctance to talk about evil. This, he surmises, is sometimes because of an unease about the religious associations of the term and sometimes because of a concern that contemporary fanatical groups "employ a language of evil to identify what they despise and want to destroy."[107] Yet it remains true, Bernstein argues, that many nevertheless now find the idea of evil compelling, sometimes unavoidable, as a way of thinking about actions that exceed, even overshadow, what the language of injustice can describe or the institutions of justice can address. We need, therefore, he says, to find a vocabulary that is "deep, rich, and subtle enough" to capture those scarcely nameable experiences of wrong that we feel moved to call *evil*. And it is here that Arendt assumes a magnifying importance for him. Arendt, he believes, is one of the few thinkers to have explored the features of twentieth-century evil, and to have done so in a way that evades theological language. Significantly, Bernstein does not suppose that Arendt should necessarily be thought of as the *last* word on evil, for "despite her perceptiveness," he argues, she "raised many questions concerning evil that she did not address."[108] What these questions are and whether or how Bernstein aims to address them will be important to consider in what follows.

The project of *Radical Evil* is to participate in the *regeneration* of a moral vocabulary of evil and to situate Arendt in that endeavor as (so far) evil's most eloquent and decisive interpreter. Significantly, and in contrast to others such as Lara, Bernstein does not think this entails the pursuit of something like "a new 'theory' of evil." He is quite explicit about this. In part it seems, Bernstein's reason is that it is a simple but steadfast hermeneutic principle that one should avoid theory's presumption of conceptual closure (an instance of his

120   PART II

commitment to a hermeneutic of fallibilism). But in part it also seems to stem from his recognition, disquieting but persistent, that there is "something about evil that resists and defies any final comprehension."[109] These are "thought-trains" to which Bernstein returns in his sage and penetrating concluding remarks.

As should be clear from chapter 1, I share much of Bernstein's apprehension of a palpable discrepancy between our experience and our conceptual languages, and with it the sense of urgency to imagine forms of open-ended critical inquiry appropriate to the appalling wrongs that we aim to understand. But what I do not share, as I indicated earlier in this chapter, is the reification of the "horrendous twentieth century" through which Bernstein creates his picture of the contemporary problem about evil and the historical reason that is supposed to ground it. For him, as for others, the twentieth century is supposed to be the *exceptional* age of atrocity. "Many people believe," he writes, axiomatically, without even a moment's reflexive hesitation, "that the evils witnessed in the twentieth century exceed anything that has ever been recorded in past history."[110] (Because he offers no qualification, presumably we are meant to count him among these "many people.") This by now familiar conceit regarding the preeminent place of the twentieth century in the world-history of evil is then updated by the assertion, offered equally with a confident absence of reflexive hesitation (again, interestingly, in line exactly with Susan Neiman's views), that the September 11, 2001, attacks against the United States represent "the very epitome of evil in our time."[111] I think few would doubt that the attacks of 9/11 should be described as acts of evil, but many too (myself included) might well wonder whether there aren't other acts, perpetrated perhaps in parts of the world about which Bernstein may not often think and by forces or regimes he might be loath to consider capable of evil, that should also count as "the very epitome of evil in our time." As before, in Bernstein we find an erudite guide to Arendt's ideas on evil, but we also find a philosopher well within the canonical circle of those unable to see beyond the horizon of an uncritical exceptionalism.[112]

As I have suggested, the chapter on Arendt in *Radical Evil* draws significantly on the discussion in *Hannah Arendt and the Jewish Question*. Here, too, Bernstein turns to Arendt's published correspondence to demonstrate the meaning of her idea of radical evil and its relation to the banality of evil, and to show that these ideas are not, in fact, incompatible with each other. To begin with, citing the exchange between Arendt and Karl Jaspers that took place in 1951 when Arendt sent Jaspers one of the first copies of her new book, Bernstein underlines the central place of "superfluousness" in her idea of radical evil in *The Origins of Totalitarianism*. He reminds us that superfluousness is in fact a theme—almost a *motif*—throughout this book. The section on imperialism, for example, is memorably about "superfluous wealth" and "superfluous men." However, clearly the most destructive dynamic of superfluousness is the one connected to radical evil that comes to be manifest in the distinctive powers of the Nazi death camps. In "Totalitarianism in Power," the third chapter of part 3 of *The Origins of Totalitarianism*, Arendt famously suggests that totalitarian power aimed systematically at transforming people into "superfluous" beings, and the death camps were the ultimate site of this multifaceted project. For Arendt, there were three stages over which the domination of the camps unfolded, each destroying a specific dimension of the humanity of the camps' victims. As Bernstein recounts, the first stage was the destruction of the "juridical person," a process that preceded the establishment of the camps and that was directed at stripping the person of all legal rights, depriving them of the protection of the law. The second stage involved the "murder of the moral person in man"—that is, the destruction of the conditions in which conscience and trust were possible, and with it the corruption of such elementary modes of supportive cooperative moral personhood as solidarity and sacrifice. But it is the third and final stage of dehumanization that was the most pernicious—namely, the destruction of human individuality and the transformation of human beings into "marionettes with human faces." It is at this stage that "human beings as human beings" are rendered superfluous. This dimension of the camps' powers of domination involved, as Bernstein says, "the attempt to transform human beings, to destroy any vestige of human individuality and spontaneity—and consequently, any vestige of human freedom and solidarity."[113] It was especially this last step, Arendt suggests, the final destruction of human dignity, that allowed millions of Jews to be marched to their deaths in the gas chambers.[114]

As I have indicated, it is enormously suggestive and important that Bernstein focuses our attention here less on the gas chambers themselves (the purely eliminationist objective of the Nazis, and the technology of killing they employed) as the mark of totalitarian evil than on Arendt's return again and again, in an often speculative language to this *process* of making people superfluous, of systematically stripping them of their recognizable humanity, of rendering them little more than living corpses, with neither legal nor moral identity. Of course, Arendt referred often enough to the camps as "death factories," but Bernstein reminds us that for her the specificity of evil lay at least as much in the destruction of the moral personhood of the Jews as in the end of death itself, the destruction of their physical selves.

However, profound and significant as this argument about the relation between evil and superfluousness was, Bernstein maintains, there was nevertheless something vital "missing" from Arendt's account—namely, deliberation on the "troubling questions about intention and motivation." Intention, Bernstein reminds us, not only was central to Kant's idea of radical evil (the free and willed adoption of evil maxims) but also was widespread as a general assumption regarding the motivated quality of evil deeds: that is, actions could only be evil if evil was their *intention*. But what does Bernstein mean by "missing" (as though it should have been there but wasn't, like a lamentable lapse)? As with Lara, he too reads the past as though it was deprived of something—some good, some truth—that is only later supplied. But from what perspective was "intention" missing? When Arendt speaks in *The Origins of Totalitarianism* of the camps as "laboratories" and therefore obviously as sites of self-conscious experimentation on human nature, isn't she in fact thinking about "intention"? Not surprisingly, Bernstein maintains that this putatively missing element became precisely the pivotal issue in *Eichmann in Jerusalem*. He argues that Arendt's "introduction of the controversial notion of the banality of evil must be understood in the context of her thought-trains about the meaning of the intentionality involved in committing evil deeds."[115]

What Bernstein seems to be saying here is not that Arendt had *no* working conception of intention in *The Origins of Totalitarianism* and only developed one in *Eichmann in Jerusalem* but rather that in the latter book she is trying to *divest* the idea of intention in the commission of evil of its conventional demonic character, a sense of evil one might easily have from the former book. By examining a fascinating exchange of letters between Arendt and Jaspers from 1946, Bernstein shows that the problem of intention was present to Arendt's mind not only prior to the publication of *Eichmann in Jerusalem* but also prior to the publication of *The Origins of Totalitarianism*. In her letter to Jaspers after reading the manuscript of his famous postwar book *Die Schuldfrage* (published in 1947 and translated as *The Question of German Guilt* in 1948), Arendt expressed a doubt about his description of the Nazi policy in terms of criminality. The "monstrousness" of

Nazi crimes, she says, "explode the limits of law," and "no punishment is severe enough."[116] Jaspers, in his reply, offered a sobering worry about this direction in Arendt's thinking, holding that the idea of "a guilt that goes beyond all criminal guilt inevitably takes on a streak of 'greatness'—of satanic greatness—which is, for me, as inappropriate for the Nazis as all talk about the 'demonic' element in Hitler and so forth." "It seems to me," Jaspers goes on, "that we have to see these things in their total banality . . . , in their prosaic triviality, because that's what truly characterizes them."[117] Arendt, Bernstein says, was largely persuaded by Jaspers and expressed as much to him, agreeing on the need, in speaking of evil, to "combat all impulses to mythologize the horrible" by attributing to it a monstrous intention.[118]

It is this sensibility, Bernstein argues, that surfaces fully in Arendt's account of Adolf Eichmann. Arendt was plainly baffled by what she witnessed of his behavior in the courtroom during the trial in Jerusalem between April and December 1961. As she says, he spoke in vivid commonplaces about his role, emphasizing, among other things, that he was neither a hater of Jews nor a murderer but only an obedient servant of the Nazi cause.[119] Even when he invoked Kant, as he did, he was only mouthing clichés, Arendt says, neither being learned nor reflective. In rounding up Jews to be deported to an almost certain death, he was, he claimed, simply doing his job, simply trying to get ahead in a familiar bureaucratic way. Without diminishing the magnitude of his crime, Arendt felt obliged to agree with him that he was not the "monster" he was made out to be by the prosecution and (especially Jewish) public opinion.[120] Eichmann was neither diabolical nor corrupt nor pathological. His undoubted wrongdoing was not the result of anything metaphysical or ultimate. There was nothing profound about him, nothing "radical" about his deeds. What characterized him was precisely the absence of an evil *intent*; indeed, he seemed precisely without autonomous or self-directed motivation, merely carrying out a function with no evident utilitarian purpose as part of a project that was in any case larger than him—or *anyone* like him, for that matter. Above all, as Arendt writes, it was "thoughtlessness" that defined Eichmann.[121] And it was this quality of his mind and character of his actions that the phrase "banality of evil" was meant to capture. If Eichmann's crime was extraordinary, he himself was merely *ordinary*. This was the paradox that confronted Arendt. As she writes in the book's epilogue, the trouble with Eichmann "was precisely that so many were like him, and that the many were neither perverted nor sadistic, that they were, and still are, terribly and terrifyingly normal."[122] Arendt, Bernstein suggests, clearly meant to identify here a

124 PART II

register that inscribed evil at the level of the routine, the commonplace—a register that qualified any trace of the metaphysics that appeared to surround the idea of radical evil.

However, moving in the reverse direction, as it were, in Bernstein's view this account of Eichmann does not preclude the continuing relevance of the idea of radical evil. He acknowledges another notable letter of Arendt's, this time to Gershom Scholem in 1964, in response to his withering criticisms of *Eichmann in Jerusalem*. In this letter, Arendt claims to have "changed her mind" and to "no longer speak of 'radical evil.'" Evil, Arendt now says, is "extreme" but never "radical," for it possesses "neither depth nor any demonic dimension."[123] Bernstein believes that this disavowal of the idea of radical evil on Arendt's part is misleading, or at least, necessarily, it has to be qualified. Arendt, he argues, "*never* repudiated the thought-trains that went into her original discussion of radical evil, especially her claim that radical evil involves making human beings as human beings superfluous, as well as a systematic attempt to eliminate human spontaneity, individuality, and plurality."[124] The idea of the banality of evil *presupposes*, he maintains, this understanding of radical evil; it is precisely the banality of Eichmann's work that contributed to the bureaucratic engine by which people were made superfluous. What Arendt rejected, rather, was the idea that such evil has metaphysical "depth" (in Kant's sense of "radical") or "demonic dimension" (in a theological or gnostic sense). To the extent that Arendt shifted her thinking, Bernstein says, she did so in regard to the question of the relation between intention and evil. "Previously, she had insisted that radical evil could not be explained or deduced from humanly comprehensible motives. When confronted with Eichmann in the Jerusalem court, she concluded that he committed monstrous deeds without being motivated by monstrous evil intentions."[125] Thus it is the clarification of the conceptual place of intention that defines Arendt's later thinking about evil.

Admirably, the direction of Bernstein's intervention is to overcome the impasse that characterizes the familiar debate about radical evil and the banality of evil in Arendt circles. But reading for the *point* more so than for the meaning, I am not so certain about his confident conclusion regarding the resolution of the seeming contrast between Arendt's earlier and later formulations of the idea of evil.

The question Bernstein set out to answer, as we have seen, is one derived from the pervasive assumption held by many (from Gershom Scholem in the 1960s to Elisabeth Young-Bruehl in the 1980s to María Pía Lara and Susan Neiman more recently) that the idea of radical evil and the idea of the banality of evil are incompatible and, moreover, that in offering the later idea Arendt had not only changed her mind but sought to propose a more *advanced* formulation, more philosophically complex inasmuch as it evaded dependence on an assumption about evil intentions. Bernstein, as we have seen, does not completely share the view that Arendt's two ideas of evil are incompatible, but he joins others of Arendt's chief interpreters in thinking that the banality of evil idea is a conceptual *improvement* over the earlier notion of radical evil. As he says, something was missing in the earlier account that is introduced into the later one—namely, a more forthright appreciation of the problem of intentionality.[126] Evil action, Arendt had apparently come to recognize, can be evil action without the evil being the malevolent motivation prompting the action. Now whether this is a close interpretation of what the later as opposed to the earlier Arendt *meant* by evil I am not prepared to guess, but it is curious that Bernstein offers little justification for the assertion of the conceptual or moral priority of unintended as opposed to intended evil. Nor does he trouble himself with wondering whether "thoughtlessness," or the absence of a reasoned, reflective motivation, is an adequate way of thinking about Eichmann's actions. To speak of evil intention, for Bernstein and many others, seems to imply monstrousness. But why should it? Surely, one can be motivated by an intention to commit evil actions without being demonic in some all-encompassing or characterological way; that is, without suggesting a diabolical personality in the perpetrator of evil—like Thomas Jefferson in his commitment to enslaving people, or Harry Truman in his commitment to destroying innocent Japanese lives on the pretext of ending the Second World War.[127] No one need argue that Jefferson's evil slaving or Truman's evil bombing implies that they themselves were monstrous men. Laurence Thomas, whose work I discuss in chapter 3, has something to say about this.

What is puzzling about Bernstein's interpretive account, outstanding though it quite clearly is, is that in extracting the passages he takes from Arendt's texts in order to excavate the real meaning of her ideas, he seems uninterested in what she might have been *doing* with these terms in the passages in which they are embedded. The rhetorical casting or construction of the question of evil in Arendt's texts appears to lie outside the range of his sleuthing radar.

126   PART II

For example, in the letter to Scholem that Bernstein quotes, when Arendt says she has "changed her mind" about evil, quite apart from the deep question of her own obscure intention, might she not be read less as changing her mind about the *answer* to the problem of evil than as changing her mind about the appropriate *question* to ask about evil in her new circumstances? Indeed, in Bernstein's earlier book, *Hannah Arendt and the Jewish Question*, from which, as I have indicated, much of the discussion about Arendt in the later book is taken, Bernstein does suggest that after witnessing Eichmann at his trial in Jerusalem she came to be animated by a "new and different question."[128] In my view, this is a perceptive observation. But, notably, Bernstein does not pursue the implications of this insight—namely, that this new and different question might well be embedded in a new and different moral-historical-political conjuncture or problem-space for problematizing evil. And if this is the case, might it not follow that *The Origins of Totalitarianism* and *Eichmann in Jerusalem* could not possibly belong to the same problem-space of questions about evil? Why should it be assumed, as it typically is, that these books can be implicitly compared as like and like, that their respective ideas can simply be read off against one another in respect of epistemic or moral complexity? Aren't *The Origins of Totalitarianism* and *Eichmann in Jerusalem*, in important ways, manifestly *not* the same kind of book, thematically or conceptually or organizationally? Isn't there something to be said about the internal formation of their respective arguments and the ideological-political-conceptual conjunctures in which they were conceived and written and published? If this is so, might it not have been more instructive to ask less whether or to what extent these formulations—radical evil and the banality of evil—have something in common with each other or can be conceptually reconciled in the evolution of Arendt's thinking than whether or to what extent they are answers to different questions that contingently emerged for her in different historical conjunctures? Indeed, wouldn't this be exactly the conceptual upshot of the kind of critical historicizing hermeneutic of which Bernstein has been an admirable advocate?

EXCEPTIONALIZING EVIL

I want to underline that my aim throughout this chapter is primarily to observe the curiously unexamined way in which Arendt is often read—not least concerning her ideas about evil—even by her best interpreters and to urge that we pay as much attention to what she might have been doing with her ideas in the texts in question as to what she might have meant, or rather, that concern with her meaning be more closely connected to concern with her *point*. I also wish to underline that this is especially pertinent where we are expressly seeking to read her from her own conjunctures into ours. I want to turn finally to aspects of one way in which Arendt rhetorically constructs the image of evil in *The Origins of Totalitarianism*. Specifically, I want to observe not only that evil is linked to the Nazi death camps but also that the evil of the death camps is itself constructed in a spuriously hierarchical way so as to diminish the evil of other atrocities, not least of all slavery.

Arendt's discussion of the death camps in the original edition of *The Origins of Totalitarianism* takes place most prominently in the last section—"Total Domination"—of chapter 12, "Totalitarianism in Power," which is the grim finale. As is well known, this section is devoted to a discussion of the character and function and effects of the camps and is based, to some extent, on survivor accounts, such as those by David Rousset, Eugen Kogon, and Bruno Bettelheim.[129] It is, of course, this section that closes with the all-important outline of the successive stages of the process of making human beings as human beings superfluous and upon which, as we have seen, Bernstein rightly focuses his discussion of radical evil. The section is characterized by an intense sense of almost bewildered shock at the near-inexplicable phenomenon of the death camps. Arendt opens her account by repeating and elaborating her argument that the "concentration and extermination camps of totalitarian regimes serve as the laboratories in which the fundamental belief of totalitarianism that everything is possible is being verified."[130] This idea that the camps were "laboratories" and thus essentially sites of experimentation on the humanity of human beings (the attempt, that is, to transform human nature) is central to Arendt's conception of the distinctiveness—and evil—of totalitarian power.

The first and in some sense *framing* point Arendt seems concerned to make about the camps is that they are at once a singular index of the "omnipotence" of the totalitarian dictator and, at the same time, "so horribly far removed from the experience and understanding of the nontotalitarian world and mentality" as to be barely conceivable, scarcely believable. The camps, for Arendt, are fantastical—and yet unrelievedly *real*. They are an inescapable fact, and yet they lie *beyond* the realm of reliable comprehension. So much so, she says, that even those former inmates who "returned to the world of the living" and tried to

128   PART II

articulate their experiences often found themselves "assailed by doubts with regard to [their] own truthfulness, as though [they] had mistaken a nightmare for reality." Confronted with this "intrinsically incredible" enormity, Arendt writes, the great and completely understandable temptation is to try to "explain it away" with "liberal rationalizations." But these rationalizations are, in the end, hopeless in the face of experiences that "simply surpass our powers of understanding." As she asks: "What meaning has the concept of murder when we are confronted with the mass production of corpses?" We try to grasp the phenomenon psychologically, she says, when "the first thing that must be realized is that the psyche *can* be destroyed even without the destruction of the physical man," and the final results of this dehumanizing process are "inanimate men, i.e., men who can no longer be psychologically understood, whose return to the psychological or otherwise intelligibly human world closely resembles the resurrection of Lazarus."[131] (In the Gospel of John, remember, Christ's restoration of Lazarus to life four days after his death is taken as the last and greatest sign of his power.) Yet one feels bound to ask: Why should the camps have been *so* shocking as to defy description let alone explanation? Why isn't this a question put to Arendt by her interpreters? What historical blindness to other atrocities does it depend upon? It will be recalled (by some at least) that in *Discourse on Colonialism* part of what Aimé Césaire polemically indicts postwar European intellectuals for is precisely that their shock at the Nazi atrocities was not the result of some perceived crime against a part of humanity but rather that methods hitherto applied to the non-European world were now being turned on White Europeans.[132] Should we also think of Arendt's shock in this way? Where was her shock at the brutal crimes committed against colonized peoples, say, the campaign of extermination carried out against Herero and Nama people in German South West Africa between 1904 and 1908? There is an odd sense in which the White violence against non-White peoples can be rendered a mere prosaic occurrence that never rises above the level of mild discomfort.

In any case, it is in the context of this depiction of a psychological and physical destruction of European Jewry said to far exceed anything the human imagination could possibly embrace that Arendt sets out the claim for the incomparable status of the camps. "There are no parallels to the life in the concentration camps," she writes. "All seeming parallels create confusion and distract attention from what is essential. Forced labor in prisons and penal colonies, banishment, slavery, all seem for a moment to offer helpful comparisons, but on closer examination lead nowhere."[133] In reading such passages, it is perhaps necessary to start by reminding ourselves that Arendt is writing here almost at the same time as she is reading the emerging accounts of the liberated concentration and extermination camps—and therefore with barely any mediating analytical distance within which to digest and properly situate the full extent of the horror.

Still, it is worth noting that this passage, and those others to which it is connected in this section of *The Origins of Totalitarianism* is, in respect of its rhetorical construction, less a description of the empirical facts concerning the camps than an axiomatic *declaration* of, effectively, *moral* facts. The passage is meant to peremptorily foreclose rather than invite meaningful comparison—even discussion about the very idea of meaningful comparison—with any other form of atrocity. Possible parallels—forced labor camps, banishment, slavery—are only *seeming*, nothing more. Where, at first sight, they might have appeared relevant, she says, "on closer examination [they] lead nowhere." Of course, needless to say, Arendt does not offer any such "closer examination," not even a clue as to what such an inspection would entail were it to be carried out by her or anyone else. To Arendt, we can only surmise, this is unnecessary. True, it could very well appear churlish to expect that there should have been reasons let alone justifications from her, given her proximity (moral and temporal) to the catastrophe she is endeavoring to write about. But it might not be unreasonable to have expected that later commentators and interpreters interested in Arendt's idea of evil would have inquired into this figuration of the exception of the death camps and the contrasts upon which it feeds.

In the following paragraph, Arendt pursues the theme of the meaninglessness of any comparison between the death camps and other atrocities, including slavery, offering this time something more of what she understands the characteristic features of the respective dominating powers to have been:

> Forced labor as a punishment is limited as to time and intensity. The convict retains his rights over his body; he is not absolutely tortured and he is not absolutely dominated. Banishment banishes only from one part of the world to another part of the world, also inhabited by human beings; it does not exclude from the human world altogether. Throughout history slavery has been an institution within a social order; slaves were not, like concentration-camp inmates, withdrawn from the sight and hence the protection of their fellow-men; as instruments of labor they had a definite price

130 PART II

and as property a definite value. The concentration-camp inmate has no price, because he can always be replaced; nobody knows to whom he belongs, because he is never seen. From the point of view of normal society he is absolutely superfluous, although in times of acute labor shortage, as in Russia and in Germany during the war, he is used for work.[134]

Though Arendt mentions here that the concentration camp inmates were sometimes used to fill a labor function, the main point for her is their economic *uselessness*. The only economic function of the labor camps, she says, was to finance their own bureaucratic apparatus. So from an economic point of view (that is, the point of view of *utility*), they existed solely for their own sake. This general purposelessness of the camps only enhanced the sense that their real raison d'être was sheer terror. As Arendt says: "The incredibility of the horrors is closely bound up with their economic uselessness." The camps served no purpose other than to mass produce corpses. And Arendt goes on to say: "In the eyes of a strictly utilitarian world the obvious contradiction between these acts and military expediency gave the whole enterprise an air of mad unreality."[135]

Again, notably, the rhetorical form of Arendt's remarks about the unparalleled nature of the camps reflects more her motivation to *declare* the singularity of the death camps than anything else—certainly she is not motivated by *meaningful* comparison. What interests me, especially, is the way slavery is pictured in these accounts—namely, as embedded within a rational and utilitarian logic of power (that is, fulfilling an economic function) and *consequently* well within the range of human comprehension. Whatever slavery was, it was apparently not enveloped in "an air of mad unreality." It was perfectly rational and comprehensible. This *intelligibility* of slavery serves to diminish its evil and helps to secure the authority of the limit-character of the death camps as an exception.

Should it matter to Arendt's latter-day interpreters that slavery is characterized in such carelessly spurious terms? To begin with, the underspecification of "slavery" in the passages quoted may give rise to an ambiguity about exactly what the picture is of slavery as a structure of domination that she is drawing on explicitly or implicitly. Because, however, she refers to slavery "throughout history," we may assume that she at least includes modern American (or New World) slavery within the ambit of her contrast. In this context, a number of questions can be raised, if only as a way of underlining how invidious the contrast is that she presents so authoritatively. Quite apart from the question whether or to what extent the death camps are aptly described as existing outside rather than within a social order (were the camps not, minimally, within a Nazi social and political order of radical exclusion, whatever their physical spatial seclusion?), it is certainly unclear what it means to assert, without further elaboration let alone substantiation, that "throughout history slavery has been an institution within a social order." What idea of the *social* is at work here? How should we describe that social *order*? The rhetorical implication here, for Arendt, is obviously that being "within a social order" somehow mitigated, lessened, the destructive powers of the enslavers and the harm suffered by the enslaved. But even if she is right that slavery was within a social order, why couldn't just the opposite effect be the case? That is, why couldn't a perverse intimacy, made possible by social relations of relative proximity, have produced a *more* adverse effect on the humanity of the enslaved? None of this is explored. In her readiness to claim the exception for the historical experience of the Jews, Arendt surrenders the opportunity to ask more pertinent and productive questions—for example, whether other total institutions, such as the slave plantation, might also have reduced its victims to superfluousness, and precisely through the legal, moral, and political processes she describes for the camps. Needless to say, her many contemporary commentators and interpreters have scarcely repaired the conceit.

It remains, therefore, to ask once more what the picture is of slavery Arendt was depending on in these passages from *The Origins of Totalitarianism*. In what sense were slave formations in the Americas (across their regional variety) "integrated" into a social order? From what ideological picture of the lives and forms of life of the enslaved in the Americas might this assumption be derived? It is worth remembering that until the publication of Kenneth Stampp's *The Peculiar Institution* in 1956 the dominant picture of the regime of American slavery and the lives of the enslaved, at least among White intellectuals, was shaped by Ulrich B. Phillips in books such as *American Negro Slavery* and *Life and Labor in the Old South*, published in 1918 and 1929, respectively.[136] In both of Phillips's books, memorably, what emerges is precisely the benign image of the contented and integrated social life of the enslaved. By contrast, however, the fundamental fact about the forms of life of the enslaved in the Americas in the critical work of Black intellectuals to whose books Arendt would have had access in the 1940s, had she chosen to acquaint herself with them—among them, Carter B. Woodson's *The Mis-education of the Negro* (1933); W. E. B. Du Bois's *Black Reconstruction* (1935); and C. L. R. James's *The Black Jacobins* (1938)—was one of pervasive exposure and

132   PART II

vulnerability to violence and violation in a context in which the (personal and political) powers of enslavers was as good as sovereign.[137] It is the precarity and not the integrity of slave life within the regime of slavery that is most prominent in their work. These, though, were not thinkers within Arendt's range of reference. It is a telling fact that, according to Richard King, the only book on New World slavery in Arendt's library was Stanley Elkins's *Slavery: A Problem in American Institutional and Intellectual Life*, a work that would quickly become controversial, as I explore in a later chapter.[138] In any case, it is hardly credible to suggest, as Arendt nonchalantly does, that the enslaved could count on the articulated solidarity and even the "protection" of their fellow-enslaved. Finally, in what sense, it is to be wondered, did the status of the enslaved in the Americas as fungible chattel with a negotiable "price" and branded ownership make them invulnerable to replacement? The very fact of the lucrative transatlantic slave trade and the potential for endless replenishment of the population of enslaved peoples makes a mockery of this uninformed assertion.

These, however, are not details about American slavery that unduly trouble Arendt, intent as she is on fixing the exception of the death camps—on the grounds of the absolute superfluousness of its victims contrasted with the presumed "value" of the enslaved. In my view, however, they should at least be details relevant to those interpreters of Arendt who seek to establish the exceptionality of her thinking about evil. Neither Bernstein nor any other of her distinguished commentators, so far as I am aware, has taken much notice of this. Again, I offer these remarks not in the spirit of diminishing Arendt's insights (it is obvious enough that here, as elsewhere, my own thinking has been deeply informed by hers) but as a way of urging that in addition to asking what her words and ideas *mean* we also ask what the *point* was of the contrasts through which the authority of those meanings was established. For surely there is room to suggest that the death camps were horrific without invidiously claiming that they were also *more* so than any other historic mass atrocity.

To sum up: In chapter 1 my aim was to sketch in broad strokes the overall arc of a moral and reparatory approach to the past in the present, and the place within it of the idea of evil, whereas in this chapter I have been concerned with critically exploring some of the assumptions that have shaped a quite prominent arena of discussion about a secular, postmetaphysical idea of evil. At the center of my concern here has been to notice the peculiar way in which this whole discursive arena is established and reproduced, club-like, around a revolving set of unexamined historiographical *conceits* and conceptual *exceptions*. I noted, to begin with, the remarkable (and remarkably unreflexive) way the twentieth century is accorded a *normative* privilege in these discussions of evil, as though the modern evils perpetrated then were somehow more heinous, more atrocious, more despicable, more odious, more wicked, more . . . whatever than those evils perpetrated in previous centuries of the modern age—let alone evils from other eras of human history. I believe this *presentist* hypostatization of the twentieth century as the exemplification of an age of atrocity is not an accidental but rather a *motivated* characterization that stems from the way one particular twentieth-century event of undeniable evil has come to stand in a hegemonic way for evil itself—namely, the (still) shocking mass murder of Jews carried out by the Nazi regime during the Second World War as a project of planned extermination. The Holocaust, as that event is now universally known, exerts a peculiar force on the contemporary imagination of evil inasmuch as it is often perceived not just as *one* among evils, with its own specificities and distinctive qualities of harm, but as the *first* among evils, a meta-evil, and therefore as in fact the very definition of what evil is. What is troubling in this scenario is that other admitted evils, New World slavery among them, can scarcely appear as anything but merely historical or empirical evils, occupying perhaps a place in the serially expanding list of similarly historical and empirical instances, but never conceived as defining the theoretical class of evil as such, or as a whole, and consequently forever dependent on the meta-evil for its larger moral significance. Without seeking in any way to undermine the aggrieved sense of the enormity of the slaughter of Jews, or even the appropriation of the idea of a "holocaust" as the name for one and only one historical event, I have been concerned to learn from those who have shown that the picture of the Holocaust that supports this account of absolute singularity, though often enough presented in ahistorical fashion, is actually a *historical* one inasmuch as it emerged in a specific conjuncture. That is to say, how the Holocaust became the Holocaust is partly a historical question of knowledge and power. I have also noted that the link established between the Holocaust as an event and the twentieth century as the age of atrocity projects a conception of evil thought of principally in relation to the perpetration of mass killing or genocide. What victims of evil suffer above all is violent and unwarranted, inexcusable *death*. No other form of violating power has the same—even nearly the same—impact as a representation of the harm of systematic wrong.

Hannah Arendt is the key figure in the establishment of this normative paradigm of evil. More than any other thinker, it is Arendt who is taken to carry out the authorizing role of setting the terms of the postmetaphysical discussion of evil in motion. Certainly, her work has been authoritative in establishing the status of the Holocaust as exception and the death camps as the ultimate evil of totalitarian power. In a sense, within the circle of Arendt scholars, Arendt is treated as *herself* an exception, certainly as exemplary, and the exceptions she constructed are invariably ignored, taken for granted, and in effect, naturalized. Arendt's work, I believe, has produced an ideological image that has, in a new post-post-Cold War conjuncture (to use my terminology from the previous chapter), become hegemonic. Arguably, it is one thing for Arendt to have understood the world and written about it as she did from within the problem-spaces of her own experience, but it is quite another for her contemporary authorizing interpreters to merely naturalize and normalize these exceptions as though they inhabited the same experience as she did, as though her problem-spaces are also theirs. By and large these commentators and interpreters read Arendt as though they look out on the same world she did, or from the same conjuncture, as though her questions could possibly be theirs, as though therefore all that was required as a hermeneutic endeavor was to discern the best meaning to attach to her various ideas, including her ideas about evil. Arendt to them is an interpretive puzzle to be solved by moving the pieces of her thinking from various parts of her oeuvre (her "thought-trains") around until a seemingly cogent picture emerges.

Where evil is concerned, the deep and confounding conundrum among Arendt scholars has been the seemingly irreconcilable tension between her two famous ideas about evil, the earlier *radical* evil from *The Origins of Totalitarianism* and the later *banality* of evil from *Eichmann in Jerusalem*. I have argued that Richard Bernstein, our best guide to Arendt on evil (perhaps our best guide so far to any part of Arendt), has reconstructed the puzzle of evil in her work in the manner of a philosophic detective, tracking down the (sometimes informal) sources of meaning Arendt gave respectively to radical evil and the banality of evil in such a way as to reconcile these two ideas about evil and produce a remarkably coherent picture of her thinking on the topic. I have learned a lot from Bernstein's intellectual generosity and erudition, but I have also expressed a modest doubt about much in his way of reading both Arendt and evil. Like many of his fellow Arendt scholars, Bernstein is troubled neither by Arendt's exceptions *nor by his own*. The subject-position from which Arendt addresses issues related to Black people gives him pause, but not enough of a pause to oblige him to think again about her possible complicities if not in White supremacy then at least in White normativity. Arendt's ideological image is not a matter of concern for Bernstein. Naturalizing the conceit that the twentieth century was the unparalleled age of atrocity allows him to offer Arendt to us as the exemplary thinker for whom evil was always "fundamental" and whose controversial ideas about evil are therefore crucial to interpretively reconstruct. What did Arendt *really mean* by evil? is Bernstein's question. My doubt, as I have said, is that in reading in this way, Bernstein takes *The Origins of Totalitarianism* and *Eichmann in Jerusalem* (and the letters that offer perspectives on them) as occupying one and the same problem-space, that across them Arendt is merely asking the same questions and therefore that, as ideas, radical evil and banality of evil might only be different answers to the same questions, answers to be compared and contrasted as like and like. In this affirmative reading, Bernstein can therefore ignore the curious fact (surely a matter for a discerning philosophic detective) that in neither of these books is evil Arendt's conceptual starting point, and that evil in fact emerges more as a way of summing up (often allusively, certainly not elaborately) an already capacious analysis governed by other conceptual terms.

This is not to suggest, to the contrary, that evil should be thought of as insignificant for Arendt. Rather, it is to urge that we read her at least as much for what she might have been *doing* rhetorically with evil in her texts as what she seemingly meant by evil in them. Perhaps if we did so, other aspects of the texts might emerge with equal force. Perhaps Bernstein and others might have noticed the rhetorical device of *exceptionalism* that pervades them. In particular, perhaps they might have noticed how the exception of the death camps (the special site of Nazi evil) was established by means of spuriously diminishing the evil effects of other admitted historical atrocities, New World slavery not least of all.

CHAPTER 3

INCOMMENSURABLE EVILS

MORALLY INVIDIOUS COMPARISONS

New World slavery, too, was a form and expression of moral evil. But it was an embodiment of moral evil quite differently organized than the evil embodied in the Holocaust—in relation to much, including in relation to the deliberate perpetration of undeserved death. It is uncontroversial that New World slavery was a transgenerational structure of social relations of domination built on a ubiquitous systemically generated violence in which death from wanton killing or deliberate neglect was common. From the kidnapping of men, women, and children from their ancestral villages, their forced march in coffles to the West African coasts, and their captivity in the dungeons of the slave forts; through the literally unforeseeable and unimaginable horrors of the Middle Passage across the Atlantic they were made to face; to their humiliating commercial sale on the auction blocks in the slave markets of the Americas, their coerced transformation into permanently enslaved people, and the endless brutality of plantation labor—social and personal violence and death were not isolated events but endemic and pervasive throughout the New World slave system. The enslaved were, by definition, persons whose legal and existential status systemically *exposed* them to the continuous possibility of naked violation, whether routine or random, including violent death. As a function of the near-sovereign powers invested in, or appropriated by, enslavers within the complex interconnected system of New World slavery, the enslaved could be disposed of by and large at will and more or less with impunity—and often enough they were.

Think no further in this regard than the infamous episode of the British slave ship the *Zong*, about which much has been written. In the historiography of New

World slavery, the story of the *Zong* constitutes an important chapter, not only in the larger history of the violence of the slave trade but also in the history of the rise of British abolitionism in the late eighteenth century. Indeed, it is in the context of the nascent antislavery movement in London that the legal case involving the *Zong*, presided over by the somewhat ambiguous figure of Lord Chief Justice Mansfield, became something of a *cause célèbre* in 1783.[1] As a reminder: In September 1781, the modestly sized slave ship *Zong*, recently purchased by the prominent William Gregson syndicate and registered in the great slaving port of Liverpool, was making its Atlantic journey from the coast of West Africa to Jamaica under the command of a reportedly inexperienced captain, Luke Collingwood, formerly the surgeon on the slave ship *William*. Overladen with a complement of more than four hundred and fifty enslaved people chained below deck, in undoubtedly unspeakable conditions, the Middle Passage voyage of the *Zong* appears to have been a colossal disaster from beginning to end, a combination of ineptitude, irresponsibility, recklessness—and deliberate *evil*. The rich and monstrous historical details need not overly detain us here. Suffice it to say—I am largely following James Walvin's reconstruction—that within Caribbean waters, and what should have been but days away from Black River on Jamaica's southeastern coast, the *Zong* appears to have lost its way, navigationally. In a panic about existing reserves of fresh water, and seeking to preserve an acceptable margin of profit, the decision was made (by *whom*, exactly, remains unclear because by then effective charge of the slaving vessel seems to have passed from the apparently infirm captain) to begin the "disposal" of weak and sickly slaves, on the theory that these slaves endangered the well-being of the remaining healthy slaves and that the protection of "cargo" was covered by insurance. With one possible exception, no serious objections from among the crew seem to have been offered to the decision to murder the enfeebled captives.[2] And so, in order to satisfy this plausible financial wager, over the course of a few days beginning on the night of November 29, 1781, somewhere in the vicinity of one hundred and thirty live, enslaved people—men, women, and children—were flung overboard by the crew, in small batches, to what can only have been an appallingly frightening death, hard to conceive even with the inspired visual art and literary fiction, from William Turner to Fred D'Aguiar and M. NourbeSe Phillip, that have emerged around the event.[3]

In the annals of New World slavery, the *Zong* is an indisputable *emblem* of the callous and calculated forms of murder that enslavers were capable of

138   PART II

perpetrating on the enslaved—and did perpetrate on the enslaved. As Walvin, puts it: "The very name—the *Zong*—quickly entered the demonology of Atlantic slavery, and came to represent the depravity and heartless violence of the entire slave system."[4] In a sense, the *Zong* event has the symbolic status of synecdoche in the historiography of New World slavery that Auschwitz has in the historiography of the Holocaust; it stands figuratively for the horror of the whole slavery era. It is, unambiguously and incontestably, an instance of moral evil: not only in terms of the *motivated* decision to knowingly commit these unprovoked, inexcusable harms, but also in terms of the culpable actions of those who, without making the decisions themselves, nevertheless participated in carrying out the order. The historical episode of the *Zong* was an evil *event*, moreover, that was situated within the larger context of an evil *institution*, which it supplemented and aggravated and magnified—namely, the evil already systemically embodied in the far-flung network of New World slavery, by then in operation for nearly a century and a half.

The harm of undeserved death by violent killing, in short, was clearly an *integral* and not an incidental feature of New World slavery. No enslaved person who survived the Middle Passage could look forward to a life free of the constant menace of wrongful death. The perpetration of arbitrary death, and the inculcation of the fear of imminent death, were dimensions of the tyranny exercised over the enslaved by their enslavers. Yet, just as certainly, one pronounced feature of New World slavery was that institutionally— that is, in the reproduction of its social relations of domination—it depended as much, or more, on a sustained *form of life* as on regular forms of death. Slavery, though surrounded by death, relied on life. Or rather, to put it more accurately perhaps, New World slavery depended on both the permanent *destruction* of the conditions for the production and reproduction of the forms of life to which those kidnapped and transported to the Americas were accustomed (the traditional lives of their ancestral villages) and the *construction* of a new form of life—the unfree, disposable, and distorted life of plantation enslavement—into which they were forcibly inserted. If New World slavery required at least the ever-present *threat* of violent death as part of the visible structure of intimidation and coercion, it also required a technology by which to *recondition* the lives of its captives ("seasoning," as it was called, "breaking in") so as to *make* them into the slaves needed to sustain and enhance the enterprise of colonial enrichment. Thus, over multiple generations, over hundreds of years, the populations of the enslaved in the Americas suffered displacement, loss, affliction, hardship, cruelty, mutilation, violation, disfigurement, and death. Many survived, many endured, some escaped; none, however, lived or died against the intelligible background of the organized cultural context of their ancestors, but rather in the *novel* context of the modernizing and protocapitalist slave Americas. The enslaved may not all have been systematically dispossessed of bare biological life itself by the institution of slavery (Africans were not enslaved *in order to be* exterminated), but they were *all* systematically dispossessed of something else perhaps as precious, perhaps less immediately visible—namely, the possibility of living in the traditions that they (or their forebears) would have thought of as contributing to a recognizably meaningful life. Recalling my discussion in the prologue, the enslaved were dispossessed of a lifeworld and form of life. They were deliberately and coercively deprived of the background social context of tacitly understood traditions that constituted the ground of a common life and were coercively inserted into a form of life of domination and distortion that had to be learned, adapted, resisted, accommodated, and sometimes rebelled against.

But does the coercively imposed and institutionalized social structure of a dominated lifeworld and form of life in which human flourishing is constrained, deprived, violated, and disposable warrant being thought of as evil just as much as the willful perpetration of genocidal death—one a coerced production and reproduction of distorted life, the other a subtraction and elimination of it? Against the reification of violent death as *the* ultimate evil one can suffer, the answer, I believe, is *yes*. Being forced to live a certain kind of life can be an ultimate evil as well, and part of the challenge of thinking about New World slavery in terms of a moral and reparatory history is offering a sense of why this is so. My concern here is to describe or *redescribe* the institutionalized destructive-constructive powers of New World slavery in such a way as to enable us to recognize an order of evil that is evil not simply for how it stands in its relation to undeserved death but for how it stands in relation to a coerced life.

<hr />

In this chapter, I spend some time thinking about this challenge by considering an approach developed by the moral philosopher Laurence Mordekhai Thomas, principally in his insightful but curiously neglected book *Vessels of Evil: American Slavery and the Holocaust*, published more than two-and-a-half decades ago, in 1993.[5]

140 PART II

To my mind, *Vessels of Evil* is one of the most outstanding discussions of evil available and the only one (to my knowledge, anyway) that takes seriously and systematically the specific problem of *slavery*'s evil. For a number of years, I have reflected on and wrestled with its challenging argument, its sensibility, and its vision, learning a lot but in the end doubting (though not fatally) some of its formulations. Growing partly out of a concern for the often-embattled contemporary relationship between Blacks and Jews in the United States, *Vessels of Evi* is a provocative and generative meditation on the *contrasting* evils embodied in the two institutions—American slavery and the Holocaust—that constitute the "watershed historical experience" of these respective groups of persecuted people. As intellectually and personally attuned as he is to the distinctive moral pain produced by these historical experiences, Thomas aims to critique and displace the pervasive inclination among many—including, indeed especially, among Blacks and Jews themselves—to *compare* the atrocities perpetrated against them in terms of which of the two, American slavery or the Holocaust, was the greater evil and who, therefore, suffered more, Blacks or Jews, by the wrongdoing perpetrated against them. One central feature of this whole exercise of motivated comparison of historical suffering concerns assumptions about intentional death as the ultimate evil. Thomas argues against such morally invidious comparisons between American slavery and the Holocaust, which, in the end, he rightly says, serve only to trivialize and impoverish our understanding of each historical experience. Thomas urges that evils, not least such evils as American slavery and the Holocaust, are "cognitively *sui generis*"—that is, being historically unique they do not admit of such comparative ranking and weighting.[6] American slavery and the Holocaust are *incommensurable* evils, and there should be ways to speak of them intelligently without magnifying or diminishing the moral horror of either with reference to the other. It will be important to recognize, however, that Thomas's intervention aims less to undermine the idea of comparison per se than to "diffuse the rhetorical force" of the indignant claims to moral precedence that typically motivate such comparison. Notably, too, in seeking a path beyond this "obnoxious" desire to structure a competition between the evils of American slavery and the Holocaust, he is also seeking a path beyond the invidious—or anyway, misplaced—need to think of intentional violent death as *the* single and ultimate measure of evil. Ultimate evil, he suggests, has more than one face.[7]

Thomas's concerns in *Vessels of Evil* are oriented by a number of significant background influences that are worth noting, however briefly. In one sense, the book is written in the discursive context of a much wider conversation with other Black philosophers—among them, Michelle Moody-Adams, Bernard Boxill, Tommy Lott, Howard McGary, Bill Lawson, and Charles Mills—who have sought to address certain aspects of New World slavery or the wider Black experience in an explicitly *philosophical* idiom.[8] It has often been remarked how odd and perhaps telling it is that so foundational an institutional injustice as New World slavery should remain so invisible to Anglo-American moral philosophy. How have normative philosophic languages of rights and liberties been so blind to the historic *relationship* between the enfranchisement of White subjects, including their endowment with the perquisites of personhood and voice, on the one hand, and the disenfranchisement and dispossession of Black subjects, with their relegation to subpersonhood and voicelessness, on the other? Is this ignorance or disavowal? In response to this systematic neglect, there has been a concerted effort among Black philosophers to constitute modern slavery as a serious object of moral theory. Notably, however, while these philosophers have focused mainly on developing an engaged philosophic language for thinking about historic racial injustice, including the philosophic case to be made for Black reparations for slavery, they have not been directly concerned with the moral concept of *evil*, as such, as one way of describing the wrongful harm slavery inflicted on the enslaved. For Thomas, by contrast, slavery was not merely one among several kinds of injustices or wrongdoing but an evil—taking evil as a morally evaluative term assigned to wrongdoing of a peculiarly harmful nature. In this way, he joins a number of other contemporary moral philosophers who have begun to revisit and explore the idea of evil as indispensable for thinking about wrongdoing and wrongful harms. Thus fundamentally, Thomas inserts the problem about slavery into an arena of moral consideration not covered by the typically rights-oriented "slavery and racial injustice" debates.

In another direction, *Vessels of Evil* takes up some of the themes of moral motivation and its conditions explored in Thomas's earlier (almost equally neglected) book, *Living Morally: A Psychology of Moral Character*, published in 1989.[9] In contrast to his later focus on slavery, however, in *Living Morally* his concern is with the more virtuous or meritorious institutions of family and friendship, doing good (altruism) rather than doing evil. *Living Morally* offers an account of how individuals come to have and sustain a good moral character, the kind of moral reflective learning and supportive environment (not least the intimate interactive parental environment) that is involved in the generation of loving, caring, trusting,

142   PART II

receptive, autonomous moral sensibilities. Arguing against the model of human beings as self-interested maximizers, Thomas is guided by the informed intuition of the centrality and, indeed, priority of love in our lives. "I believe," he says, "that love gives morality a place in our lives that it would not otherwise have. If you will, love anchors morality in our lives; for it is in virtue of love that doing what is right has ontological priority in our lives."[10] Above all, one might say that what captures Thomas's attention is the problem of moral flourishing—or as he put it, the inextricable link between moral flourishing and human flourishing. As we will see later in this chapter, these are intuitions and modes of philosophic attention that also shape his exploration of moral evil, and in particular his resolute conviction about the moral goodness and rightness of forgiveness for past evil.

As I read him, Thomas's philosophic commitments in *Vessels of Evil* are animated and oriented more by an Aristotelian sensibility for the virtues and the contexts of their cultivation, than, say, a Kantian one undergirded by a rational rights-based liberal individualism. Or anyway, it is the virtue of the good rather than the priority of the right that focuses Thomas's inquiry. As important, and not unrelated I believe, an overall philosophic modesty and understated minimalism characterizes his ordinary language and practical reasoning attitude toward addressing moral questions, one that felicitously takes our best intuitions as a starting point for conceptual analysis. In some ways this approach helps to guard against the all-too-familiar and all-too-impoverishing exorbitance of overly technical philosophic jargon. *Vessels of Evil* is learned and thoughtful without being verbose or pretentious; it appeals less to a schema of doctrine than to what we might reasonably hold in common in our basic understanding of our shared moral world. Of course, in taking this particular liberty Thomas runs the unavoidable risk that *his* intuitions, largely unexamined (or examined *only* as to their rational plausibility rather than, say, their historiographical intelligibility), are no more than settled ideological conventions or normative devices. So, for example, it is important to Thomas that the aim of *Vessels of Evil* is not to *add* anything new sociologically or historically to what we already conventionally "know" about American slavery and the Holocaust. Rather, taking these in terms of "what is unshakably there" or "what is commonly agreed" about them, he offers instead a deliberately *philosophical* project. This project has the express aim of *making sense* of the *concepts* and *attitudes* concerned with these atrocities in order to try to discern the *differences* that shaped the hostile and harmful historical experiences of Blacks and Jews.[11]

Now, needless to say, I can easily see the heuristic point of bracketing a deep social-historical engagement with the details of American slavery and the Holocaust so as to bring the conceptual concerns at stake more sharply and provocatively into focus. One cannot, obviously, see everything all at once; insight always *entails* blindness—or anyway, selective seeing. This is a principle I too endorse. But I am not as sure as Thomas seems to be that the "philosophical" can *always* be so cleanly cut away from the histories that shape the authoritative discourses, the very conventional and normative idioms, in which the institutions of New World slavery and the Holocaust are given to us as *given* institutions as such (these are doubts similar to those I expressed earlier regarding Jonathan Lear). Histories and concepts are sometimes quite entangled. This, after all, is the whole point of Jeffrey Alexander's critique, considered in chapter 2, of the idea of the "Holocaust" as a compact bundle of unexamined and authoritative assumptions. The historiography of New World slavery is a no less *contested* arena of debate. Indeed, as we will see, in the course of his account, Thomas soon finds himself in the middle of some not uncontroversial claims about the character of slavery and its effects on the enslaved.

The respective historical suffering of Blacks and Jews, Thomas argues, has often been the subject of more or less explicit invidious comparison between slavery and the Holocaust (we have seen this in Hannah Arendt) that seeks to determine or make a claim about which was the more cruel or destructive of the two, which was *eviler*. The whole project of *Vessels of Evil* is animated by the apprehension that there is something deeply misguided and impoverished in such comparisons between American slavery and the Holocaust. Thomas's aim, he says, is to think the "conceptual differences" between American slavery and the Holocaust without lapsing into the kind of comparison between the two historical atrocities that concerns itself (implicitly or explicitly) with who suffered more and who less, Blacks or Jews. American slavery and the Holocaust, Thomas argues, were *both* profoundly evil, but they were evil in "radically different ways."[12] Their evils, he maintains, are "incommensurable" with each other. So that, contrary to what is suggested, for example, in Arendt's remarks on the death camps referred to in chapter 2, slavery and the Holocaust cannot be compared, strictly speaking, on any *scale* of harms. They cannot be measured against each other. They were different institutionalized practices involving different ideological conceptions of their victims and different rationalities and technologies of evil. And yet, even so, he urges, it is worth *juxtaposing* them as he does

144   PART II

for no other reason than that the ways in which they differ are illuminating for deepening and complicating our thinking about the varied practices of evil.[13] What is at stake for Thomas is to "articulate the conceptual differences between the Holocaust and American Slavery rather than to compare the atrocities of one with the other."[14]

Early in *Vessels of Evil*, Thomas puts the fundamental difference between slavery and the Holocaust in the following way: "The very telos of Slavery was to bring about the utter dependence of blacks upon slaveowners. The very telos of the Holocaust was the extermination of the Jewish people." In Thomas' view, these contrasting features do not indicate a hierarchy of evils between the Holocaust and slavery. Although it might be thought, he says, that because the aim of the Holocaust was extermination, which was not the case with slavery, then *consequently* the former was the worse evil, this conclusion does not follow. As he clarifies: "This is not because wrongful death fails to be the ultimate form of harm we take it to be. Rather it is because death is not the only ultimate form of harm that a person may endure."[15] Far from downplaying the idea of wrongful death as an ultimate harm, Thomas simply aims to hold open the possibility of other forms of grave, systematic harm, equally evil but that do not necessarily have the deliberate perpetration of death as their telos and sustaining raison d'être.

There is, I believe, an admirable sense of balance and judiciousness that shapes Thomas's handling of these instances of historical evil, slavery and the Holocaust. By and large, Thomas is not a polemicist. Nevertheless, I read *Vessels of Evil* as a philosophic *intervention* that challenges and decenters the conventional assumption that the physical death involved in extermination (unpardonably horrific as that clearly is) is the *only* or *privileged* paradigm of evil. If we take physical death to be the hallmark of evil, slavery's evil can appear only contingent and therefore diminished. Part of the critical value of *Vessels of Evil*, therefore, is precisely that it offers a vantage point from which to question the seeming self-evidence of the prevailing *death-centered* paradigm of evil that we have already seen at work. A good deal of the book's emphasis is oriented toward enabling us to appreciate that while death by *mass extermination* is undoubtedly an instance of *ultimate* evil, it need not by any means be the *only* one—so too might the evil embodied in the coerced production and reproduction of a distorted *form of life*. In this, Thomas is guided by the idea that there "is no true understanding of a people without a grasp of its moral pain." This idea of moral suffering is central to him, and in particular the idea that no peoples' suffering should be taken to be morally definitive of the suffering of humankind as such. Indeed, in aiming to make sense of the moral pain of Jews and Blacks, Thomas writes "with the conviction that the moral pain of neither can be subsumed under nor assimilated into the moral pain of the other."[16] This is an invaluable perspective. Notably, therefore, what we won't find in Thomas's book is anything like a general *theory* of evil.[17] What we will find, rather, are so many moral philosophic exercises in the attempt to make sense of the manifest evil at the heart of these two historical institutions. In short, I read *Vessels of Evil* as a critique of the ideology of *exceptional* evils of the sort that we have already encountered.

In what follows, I have a limited and largely selective and exploratory itinerary. Although I aim to reconstruct a good deal of Thomas's argument in *Vessels of Evil*, I do not intend to engage this book comprehensively—there is much in it that I leave aside. To begin with, however, I briefly set out aspects of the conception of evil developed by two eminent philosophers who are worth thinking about alongside Thomas—namely, John Kekes and Claudia Card. These two very different philosophers engage the problem of evil in ways that offer suggestive points of contact as well as contrast with each other—and with Thomas. Against this background I discuss dimensions of Thomas's conception of evil as set out in *Vessels of Evil*. My aim is to better discern the distinctive character of his idea about the nature of human vulnerability to evil action, an idea that he develops in conversation with Martha Nussbaum's influential *The Fragility of Goodness*.[18] Importantly, Thomas is especially interested in large-scale evil, in *atrocities*, and in the institutional—or institutionalized—evil that produces and sustains them. I sketch out his characterization of the evil of New World slavery specifically in contrast to that of the Holocaust. My own overall interest, as I have indicated, is to ask what the critical question about New World slavery ought to be in the current moral-political conjuncture. Consequently, my attention to Thomas's description of the Holocaust is driven largely by the extent to which it enhances our sense of the distinctiveness of slavery's evil. Notably, Thomas derives his idea of this distinctiveness in part from Orlando Patterson's conception of "natal alienation" as the essential defining feature of slavery.[19] Thomas offers a specifically *narrative* redescription of Patterson's sociological argument that, I suggest,

146   PART II

offers significant insight into the moral evil of slavery but at the same time obscures something vital about slavery's character as an institutionalized social relation—namely, the sense of slavery as a *form of life*. (Patterson's work is the subject of chapter 4.) Finally, I explore Thomas's ideas about forgiveness in the context of evils such as New World slavery. This is not an argument he makes in *Vessels of Evil*, but he does so elsewhere in what I take to be a connected discussion.[20] Although in many ways cogent and humane, and attentive to the senses in which people can, without malign intention, get caught up in a "moral climate" of evil, I suggest that the questions of forgiveness and redemption are not so much insufficient to meet the challenges of the evil perpetrated by the *institution* of New World slavery as *irrelevant* to them.

CONTRASTING APPROACHES TO EVIL

If the moral challenge of the theological problem of evil (that is, theodicy) was to account for how an omniscient, omnipotent, and benevolent creator could allow the innocent to suffer, the moral challenge of the secular problem of evil is to consider the prevalence of severe wrongdoing and harm in the world given a naturalistic conception of the human condition. The field of secular theoretical discussion of moral evil—that is, evil involving *human* agency—is crossed by a rich number of hard questions, not all of which are addressed in this chapter but ought, nevertheless, to be borne in mind. Among these questions are the following: Is evil a moral concept that continues to have critical theoretical use-value, or is it more confusing or ambiguous than it is worth? What is the relationship between evil and other concepts of negative moral evaluation such as "bad" or "wrong"? Is evil simply an extreme form of these, or is there a discernible and relevant qualitative difference? What is an evil action? Should persons or their characters also be described as evil, or only deeds, intentions, and motivations? Can an institution be evil? What kinds of harms or human suffering count as evil? What is the relationship between the occurrence of evil and the nature of the human condition? If evils are what they are, in what sense are they reparable?[21]

Against the background of these questions, I want to look at two prominent and contrasting philosophical accounts of evil with which Laurence Thomas's approach both converges and diverges—those of John Kekes and Claudia Card.[22] These are both philosophers who, like Thomas, are concerned to construct a secular conception of evil and who seek to do so at least in part by taking some distance from Kant's formulations, with respect to his idea of "radical evil' specifically (sketched in chapter 1) but also more generally with respect to the broader moral philosophy of autonomy and self-determining will that underpins this idea. Which is not to say, however, that the heritage of (or at least the argument with) Kant is completely absent in either. To the contrary. Both Kekes and Card, and Thomas as well, seek to "deromanticize" evil; that is, they seek to call into question the focus on diabolical agents of evil, "moral monsters," while themselves preserving room for the deep sense of a capacity—if not an innate propensity—in human beings to commit evil. This debate is part of the inheritance not only of Kant, of course, but of Hannah Arendt as well—or of Kant via Arendt. At the same time, notably, though not surprisingly, neither Kekes nor Card offer, or are concerned to offer, the kind of *historicized* conceptual account that might suggest what it is about the current conjuncture that gives the moral criticism they develop its particular purchase or value. The world (including the philosophical world) they both intervene in has no specifiable, historical-ideological shape, apart from being a moral world in which evil is perpetrated and suffered. To them, evidently, evil is not only a timeless philosophical problem but also a problem whose philosophical contours (and philosophical urgency) have no distinguishable or relevant historical conditions. As should be clear from what I have said in chapter 1 of this book, I am interested precisely in the problem-space in which evil emerges as a cogent moral category of severe disapprobation. In this respect, that Kekes and Card and Thomas all begin publishing their work on evil in the 1990s and 2000s is not surprising or irrelevant.

In chapter 4 of *Vessels of Evil*, "Characterizing Evil," in the course of his discussion of the features that characterize evil Thomas offers a somewhat enigmatic footnote in which he expresses disagreement with Kekes's idea that evil is essentially "undeserved harm." To be sure, as we will see in a moment, this idea *is* indeed central to Kekes's overall argument. But Thomas's reasoning for dissenting from this view is curiously obscure—*curious* because, as I have said, obscurity is not an especially prevalent hallmark of his writing. According to Thomas, the view that evil is undeserved harm "gets the discussion off on the wrong foot" inasmuch as it "makes it more difficult than [Kekes] realizes to talk about purely secular evil rather than religious or metaphysical evil."[23] My suspicion is that Kekes would be surprised indeed to hear this about his book, *Facing Evil*. And unfortunately, in his otherwise carefully and attentively staged argument Thomas offers nothing

148 PART II

by way of a considered account of this disagreement. In what way does the idea of "undeserved harm" get the discussion of evil off on the wrong foot? Which foot is that, specifically? Is it this idea by itself or the specific way in which Kekes uses it? Why should the idea of undeserved harm disable a distinctly secular conception of evil? None of this is spelled out or even indicated. I have reason to wonder whether, to some extent anyway, Thomas's *Vessels of Evil* shouldn't be read as a (tacit) response to Kekes's *Facing Evil*, and as offering an implicitly rival conception of evil.

John Kekes is a thoughtful philosopher who has been systematically developing his ideas about evil over a number of years and in a number of books, beginning with *Facing Evil*, the argument of which was revised and extended in *The Roots of Evil*, published many years later.[24] It is the first of these two books that especially interests me. For Kekes, evil is not an isolated moral-philosophical concept; rather, it forms a generative dimension of his broader political-philosophical thinking—for example, about the question of liberalism (in *Against Liberalism*) and of the virtues of conservatism (in *A Case for Conservatism*), and it shapes his considerations of the essential conditions of human life and human welfare (in *The Human Condition*) and much else.[25] Part of what is interesting to me about Kekes is that he develops his ideas about evil in relation to a wider set of moral-political conceptions that help to cast doubt on the self-evident privilege of the Enlightenment and of liberal reason: the conception, for instance, of a moral tradition (connecting his work to that of Alasdair MacIntyre), the conception of value pluralism (connecting his work to that of John Gray), and perhaps most important, the conception of the tragic (connecting his work to that of Martha Nussbaum).[26] In Kekes, then, there is an instructive critique of some of the prevailing normative tenets of the Enlightenment and specifically liberal rationality and moral and political sensibility—not least, the role of choice and character and autonomy in thinking about human harm, human wrongdoing, and human flourishing.

At the same time, however admirably sensitive Kekes is in *Facing Evil* to the historical problem of evil, he works with a remarkably conventional and restrictive picture of the *instances* of evil that appear to be its *exemplifications*. It is not surprising that Stalin and Hitler head the list, presumably because they appear to require no further justification. But why do they appear to be such self-evident exemplars? Why doesn't Kekes feel obliged to *make* the case that these are indeed evil's quintessential examples? In what ideology does this stance partake?

Why does the demonology that so resolutely casts Stalin and Hitler as stereotypical figures within the malign aura of evil not even touch, for instance, the figure of Harry Truman, the U.S. president who gave the order to use the atomic bomb against Japan in August 1945? Were the bombing of Hiroshima and Nagasaki not also atrocities, acts of culpable evil? Or are war's victors immune to, or excused from, this damning ascription? Elizabeth Anscombe did not think so, to her credit, and was willing to speak out about it.[27] Kekes then names the massacres of "Armenians, Cambodians, Gypsies, Indonesians, Jews, kulaks," all shocking and reprehensible acts of evil. But, allowing that he couldn't possibly name *every* massacre in recorded history, how has he chosen these as the standout examples? Is it odd that the evils that founded the republic that is an essential part of the very conditions of possibility of the book Kekes writes are overlooked? The genocidal killing of Native American people, the systematic expropriation of their lands, and the destruction of their forms of life—this history of evil does not make it onto his list. Nor, needless to say, does the history of the enslavement of Africans and their descendants, their perpetual racial bondage, coerced acculturation, and the appropriation of their wealth-producing labor. The disavowing silence that naturalizes the invisibility of these evils might (or *should*) itself be part of a history of evil in the modern world.

These caveats aside, Kekes's work certainly deserves considered attention. Evil is a *moral* problem, he says in *Facing Evil*, because it threatens and ultimately undermines our aspiration to lead good lives. But more than this, evil is a *prevalent* moral problem; it is not merely incidental or passing or superficial but is an insidious and profound and quite likely permanent feature of the human condition. Consequently, the problem of evil demands our urgent moral and political attention. We need, Kekes argues, to *face* evil undauntingly and not turn away from its moral ugliness or hide behind a facile faith in human goodwill. Only by appreciating the depth of evil's claim on our lives can we hope to adequately grasp what is required of us as moral agents if we are going to be able to ameliorate, if not completely eradicate, its baleful effects. This is the daunting project of *Facing Evil*.

Now, in this book, as we have just seen, Kekes defines evil as "undeserved harm inflicted on human beings"—that is, harm that has no discernible justification, no warrant, no moral foundation.[28] It is inexcusable. Kekes recognizes, he says, that the popular idea of the banality of evil drawn from Hannah Arendt is one way of "deromanticizing" evil, of stripping evil of the demonic grandeur

150   PART II

of *intentions*. Without necessarily disagreeing with Arendt's approach, however, he urges that there is an older and deeper approach whose conceptual resources should be explored: namely, the one found in the idea of *tragedy*. Animated, as I have suggested, by Nussbaum's book, *The Fragility of Goodness* (though eventually taking a sharply critical distance from it), Kekes maintains that what tragedy shows us is that our lives are shaped to a significant degree by factors over which we have little or no control. It shows us the extent to which the familiar assumption that we are the masters of nature, including our own natures, and can fully determine the outcomes of our actions, and thus the realization of the good, is an illusion, and moreover a dangerous illusion. Tragedy undermines the seductive pretense of the sovereignty of the rational and autonomous will. As Kekes writes in a measured and clarifying passage:

> Tragedy shows our vulnerability to evil. We learn from it the contingency of human existence, the indifference of nature to human merit, and the presence of destructive forces as part of human motivation. But the most painful lesson of all is not that our vulnerability to evil is merely the consequence of adverse external causes but that we ourselves are also agents of the contingency, indifference, and destructiveness that jeopardize the human aspiration to live good lives. The tragic view depicts human motivation as the arena in which our virtues and vices wage their endless battles, and it forces us to recognize that the issue remains undecided. Thus, tragedy prompts us to see human character as fundamentally flawed. The flaw is not a specific vice, like selfishness or intemperance, but a general propensity to live in a state of tension between our virtues and our vices.[29]

Thus the wisdom of tragedy is that it offers us at once a more modest and a more realistic picture of ourselves and others, a picture of ourselves and others that appreciates the fact that no one is immune to reversals of fortune, that the just and virtuous sometimes suffer and fall from grace while the unjust and vicious are sometimes those who prevail and thrive. If this view is right, Kekes argues, there is no point saying that what we need is better *reason* and more *resolve* because these too are always-already "infected" with the very conflict they are meant to overcome. The tension between our vices and our virtues is *constitutive* and *ineradicable*. "According to the tragic view, we are tainted through and through, and this is one main reason (though not the only one) why evil is prevalent and why human aspirations to live good lives are so rarely realized."[30]

Kekes observes that such a tragic point of view is not widely accepted in contemporary moral thinking; it is in fact widely rejected. It flies too much in the face of the ideal (whether Platonic or Kantian in origin) that we are, or can be, or certainly *should* be, arbiters of the good to which we aspire. There is a deep antitragic dimension to the social and individual constructionism that animates Western humanism. Antitragic moral thinkers, Kekes argues, are especially reluctant to allow so profound a role as *character* has in the tragic point of view, as well as the radical implication that important instances of evil can be thought of as *unchosen*, insofar as they derive less from willed decisions to commit evil than from underlying vices—and therefore it is not merely the actions of these agents that should be judged as evil but also the character-constituting *agents* themselves.

People who are reluctant to see character as crucial to thinking about evil, Kekes says, demonstrate a "soft" reaction to evil. For them, by and large, evil is not evil unless it is action freely chosen by agents. The background morality from which the soft reaction to evil flows is what Kekes calls "choice-morality." Choice-moralists aim to make a sharp distinction between the actions of agents and the agents themselves. On this account, people are not evil, only *actions* are. Choice-moralists maintain that to call people evil is to unhelpfully demonize them. Only in extreme circumstances should both agents and their actions be described as evil (Stalin and Hitler, presumably). For Kekes, of course, evil *can*, certainly, be chosen, and chosen evil is particularly egregious. But the tragic view shows that much, maybe *most*, evil is not of this sort—it is unchosen. Choice-morality also depends on the view that the primary potentiality in human nature is for the development of the virtues, the realization of the good, and that vices (including evil) result from the corruption of the virtues, the subversion of the good. Famously, this is basically Kant's view and has been taken for granted in a large swathe of contemporary ethical thinking. Kekes thinks that tragedy enables us to see that this view is deeply mistaken. Our propensity for wrongdoing and evildoing, he maintains, is an independent and rival potentiality to that of our propensity for virtuous actions.

Kekes believes that the choice-morality of the soft reaction to evil fails to adequately account for the fact that evil is so prevalent. The alternative to this view is, not surprisingly, a "hard" reaction to evil. The background morality that

152 PART II

supports this hard reaction to evil—the one that Kekes commends and defends—
is what he calls "character-morality." On this view, actions as well as agents are
potentially evil. People who hold a "hard" reaction to evil, Kekes maintains,
believe that a good deal of the evil that threatens and undermines our aspiration,
and our ability, to live good lives is caused by the "characteristic but unchosen
actions of human beings." These unchosen actions grow out of vices that have
become ingrained in character. As Kekes puts it, "People cause evil when they
act naturally and spontaneously, without much thought or effort, in accordance
with the vices that have achieved dominance in their characters. They may be
cowardly, lazy, intemperate, thoughtless, cruel, vain, or envious, and these vices
are reflected in their actions. They do not choose to act in these ways. They pre-
dominantly are in the ways shown by their actions."[31] Of course, Kekes recognizes
that character is itself *formed* over time. Therefore, there is to some extent, early
in life, a choice in the matter of who one eventually becomes.[32] But as adults,
when our characters are more established and motivated, we act in largely characteristic habitual ways. Thus the "primary fact is that many people have vices of
which the evil actions are the predictable outcome." In such people, evil actions
are the unchosen effect of "vice-driven" and habit-patterned action. If this is
true, Kekes argues, then the relation between agents and their actions cannot
be as choice-morality supposes: "If evil is undeserved harm and if these people
habitually cause undeserved harm, then the hard reaction prompts us to regard
as evil not only their actions but also the agents themselves, insofar as they are
the causes of evil."[33]

The secular problem of evil, Kekes repeats throughout his book, resides in
the unresolvable tension between the essential conditions of human life and the
aspiration to live morally. The tragic view reveals this permanent tension and
helps us to see that ineluctable contingency is an ineradicable part of human life.
The tragic view helps us, therefore, to recognize the conceit of choice-morality's
ideals of autonomy and mastery. It helps us, he says, to look at evil "unflinchingly,"
and it helps us to see that "we are among the causes of our own vulnerability to
evil."[34] But still, in the end, for Kekes the tragic view is not enough. It functions
well as a kind of "diagnostic" of our moral condition; but agreeing with the diag-
nosis should not commit us to the "hopelessness" that follows from the tragic
point of view. There remains an area of "control," he suggests, somewhat surprisingly, that offers "the prospect of modest but true hope."[35] Here we see the
role in Kekes's thinking of an almost voluntarist idea of responsible agency. If

we cannot eliminate altogether the essential conditions of human life, we can nevertheless act to minimize the damage that they potentially cause. What we need, Kekes argues, is to cultivate a "reasonable response" to the tension between our aspirations and the given circumstances of our lives. Central to what is required for such a response is to "enlarge our understanding of the essential conditions" and to adopt a different attitude to them, one shaped by what he calls a "reflective temper." Such an enlarged understanding urges us to recognize that it is a simple fact of human existence that we do not have total control over the course of our lives. But tragic situations, Kekes maintains, unexpectedly, are only tragic because of our attitude and response to them. "Tragedy is not intrinsic to the world; we collude in producing it."[36] The problem, he says, is that we have the "expectation that contingency, indifference, and destructiveness will be overcome by reason and decency, and our expectation is disappointed." The result of this disappointed expectation is that we "come to see our lives as tragic, and we are assailed by hopelessness."[37] What we need to do is to reflectively bring this expectation within a different and, in effect, more *tempered* and *modest* perspective. By reflectively acknowledging the pervasive force of these essential conditions, we can create the possibility of reducing the weight of this expectation of promethean mastery over adversity and of unmitigated success in our projects. "This enlarged understanding, leading to reduced expectation, is the ground for true hope"—that is, a constrained or "chastened hope."[38] (One is tempted here to see a connection between this view and Albert Camus's idea of an "absurd" hope.) For Kekes, part of the value of the idea of character-morality is that—though it is attuned to the tragic sense of contingency, indifference, and destructiveness in human life—it is not reducible to the sense of paralysis and doom it can induce. By urging the cultivation of the virtue of the sort of enlarged and reflective understanding of the conditions of our lives he commends, the view from character-morality aims to offer positive resources for responding to the secular problem of evil.

As I have suggested, one of the principal texts through which Kekes seeks to demonstrate what he means by a reasonable response to the problem of evil is Martha Nussbaum's *The Fragility of Goodness*, a book to which Kekes's own work is manifestly and avowedly indebted. However, Kekes sees in Nussbaum's book *both* an inspiring opening toward *and* a disappointing turning away from an adequate understanding of tragedy—and therefore evil. In her description of human life and its conditions of contingency, indifference, and destructiveness,

154   PART II

there is much with which Kekes straightforwardly agrees. He notes, though, that in these descriptions Nussbaum demonstrates an intolerable inclination to consider the jeopardies humans face not as limits thwarting their aspirations but as "spurs to human greatness."[39] For her, our vulnerability is not merely a lack or a deficit but precisely a dimension of human experience that enriches and ennobles our excellences and achievements. Thus Nussbaum offers, Kekes says, a "romantic" response to the tragic problem of evil, and this he argues is flawed and even dangerous insofar as it hampers our ability to properly face and cope with evil (he also negatively considers Sidney Hook's "pragmatic" response and Thomas Nagel's "ironic" approach). The sense that what is good about human excellences "just is its vulnerability to conditions that both call it forth and threaten to destroy it" strikes Kekes as incoherent and misguided. Nussbaum, he argues, "illegitimately passes from the true claim that without inhospitable essential conditions of life there would be no need for human excellences to the false claim that human excellences are partly constituted by our vulnerability to these adverse conditions."[40]

I am not as sure as Kekes is that it is a "false" claim to hold that the qualities of admirable human achievement especially stand out against the adversities in the face of which they are won; or that it is ill-judged to think that it is partly the fact of the adversity that helps to constitute the excellence of that achievement. This seems to me a crucial idea for a tragic ethics of contingency. But Kekes demurs: he sees a short distance from the insight regarding our vulnerability to evil to "an attitude that embraces evil as good."[41] Now, again, arguably, this seems like a tendentious reading of Nussbaum. But what it clarifies, perhaps, is that for Kekes, contingency, indifference, and destructiveness are more than mere *conditions* of evil; they are themselves evil—or almost so.[42] As clinching the argument against Nussbaum's alleged romanticism, Kekes proposes her characterization of Polyxena's death in Euripides's profoundly unsettling play *Hecuba*. Readers of Nussbaum's elaborate discussion of *Hecuba* will remember that, for her, central to the play's tragic dynamic is the theme of the violation and betrayal of a "child's trusting simplicity," specifically Polyxena's. Famously, Troy is defeated, and Hecuba and two of her children, Polydorus and Polyxena, are captives of the Greeks. Polyxena believes she is to be given as a prize to one of the Greeks, but Odysseus has demanded otherwise—namely, that she be offered as a sacrifice to appease the anger of Achilles's ghost. Undaunted by this turn of events, the ruthlessness of the betrayal, she "responds with remarkable courage and dignity,"

Nussbaum says, going to meet her "death willingly, saying that death is better than a slave's life."[43] And a bit later, Nussbaum writes: "Most touching of all, perhaps, is her final display of maidenly modesty. As she fell in death, reports the incredulous herald, even at that ultimate moment she took thought to arrange her skirts so that her body would not be revealed in an immodest way."[44] Kekes finds this focus on Polyxena's attitude of bravery and modesty in the face of her unchosen predicament, rather than the perpetration of the evil that is about to overcome her, a "skewed judgment."[45] It is the latter rather than the former that Kekes thinks is the true meaning of the tragic in Euripides's text. Somewhat obscurely, he holds that Nussbaum's judgment is informed by an "attitude" of "passionate love of life—a love that makes one open, vulnerable, and receptive; a love that is oblivious to risk and danger, disdains safety, and concentrates on its object with an intensity that relegates everything else to insignificance."[46] Supposedly, this is the attitude she finds in Polyxena. But it is a misplaced attitude, Kekes declares, not only because it does not properly belong to such a "half-formed child-woman" as Polyxena but also because it is an attitude that obscures the reality of evil, and more, that weakens our capacity to adequately respond to evil. But why should this be so? Kekes does not clearly say. It seems to me, however, that a more useful and discerning and generous conclusion for him to have reached might have been that he and Nussbaum are really looking at the same predicament or event from different perspectives: she from the side of the victim, he from the side of the perpetrator. Kekes's focus is the tragedy of becoming an evildoer, whereas for Nussbaum the issue is the tragedy of becoming an evil sufferer.

The work of Claudia Card on evil, especially the work embodied in her seminal book *The Atrocity Paradigm*, published in 2002, offers an instructive contrast to Kekes—and, as I will suggest, an instructive point of contact with Thomas, who in fact she has sometimes cited. Card shares with Kekes the general view (as participants in the heritage of Arendt) that the appropriate target of secular moral considerations of evil should not be "moral monsters"—that is, those exceptional and perhaps anomalous individuals whose lives appear to be unequivocally reprehensible and blameworthy. At the same time, Card writes self-consciously in criticism of what she sees as Kekes's one-sided focus on *evildoing* rather than

156 PART II

evil-suffering. If she does not completely neglect the issue of evildoing, for her it is the standpoint of the victim of evil rather than the perpetrator of it that should be the central axis of theorization.[47] On the whole, perhaps, Card is not so interested in the tragic question about the contingency of the human condition and how good lives sometimes go bad—though, like Kekes, she has clearly been influenced by Martha Nussbaum's criticism of the Stoic conceit of self-mastery[48] Above all, what is of conceptual interest to her is the harm experienced by those *against* whom wrong has been done.

Claudia Card (who died in 2015) was a profound and admired moral philosopher who came to her late and influential work on evil from many years of philosophic thinking centered on the intersection of ethics, gender, and oppression. So, to begin with, not only the philosophical orientation of her work but the whole tone and sensibility offers a marked contrast with Kekes. Card was, from the 1970s, a philosophic protagonist in the development of feminist pedagogies, and specifically a feminist ethics, urging a concerted focus on rethinking debates around moral responsibility, moral agency, voice, and character in the context of sexist indifference, hostility, and domination. This was the starting point of her well-known edited volume *Feminist Ethics*, published in 1991.[49] Her collection of essays, *Lesbian Choices*, published a few years later, in 1995, offered a courageously personal and pathbreaking reflection on the ambiguities and moral complexities of choice involved in lesbian identity, sexual agency and preference, and friendship.[50] The following year she published *The Unnatural Lottery: Character and Moral Luck*, which offered an intervention into the famous debate about "moral luck" initiated by Bernard Williams and Thomas Nagel. If there is a "natural lottery" from which our allotment of physical and psychological assets and liabilities are derived, Card argued, we need also to consider that there is, for people in certain social circumstances and historical contexts, an "unnatural lottery," in which the decks are stacked in such a way that degrees of good and bad luck are structurally and institutionally overdetermined.[51] It is not surprising, given these background preoccupations and commitments, that Card brought to her thinking on evil, in particular her thinking on twentieth-century evils, both a sensibility of moral and political outrage at a range of experiences of domination and violence and the insightful perspective of an ample philosophical synthesis.[52]

Part of Card's project in *The Atrocity Paradigm* is to situate the secular problem of evil she is seeking to define and theorize in relation to dominant strands in contemporary moral philosophy—in particular, the divergent heritages of utilitarianism (with its calculus of harms and pleasures) and Kantianism (with its focus on willful wrongdoing). Indeed, she considers her work a synthesis of what is most useful in each strand, and this modest sense of seeking to strike a pathway between contending philosophical positions is one of the attractive features of her work.[53] But, notably, her first theoretical move in setting out the terms of her investigation is to release the *substantive* moral problem of evil from the influence of Nietzsche's genealogy—to challenge what she calls Nietzsche's "denial of evil" in both *Beyond Good and Evil* (1886) and *On the Genealogy of Morality* (1887). Card worries that much contemporary moral philosophy has followed Nietzsche, not necessarily in the detail of his views about the origins of the judgment of evil (namely, in the *ressentiment* of the weak, in the abject morality of the slave) but in the general genealogical orientation that refrains from *evaluative* judgments about evil or that questions (sometimes belligerently, sometimes ironically) the motive—varieties of the "will to power," typically—that drives such judgment. Nietzsche's critique, she writes, "has helped engineer a shift from questions of what to do to prevent, reduce, or redress evils to skeptical psychological questions about what inclines people to make judgements of evil in the first place, what functions such judgements have served." Card's project is to "reverse" this Nietzschean shift, not because she uncritically endorses the "hatred and revenge" of the wronged (indeed, she explicitly does *not*) but because "evils, the worst wrongs people do, deserve to be taken seriously and to receive priority over lesser wrongs, which are usually easier to talk about and easier to fix."[54] This whole orientation that sees evil—the *worst* wrongs—as having moral precedence over other wrongs inflects and sustains Card's argument.

I think Card has a legitimate worry here, though I do not fully endorse her formulation of it. I think it is indeed arguable that the strategy of genealogy (whether in the name of Nietzsche or Michel Foucault) has *both* opened up a universe of hitherto unasked questions about the will to power embodied in moral and political knowledges *and*, simultaneously, and precisely in so doing, obscured or disabled pertinent questions about how to make new or alternative moral and political judgments, however provisional and admittedly fallibilistic, about the wrongful harms of certain actions and institutions.[55] It is true that, in some sense, genealogy has itself become a *normalized* strategy of criticism, foreclosing some directions even as it commends others. Therefore, Card is entirely right to suggest that genealogy can be "turned back on Nietzsche" and that we can

158 PART II

inquire into "what functions or interests are served by his shift of focus from evils to those who judge."[56] And yet, of course, even if one agreed (as I do) that there is virtue in posing the questions she now aims to pose about evil, Card would be mistaken to believe that she herself can evade at least one version of the genealogical inquiry—namely, what is the contemporary problem-space that makes the new questions about evil she raises so seemingly pertinent? Unfortunately, like Kekes, Card does not ask herself this question. As I have suggested in earlier chapters, this is an important question to ask if we are to grasp the significance of the moral turn that shapes our present concern with evil, the conceptual-political contours that animate this direction of inquiry.

Unlike Kekes, Card is not principally interested in isolated incidents of evil or in our individual propensity to commit acts of evil, however heinous. She is principally interested in *atrocities*—that is, publicly known, and typically large-scale and collective acts of evil. She has in mind such phenomena as "genocides slavery, torture, rape as a weapon of war, the saturation bombing of cities, biological and chemical warfare unleashing lethal viruses and gases, and the domestic terrorism of prolonged battery, stalking, and child abuse."[57] It is a varied list, she acknowledges, but these diverse institutions and practices index the scale and profundity and urgency of the problem of evil she aims to describe. Importantly, Card's interest in atrocities is not merely empirical, although historical cases are certainly material to her theoretical concern. Rather, her interest is, above all, *conceptual*. For Card, atrocities are *paradigms* of what evils are. They are not merely extensions of individual acts of evil; they are themselves orders of evil that help us to better grasp the essential features of evil, including the role of human agency in the commission of evil. This is why Card distinguishes between *catastrophes* and *atrocities*—the former simply happen, they occur, they are acts of God. By contrast, atrocities are *perpetrated*. They typically extend over time, involving multiple actors differently positioned in relation to the perpetration of harm, and therefore embody multiple levels of intention and motivation, and planning and decision-making, and culpability and blameworthiness. Moreover, as Card suggests at one point, thinking through atrocities helps to focus our attention on concrete *evils* rather than on evil as an abstraction and therefore helps to orient us away from the suggestion that evil is a manifestation of dark or metaphysical forces. On her account, atrocities are conceptual paradigms of evil, but this is not simply because they are often spectacular occasions or events or processes; they are conceptual paradigms of evil because they are *indisputable* evils, because they "deserve priority of attention," and because the "core features of evil tend to be writ large" in them, "making them easier to identify and appreciate."[58]

Atrocities, Card argues, help us to identify and appreciate the two cardinal facts about evils: they are *perpetrated* and they are *suffered*. Thus she begins with what she thinks of as a "simple abstract definition" of evils—namely, as "foreseeable intolerable harms produced by culpable wrongdoing." She goes on to clarify (perhaps with Kekes in mind) that on her theory it is the "nature and severity of the harms, rather than the perpetrators' psychological states" that matter for distinguishing evils from ordinary wrongs.[59] On this definition, evils have two basic components: they are composed of, first, foreseeable intolerable harm, and second, culpable wrongdoing. These are the basic components of Card's theory. In her view, neither wrongdoing nor the suffering of harm are sufficient in themselves for the presence of evil. In evil, both occur together. The idea of foreseeable intolerable harm speaks to the sense in which evil should be differentiated from other more minor forms of wrongdoing. Not all harms are evil—although all evils by definition, harm. To say of an action or a deed that it is evil is to point to some profound, grave, or egregious damage that it has done to another human being. Evils *ruin*, as Card puts it. They not only oppress or exploit human beings (disagreeable as that might be) but also destroy something integral to the humanity of human beings. On this view, evils are not merely "very bad" deeds, they cross a threshold of what is supportable; they deprive people of the possibility of flourishing, the "opportunity to live out a meaningful life."[60] It has been an important part of the urgency of Card's argument regarding evil that she maintains it should be distinguished from other wrongs, such as "unjust inequalities," for example. In this context, she has argued, controversially, as one can well imagine, that feminists would do better to target the evils of domestic abuse as having greater priority over gender equality.[61]

The second component of Card's conception of evil in *The Atrocity Paradigm*—namely, culpable wrongdoing—speaks to her concern with the moral agency that evil actions presuppose. Evils, for Card, can be perpetrated and maintained only by human beings who, at least in principle, have the capacity for moral reflection on their actions, who therefore have the potential to act otherwise than they do, and who consequently can be held accountable for their acts of commission and omission. To repeat—in her view, atrocities are not catastrophes. They do not merely happen. Note, in this regard, that the idea of culpability in relation to evil is meant to encompass actions that are not necessarily motivated by intentional

160   PART II

wrongdoing, by deliberately willful acts (such as torture or rape, for example). As she writes (again, surely, with Kekes not far from her mind), "Evildoers . . . are not necessarily malicious. Oftener they are inexcusably reckless, callously indifferent, amazingly unscrupulous. Evildoers need not be evil people, although they may become so over time."[62]

One other feature of Card's discussion is worth highlighting because it has a bearing on Thomas's argument—namely, the question of *comparing* evils. Evils are the worst wrongs, she says, but some evils are worse than others. Card recognizes that this is a slippery slope, that the yield from such comparisons may be a good deal less than the effort is worth. Comparing atrocities, she acknowledges, can be a "morally sensitive issue," but in her view a theory of evil should in principle be able to make sense both of degrees of evil and of the resistance some people feel to making such comparisons.[63] Card lists a number of dimensions along which comparisons might be made—severity of harm, for example, that might be a function of intensity of suffering, duration of suffering, or number of victims— but admittedly none of this is straightforward. Indeed, in the end it is not clear how committed Card is to establishing such a framework of comparison. She writes, on the one hand, "An atrocity is already so evil that in some contexts it seems disrespectful of victims to point out that another was even worse. For the individual, intolerable is intolerable." And, on the other hand (later on the same page), "The atrocity paradigm is compatible with the idea that some evils are worse than others without committing us to the idea that, even in principle, large-scale atrocities can always be ranked."[64] This seems to me somewhat confused: atrocities are conceptually comparable but their comparison may be morally illegitimate. Although Card does invoke Thomas's disapproval of such ranked comparisons where slavery and the Holocaust are concerned, it is not clear that she has grasped either the motivating sources or the full force of his dissenting argument.

In later work, embodied in the book *Confronting Evils: Terrorism, Torture, Genocide*, published in 2010, Card introduces a number of revisions, at least two of which are especially pertinent to my concerns here with Thomas specifically, but also with the theme of slavery and evil more generally. To begin with, for a complex of reasons Card modifies her working definition of evil to encompass the view that evils are "inexcusable," not just "culpable"—indeed, that evils are perhaps more importantly inexcusable than culpable. Thus the revised formulation offers: "Evils are reasonably foreseeable intolerable harms produced by inexcusable wrongs."[65] Part of the rationale for this shift (again, underlining the importance to Card of evil *suffering* as against evil perpetration) is to better capture the distinctiveness of evil embodied in institutions. The idea of evil as culpable, Card now suggests "works best for evils perpetrated by individuals acting independently" but less well for institutions that embody evil practices.[66] Culpability is less relevant for identifying the evils of institutions. She argues that even where there is no identifiable culpability it is still plausible to characterize an institution as evil. It is not, Card emphasizes, that answerability is nonexistent in such practices of evil. This would be very unlikely. Rather, it is that it is not *necessary* for the identification of evil—and moreover, she writes, the "role of culpability in institutional evils, where it does exist, is more complex than the role of culpability in individually perpetrated evils." It is the lack of moral excuse that best helps us recognize the evil of institutions:

> An institution is not evil simply in virtue of causing intolerable harm. I still believe the harm must be reasonably foreseeable at the point at which the institution is an evil (rather than, say, just a disaster). Further, rules that, when implemented, produce intolerable harm are not simply morally unjustifiable: if they are evil, they are inexcusable. They are evil, that is (rather than simply unjust or unnecessarily stringent), when they lack even a partial defense in terms of moral values. That is not to say they lack humanly understandable explanations, only that the explanations do not begin to justify the rules, morally speaking.[67]

Needless to say, this is a very helpful revision for thinking through the distinctiveness of slavery's evil, which embodies both culpable individuals as well as inexcusable institutional practices.

Another development of significance for thinking about slavery's evil is Card's adoption of Orlando Patterson's idea of "social death," from his 1982 book *Slavery and Social Death*, to describe the evil of genocide.[68] (As we will see in chapter 4, where I discuss his work in some detail, Patterson repays the favor in his revised conception of slavery as a slow and protracted genocide.) As early as 2003, the year following publication of *The Atrocity Paradigm*, Card published an essay titled "Genocide and Social Death" in the feminist journal *Hypatia*, which would be revised and suggestively retitled "Genocide Is Social Death" when published some years later as a chapter in *Confronting Evils*.[69] Notice how the relationship

162   PART II

between genocide and social death is here recast as no longer one merely of coordinating conjunction but of *identity*, and this is Card's point. The later essay opens provocatively: "Social death is not necessarily genocide. But genocide is social death." In Card's view, social death is a condition with many sources in different kinds of deprivation. It need not be evil, but it can be, "depending on the harm it does and whether it results from inexcusable wrongs." The central evil of genocide is the "intentional production of social death in a people or community." Social death is what defines the evil of genocide. On Card's wide interpretation, social death is essentially the extinction of the "social vitality" of a people or community. Such social vitality, she argues, "exists through relationships, contemporary and intergenerational, that create contexts and identities that give meaning and shape to our lives."[70] When these relationships break down, for whatever reason, members of the community in question suffer a loss of vitality, and the creation of reasonably foreseeable conditions that produce this intolerable loss of vital social flourishing is evil.

Now, importantly, for Card not all mass murders aim at the loss of social vitality. The point about genocide for her, however, is that it does precisely that whether or not a homicidal intent is part of its program. Casting social death as a—as *the*—central dimension of genocide, Card argues, shifts attention away from "body counts" and concentrates our focus on the *relationships* that constitute the relevant community and establish the relevant contexts of life and death. As a result, it helps to destabilize the assumption that genocidal acts are necessarily directed at mass murder. Forcibly sterilizing the women and men of a targeted group, or forcibly separating children from their parents to reeducate them into a new form of life, or, again, presumably, the kidnapping and transplanting of a "racial" group of people into conditions that destroy their connection to an ancestral culture—all of these are modes of genocidal social death. In this sense, Card argues, the "Nazi genocide was not only a program of mass murder but an assault on Jewish social vitality."[71] And that assault, she further reminds us, though carried out within a relatively short span of time, was nevertheless carried out not all at once in a single fashion but over various stages. The social vitality of the Jews was undermined and constrained before the concerted attempt to extinguish their very physical vitality as a people was formally put into operation. Although she does not say so explicitly, it is easy to see that, in this formulation, Card is reading Orlando Patterson *with* Hannah Arendt's idea of radical evil in mind, in particular the famous chapter on "total domination" in

The Origins of Totalitarianism (discussed in chapter 2), in which Arendt describes the progressive stages by which Jews were transformed into "superfluous" people. Certainly, Arendt's impact on Card, perhaps more so in Confronting Evils than in The Atrocity Paradigm, is broad and deep.[72] In any case, it is in this context of the specification of the evil harm done to Jews by the Nazis that Card expresses some disagreement with Thomas, to whom I now turn.

TRAGIC CONDITIONS, EVIL ACTIONS, AND PEOPLE OF ORDINARY DECENCY

Claudia Card has praised the analysis Laurence Thomas offers in Vessels of Evil as "philosophically groundbreaking."[73] It is not difficult to see why. The first part of Vessels of Evil is concerned with a general outline of his approach to the problem of evil. Not unlike Kekes's starting point, Thomas's project is explicitly to make the case for a place within "the human condition" of a conception of evil that does not depend on any vestige of the recurrent idea that some people are naturally evil (though, frankly, it is not clear whom he has in mind here as formally defending this view). Thomas recognizes, of course, that there are people—exemplars so to speak (and the suspects, tiresomely, are the usual ones)—whose lives appear to be the very embodiment of an innate and inexpungable evil. But he is less concerned with these examples of extreme depravity than with the ordinary people, otherwise reasonably well intentioned or well adjusted, who nevertheless commit, or allow to be committed (his real interest), moral horrors such as New World slavery and the Holocaust. In tune with Card, Thomas maintains that deliberately wicked or reprehensible motives do not always account for evil actions, especially those actions embodied in institutionalized or protracted practices of evil such as these. Ordinary people can commit evil, or anyway can stand aside and allow evil to be committed and sometimes can even benefit from that commission of evil. "Any account of evil," Thomas says, "must be true to the reality that people of ordinary moral decency can be swept up by social tides, and that, as a result, people of ordinary moral decency can come to do what would hitherto have been unimaginable even in their own eyes."[74] How is it that in the Germany of the late 1930s and early 1940s and in the England and France of the seventeenth, eighteenth, and nineteenth centuries so many people of presumably ordinary moral decency can have actively participated, or allowed themselves

164   PART II

to be swept up, in such evils as the extermination of Jews or the enslavement of Africans? This is Thomas's question—indeed, the question that, from the beginning, has shaped his interest in evil.[75]

The alternative to the idea of a conception of natural evil, one that takes into consideration the contingences and conditions in which evil emerges and comes to be sustained, Thomas suggests, is one based on what he calls the "fragility-goodness conception of human beings."[76] Human beings are naturally neither good nor bad: they are *fragile*. This is a moral-psychological perspective on human ontology that is deeply generative for Thomas, motivating, for example, his interest in children and the parent-child relationship. In this instance, however, it informs a *tragic* conception of the human condition indebted, not surprisingly, to Martha Nussbaum's *The Fragility of Goodness*.[77] Again, the implicit argument with Kekes is notable. Readers of Nussbaum's book will remember that she offers an account of the ethical implications of the ineradicable fact of vulnerability of any human life—not least a human life that aims to be a good life—to factors beyond its rational control. She gives us a picture of human beings endlessly grappling with the impossibility of entirely banishing contingency or luck from their moral lives, and therefore forever exposed to unexpected turns of events. Thomas's idea of the essential precariousness of human being draws on these ideas. In his account, human beings are intrinsically fragile because whatever may be their propensity for moral wrong, their inclination to even a modest goodness can easily be derailed by conflicting values between which, without any necessary self-deception, one can choose deplorably, abominably. If evil is not helpfully understood as innate, it cannot be adequately thought of as merely a failure of right reason or a breakdown in one's commitment to moral virtue. What intrigues Thomas is the idea that very often persons who commit evil do so *not* because they are evil (nor because their character vices lead them to evil actions, as Kekes believes) or out of any explicit desire to do what is morally wrong but because they *find* themselves in conflicting circumstances—he calls these "obliging interpersonal contexts"—that constrain them to make *choices* that commit them to evil actions. The larger phenomenon here, of course, is the one explored, on the terrain of experimental psychology, by Stanley Milgram in his seminal work *Obedience to Authority* and more recently by Philip Zimbardo in *The Lucifer Effect*.[78] It is not hard to imagine circumstances in which such compliance, acquiescence, conformity, or submission take place: fear, gratitude, greed, and self-deception are surely among the motivating sources of such action.

The tragic idea of human fragility allows for the paradox that morally decent individuals, for reasons that in some circumstances could even be construed as morally commendable, or at least morally neutral, can end up committing acts, or supporting acts, that are morally odious. Unlike with Kekes, for Thomas the tragic conception of human fragility and vulnerability does not yield a focus on unchosen action but rather a focus on the morally ambiguous, paradoxical, or conflicting circumstances that can constrain one to choose evil or to choose complicity with evil.

Notably, Thomas is particularly interested less in single isolable acts or events of evil than in evil that has taken root in a society, evil that has come to take an identifiably social and collective form directed at certain people or certain categories of people. This is evil as embodied in an institution, structure, or pattern of social practices. They are evils that, characteristically, have large-scale and significant duration. They are often enough carried out in public view and elaborated in a social ideology. These are the evils that Card calls atrocities. It is a central dimension of Thomas's conception of this sort of evil that it requires a supporting or underpinning social-psychological context, what he calls a *moral climate*. For evil to flourish, Thomas argues, it needs more than people inclined toward evil; it needs, in addition, a conducive, facilitating environment. It needs somehow to find a *footing*. For evil to gain a grip on any social world, it has at least to be *encouraged*, or at all events *not discouraged*, by substantial enough numbers of participants in that world. How can it happen, Thomas asks, that persons of ordinary moral decency, of ordinary civility, people who ordinarily would never dream of committing acts of gross cruelty, can nevertheless find themselves in a moral climate in which such cruelty is, if not deliberately advocated, then at least tolerated? To flourish, evil requires an obliging, cooperative, or at least complaisant social environment. For long-lasting evils such as the Holocaust or New World slavery to have occurred and been perpetuated in the forms that they were, they had to gain a foothold, a point of anchorage, in conditions that promoted or at least sheltered them.

What is the form of moral community that enables—or minimally, that fails to disable—such evil that results from our fragility? Here Thomas describes a "common sense morality" that is typical, he suggests, of certain liberal societies— what he calls "laissez-faire common-sense morality"—that can be a significant factor in the emergence and spread of evil. This is a form of moral community in which people are only loosely connected to each other and feel under no obligation to inconvenience themselves on behalf of others, especially on behalf of those they consider strangers, those who do not belong or can come to be perceived as not belonging, to one's community. The issue is not necessarily that such a community openly or explicitly incites or encourages the "callous indifference" of its members toward these ("religious" or "racial") others but that t offers little incentive for anything more than a passive, nominally concerned attitude of "distracted indifference" toward them. Within a community organized around this weak idea of commonsense morality, Thomas says, being a person of ordinary moral decency is perfectly compatible with allowing harm to be perpetrated and perpetuated, or at least is compatible with not actively preventing it from being perpetrated and perpetuated. As he says, "Common sense morality does not require that people take a stand to prevent the occurrence of evil."[79] Furthermore, this sort of morality provides at least a fertile context for what he calls "moral drift"—that is, a context in which more and more people over time become inured to the occurrence of evil in their midst, or anyhow more and more people grow less and less surprised by the frequency of occurrence of evil and are eventually able to simply shrug their shoulders in the face of it. In this way a *society* might even be said to *become* evil, or to become indifferent to the perpetration of evil in its midst (which amounts to the same things).[80] Note again a tacit argument with Kekes. Where Kekes aims at a moral theory of individual character, Thomas aims at a moral psychology of social life. Both, I think, worry that evil can find a home in liberal forms of society, but Thomas perhaps does less—at least less in *Vessels of Evil* than in earlier work—to specify the political form of liberal society most likely to be implicated in evil. Needless to say, what he describes certainly resembles procedural republics of rights-based liberalisms.[81]

The question now arises, what kinds of action count as evil? When do actions cease to be merely bad and cross the line into evil? Is evil a special sort of wrongdoing? Thomas takes up questions such as these in chapter 4, "Characterizing Evil." What is his conception of evil? Or perhaps better: What is the domain of issues that an idea of evil is meant to evoke? For it is soon clear that for Thomas—unlike for Kekes and Card—evil does not admit of a straight definition but solicits, rather, approximations of characterization. For Thomas, thinking about evil is not a matter of theorizing evil as such but of offering successive elaborations of it. From a moral point of view, he says in respect of evil acts, the only harm worth seeking to explain is the harm that moral agents perpetrate.[82]

To begin with, then, minimally, an evil act is a wrong act that harms another living creature. In certain circumstances, refraining from the commission of an act can also be evil inasmuch as it causes harm. But clearly an evil act is *more* than a merely wrong act. Not all wrong acts are evil.[83] A number of other features of an act have also to be taken into consideration: in particular, such features as magnitude, moral gravity, intention to harm, and of special social significance, the deadening of moral sensibilities. These are all crucial features, though none by itself is exclusively definitive.

Kekes, remember, insists on speaking of evil *people*. Such are people whose underlying character vices *incline* them toward the (regular) commission of evil. For Card, the idea of an evil person, though not by any means completely irrelevant, is for all intents and purposes dispensable. In general, Thomas is not disposed to speak of evil persons, but he does admit the idea of persons with an evil character. The difference between evil people and people with evil characters is not exactly clear. For a person with an evil character is (as with Kekes) simply a person who is "prone to do evil acts"—that is, a person whose character is so formed and established over time that there is every likelihood that they will commit acts of evil.[84] For Thomas, it seems though, the worry is that the idea of an evil person is assumed to be the idea of a person who is, as he puts it, evil "through and through."[85] Such people are hard to imagine, he says. People are not likely to have—or lack—*all* those sensibilities *all* the time that would make them evil through and through. Is this, perhaps, what Thomas means by asserting that Kekes gets the discussion of evil "off on the wrong foot"? What interests Thomas, rather, are people who are, as he calls them, "morally bivalent"—that is, whose lives exhibit *both* good and evil behaviors and good and evil characters. These people are at once more common and harder to understand. Few of us are either entirely good or wholly evil, and it is therefore the *relationship* between these dispositions or propensities that invites considered reflection. Crucial to understanding such morally bivalent persons, Thomas argues, once again underlining the *social* dimension of the production of evil, is the idea of a "moral audience"—that is, the moral community with which a person identifies and within which the authoritative affirmation or disaffirmation, approbation or disapprobation, of their moral selves takes place. Moral audiences are important because they reflect back to us an approving or disapproving sense of ourselves and therefore help to shape the conditions of restraint and opportunity for one kind of action or another. In general, Thomas thinks, "few people are willing, and

168   PART II

fewer still can afford, to run the risk of widespread moral disapprobation, and the alienation that it can give rise to."[86]

It is not difficult to see the value of this idea of connecting moral climates, ordinary moral personhood, and moral audiences. As I will suggest in chapter 4, the literature on New World slavery, nonfiction as well as fiction, is replete with White people who display a bivalent character. These are people, for example, who arrive in the slave Americas from Europe (as bookkeepers or overseers, say; middling types, usually) with a determination not to participate in the morally debased behavior of the slave-holding society—the debauchery, the violence, the exploitation, the greed, and so on—but who find (sometimes to their alarm) these decent and upright propensities disaffirmed, even openly ridiculed, by the dominant White moral audience. Gradually, they are less and less able to reconcile the gap between who they take themselves to be and who they are perceived to be by their new moral community; it grows difficult to consistently hold onto their righteous sense of indignation at the prevailing modes of conduct, and they find themselves, sometimes a little guiltily, sometimes not, yielding to the normative conventions of the White supremacist society. They are not necessarily changed entirely, through and through, as it were, but are changed enough for us to recognize different, less agreeable, dimensions of their character. *These* are bivalent people, Thomas would say, whose initial restraint is received with disapprobation by the moral audience that counts for affirming their identities as slaveholders, and whose moral compass, as a consequence, is reoriented toward the expected behavioral norms of White people in respect of the Black enslaved. Such people are not incapable of personal or familial generosity or goodwill; they can well be, in certain domains of life, attractive persons of virtue, respectability, and even high principles.

Perhaps not surprisingly, Thomas Jefferson is one of Laurence Thomas's prime examples of moral bivalence, someone whose character manifestly exhibited both good and evil behaviors. Jefferson was a man of "honor and integrity," Thomas says, and at the same time a man who demonstrated an acceptance of the evil institution of slavery, happy to indulge in the social, economic, and sexual privileges of the southern slaveholder. Now, arguably, Thomas Jefferson may not have been Thomas Thistlewood, his slightly older contemporary in British colonial Jamaica, and a man of lesser social standing and openly predatory sexual inclination toward the enslaved women under his command.[87] But is it self-evident, within the terms of bivalence that Thomas offers us, how to grasp a difference between them that matters? Might Thistlewood also be described as morally bivalent? Was his relation to Phibbah any less virtuous or any more notorious than Jefferson's to Sally Hemings?

On Thomas's account, it is possible for someone to have a moral audience that extols a certain evil behavior and at the same time have a range of concrete experiences that are at odds with the judgment of this moral audience—to be bound to a moral community for whom the enslaved are *formally* less than human and yet have personal experiences with the enslaved that depend on the tacit recognition of their humanity. This is a familiar and intractable paradox of slavery's powers of coercion and intimacy, and such, Thomas thinks, would have been the case with Jefferson. But not only Jefferson. Thomas thinks this was the case for all slaveholders insofar as they lived the inescapable contradiction, or at least the unavoidable tension, between the formal standards of their community (acceptance of slavery's assumption of the subpersonhood of Blacks) and their own inexorable existential experience (of the humanity of the enslaved). Jefferson is an especially interesting instance, Thomas argues, in that his standing among the members of his principal moral audience was perhaps less tethered than is typically the case to their conventional standards of moral attitude and behavior. In Thomas's view, Jefferson was at least able to "acknowledge the voice of humanity in his slaves," and therefore his experience was psychologically more "tumultuous" than for others who were better able to drown out these voices—that is, to successfully disavow that experience of mutual humanity.[88] As Thomas says, "Just as flaunting a rule presupposes the very existence of that rule, so taking steps to prevent the humanity of others from operating at a conscious level in one's life necessarily presupposes a recognition of their humanity."[89] This is an instance, he claims, of a general principle—namely, that human beings are "sui generis." They "constitute a manifestly evident natural kind"; the behaviors of human beings are "manifestly evident as such to all like human beings."[90] Therefore, it is not possible to deny the humanity of other human beings without "significant and sustained psychological maneuvering," without severe compartmentalizing. Thus Thomas concludes, "It takes great effort to deny the ongoing reality of fundamental human experiences. It is only in the context of a community that any psychologically healthy human being has a chance at succeeding in doing so."[91] (The discussion of "psychological doubling" in the case of Nazi doctors' doing both good and evil is a special instance of such compartmentalizing.[92]) What the discussion of Jefferson shows is the relation between bivalent characters and

170   PART II

disavowal and self-deception. To return to the contrast between Jefferson and Thistlewood as bivalent characters, it is arguable that disavowal was a more turbulent experience for the former than the latter, but in no way less consequential, perhaps, for their respective victims.

CONTRASTING EVIL INSTITUTIONS: EXTERMINATION AND NATAL ALIENATION

In part 2 of *Vessels of Evil*, titled "The Institutions," Thomas turns from his discussion of the microlevel of evil *actions*, their conditions and characterization, to the macrolevel of the evil *institutions* that are at the center of his concern, American slavery and the Holocaust.[93] Evil actions and evil institutions are undeniably linked to each other, but they are not simply isomorphic with each other. Institutions are not merely extensions of actions; they are not merely actions writ large. Not all evil actions have an institutional context much less character; and within the nexus of relations that constitute an evil institution, not all individuals are direct perpetrators of evil actions, even where their actions are culpable inasmuch as they contribute to the larger production and reproduction of the institutional practice. Claudia Card points to this insightfully (in reference to rape) when she writes that one reason some evils are not easily recognized as the evils they are is that "the source of the harm is an institution, not just the intentions or choices of individuals (many of whom may not share the goals of the institution, even when their conduct is governed by its norms)."[94] In *Vessels of Evil*, Thomas is mindful of this irreducible relation between individuals and institutions.

Evil institutions, Thomas suggests, can be described with reference to two dimensions: the *conception* they have of their victims and the *treatment* to which these victims are subjected. In the first of this section's two chapters, "American Slavery and the Holocaust," Thomas focuses on two ways in which the institutions of American slavery and the Holocaust were "fundamentally different from each other" with respect to the conception each had of its victims and the way each institution treated victims. In a characteristically clarifying and qualifying gesture, Thomas reminds us that he is less interested in the exceptions than the *rule* regarding these institutions. Thus, he says, his descriptions of American slavery and the Holocaust are meant to imply no indictment of every White person or every German who lived within their respective evil moral-historical environments. What he is after, he maintains, is a picture of the "evil moral climate" that supported these institutions and that was 'embraced to varying degrees by the members of the society in question."[95] Similarly, he goes on, he does not imply that every Black or every Jew was treated in the ways he describes. The measure of a moral climate, he argues instructively, 'is not found in its exceptions." Rather, he says, "An evil society is no less evil if it fails to abuse every member of the class of persons treated evilly, any more than a just society is any less that because of the occasional miscarriages of justice."[96] I think this is right on the whole, though we may wonder whether the justification for the latter might not depend, at least in part, on which kind of miscarriage of justice is in question and how "occasionally" it occurs.

Beginning with American slavery, Thomas offers that the term that best characterizes the institutional *attitude* of slaveholders toward the enslaved in the United States is 'moral simpleton."[97] That is, the Black enslaved were taken by and large by White slaveholders to be people of inferior intellectual and onto-logical standing within humanity: not nonpersons so much as moral subpersons. Not surprisingly, and not without justification, Thomas immediately recognizes that for some of his readers this term—*moral simpleton*—will carry altogether unsavory connotations, that it is necessarily burdened by disagreeable racial allusions regarding Whites' perceptions of Blacks. But Thomas is prepared to defend it with respect to other possible ways of characterizing how slaveholders routinely viewed their slaves. For example, "paternalism" is one way the attitude of slaveholders in the United States has been described, perhaps most famously by Eugene Genovese in his classic book *Roll, Jordan, Roll*; the idea of the "Sambo personality" offered by Stanley Elkins in the controversial work *Slavery: A Problem in American Institutional and Intellectual Life* is another.[98] Thomas does not deny the value of either of these descriptions for talking about the ways slavery as an institution viewed the enslaved, but he urges that his idea of "moral simpleton" allows for a much wider range of relevant moral description than "paternalism" and avoids the ideological implications of "Sambo." This may well be a matter of debate, and it suggests again that, contrary to the view Thomas appears to hold, descriptions of evil institutions are not morally or ideologically neutral. But Thomas could hardly be uninformed on the matter. Indeed, in using the idea of moral simpleton, he also intends to register the deep cultural-historical resonance of a racist perspective that accords with the place Blacks have traditionally held in Western culture—which, as he sardonically quips, "is essentially no place

172 PART II

at all."[99] As everyone knows, during the period of American slavery, Africans were not regarded as having a role of any significance in the history of Western moral and intellectual thought (perhaps, indeed, in the history of *any* moral and intellectual thought worth the name). In this sense, they were moral and intellectual simpletons, a view, of course, that still persists to this day, if not always expressed in quite the same bald terms.

It is soon clear, however, that the term *moral simpleton* is also useful to Thomas because it offers a crucial point of *contrast* with the story of the perception of Jews both by the Nazis and by anti-Semites more widely. As a group, Jews were not typically viewed as moral simpletons. Indeed, notably, the Nazi conception of the Jews was not usually aimed at their *cultural-intellectual* capacities or competences as human beings. Their ontological personhood was not generally in doubt. Rather, anti-Semitism's prejudicial conception was aimed at the *moral character* of Jews and more specifically at the perverse and ineradicable vices that these characters allegedly embodied (this is the familiar stereotype of the Jew as sly, crafty, greedy, and so on). Jews, Thomas proposes, were seen as the embodiment not of the characteristics of the moral simpleton but of "irredeemable evil."[100] Jews carried a threatening moral *stain* that was perceived as pervasive across all Jews and that could not be corrected or improved much less removed.[101]

Thomas's point in drawing this contrast as he does is to invite us to recognize that the respective prejudicial institutional idioms through which the enslaved and Jews were perceived are not, strictly speaking, comparable. "Moral simpleton" and "irredeemable evil" make, he says, for an "incoherent pair"—that is to say, they inhabit different and indeed *incommensurable* conceptual registers. As he writes: "Moral simpletons might do what is wrong often enough. It might even be characteristic of moral simpletons that they are lazy. But the very idea of a moral simpleton excelling at being evil is untenable."[102] Likewise, the idea of an irredeemably evil people being moral simpletons seems doubtful, like a contradiction in terms, because such evil is presumed to depend on a measure of resourcefulness and cunning, and therefore on a scheming, threatening mode of intelligence. In other words, these characterizations are not simple "extensions" of each other. This underscores for Thomas the sense in which American slavery and the Holocaust were very different *kinds* of evil institution—if nonetheless *equally* evil institutions. Here he points to the implications of the contrast in terms of the practices characterizing these evil institutions: "While a society might very well have some use for moral simpletons, it is not at all clear what use a society could have for the irredeemably evil. The main difference between the Holocaust and American Slavery reflects just this fact: extermination versus the utter dependency of slavery, respectively."[103] Again, part of Thomas's point is to signal the danger in a certain kind of comparison, one that sees intentional death as the *only* ultimate form of evil. There is the temptation, he says to conclude that because the aim of the evil powers of the Holocaust was death, whereas that of American slavery was the absolute dependence of the simpleton, it is obvious that the former was eviler than the latter. But as he says, "How one survives makes all the difference in the world. As a matter of conceptual truth, it is simply false that surviving is always rationally preferable to death."[104]

If the conception American slaveholders held of their slaves was that of moral and cultural simpletons, Thomas argues, the practical aim of the institution of American slavery was what he calls the "cooperative subordination" of the enslaved. The institution of American slavery worked by means of obliging the enslaved to cooperate in their own domination. Now, once again, as with the idea of the slave as a moral simpleton, Thomas is acutely aware that this description may not be entirely acceptable to some inasmuch as it may "seem incompatible" with the undeniably "deep cruelty" of slavery.[105] The institution of American slavery, Thomas maintains, sought to integrate the enslaved into certain subordinate and dependent roles within the dominant structure of White society in order to secure their cooperation. Without this cooperation, Thomas holds, the system of slavery would have collapsed. As he puts the matter starkly: "American Slavery would not have succeeded had not a significant number of blacks to some extent adopted an internal point of view toward—that is, some measure of acceptance of—the very institution that oppressed them; this internalization made possible limited but nonetheless genuine and significant cooperation between slaves and slaveowners."[106] Thomas recognizes, I think—in some sense he could scarcely *not* recognize—that this idea of Black cooperation in their own domination runs against the grain of a whole revisionist orientation in the historiography of American slavery, beginning in the 1970s with works such as John Blassingame's *The Slave Community*, that explicitly opposed the notion of (passive) cooperation and submission and highlighted, by contrast, the creative cultural integrity of the social worlds of the enslaved, including the varieties of resistance.[107] Not surprisingly perhaps, Thomas spends a good deal of time clarifying that his view of cooperation is not incompatible with the idea that Blacks

174 PART II

were discontented or indeed that they resisted their domination, sometimes with armed rebellion. Thomas's *emphasis*, however, lies elsewhere. "It is the unadorned truth that Slavery lasted some three hundred years—a very long time," he writes. "It is simply not plausible to suppose that throughout those years every black was daily plotting the way to freedom, let alone the freedom of all blacks, even as we acknowledge that most blacks regarded Slavery as a gross injustice and that some struggled valiantly against it."[108] In short, Thomas holds that slavery depended on forms and relations of trust, loyalty, and cooperation (the cook, the nursemaid, the coachman being the familiar examples), and it is unhelpful *not* to see these as contributing to the relative longevity of the institution. It is interesting, incidentally, that he doesn't add that such trusted slaves were very often precisely those who would come to be central to the development of revolts, inasmuch as they felt most keenly the sting of humiliation and abjection, and moreover were often best placed to gain intimate and strategic knowledge of the workings of the system. But it is less the moral psychology of resistance that interests Thomas than the moral psychology of *accommodation*.

For Thomas, the simple fact of the matter is that, bitter and unpalatable as this may be to those who have a misguided notion of slavery, the majority of the enslaved accommodated themselves to the institution, "albeit with great uneasiness."[109] Here Thomas is sharply pointed, even remarkably polemical: "To insist otherwise is, I fear, to make the fundamental mistake of assessing the lives of the slaves not from their vantage point but from ours. Of course, there were revolts and other subtler forms of resistance on the part of the slaves. But the continued existence of slavery makes it clear that not every slave so behaved. If every slave had refused to do the bidding of slaveowners, then slavery would have been no more." Those who believe that "freedom was the highest priority for every slave" are very much mistaken.[110] American slavery, Thomas reiterates, was a system of coercion built around the "cooperative subordination" of "moral simpletons." Although clearly brutal, its deep cruelty was embodied not only in its physical violence (certainly not to be discounted) but also in the "nexus of attitudes" it developed, particularly in the ways in which it solicited a perverse loyalty and obedience from the enslaved while failing to acknowledge, in even basic ways, their humanity, often demonstrating a callous disregard of elementary forms of gratitude. This monstrous "moral incongruity" is one of the forms that slavery's evil takes. As an instance, Thomas points to Frederick Douglass's famous description of the ingratitude that his grandmother's slaveowner showed her in response to her unfailing dedication to him. It is in this perverse incongruity that the basic inhumanity of slavery is to be found: slaveowners took a depraved delight in the goodwill of their slaves while showing no gratitude toward them in return.[111]

In contrast with his description of the treatment of the enslaved within the institution of American slavery, Thomas's description of the treatment of Jews in the Holocaust requires fewer pages. Straightforwardly, the Holocaust was "a purely coercive institution."[112] Jews were not really expected to cooperate in their own destruction. Even the supposed cooperation of the Judenräte with the Nazis, Thomas says, cannot properly be called cooperation inasmuch it was not in any way expected to lead to the integration of Jews into Nazi society. (But surely, one might suggest, it is at least controversial whether slave cooperation was expected to lead to their "integration" into White slaveholding society. A good deal may hang here on just how one understands the moral sociology of slave society, on which there is more in chapter 4.) The Holocaust did not aim to make Jews internalize the ideals of the Nazis. Because the Jews were irredeemably evil, and because there was no point in seeking to improve or rehabilitate them, the aim of the Holocaust was extermination, pure and simple. Consequently, any complicity was merely incidental and did not affect the overall rationality of the Nazi project or the fate of the Jews over whom they exercised power.[113]

In chapter 7 of *Vessels of Evil*, "Murderous Extermination and Natal Alienation," Thomas continues to develop and deepen the contrast spelled out in chapter 6. His specific aim here, though, is to deflate the seeming privilege given to intentional killing as the ultimate wrong that one can suffer. Thomas's chief point is to resist this reification of death as evil. He does not want to diminish the distinctiveness of the evil of wrongful death; but at the same time, he wants to open some room in which one can see it as but *one* among possible absolute evils. The special "moral horror" of the Holocaust, he says, is undeniably accounted for by the "killing of six million Jews."[114] Intentional killing of innocent people is obviously morally opprobrious, and given this moral agreement no one doubts that the Holocaust "represents an ultimate form of evil." By contrast, despite such instances as the events aboard the *Zong* mentioned earlier, American slavery was by and large not a project of concerted mass murder Extermination

176   PART II

was not its *aim*. "Dead people do not make good slaves," as Thomas dryly puts it (though he could have gone on to add that publicly displayed mutilated and murdered slaves nevertheless made good examples to living slaves of what the cost of insubordination or resistance might be). Death certainly forecloses virtually every kind of possibility, but death is not the only evil that forecloses possibility. And as Thomas cautions, evil is not "impoverished" by not being associated with the explicit aim of mass death.[115] To the contrary, our understanding is only enhanced by being open to other ways of thinking about ultimate evil.

One way of talking about evil in relation to the institution of slavery, Thomas suggests, is by way of mobilizing the idea of "natal alienation" from Orlando Patterson's now-famous *Slavery and Social Death*. I have already mentioned Claudia Card's engagement with this book in recharacterizing genocide and will come in a moment to her disagreement with Thomas—as well as his tacit response to her. This move to Patterson's work is perhaps not entirely surprising. Over the last two decades, Patterson's thinking about slavery and particularly the idea embodied in *Slavery and Social Death* have gained an influence in the historiography not only of modern slavery but, to some degree, of ancient slavery as well.[116] Memorably, in Patterson's view, natal alienation is the central *estranging* social process to which the enslaved were subjected by the coercive institutional technologies and rationalities of slavery—one of the constituent powers of the slave relation of domination by which the end condition of social death was imposed on the enslaved. More specifically, natal alienation was the process by which the enslaved were systematically *detached* from any birthright claim to legitimately belong to an intergenerational social order and cultural lifeworld. As Patterson writes in a well-known passage:

> Not only was the slave denied all claims on, and obligations to, his parents and living blood relations but, by extension, all such claims and obligations on his more remote ancestors and on his descendants. He was truly a genealogical isolate. Formally isolated in his social relations with those who lived, he also was culturally isolated from the social heritage of his ancestors. He had a past, to be sure. But a past is not a heritage. . . . Slaves differed from other human beings in that they were not allowed freely to integrate the experience of their ancestors into their lives, to inform their understanding of social reality with the inherited meanings of their natural forebears, or to anchor the living present in any conscious community of memory.[117]

Importantly for Patterson, then, one could say that what was destroyed by New World slavery was the continuity of generational institutions of heritable traditions by which individual slaves implicitly oriented themselves in relation to an intelligible temporal structure of past-present-future that belonged to them. Patterson does not put it this way, but I would say that what the natal alienation of the enslaved destroyed were the conditions of possibility of continuity of traditions of *forms of life*.

Thomas draws on this idea to shape his moral theorization of slavery's evil. He is aware, he says, that he has not literally translated Patterson's moral-sociological ideas into his philosophy but hopes at least to be in tune with Patterson's overall intentions. This is a significant caveat because, arguably, Thomas offers a somewhat limited interpretation of Patterson's idea of natal alienation. In particular, Thomas is concerned to introduce such "refinements" into Patterson's view as might relieve the original idea of its seeming *catastrophic*, or "all-or-nothing," character. Thus Thomas agrees that there is natal alienation when members of an ethnic group are forcibly prevented from participating in their historical traditions. However, he also highlights that the problem is not merely this founding suppression of their heritage but, in addition, the perpetuation of their ongoing exclusion from equality of membership in the dominant society. This refinement, Thomas argues, "is meant to allow for the theoretical possibility that a people who have been prevented from participating in their own historical-cultural traditions may yet flourish as equals in a society."[118] Perhaps against the grain of Patterson's account, Thomas's point is that natal alienation can, at least in principle, be arrested or reversed—that is, natal alienation is potentially *reparable*. Historical-cultural traditions survive insofar as individuals can fully participate in the practices that define them. Practices and institutions that preclude this cultural reproduction potentially impose conditions of natal alienation. The longer an ethnic group is exposed to such oppressive rupturing practices and institutions, the more likely it is that they will become natally alienated. Thomas suggests that beyond seven generations few if any in the population of the enslaved would have carried what he calls the "imprimatur" of their original culture. In the first generations, there were slaves with "first-hand memories of their past, whose lives thus bore the full imprimatur of their African historical-cultural traditions."[119] But gradually, across the generations, this would have changed until there was very little remaining of any but the most distant and tenuous contact with that past. Thus what was broken in slavery,

178   PART II

Thomas argues, was the continuity of a cultural *narrative*.[120] To produce natal alienation in a people, he says, is to render them without a story form, and this itself is a kind of evil. Thus natal alienation is an evil, Thomas argues, because it disables something fundamental in human life—namely, the capacity to give collective and personal life moral coherence and integrity through an affirmative cultural narrative.

This seems to me a plausible but limited social and cultural theory, perhaps too much a philosopher's view of society. It too easily misses or overlooks a dimension central to Patterson's account—namely, the institutionalized relations of domination that structured the new contexts of enslaved life. Thomas is, of course, right to point to the importance of the rupturing of narrative and memory in the natal alienation of the enslaved. But the idea of narrative and memory may offer too narrow a picture of the kind of catastrophic loss enslavement in the Americas entailed. It may be better, as I emphasized earlier, to think of what was ruptured and lost as not just a narrative but the conditions of a *whole* form of life. The coherence and integrity of human flourishing depend on a people's capacity to organize their social and individual lives in ways that enable these narratives and memories to have the point and purpose they are meant to have within the cultural traditions from which they derive. A form of life organizes the common goods to be pursued; the institutions within which these goods are located and reproduced; the structure of social, aesthetic, and moral values that make these pursuits worthwhile; the social roles that carry out the obligations that shelter these values; and so on. An imprimatur is only an imprimatur to the extent that it is embedded in a lived form of life. Therefore, it is really a whole form of life that was lost by enslavement, not only narratives and memories. It was a form of life that could not be reproduced in the New World conditions of enslavement, and it was the destruction of this connection to a form of life that produced the first conditions of natal alienation. This is not to say, obviously, that there weren't individual slaves, specialists of one sort or another who didn't carry with them to the Americas specialized cultural knowledge from the societies from which they were forcibly taken—stories, techniques, personal names, cures, gods, rituals, wisdoms, ways of doing things and ways of not doing things, prohibitions, and so forth. And it is easy to imagine that, even in the constrained circumstances of slavery, these specialists might have passed on their knowledge to others within their community. These were undoubtedly profound figures, treated with esteem by their fellow enslaved (indeed, in chapter 4 we will encounter one such figure, albeit a fictive one). But they were also figures who exuded a certain pathos, for what we immediately recognize about them is that, though they might indeed have admirably *remembered* knowledge and cultural techniques, they lacked what was in effect most crucial—namely, that social and cultural matrix of institutionalized practices that would have given *sustaining* point to these traditional knowledges and techniques—that would have given tacit meaning to how things are done and *why*. These practitioners might have retained remembered narratives, but they could not have retained the conditions necessary for the continuity of the traditions in and through which generations are integrated and socialized into the totality of a form of life.

In any case, this conceptual quibble aside, the contrast with the case of the Holocaust is stark. The Holocaust, Thomas argues, was not an institution of natal alienation for Jews. This is because the central tenets of Judaism—its defining traditions—endured in spite of Hitler's every intention to destroy their human condition, the Jewish people themselves. The continuity of the narrative that bound the institution of Judaism into a coherent whole remained unbroken. No Jew who survived the Holocaust, Thomas says, was at a loss as to how to recover the traditions of Judaism.[121] After the Holocaust, the Jewish tradition was left very much intact. This, of course, was not the case for Africans kidnapped and transshipped into New World slavery where there was no possibility of recovering the traditions that secured their former forms of life. But here is where Claudia Card begs to differ. For her, Jews no less than Blacks were made to suffer a loss of "social vitality" as a consequence of the atrocity they endured. Against Thomas's focus on narrative traditions as such, she holds that "the question . . . should be not simply whether the traditions survived but whether individual Jewish victims were able to sustain their connection to these traditions."[122] She goes on to argue that "sustaining these connections meaningfully" depended not only on abstract doctrines of tradition but also on concrete relations of family and community settings of religious observance. Jews who escaped to the United States and Australia might have had a chance to escape social death, she says, but many were not so fortunate. Of course, in reply, Thomas could well argue that it is precisely the United States that he is talking about because it is the contrast between how Blacks and Jews survived their respective catastrophes there that interests him. Moreover, he underlines (in a passage that reads like a direct response to Card though he does not mention her by name) that if he agrees that much pertaining to Jewish culture may have been lost, the "deeper concept

180 PART II

of being a Jew" was not: "It is not Jewish culture that defines Judaism. There is one Judaism per se, which admits of many cultures."[123] Now, I have no interest in adjudicating between Card and Thomas here. Arguably, they are in part responding to different provocations, which, unfortunately, neither identifies. It is notable, however, that in *Vessels of Evil* Thomas does not talk about "social death"—that is, the *condition* that results from the *process* of natal alienation. It is the latter that shapes his focus, whereas for Card it is largely the reverse. In a sense, Thomas's interest in natal alienation is driven by his aim to construct a background story of American slavery compatible with what he sees as the contemporary condition of U.S. Blacks—namely, a lack of "group autonomy" (this is the subject of part 3 of his book, which I do not discuss). Natal alienation, in his view, has undermined the capacity of Blacks to produce a sturdy and enduring pattern of affirmative and collective self-determination.

Be that as it may, the conclusion to be drawn between these contrasting forms of evil, Thomas argues, "is not that natal alienation is on a par with extermination, but that natal alienation is, or certainly can be, an extraordinary evil that has nothing whatsoever to do with death."[124] Slavery and the Holocaust, he concludes, are both "ultimate" evils, differently organized, with one depending on death, the other on the construction of a particular kind of life, a fundamentally alienated one. There are two ways of understanding the claim that an institution is an ultimate evil, Thomas maintains: one is that there is no evil that can be more horrible than this institution (a conception that allows, he says, that at least one and possibly more institutions might be at least *as* horrible), and the other is that *all* other evils are less horrible than this institution (in which conception there can, in effect, be only *one* ultimate evil). For Thomas, slavery and the Holocaust must be spoken of in the first sense, as ultimate evils *both*.[125] This way avoids invidious comparison, he holds, and retains the conceptual virtue of thinking contrastively.

FORGIVENESS AND REDEMPTION

I close this chapter by briefly discussing an essay, "Evil and Forgiveness: The Possibility of Moral Redemption," published some years after *Vessels of Evil*, in a collection dedicated to the work of Claudia Card, in which Laurence Thomas reflects on the role forgiveness and redemption should play as a response to evil.[126]

Notably, *Vessels of Evil* itself offers no account of the appropriate response to evil (rather, the book closes with a discussion of survival beyond evil), though elsewhere Thomas has shown himself not to be persuaded by arguments for reparation or compensation. American slavery and the Holocaust, he says, are "irrecoverable harms" and there is "no future action that can make up for the wrongs that were done." In particular, what worries Thomas is the attempt to assign a monetary value to past wrong, or more specifically that such an assignment will delude us into thinking that some moral repair has thereby been realized: "We distort the very evil that was done when the alignment between money and wrong is made so strong that it would seem as if something morally important has been recovered should sufficient money be awarded."[127] I agree that American slavery and the Holocaust are *irrecoverable* wrongs, not because of their pastness but because nothing can be done to completely, morally, right them. In this sense they are irreparable. Yet it seems to me that there is an appropriate reparatory response—both moral and material—to be made when generations of life chances have been blocked and distorted for the sake of the systematic enrichment of others.

In "Evil and Forgiveness," Thomas takes up Card's idea in *The Atrocity Paradigm* that victims of evil need not be thought of as virtuous, insofar as they themselves can turn out to be unscrupulous, even vicious, sometimes to the point of ceasing to deserve apology much less reparation from their wrongdoers.[128] This is a strong, undoubtedly controversial claim, but its importance lies in seeking to demythologize the status of victims. After all, victims are human beings too, given, like everybody else, to dubious responses and questionable attitudes. They need not be thought of as completely powerless or completely unimpeachable. Card's argument brings to the fore the question of the moral powers with which victims respond to the wrongs they have suffered. Specifically, Thomas is interested in the moral conditions in which victims can, or indeed should, forgive wrongdoers who are, in some relevant sense, deserving of their forgiveness. Are there conditions in which victims of wrong can be morally obliged to not withhold forgiveness from their aggressors? This is the question, baldly put. Suffering wrong understandably breeds resentment and anger on the part of victims, and often a quite reasonable reluctance to forgive those who have wrongfully harmed them. Indeed, some would argue that resentment has its virtues. Not Thomas, however. For him resentment falls among the morally unworthy sentiments. He follows Jeffrie Murphy in holding that what defines forgiveness is, precisely, *foreswearing* resentment.[129] To those who resentfully or otherwise withhold forgiveness from their wrongdoers, Thomas poses the question: "Does a victim's steadfast refusal to forgive her or his wrongdoers, if the wrongdoers are unequivocally deserving of forgiveness, constitute unscrupulous or abusive behavior on the part of the victim?" Clearly this is a deeply sensitive question in many circumstances, including those explored in *Vessels of Evil*. It is one thing to think of the refusal to forgive as churlish or ungenerous; but some might say that to call it "unscrupulous or abusive" is to go too far. Again, notably, ever the provocateur, Thomas does not shy away from exploring positions (sometimes through analogies) that might, from certain perspectives, appear to hold victims of wrong to too high a moral standard. An affirmative answer to his question, Thomas says, yields the thesis that victims "can have a moral obligation to forgive those who have wronged them if these wrongdoers are now deserving of forgiveness."[130] Just because one has been a victim of evil does not give one the moral right to withhold forgiveness from those who demonstrate the appropriate *contrition* for their evil actions. This is the center of Thomas's claim, and it is a claim about moral personhood. As he put it elsewhere: a "transgressor's sincerity of contrition" should be the focus of arguments for or against forgiveness.[131] If moral change for the better—sometimes imagined as a kind of *conversion* experience—has taken place in the wrongdoer, the victim is morally obliged to acknowledge this and act in such a way as to relieve the moral burden the transgressor carries.[132] Needless to say, for some victims perhaps more than others, or the victims of some evils more than others, this may be a bitter, even impossible, pill to swallow.

As in *Vessels of Evil*, Thomas is specifically interested here in forgiveness for what he calls "communal" as opposed to "autonomous" atrocities—that is, atrocities (such as slavery and the Holocaust) in which members of one group act in concert to wrongfully harm members of another stigmatized group. He is not talking about atrocities in which, as with serial killers or rapists, the wrongdoer is typically acting on their own against other individuals.[133] The former, remember, consists of evils that are perpetrated within a "prevailing moral climate" in which people who might not be otherwise thought of as evil are swept along and either commit grave, inexcusable wrongs themselves or stand by and do nothing to prevent or punish them when they occur. Now, Thomas does not specify what sort of communal atrocities these are, whether they are of long or short duration, or whether or to what extent they are integrated into a wider social, economic, and political order, that is, a form of life. In any case, the idea of a prevailing

INCOMMENSURABLE EVILS   183

and enabling moral climate is especially important to Thomas's consideration of forgiveness because he wants to underline humanity's ontological fragility and, consequently, the contingent vulnerability of everyone to the commission of wrong. He does this by commending the *redemptive* moral attitude of humility captured in the remark, attributed to the sixteenth-century English reformer John Bradford: "There but for the grace of God go I." That is to say, but for God's benefaction, I might have found myself in the shoes of the evildoer. For Thomas, forgiveness and redemptive humility are two sides of the same moral coin.

I am not going to spell out Thomas's argument in full here. Suffice it to say that he urges that there are a number of basic conditions the fulfillment of which not only makes a wrongdoer deserving of forgiveness by her or his victim but also makes that victim a wrongdoer if forgiveness is withheld. Among these are that the wrongdoer seeks forgiveness of his or her own accord; the wrongdoer fully and willingly acknowledges the wrongdoing, not only privately but also publicly; the wrongdoer expresses genuine remorse, articulated with shame and regret; and the wrongdoer furnishes evidence over time that he or she is unfailingly committed to righting the wrong done. When these conditions of *righteous* contrition have been met, the wrongdoer not merely deserve forgiveness but is *owed* forgiveness; the victim now has a moral obligation to forgive the wrongdoer. What the evil wrongdoing is seems to be immaterial to Thomas. Evidently *all* evils, including radical evils, are readily forgivable in a context of sincere contrition. I think this is an untenable view, and I return to it in the epilogue

Slavery, curiously, does not directly appear in Thomas's reflections on forgiveness—only indirectly, in the case of George Wallace, which he focuses on. Thomas thinks that Wallace, former governor of the U.S. state of Alabama and former Democratic presidential candidate, is a model for what he is talking about. As is well known, Wallace was a notorious racist and an avowed segregationist ("Segregation now, segregation tomorrow, segregation forever" was his famous 1963 battle cry against the civil rights movement), in many ways the very personification of the institutionalized White supremacy in the Old South. Thomas does not tell the story in full but in 1979, seven years after the 1972 assassination attempt on his life that left him paralyzed from the waist down, Wallace became a born-again Christian and publicly expressed remorse for the pain he had caused Blacks. Indeed, he sought—and apparently received—forgiveness from many Blacks in Alabama.[134] In his 1983 bid for governor, so it is said, a record number of Blacks voted for him, and in turn, with his victory, he

184   PART II

appointed a record number of Blacks to state positions. Here, says Thomas, is a genuine instance of righteous remorse for evil on the part of a notorious individual, and perhaps a genuine instance of individual Blacks in Alabama feeling that a debt had been paid with sincerity. In this case, Thomas argues, forgiveness s clearly owed.

I wonder, however. It is notable that Thomas's concern is a purely *interpersonal* one. He does not stop to inquire about the status of Wallace's evil historical actions with respect to the larger structure of domination and enrichment of postslavery White supremacy in the Old South. Remember that, on Thomas's own account, we are explicitly talking here about *communal* and not individual evils. Shouldn't it matter, as it seems to in *Vessels of Evil*, whether communal evils are institutionalized, entrenched in the conditions of production and reproduction of a social form of life? In the context of the entrenched and transgenerational atrocity of American slavery and the formalized postslavery segregation it gave rise to after Reconstruction, who is to determine what the conditions of forgiveness are, when they have been met, and to whose satisfaction? Can one forgive a contrite wrongdoer but withhold forgiveness for the evil wrongdoing itself—that is, forgive the actor but not the act? What is the wrong that individual Blacks can forgive Wallace for? What does the charity of their forgiveness amount to in the context of the continuing legacies of postslavery Black life in the Old South? What is the status of an individual's righteous contrition for wrong if that wrong is not repaired? What is forgiveness, in other words, that forgoes repair? Perhaps part of the issue here is the conceptual *register* of Thomas's concerns: he is focused primarily on the moral psychology of interpersonal relations to the effective neglect of the *moral sociology* of the institutional and structural conditions of flourishing Black lives.

As I have suggested, the real thrust of Thomas's argument in "Evil and Forgiveness" is to disapprove of the moral arrogance he sees expressed by victims of egregious harm who withhold forgiveness in circumstances in which none of us is exempt from the commission of evil. This follows in part from his idea of the tragic dimension of the human condition that he sets out in *Vessels of Evil*. When a climate of moral evil prevails, he argues, few of us have any good reason to believe that were the shoe on the other foot, so to speak, we might not ourselves have committed the evils characteristic of the period, and consequently stand in need of the forgiveness of our victims. This is the attitude he sees captured in Bradford's poignantly pious remark, "There but for the grace of God go I."

INCOMMENSURABLE EVILS 185

The fact that one has not oneself fallen to the path of evil is not simply owing to one's own virtue and effort but in large part owing to the divine grace of God—that is, to luck. Therefore, in the face of the evil to which we are all susceptible, it is wise and humane and good (if not to risk committing the sin of pride) to exercise humility and, in recognizing our own fragility and vulnerability, attend with compassion and mercy to the moral fragility and vulnerability of others. In such circumstances, Thomas concludes, forgiveness is a morally redeeming force.

Certainly, it is hard not to appreciate how compelling this claim is for the virtue of forgiveness, the generalized humanitarian good of standing ready to forgive those who trespass against us that we too may be forgiven if or *when* we trespass against them or others. But at the same time, surely something is askew in Thomas's formulation, in particular the systemic asymmetry between perpetrators and victims that it obscures: there is a presumption that these subject-positions are strictly and readily interchangeable. But within structures of evil domination of the sort that would unambiguously count as communal evils, surely not everyone stands in the same moral relation to the potential commission of the systemic evil that characterizes the institutional atrocity in question. In the context of New World slavery, for example, it might well have been a morally high-minded act of humility for Lord Chief Justice Mansfield, listening to the evidence presented to him of what the slavers on the *Zong* perpetrated, to have reflected on his own moral luck: there but for the grace of God go I, he might well have said. Given the pervasiveness of slaving interests in eighteenth-century British society (interests that in fact touched him directly and intimately in the person of his Black great-niece, Dido Elizabeth Belle), it is not implausible to imagine that in other circumstances he could well have been a slaver too and found himself in a situation in which, swept along within the moral climate of racial indifference to the lives of Black people, he could have ordered the murder of some one hundred and thirty enslaved persons.[135] But would it have been coherent to say the same of his Black contemporary, Olaudah Equiano, the former slave and abolitionist who triggered the movement to bring the *Zong* case to trial?[136] As a deeply pious man of wide experience, we can well imagine that he was keenly and gratefully attuned to the redeeming rationalities of the grace of God and the sins it must have spared him. He had, after all, briefly participated in slaving too, but not, as he recognized, from a position of racial security (in an Atlantic world where Blacks were by definition *enslavable*) and not without a semblance of racial solidarity. In other words, whatever interpersonal grounds there might have been for mutual recognition, Equiano and Mansfield occupied rather different and mutually exclusive structural locations within the social order that sanctioned the institution of slavery, and neither could have said with respect to the other, except of course with bitter irony, "There but for the grace of God go I."

<hr>

To sum up: In chapter 2, my concern was to throw light on the whole ethos and ideology of exceptionalism that surrounds the evil of the Holocaust—that includes the twentieth century as the paradigmatic era of evil; the mass killing of European Jews as the meta-evil, the evil that defines all evil; and Hannah Arendt as the unimpeachable theorist of evil. Part of what interests me, I noted, is the way in which, within this regime of exceptional evil, the evil of other atrocities, New World slavery, for example, is obscured—or rendered visible only as merely *empirical* evils and therefore without claim to the moral universality of a shaping role in defining what evil is in the modern world. I would say that this is an instance of a wider systemic racism that governs the construction of authoritative knowledges about Black experience. It is a form of racism to assume that Black experience is only ever merely empirical, never an exemplary instance of universality.

In this chapter, by contrast, my central concern is with the work of one philosopher, Laurence Mordekhai Thomas, who has offered a cogent conceptualization of evil worth thinking about in relation to other prominent theorists of evil, John Kekes and Claudia Card, for instance. In his book *Vessels of Evil*, Thomas seeks to respond to, and indeed to *disarm*, some dimensions at least of the exceptionalism that animates the invidious comparison between evils, such that the evil of mass killing can appear as *the* ultimate evil. The undoubted evil of mass extermination need not be thought of as the *only* ultimate evil. The idea of evil, as Thomas mindfully puts it, is not diminished or degraded by not being associated with extermination. There are other atrocities at least as evil as—if nevertheless *differently* evil than—extermination, among them the enslavement over multiple generations of a "racial" or "racialized" population.

Thomas, I noted, mobilizes Orlando Patterson's famous idea of the natal alienation of the enslaved to suggest that the systematic destruction of the cultural narratives that gave heritable coherence to the enslaved is *also* an ultimate evil.

I, too, find this a compelling idea. But perhaps more persuaded than Thomas is by the moral *sociology* of social domination that grounds Patterson's account, I argued that what is important in that proposal is less the loss of narratives of cultural identity per se than the irreparable destruction of the conditions of attachment to a background form of life that would have given point and function to these narratives (the reader will recognize, I hope, the resonance with my earlier discussion of Jonathan Lear). It is this destruction—together with the concomitant construction of a slave form of life in which their possible forms of self-determination and autonomy were constrained and distorted—that institutionalized natal alienation and rendered social death the evil it was.

Thomas, as I have read him, is a philosopher of capacious humanity, and it is not surprising that in other reflections directly connected to *Vessels of Evil* he should propose a strong argument for an attitude of redemptive forgiveness in cases of atrocity. Indeed, as we saw, his argument is not simply in favor of forgiveness for evil but *against* the unacceptable wrong of *withholding* forgiveness in cases of sincere apology for evil harm. I have expressed some misgivings about this argument. Beyond minor quibbles with what appear to me to be internal inconsistencies in his argument, my main concern is that if the conception of evil as institutionalized natal alienation in *Vessels of Evil* is right (at least as I have construed it) interpersonal forgiveness is not so much impossible as *irrelevant*. It would be an act of misplaced and essentially vacuous generosity for individual Blacks to forgive individual Whites, or Blacks as a whole to forgive Whites as a whole (whatever moral communities these conventional terms are understood to encompass). Such forgiveness would alter nothing about the moral or material world of White supremacy in which we live. The evil of New World slavery as a multigenerational and institutionalized historical atrocity, as I keep repeating, inheres not only in the irreversible destruction of a social group's attachment to and embodiment of historical forms of life (a ruthless evil by itself); rather the compounded evil of New World slavery inheres also in the inscription of this group of people within, and their conscription to, a new form of life—namely, enslaved subordination within a structure of racialized domination fueling the expansion and transformation of modern global capitalism. Governing this structure was, on the one hand, a regime of extreme extraction that led to the permanent enrichment of the slaveholders and their descendants and beneficiaries and the systematic impoverishment of the enslaved and their descendants and beneficiaries; and on the other hand, an ideology of White supremacy that

188   PART II

has justified and rationalized this modern global world order. It should be clear that this pernicious structuring of the modern world is not simply a matter of narrative, however important narrative is to the human condition, just as its reversal or undoing cannot simply be a matter of the individual goodwill that animates redemptive forgiveness. Thomas undoubtedly will not agree, but in my view, a more adequate response will have to build on political mobilization and the sustained organization of political struggle shaped and argued over by an antiracist and anticapitalist philosophy of change, the scope and depth of which have yet to be fully articulated.

PART III

PART III

CHAPTER 4

SLAVERY'S EVIL LIFEWORLD

QUASHEBA'S DEATH

Quasheba is an enslaved woman on an eighteenth-century sugar plantation in British colonial Jamaica, arguably (as I have described earlier) one of the most brutal systems of modern slavery in the Americas. When we first meet her in the dramatic opening pages of Orlando Patterson's 1972 novel *Die the Long Day*, she is in desperate flight and in fact but moments away from her violent death at the hands of slave-catching Maroons.[1] A Creole woman of extraordinary character—willful, defiant, reflective, courageous, bad-minded, self-possessed; in a word, *own-way*, as Jamaicans say—Quasheba has attempted (unsuccessfully, she rightly, regretfully suspects) to right a wrong by killing Busha Pickersgill, the White overseer of a neighboring plantation who, disfiguringly diseased though he and everyone else (enslaved and free) knows he is with a degrading and fatally infectious syphilis, has nevertheless laid sexual claim to her precious daughter Polly. Quasheba understands, as well as any of her fellow-enslaved, the evil nature of the social and sexual organization of domination within which she lives, the routinely coercive and humiliating powers that define the parameters of her enslavement, that injure and undermine her basic sense of human flourishing and severely diminish and constrain her avenues of effective response, much less dissent and refusal. She has tested their limits many times after all, sometimes only narrowly escaping, for the least infractions, the vengeance of the driver's whip or, worse, the retribution of the magistrate's punishing treadmill.[2] But Busha Pickersgill's predatory demand and the lengths to which he is prepared to go to satisfy his pernicious desire and sadistic will—he has already tried, and failed, to rape Polly—are of another order. To Quasheba his demand has a special

192 PART III

quality not only of debasement but of *dishonoring* an elemental maternal claim. It therefore crosses a *moral* line such that what was all along a barely tolerable burden of harmful wrongs now becomes simply insupportable to her.

It is important to the novel's point, I think, that it is not just the *fact* that sexual favors are demanded of her daughter by a powerful White man that precipitates Quasheba's drastic course of action. Appalling as this structure of sexual domination might have been, Patterson suggests, such demands were a recognized social fact of enslaved female life. As chattel, Black enslaved women had no rights—least of all rights in their bodies—that any White man needed to acknowledge much less heed. But sometimes, where opportunity permitted, such relations of asymmetrical intimacy were to be manipulated by enslaved women and used to their advantage—as Phibbah seems to have done with Thomas Thistlewood.[3] Indeed, Quasheba's hope is precisely that Polly will find a desirable—or at least a workable, livable—liaison with an agreeable White man (she has her eye on the new bookkeeper, McKenzie) who can protect her from the worst features of enslavement and perhaps even offer some prospect of upward social mobility, however circumscribed, and if not for her then at least for any children she might bear. The issue for Quasheba is that the White man in question is not merely undesirable but undesirable in an offensively contaminating and demeaning way, diseased with syphilis, itself a sign of his sexual depravity, and almost certain to infect and destroy her beloved daughter. There is therefore *nothing*, either personal or social, to be gained from such a relationship and *everything* to lose. Quasheba's own mother, in fact, had been infected by syphilis and wasted away in a painful death. Quasheba is therefore faced with a dilemma. Although she is urged by her fellow-enslaved to yield to the demand Quasheba finds herself bereft of the moral-psychological resources that would enable her to subserviently submit to this particularly humiliating and undermining degradation. Before the two sniggering bookkeepers, she appeals to her master, the overseer Busha Gregory, in the stereotypical fashion, in a carefully choreographed display of flattery and coaxing and ingratiating obsequiousness. But alas, this fails. It turns out that, for an enslaved person, even behaving *like* a slave in the expected slavish way the familiar institutionalized roles require does not guarantee success in securing the desired solicitous effect. Quasheba is not only mere chattel. The social form of her bondage is such that she has no authoritative claim in her own kin, no claim that rises to the level of legitimacy. Not surprisingly, then, she is unable to persuade her master against handing her daughter over to Pickersgill's sickening embrace. Now it is true that Busha Gregory has no special desire to meet his fellow overseer's licentious request that he hire Polly out to him, but he knows that the first principle of White supremacy in eighteenth-century Jamaica is racial solidarity (a rough-and-ready internal sense of reciprocity, hospitality, liberality, and egalitarianism against the mass of captive, barely governable Blacks) and, moreover, in this instance he finds himself frustrated by mounting debt on the plantation he manages and hopes the transaction will offer a means of meeting some part of his immediate material need. Infuriated by Quasheba's importunate behavior, Busha Gregory only further berates and ridicules her, and when she blurts out the public secret driving her worry—namely, Pickersgill's syphilitic condition—he physically abuses her for her insolent presumption.

This implacable disregard of what appears to Quasheba so basic and so meager a plea is too much for her to bear; it is an affront to the last shred of self-worth and dignity she possesses. For her it is, abruptly, the end of the line. Something *gives*. If, by and large, Quasheba has managed to accommodate herself to her enslaved life, still she cannot reconcile herself to the foul and perversely single-minded cruelty embodied in this denial to herself, even as a slave to whom almost *everything* is already denied, of this last domain of bare human entitlement—the protection of her daughter from threatened violation. When Cicero, her well-meaning but fretful lover, imploringly reminds her as she sets off to commit her deed that after all she is only a Neager, she responds incisively: "True me is a Neager. But me is human too and is only one time they can kill me."[4] It is intriguing to speculate what Quasheba might have meant by this searing, poignant (and, it would seem, very *modern*) remark or, rather, what the self-reflective, moral-psychological process unfolding in her is to which Patterson aims to direct our attention. The obvious particular *social* fact of her racial enslavement, Quasheba suggests, does not diminish, let alone extinguish, the universal *moral* fact of her equal worth and inalienable humanity and the affirmations and entitlements that *should*, in principle, follow from this. Even if she is property, she is also a person. She is *not* nobody. She *is*, despite the powers that ruthlessly seek to deny it, somebody—or anyway, *smaddy*—embodied in her own distinctive Creole ontology of personhood.[5] What grounds and motivates Quasheba's profound recognition of this colliding contrast between her contingent historical predicament and her self-affirming claim to universality, and what serves to propel the *tragic* action that leads, so seemingly inexorably, to her doom? Here, for Patterson, arguably, is one beginning of Quasheba's *moral*, if not political, freedom (the distinction, I believe, is crucial to his purposes), the moment that decisively demarcates the end of an old condition of docile submission to evil wrong and the commencement of the explicit avowal of a value, henceforth inexpungable, of self-possession and self-respect. Is Patterson's suggestion here that this is, in perhaps some inchoate measure, an inaugural *experience* of individual freedom? That is, is this one dimension at least of the birth of the paradoxical relationship between slavery and freedom that his later work would explicitly explore? Compelled by Quasheba's sense of foreclosed alternatives, the mocking silence of the obdurate world, she cannot now *not* act to salvage something of the moral value of her personhood and her maternal claim in the personhood of her only daughter, even if it means her own certain death—which, of course, it does.

When we encounter Quasheba, alone and abandoned with her final memories and her last reflections—the reasons and desires and deliberations and judgments that propelled her dire action or guided her conduct, and the decisions and contingencies that brought her to this pass—she is hiding precariously from her pursuers in the faint light of the early dawn. Who is she? What is her story? In the way Patterson draws the grim picture of her desperate circumstances, there is something allegorically still and quiet and terrifyingly fragrant with foreboding that permeates the landscape around her, an environment ineffaceably inscribed by the evil social relations of slavery. It is morbidly sublime. The moist blue light is as much a sign of fertile lushness as of rot and horror and putrid mortification. Dawn is less a new beginning than an already ruinous end—for the enslaved, an end, in fact, without end. Quasheba is waiting to die. She knows she has no good options to choose between. On the one hand, there are the dense and verdant hills now traversed by Maroons, themselves formerly enslaved people. The early eighteenth-century treaty they won from (or conceded to) the British colonial powers in their protracted war gave them unprecedented internal sovereignty, but it also bound them to slave-catching, and they now had at best an ambiguous—and at worst a treacherous—relation to those still enslaved.[6] Quasheba despises the Maroons. She cannot trust them; and in any case, she has now killed one of them in her bid to escape, and she knows with certainty they will not spare her. Caught by them, she will meet a swift and brutal end—and secure them their reward. On the other hand, there is the familiar world of the plantation, Richmond Vale, with its sugar works and cane fields and great house and slave village, that she can just about make out in the sleeping valley below. It is the deceptive scene of a degraded and violated life in which the rationalities and technologies and mentalities of almost total social domination are designed to disable and erase the traditions of her forebears, limit and curtail and deface any articulation of personal and social autonomy, and preclude even the prospect of righting the wrong to which she has been subjected. Even if by some miracle she could make it back to the plantation's precincts, she knows her enslavers will no more spare her life than will the Maroons; they will simply exercise the absolute sovereignty they hold over her life and death in a fiendishly protracted way so as to make a public example to her fellow-enslaved of the fate of those who dare to exhibit such audacity as she has. Her situation is parlous, near hopeless. Strictly speaking, she has only an absurd choice between equally impossible options. In the end, precipitated by who knows what impulse—a resolute realism or a resigned fatalism—she decides to make for the plantation she knows. But alas she is intercepted by the small band of Maroons tracking her, and they have at her exhausted and defeated body with unforgiving ferocity.

Die the Long Day, I believe, is a philosophic novel, an exemplary work of *moral* literary fiction. I emphasize "moral" fiction here because (in tune with the larger concerns of *Irreparable Evil*) what interests me about Patterson's novel is less its literary merits (however those are determined by professional critics) than the way in which it offers us a *possible* lifeworld of New World slavery as an incitement to critical reflection on the thinkable moral experience of the enslaved, their plausible organization of a meaningful way of living *with*, and sometimes living *against*, the extreme social form of domination within which they found themselves as the overwhelming coercive context of their lives. As I have described it in chapter 3, New World slavery was an unremitting structure of evil not so much for its perpetration of genocidal death (though I note that Patterson has now moved provocatively in the direction of this language) as for its institutionalization, over multiple generations, of a distorted social formation of relations of domination that knowingly violated the enslaved in physical and spiritual ways and that deliberately thwarted, indeed often prohibited, their reasonable prospects for human flourishing, individual, familial, and social. Slavery constituted a perverse form of life in which individual enslaved life was deemed of little human (moral) value: the enslaved constituted a community of invalid and disposable persons whose lives could be commanded, subjugated, assaulted, and discarded at the whim of their enslavers. This was the mode of its radical social-cultural devastation, and absolute evil.

And yet part of what is instructive about Patterson's fictional Quasheba is that, set against the adversity of this unpropitious background environment, we are invited to see her excellences as a human being, the virtues that shape and vivify her moral personhood, the actions that grow out of the articulation of her pronounced sense of self-possession, the reasons and reasoning that sustain and animate those actions, and the moral goods and motivated ends toward which she progressively directs herself. It is in this sense of personhood, Patterson suggests, that her poignant beauty, her dignity, and her grace lie—not to mention the radical universality she claims is hers. Quasheba's tragic doom is a consequence of the tension, or rather the *conflict*, between her instinct for self-determination and the constraining obligation to choose between distorted options: the asymmetrical and unyielding relation between what is up to her to make of her enslaved world and what is indifferently given to slavery's powers to make of her. But *Die the Long Day* shows us more than a social regime of routine or banal evil, a social formation organized in such a way as to systematically strip human beings of their dignity by normalizing their degradation and humiliation. For, notably, what Quasheba encounters in Busha Pickersgill's demand of her and her daughter, and in Busha Gregory's mean, acquiescent complicity in it, is an especially perverse and vicious and cruel form of moral *wickedness*. These White men are not simply passive characters in an evil social order, complaisant beneficiaries, so to speak, of the institution of the slave plantation in which they *find* themselves; they are themselves actively, wantonly, knowingly, culpably, evil. It is their perpetration of evil that Quasheba and her fellow-enslaved are obliged to navigate.

Orlando Patterson often identifies himself as a historical sociologist, and this is apt in its way. After all, it is the historicity—the internal historical rationalities—of social and cultural forms and practices that most concentrate his attention.[7] But as important as this description is, I suggest that it is too modest, too circumscribing. It offers too limiting a picture of the real scope and animating character of his interpretive work. Patterson, I believe, is also a *moral* sociologist; indeed, more broadly he is a moral realist and a public moralist, one moreover whose conceptual work lends itself (as the reader might have already guessed) to a discussion of the moral evil of New World slavery.[8]

It is true, of course, that no more than a cursory glance at the dense archive of the long arc of Patterson's work is needed to confirm his commitment to the fundamental labor of historical reconstruction. Patterson is an unsentimental materialist by temperament and overall intellectual orientation. The ascertainable evidence of the historical record—the "data," as he sometimes says, like a true sociologist—is for him an indispensable resource and guide. Although Patterson is a critic of positivism, truth matters to him. Moreover, it is not insignificant that the historical reconstruction to which he has leant his empirically grounded sociological imagination has sometimes been directed beyond the relatively secluded and rarefied air of the academy toward the rough-and-ready ground of directly shaping public policy. Patterson has been not only a university-based scholar of undoubted distinction but also an advisor to governments (principally, but not only, in Jamaica). In each of these registers of intellectual inquiry, what is important to him is what the *point* is of the exercise—the *normative* point, one might say. What has motivated and propelled Patterson, in some sense, is the conviction that social-historical inquiry worth the name should have the "nerve"—as he put it, borrowing from David Riesman, his Harvard colleague and interlocutor for many years, and a moral sociologist if there ever was one—to engage and challenge conventional assumptions, to go against the grain of the prevailing shibboleths governing our cherished concerns and beliefs, especially when these misguided or impoverishing ideas are promoted by people with whom one might be expected to feel a sense of solidarity or common cause.[9] Like Riesman's, Patterson's intellectual voice—exploratory, experimental, boundary-testing—has been directed at forcing us to see in a stark and sometimes provocative way the historical routes and contemporary contours of our moral predicament and social discontent.

Notably, therefore, Patterson's well-known historical sociology of slavery and freedom, embodied in the monographs *The Sociology of Slavery*, *Slavery and Social Death*, and *Freedom in the Making of Western Culture*, has not only depended on the solid ground of hard data; it has also been emphatically shaped by a Weberian *Verstehen* approach to human action that illuminates *existential* concerns (with dishonor, alienation, violation, dehumanization, and so on) and their *normative* implications (comprehending and commending the significance, for example, of responsibility, freedom, autonomy, and will).[10] But more than this, even as this scholarly work mines the complex tension between an empirical and a moral sociology (and the methodological pathways by which one informs the other), he has also exhibited a ready sensitivity to the very *limits* of sociological explanation as such and a corresponding attunement to at least one other interpretive means of articulating the moral shape of human experience, in particular the human experience of extreme domination—namely, narrative *fiction*. Patterson has been not only a practicing sociologist and social policy advisor but also a practicing novelist, and within Caribbean literary history a formative and distinctive one, part of the first wave of postindependence literary creativity in Jamaica.[11] He is the author of three books of fiction between 1964 and 1972—*The Children of Sisyphus, An Absence of Ruins,* and the already-encountered *Die the Long Day*.[12] These realist narrative fictions undoubtedly depend on a rich historical-sociological knowledge, but in their figurations of character and moral agency they carry the burden of a distinct existential and moral-psychological project as well. They aim to grapple with the problem of evoking and exploring registers of lived experience—not least Black, enslaved experience—that lie beyond the representational capacity of the sociological monograph.

To be sure, then, with so complex a range of intellectual and creative dispositions, Patterson is not an easy thinker to characterize or categorize in any readily available terminology (despite a desire on the part of many to do so) He has never, for example, easily fit into any political or ideological camp: left liberal, or conservative. If culture and decolonization are not irrelevant to him. he has never been a cultural or an ethnic *nationalist*. If Marx has always been a touchstone for his social theory, Marxism has held no *programmatic* political appeal to him. Perhaps what his literary-sociological imagination has offered him are resources with which to resist a certain kind of *dogma*, White or Black, radical or otherwise, especially when these dogmas turn (tacitly or not) on assumptions about an essential *identity* that authorizes authenticity or truth.[13] It is not surprising, therefore, that Patterson's work has been much misunderstood (sometimes scarcely properly *read*), with his ideas often appropriated out of context and drafted into formulations and conceptions far removed from his own projects. And such projects have been various. But across the several directions he has taken one can discern a certain consistency in the questions he poses— about slavery, for example, as a structure of domination and in the historical vision that shapes his understanding of Black experience in the New World. In particular, I suggest, there is a hermeneutic strand within Patterson's work, running through the fiction and nonfiction alike, the older as well as more recent work, the studies of Jamaica no less than those of the United States. This interpretive thread grows out of his permeating sense (unaltered throughout the tumultuous and sometimes acrimonious years from the late 1960s through the 1970s of the alliance, as he might think of it, between Black cultural nationalism and White liberal revisionism) that New World slavery was a fundamental, unremitting, and irreversible *catastrophe*, precisely in the measure that it not only destroyed forever the connection to the moral and social fabric of relations in which the lives of the Africans captured and transported into enslavement in the New World had been embedded, but also persistently undermined and deformed the social and cultural conditions in which alternative heritable and legitimate forms of familial relations and individual personality could be reconstructed and sustained in the context of the slave plantation.

At least until very recently, Patterson has not explicitly and systematically linked his thinking on New World slavery or Black experience more generally to the idea of moral *evil*, as I have used the term in earlier chapters. Moral sociologist though he is, this has not been his favored moral-conceptual language.[14] Which is not in itself surprising because, as we have seen, until recently evil has not been a moral language of widespread philosophic (much less sociological) acceptance. Clearly enough, however, part of what is generative about Patterson's thinking on slavery in terms of *catastrophic experience* is that (as I noted with Laurence Thomas's invocation of him) it also invites thinking in terms of the *atrocity committed*. And atrocities, as Claudia Card taught us to see them, are the *first* of moral evils. No wonder, then, that in recent reflections—and rereflections—on slavery Patterson has been drawn in precisely this direction. For example, in "Life and Scholarship in the Shadow of Slavery," his long introductory essay to the second edition of *The Sociology of Slavery*, Patterson now urges a conceptualization of Jamaican slavery as a form of "protracted and slow-moving genocide on a scale that approaches the Jewish holocaust in Nazi Germany."[15] I am not so sure about the comparative dependence gestured at here (I take seriously the worry Thomas expresses about such slavery-Holocaust formulations of comparison). But it is important to recognize that Patterson's argument grows out of his long-held view (to which I come in a moment) of "the peculiar savagery of the condition of enslavement in Jamaica" in which the enslaved were deliberately overworked and underfed on the slaveowner's calculation that it was cheaper to work a slave to death and import fresh numbers than to produce the social

200   PART III

and material conditions that might have encouraged the enslaved to reproduce themselves.[16] Jamaica was notorious for the fact—in contrast with North America and Barbados, the counterfactual instances Patterson mobilizes to analyze the slave trade database—of a persistent demographic decline in its slave population. A modicum of population increase more in line with these other slave societies might have been possible had the "proto-Leviathan" slave regime in Jamaica not pursued the "Hobbesian demographic strategy of buying, mercilessly over-exploiting and replacing their enslaved from the slave trade."[17] There were alternatives, in other words, that were decided *against*. Consequently, this Jamaican slave-owning strategy was, as Patterson puts it, a "clear choice."[18] One might even say an *evil* choice.

Pressing the question of demographic decline in this direction Patterson aims to show that had Jamaican enslaved people been able to increase in the manner of the enslaved in, say, Barbados, the slave population in Jamaica would have stood at five million more souls than was the case in 1830, on the eve of abolition. For Patterson, these five million dead represent the missing enslaved people whose absence is the direct result of the "deliberate curtailment" of Jamaican slave lives, and their staggering number constitutes irrefutable confirmation that Jamaican slavery was a form of genocide—longer in duration and differently organized than the Jewish Holocaust, to be sure, but a genocide nonetheless.[19] In making this argument, Patterson has been influenced by the fact that a number of scholars of the Jewish experience have made use of his idea of "social death," among them Marion Kaplan and Daniel Goldhagen. Of special interest, in this respect, is that, as mentioned in chapter 3, Claudia Card makes use of it as well, arguing (in a phrase Patterson appreciatively invokes) that "social death is utterly central to the evil of genocide."[20] Agree with this reconceptualization and the comparison with the Holocaust it entails, or not, what is interesting is that in the new conjuncture marked by the moral turn and the new critical discourse about moral evil Patterson can now *resituate* his work in this critical idiom and even align it with reparatory claims.[21]

For Patterson, I might say, slavery's evil is to be found both in the genocidal physical brutality that characterized an undeniably cruel system of human bondage and also in the all-embracing *destructive-constructive* powers that produced and reproduced over nearly two hundred years of British slavery in Jamaica a *perverse* and systemically *distorting* social formation to which the enslaved were collectively and individually obliged to *accommodate* or *adjust* themselves and learn to negotiate and evade and resist and survive as best they could. Indeed, these registers of evil are inseparable. "Natal alienation" and "social death" are the connected moral-historical concepts he later developed to capture the effects of these destructive-constructive powers. To subject people to natal alienation and social death is to commit evil; and institutions that produce and reproduce natal alienation and social death are evil institutions. And for Patterson, significantly, both figuratively as well as substantively, as much personally as intellectually, eighteenth-century colonial slave-plantation Jamaica has long served not only as his scholarly starting point but as the *exemplary* instance of the kind of social formation made by the evil rationalities of slavery—namely, a social formation that never did, and perhaps never could, add up to the *normative* order of a coherent and internally integrated Parsonian society.[22] Even as he would endeavor to conceive a *general* moral-social theory of the conditions of enslavement—to construct the idea of social death as the general answer to the general question about slavery—the trace of Jamaica, the ghost of Quasheba, you might say, could be discerned as the muted background of his thinking about the experience that rendered New World slavery a distinctive form of evil dehumanization and powerlessness. Or so, anyway, I argue.

In this chapter my limited itinerary is as follows: The overall direction of my concern—where I'm headed—is a reading of the moral complexity of *Die the Long Day*, the sense of the novel as a reflection on the institutionalized moral evil of New World slavery and the responses of the enslaved and enslavers to this evil. But to understand *Die the Long Day*, I believe one has to have a view of what Patterson is doing in his first historical-sociological study of slavery, *The Sociology of Slavery*. As I've already hinted, the argument about natal alienation and social death set out explicitly in his magnum opus *Slavery and Social Death* has genealogical roots in this earlier work. If Quasheba is the inaugural figure of social death and moral freedom, the contours of her condition and action are already adumbrated in the early monograph. Indeed, I would venture to argue that it is *The Sociology of Slavery* that in effect sets out the essential *problem* about slavery that seeds *all* of Patterson's later work.[23] It is here, I think most incisively, that he first conceptualizes the catastrophic social and social-psychological nature of New World slavery and locates slavery's moral harms both in the

202 PART III

violent brutality of the slave plantation and in the violating systemic order (or disorder) it produced and reproduced. Thus my first challenge is to properly situate *The Sociology of Slavery* within the particular postcolonial problem-space of discourse about slave and postslave Jamaica, and to sketch Patterson's central concern to answer a number of fundamental interconnected questions about slavery as an *institution* of relations of domination: What were slavery's distinctive powers? What did these powers *do* to the enslaved? How did the enslaved *adjust* or *accommodate* themselves or otherwise respond to these powers? Note that these are less legal questions about property than social and psychological questions about the mode of personal and social experience of an extreme form of domination. Crucial here is the picture of the Jamaican colonial and postcolonial social formation inherited from slavery, in terms of both its racial structure and its stark artificiality—that is, its dependence for stability and order, more on the pervasive coercion of the state than on the building of a common core of shared values. This is the problem, of course, that M. G. Smith's theory of pluralism sought to address, and it leaves deep traces in Patterson's picture of slavery as a form of domination.[24]

Also crucial to Patterson's picture of the institution of slavery is Stanley Elkins's pivotal 1959 work *Slavery: A Problem in American Institutional and Intellectual Life* and the debate about the moral personality of the enslaved it provoked.[2] Regrettably, in my view, *Slavery* has all but disappeared from discussions of New World slavery, because part of what it explicitly sought to do (as its subtitle indicates) was precisely to pose not merely a historical question about slave personality but a *historiographical* one about the nature of the debate itself concerning the *problem* of New World slavery. The exploration of the former was an effect of the conundrums introduced by the latter. In any case, Patterson has had a long and embattled relation to Elkins's work, which requires exploration. This theme of slavery's impact on the moral personality of the enslaved is moreover illuminated in a vital way (not explored by Elkins, it is true) by the question of the slaves' refusal of their enslavement. Needless to say, this was (and understandably has remained) a vital arena of discussion and theorization about the New World slave past, especially for Black scholars. What is especially interesting in this respect is Patterson's concern not only with the political organization of resistance (the focus, for example, of C. L. R. James's *The Black Jacobins*) but also with the moral and existential limits to subjection, the point at which the individual slave in effect says *no*—no more, enough is enough. It is here that the influence of Albert Camus is poignantly felt, not only from the theory of the absurd in *The Myth of Sisyphus* but also from the theory of refusal in *The Rebel*. Finally, in the same way that Elkins's book was pushed aside in the mid- to late 1960s and early 1970s, with the rise of cultural history and the militant cultural nationalism it informed (and was informed by), so, in a certain sense, *The Sociology of Slavery* came to be all but displaced by the rise to prominence in the 1970s of Kamau Brathwaite's cultural theory embodied in *The Development of Creole Society in Jamaica*. Patterson may now be perceived as a protagonist of a *cultural* sociology, but this is not quite the conceptual problem-space in relation to which the intervention of *The Sociology of Slavery* was framed.[26] As with other cultural nationalists, Brathwaite had no time for what came to be perceived as the "damage" theory of slavery and its aftermaths, and in contemporary Carib-bean scholarship Brathwaite's Creole theory remains in many respects the pre-vailing orientation to the slave past. I shall suggest that this should be challenged.

Arguably, however, nowhere does Patterson more powerfully and poignantly and vividly reflect on these questions—the brutally coercive structure of the slave world, the complex moral personality of the enslaved, and the relation between accommodation and refusal—than in the novel *Die the Long Day*, pub-lished just five years after *The Sociology of Slavery* and in many ways its fictive companion. *Die the Long Day* is his only work of historical fiction, and its pro-tagonist Quasheba, I repeat, haunts all of Patterson's work.[27] Neither Euripides's Hecuba nor Sophocles's Antigone, though bearing strong resemblances to both, Quasheba nevertheless embodies powerful and conflicting moral-social forces in her tragic—and emblematic—transfiguration of natal alienation and social death. Like others I too am drawn to literature, narrative fiction in particular, as a space where moral thinking, not least moral thinking about evil, finds a dramatic and therefore complex and especially clarifying footing.[28] An attentive reading of *Die the Long Day* for its moral illumination of the evil of slavery will therefore form the horizon of my concerns in this chapter. In its fictive phenom-enology, *Die the Long Day* describes the *possible* moral world of enslaved life on an eighteenth-century Jamaican slave plantation. As literary fiction, it imagines, and invites us to imagine, the actions, personalities, and scenes and contexts of a profoundly distorted social order. Above all, it imagines, and invites us to imag-ine, the moral personality, agency, and judgment of one outstanding enslaved woman, Quasheba, headstrong to a fault and doomed, a woman negotiating the intolerable debasement and dishonor and powerlessness of her condition

204   PART III

in the effort to protect her girl-child from the sexual predation of a debauched, diseased, and culpably evil enslaver—and thus, in the process, to defend some region of value and honor, some dimension of nonnegotiable moral personhood. *Die the Long Day* fictively imagines, and invites us to imagine, the social lifeworld of the evil of slavery's social death.

A MONSTROUS DISTORTION OF HUMAN SOCIETY

The Sociology of Slavery, published in 1967, was a revised version of Patterson's doctoral thesis at the London School of Economics, where he was a postgraduate student between 1962 and 1965.[29] It is shaped by a distinctive problem-space of conceptual and historical questions. As I have already suggested, all the major themes that would subsequently preoccupy Patterson, not least those of social death and moral freedom, are already to be found adumbrated in this early work in the sociology of Jamaican history.

Notably, Patterson belongs to the first generation of West Indians trained as social scientists at the still relatively new University College of the West Indies, Mona, Jamaica (completing his degree at the same time that it became a fully fledged independent university in its own right, the University of the West Indies).[30] The question of the social sciences—economics, sociology, social and cultural anthropology, and social psychology, principally—had emerged as one of urgent significance in the Jamaican post-1938 years of gradual constitutional decolonization, in response to both a colonial and a nationalist anxiety about the character and stability of a social formation that was, essentially, and self-evidently, the peculiar, contrived, and distorted product of colonial plantation slavery. This was the point, for example, of the West Indian Social Survey (1947–1949), funded by the Colonial Social Science Research Council, and the scholarly studies that came out of it.[31] Work such as the social psychologist Madeline Kerr's *Personality and Conflict in Jamaica*, published in 1952, and, a little later, the social anthropologist Edith Clarke's iconic *My Mother Who Fathered Me*, published in 1957, are products of the West Indian Social Survey project. Importantly, both were informed by the prevailing and intersecting "individual and society" and "culture and personality" conceptual orientations of Anglo-American social science in the 1950s.[32] How do individuals *adjust* to society, especially a society as historically conflicted and hierarchically structured as Jamaica? How is *conformity* to authoritative social norms secured and reproduced? What is the impact of *culture* on individual *personality*, above all where cultural groups, as Kerr put it in a phrase soon to become resonant, "live alongside each other but not together"?[33] Kerr and Clarke were inspired by the incipient idea that one could, as it were, read the historical "mark of oppression" (in Abram Kardiner and Lionel Ovesey's poignant phrase) on the *social* form of the family and the *individual* form of personality of the Jamaican freed people and their progeny down through the generations.[34] Their books would have a large impact on the conceptual vocabulary of Patterson's thinking in the 1960s, in his fiction as much as in his nonfiction. Part of what he inherits from them, and the larger intellectual and political milieu out of which they come, is an attunement to the moral sociology of personality formation. Against the backdrop of the gathering momentum of decolonization and all that it implied about the hope of building an independent society of productive, integrated citizens, the question that confronted Patterson was: How should we understand the divisive racial, social, and social psychological structure inherited from plantation slavery?

The Sociology of Slavery was the first scholarly book on Jamaican slavery by a Jamaican scholar to be published in the context of postindependence Jamaica. It was also the first to make use of the archives of the famous—or infamous— Worthy Park estate, a plantation in continuous sugar production since 1670.[35] It is not surprising, then, that *The Sociology of Slavery* was animated as much by the evil past of which it spoke as by the unresolved present in which it was written. Along with many of his generation who came of age as the colonial order was winding down, Patterson sensed that political independence in 1962 was far less than it should have been. Significantly (and something not often remembered), the book is dedicated to the great Marxist savant of Caribbean letters and politics C. L. R. James, who in early 1960s London was a formidable presence for West Indian students like Patterson (and his friends, Norman Girvan and Walter Rodney) and whose 1938 study of colonial Saint-Domingue and the Haitian Revolution, *The Black Jacobins*, provided a sort of model for a critical historiographical orientation.[36] James was undoubtedly an inspiring and authoritative figure, but he wasn't, after all, a *social* theorist in the Durkheimian and Weberian and, especially, Parsonian senses.

Perhaps the more profound and permeating influence on the conceptual structure and project of *The Sociology of Slavery* was the "plural theory" of the Jamaican poet and social anthropologist, M. G. Smith, who was in fact one of

206   PART III

Patterson's principal teachers at the University College of the West Indies.[37] Smith, a student of Daryl Forde's at University College, London, had conducted fieldwork in northern Nigeria in the late 1940s.[38] He had become much influenced by the reformist thinking of J. S. Furnivall, the British-born colonial civil servant and author of, among other works, the influential *Colonial Policy and Practice*, published in 1948.[39] Smith returned to Jamaica in late 1952 and soon drew close to the maturing nationalist movement around Norman Washington Manley and the People's National Party in its moment of historic compromise away from its formative radicalism. From 1953 through the early 1960s, the decisive years of constitutional decolonization, Smith would publish a number of vital analytical essays on the structurally and institutionally "plural" character of the Jamaican social order.[40] The prominent and indeed driving idea in these essays was that the Jamaican historical social formation, evolving out of the conditions of racial plantation slavery, was made up of three conflicting social and cultural sections, "White," "Brown," and "Black" (in the vividly literalist and reductive nomenclature of Jamaican racial discourse), each with its own, largely exclusive, institutional practices that were held in place not by collectively shared values but, and only *functionally*, by the overarching coercive presence of the state— first, the colonial state, and subsequently, its successor, the neocolonial state.[41] This insight of Smith's *tragic* anthropology (as I have elsewhere called it, for its grim and trenchant sense of an unrelenting reality of constitutive antagonism) shapes the core of Patterson's ideas in *The Sociology of Slavery*.[42] I do not say that Patterson entirely shared Smith's views about the fixed tripartite divisions of a plural society—he did not. But what he and Smith did share was a deep sense of the *founding* and *enduring* catastrophic impact of New World slavery on the social formation inherited by modern Jamaica. Neither Smith nor Patterson should be understood, strictly speaking, as historians of the Jamaican past but rather as historically informed *theorists* (anthropological and sociological, respectively) of the past of the present of Jamaica's social structure.[43] Like Smith, Patterson was expressly concerned with the peculiar character of Jamaica's social formation: its starkly, perhaps cynically, fabricated and instrumental character.

The Sociology of Slavery formally covers the entire period of the one hundred and eighty-three years of British slavery in Jamaica, but the picture it draws is deeply informed more by the formative middle decades of the eighteenth century. For Patterson, given the particular history of slavery, there was little that was organic about the social formation, little that had evolved out of any shared inner complex of interconnected norms and values. In his view, as he put it early in the book, Jamaica was historically unique in that it presented "one of the rare cases of a human society being artificially created for the satisfaction of one clearly defined goal: that of making money through the production of sugar."[44] In this sense, unlike British North America, colonial plantation Jamaica was *never* a "settler" colony in any proper sense of the term—a fact underlined by Trevor Burnard in his more recent historical work.[45] Despite meager attempts to encourage English settlement—and all that such settlement entailed in terms of the establishment of the institutionalized social and cultural forms that would enable the reproduction of a permanent *society*—Jamaica remained throughout the eighteenth century largely a colony of *extraction*. The English who came voluntarily after 1655 (and in the early years many did not come voluntarily but came as indentured servants) had no intention of staying but sought, rather, to make quick fortunes followed by, as rapidly as possible, an enhanced return to England.[46] They had not come to *found* a new society of civic and political order. Even the economic system they set in motion was meant to be a wholly short-term enterprise of relentless monocrop agricultural exploitation. It was not meant, for example, to provide the conditions of a new *home* much less a new *idea* of home—the *vision* of a new order. This was neither Virginia nor Massachusetts, nor Barbados for that matter.[47] Patterson writes: "After the first fifty hectic years of indecision during which an unscrupulous few may have fulfilled their dreams, Jamaica developed into what it would remain for the rest of the period of slavery: a monstrous distortion of human society."[48]

Here in a nutshell is Patterson's fundamental (and fundamentally *enduring*) point about Jamaican slave society—it was not a human *society* at all, properly speaking. He goes on to underline that the violence of plantation slavery lay less in the obvious prevalence of wanton bodily harm and indifferent death than in the disfigured mode of community: "It was not just the physical cruelty of the system that made it so perverse, for in this the society was hardly unique. What marks it out is the astonishing neglect and distortion of almost every one of the basic prerequisites of normal human being."[49] In short, for Patterson, Jamaica posed a specific historical problem for the normative sociological theory of social order. For, as he says starkly, few systems have more resembled "the Hobbesian state of nature."[50] To be sure, the rationale for underlining this character was not

208 PART III

merely the critique of normative Parsonian sociology. *The Sociology of Slavery* was also meant as a critique of the imperial history of colonial administration and an internal critique of Jamaica's "recently emerged bourgeois intelligentsia" and their nationalist idea of an integrated multiracial society.[51]

Thus, *The Sociology of Slavery* was an intervention simultaneously into several domains of debate, and to carry out its agenda it sought to analyze, in an unprecedented way, the social organization of the lifeworld of Jamaican slave society: the "nature of the society which existed during slavery in Jamaica, and in particular, to concentrate on the mass of the Negro people whose labour, whose skills, whose suffering and whose perseverance and, at times defiance, managed to maintain the system, without breaking—like the Arawaks under their Spanish masters before them—under its yoke."[52] Across its ten chapters, the book traverses an itinerary that offers, in succession, accounts of the socioeconomic structure of the slave-plantation system, the treatment of the enslaved in law and in custom, the sociological portrait of the enslaved, their socialization and their personality, their social institutions, and the mechanisms by which they resisted their condition of enslavement. It is in the structuring of the *social*, therefore, that one principal dimension of slavery's moral evil inheres. In effect, *The Sociology of Slavery* poses the following questions: Who were these enslaved men, women, and children? What were the legal and institutional conditions that *transformed* them into slaves? How did they *adjust* to the coercive conditions imposed on them? What kinds of personality did they produce in these circumstances? What institutions did they develop among themselves (religious, familial, economic, recreational, birth and death, and so on), and how did these shape the lives they led? What were the mechanisms by which they resisted domination? Is there a relation between the forms of personality and the modes of resistance? How are we to understand the moment when the enslaved person says no, enough is enough? These are crucial questions because they point in the direction of one overarching preoccupation that might be summed up in the following questions: What did slavery *do* to the enslaved? Beyond the obvious fact of brutality and cruelty of an unspeakable kind, what did slavery's characteristic *powers* do to the enslaved as persons and as a group of persons? In what ways did these powers—and their attendant rationalities and technologies and relations—constitute the enslaved *as* enslaved? These, in effect, are Orlando Patterson's abiding questions. They are the questions that animate *The Sociology of Slavery*, and moreover they are

SLAVERY'S EVIL LIFEWORLD   209

the questions (albeit on a wider more generalized terrain) that would come to animate the later *Slavery and Social Death*.

Instructively (and not so surprising given the "individual and society" framework they both inherited), to some extent the questions that concerned Patterson were also those that occupied Stanley Elkins in his controversial book *Slavery: A Problem in American Institutional and Intellectual Life*. Patterson engaged this work in an important chapter in *The Sociology of Slavery* on "socialization and personality structure" among the enslaved in Jamaica.[53] Elkins's *Slavery* was a provocative intervention when it appeared, aiming, as its subtitle suggests, less at the substantive history of the past of slavery than at the intellectual *historiography* in the United States in which slavery so profoundly appeared as a problem as such. (It is too often forgotten, or overlooked, that Elkins was seeking to step back from the inherited paradigms and offer a provisional, *conceptual* account rather than a definitive and substantive history.) Above all, Elkins was seeking to alter the twentieth-century terrain of the debate about racial slavery in the United States (from Ulrich B. Phillips to Kenneth Stampp), in part by displacing the moralizing preoccupation with slavery's brutality and unfreedom (which were undeniable) and developing a conceptual framework for understanding the varied *powers* involved in the social-psychological organization of the domination of the enslaved—exactly what interested Patterson. And within this conceptual framework, *personality* was the governing problem. What was the impact of slavery on the personality of the enslaved? How, in social psychological terms, did the enslaved *adjust* to slavery's institutionalized powers?[54] Famously, building on Frank Tannenbaum's comparative approach in *Slave and Citizen* of a decade before, Elkins offered a self-consciously *heuristic* contrast between two kinds of slave systems in the Americas: on the one hand, the constitutively secular-liberal, Protestant, and capitalist culture of the southern United States and, on the other, the conservative, paternalistic, and Catholic culture of the Spanish and Portuguese New World colonies.[55] Such schematic contrasts, obviously, are limited and depend to some extent on a stereotypical binary—but Elkins (though relentlessly accused of reductionism) was not unaware of the abstraction he was seeking to put to conceptual use. Without denying the violence inherent in all slave systems, Elkins was more interested in this provisional contrast for what

210   PART III

it potentially illuminated about the *organization* of the *powers* by which the lives of the enslaved—including, significantly, their personalities—were *shaped*, and in particular the range of institutions (whether narrow or wide) through which enslaving powers defined the constraining context of enslavement. In a Cold War conceptual typology that was becoming increasingly attractive across several intellectual and political areas of discussion (against the background of the new and pressing problem of *totalitarianism*), Elkins found that the slave system of the continental United States was relatively "closed" compared to those of the Spanish and Portuguese colonies that were relatively "open."[56] His informed intuition was that the more diverse the institutions and symbols of authority (that is, the more open the system), the wider and more varied the possibilities for the *personality adjustment* of the enslaved. Perhaps not unexpectedly, it was the relatively closed system of U.S. slavery that produced the "personality type" historically known as "Sambo": stereotypically docile but irresponsible, loyal but lazy, simple but crafty, and so on. This racial figure, Elkins argued, was to be found neither on the African continent nor in the slave systems of the Spanish and Portuguese New World colonies and therefore appeared to be strictly an *effect* of the distinctive authority structure of the type of slavery found in the United States.[57]

Memorably, in order to inquire into the *mechanisms* by which the enslaved adjusted to the near absolute power of the antebellum slave system, Elkins drew on two kinds of material, both again very much part of the intellectual environment of the postwar United States of the 1950s: on the one hand, the emerging literature on the psychological effects of the Nazi concentration camps, as a way of thinking not simply about extreme violence but about *totalizing* forms of institutional power; and, on the other, psychoanalytically informed theories of personality that provided a conceptual language for mapping the social development of the psyche and its internal modes of response. It is important to underscore (against some of his critics) that Elkins did not believe that the slave plantation *was* a sort of concentration camp. But what intrigued him (as it did others such as Hannah Arendt) were informed accounts, such as supplied in the influential work of Bruno Bettelheim, of the seemingly rapid development of "infantile personality" traits in adult inmates adjusting to powerlessness and dependence.[58] The camp analogy, therefore, offered (again) a heuristic way of thinking about the psychological effects on personality of relatively closed, total, and inflexible forms of power and authority. As with others in that postwar historical conjuncture, Elkins was inspired by the suggestion in psychoanalytic theory of how an authoritarian father figure (in the form of an SS guard, for example) might induce "identification with the aggressor." In a connected way, Elkins was intrigued by the suggestion in Harry Stack Sullivan's interpersonal psychology of how personality formation (or re-formation) depended on interactions with "significant others," including the internalization of authority; and similarly, in role psychology he was interested in the way the assignment of certain functional places in the system shaped how people came to see not only others but themselves as well. For Elkins, these were powerful social-psychological *tools* that suggested a *direction* of thinking conceptually about the impact an organization of power such as the slave plantation could have had on the enslaved, and in this way he sought to *reorient* the historical study of American slavery.

As we know, this project was largely a failure. Perhaps Elkins could not have anticipated the almost crusading storm of militant dissent his book would provoke.[59] In a sense, *Slavery* was the embodiment of a paradigm of scholarship that belonged to a conjuncture on the eve of dissolution and displacement. In the emerging problem-space created by the rising tide of racial feeling in the United States, as the 1950s civil rights movement gave way to the 1960s cultural nationalism of Black Power, the very *terms* of its discussion were seen not only as antiquated but even as racially offensive and unwelcome. In the discursive context of the broader cultural turn vivifying the *Weltanschauung* of the 1960s and the corresponding emergence of the political idea of *Black culture* as a generative, creative, and integrating whole, Elkins's conceptual vocabulary seemed to suggest too much the idea that slavery had induced nothing more than a pathological victimhood in the enslaved.[60] Patterson had a different assessment; although not uncritical of *Slavery*, he was not hostile to Elkins.[61] Strongly influenced, as I have suggested, by the 1950s work on the social psychology of personality, Patterson's chapter "The Socialization and Personality Structure of the Slave" in *The Sociology of Slavery*, especially the section "An Analysis of 'Quashee,'" concerns itself with precisely the kinds of "adjustments" to slavery the enslaved were obliged to make, and the personality traits the system appears to have induced. As Patterson understood it, the overseer more so than the slaveowners proper (who in the Jamaican case were often enough absentee proprietors) was the crucial authority figure on the plantation. As Patterson put it, "[The overseer] may have stimulated fear and terror, but never respect or co-operation. To the slaves he was an enemy never to be trusted, and to be foiled at every opportunity."[62] It was under the eye of the overseer that the slave spent most of his or her working life.

212   PART III

Thus Patterson writes, "All the psychological techniques which had to be employed in outwitting him and thwarting his every action were constantly in use and eventually became 'a kind second nature.'" It was primarily in the context of the overseer-slave relationship, he says, that the "peculiar personality traits of the slaves . . . came about and functioned."[63] Much the same could have been said of the bookkeeper as well, a subordinate White who answered to the overseer. Both overseer and bookkeeper are central figures in the lifeworld fictively described in *Die the Long Day*.

Thus Patterson found that Elkins's Sambo figure resembled the "Quashee" figure in the Jamaican literature. That the historian Edward Long used it, for example, in his *History of Jamaica* suggested to Patterson that by at least the beginning of the second half of the eighteenth century the term had come to "designate peculiarly Negro character traits"—crafty, artful, deceitful, lazy, lying, evasive, capricious, distrustful, and so on.[64] Therefore, Patterson writes, there is no doubt about Quashee's existence: "The problem is to ascertain how real, how meaningful, this psychological complex was in the life of the slave."[65] It is here that he resists what he thinks of as Elkins's normalization of this docile figuration of the enslaved person. To explore this question in the depth that it required, Patterson maintains, would require going into existential and role psychology, which was outside the scope of his historical-sociological work. In a certain sense *this* came to be the labor of the novel *Die the Long Day*. In the context of *The Sociology of Slavery*, he argues, Quashee existed on three levels at least: first, as a stereotype held by Whites of their slaves; second, as a response to this stereotype on the part of the enslaved; and third, as a psychological function of the real-life situation of the slave. These levels were interconnected and mutually reinforcing—the enslaved lived in a *total* world. The real-life situation of the slave was one in which there was a complete breakdown of all the major institutions—marriage, family, religion, and organized morality. This was made worse by the fact that the Whites offered no viable alternative mores and institutions but were themselves socially disorganized: "There could be no kind of guiding principle, then, in the socialization of the slave, except that of evasion, which he learned from hard experience."[66] A good deal of the personality traits of the slave—laziness, irresponsibility, for example—can be explained "in situational terms," Patterson argues.[67]

But not everything could be accounted for in this way. The basis of some of what have been identified as Quashee's traits—evasiveness, dissembling, pathological lying, for example—must be sought elsewhere; namely, in the stereotypes the Whites produced of Quashee as a way of rationalizing the brutality and exploitation of the system. Moreover, since the slave-masters had almost absolute control over their slaves, they were able to create the conditions that would actualize the very stereotypes they had of their slaves—thus making for a case of Robert Merton's famous idea of a "self-fulfilling prophecy."[68] Patterson was quite taken by this social-psychological idea; but he added a supplementary dimension to it. Besides being forced into situations that produce the behavior the stereotype describes, Patterson argues, the slave also responded directly to the stereotypes "by either appearing to, or actually, internalizing them": "The slave, in fact, played upon their master's stereotype for his own ends." And playing the stereotype had a number of functions. First, the slave could see that however much the master might protest at his stupidity he was pleased by the slave's offering proof of his rationalizations. Here the slave was exploiting the "see-what-I mean" mentality of the master. Second, by playing the stereotype, the enslaved were able to disguise their true feelings, which was crucial in a situation in which it was nearly impossible to easily trust anyone. The enslaved had the satisfaction of "duping" the master, "playing fool to catch wise," as the Jamaican saying goes. And third, there was the function of exasperating the master with sheer inefficiency, bungling, and stupidity.[69] Patterson was to extensively explore *all* of these dimensions in *Die the Long Day*.

Consideration of the socialization of the enslaved and the forms of personality this social-psychological "adjustment" engendered are part of the background for Patterson's penultimate chapter concerned with "the mechanisms of resistance to slavery."[70] The question of the resistance to slavery formed an important, though to that point not yet central, concern in the historiography of New World slavery. The question that animated Patterson was how the impulse to resist could have emerged within an institutional form of domination so totalizing and overwhelming as plantation slavery. As he writes in the opening sentence of the chapter: "Despite the rigours and severity of slavery, despite the all-embracing nature of the exploitation by the master of his slave and the totality of his domination over him, the latter, nonetheless, was never completely subdued. In one form or another the slave expressed his resentment of his lot, sometimes in a covert, indirect and relatively mild manner, at other times in direct revolt against the object of his oppression."[71] Given perhaps his novelist's sensibility and attunement, Patterson was acutely aware that an empirical

214   PART III

sociological analysis was faced with certain limitations in its ability to respond to the question: "From whence arose the spirit of rebellion in the slave?"[72] This is Patterson's *final* question. The ultimate answer to that question, he says (and it is important to recognize that it was a *question* for him), lay *outside* the framework of a sociological inquiry and entailed something more akin to a moral-existential speculation on the limits of human endurance. The chapter discusses the modes of passive and violent resistance, and comes in the end, in its concluding paragraph, to the perplexing question toward which it had all along been heading. Here consequentially, Patterson draws explicitly on Camus's *The Rebel*: "What, then accounts for the presence of this need which seems to survive under conditions which in every way conspire to smother it? Every rebellion, Camus has written, 'tacitly invokes a value.' This value is something embedded deep in the human soul, a value discovered as soon as a subject begins to reflect on himself through which he inevitably comes to the conclusion that 'I must become free—that is, that my freedom must be won.' In the final analysis it is the discovery of this universal value which justifies and stimulates the most tractable of slaves to rebel."[73] It is *this* question that Patterson sought to pursue in fictive form in *Die the Long Day*.

The presence of Albert Camus in Patterson's work bears reflection, less for the faithfulness of his rendering of it than for the uses to which he commits it in grappling with his own conundrums—broadly, the predicament of the Black individual, slave and postslave, confronting and navigating the opacity of an unyielding and implacable plantation and postplantation world of social-racial domination. As I have already indicated, Patterson is most directly influenced by Camus's two major books of philosophic inquiry, *The Myth of Sisyphus* and *The Rebel*. These books are indeed central to any understanding of Camus's thinking, the former published in 1942 in the midst of the Nazi occupation of France, the latter in 1951, during the escalating Cold War, as French intellectuals, scarred by the trauma of what he called the "French and European disaster" but inspired by the Résistance, worked out rival approaches to the question of Marxism and the Soviet Union, the problem of political violence (or sanctioned murder), the role of history (or historical determinism), the significance of collective action and solidarity, and so on. For Camus, *The Rebel* was to be read as a successor to *The Myth of Sisyphus*, or at least as a book that sought to take up and complete the unfinished work of the philosophy of the absurd.[74]

Now, memorably, for Camus in *The Myth of Sisyphus* the idea of the absurd is meant to capture an intractable and irreducible dimension of human existence—namely, the inaccessible muteness of the world in the face of our expectations of intelligibility, transparency, and coherence. We confront the world with an ontological need for meaning and value and with an anticipation that the world won't abandon us, that it will make sense to us in a stable and solid way. But the world—without God, without System—turns to us only a mocking face of blank indifference. Note that it is neither the world itself nor ourselves as such that is absurd. Rather, it is the awakening *awareness*, sometimes slow, sometimes sudden, of the irreconcilable gap between the two that is the birth of the absurd as a kind of consciousness. But if there is this permanent rupture or insurmountable void between the world and our consciousness of the world, how do we assure ourselves of a reliable ground of value, and a bulwark against the downward spiral of nihilism? For Camus, of course, there are no guarantees, only the grim, unending repetition endemic to life, certainly oppressed life. This is the savage beauty and stoic grace of Sisyphus, the scornful self-possession with which he shoulders his unasked-for burden up the hill and makes his way down again only to resume his thankless lifelong labor. For Camus it is important that Sisyphus resists *both* the temptation to a transcendent faith, what he calls "philosophical suicide," as well as the temptation to a faithless self-renunciation—that is, physical suicide, the abandonment of life itself.[75] It is not hard to see, I think, how the dire poetics of this picture of the human condition would appeal to Orlando Patterson, seeking as he is to grapple with the confrontation between the diasporic Black subject (slave and postslave) and the unforgiving heedlessness of an oppressive world. Readers of his first novel, *The Children of Sisyphus* (completed in the same years as his dissertation was being written), will remember the Rastafarian intellectual Brother Solomon who, having failed at philosophical suicide (the eschatological hope in divine rescue from Babylon he encouraged in his followers), deems his own life no longer worth living and commits physical suicide by hanging himself. In so doing, Patterson suggests (following Camus), Brother Solomon surrenders the courage upon which the moral principle of the absurd depends.

In a sense, not surprisingly, this conception of the absurd appeared to many only to motivate a philosophy of resignation, even fatalism. This was certainly not Camus's intention—nor indeed is it Patterson's. Camus wanted us to see what remains sublime in the paradox of a hopeless fortitude. Recall the final sentence

216   PART III

in *The Myth of Sisyphus*: "We must imagine Sisyphus happy."[76] In any case, Camus had always believed (it was the basis, after all, of his early criticism of Jean-Paul Sartre's existentialism) that the real issue is how to positively respond to the ineluctable experience of the absurd. This is the task of *The Rebel*. As Camus's commentators have suggested, the complex arguments of *The Rebel* have to be situated in the antagonistic discursive context of the French intellectual landscape of the postwar mid- to late 1940s—in which, central among the conflicted issues was the legitimacy of the use of violence in the service of putatively progressive causes. When is murder permissible? What conception of history allows one to judge when killing is justifiable or whose life is worthy of life? Famously, Maurice Merleau-Ponty's 1947 *Humanism and Terror* was one very influential Marxist attempt to justify violence on behalf of progressive history—and one with which Camus fundamentally disagreed.[77]

Needless to say, this discursive context would not have been entirely irrelevant to Patterson in the early postcolonial years of the 1960s, thinking about the moral legitimacy of collective violence—revolutionary, or at least rebellious violence—in the service of radical political action. After all, the reemergence of interest in James's *The Black Jacobins* together with the wider emerging focus on slave revolts in the historiography of New World slavery takes place in the context of an anticolonial and Black rethinking of the means-ends relationship in political action.[78] This moreover is also the moment of the publication of Frantz Fanon's *The Wretched of the Earth*. But clearly, as can be seen from the passage Patterson quotes from *The Rebel*, what especially caught his attention in Camus's thinking was less the attempt to come to terms with the political organization of resistance than the formation of the moral *moment of refusal*. What is the point at which an individual no longer "agrees" to be dominated? What precipitates the crisis in which it is no longer possible to accept what has for so long been endured? And what are the moral *implications* of this moment? Is this act merely a (negative) instance of refusal of the prevailing condition, or is it also, and in the very same gesture and in exactly the same measure, an instance of the *affirmation* of a new value? These were not antihistorical questions, but they were not ones that Marxists typically posed (whether in respect of France or Jamaica). Furthermore, it was undoubtedly of central importance to Patterson that in posing these questions about the act of rebellion in contrast with the organization of revolution (a tension in the slavery debates as well), it was the figure of the slave that Camus mobilized. Not, of course, so far as we know, that Camus had any interest in New World slavery. Indeed, he was only offering his own intervention into the postwar French Hegelianism inspired by Alexandre Kojève's lectures on Hegel's *Phenomenology of Spirit*, in which the master-slave dialectic figured prominently. Camus was not necessarily hostile to Hegel, but what concerned him about this emergent reading of Hegel (informing Merleau-Ponty as much as Sartre and others) was a certain reification—or deification, as he put it—of the movement of History.[79] For Patterson, too, although slavery was certainly no mere instance in a *metaphysical* binary, the fictive illumination of the moment of the slave's moral refusal was a way of critically engaging prevailing positivist and determinist renderings of history.

<hr>

The Sociology of Slavery might be described as a social phenomenology of the lifeworld of Jamaican slavery, in particular the lifeworld of the enslaved. Its problem-space is the early postcolonial conjuncture in Jamaica in which the stark reality was that the anticolonial project had not produced—and political independence likely *would* not produce—even the semblance of a decolonized national society out of the divisive and chaotic slave and postslave colonial pasts.[80] From the standpoint of its "plural" present, *The Sociology of Slavery* sought to inquire into the impact that the powers of New World slavery—the social, institutional, and social psychological powers, most particularly—*had* on the enslaved. It sought to think about the impact of these powers on the conditions of their *ways of life* and on the conditions of their moral *personality*. The direction of the answer offered by *The Sociology of Slavery* is that slavery's powers of domination produced a lifeworld of cultural devastation and social psychological disorganization: it produced Quashee as a dimension of personality as much as it disclosed the latent existential possibility of the rebel. Crucially, then, for Patterson, what slavery's powers constructed was not a lifeworld that could, properly speaking, be called a normative "society." In his view, the authoritative perspective of Elsa Goveia notwithstanding, the idea of a "slave society" was somewhat oxymoronic.[81] Of course, Patterson does not mean by this that slavery produced no social structure, no reproducible social *pattern* of racialized asymmetry; he means, rather, that what was produced was a contrived and artificial structure and pattern—there was no engine internal to that structure or pattern that generated the organic telos of a viable norm of social organization. Again, disagree

218   PART III

though he might have with some of the details of M. G. Smith's theory of pluralism, *this* is what he has in mind here. Slavery's powers not only subjected the enslaved to endless physical brutality and coercion but also institutionalized a mode of systematically stripping the enslaved of their former ways of life, while at the same time distorting and disabling the conditions in which any new modes of individual and familial and social flourishing could have been created. In retrospect, I believe one can recognize in this early monograph the enslaved form of life that Patterson would later come to call *social death*—for what social death entails, remember, is precisely this stripping away of the elementary social forms that give human life the meaningful generational context of temporal depth and an assured normative network of social vitality. Again, recapitulating Card, understood this way, social death is indeed a form of *evil*—it is the social suffering of an avoidable harm produced by a perverse and systemic moral wrong.

Notably, as with Elkins's *Slavery* in the United States, the Jamaican conjuncture that produced *The Sociology of Slavery* was soon challenged and, in effect, displaced in its centrality by another conjuncture that, in certain respects, made Patterson's argument seem, to some, wrongheaded, even anachronistic, possibly reactionary. In 1971, Kamau (then Edward) Brathwaite published *The Development of Creole Society in Jamaica*, which, in framework as much as in ethos and vision, offered a very different picture altogether of plantation slavery and of the relationship between the enslaved and their enslavers. *The Development of Creole Society in Jamaica* can be read as a direct response to *The Sociology of Slavery*, offered in terms that were not completely unlike those leveled at Elkins's *Slavery*. Already in 1968 (a watershed year for Black diasporic critique), and barely a year after the publication of Patterson's book, Brathwaite wrote a sharply critical review essay on it that in many ways forecast the argument elaborated in his own soon-to-be-published monograph and introduced us to the elements of his emerging idea of a specifically "Creole society" (an idea he borrows from Goveia).[82] Two dimensions of critique principally animated Brathwaite's reading of *The Sociology of Slavery*. The first had to do with what he thought of as the "static" character of its sociology. In Patterson's account, Brathwaite argued, the tension between sociology and history was finally resolved in favor of the former, so that what emerges is a picture in which the "social institutions of the slaves are seen from a generalised fixed viewpoint, with little indication of the operation upon them of the dynamics of change."[83] In Brathwaite's view, Patterson's historical sociology was more sociology than history. As a consequence of this, he found Patterson's vision lacking a sense of the "living wholeness" of Jamaican Creole society—an exemplary demonstration of which he found in Goveia's 1965 monograph, *Slave Society in the British Leeward Islands at the End of the Eighteenth Century*.[84] Brathwaite rightly discerned in Patterson's *structural* orientation the trace of Smith's pluralism—which he and Goveia would criticize in quite similar terms.[85] Brathwaite recognized that for Patterson "Jamaican slave society was a non-society, a mere agglomeration of plantations" held together by coercive force rather than by any *integrative* values or norms (dominance rather than hegemony, to use a different nomenclature). And this is what he disagreed with—what he called a "disintegrationist concept of society."[86] For Brathwaite, to the contrary, from various social groups (Whites and Coloreds most, but Blacks as well), and at certain historical periods more than others (1800s more than 1700s), and within certain institutions of social life more than others (education, but even marriage), there were ongoing *integrative* processes pushing (progressively, if unevenly) in the general direction of *creolization*.

The second dimension of Brathwaite's critique had to do with the *cultural* significance of the African presence in slave-plantation Jamaica. Brathwaite argued that Patterson was (at best) "ambivalent" about the presence of African cultural retentions, between what are "survivals" and what are "reinterpretations," and how to understand the relations between these and the directions of cultural change. Patterson, he suggested, was inclined to see the cultural practices of the enslaved more as compromise adjustments *to* European institutions than as resistant creative adjustments *of* African practice.[87] More precisely, *The Sociology of Slavery* lacked (as Brathwaite might also have said of James's *The Black Jacobins*) a positive—that is, *anthropological*—account of African culture in New World slave society. In this respect, the influence on Brathwaite of the 1960s revival of the work of Melville Herskovits and the anthropology of acculturation is very evident. Herskovits's great work, *The Myth of the Negro Past*, was originally published in 1941 (as part of the Carnegie Corporation's project on American Negro life); but given the wider assimilationist paradigm of the moment (of which Gunnar Myrdal's 1944 *An American Dilemma: The Negro and Modern Democracy* is the classic instance), its impact as a groundwork of Black cultural difference was relatively negligible.[88] However, when it was reissued in 1958 (the year before Elkins's *Slavery*), Herskovits's rejection of the prevailing idea that African Americans had lost their African culture as a consequence of the deculturing predations of slavery acquired a new salience. In the slavery debates that emerged in the 1960s

220   PART III

The Myth of the Negro Past helped to shape the Black cultural nationalist argument for the continued African presence in the Americas. This is partly Brathwaite's generative discursive context. In 1971, the same year as the publication of *The Development of Creole Society in Jamaica*, Brathwaite would publish an approving introduction to a reissue of Herskovits's 1937 Caribbean classic, *Life in a Haitian Valley*, reiterating the gist of that anthropologist's idea that "African culture was an autonomous entity, though diverse within itself, with its own norms and structures which could be externally observed, appreciated or devalued, but could not be understood apart from its own ground and environment."[89] Understandably, then, on Brathwaite's reading, Patterson's account of slavery was characterized by a relentlessly negative (and pessimistic) vision of fragmentation and cultural loss—even though, as Brathwaite put it in what he took to be a closing clinching remark, the very demonstration Patterson offered of the slaves' adjustment to the system should have "disrupted" this thesis "of a disintegrated society of masters richly absent or presently debauched, [and] of slaves prostituted and trauma ridden."[90] For Brathwaite, in other words, social adjustment was itself the sign of *Creole* cultural transformation.

This was a conceptually powerful critique. And in the context of the cultural-political radicalization of the Jamaican (and Caribbean, indeed, Black diasporic) 1970s, Brathwaite's Creole society thesis came to seem very appealing to many—and *still* does. It certainly resonated with the post-1968 postcolonial problem-space that was being reshaped not only by the emergence of discourses of radical social transformation (varieties of Third World socialism, including Michael Manley's) but also by the rise of an assertive Black *cultural* consciousness in which the African (Caribbean) subject was seen not as the reactive or adjusting victim of White domination but a *self-determining*, subaltern, hermeneutic agent of cultural creativity and cultural change. Think of the contrast, say, between the figure of Rastafari in Patterson's 1964 novel *The Children of Sisyphus* and in Brathwaite's poem "Wings of a Dove" from the 1967 collection *Rights of Passage*—the former rich with existential foreboding, the latter, the embodiment of militant cultural integrity.[91] In the new (Creole) paradigm of New World slavery that emerged from Brathwaite's work, it is less social or institutional *power* that is of interest (it is not the question of what coercive power did to the enslaved that needs answering) and more the languages of cultural *process* of creolization (the question of how the enslaved creatively enacted an intelligible life). Similarly, for Brathwaite, it is not the personality of the enslaved that is of critical consequence (he has no interest whatsoever, for example, in Stanley Elkins's thesis or the debate about it) but the "folk culture" of the enslaved understood as a dynamic, African-based process interacting with European (and later other) influences in a fluid, or at least constantly changing, environment. In an important sense, Brathwaite's intervention in Caribbean historiography was similar to John Blassingame's in the United States.[92] Both interventions signaled a *paradigm* shift, marked by a decline in the role of psychology in the social sciences and a *turn* to culture (in an Africanist *agential* sense) as a determining factor in slave and postslave Black life.

One may wonder whether we are not now, in the current New World Black conjuncture of the early twenty-first century, witness to another paradigmatic turn in which the critical conceptual value of this subaltern "culture" argument of which Brathwaite was a protagonist has very much diminished. and in which part of what is necessary is to reconstruct an analytic of power and domination, which would entail rereading Patterson's contribution.[93]

It seems to me important, however, *not* to see these rival conceptions of Jamaican plantation slavery in progressivist terms, as is very often the case—that what Brathwaite produced in his integrative Creole theory of the 1970s in effect *bested* (because it was conceptually superior to) Patterson's disintegrative plural theory of the 1960s. It is too simple to say that one offers a *true* picture of plantation slavery and the other a false picture. Again, as I argued in chapter 1 of this book, the purchase of a theoretical proposition does not stand like an abstraction in a vacuum but depends on what question it is (tacitly) trying to answer—it depends, in other words, on the problem-space or language-game in relation to which it was formulated. Patterson's *The Sociology of Slavery* and Brathwaite's *The Development of Creole Society in Jamaica* manifestly belong to different conjunctures and different language-games. It may be more helpful to see the visions articulated in these books as, in some respects, rival sides of the same coin of the larger problem of Caribbean slave and postslave society, and to imagine Patterson and Brathwaite as thinkers holding onto opposite ends of the same paradox that constitutes the making of Caribbean society. In this sense, the *fragment* and the *whole* may be of a piece, integration and disintegration not mutually exclusive processes but *dimensions* of a historical Caribbean reality coming contrastingly into perspective in different historical conjunctures. There is a sense, in my view, in which the 1970s Jamaican conjuncture that gave Brathwaite's Creole theory its lease on life was concerned to assert the primacy

222   PART III

of an optimistic synthetic cultural consolidation. But in the Caribbean present, this momentum has certainly waned significantly, if not vanished altogether, and conceptually therefore the argument for a progressive movement of integration of the social and cultural elements of the society is less persuasive now than it might once have been. If this is true, then the justification for rethinking the resonance of the theory of pluralism is not far to find in a contemporary Jamaica in which the grammar of conflict and division has once again supplanted the poetics of Creole integration.[94] In this context at least, Patterson's work should assume a new (if not exclusive) relevance because it brings into sharp relief the constitutive rupture that founds Caribbean history. At the same time, however, I think it is important to conceptualize this rupture of cultural devastation that derives from the catastrophic effects of slavery's powers not only in the old historical sociological terms, but also in terms of historical atrocity and moral evil.

SLAVERY'S EVIL LIFEWORLD

Patterson's preoccupations in *The Sociology of Slavery* with social and personality organization in the context of the dominated world of the enslaved in colonial Jamaica, with the totalizing powers of the plantation regime and the modes of response of the enslaved (the blurred continuities between accommodation and resistance), are refracted in fictive form in his novel *Die the Long Day*.[95] We have already briefly encountered the dire predicament of the novel's protagonist, the inimitable Quasheba, and the horrific events that bring her relatively short life to a violent end—events that form the novel's backdrop, that set the tone of the general moral atmosphere in which the dramatic action unfolds, and that drive and rationalize its overall narrative telos. *Die the Long Day*, I've said, is helpfully thought of as the fictive companion to *The Sociology of Slavery*.[96] I do not mean by this, of course, that Patterson's novel is merely derivative of, or decorative in relation to, his monograph, the sociologist playing at literary art.[97] That idea depends on the false—or anyway certainly impoverishing—assumption of a fundamental divergence between these discursive forms on the grounds of some idea of truth. Rather, it seems more helpful to think of each—novel and monograph—as having its own respective constraints as well as capacities, neither form giving you everything you hope for hermeneutically or poetically but each giving you something insightful.

In this respect, we have seen in *The Sociology of Slavery* that Patterson is acutely aware of the limits of the monograph's modes of intelligibility. On the account I would commend literature too *thinks*, not, it is true, in explicitly propositional language but in imaginative and exploratory—yet still *conceptual*—ways not easily available to the form of the sociological text.[98] One conceptual way that literature thinks is *morally*—that is, in and through the *conduct* of the characters it portrays in the fictive-but-realistic lives they are shown to lead. Thus I take the form of the novel, or anyway of the social realist novel (of which Patterson's *Die the Long Day* is an instance), as a creative discourse that builds up a phenomenological and existential and specifically moral lifeworld.[99] The novel offers a "possible" world in which, through an organization of plural and very often conflicting interconnected actions, personal and social relations are set in temporal motion and spatial extent; and cognitive and affective life, the life of diverse reasoning and desiring moral agents navigating varied dilemmas and conundrums, is concretely evoked and plausibly portrayed. In its moral dimension the social realist novel invites us to consider these actors in terms of the presence or absence of *virtues* or qualities of personhood, the broad, given, social-historical *circumstances* in which they are made to find themselves as well as the more contingent *situations* that are partly within and partly beyond their shaping control. We are invited to witness as these actors navigate unfolding states of affairs, to consider how they act and why, what ends they aim for and how they justify these ends to themselves and others, which values and standards they approve or commend or seek to embody and which values and standards they condemn or resist or reject.[100]

I think of the novel, then, as a dynamic moral field, and as such, as inviting a moral reading. It is hardly surprising, consequently, that the novel is sometimes seen not only as a paradigmatic site for thinking about moral conduct in general (including conduct involving both relatively ordinary virtues and relatively ordinary vices) but also an exemplary site for thinking about moral evil specifically—that is, a site for an exploration of the enormity and complexity and prevalence of evil, in evil characters, evil actions, and evil conditions, and of the relations among them. Indeed, given the realistic lifeworld of irreducible relations it creates, the novel potentially enables us to explore some of the difficult moral questions about evil, questions (as described in earlier chapters) that philosophers like Claudia Card and John Kekes and Laurence Thomas do not necessarily agree about because they are questions that, by their very nature, do not lend themselves to clear-cut or hard-and-fast answers. These are questions

224 PART III

about, for example, the relation between evil and intentionality (whether an intention to cause intolerable moral harm is a necessary component of evil), about moral monstrosity (whether it takes a moral monster to commit indisputable evil or whether people otherwise perceived to be of ordinary moral decency can get "caught up" in evil); about distinctive forms of human suffering and harm (whether deliberate mass killing need be assumed to be *the* ultimate definition of evil); about the distinctive sources of evil (whether wrongful harm belongs only to the actions of individuals or whether it can be located also in social and institutional relations), and so on. The value of the novel is that it need not commit us, or reduce us, to any single or one-sided dimension of appreciation, and therefore it affords us an expansive yet realistic space for thinking through evil.

Along these lines, I am going to suggest that Patterson's *Die the Long Day* is one literary site in which to explore precisely the evil of New World slavery.[101] In the novel, Patterson provokes us to explore a range of features of slavery's evil, the deliberate practices of cruelty and humiliation and wanton violence perpetrated by White enslavers on the Black enslaved. But what is especially interesting to me is the way he pictures these in relation to the slave plantation imagined as a distinctive kind of intersubjective lifeworld—a relatively closed, total, and radically distorting one—in which these vices are not only contingent but also viciously *endemic*. In this way, one can see that the evil of slavery was to be found not merely in any given spectacular act or event of violation but in a routine, systemic form that reproduced violation as a behavioral and institutional norm.

As its title suggests, the action in *Die the Long Day* takes place over the temporal arc of a single day, or at least a roughly twenty-four-hour period, from dawn to dawn, between the death of Quasheba and the ritual ceremony performed by her fellow-enslaved to send her spirit home to Africa. By organizing the social time of the novel in this way, Patterson deliberately sets us down, unsentimentally, in the middle of the prosaic social and economic life of a working (if, as it happens, not very prosperous) sugar plantation. The shadow of debt and decline are already haunting the late eighteenth-century Jamaican plantocracy, and the fictional Richmond Vale is not in sound financial order.[102] No one there yet knows Quasheba's fate as day breaks. There is, as a consequence, a pervasive atmosphere of ordinary everydayness. We are encouraged to imagine a lifeworld in which people, in particular the enslaved, take their circumstances more or less for granted, which is obviously not to say they accepted this condition. Slavery is simply the habituated form of life within which they live—and have lived for several generations. Indeed, it is an unexceptional day in August, the hottest month of the Jamaican year, when the newly burned canefields are being turned and readied for planting. But this routine fact only intensifies the onerous rhythms of repetition in the lives of the enslaved we witness. Internally, therefore, within the phenomenological lifeworld the novel describes, nothing is particularly unusual about the day. There is a given round of ongoing activity that marks the tedious regularity of the labor, the endless feeling of exhaustion the enslaved experience; there are the prescribed social roles, with their more or less internalized expectations, and the performances that structure the interactions between enslaved and enslaver. The world is what it is. We know, of course, that this is a structure of institutionalized brutality, cruelty, and humiliation, but its vicious powers are inscribed into the warp and woof of the naturalized and normative fabric of the social background. As grievous as they are, the harms barely stand out; the evil is routinized, almost banal.

For Patterson, as we know from *The Sociology of Slavery*, the structure of the social world brought into existence by the plantation regime scarcely constituted a "society," properly speaking. True, there were interpersonal relations of varying degrees of intimacy and filial meaningfulness among the enslaved. But none of these were stable or secure. True too, there was a semblance of shared "cultural" sensibility (later registered, for example, in the general anxiety around ensuring that Quasheba is given a proper burial) and a shared "cultural" idiom (registered, again, in the collective intelligibility of the funerary practice itself).[103] But what stands out most prominently in the lifeworld presented by the novel is the closed and rigid social order of domination in which the power exerted over the powerless is manifestly maintained entirely within a framework of coercion rendered palpable by the presence of the overseer, the bookkeeper, and the driver. It is significant, I believe, that within the lifeworld of the enslaved there is barely any self-consciousness of an *alternative* world—notably, marronage appears more as a threat than a solicitous possibility, let alone a positive hope.

The social world of the novel, in other words, is a world of near total power, on the one hand, and near total powerlessness, on the other. And what interests Patterson most is how to think about the enslaved navigating this structure, the social psychological resources that might have been brought to bear on living

226 PART III

in such circumstances of institutionalized domination. This is why the central question posed by the novel deals with the rationality of *accommodation*: the capacity of the enslaved to adjust to a form of life, to make it, in some relevant way, their own. In a certain sense, accommodation is the behavioral conundrum *Die the Long Day* explores. In this respect, the novel is a prolonged meditation on a single Jamaican maxim: "Play fool to catch wise." Its importance is signaled by the fact that it is one of the two epigraphs used to frame the book as a whole.[104] The proverb had appeared before, in *The Sociology of Slavery*, in Patterson's effort to *de-essentialize* Stanley Elkins's claims about the Sambo personality. For Patterson, remember, Elkins has a point, but it's one that needs a conceptual nuance disclosed in the semiotic implications of this popular Jamaican saying. As Patterson understands it, the aphorism testifies to something like a lived *rule of conduct* of the powerless—the "hidden transcript" informing a creatively defensive "art of resistance," James Scott would say.[105] To "play fool" in order to "catch wise" is to feign ignorance or incomprehension or even stupidity so as to foil or deflect or parry attempts by those with the coercive power to injure or damage one's body and degrade and humiliate one's soul—in the process sometimes extracting some small measure of gain or advantage or pleasure from the exposed vulnerabilities of the powerful. There is perhaps a ludic or *ironic* element involved in this artful conduct: one is, after all, "playing" at a mode of being the subperson one is presumed to be in the eyes of the powerful. Patterson wants to suggest, however, that what this maxim shaped was not merely the rational, reflectively self-conscious code of conduct of the enslaved (though it was likely that too, in part) but a dimension of their embodied *habitus* as well.[106] It shaped a more or less gradually cultivated *disposition* that could, almost without conscious thinking, unpremeditatedly, come into play in diverse situations of threat or menace for the enslaved. As one might put it, to "play fool to catch wise" constituted a practice of moral and practical *learning* that was also a *habit-forming* practice of self-making. All of the enslaved characters in *Die the Long Day* have embodied this virtue ethics of loquacious opacity if for no other practical reason than to survive.

Significantly, I believe, this concern with the everyday social psychology of accommodation helps to explain why dissent and resistance appear in the novel as they do, not as the political organization of collective revolt against the slave regime but as an ordinary ethics of exemplary personal refusal of evil.[107] Patterson is certainly not uninterested in the historical sociology of slave revolt, but these exceptional events are not the focus of his attention in the novel.

Notably, *Die the Long Day* has no telos toward a coming horizon of revolution in relation to which the "progressive" social consciousness of the enslaved can be judged. The novel isn't framed around the promise of general slave emancipation. And yet *Die the Long Day* is nothing if not a meditation on the meaning of *refusal*. What else is the extraordinary figure of Quasheba if not a momentous instance of uncompromising rejection of dehumanization? Of course, this refusal of slavery's evil is not aimed at an explicitly *political* horizon. Quasheba is not seeking to liberate herself, much less her fellow-enslaved. Her aim is not the end of slavery as a social and economic *system*. She does not explicitly envisage a new world. Quasheba, in other words, is not meant to be a militant like her near-contemporary Tacky, the great eighteenth-century enslaved man who has been figured as a profound political and military strategist of slave revolt.[108] To the contrary, Quasheba has *murder* on her mind, not liberation. But even so, the question Patterson raises by her action is whether this attempted murder of an unquestionably vile and wicked slave master is not only justifiable but also in itself an affirmative act of *moral* freedom—or at least, an act of vindication or reclamation of a part of herself, her personhood, that has been systematically denied. In the face of so nightmarishly evil a condition, can murder be the exercise of virtue?[109] This is Patterson's question. What interests him, then, is less the political than the moral or existential question—less the question of the collective rebellion of the enslaved against the system of slavery than the question of the individual enslaved person's arrival at a point beyond which the existing norm is insupportable because it has undermined a part of the self that it is, simply, unpardonable to violate. In a curious way, in this respect, Patterson seems to waiver between the speculative concerns of *The Myth of Sisyphus* (the recognition of the world's blank indifference) and those of *The Rebel* (working out the moral-political implications of that oppressive, burdensome indifference in the context of murder). True, Patterson invites us to imagine Quasheba as becoming acutely aware of the absurdity of her condition—the intractable relation between her self-consciousness (her recognition of her universal humanity) and the callous obliviousness, the unjust silence, of her universe (her abject status as a powerless slave). Like Camus's rebel, what Quasheba arrives at is a "borderline" point at which she is no longer willing to be what she has been made into by the systemic evil that dominates her, and in that act of refusal she affirms the intrinsic dignity of her humanity. However, though she acts on a moral claim that her fellow-enslaved will admire and even identify with, unlike

228   PART III

Camus's rebel Quasheba is not seeking a principle of *solidarity*, a common way of grounding collective action against the unresponsive wall of domination.[110]

✦

Die the Long Day is constructed around a series of characters, sketched in more or less detail in various episodes and through whose conundrums, actions, and personalities we catch a glimpse of the social and social-psychological organization of the lifeworld of a slave plantation. I focus on four of the novel's characters—three are enslaved, and thus allow us to think about responses to the evil they suffer; and one is an enslaver, and thus allows us to consider aspects of the perpetration of evil harm in the context of New World slavery.[111]

To begin with, there is the central figure, Quasheba, whom we meet at the moment of her death as the novel opens. It is noteworthy that Patterson stages his drama around the figure of an enslaved woman and her relationship with her daughter. For him, this dyadic relationship is deeply symbolic of both the powers as well as the enduring wound of slavery.[112] Quasheba is on the run for attempting (unsuccessfully, it turns out) to kill the syphilitic slave master Pickersgill, who is trying to coerce her daughter, Polly, into a sexual relationship with him. Note that Pickersgill does not want to directly force Polly to have sex with him (though he has tried that). Perhaps with other enslaved women he, like Thomas Thistlewood, simply imposes a will sanctioned by the White male order. But in this instance Pickersgill is asking for something more perverse. He wants Polly to *agree* to sex with him—as though to construct the fiction of her sexual desire for him. In any case, it is the deliberate act of refusal of this pervasive form of moral evil during slavery—the institutionalized powers that gave White men nearly unfettered access to the bodies of Black women—that propels the narrative arc of the story.

Now, perhaps not surprisingly, Patterson has given his protagonist the name Quasheba, the feminine form of Quashee (which he had examined in *The Sociology of Slavery*); so there can be no misunderstanding what is at stake for him in the description of her character—namely, the exploration of the personality of the enslaved and, in particular, the controversial question of whether or to what extent the enslaved can be said to have accommodated themselves to the evils of their enslavement (and therefore, again, he is intervening in the Elkins debate). Quasheba is presented as an extraordinary person. She is a strong-willed, own-way woman going about her business in both the secular and the spiritual worlds in which she traffics. She is *exceptional* in many respects: envied by some, feared by others, admired by all. But in her relative powerlessness, she too is obliged to navigate her way precariously through the matrix of injurious coercive relations—the endless possibility of physical violence and humiliating violation— with as practiced a sense as any for playing the expected role of the "enslaved" in order to sustain herself and make the best of her severely limited options. She too can play fool to catch wise. But nothing in her personality suggests that this is all there is to her. Indeed, her self-possession suggests that enslavement is purely *accidental* to who she is, an external fact of her contingent circumstances. She is a self-directed, if not self-determining, woman who *happens* to be enslaved. Not all of her fellow-enslaved are like her; many, perhaps most, are determined—or *overdetermined*—by their enslavement.

Quasheba is an exemplary moral and practical reasoner. She appears to us as a woman forever asking herself what she should do, how she might best achieve the limited ends she has in view (primarily the good of her daughter's welfare and advancement), how she might choose between options that, given the pervasively evil conditions of her life, are not simply unfavorable but in a sense very nearly impossible to positively embrace. The choice Quasheba finally makes is a *tragic* one. Aroused to a righteous rage, her decision to act in the way she does precipitates an unfolding sequence of actions—none of which, once enacted, can be reversed or undone—that lead in the end to her terrible suffering and destruction. As Martha Nussbaum memorably suggests in *The Fragility of Goodness*, there is a grave and frightening and yet ennobling human beauty in certain instances of tragic choice, when an exposed and vulnerable person is compelled to act in the face of desperately inhospitable or brutally cruel and pitiless circumstances.[113] Quasheba knows the odds are not good for her survival if she acts as she thinks she must in defense of the value, the fragile good, in fact the duty, that she feels is absolutely at stake. Yet the question that seems to torment her is not *should* she act but how can she *not* act? So she does act, propelled by passional reason, and for it she pays the price. For Nussbaum, remember, there is a tradition of moral thinking, associated (differently perhaps) with the heritage of Plato and Kant, that believes that autonomy and immunity to the incursion of chance are absolute goods, indeed the only path to the good life. In Quasheba, Patterson shows us an extremity in which a person's aspirations to a human good (the duty to her daughter) is almost entirely circumscribed by forces beyond her control.

230 PART III

Her vulnerability is nearly all that there is, and her moral beauty inheres in the manner in which she accepts the suffering she cannot escape. Patterson, I think would like us to ask ourselves how we should understand Quasheba's dilemma and the reflective consciousness she demonstrates, and what we should make of her as a moral agent navigating the unyielding evil she is up against.

In the episode in which we are made to witness Quasheba agonizingly arrive at the desperate and tragic decision she takes (and it is a moral decision she *makes*, not a spontaneous, let alone random, act), it is notable how Patterson sets up the moral and existential picture of her anguish and the motives that shape the evolution of her conduct. He invites us to witness a relatively brief but catalyzing moment within the lifeworld of a form of sociality, lacking firm legitimacy or standing and therefore avenues for redress and awash with contending moral emotions—helpless anger, empathy, spitefulness, frustrated hatred—that are all constrained and animated by the fact of a barely supportable domination. Quai, an enslaved man on Pickersgill's plantation, Majesty Valley, has come with news for Quasheba about Polly's predicament. Cicero, Quasheba's lover or "husband" (and about whom more in a moment), does not want Quai to recount to her all that Pickersgill has done to punish Polly in his effort get her to have sex with him because Cicero knows it will only inflame Quasheba further. He urges more restraint, but Quasheba insists on hearing everything in all its excruciating detail. With evident irritation, she tells Cicero to keep out of it; Polly, after all, is not his child. And so Quai, taking his own perverse pleasure in observing Quasheba's growing torment, proceeds with his account. First, he says, Polly was relegated to the kitchen, to gather firewood and mind the stove, work so dirty her "pretty brown skin . . . became as black as any saltwater Neager" (27). The kitchen staff, Patterson tells us later, are the lowest and typically the darkest of the household slaves (89). Polly's rival, Desdemona, a mulatto, had earlier been consigned to the kitchen staff at Richmond Vale and "lost caste" as a consequence (90). This kitchen-work punishment was clearly aimed less at harming Polly physically than at breaking her *spiritually*, at destroying her self-esteem—a self-esteem, of course, based on a warped and insecure pride in her place in the hierarchy of color in Jamaica's racial order. But the punishment didn't end there because Polly continued to refuse Pickersgill's sickly advances. Consequently, she was sent to join the washerwomen's gang and even put in the stocks for a day. Still, Quai recounted, she refused to comply with Pickersgill's wishes. And as Quai pauses, we witness Quasheba's visible distress intensify as though she can

SLAVERY'S EVIL LIFEWORLD   231

anticipate what is to come next. Because she remained so unwilling, so noncompliant, Polly was subjected to the ultimate punishment that an enslaved woman of her color and sexual desirability could suffer—she was sent to the field "with a hoe like every other field Neager" (27), and the driver was ordered to beat her as he would other field slaves who fell short on their tasks.

This is more than Quasheba can bear. *This* is the last straw: the *reduction* of Polly to the status of a *mere* field slave. But why? Why is this the irreversible rock bottom for Quasheba? Again, it is not simply her daughter's potential exposure to the *physical* violence of the driver's whip or the onerous hardship of cutting cane that undermines Quasheba's equanimity, her ability to reconcile this punishment to her and her daughter's general status as powerless enslaved women. Rather, it is what Patterson, in *Slavery and Social Death*, would call the "symbolic" violence of the punishment that overwhelms her. It is that this defenseless exposure to the whip and field labor are the very toxic mark of the *degradation* and *dishonor* of the enslaved, a degradation and dishonor from which she had sought, against almost impossible odds, to shelter her precious daughter. What little maternal pride Quasheba had been able to accumulate in the incongruously distorted hierarchical regime of skin-color value, one of the enduring evils of plantation slavery, what little sense of privileged difference she has been able to win in the viciously and precariously competitive environment *induced* among the enslaved themselves by the ideological apparatus of racial slavery, had now been precipitously, irrevocably undermined, invidiously subverted. Thinking again about my earlier remarks concerning the politics of solidarity, it is notable that Patterson is not concerned here to unfavorably *judge* Quasheba for not standing—say, politically—*against* the color hierarchy to which she and others are subjected, and which she and others have internalized, and within which she is losing her dubious, never entirely assured footing. Her pride, and the conceit it inspires in her, may well be misplaced, Patterson seems to suggest, but they are *all* she possesses, the thin edge of the wedge of the social death she inhabits. Indeed, her fierce and haughty attachment to her pride is a large part of what makes her (ambiguously, it is true) admired by everyone around her—including her enslavers. But it is also what grievously exposes her to the downfall of shame and humiliation. Natal alienation inscribes this inescapable vulnerability in the lifeworld of the enslaved. Quasheba has been grievously *humiliated* by her abject powerlessness to secure the prerogative of a basic maternal legitimacy. She has been made to suffer a ridiculing abasement so undermining that it stands beyond repair.

232   PART III

For the enslaved, Patterson repeatedly suggests, the evil of enslavement lies not only in their continuous exposure to physical brutality but also in their continuous exposure to the symbolic violence of humiliation and dishonor. Nothing demeans, nothing undermines a basic sense of humanity, like the mortification that comes with the abject powerlessness of public humiliation. In several consequential scenes in *Die the Long Day*, a weaponized humiliation is vividly on display—even among the enslaved themselves. Quasheba herself roguishly mobilizes it against her quadroon cousin Benjamin, whom she seduces in order to extract money from him (57–60). But its profound destructive, even psychopathological potency is fully revealed in the case of Chantoba, who is permanently scarred, to the point of madness, in a shocking episode in which the seasoned bookkeeper David, a man of base cynicism whose specialty is making an art of humiliation, deliberately shames her—instead of beating her—when she is caught stealing corn (106–8). This is not Quasheba's fate. To restore a modicum of dignity, to prevent the enslaver's sexual trespass, she acts defiantly and suffers the fatal consequences.[114] Quasheba chooses murder as the defensive exercise of parental virtue.

The institution of slavery has dispossessed Quasheba of her ability to carry out her duty to her daughter. This is the problem of slavery's evil that Patterson highlights: the distortion of a structure of social relations that systemically evacuates the prospect of stable, assured, and heritable obligations between kin. This is one way that the rupture of natal alienation is reproduced. Quasheba's sense of her elementary maternal obligation to her daughter is treated with contempt and disregard. In the context of the total institution of domination she inhabits, she does not have many options by which to right the wrong inflicted on her, by which to achieve justice. No normative institution or apparatus will afford her protections and safeguards or avenues of redress. She has no rights (indeed, to invoke Hannah Arendt, no right to have rights). She has appealed in the required way to the only potential source of relief for the injustice she suffers—the overseer, the effective sovereign—and she has been roundly rebuffed precisely as a reminder that all she is to the powers of enslavement is a racialized slave, a Neager. But what Patterson suggests is that it is precisely in and out of this moral dead-end that, reflectively, perhaps as a matter of learning, Quasheba arrives at the astonishing revelation about herself that she utters to Cicero, that there is a dimension of her being that is equal in value to this dimension in everyone—anyone—else, including her slave masters, that she possesses an intrinsic worthiness that is incomparable, one that she has not acquired but that is simply the gift of her inalienable humanity. She is smaddy. Her self-respect demands that Pickersgill must pay for his transgression of this dimension of her being.

In expressing her defiance, recall that Quasheba says to Cicero (rebutting his entreaty) that yes, she is a "Neager," but she is also "human," and like all humans she can be killed only once (30). This is a profoundly arresting quasi-philosophic statement, and it is worth exploring what Patterson might be inviting us to consider by placing it in Quasheba's mouth at this particular dramatic moment. In a certain sense, this now-familiar phrasing (with its Enlightenment resonances and distinctions) marks her as a conscript of modernity, a dominated subject of modernity's powers who has come into a language of self-description with which to assert an intrinsic value irreducible to her instrumentalized condition as enslaved. It is indeed notable that Quasheba does not disavow her degraded, subservient status as an enslaved Black person, a mere means for a slaveowner's aggrandizement; on the contrary, she readily acknowledges this identity. How could she *not*? Enslavement is her given historical reality. But this social fact of her circumscribed status does not preclude or erase, Quasheba holds, the transcendent quality of what she unconditionally *is* in her personhood—namely, a human being, and therefore a self-evident member of the larger moral family of humanity. The moment has an almost Kantian inflection that I think is deliberate on Patterson's part. Quasheba asserts that her status as enslaved cannot alter the humanity in her person. This is inviolable; she is an embodiment of this moral entitlement, and it is the source of her autonomy and her dignity. In this respect, she is an *end* in herself, and this ontological value takes precedence over her *social* status in her assessment of how she has been wronged, the nature of the harm that has been perpetrated, and the justification therefore of the vengeful action she has set out to commit. It is in her humanity that she has been wronged and, as she suggests to Cicero, it is in her humanity that she will respond.

◆

Instructively, no other enslaved person in the novel is quite like Quasheba in this quality of self-recognition of nonnegotiable personhood; none of them quite rises above their abject condition of a slave, whatever other virtues they may possess. Cicero, for example, offers an illuminating contrast to Quasheba and shows us

234   PART III

a response to another, pervasive side of slavery's evil, the perpetually intrusive shadow of dehumanizing violence. Even though, significantly, Patterson names him after the slave-owning Roman statesman and orator and philosopher of, among other things, dignity (and indeed New World slaves were, often-enough ironically, so named), it is in a sense in Cicero that Patterson takes a sustained look at the complexity of the Quashee personality, that figure of the enslaved who has seemingly accommodated themselves to the evil of enslavement through the internalization of subservience. At first, indeed, Cicero appears not an especially profound character, a "moral simpleton" in Thomas's terminology, hardly an intellectual match for the vividly rebellious Quasheba.[115] He lacks her audacity. Although industrious in his kitchen garden and diligent in his care for his mother and great-aunt, he lives seemingly with no spirit of defiance, in as constrained and cautious and unobtrusive a way as possible, doing the next thing, and then the next thing, in order to carry on within the vicious, mind-numbing context of his enslaved life. But this is not the whole picture, for survival itself may have been the first and most basic act of refusal. Patterson takes care to invest Cicero's seemingly simple-minded acquiescence with existential folds of reflexive self-consciousness that make his character richer and more paradoxical than might otherwise appear to be the case.

When he wakes up on the morning of Quasheba's disappearance, for example, to the stirring, rude intrusion of the loud crack of the driver's whip and the limp, weary crowing of the rooster, Cicero is momentarily seized by an unsettling but vaguely familiar tension. It seems to us scarcely a cognitive moment; it barely rises to the level of what the phenomenologists might call *mindfulness*, that quality of active, oriented self-awareness.[116] It is mute and *almost* entirely embodied. But it is not a state of complete unawareness. It is not lacking in sense-making, even a faint kind of conscious *thoughtfulness*. It is, Patterson writes, "his only conscious response to the reality of his existence *as a slave*: the only time he dared to even think about it and allow himself the freedom of responding naturally to his awareness of what his life meant" (19). The transcendent sensation of freedom passes quickly: "a trained forgetting of what was central to his existence" (20). It is an intriguing and deeply significant description. Notice that Cicero is not woodenly unconscious. To the contrary, Patterson makes him a fully *ethical* self in Michel Foucault's late sense that he has (over the course of time, we can assume) worked on himself in such a way as to produce a mode of being able to cope with the brute reality of his enslavement.[117] Cicero has painfully, painstakingly, *learned* to live as a slave, cultivated the mode of being of a slave. Foucault, perhaps infamously, had only a narrow picture of slavery as an institution of totalizing power and, within it, of the lifeworld of the enslaved, but his idea of "subjectivation" as a self-forming moral activity is not irrelevant here, however constrained the conditions in which it might take place.[118] Cicero has strived (undoubtedly by more *and* less conscious means) to inculcate in himself an active practice of forgetting such that it has now become routine, a *habit*; merely a repetitive dimension of his enslaved *habitus*. But the moral labor of that practice has nevertheless left an indelible (negative) *trace* of precisely what he has sought to forget—namely, the dim awareness of a self whom he *could* but should *not* be, the faintly apprehensible gap between an imagined nonslave self momentarily aroused as he awakens and the self that is in fact, in his conscious reality, enslaved. That possible self merely marks the line that Quasheba, but not Cicero, crossed (indeed, one of the things that attracts Cicero to Quasheba is precisely her willful, ungovernable, *tarrying* with that line). For Patterson, then, Cicero's liminal experience is not utterly, morally, and intellectually vacuous. Yet it is so fleeting, so fugitive, as to have no tangible duration. It just flashes up as an almost involuntary movement in the hollow of Cicero's daybreak awakening, as his mind spontaneously gropes toward consciousness, and has as quickly to be suppressed in order to fend off the crushing reality of what he actually is—namely, a slave. There is, though, Patterson suggests about Cicero, the glimmer of a moral freedom the practice of which is not completely beyond his recognition or reach (some of which we see in the court scene when he comes to Quasheba's aid [130–32]). Perhaps it is in some such shapeless, inarticulate *sense* of unfreedom that Patterson would later, in *Freedom in the Making of Western Culture*, come to see precisely the slave beginnings of the moral story of freedom in Western discourse Cicero, too, is paradigmatic for Patterson.

For accommodation is never-not paradoxical. Cicero routinely plays fool to catch wise. With him it is almost completely habitual. Indeed, the whole ethos of this proverb is spectacularly on display in his encounter with the new bookkeeper, McKenzie, in which the behavioral features of the practice of subservience are brought into play, almost automatically, by coming face-to-face with a figure of plainly banal but absolute power. Seeking information about Quasheba, who has not turned up for work, McKenzie rides up and intercepts Cicero as he leaves the field for his morning breakfast. McKenzie has not yet adapted to the dialogical maneuvers—the "congo saw" or "Negro talk"—that

236 PART III

the enslaved employ in navigating asymmetrical verbal encounters with their enslavers, so he is particularly vulnerable to these devices, and he knows it. Not surprisingly, then, within the first moments of the exchange (if that is what we should call it) the encounter goes completely awry and soon descends into a brutish violence. McKenzie begins, innocently enough he thinks, by asserting "You are Quasheba's paramour, or what I think you call husband." For Cicero however, the sociology of such relationships is much more complicated than is captured in the bookkeeper's reductive terms. Quasheba, he clarifyingly responds, has not *yet* become his "full wife." McKenzie, puzzled, decides to leave this kinship detail aside and goes straight to the point. "Well, where is she?" he demands, barking in a suitably peremptory tone to reaffirm his authority. "Who, Massah?" Cicero answers with seeming guilelessness. "The woman!" the bookkeeper retorts harshly, his temperature clearly rising. "You mean—," Cicero starts to reply. "Yes I mean Quasheba," McKenzie interrupts, with growing, perplexed exasperation. "Ohhh, Quasheba," concedes Cicero cheerfully, as though he has only now realized who the bookkeeper is talking about (71). In Patterson's account, this is Cicero "playing fool to catch wise." His puzzlement and ignorance are a deliberate, practiced pretense. He begs pardon. He shuffles. He accepts that he is no more than a slow, stupid slave. In this way, he marshals the appropriate demeanor of abject, baffled subservience. It is a pretense, yes, but it is also a habit. Noticeably, there is no interval of reflection before the conduct is brought into play.[119]

Needless to say, McKenzie is frustrated and disconcerted by this behavior, because he cannot properly discern whether he is being taken advantage of or whether Cicero's behavior is transparently sincere. Patterson writes: "McKenzie looked down at the babbling creature before him and wondered what to make of him. Was the black serious? Were they really that stupid? But what other explanation was there? It took a lot of cunning and downright nerve for this creature to stand there and consciously try to make a fool of him. He found it difficult to believe that he had the intelligence to be that cunning, or the courage to be that impudent. But if the black was really as stupid as he seemed to be what chance did he have of getting the information he wanted from him?" (72). It is a feature of the kind of near-absolute power that enabled the enslaver to almost completely dominate the enslaved with impunity, Patterson suggests, that also left the enslaver unable to make sense of the lifeworld of the enslaved. The enslaved remained (or, a moral-psychological *dimension* of the enslaved remained), if not passively, then with a kind of negative resolution, impenetrable, impregnable to the enslaver's crude linguistic coercions. In any case, by now in the encounter McKenzie is almost at his wits end. But for the sake of the information about Quasheba he positively needs in order to carry out his duties, he decides he must try again. This is power's blindly obsessive, extractive conceit—and we witness its vulnerability to the slave's own, scarcely negligible counterpowers of opacity. But the situation only gets worse, more inanely convoluted, more hopelessly opaque, more impossible. They are only talking passed each other. And then, precipitously, it is just too much for McKenzie. He loses control. He snaps. As Patterson writes in a revealing passage that captures the extreme perversity of evil: "He looked down at the creature standing before him and hated him. Hated his stupidity. Hated his savagery: his blackness; his dissemblance. He hated him for being part of the reason, perhaps the main reason, why he was tempted to this ghastly island. Most of all he was outraged by his inaccessibility, for the barrier he dared to keep around him by his very subservience." The whole exchange is almost Hegelian in its dialectic of asymmetrical reciprocity, recognition, and dependence: "Without thinking, and with a rage that had never before so consumed him, he held up his whip and lashed the brute. Over and over again he struck him. Cicero groaned, screamed and struggled as the whip cut into his face, his neck, his back and sometimes his hands as he tried to bar the blow" (74).

I return to McKenzie in a moment, but part of what is crucial in the description of this encounter is that while Cicero is feigning dumb incomprehension and so on, Patterson does not present the moral psychology of it as a matter of purely cunning calculation. Not that Cicero is incapable of this (as, again, we see in his exchange with the magistrate when he is seeking to save Quasheba from punishment and thus demonstrate his commitment to her [128–34]). But here he is clearly too distracted by worry about Quasheba's whereabouts to be self-consciously strategic. It is true that when Cicero notices McKenzie approaching him he braces himself for the interrogation he knows is coming, but it is almost an unconscious tightening of his muscles—as Fanon taught us to recognize as an embodied reflex of the colonized.[120] When the exchange begins, there is nothing noticeably premeditated in the style of his linguistic performance. He is not baiting McKenzie, nor goading him. He is not deliberately mocking him either, so far as we can tell. He has not set out to deceive McKenzie. Whatever is motivating Cicero (if *motivation* is the right word here), his behavior is more

238   PART III

or less spontaneous, unformulated. It seems to proceed by way of largely embodied or ingrained sociolinguistic rules of evasion. Thus, notably, after the brutal encounter is over and Cicero recovers himself, such as he can, there is no visible sense of emotional satisfaction or moral triumph at having, say, thwarted the enslaver's wickedness. There is not the merest sense of achievement—or resentment, for that matter. It is a routine response to a banal evil that is part of the lifeworld of the enslaved. Cicero merely staggers on toward his grand-aunt's hut, where she tends his wounds, gives him a reviving salve of rum, and roundly berates him for falling afoul of the bookkeeper McKenzie on account of his foolhardy relationship with that no-good Quasheba. What Patterson is interested in here is the way in which the very *expectation* of violence produces a bodily alertness or anticipation and unselfconsciously activates the appropriate embodied, including verbal, form of response.

Another somewhat more self-conscious version of the practice of playing fool to catch wise can be seen toward the end of the novel in an encounter between the enslaved man, Africanus, and Busha Gregory, the overseer of Richmond Vale, when Africanus is caught attempting to steal a rooster. Africanus is a wise old man, an African, as his name suggests, not a Creole slave as Quasheba and Cicero are. His role in the novel is a mediating and tempering one. He is a trusted healer, even a kind of ethical thinker and ethical teacher, who embodies the best values among the enslaved. There is little he has not seen in his long life. With Africanus, survival is a moral good, a guiding principle—and not just individual survival (though that too) but also the *collective* survival of the enslaved as a whole. A self-conscious practical reasoner, it is the long run that matters to him. As he instructs a young enslaved man given to malingering that is attracting the overseer's attention: "Never stand out. Live like a lizard. Blend so much with every movement. Laugh when the rest laugh. Cry when the rest cry. Be nobody and you remain somebody till your dying day" (51). Or again later, when he counsels Cicero against doing something rash that will get him killed: "You must live. All of us. We must live. No matter what it take, we must live. . . . We must live and bear the burden" (181).

Like everyone else, Africanus is an admirer of Quasheba, of her strength of character as well as her alluring beauty. He once healed her when she was gravely ill, and in thanks she offered him her body, which he gratefully (if, initially, diffidently) accepted. But we really get to know Africanus's moral depth as news of Quasheba's death spreads, and it is heard that Busha Pickersgill—who, it is now known, had set the Maroons on her and ordered them to bring her back dead or alive (160)—is planning to have her body strung up on the side of the road as a lesson to the enslaved and for vultures to pick over (177). The enslaved are collectively outraged at this prospect. It is a deep indignity. It also inspires anxiety and fear because the absence of a proper funeral would mean that Quasheba's damaged and unreconciled spirit will not return home to Africa but restlessly roam the slave village and haunt them. It is imperative, therefore, that she receive the appropriate send-off. Pickersgill has asserted rights to the body even though she is not his property because it is him she tried to kill, and he will not change his mind unless Polly agrees to (voluntarily) give him the sex he wants. But Polly remains steadfast in her refusal. What would her mother have died for if this submission to Pickersgill's demand is to be *her* end? With great authority and subtlety, however, Africanus endeavors to persuade Polly that though her refusal is understandable given Pickersgill's diseased condition, this is not the right moral perspective from which to think about the decision at hand. In life, he says eloquently, Quasheba tried to redress the wrong that had been done both to Polly and to her as Polly's mother; she failed, unfortunately, and she paid a terrible price for that failure. Now in her death her fellow enslaved owe her, minimally, as a matter of common *duty*, the dignity of a safe passage home—whatever it takes, no matter the sacrifice. A responsibility lies with the *community* left behind. It is neither vengeance nor justice, but it is nevertheless necessary and binding for collective moral closure. In the end, Africanus is able to persuade Polly to do what is needed both for the common good of the slave community and for her mother's postmortem journey. And everyone is relieved, including the overseer, Busha Gregory, because this will save him the disruption of discontented slaves and interruption of planting the new cane shoots, and will also win him the favor of his better-off neighbor.

Until this point in the story we see Africanus in his role as a deftly skillful diplomat, principled to a fault. Hardly a "slavish" personality, he is respected by all—enslaved *and* enslavers—on the plantation. But he too has his moral-psychological limits. He too can play fool to catch wise, both for his own purposes and for the collective good. Africanus decides that the rooster to be killed for Quasheba's funeral must come not from his own chicken coop but from the overseer's.

240 PART III

Busha Gregory should be made, in some small measure, to pay for his betrayal of *his* slaves in allowing Busha Pickersgill to dictate the terms of release of Quasheba's body. Only the blood of his prized cock "would feed her soul" (191). Africanus decides he will steal the rooster. For a man with his sense of prudence and circumspection, it is a weighty decision, but once made he has no qualms about carrying it out. He sets off on his mission. Needless to say, he is caught by the night watchman who is startled and dismayed that it is old Africanus he finds in the act of stealing his master's rooster. But curiously, whether it started out like this or not, it soon begins to look as though Africanus was at least prepared to be caught, even *wanted* to be caught, so as to have the opportunity to encounter and deliberately undermine the conceit of his master's racist idea of him and his fellow Blacks (192–93). Indeed, Busha Gregory can hardly believe the watchman when he tells him that Africanus was found in the chicken coop attempting to steal a rooster. Something of his idea of Africanus has been threatened, destabilized. "You're not a slave, Africanus," the overseer had earlier said to him, sentimentally but incongruously, when Africanus had persuaded Polly to sleep with Pickersgill. "Not in my book. You're a slave only in name" (189). But now a more congruent view emerges: "Africanus, am I hearing rightly?" he asks with seeming incredulity. Africanus affirms "almost with a sense of pride" that it is true: "His voice . . . suitably low and shameful, his head hanging. He anticipated the Overseer's anger and waited with subdued impatience." Africanus knows exactly how the abusive discourse will unfold, beginning with the condemnation of his race, and he acts in such a way as to solicit, invite, summon it—not, of course, for the pain but for the sweetness of the infrequently enjoyed power of the powerless. "He waited in eager anticipation for the next course in this rarely savored feast of abuse which he had got his master to serve him." Africanus is a master of the poetics of recognition, of the subversion of the master-slave dialectic. "My God," the overseer blurts out, "I've lived among you no-good black bastards for more years than I care to remember and the more I see of you the more you prove what a lowly, base lot you all are. Look at you, just look at you! A man of your age. A man we all trust" (195). The overseer's genuine shock nicely discloses the delusion that total power is ever omnipotent, omniscient. But it is not over. Africanus is still waiting for the overseer to utter the racist characterization that the occasion really demands. He produces more "slave" behavior, and finally, predictably, Busha Gregory angrily asserts the old sanctimonious racist cant: "Show me a Negro and I'll show you a thief, it's said. And every word of it is true. It's in your blood, you bloody black bastards. You spend a lifetime suppressing it, but like hogs being drawn to a sty it must come out someday. You're a pack of thieving animals, you hear me!" In a sense, Africanus has gotten exactly what he sought: he will presumably walk away with the rooster, and he has demonstrated that if the enslaver can solicit the racial stereotype from the enslaved so the enslaved can solicit the racial stereotype from the enslaver. "As he stood before the angry master going through the motions of servility he felt a deep sense of satisfaction. His soul felt purged of the restlessness that had haunted him all day. He was at rest again" (196).

Not so his master, Busha Gregory. As I have suggested, on many slave plantations in the Caribbean, like the fictive Richmond Vale, the overseer was the dominant figure of White power, the embodiment of the institutional evil of slavery, the virtually sovereign decider in matters concerning the work and punishment and the life and death of the enslaved. Whether or not the overseer was distinctly evil, more evil than warranted to carry out the ordinary functions of the slave plantation within the overall evil climate, he was certainly the principal point of articulation of slavery's evil. Busha Gregory is an undistinguished man, a man of forgettable mediocrity ("one of the many who hadn't made it" [172]). Faced with Africanus's deed, he seems quite unable to get beyond his agitated incomprehension, the exposure of the powerlessness at the center of total power. All he can manage now is to resort to the familiar brute violence stereotypically available to the slave master. He slaps Africanus, who, somewhat theatrically, falls to the ground in a prepared gesture of groveling submissiveness (196).

<hr />

So far we have been looking at the exploration in *Die the Long Day* of the way slavery's institutionalized evils were lived and responded to by the enslaved. We would do well to remind ourselves that in the novel these episodes—involving Quasheba or Cicero or Africanus—are meant to appear as routine, not as spectacular or exceptional but merely as part of the very fabric of a transgenerationally perpetuated structure of domination. But let us turn now to the novel's exploration of the way these evils were embodied and lived and perpetrated by the enslavers. Here I focus on the new bookkeeper, McKenzie, the most developed of the four principal White men who figure in the novel. McKenzie is interesting because he is meant to show a contrast: he is not as self-evidently callous

242   PART III

and mean as his colleague, the other bookkeeper, David; nor is he as self-interestedly cynical or crudely insensitive as Busha Gregory, for whom he works; nor again, is he as wantonly debauched or depraved as Busha Pickersgill. Or, anyway *not yet*. These are White men who are now part of the taken-for-granted world of slavery. McKenzie is meant to be a *thoughtful* man, not generally or typically motivated by base violence or shallow gratification or greed. How, then, should we think of his conduct and character in relation to the wider institutional evil of slavery? The vicious beating to which he subjects Cicero when frustrated by his inability to extract the necessary information from him is indisputably an act of evil wrongdoing, inflicting on the defenseless slave a grave and undeserved harm. But I take there to be a deeper question about the evil of plantation slavery at stake in Patterson's description of McKenzie's behavior in this encounter with Cicero, and also, in a different context, in his tormented encounter with the enchanting mulatto, Desdemona, who is tempting him into a sexual relationship. Should we think of McKenzie himself as evil? Is he an evil *person*? Or is he someone within the range of ordinary moral virtue who has merely succumbed to the moral climate (in Thomas's terms) of wickedness endemic to an evil system? How does someone *become* evil? Does it matter one way or the other for our consideration of the evil of plantation slavery if the perpetrator of an evil act has an evil character, is habitually evil (as John Kekes might say), or has only been incidentally drawn to evil by contingent factors? *Die the Long Day* invites us to consider these moral questions.

McKenzie is new to Jamaica; indeed, he has been there only five weeks. Unlike his colleague David, he has yet to adjust to the norms and customs of slave-plantation society. After fleeing the scene of his fit of explosive and brutish violence inflicted on Cicero, McKenzie rushes home to his cabin and flings himself down on his bed and buries his head in his pillow. That was decidedly not the behavior he expected from himself, a man (as he considers) of evident refinement and Christian civilization. As he tries to pull himself together, though, what he feels is not contrition or regret for what he has done to Cicero but a mild sense of shock at the change that is clearly overcoming *him*. As his fellow Whites have told him, it was bound to happen: the "blacks changed you, whether you wanted to change or not" (80).[121] He has already detected his own gradual "coarsening" as a consequence of Jamaica's moral climate (87). Interestingly here, there is tacit acknowledgment of the wrong he has done to Cicero, but the self-justification is that the corrupting influence comes not from himself or even the mores of the institution but from the enslaved. It is *they* who have brought the evil upon themselves. Self-deception, as Thomas teaches us, is a "handmaiden of evil."[122]

Notably, McKenzie is a Scot (whereas David is an Irishman who, in the racial hierarchy of the colonial imagination, is but a half step from the Blacks).[123] In a familiar story, McKenzie has gone out to the colony to repair his severely damaged fortune. Indeed, one might imagine him reading Edward Long's *History of Jamaica*, which was conceived in part as a means of encouraging those in similar circumstances to partake in the boom of the post-1740s Jamaican slave economy. His father's untimely death meant that he had to give up his pursuit of a law degree at the prestigious University of St. Andrews in Scotland (one of the oldest universities in the English-speaking world) to look for work. Fallen on hard times though he has, McKenzie nevertheless takes himself seriously as an educated man of the rational pedigree of the Scottish Enlightenment, not one of those "vulgar, semiliterate absentee landlords whose ostentation had been the source of much mirth among his friends" (37). Nor would he, presumably, think of himself as quite of the station of his contemporary Thomas Thistlewood, also a man of some learning and few means. Indeed, not insignificantly, McKenzie sees himself as a fierce antagonist of David Hume's views concerning the priority of the passions over reason in governing human behavior. We can imagine, then, that it is with a good deal of resentment toward—and ill humor for—Jamaica, a "hot, steamy, fever-ridden slave camp," that he has left his "beloved Edinburgh" to live "amid a wilderness of alien godless savages and uncouth money-grabbing whites" (36–37). No doubt, he has vowed to keep himself as far away as he can from the insidious and demeaning atmosphere. But, alas, no sooner has he become part of the social life of the plantation than he begins to sense, with a degree of alarm and a sinking feeling of inevitability, the fragility of the armor erected around his civilized self. As he succumbs to the enervating moral climate, he rapidly grows less and less certain of his vaunted immunity to the evil degradation surrounding him, to the temptations to physical violence and sexual violation that he more and more finds irresistible. He has a growing apprehension that soon enough he too will have acquired what his fellow Whites called "the custom of the country" (37)—that is, he too, whether resignedly or with enthusiasm, whether with disgust or pleasure, will have embraced slavery's evils as merely how things just *are* in a slave-plantation society.

Instructively, as a device for opening up his character's interiority for our scrutiny, Patterson has McKenzie keep a personal diary (the convergence and

244 PART III

contrast with Thistlewood is again notable). It is evidence in him of a certain kind of enlightened self-consciousness. McKenzie is not only a man of reason but a man of *reflective* reason, a man in the habit, since St. Andrews, of exposing his soul to self-examination. Still, as the hard weeks in Jamaica wear on, he begins to feel that there is "something incongruous about being a bookkeeper and keeping a diary," a conflict between the "refined habits of a civilized man" that diary-keeping presumed and "his increasing degradation and the continuous blunting of his sensibilities" (81). Now, in the aftermath of the beating he has given to Cicero and having taken an unsettling lunch with his fellow Whites and retiring to his room, McKenzie feels a desperate need to pour his soul into the diary's pages. His steep moral decline—and his self-consciousness of this moral decline—offer him a rare picture into the nature of the slaving civilization of which he has become a part. As he says, with a fervent, almost eloquent lucidity:

> I have never been so confused in all my life. I feel that something awful is happening to me. I am being overcome by something monstrous and evil. Yet I seem unable to do anything to fight against it. At times I seem to be even unconsciously helping it along. It has been said that man is naturally evil, basically depraved. I had never before accepted this view. But now I am beginning to change my mind. We are all evil. The natural state of man does seem to be savagery and the gross indulgence of his passions. It has taken me until now to find out what civilization is all about. It is something which comes between man and himself. Something which emancipates him while it shields him from the chains of his own base passions which would seek always to enslave and destroy him. Now that I live in a land where this shield is absent, it is easy to recognize its worth. (151)

Reason, he now discovers, is no protection against his debased desires. To his chagrin, the suspicion is growing that the poisonous views of the "heretic, David Hume," that "reason does what the passions bid it," might be the unavoidable truth (152). He cannot but acknowledge his twisted obsessive desire for Desdemona (which he eventually consummates in a prolonged and tortured scene of resistance and submission [223–30]). And he candidly reveals that the beating he earlier gave to Cicero has altered his relationship to the enslaved, not only in the sense of removing any inhibition he might hitherto have felt to treating

them *as* slaves but also in the sense of inscribing him uncannily in an inseparable bond *with* them.

> I am no longer able to detach myself from them. In making them my slaves,
> I make myself their master. And being their master seems to have become
> everything. . . . How ironical and absurd it is that being a master should itself
> be a form of enslavement. For this is what I am becoming, just like the rest
> of them. Outwardly, a slave to the very condition I master; inwardly, a slave
> to my passions which comes about as inevitably as death, by the fact that my
> outward enslavement to the role of master destroys the barrier of civiliza-
> tion, leaving me helpless and impotent before the fetters of my base nature.
> (152–53)

In this suggestive Hegelian formulation, Patterson marks the moment of an
emergent dialectic of recognition in which McKenzie crosses a line that all
Whites in slave-plantation Jamaica eventually cross, from being a seemingly
innocent outsider to the constituting subject/object rationalities of plantation
slavery to being an implicated and constituent insider to the mutually inter-
locking shaping of master and slave.

By casting McKenzie's character, educational background, and social circumstances as he does, Patterson suggests a complicated picture of the evil that we
witness him perpetrate. On the face of it, McKenzie is not likely a habitual
evildoer. Perhaps his fictive character would have been morally uninteresting
if he was. McKenzie does not appear to have arrived in Jamaica *motivated* by
a desire to cause any more harm to the enslaved than is already their lot as a
consequence of their enslavement. McKenzie, so it seems, is *corrupted* by the
evil moral climate of the slave plantation. He *becomes* evil, perhaps. Certainly,
in his own eyes he has been *seduced* into evil by social forces larger than himself,
forces he has found, in the end, too overwhelming to resist with his own meager
moral-psychological resources.

And yet, of course, this is not the whole story, Patterson suggests. Acts of
evil, as John Kekes likes to remind us, are performed by human beings—they are
often moral acts perpetrated by actors whose character, by ingrained vices, has
disposed them to evil. Evil, therefore, is never simply reducible to the *external* or
circumstantial conditions in which it occurs. McKenzie's disposition is certainly
such that it is easy to see that he would likely eventually descend into the evil

246   PART III

he misconceives as tempting him. After all, he is drawn to the evil as much as the evil beckons him. He is a dogmatic and racially prejudiced man who, like dogmatic and prejudiced people generally, believes in the absolute sanctity of his dogma and prejudice. Patterson, as I mentioned, makes McKenzie out to be an antagonist of Hume's views on the passions, one who is beginning, perhaps, in the light of his own experience, to revise that blanket hostility. But he was likely in complete agreement with Hume's bigoted views about Black people, as expressed infamously in the 1753 footnote he added to his essay "Of National Characters." One can imagine McKenzie being intrigued, on reflection from Richmond Vale, by Hume's doubts about a certain "negroe" in Jamaica who is said to be "a man of parts and learning; but 'tis likely he is admired for very slender accomplishments, like a parrot, who speaks a few words plainly."[124] Would McKenzie have heard of Francis Williams, the free Black Jamaican poet to whom Hume is here alluding? And if so, what might he have thought of him and his achievements?[125] But even as McKenzie holds his views like an impregnable shield around himself, he is not completely unaware of his inclination to self-deception, that he is protecting himself less against the enemy from without than against his own despised impulses, desires, and suppressed vices. The abstract revulsion he feels against Black people is only amplified and given direction in the context of the slave plantation. Even as he unleashes his ferocity against Cicero and lustfully devours Desdemona, he has a more than dim consciousness that part of what he hates in Cicero and despises in Desdemona comes from within himself—his sense of his own inadequacy and failure, his need for what these enslaved people can afford him in remaking his fortune and self-worth, the negative mirror to his own predatory civilization. Arguably, then, one can read Patterson as suggesting that if there is undoubtedly something about the institutional powers of slavery that corrupts and seduces even the most seemingly steadfast model of a civilized man, then there is also a *readiness* to evil, so to speak, a disposition habituated to prejudice and racial dogma that realizes itself in the abundant opportunities that slavery presented for violence and violation.

Orlando Patterson's *Die the Long Day* is an exploration of the moral psychology of the evildoing and the responses to evil that manifest within the wider context of the routine institutional evil of colonial slave-plantation Jamaica. I have been less concerned with the novel's putative literary value than with the intimate portrait of the phenomenology of the lifeworld of the enslaved it draws, the portrait of the enslaved making and navigating a social and individual life against the backdrop of the form of life of the colonial slave plantation. This fictive phenomenology of a day in the life of the enslaved, as I have said, is informed by the moral sociology of its nonfiction companion, *The Sociology of Slavery*. It is easy to see that fundamental to Patterson's account is the idea that this lifeworld is almost totally dominated by the structuring powers of the plantation; for him, the slave plantation was a total institution, an institution with near sovereign power over the lives of the enslaved—powers capable of coercing, sexually violating, humiliating, mutilating, and killing with relative impunity. Such powers, therefore, severely constrained the arenas in which the enslaved might construct modes of ordinary everyday response. In this context the line between accommodation and refusal was never necessarily transparently clear. Patterson shows that, in its habitual techniques of evasion, seeming docility and stupidity, and impenetrable opacity, playing fool to catch wise was one of these ambiguous linguistic techniques of the self that were learned (or invented) by the enslaved to navigate the continuous threats of violence and violation in every encounter with representatives of White plantation power. Every enslaved person was obliged to some degree to learn to live with what playing fool to catch wise enabled and disabled. But there were exceptions. Quasheba was one. In the context of a structure so total, so overwhelming, and so relentless as New World plantation slavery, where can the moral psychological resources come from to refuse even the ironic gesture involved in playing fool to catch wise? This is the question *Die the Long Day* asks us to ponder. Quasheba shows that she had learned how to grovel in subservience like any slave. But she also shows that there may be a line, more an internal moral line having to do with the dignity and humanity of her person than an explicitly political line to do with her social emancipation, a line, moreover, not always definitive or conclusive or foreseeable but a line nevertheless beyond which carrying on as enslaved simply becomes no longer humanly supportable.

To sum up: Contemporary theorists of evil are right to think of evil as not merely action or character that is recognizably bad. Evil, they urge, is more than ordinary wrongdoing. Their differences aside (differences that turn on the role they assign, for example, to character or agency or circumstances), such theorists agree that evil constitutes a distinctly pernicious and destructive quality of action

248   PART III

that strikes at the heart of human being, at the integrity of a basic mutually
recognizable sense of human well-being and human flourishing. But we have
also learned, especially from moral theorists such as Claudia Card and Laurence
Thomas who have thought about *atrocities* as a distinctive category of evil, that
the evil in human action need not necessarily be solely individual or autonomous
or interpersonal, it need not reside only in the action of one person in relation
to another. Individuals, as individuals, certainly *commit* and certainly *suffer* evil,
but sometimes they commit and suffer evil not only by—or in—themselves as
individuals but also *collectively* in the context of evil societies or evil structures or
evil institutions. Such evil takes place, as has been argued, within pervasive moral
climates that encourage or at least fail to discourage one group of people perpetrating ongoing harm on another group of people (in the name of race or ethnic-
ity or religion or some such ideology of collective identification or vilification).
For such moral climates of evil to perpetuate themselves, of course, for them to
produce and reproduce their effects, they have to be *embedded* in structures and
institutions—that is, inscribed in asymmetrical social, economic, and political
relations of domination. Again, such systemic and institutional evils need not
always be *spectacular* in manifest form—murders, rapes, mutilations, and so on.
They may not take the form of events that stand out against the background of
what is taken for granted within such institutions. Precisely because they are
systemic and institutional, such evil is often embedded in *routine* actions and
relations (that is, actions and relations that have come, over time, to be routine,
if no less coercive for their routinization and naturalization), sometimes barely
visible, coming even to be assumed by actors (perpetrators and victims) as simply
part of the given form of life. The evil in this case is not incidental or contingent.
It does not depend on whether there are particular agents who dramatize or
magnify the evil, the adepts, so to speak, who more than others embody the vices
that characterize the social and moral relation. In some historical instances, such
systems and institutions have not been transformed by evil; they are *founded* in
evil, and *for* evil. Such institutions are sometimes not transitory, emerging and
disappearing within the temporal duration, say, of a generation or less. Sometimes
they are in fact *the* basic institution that *constitutes* a form of life for groups of
people over multiple overlapping generations. Here we are tempted to speak not
only of an evil institution but also (with Laurence Thomas) an evil *society*. And
this longevity is basic to the harm that these institutions and systems perpetrate
and perpetuate. Where this kind of evil is concerned, the evil suffered is not

only—is perhaps not even primarily—the evil of physical abuse and violation but also the spiritual evil of the harm done to a basic sense of dignity and self-worth. The historical example of New World slavery confirms this.

I've been saying in this chapter that the work of Orlando Patterson gives us some language with which to articulate the systemic and transgenerational institutional evil embodied in New World slavery. Although he does not mobilize the conceptual idiom of evil systematically, I argue that a good deal of his work—the novels as well as the sociological monographs—is shaped by a pronouncedly moral preoccupation, in particular with power and its social and social-psychological modes of domination. For Patterson, New World slavery was, first and foremost, a moral and material structure of coercion built on generations of systemic and symbolic violence and violation. On his account, this structure of domination was nothing less than catastrophic, in a *foundational* and *continuous* way, as much for those kidnapped into its system through the transatlantic slave trade, and so deprived of a prior experience of freedom, as for those born on the plantations of the Americas and whose idea of freedom would consequently have to be imagined against their enslavement. As I have understood them, Patterson's central questions concerning slavery's powers have been persistent and enduring, in the monographs from *The Sociology of Slavery* through *Slavery and Social Death* to *Freedom in the Making of Western Culture* and in the novel *Die the Long Day*. His later theory of natal alienation and the social death to which it subjected the enslaved is, in a sense, only his most elaborate and *general* way of framing his discussion of slavery's powers and the resources with which enslaved life constituted itself. What is insidious about natal alienation is that by radically and permanently rupturing the collective heritability of the past and the norms and forms—that is, the embodied traditions—of social and familial and cultural organization that enable such pasts to structure an authoritative coherent lifeworld in the present (including the imagination of dependable futures), it forever impoverished the social, cultural, and moral psychological lives of the enslaved—both those kidnapped from their African villages and held captive at the coasts to be transported across the Middle Passage into enslavement and those born into the institution and who therefore knew no other form of life but that of plantation slavery. Simply put, an institution so organized that it systematically and deliberately produced and reproduced natal alienation across multiple generations is an evil institution, and when that institution is the central shaping force in a social formation, it makes for an evil society—whatever the moral character of those

250   PART III

who actually owned or managed the plantations and the enslaved and those who governed the polities that framed and legitimized these activities.

Moreover, as I have suggested, the questions about New World slavery's material and moral powers and the responses of the enslaved that have animated Patterson's work are questions with at least one recognizable provenance in a founding debate concerning colonial and postcolonial Jamaica. This is why, I believe, the historical instance of Jamaica has been both substantive and figurative for his imagination of slavery. Eighteenth-century colonial slave-plantation Jamaica was as close to a *total* slave formation as one might imagine, a more or less closed structure of authoritarian governance. Patterson asks: How might we best imagine what conditions of subjectification—or what conditions of personality formation—such total authoritarian structures imposed and induced? What modes of response did they encourage in the enslaved? These were Stanley Elkins's questions as well, but they are scarcely questions that animate the contemporary historiography of New World slavery. I think they *should*. I have suggested that, above all, Quasheba, the unforgettable tragic protagonist of *Die the Long Day*, is quintessential for Patterson, simultaneously embodying the evil relations of slavery as well as their *refusal*. For in Quasheba we see an enslaved woman whose basic sense of herself as the protector of her girl-child has been violated beyond repair and who arrives at an irreversible decision to refuse to accept any longer what she has been made into, to choose her dignity even if it means to sacrifice her life. It is not revolution; it is not even an incitement to social rebellion. It is an individual quest. But in the flash of Quasheba's momentary *experience* of freedom—in the categorical denunciation of the evil to which she was subjected and the existential affirmation of her humanity—she gives birth to a fleeting idea and an unstable possibility. For Patterson, she is not merely a marginal figure through whom a local instance of enslavement can be characterized but also a seminal figure through whom, arguably, one iteration of the world-historical problem of freedom emerges.

CHAPTER 5

EVIL ENRICHMENT

EUROPE'S COLONIAL SLAVE DEBT

New World slavery was not only a structure of distorting and dehumanizing social relations of power *within* the slave plantation colonies—an internal structure of evil social relations of degrading power that undermined the capacity of those enslaved to live flourishing individual and collective lives, let alone the lives their forebears had lived (see chapter 4). It was also a generative and transformative dimension of an evil *colonial* relation integral to the making of the modern capitalist world as a whole. New World slavery, in other words, was no mere appendage to the emerging modern capitalist world order of the eighteenth century; it was at least one significant dimension of the dynamic process that stimulated and drove that world-historical emergence. New World slavery was integrally and not contingently or incidentally connected to that modern capitalist world, and consequently it cannot be separated or extracted from its moral and political story. In this context, New World slavery was a source not only of the opulent (sometimes generationally class transformative) wealth of individual slave traders and slaveholders (and the merchant and other commercial interests involved in the far-flung slavery business) but also of the spectacular enrichment of the modern European states and societies involved in the slaving enterprise. What New World slavery produced was identifiable, heritable private wealth that enriched specific families through the generations; but it was also the basis for a generalized (if unevenly, unequally accessible) wealth of institutional and infrastructural development and diversity (governmental, civic, recreational, educational, religious, artistic, and economic) in European polities.

252 PART III

However, this well-enough-known historical fact captures only a part of what is important about the colonial relations of power in which New World slavery was instituted and reproduced. It leaves out a central *dynamic* of that power. New World slavery was not just a dimension—even a leading dimension—of modern capitalist development. More significantly, it was historically structured into the commercial capitalist world in an *asymmetrical* relationship between the dominant European centers of capital investment, accumulation, and expansion and the colonial peripheries of resource and labor extraction. Colonial metropolis and colonial periphery were constituted in an *inverse* relationship. The magnificent splendor of Europe enabled by the profits from the slave trade and plantation slavery was but *one* side of an internally interconnected formation, the other side of which was the misery and want and totalizing violence of plantation societies in the colonies. Brutal labor extraction at one end of the colonial chain was realized as fabulous profits at the other. New World slavery, in other words, was an atrocity in Claudia Card's sense (discussed earlier), but this atrocity was not instituted and sustained by itself in the colonies for their benefit. It was instituted and sustained by an evil colonial *relationship* that guaranteed the enrichment of Europe at the expense of the colonial periphery. The questions that shape my concern, then, are these: What should be the contemporary moral-political implications of this historical colonial relationship of evil? What moral responsibilities and obligations of redress should follow from the historical wrong of colonial slavery? What is owed by the former slave powers to the postcolonial states of the former enslaved? Moreover, from the reflective consciousness of our postcolonial present, how should we think (or rather, *rethink*) the anticolonial response to the colonial slave past—that is, the moral-political demand that seemed to *follow* from the anticolonial construction of the problem about colonial historiography and that forms an authoritative dimension of the Caribbean intellectual tradition we have inherited?

It is well known—or it *should* be—that part of the moral-political point of the intervention that C. L. R. James makes in *The Black Jacobins* is to reverse a familiar European historiographical conceit concerning the *sources* and *vector* of world-historical development and world-historical relevance. Arguably, until the publication of James's pioneering book in 1938, the common assumption was that such development and relevance *emanated* from the European capitals of the colonial enterprise (London and Paris, most especially) out toward the backward colonial peripheries. Seen from the perspective of Europe, it was the colonial centers that *made* these colonial peripheries and accorded them *value*. These peripheries, so it was assumed, would not have had a measurable worth were it not for the moral-material substance imparted to them by the colonial system. A crucial part of the point of *The Black Jacobins* is to subvert precisely this racialized, *racist*, colonial presumption. James aims to underscore that the colonial slave plantation economies of the West Indies were not merely integrated into the European centers of the emerging modern capitalist order but that the latter were in fact *dependent* upon the former, not the other way around. It is not Europe, in other words, that facilitated the development and relevance of the colonies but rather the slave colonies that enabled the emergence and enrichment of modern Europe. It is by extracting resources from the colonies that Europe produced its phenomenal wealth. James makes the point sharply in an often overlooked or unexamined passage in *The Black Jacobins* that in fact opens the preface to the first edition of the book. Here is what James writes:

> In 1789 the French West Indian colony of San Domingo supplied two-thirds of the overseas trade of France and was the greatest individual marked for the European slave-trade. It was an integral part of the economic life of the age, the greatest colony in the world, the pride of France, and the envy of every other imperialist nation. The whole structure rested on the labour of half-a-million slaves.[1]

What is James trying to do in drawing this picture of the *relationship* between slavery in Saint-Domingue and the wealth and splendor of eighteenth-century France? What should we name as the colonial provocation to which his pointed assertion of a perverse asymmetry might be construed as an anticolonial answer? And what, for James, are the moral-political implications of this gross structure of exploitation? Contrary to the shibboleths of the hegemonic story told by imperial history, far from France being its own sui generis invention, it is the enslaved African labor in the plantation colony of Saint-Domingue that produced a significant share of its prosperity and power, that provided the basis from which its greatness emerged. Moreover, James suggests, what those half a million enslaved people in Saint-Domingue made possible, or more precisely, what was brutally extracted from their exhausted bodies, was not simply the fantastic fortunes of various *individual* slaveholders but also the dispersed and *generalized* infrastructural wealth of the modern capitalist world as a whole.

254 PART III

Now, admittedly, though *The Black Jacobins* certainly sheds light on the centrality of the economic factors shaping the relation between Saint-Domingue and France, it is not here specifically that the book made its historic anticolonial mark. Rather, in the narrative he constructs of his great hero, Toussaint Louverture, James is more focused on responding to another dimension of the wider colonial historiographical disavowal, to the effect that the enslaved played no significant role in the destruction of the slave system, that their emancipation was a European humanitarian gift, a boon altruistically given, not a right fought for and taken. That is, for the revolutionary James, the moral-political rejoinder to this colonial denial of the liberationist agency of the enslaved was a vindicationist account of the struggle of the colonized for the right of self-rule. This is the telos of *The Black Jacobins*.

But if James had formulated the crux of the anticolonial problem, the argument concerning the role of West Indian slavery in the development of European capitalist modernity was, famously, developed in a sustained way by his former student and erstwhile friend and political associate Eric Williams in his book *Capitalism and Slavery*, published in 1944.[2] *The Black Jacobins* and *Capitalism and Slavery* are two of the great inaugural texts (perhaps *the* two great inaugural texts) in the anglophone Caribbean intellectual tradition inasmuch as in them the *anticolonial* problem about colonialism—or more precisely, the anticolonial problem about colonial *slavery*—is first formulated in a way that continues to be recognizable and even *resonant* today. They pried open an intellectual-political door, and not just on account of the incisive political-economic critiques of colonial power in the Caribbean they offered. Rather, *The Black Jacobins* and *Capitalism and Slavery* are what they are—namely, formative anticolonial interventions—because they *refused*, with penetrating vision and eloquently indignant voice, the marginality to which the Caribbean had been relegated, and *retold* the story of the Caribbean as world-historical, as a fundamentally inaugural dimension of the making of the modern world in which, therefore, enslaved Black Caribbean subjects were not miserable, minor supplicants but principal participants in a modern global world. In so doing, they helped to shape the radical anticolonial demands on the colonial present they wrote against. This is why there is no critical reconsideration of Caribbean pasts (certainly not Caribbean slave pasts) in relation to possible alternative Caribbean futures that isn't obliged to refer to their stage-setting formulations. And yet, of course, the relation between the respective arguments of *The Black Jacobins* and *Capitalism and Slavery*, and the moral-political implications that can be drawn from these arguments, are anything but uncomplicated. They are not identical interventions. In a sense, though written within roughly the same Caribbean anticolonial conjuncture or problem-space of questions—concerning the hegemony of the colonial historiography that authoritatively mapped the past-in-the-present of the Caribbean, that constructed a picture of the problem about the Caribbean—*The Black Jacobins* and *Capitalism and Slavery* offered different, indeed perhaps even *rival*, perspectives on how to respond to it. *The Black Jacobins* and *Capitalism and Slavery* are companions, kin of a sort but antagonistic ones; they are at once deeply, richly interconnected and yet as deeply and richly divergent, simultaneously joined at the hip and yet at variance with each other.

Needless to say, the contrasts and resemblances between *The Black Jacobins* and *Capitalism and Slavery* have a good deal to do with the temperamental and ideological contrasts and resemblances between their respective authors, C. L. R. James and Eric Williams. Born in Trinidad ten years apart, in 1901 and 1911, respectively, and of similar lower-middle-class social backgrounds, James and Williams belong to an early conjuncture in the formation of an anglophone Caribbean intellectual tradition. They stand in the shadow of their eminent countryman, the late-nineteenth-century figure John Jacob Thomas (c. 1840–1889), schoolmaster, scholar, and civil servant, whose indignant takedown of the racist pretensions of James Anthony Froude—*Froudacity*—was published in 1889.[3] *The Black Jacobins* and *Capitalism and Slavery* can be read in genealogical relation to Thomas's book and the tradition of critique it inaugurates. James and Williams knew each other from early in their lives, and they would go on to have a complex, intense, and competitive intellectual-political relationship. Their trajectories were both similar and contrasting, both intersecting and diverging.[4] Each left colonial Trinidad for metropolitan England in 1932, one for life as a writer (very soon to evolve into a revolutionary political thinker and organizer), the other to pursue an academic degree. For both, England (where they appear to have met regularly) would be a site of rapid and tremendous intellectual-political learning and transformation.[5] Then, at the end of the 1930s, they each left Old World England for the New World of the United States (James in 1938 after the publication of *The Black Jacobins* and Williams in 1939 the year after defending his dissertation)—again traveling along connected but significantly different paths: James for New York and the battlefield of Trotskyist and Black political writing and work, and Williams for Washington, D.C., and an academic position

256   PART III

at Howard University. The United States, where they resumed their apparently warm friendship, offered an environment of possibilities and constraints significantly different from those in colonial England, and not least because of its racial history and racial politics. Each would leave the United States under contrasting circumstances (James back to England in 1953, under Cold War immigration pressure, and Williams back to Trinidad in 1947, to continue his work for the Caribbean Commission), but they connected again when James returned to Trinidad in 1958 at Williams's invitation to participate in the nationalist project under the leadership of his People's National Movement. Here, alas, their always latent disagreements and conflicts, their contrasting temperaments and political orientations, led to a final break, with James returning to England in 1960.[6] It marked the end of a remarkable intellectual association.

In later years, James and Williams would offer different appreciations and assessments of the other, not least with respect to their already famous books. On James's account (offered in an interview published in 1972), he had had, from early on, a sort of mentoring relation with the younger Williams.[7] He had not only played a formative role in shaping Williams's scholarly direction but had given him the basic outline of his doctoral dissertation. Here is how James puts it in a not implausible description:

Williams used to come to my house in London and spend his vacations with me. Frequently I used to go up to Oxford and spend some time with him. When, working on *The Black Jacobins*, I went to France to do work there (investigating documents and so on), Williams would go with me. I knew him very well and he knew me well. . . . Then he came to me, as he usually did, asking me questions. He said: "I am to do a doctorate. What shall I write on?" That was very plain. I told him, "I know exactly what you should write on. I have done the economic basis of slavery emancipation as it was in France. But that has never been done in Great Britain, and Britain is wide open for it. A lot of people think the British showed good will. There were lots of people who had good will, but it was the basis, the economic basis that allowed the good will to function." He said, "Do you think that will be good?" I said, "Fine." He said, "Well, what shall I say?" I said, "Give me some paper!" and I sat down and wrote what the thesis should be with my own hand, and I gave it to him. He must have copied it down, and took it to the Oxford authorities. Later he told me they said it was fine. And he went on from there. I saw the manuscript quite often, I read it about three or four times. The facts themselves and the road he was to take, I wrote that for him. I don't see why I shouldn't say that now, it isn't a crime on my part.[8]

It is a quite extraordinary account. There is the sound in it of grievance and wounded indignation. But it is hard to imagine that Williams did not learn a lot from James; and it is easy to understand that James would resent the excision of his presence from the intellectual life of the younger but clearly now more powerful man.

Indeed, Williams seems to have been determined to erase any trace of James's influence on his intellectual-political formation. In the mid- to late 1960s, by then prime minister of an independent Trinidad and Tobago, Williams offered less an account of his personal relationship with James than a reflection on James's intellectual contribution. Notably, there is no hint of friendship or political association. Intriguingly, in his memoir *Inward Hunger*, in his fond recollections of Queen's Royal College he makes no mention at all of James, among either his teachers or his acquaintances.[9] He does, however, offer a sharp and revealing contrast between his own preoccupations and orientations and those of James and George Padmore, both of whom, Williams says, had basically deserted the West Indies—Padmore for Africa, and James for "the absurdities of world revolution."[10] Between the wars, Williams writes in *British Historians and the West Indies*, published shortly before the memoir, three exceptional West Indian anticolonial writers had emerged—all, as it happened, from Trinidad—to fundamentally challenge the shape of British colonial historiography: he names himself along with James and Padmore. They were the "trinity" of Trinidadians who would reconceive the problem about colonial history. Of the three, Williams writes, only *he* had completely devoted himself to the West Indies. Although he praised James's *The Black Jacobins* as the book that "rescued" the Haitian Revolution and Toussaint Louverture from historical oblivion and offered one of the "first challenges to the British interpretation of the abolition of the slave system," he nevertheless goes on to underline that this was merely the exception to an otherwise almost irrelevant intellectual life. However important *The Black Jacobins* was on its own, Williams writes, this "incursion into West Indian history was only a temporary deviation from the author's preoccupation with Marxism and the world revolution that was so confidently expected in the Bloomsbury set of the thirties."[11] Bloomsbury here signifies a certain vacuous infatuation with

258   PART III

radicalism associated with the cosmopolitan and radical writers—among them, Virginia Woolf, Leonard Woolf, Maynard Keynes, E. M. Forster, and Lytton Stratchey—who met in the Bloomsbury district in London's West End and with whom James was associated.[12] Williams felt that he, James, and Padmore were indeed exemplary cosmopolitan and radical Trinidadians, but only he was the *authentic* West Indian because only he had used that cosmopolitan experience to shed light on specifically West Indian affairs. As Williams puts it (speaking of himself in the third person), "Where James and Padmore forsook the West Indian backyard for the international stage, Williams sought to illuminate the West Indian scene by international experience." And in this respect he saw *Capitalism and Slavery* as a more radical intervention than *The Black Jacobins*. And not insignificantly, in his view, he suffered for it. He continues: "The full force of British hostility was reserved for Williams, himself a product of Oxford, as a rebel against the British historical tradition which Oxford had done so much to develop."[13] Indeed, such was this hostility that even James's radical publisher, Frederic Warburg, refused to touch the dissertation, saying, according to Williams, "I would never publish such a book. It is contrary to the British tradition!"[14] For Williams, in other words, something of what he was doing, and what he represented as an anticolonial rebel, went more deeply or more dissonantly against the grain of the culture of colonialism than the pronouncements and activities of his seemingly more revolutionary countrymen, James and Padmore.

This is hyperbole, of course, though not without a measure of truth, and it highlights something important, at least for our purposes—something perhaps of lasting relevance for successive generations of the Caribbean intellectual tradition. It is true that neither James nor Padmore, though anticolonial in political perspective, were nationalists of the sort that Williams was. They were anti-imperialists as much as anticolonialists, with an *internationalist* orientation formed by an antibourgeois Marxist heritage. And in this sense, arguably, *Capitalism and Slavery* was inscribed more narrowly than *The Black Jacobins* in the specific contours of Caribbean anticolonial nationalism.

In this chapter, my aim is to reflect on the anticolonial assertion that, structurally, European prosperity rested on the labor of colonial slaves in the West Indies. My focus will be on *Capitalism and Slavery*. Although neglected for many years after its initial publication (a complicated story in itself), *Capitalism and Slavery* is now the subject of a good deal of scholarly discussion and debate. Perhaps not surprisingly, much of this discussion (the so-called Williams debate) has concerned itself with the plausibility or historical accuracy of what are seen as its central empirical claims: one, that the slave-trade-driven commercial capitalism (or mercantilism) of the seventeenth and eighteenth centuries provided the primitive capital accumulation for the emergence of nineteenth-century industrial capitalism; two, that this rise of industrial capitalism and its ideology of free trade in turn undermined the importance of the monopoly system in which slavery was embedded and helped to precipitate its decline; and three, that it was this and not the moralizing of the abolitionists that was the crucial factor in bringing down the slave trade in 1807 and West Indian slavery itself between 1834 and 1838. I do not discount this debate, but in contrast with its protagonists, I am less interested in the plausibility or otherwise of the central historical theses of *Capitalism and Slavery* than in the moral-political *project* in which the book's claims are embedded, the anticolonial *historiographic* intervention it is making.

In an instructive essay of a number of years ago, the African American economic historian William Darity Jr. raised the question of whether one could speak of a "distinctly West Indian viewpoint in the historiographical literature on slavery," and more specifically whether or to what extent Eric Williams had contributed to this perspective.[15] Is there a "Caribbean School" of thought on slavery? he asks. To my mind, Darity has been one of the most sensitive commentators on Williams's *Capitalism and Slavery*. Certainly, he is one of the few North Atlantic interpreters of Williams to bother to recognize that there may be other contexts than the "Williams debate" that matter for understanding what *Capitalism and Slavery* is all about. Indeed, in the course of a number of insightful essays, Darity has been concerned less to defend or criticize Williams's argument than to situate it in its historical and conceptual contexts. This seems to me a refreshing approach. Darity's question about a Caribbean School is clearly allied to mine but not identical to it. I, too, would argue that there is a Caribbean intellectual tradition of questions concerning slavery. But notably, what Darity aims to reconstruct is really what he takes to be the "antecedents" to *Capitalism and Slavery*, the ideas out of which it might have emerged, and what he finds in the end is that the "central theses" of the book "do not have an exclusively West Indian origin."[16] Fair enough. Importantly, for example,

Darity shows how the work of Abram Harris and his student, Wilson Williams, developed a conception of the contribution of Africa and New World Blacks to capitalism that Williams very likely knew of and that very likely influenced him. However, I am not sure how exactly one establishes such exclusive origins.[17] Like Darity (to whom I return later), I am interested in what Williams might have been reading as well as the contexts in which he might have been reading. But what I am aiming to understand is not whether his perspective is uniquely West Indian but what the (anticolonial) moral-politics is that shapes his concerns. Whatever else it is, *Capitalism and Slavery* is also a *polemic* against a founding constitutive presumption of imperial historiography—namely, the presumption that erases the presence of the Black enslaved and their material contribution to the making and, more, the prosperity of the empire, and with that erasure, the disavowal of any moral-political responsibility and historical obligation on the part of Britain. As I will argue, *Capitalism and Slavery* is a book about conjunctures of crisis and how shifts in moral and political thinking emerge in relation to changes in material circumstances. It is as much a book about historical processes as about the moral-political *imagination* of history; it is as much a book about the slave past as such as about the colonial *present* from which Williams is writing and the implications for the postcolonial *future* he aspires to and is writing toward.

My agenda in what follows is relatively restricted. To begin, I will partially reconstruct the problem-space of *Capitalism and Slavery* and, in particular, aspects of the distance Williams traveled between his Oxford University doctoral dissertation submitted in 1938 (and only recently published), *The Economic Aspect of the Abolition of the West Indian Slave Trade and Slavery*, and his *Capitalism and Slavery* that appeared six years later.[18] What was the distinctive question that *Capitalism and Slavery* aimed to answer? What was the problem about the prevailing colonial historiography of the Caribbean past, and the Caribbean slavery past especially, that animated and propelled Eric Williams in the wake of the completion of the dissertation and his departure for the United States?

Second, I will reconstruct aspects of the rhetorical structure of *Capitalism and Slavery*. What is its tropic economy and to what *effect* does it work? I will suggest that in contrast to the plot of Romantic vindicationism of James's *The Black Jacobins*, for example, it is the poetic trope of *irony* (parodic irony, often) that prefigures the conceptual-political work of *Capitalism and Slavery*. The question is: What is irony *doing* in Williams's argument about the relationship between West Indian slavery and European capitalism? My overall aim in these two directions is to think about the horizon of politics in relation to which Williams's book should be understood. Although the anticolonial Williams understood the colonial relation between the slave plantation peripheries and the European metropolitan centers as a relationship of *debt*—in other words, that something was *owed* in respect of what had been usurped or wrongly taken—it is a significant fact that that something was sovereignty, not reparation, at least as understood today. What are the implications of the fact that *Capitalism and Slavery* was informed by, and in turn informed, a *sovereignty* project and not a reparatory one? Obviously it is imperative to read and explicate Williams's book in terms of his own anticolonial conjuncture, but what is entailed in *rereading* it in a conjuncture in which this sovereignty project no longer defines a plausible moral-political horizon? What might it mean to read *Capitalism and Slavery* for its implications for a moral-political present shaped by a reparatory claim on the colonial slave past?

In this context, third, I offer a brief critical discussion of the first formal attempt to write an explicitly reparatory Caribbean history—namely, Hilary Beckles's *Britain's Black Debt*, published in 2013. Beckles thinks of his book as situated in the Caribbean historiographical tradition of Eric Williams, and this is fair enough as far as it goes. But how far is that? *Britain's Black Debt* is a flawed book, in argument as well as execution. However, it has the virtue of offering us an excellent opportunity to think aloud about how Caribbean reparatory histories might link pasts of atrocity to presents as a matter of historical responsibility and moral-political obligation. In its human rights framing (however thinly articulated), *Britain's Black Debt* makes an argument on specifically *juridical* premises—namely, the illegality of slavery—and it asserts on this basis the justification in international law to make a legal claim in the International Criminal Court at The Hague against the perpetration of the historic crime of slavery. Besides the ambiguity surrounding the formal status of West Indian slavery as a crime in British positive law in the eighteenth century, it will be worth wondering whether in the political context of the contemporary Caribbean the liberal legalism that underlies Beckles's commitments—and the elite, neoliberal regimes that shelter them—can have much more than a symbolic or palliative effect on the material and spiritual legacies of colonial slavery. Perhaps what is needed is to rethink both reparation and sovereignty in relation to each other.

262   PART III

THE PROBLEM-SPACE OF *CAPITALISM AND SLAVERY*

What is the problem-space of *Capitalism and Slavery*? What were the shaping provocations that it can be read as responding to? What questions—about colonial power, say, or slavery or race—is it an answer to? Notice that I am not asking what the substantive *theses* are that Williams advances in *Capitalism and Slavery*, which are the preoccupation of those involved in the Williams debate. These, too, are important questions, but in my view they should be considered in relation to the *prior* question concerning the problem-space that motivated and propelled Williams's research agenda and the moral-political horizon of his critical project. Needless to say, there are multiple contexts of intelligibility in relation to which *Capitalism and Slavery* can be situated. Necessarily, in what follows I will not only be both brief and schematic but also selective, inasmuch as *my* excavating questions about Williams's questions are shaped by the reparatory provocations, so far as I can make them out, that animate my own problem-space (see chapter 1).

Perhaps the first context of intelligibility of note concerns the colonial and anticolonial context of the British West Indies, and in particular of Trinidad, in the early decades of the twentieth century, that marks out the contours of Williams's early intellectual formation. Trinidad, a relatively late British colonial acquisition (formalized in 1802 by the Treaty of Amiens), was incorporated into the empire as a Crown Colony, ruled directly from Britain through its appointed colonial governor. Crown Colony rule, perhaps more so than the older "representative" regimes of colonial government, such as in Barbados and Jamaica, was designed, as Gordon K. Lewis suggests, to stifle local political initiative, not to speak of anticolonial dissent. Trinidad, in the early twentieth century, he says, was "in almost every sense, the perfect model of a colonialist body politic."[19] Still, in the years following World War I, and not least in response to the shock of naked racial discrimination experienced by the loyal soldiers of the West India Regiment, organized expressions of anticolonial discontent began more systematically to emerge. In Port of Spain in the 1920s and early 1930s, this incipient social and political protest centered on the remarkable figure of Andrew A. Cipriani, the "Captain," as he was affectionately called, and about whom C. L. R. James would write an admiring portrait in his fledgling attempt to urge a politics of self-government in Trinidad.[20] Cipriani, a White Trinidadian of Corsican descent, became the defiant and self-proclaimed champion of the "barefoot man," attacking various forms of discrimination and demanding social and political reforms. But as Lewis maintains, Cipriani was perhaps less against colonialism as such than against its unenlightened practice; and in the 1930s, his old-style Tory radicalism would be displaced by the more aggressive Black working-class politics of Uriah Butler.[21] Certainly, this inchoate atmosphere of discontent and challenge to the colonial status quo would have directly entered Williams's family household through his father's friendship with the great Grenadian patriot, T. A. Marryshow, who, notably, was Williams's godfather and perhaps an early mentor of sorts. Williams remembers him taking an interest in his future plans.[22] Moreover, alongside and entangled with this political public sphere there also emerged a literary-cultural public sphere, notably around Alfred Mendes, Albert Gomes, Ralph de Boissière, and James. In 1929, Gomes and James launched the short-lived literary magazine *Trinidad*, devoted primarily to the publication of short fiction. And in 1931, Gomes, James, and Mendes introduced the sturdier more politically mature magazine the *Beacon*.[23] In his memoir, Williams, who was no cultural illiterate, takes no notice of these developments in describing the environment of his youth. However, it is clear enough that Williams was growing into adolescence in a world being reshaped by an incipient oppositional intellectual culture of colonial discontent and self-redefinition in which there was not only a growing resentment at colonial exclusions but also a marked self-consciousness of colonial deceit, hypocrisy, and disavowal concerning the hegemonic story of colonialism.

Williams was born in 1911 into the aspiring Black Catholic lower-middle class in Port of Spain, a class constrained on all sides by a lack of the social and financial resources necessary for advancement.[24] His father was a postal clerk who doubled as an accountant on the side, and his mother, was a homemaker who baked and sold cakes to help make ends meet. As the eldest child, Williams was drafted as "principal assistant" to both his mother and father. With a seemingly ever-expanding family, the Williamses, like other families of their social class fragment, lived in a chronic state of economic precarity and with an acute sensitivity toward the racial exclusion, humiliation, and marginalization to which they were constantly exposed. They lived the ambiguous moral pain of thwarted Black aspiration. In such a context, the only narrow path of social mobility (principally into the professions) was education, and Williams's parents spared no sacrifice to enable their eldest son to avail himself of every opportunity. Williams, a clearly motivated and independent-minded "young colonial," made good, moving from

264   PART III

the study disciplines at Tranquility to the rigors of the prestigious Queen's Roya
College, a secondary school, as he put it later, that equipped him better than any
English public school could have done for his coming success at Oxford.[25]

To his father's disappointment, Williams had decided early on to pursue the
study of history at university, and the island scholarship he won in 1931 took him
to Oxford University and into the heartland of British imperial history. During
the years when Williams was a student at Oxford (1932–1938), the leading expo-
nent of the study of imperial history was Sir Reginald Coupland (1884–1952). As
Williams put it, Coupland was the very embodiment of the "tradition of British
historiography as established in the nineteenth century by [Bishop William]
Stubbs in particular, sharpening this tradition in order to face the increasing
criticism to which imperialism was subjected" in the early twentieth century.[26]
Under Coupland, imperial history came of age as a respectable dimension of the
wider discipline of British history, as a means by which to refurbish the image
of the project and purpose of the British Empire. Coupland had been appointed
Beit Professor of Colonial History at Oxford in 1920, succeeding Hugh Egerton,
who had held the post since 1905. Although Coupland had not published much,
there was an expectation that he would bring a "first-class mind" to thinking
about the empire in a moment of imperial doubt and the early stirrings of the
anticolonial demand for self-government. And indeed, Coupland did not disap-
point. An "Edwardian of sensibility and imagination," as J. D. Fage writes with
sympathy and without irony, Coupland sincerely believed in Britain's moral
responsibility to the "backward peoples of the Empire."[27] The interwar years have
been referred to as "the Coupland era in imperial history" because he bestrode
those years with a magisterial air of vision and vocation, concerning himself not
only with the West Indies but also with East Africa and India (as well as with
Britain).[28] Moreover, Coupland was not merely a passive academic scholar of
colonial history lecturing to undergraduates. To the contrary, he busied himself
with the practical affairs of the empire, with the recruitment of students into the
colonial service, and with his own contributions to colonial assessment and policy: he was a member of royal commissions on India (1923–24) and on Palestine
(1936–37). In 1936 he visited Trinidad, where he delivered the inaugural lecture
for the Historical Society of Trinidad and Tobago, titled, notably, "The Value
of History."[29] "Coupland was an idealist," Wm. Roger Lewis writes. "He believed
in the moral capacity of the British Empire to shape a better world and to help
dependent peoples to advance toward self-government. He was almost, but not

quite, as unabashed as Macaulay in believing in the history of the Empire as the story of unfolding liberty."[30] Or, as Fage puts it, in similar tones:

> Although [Coupland] had lived into the period in which imperial policy was mainly concerned with the transition from colonial dependency to self-government, and although he himself helped in this shift of policy, he was not one to believe that imperialism was generically evil. He retained his belief that a nation as wealthy, as strong, as advanced, as was Britain in the Victorian and Edwardian eras, had a moral duty to aid less fortunate peoples, and that sometimes this duty could only be fulfilled by interference in, or control of their affairs.[31]

Coupland clearly saw the imperial project as a grand benevolent act of humanity. It may not be hard to imagine, then, that it was precisely this colonial conceit of empire as a progressive humanitarian endeavor bearing the gift of a civilizing freedom to the backward natives, without the merest reflection on the contribution of these natives to imperial wealth, strength, and advancement, that would have fueled the intellectual outrage of a colonized subject such as the young Williams. Nor should it be surprising, given his assumption of a tough but essential benevolence, that Coupland would be much embittered by what he perceived to be, as Frederick Madden writes, "Williams's personal attack on him in *Capitalism and Slavery*."[32]

Where the West Indies is concerned, Coupland had made himself a specialist on the history of the slave abolition movement and in particular of its great hero, William Wilberforce. Coupland's *Wilberforce*, perhaps his inaugural statement on imperial history, was published in 1923, but it is his general study of the abolition movement, *The British Anti-Slavery Movement*, that offered an overall account of slavery and the great moral struggle against it.[33] *The British Anti-Slavery Movement* has its origin in a series of lectures Coupland gave at the Lowell Institute in Boston in 1933, significantly the centenary of the Abolition Act and a year of celebration in Bristol and Liverpool, as well as in Wilberforce's birthplace, Hull.[34] For Coupland, antislavery was the heroic campaign against "the greatest crime in history," one he describes with a certain sensitivity for the material as well as moral harms it inflicted on Africans and their descendants (and also on Whites, he occasionally adds). At the same time, notably, Coupland wrote from within the familiar White supremacist sensibility of early twentieth-century scientific racism, in which Africans were savages and brutes—and therefore, quite understandably (but, still, unjustifiably), *enslavable*. Africans, Coupland tells us nonchalantly, had been "secluded" from the main "stream of civilization" to be found in Europe and Asia, isolated in a tropical environment that had made it "easy for them to live, but difficult to do more." "Here and there," he continues, "a vigorous tribe attained a substantial measure of military and even political organization; but there was nothing remotely comparable with the social and cultural achievements of Europe and Asia." It is not surprising, then, that "the great mass of Africans . . . stayed sunk in primitive barbarism, the most backward of all the major races of men."[35] With no social or cultural accomplishments to their credit, Blacks had only one thing to recommend them, their capacity to labor. Here again is Coupland:

> To more fortunate and forward folk in other continents they seemed at first contact little more than animals; and centuries were to pass before they were allowed the opportunity of proving their capacity to take their place in the march of human progress. But in one thing, it seemed from the outset, they excelled—in their physical strength. They could work, or be made to work with a whip, both hard and long. If slaves were needed, therefore, they provided the ideal material.[36]

Moreover, it was said, Africans already practiced slavery. It was a "normal feature of African life," and African tribal chiefs had no qualms about providing slaves to European traders from among their own people, or about acquiring slaves by raiding their neighboring villages.[37] So, in the course of time, a whole network of slave-trading was established to nourish the European demand.

Against this background, the story of the antislavery movement that unfolds is that of the progressively achieved realization within British public opinion and parliamentary politics in the late eighteenth and early nineteenth centuries that slavery was a grievous wrong that had to be ended. The fact, Coupland writes in a voice of contrition, that the slave trade and slavery were "not only tolerated but more or less actively supported by public opinion in all the maritime states of Western Europe for three or four hundred years and were only abandoned at last in the course of the nineteenth century" is a "startling comment on the process of civilization."[38] That Britain could have "suffered" such a system to exist is not a story to be looked back upon with pride but rather with surprise and incredulity.

It is a past that can be explained, Coupland offers, only by the fact that "modern humanitarianism' was only just emerging in the mid- to late eighteenth century. Furthermore, he holds, the ordinary Englishman was too far removed from proximity to the actual scenes of slavery: "He did not see the slave-ships on the 'Middle Passage,' nor hear the cracking of the whips which called the slaves to work on the plantations."[39] The whole project of the "Emancipators" was to effect an enlightening change on this situation, such that, over the course of a relatively short span of a few decades "educated Englishmen were learning more and more about Slavery and becoming for the most part more and more averse to it."[40] For Coupland, it was left only for the right man to appear who could translate this great upswell of popular antislavery consciousness into a sharply articulated parliamentary opposition in order to secure the necessary legislation for abolition. And of course, by a remarkable coincidence, such a man indeed appeared at just the right time in the incomparable person of William Wilberforce.

From here on, in Coupland's narrative, the generative spine of the story of slave abolition is largely that of the singularity of Wilberforce—his dynamic strength of character, his passionate eloquence in the House of Commons, his willing sacrifice of health and money, and his undaunted sense of the righteousness of his purpose.[41] The first plank of this purpose, the Bill for the Abolition of the Slave Trade, was finally accomplished in 1807. But while the abolition of the slave trade was in itself a great achievement, it was only the first stage of what was perceived by the Emancipators (Coupland maintains) as a wider campaign against the entire system of slavery. Although Wilberforce was now retired from parliamentary leadership of the campaign (which had passed to Thomas Fowell Buxton) and in failing health, he was undeterred by attacks from the weakening but still effective proslavery lobby and the intransigence of the Jamaica House of Assembly, and remained committed to the ultimate goal. As is well known, James Stephen, son of a famous father in the abolitionist movement and the legal advisor to Colonial Secretary Edward Stanley, "drafted the Bill in two days and a half—one of the two sole occasions in his life on which, true child of the 'Clapham Sect,' he consented to work on Sunday."[42] Introduced on July 5, the Slavery Abolition Act became law on August 29, 1833. "By a dramatic coincidence," Coupland writes of this climactic moment, "the great veteran of the cause lay dying." His life's work was accomplished, and he could leave this world with a just sense of satisfaction. "Thank God," Coupland quotes the unimpeachable abolitionist "Saint" as saying—in moral triumph, notably, not irony—a few

268 PART III

days before his lamentable death on July 29, 1833, "that I should have lived to witness a day in which England is willing to give twenty millions sterling for the abolition of Slavery."[43] The Act for the Abolition of Slavery would go into effect on August 1, 1834, and with this chapter the central focus of Coupland's story comes to an end. The remainder of his book is concerned with the extension of the campaign for the abolition of the foreign slave trade and of slavery itself beyond the British Empire.

Here, then, in Coupland's *The British Anti-Slavery Movement*, was the authoritative story of the abolition of the British slave trade and British West Indian slavery that defined the discursive space with which Eric Williams was faced in Oxford in the 1930s. It purported to show the leading role not only of abolitionism in the destruction of the whole slavery enterprise but also of abolitionism itself as the expression of a pure humanitarian ideal that animated the inner ethos of the imperial project. In it, imperial Britain emerged as a paragon of virtue, an exemplary proponent of the highest principles of moral conduct, blemished perhaps, as paragons often are, and therefore not completely blameless, but nevertheless unmistakable in the overall benevolence of its motivations and magnanimity of its powers. Understandably, as the story of the making of the Black Caribbean world out of which Williams came in the early twentieth century, it was not only a historiographical conceit but also a moral-political outrage: casually racist, insolently superior, resolutely complacent, laughably superficial, and incongruously self-congratulatory. For Williams, the history of empire, certainly the part of the empire in which he was condemned to be a colonial subject and in which, consequently, he had a stake, could scarcely be the Whiggish story of a steadily unfolding liberty.[44]

In the closing pages of his exculpatory introduction to the second edition of *The British Anti-Slavery Movement*, Fage turns to what he calls, in a somewhat wounded way, the "savage attack" on Coupland and his book "contained in Eric Williams's *Capitalism and Slavery*." "Dr. Williams," he writes, drawing a revealing (perhaps unselfconscious) contrast, "is a distinguished Negro scholar who was later to become Prime Minister of his native Trinidad." The book he wrote, Fage continues, with strained resentment at the evident ingratitude, was "to a large extent the result of research done in Coupland's own university."[45] Fage then goes some way in seeking to determine where each—Coupland and Williams—might have been right and ends on the following illuminating reflection on their contrasting perspectives:

> Looking back twenty or more years, one may wonder why Dr. Williams felt impelled to attack Coupland and his book so directly. There seems to have been an underlying lack of sympathy and understanding. Perhaps this was inevitable in the late 1930s and early 1940s when a young Negro radical from the colonies, still more one from the bitterly depressed West Indies, found himself working in the shadow of the school of imperial history that Coupland had established within the calm walls of Oxford University. In reality there was no argument. Each man was right to write as he did. Williams and Coupland were neither writing about the same thing nor writing the same kind of history. Williams was examining the place of Negro slavery in British economic history and, as an economic historian, believed that it was economic forces which determined political and moral attitudes. Coupland, on the other hand, was a historian of the British empire, whose approach to history . . . was through the individual. He was not writing a book on slavery or the slave trade, nor indeed on the ultimate reasons for the abolition of these things. His subject was the *campaign* of a group of Britons for their abolition.[46]

It is hard to say whether Fage is simply being disingenuous here, as though Coupland and Williams merely occupied different perspectives that might (as he says a moment later) in the end be reconciled. What would the rationale be for the sort of "sympathy" Fage finds missing in Williams? Notably, Fage has nothing to say about the unblushing racism that informs Coupland's book. He rightly senses the *offense* that the book has caused the "young Negro radical from the colonies," but he does not wish to imagine the basis for this. He does not wish to recognize the internal and not external—that is, the *systemic*—relationship between the "bitterly depressed West Indies" and what was capable of being established "within the calm walls of Oxford University." He can reflect only that Williams lacked the appropriate measure of grateful appreciation for what he was able to achieve at "Coupland's own university," without so much as a momentary reflection on Oxford's relationship to slavery, to the Barbados slaveowner Christopher Codrington, for a start. For him, Williams's *Capitalism* and *Slavery* is straightforwardly a *motivated* history, whereas Coupland's *British Anti-Slavery Movement* represents the equable and dispassionate account of an unquestionably worthy dimension of Britain's past. By contrast, for Williams, of course, Coupland's was not an innocent but a "romantic" account meant to offer to a British audience a self-applauding narrative of enduring moral goodness.[47] It was, in effect, an egregiously *ideological* story inasmuch as it disavowed the complex history of material enrichment and economic transformation that provided one, at least, of the *conditions* for the success of the abolitionists. It was as though now that the enslaved had served their economic purpose and, even more, now that they were hindering further enrichment and transformation, the institution of slavery could be done away with and the new ideologues of humanitarianism righteously assume the mantle of the historic defenders of freedom and, in the process, put the sordid past the West Indies represented out of mind. Coupland's book, in other words, served to absolve Britain's imperial conscience of the moral sin of its mode of enrichment—as though the evil of slavery had been redeemed by the admitted humanitarian sacrifices of the Saints in the story of abolition, Wilberforce first among them. The debt to Blacks had been paid in full, and the book on slavery's past in Britain's present could now be closed forever.[48]

In late 1938, Williams defended his doctoral dissertation at Oxford University. "The Economic Aspects of the Abolition of the West Indian Slave Trade and Slavery," as it is titled, was written under the supervision of Vincent Harlow, the author of books on seventeenth-century Barbados and the slave-owner and patron Christopher Codrington. It is often assumed by Williams scholars and others that the 1944 *Capitalism and Slavery* is merely the revised and published version of the dissertation, but this is not exactly so. Its recent publication (edited by Dale Tomich and introduced by William Darity Jr., both distinguished scholars of Williams) allows us now to better glean the convergences and divergences in concerns and structure between the two. The tone and phrasing of *The Economic Aspects of the Abolition of the West Indian Slave Trade and Slavery*, though eminently Williams, is more muted than that of *Capitalism and Slavery*; there is a constrained voice of academic earnestness and decorum in the former that, in the latter, more directly political, even polemical, will by and large be dispensed with. Furthermore, the dissertation has a narrower historical field of focus—namely, the factors involved in the abolition of the slave trade and slavery (with one section devoted to each)—rather than the rise and fall of the whole institution of slavery in relation to the story of capitalism. Indeed, significantly, "capitalism," as a political-economic and ideological category, is virtually absent from the dissertation.[49] Not surprisingly, *Economic Aspects* takes aim at the argument, chiefly associated with Reginald Coupland, that abolition was largely the result of the formidable and righteous battle waged by the humanitarians against the evil of the slave trade and slavery. Coupland himself could scarcely be avoided. Importantly, he participated in the dissertation *viva* and appears to have even offered words of praise for it. But there is evidence that Williams had been under considerable pressure from Harlow to mute the critique of the humanitarian argument, and of Coupland specifically, or at least to give some credence to their influence.[50] Thus Williams's case is carefully and cautiously made, less by frontally attacking the humanitarian apology than by demonstrating how without the economic forces the humanitarians could not have succeeded. Still, the economic argument is pointedly and unmistakably made. Attacks on the slave trade and slavery were not themselves new, Williams argues. Enlightenment European thinkers such as Rousseau and Montesquieu had excoriated both but to no avail—a claim that, memorably, James makes too.[51] This is because, Williams urged, too many "vested interests" had powerful economic stakes in continuing the institution for these humanitarian appeals to have a material impact. The abolitionists, Williams notes, with a certain mischievous intent to demonstrate the complicity of the humanitarian with the economic dimensions, had somehow to win over or neutralize these vested interests, and in the process "they were forced to accept the assistance of men who were actuated by the more sordid motives of gain and self-interest, and whose adhesion to the abolition campaign did much to sully the 'bona fides' of the humanitarian group."[52] Williams even quotes Thomas Clarkson, one of the humanitarians for whom he had great respect, as a guide to his own account. The dissertation is thus offered as a study of these material and self-interested motives that undergirded and secured the success of the humanitarians.

As I suggested earlier, over the years William Darity Jr. has been one of the most discerning commentators on Williams's *Capitalism and Slavery*. It is not surprising, then, that he has been at the forefront of the discussion about the relation between the now-published dissertation, *Economic Aspects*, and the book *Capitalism and Slavery*—the discussion concerning whether Williams *changed* his mind on the causes of abolition between the one and the other. In particular, in his introduction to *Economic Aspects*, Darity has taken issue with the historian

272   PART III

Howard Temperley, apparently one of the first scholars to take up in public the relation between these two texts and to do so with a mind to commending the dissertation and condemning the book.[53] For Temperley, a "new orthodoxy" of economic determinism based on Williams had displaced the old orthodoxy based on Coupland—or, as he cleverly annexed Elsa Goveia (the doyenne of West Indian historiography) to his cause, a new shibboleth had come to replace the old.[54] Temperley urged that there was a sharp distinction to be drawn between the presentation of the abolition argument in the dissertation, where humanitarianism is supposed to have been given a balanced and judicious role in bringing down the slave trade and slavery, and *Capitalism and Slavery*, where it is marginalized and treated dismissively. "Looking simply at Williams's dissertation," Temperley writes in the published version of his argument, "one would be justified in concluding that the author's intention was to supplement rather than to challenge the then prevailing interpretation" of the contribution of the Saints in the story of abolition.[55] As one can well imagine, Darity is incensed by this, seeing Temperley as little more than an apologist for the abolitionist position, especially because a good deal of Temperley's argument consists of seeking to rescue Coupland from the ignominy in which Williams had placed him. Indeed, Darity's suspicion is deeper still—that Temperley's is an ideologically overdetermined, not to say dishonest, reading of Williams, one often enough shared by scholars of otherwise impeccable stature and prestige.[56] "I demur," Darity writes, with a certain amount of irritation in response to Temperley's claim. "There is no difference between the abolition thesis presented in the dissertation and in *Capitalism and Slavery*; while the dissertation, unsurprisingly, is more subdued in tone and less colorful rhetorically—it is, after all, a *dissertation*—the substance of the analysis is identical."[57] Or again, in the closing sentence of his introduction: "As Williams would have had it, both in the pages of his doctoral dissertation and in the pages of *Capitalism and Slavery*, humanitarianism was merely the glove cloaking the icy calculus of British imperialism."[58]

Now, plainly, this is an iteration of the Williams debate that bloats the archive on *Capitalism and Slavery*, and I have no interest in being caught up in it. However, there is something instructive to notice here in the seeming divergence between Temperley and Darity that amounts, alas, to more of a convergence. I think Darity is perhaps right that Temperley has an ideological agenda—namely, to discredit *Capitalism and Slavery* and so perhaps to breathe new life into the old orthodoxy about the humanitarian champions of abolition. Darity is skeptical of this because he holds the countervailing interpretive position in the same debate. But I also wonder whether, in seeking to shield Williams from this attack as he does, Darity doesn't *inadvertently* obscure a crucial sense in which, as Tomich puts it in his preface to *Economic Aspects*, "the dissertation does indeed present the same argument as the book, . . . but it is a different *work*" than *Capitalism and Slavery*.[59] I think *this* is right too. To my mind, paradoxically, in his very attempt to reduce and even ridicule the scholarly significance of *Capitalism and Slavery*, Temperley pays it the backhanded compliment of seeing it for precisely what it is—namely, a *political* intervention and not simply an academic treatise. "What makes the case Williams presents [in *Capitalism and Slavery*] compelling," says Temperley in what he believes is a clinching dismissal, "is not the evidence he cites, which singularly fails to support the large claims he makes, or the logic of his arguments, since these on closer examination turn out to be incompatible, but the power of the rhetoric with which it is presented. Far from being a straightforward work of history as it might at first sight appear, *Capitalism and Slavery* is, in fact, a polemical work of great subtlety and passion."[60] Temperley recognizes, even of course as he deplores it that, "what is most notable about Williams's treatment of the abolitionists . . . is not the details . . but the rhetorical strategy he adopts."[61] (Curiously, though he seems to sense that this is precisely Goveia's point in "New Shibboleths for Old," he does not reach more deeply into the character of her admonishing critique of *British Historians and the West Indies*, in which she draws out the Williams who rhetorically affects to be concerned with one topic while really writing about another.[62])

However troubling the *direction* of Temperley's reading of the rhetorical virtues of Williams's work may be to more radical sensibilities (the negative value he attaches to its polemical character), he has put his finger on the simple salient point that, as Hayden White would have put it, as a work of historical knowledge *Capitalism and Slavery* consists of a verbal structure in the form of a narrative prose discourse and should be analyzed as such in relation to both its manifest character and purpose and its *effective* latent poetics.[63] I will return to White in a moment to help me think about the specific poetics of Williams's book, but the important point to appreciate here is that *Capitalism and Slavery* not only has a wider concern than the true causes of abolition (the central problematic of the dissertation) but also is the work of a militant anticolonial intellectual with a

274   PART III

moral-political-rhetorical—rather than a merely professionally academic—ambi-tion with respect to the Caribbean.

The six years between the submission of the academically formidable but politically (relatively) benign dissertation in late 1938 and the publication of *Capitalism and Slavery* in 1944 were years of significant *political* reorientation for Eric Williams, now no longer a student and looking to his own future. If he was already an anticolonial intellectual before the war (in Trinidad and later in Britain), the new post-PhD context of the racial United States, the problem of democracy provoked by the war against Nazism, and labor and nationalist developments in the West Indies itself gave that anticolonial politics an impetus and a direction that it did not have before. The seemingly rapid rewriting of the manuscript that would become *Capitalism and Slavery* cannot be divorced from this conjuncture. From a narrowly defined account of the economic aspects of slavery abolition, it became a wider story about the relation between the history of capitalism and the rise and fall of slavery (which amounted, therefore, to a his-tory of the relation between the systemic and exponential growth of individual and British prosperity, on the one hand, and the degradation and immiseration of the enslaved, on the other). Much of the story of these years is well known, told autobiographically by Williams himself in *Inward Hunger*, as well as by his biographers, and therefore I make no effort to be comprehensive or exhaustive.[64] I only want to map enough of this conjuncture to tease out some salient elements that, arguably, shaped the new horizon of Williams's thinking—and, indeed, his actions, for part of what is shifting in these yeas is that he is becoming not just a man of intellectual ideas but also a man of driven *political activity*.

Even before his Oxford *viva*, Williams would have been acutely aware of the labor unrest that was sweeping the British West Indies in the 1930s and in par-ticular tuned in to the formation in Jamaica, in September 1938, of the Peoples' National Party, the explicit nationalist aim of which was constitutional reform in the direction of self-government. It would be another decade and a half before Williams himself formed such a political party and made the formal plunge into nationalist politics, but these events certainly shifted the character of anticolo-nial dissent away from the mildly critical politics of Cipriani and Marryshow or even the agitational militancy of Butler. The demand for political democracy was now on the agenda across the Caribbean.[65] For Williams, however, the political question of Caribbean futures would take shape in the context of his move to the United States. Having defended his thesis, Williams was, to his chagrin, unable to secure an academic position in England; more bitterly, neither was he able (as I have mentioned) to interest a publisher in the manuscript of the dissertation. The United States, it turned out, offered better prospects for both. In mid-1939 he was offered the post of assistant professor of social and political science at Howard University, the "Negro Oxford," as he would call it, starting in the fall of that year. Thus, like James, if for different reasons (the one political, the other academic), Williams would spend the war years in the United States—and both he and James, again differently, would be engaged not only by the contrast with colonial Britain in intellectual atmosphere but also by the form of racial politics they encountered. Moreover, the position at Howard afforded Williams the opportunity to meet major Black intellectuals, among them the economist Ralph Bunche, the sociologist E. Franklin Frazier, the historian Rayford Logan, and above all, the philosopher Alain Locke, "an old Oxford man himself" who was connected to both Black literary-cultural life and Black civil rights politics.[66] Once in the United States too, Williams was able to establish fruitful contact with two historians of the British West Indies whose ideas were closer to his own way of thinking about the slave past (or at least unencumbered by British imperial attitudes to history)—Lowell Ragatz and Frank Pitman, both of whom would be crucial for his landing a book contract with the University of North Carolina Press for the manuscript of *Capitalism and Slavery*.[67]

The U.S. context afforded not only research opportunities but also a new context for thinking about Caribbean futures. In late 1940 (with the surrender of France to Hitler's armies and as the fall of Britain now seemed eminently possible) the U.S. and British governments signed an agreement according to which Franklin Roosevelt's administration would send Winston Churchill warships in return for land rights in British possessions for U.S. air and naval bases. This brought a U.S. military presence directly and materially into the Caribbean, indeed into Trinidad most prominently. But one of the results of this increased cooperation between the United States and Britain in relation to the Caribbean was the formation in March 1942 of the Anglo-American Caribbean Commission whose objective was to coordinate social and economic policy on the region. Williams, who saw an opportunity here to have an influence on emerging directions, almost immediately offered his services and

276   PART III

was soon (though not without some pressures and controversies) appointed to the commission.[68] Whatever his political ambitions were prior to his arrival in the United States, the new context shifted his overall sense of himself more and more in the direction of the relationship between his historical scholarship and policy and political action.

These dimensions of Williams's new problem-space come together in the short book *The Negro in the Caribbean*, which he assembled in 1942 in response to an invitation by Alain Locke to contribute to his Bronze Booklet series.[69] An index of the increasing U.S. strategic interest in Caribbean affairs, Williams had received support from the Julius Rosenwald Fund to enable him to travel to the Caribbean in the Summer of 1940—specifically, to Cuba, Puerto Rico, the Dominican Republic, and Haiti.[70] The trip allowed him to better acquaint himself with parts of the Caribbean he knew less well, and it made *The Negro in the Caribbean* a book not merely focused on the anglophone Caribbean but with a wider more comprehensive reach.[71] *The Negro in the Caribbean* is a much neglected book, but it seems to me an indispensable part of the context for thinking about the project of *Capitalism and Slavery* because in it Williams directly links the problem about the slave past that the latter book delineates to the political and economic *future* of the Caribbean.

After a sort of topical survey of the archipelago of islands (covering such matters as size, demographic features, agricultural products, and so on), Williams turns in the second chapter of *The Negro in the Caribbean* to the "slavery background" common to all the Caribbean. And here Williams introduces a theme that, though absent from the dissertation, will open *Capitalism and Slavery*—namely, the relation between race and slavery, undoubtedly an issue of particular feeling among people of African descent in the racist Americas (and certainly an especially acute issue for U.S. African Americans in the context of which, of course, Williams was writing). The African slave trade ("the greatest migration in recorded history") and the institution of plantation slavery it fed was a moral outrage that stood on an economic basis. Having destroyed the Native population and settled on a large-scale monocrop agricultural direction, the colonial powers recognized that a ready source of labor was required. It was the economics of labor, not the ideology of racial inferiority, that prompted the initiation of African slavery. Williams writes (the rhetorical form of the sentence suggesting the argument in which he is engaged): "This great inhumanity of man to man had its origins not in contempt for blacks or in any belief that the black man was destined for slavery. These were later rationalizations invented to justify what was in its origin basically an economic question, one which can be explained in one word—Sugar."[72] Here, in a sense, is the source of the *problem* Williams is confronted with: sugar is the crucial link in a colonial chain that holds the Caribbean in thrall. It is sugar that produced slavery. It is sugar that produced economic dependence externally and economic misery internally. It is sugar that structured racial domination within the plantation economy. Whether the enslaved were emancipated from below (as in Haiti) or from above (as in the British West Indies), they remained at the mercy of sugar. Thus, for Williams, in *The Negro in the Caribbean* as well as in *Capitalism and Slavery*, quite apart from the historical error of thinking that the ideology of race preceded the economics of slavery, what the prioritization of the former occluded was the recognition of the powers that sustained the latter—namely, the preeminence of sugar in the regime of capital.

Central to Williams's moral-political point is that because sugar would not have been possible without slavery, and sugar was a key to European wealth in the seventeenth and eighteenth centuries, the enslaved had made a large, indeed "disproportionate," contribution to the prosperity of Western civilization. This simple fact, he argues, has gone unacknowledged, has been systematically "forgotten" (he may as well have said been *repressed* or *disavowed*, to add implicating force to the claim). If, Williams says, it was sugar that made the West Indian islands "the most precious colonies known to the Western world up to the nineteenth century," then it was "the Negro, without whom the islands would have remained uncultivated and might as well have been at the bottom of the sea, who made these islands into the prizes of war and diplomacy, coveted by the statesmen of all nations."[73] Therefore, European colonizing powers, not to mention the United States, "all are indebted to Negro labor."[74] Here Williams quotes a surprising and illuminating passage from a speech given by Winston Churchill, in which, in a backhanded way, Churchill acknowledges precisely that this is a relationship of debt:

> Our possession of the West Indies, like that of India . . . gave us the strength,
> the support, but especially the capital, the wealth, at a time when no other

278   PART III

European nation possessed such a reserve, which enabled us to come through the great struggles of the Napoleonic Wars, the keen competition of commerce in the 18th and 19th centuries, and enabled us not only to acquire this appendage of possessions which we have, but also to lay the foundation of that commercial and financial leadership which, when the world was young, when everything outside Europe was undeveloped, enabled us to make our great position in the world.[75]

Williams does not tell us this, but Churchill was here addressing West Indies planters in a speech given in July 1939, on the eve of the September 3 declaration of war against Germany.

However, notably, this idea of a moral debt incurred by European colonizing powers as a direct consequence of what Black enslaved labor had made possible for its economic wealth and military strength, though explicit in Williams's mind, remains underdeveloped and fleeting. It certainly does not inform a conception of redress or an obligation to repay what might be materially owed. This is not the language-game in which his argument is conceptually organized. More precisely, what is owed with respect to this historical debt is not reparation but political democracy, and this is the direction of the arc that propels the argument of *The Negro in the Caribbean*. Against the historical background that he has outlined, the future of the Caribbean, Williams asserts, is partly an "internal" and partly an "external" problem. These were obviously connected; one could not be resolved without the other. Where the internal problem is concerned, democracy is required—that is, the right of the inhabitants of these colonial territories to decide their own affairs. "Any solution of the internal problem," Williams writes, "would be meaningless which continues to ignore the extension of full democratic privileges to the Negro."[76] He recognized, of course, as anticolonial intellectuals did in the 1940s and 1950s, that only economic emancipation would preserve the value of political sovereignty. But like all of them he believed that everything depended on the priority of political freedom. He wrote: "Full and unqualified democracy—nothing less. The true Magna Carta of these colonies is economic emancipation, but the road to economic emancipation demands political democracy."[77] The colonial debt, in other words, is charged to the account of sovereignty. In the anticolonial language-game that, like other anticolonial nationalists, Williams's moral-political imagination is implicitly embedded in, it is sovereignty that is the *horizon* of political possibility, or the horizon without which nothing else is possible. Williams is aware that there may be a tension between the nationalist middle-class politics of political responsibility and representation and the working-class politics of social and economic reform, but in his mind these seemingly diverging politics converge in the politics of decolonization from the 1930s onward. The project of the nationalist elite was to take over the reins of power and guide the way to such limited economic reform as was imagined (the essence of "doctor politics"). Arguably, as one can better appreciate in generational retrospect, this was certainly one of the conceits of the nationalist movements and of anticolonial leaders like Eric Williams.

Here, then, in an admittedly summarized and by no means exhaustive sketch, is something of the problem-space in which *Capitalism and Slavery* should be situated: the formative intellectual-political context of late 1920s and early 1930s Port of Spain in which one emerging question was how to frame a historical rationale for the anticolonial demand; the racist disavowals of British imperial history that screened away in the self-congratulatory idiom of abolitionism the gross depredations of colonial slavery and the one-way enrichment it enabled; the explosion of labor unrest across the British West Indies between 1937 and 1938 that triggered an explicit discussion about constitutional decolonization; the explicitly and antagonistically racial context of the United States in the late 1930s and 1940s that nevertheless offered, in the relatively freer academic culture of Howard University and the contact it afforded with radical Black scholars, the opportunity to develop a less constrained political-intellectual argument; the outbreak of the allied war against the racist regime of Nazi Germany, which, fought as it was in the name of democracy and self-determination, helped to undermine the justification for continued British colonial rule; and the Anglo-American Commission that explicitly put the question of the political and economic future of the British West Indies on the table. It is this discursive context, I think, that enables us to connect the historical *content* to the anticolonial *form* of *Capitalism and Slavery* as it was shaped out of the more limited project of the doctoral dissertation.

THE IRONIC STORY-FORM OF *CAPITALISM AND SLAVERY*

Toward the end of his notable introduction to the first British edition of *Capitalism and Slavery*, published in 1964, a full twenty years after the first U.S. edition, the Scottish historian Denis Brogan (who would also introduce Williams's memoir,

280   PART III

Inward Hunger, a few years later) offers the following perceptive remark: "Dr. Williams is no mere debunker, but he is an ironist with an admirably edged style."[78] Brogan was Williams's tutor at Oxford and so perhaps had been able to observe him at relatively close quarters.[79] His elaboration of this discerning comment about his former student's style is admittedly oblique and brief and underdeveloped, going on to refer only to Williams's tendency to an exorbitant language when speaking of persons who, or institutions that, had made their reputations and their fortunes in the shamefully execrable business of slave-trading and slave-owning. Still, it is by no means an indifferent observation. And it is sufficient to point us in a profoundly important direction with respect to *Capitalism and Slavery*—namely, the significance of irony in the constitution of its rhetorical force. Although not always the case, as we have seen (negatively) with Temperley, *Capitalism and Slavery* is most often read as a dry study in straightforward economic history to be assessed in relation to the quality and reliability of its data as opposed to the *form* of its story—which contrasts with the readily appreciated dramatic narrative that carries forward C. L. R. James's epic story of slave revolt. Thus it is largely overlooked that Williams's book is in fact not only replete with ironic turns of phrase and ironic reflections that serve (sometimes humorously) as parodic punctuations to an otherwise stern and relentless narrative, but also, and more pervasively, that it is constituted by a historiographically self-reflexive *story-form*, shaped by Williams's ironist's voice (that "admirably edged style"), that signals to the reader again and again that a good deal *more* or *other* than a pure statement of economic historical facts is at stake in the book, something like a *moral-political* meta-commentary on the accepted clichés and commonplaces of the prevailing imperial historiography.

Indeed, arguably, the very idea of the *economic* as the theoretical register of the determining truth-claims advanced by *Capitalism and Slavery* may very well be understood as part and parcel of the *literary* work of ironic composition in the text, part and parcel, that is to say, of its strategic rhetoric of anticolonial *subversion*. For Williams, remember, the defining trope in the contemporary imperial history of his time was Romanticism, for him the *pejorative* name of a form of willful indifference to, or self-interested disavowal of, the hard, tangible, background facts of slavery. Reginald Coupland was the paradigmatic instance of this moralizing, self-congratulatory Romanticism; Williams's economic history functioned ironically as the subaltern materialist counterpoint to the abolitionists' high-minded idealism. Williams is, in effect, staging a moral-political assault on the positive terrain of the putative economic facts. This is the truth-game, so to speak, into which he has entered, and it will need to be won on the hard, irrefutable ground of these unsentimental facts. Williams's economic determinism, if that is what it is, was by no means naive; it was a self-conscious element in a sophisticated philosophy of history that in fact he outlines at the end of the book.

As a literary-linguistic figure, of course, irony has a complex history, and a complex understanding, that cannot be rehearsed or unpacked here with any degree of comprehensiveness. It has, in any case, already been the subject of a good deal of critical considerations. Memorably, as a work of critical historiography, Hayden White's *Metahistory* turns on a struggle with irony. For White, irony is one of the four master tropes of narrative discourse, along with metaphor, metonymy, and synecdoche. But it is, in a sense, not merely one among equals but *the* most ambiguous and corrosive and perhaps hegemonic trope shaping the precritical or metahistorical *unconscious* of historical awareness. The aim of *Metahistory* is to historicize irony. On White's account, European historical thinking descended into an "ironic condition" at the end of the nineteenth century—in effect, what is generally known as the "crisis of historicism"—a condition from which, despite the great structuralist and poststructuralist wars against historicism (from Claude Lévi-Straus to Michel Foucault), contemporary historical thinking has failed to liberate itself.[80] As White reminds us, the basic, recurrent figurative tactic of the ironic consciousness, emplotted often enough in a satirical narrative form, is *catachresis*, the semantic misuse of words, the deployment of language "designed to inspire Ironic second thoughts about the nature of the thing characterized or the inadequacy of the characterization itself."[81] Irony is a provocation to reflective doubt. Now, for White, irony is linguistically disruptive but politically agnostic. More than this, though, as a figurative agent it tends to lead nowhere beyond itself. The linguistic action it produces is largely the rearguard one of debunking, deflating, discrediting, or anyway controverting received hegemonic discourse. Skepticism and pessimism are its standard postures. In an important sense, White's radical project in *Metahistory* was to find a way to release historical thinking from what Michael Roth famously called the "ironist's cage."[82] Not, notably, by overthrowing it so much as by *internally* subverting it, by being critically self-conscious (rather than naively unaware) of its linguistic-cognitive-ideological operations. *Metahistory* is itself nothing if not a great ironic text. As White puts it, the task is to *turn* an ironic consciousness against irony itself.[83] Whether *Metahistory* achieved its critical ambition to evade

282   PART III

the frustrating, at best anarchistic, relativism of irony has been at the heart of the endless debates about White's work.[84]

Eric Williams was by no means a naive ironist. His aim in *Capitalism and Slavery* was precisely to sow doubt in the authority of colonial historical knowledge, and irony was his master trope delivered in a satirical historical narrative. Thought of as a rhetorical device that registers a contradiction or at least a tension between what is said and what is meant, between the representation and the real, between the fiction and truth, irony is a recognized way of playing with the decidability—and undecidability—of meaning in language. And insofar as this instability and unreliability raise questions about the sincerity and authenticity of verbal performance (whether in speech or writing), irony has always been thought of as having not merely linguistic implications but moral and political ones as well.[85] Certainly, Williams is always saying more than he is literally saying in *Capitalism and Slavery*. A good deal of what has seemed important about irony, from this point of view, is that it can work to expose (sometimes unceremoniously, sometimes subtly), and thereby unsettle, the seeming transparency of dominant or powerful discourses. With all the appearance of granting attention and respect, irony can be an effective indirect way of challenging what is thought to be the ignorance or fraudulence, or again sophistry, of received knowledge. Above all, irony aims at undermining not just error but also *presumption* and *conceit* in the presentation of error as truth. It is the *masquerade* that irony targets. But in addition to this aspect of irony (irony as a rhetorical figure), it has also been important to think of irony more amply and capaciously as encompassing not only linguistic practice but also the attitude of an entire *personality*. In this sense, it is not just that, for example, Plato's Socrates (often thought of as the origin of irony) employed an ironic art of language in his dialogical engagements with the Sophists; it is also that this practice expressed something deeper—namely, an ironic art of living, a form of life in which his very style of living offered itself as a continuous mode of *questioning*: that is, an ironic *self*. Socrates was not only ironic in his dialogues; in his cast of mind and orientation *he* was also an ironist. Here, therefore, irony is a kind of cultivated outlook, a sensibility, a *style*, with which moral and political life as a whole is approached.

Both these senses of irony, I believe (irony as an art of language and as an art of living), are germane to thinking about Williams and *Capitalism and Slavery*. Williams was undoubtedly an ironist as Brogan observes, and much that is important has been written about his inscrutable and enigmatic character.[86]

EVIL ENRICHMENT   283

But for my purposes here—that is, the consideration of the *story-form* of his seminal book—I pay special attention to the figure of irony as a compositional strategy. In particular, what interests me is the way irony is mobilized by Williams to puncture the racist hubris and sanctimonious cant offered by British imperial historiography in its authoritative account of West Indian slavery in British history. Perhaps predictably, given its defining double-edged character, Williams's irony has a double-edged politics: it serves a clearly *critical* function in challenging the hegemonic imperial perspective on the slave past, on the one hand, but on the other, it may also serve an *elitist* nationalist function in its vindication of the promise of the educated Black and Brown middle classes and of their entitlement to rule the postslave postcolony. As a linguistic test of wits, as White would have reminded us, irony is no guarantee of radical politics.

It is not surprising, then, given its ironic (and *therefore* deliberately self-reflexive) story-form, that *Capitalism and Slavery* is simultaneously a work of history (as a study of a particular past) and a work *about* history (as a study of how to approach pasts in the present). As for James in *The Black Jacobins*, what is at stake for Williams is a *perspective* on the historical inquiry into a slave past that is (tacitly) embraced as his own. *He himself*, in other words, is the present of that past. And as with *The Black Jacobins*, the preface to *Capitalism and Slavery* is not an irrelevant part of the work as a whole, though, notably, unlike James in his book, Williams leaves his weighty reflections on the philosophy of history for the conclusion—as a meta-summation of his perspective on historical knowledge. Still, Williams's preface (dated 1943), though brief, is nevertheless written with a direct and searching sensitivity for the historical tasks as well as the historiographical stakes involved in his undertaking. In the opening sentence of the preface, Williams writes with direct historical reference: "The present study is an attempt to place in historical perspective the relationship between early capitalism as exemplified by Great Britain, and the Negro slave trade, Negro slavery and the general colonial trade of the seventeenth and eighteenth centuries." Then he goes on, in a sudden sweeping enlargement of perspective and historiographical specification, to offer self-consciously a kind of statement of purpose: "Every age rewrites history, but particularly ours, which has been forced by events to reevaluate our conceptions of history and economic and political development."[87] *Particularly ours*? Here, in a nutshell, is the problematic of *Capitalism and Slavery*. There is a general and a specific issue at stake. The book (as he repeats elsewhere) is really about the *general* relation between modern capitalism and New World slavery; the *specific* instance of British capitalism is only the natural or obvious exemplification of a broader historical process that amply illustrates the profound (and profoundly *unacknowledged*) contribution of the "Negro slave trade" and "Negro slavery" to the making of the modern world. Notably, the *racial* question is not irrelevant to Williams, even if it is not (as similarly with James) to be made the driving force of the historical account.

Williams is not an anticapitalist. However, his intervention aims to *rehistoricize* the general story of capitalism by way of a rehistoricization of the particular story of British capitalism. In the authoritative story of capitalism, he suggests, the Industrial Revolution has a canonical place in the scholarly and popular imagination as the great conjuncture of economic, technological, and social-political transformation that brings the modern European world as we know it into existence. But what is the background of this celebrated great transformation (to borrow Karl Polanyi's term)? What are its antecedents, its conditions of possibility? *Here*, says Williams, is the *foundation* story of the conjuncture of West Indian slavery with capitalist development. The relation between the two—capitalism and slavery—is a largely ignored or *disavowed* dimension of the making of the modern world. In the historiography of empire, this story of the relationship between the commercial or mercantile capitalism of the seventeenth and eighteenth centuries and the industrial capitalism of the nineteenth century corresponds to the story of the eclipse of the First Empire of the British Americas (including the British West Indies) by the Second Empire centered on British India. In some sense, what Coupland's Romantic account of abolition allows is precisely the rationalization of this closure (and forgetting) of the era of the West Indian contribution to British capitalist wealth.

However, for Williams, coming at this relation between slavery and modern capitalism is self-consciously a matter of *rewriting* history for a new and different age. The features of his conjuncture are not explicitly elaborated, and what the contrast is between *his* age and any other in which the past of the African slave trade and Black slavery might have been written is not spelled out—only alluded to in the sense that conceptions not only of history but also of "economic and political development" are at issue—presumably those that are germane to the politics of decolonization and sovereignty. Notably, there are "events" that have "forced" the reevaluation of history and development—and here the allusion is clearly to the context of the economic crisis precipitated by the 1929 stock

EVIL ENRICHMENT   285

market crash, the war with Nazi Germany, and the consequential questions those events raised together about economic and political democracy.

Importantly, though *Capitalism and Slavery* is clearly concerned with economic, political, and moral *ideologies* (Adam Smith's most prominently), Williams maintains that it is not to be read as a history of ideas or interpretation—in the way, for example, we today might think of David Brion Davis's later program beginning with *The Problem of Slavery in Western Culture*.[88] It is, Williams says, with disarming understatement or deliberate misdirection, "strictly an economic study of the role of Negro slavery and the slave trade in providing the capital which financed the Industrial Revolution in England and of mature industrial capitalism in destroying the slave system. It is therefore first a study in English economic history and second in West Indian and Negro history. It is not a study of the institution of slavery but of the contribution of slavery to the development of British capitalism."[89] This is a remarkable—and remarkably underexamined—statement for the historiography of West Indian slavery. In contrast with later *postcolonial* Caribbean intellectuals, such as Orlando Patterson in *The Sociology of Slavery* or Kamau Brathwaite in *The Development of Creole Society in Jamaica* (both discussed in chapter 4), the former concerned with the internal structure of slave society and the latter with the dynamics of slave culture, for the *anticolonial* Williams it is the *colonial relation* between Britain and the Caribbean that is at stake.

I do not intend to rehearse here in any more detail than is needed the stepwise argument that structures *Capitalism and Slavery*. Between the preface and the conclusion (to which I return in a moment), the book unfolds over the arc of twelve substantive chapters, opening with the origins of the slave trade and slavery, rising up through West Indian prosperity, heading toward the crisis precipitated by the American Revolution, and thereafter declining rapidly through encumbrance and insignificance toward abolition. Now, as I have indicated, Williams begins his story in *Capitalism and Slavery* in the same way he did *The Negro in the Caribbean* (a clue to their connection)—with a critique of the view that slavery was rooted in racism rather than the other way around, racism in slavery. Slavery, Williams repeats, was a response to a *labor* problem—that is, to the planter's conundrum of how to develop profitable large-scale agricultural production: "He would have

286   PART III

gone to the moon if necessary, for labor. Africa was nearer than the moon, nearer too than the more populous countries of India and China. But their turn would come."[90] The second chapter takes up the development of the slave trade and of its formal legitimacy in Britain, how from the privateer and slave trader John Hawkins in the sixteenth century right up until the 1780s slave-trading not only flourished but remained a "cardinal object of British foreign policy" (30). The slave trade was the driving force of the triangular trade, and the latter was the engine of mercantilism, the generative system and ideology of commercial capitalism. This is the theme of chapter 3. The discovery of America, Williams says, was essentially a mercantilist event, opening the possibility of a seemingly inexhaustible market for trade. The slave trade was the "spring" that set the whole process in motion and thereby provided "one of the main streams of the accumulation of capital in England which financed the Industrial Revolution" (52). Both this and chapters 4 and 5 are primarily concerned with the absurdly fabulous wealth of the West India planters and their mercantile supporters. But, as Williams writes, with engaging, even mocking, parody: "Cinderella, decked out temporarily in her fancy clothes, was enjoying herself too much at the ball to pay any attention to the hands of the clock" (84). Here is Williams introducing this archetypal folktale figure into his serious historical account in order to interrupt and overlay it with ironical counterpoint.

In these early chapters, Adam Smith emerges as, in a sense, the shadow theorist of *Capitalism and Slavery*. The great skeptic of mercantilism and prophet of free trade (as well as a theorist of moral sentiment, as we've seen in chapter 1), the Scottish philosopher saw more perspicuously into the underbelly of his political-economic present than most of his contemporaries did. Smith is Williams's intellectual hero in *Capitalism and Slavery*, as Marx is James's in *The Black Jacobins*, exemplars, respectively, of varieties of radical eighteenth- and nineteenth-century materialisms. *Capitalism and Slavery* is, after a fashion, an *anticolonial* reading of Smith's *The Wealth of Nations*, or perhaps more accurately, it is a reading of *The Wealth of Nations* as itself an anticolonial text. Smith, for Williams, was a foundational critic of the Old Colonial system. Memorably, *The Wealth of Nations* was published in exactly the same year, 1776, as the Declaration of Independence that opens the American Revolution. The two—the philosophy of free trade and the antimonopoly political statement and revolutionary event—are in fact inseparable for Williams, and not simply for anachronistic reasons. *The Wealth of Nations* lent itself to the philosophy of

American anticolonialism as *Capitalism and Slavery* aims to furnish a philosophy of Caribbean anticolonialism. But also *more* than this. For Williams as for Smith, "economy" is not merely a technical entity but a *moral-political* one. In the same way that Smith's classic work of the Scottish Enlightenment is not simply an economic handbook but also a moral philosophical exposé of decadent vested interests, so too Williams's classic of the anticolonial enlightenment is not only a study of slavery economics but also a moral-political exposé of the moribund interests that were still, in the 1940s, holding the Caribbean in colonial subjection.

Indeed, the subject of chapter 6 is the American Revolution. Not coincidentally, it is placed at exactly the halfway point in *Capitalism and Slavery*, for this event is precisely the *turning point* in the whole narrative. For Williams, the American Revolution marks a fundamental rupture in the whole structure of mercantilism and the beginning of the secular decline of the importance of the West Indies and West Indian slavery. As Williams puts it: "American independence destroyed the mercantile system and discredited the old regime. Coinciding with the early stages of the Industrial Revolution, it stimulated that growing feeling of disgust with the colonial system which Adam Smith was voicing and which rose to a veritable crescendo of denunciation at the height of the free trade era" (120). Furthermore, the end of preferential trade with the mainland threw the already beleaguered West Indian planters into direct competition with their French rivals, especially Saint-Domingue, the great powerhouse of late eighteenth-century slave-plantation economies. Every fallacy of West Indian privilege was now manifestly exposed—or *should* have been. For, true to form, the West Indian planters seemed blithely unaware of their precarious situation and approaching ruin. In another of the parodic asides that punctuate the narrative, Williams sums this up when he writes, "Rip Van Winkle, drugged by the potion of mercantilism, had gone to sleep for a hundred years on his sugar plantation," having no idea that he now teetered on the very brink of unavoidable and irreversible disaster (125).[91]

And so, from chapter 7 on, the arc of the story points irrevocably toward collapse and doom. We watch as, progressively, the West Indian slaveowners and the West Indies as a constituent part of the British Empire are rendered not only relatively negligible but, more, an "anachronism" (133). By chapter 8, as water power gave way to steam, as machines were increasingly made by other machines, as the cotton and iron industries expanded, and as Liverpool was displaced by Manchester as capitalism's epicenter, it looked as though (invoking none other

288   PART III

than the great seventeenth-century satirist Jonathan Swift) the Lilliputian mercantilists could no longer hold down the Gulliver of advancing industrial capitalism (135).[92] Or again, using an English nursery rhyme for even more pronounced ironic force: "The West Indian Humpty Dumpty had had a great fall, and all the King's horses and all the King's men could not put Humpty Dumpty together again" (145). As Williams makes clear again and again, in response to humanitarian ideology, the attack on the extravagant and aggravated West Indians was not simply an attack on slavery. It was an attack on monopoly. And this is nowhere more evident than in the problem that arose from the slave insurrection in the coveted French Saint-Domingue, but a stone's throw away from the economically exhausted British Jamaica. Prime Minister William Pitt, a friend of Wilberforce's although not himself so unambiguous an abolitionist, was faced with a revealing dilemma: "Either he must ruin Saint Domingue by flooding Europe with cheaper Indian sugar or by abolishing the slave trade; or he must get Saint Domingue for himself" and continue the slave trade. In the end, of course, the choice was moot: Saint-Domingue was lost to *both* France and Britain, and now posed a danger of a wholly unprecedented kind. And henceforth, Williams writes drily, with nothing to gain from more slave-trading, for the British state "the slave trade became merely a humanitarian issue" (149)—his *merely* registering the ironic subversion of the humanitarian presumption concerning the spurs of human action.

In chapters 9 and 10 the endgame is in motion—the denouement. In the familiar rhetorical contrast that shapes his narrative, Williams writes that if in the eighteenth century every important "vested interest" sought to participate in the monopoly triangular trade of the old colonial system, "after 1783, one by one, every one of those interests came out against monopoly and the West Indian slave system" (154). These capitalists, notably, were not antislavery. They were, after all, quite prepared to pour investments into support for slavery in Cuba, Brazil, and the southern United States. In chapter 11, Williams at last turns to face the humanitarians head on. It is an important fact that while, clearly, in weighing the forces that brought down the slave system, *Capitalism and Slavery* subordinates the role of the humanitarians, Williams's purpose is not to naively ignore them. For to disregard humanitarianism, Williams says, would be to "commit a grave historical error and to ignore one of the greatest propaganda movements of all time." Humanitarians were, he allows, the "spearhead of the onslaught that destroyed the West Indian system and freed the Negro" (178). The problem, therefore, is not that the humanitarians were irrelevant; the

EVIL ENRICHMENT 289

problem is that their contribution had been exaggerated by imperial historians like Coupland. On the whole, needless to say, Williams shows a marked antipathy toward them. They were ideologues; they were by and large reactionaries, where domestic matters were concerned. If Williams sometimes betrays a mild admiration for the indefatigable Thomas Clarkson, "one of those friends of whom the Negro race has had unfortunately only too few" (179), by contrast he is as openly dismissive of the most famous of the abolition saints, William Wilberforce, as Coupland is celebratory and memorializing of him. Williams can barely conceal his contempt when he writes of the exalted icon, the embodiment of everything the Black West Indian in Williams was meant to be thankful for: "There is a certain smugness about the man, his life, his religion. As a leader he was inept, addicted to moderation, compromise and delay. He deprecated extreme measures and feared popular agitation. He relied for success upon aristocratic patronage, parliamentary diplomacy and private influence with men in office" (181). In any case, Williams argues, there is a deep misconception about the project of the abolitionists with respect to the institution of slavery, for him (as a West Indian) the *deciding* question. "The initial error into which many have fallen is the assumption that the abolitionists, from the very outset, never concealed their intention of working for complete emancipation" (182). To the contrary, they did. They "repeatedly disowned any idea of emancipation" on the grounds that the abolition of the slave trade would lead, eventually, by a natural progression and without intervention, to the freedom of the enslaved. It was not until fully 1823, Williams reminds us, "that emancipation became the avowed aim of the abolitionists" (182), and then, not so much on account of the condition of the enslaved as in outrage against the treatment of the missionaries only recently allowed access to the enslaved on the plantations.

The grand finale of the book, chapter 12, was a late addition Williams tells us, inspired, needless to say, by C. L. R. James.[93] That it was added while the book was literally at the publisher suggests the deep influence James had on Williams's thinking at the time and the overall kinship, moreover, between *The Black Jacobins* and *Capitalism and Slavery*. But it also suggests that Williams had been uncertain about the justification of such an inclusion and had, perhaps, to be persuaded of its merit. For in a sense, it reads as somewhat at odds with the cast and tone of the overall conceptual structure of the narrative to this point. It would be a grave mistake, Williams writes, however, "to treat the question [of slavery abolition] as if it were merely a metropolitan struggle," as indeed might have been implied by the preceding chapters. For contrary to popular (colonial) belief, the most significant of the social forces in the colonies were not the White property owners but the Black enslaved themselves. If they have largely been ignored in the past, Williams says, this is changing because of West Indians such as James. "Modern historical writers are gradually awakening to the distortion which is the result of this" (197). The enslaved were actively involved in deciding their fates, in claiming their freedom, and certainly from the early nineteenth century it was clear that one way or another they would have it. Thus, in 1833, Williams writes in a well-known peroration, the options were unmistakable: "Emancipation from above, or emancipation from below. But EMANCIPATION" (208; emphasis in original).

This is the story Williams tells. But, as I have said, *Capitalism and Slavery* embodies a historiographical meditation that he outlines in the conclusion in the form of an explicit philosophy of history. The text of this conclusion has been much ignored by those focused on the Williams debate, but when read in relation to the ironic character of the body narrative it strikes a resonant contrast. Here the voice is intense, philosophic, setting out the rationale for the radical ambition of his intervention. Williams begins this conclusion by insisting again, if in a more elaborate way than in his preface, that while the book is indeed a study dealing with the specificity of British capitalism, the general title "Capitalism and Slavery" is the appropriate one. "British capitalism and Slavery," he writes, "while pedantically more accurate, would nevertheless have been generically false" (209). The genre, then, is *not* immaterial. For the processes at work in British capitalism (though more advanced) were also at work in capitalist development in France— that is, the fundamental centrality of the slave trade (and therefore the slavery system) in nourishing the interconnected complex of historical capitalism. The West Indian slave colonies were thus an important (if not the only) "stream" that propelled the making of the modern industrial world and the parliamentary liberal democracy that accompanied it. The other great colonial stream that "fed the accumulation of capital in Britain"—namely, the India trade—was secondary until after the loss of the American mainland colonies.

At its generative center, *Capitalism and Slavery* is about intersecting conjunctures of crisis. Again, in a more direct and elaborated way than in the preface, we recognize that although substantively focused on the crisis triggered by the American Revolution and lasting into the political settlement of the 1830s, the book is indirectly about the implications of the more *immediate* crisis triggered by the 1929 financial turmoil, the war against fascism, and the emerging politics of constitutional decolonization. In a fundamental way, *Capitalism and Slavery* is an anticolonial response to *this* conjuncture. There is thus a genealogical impulse at work in this book: Williams is thinking the slave past in relation to his own mid-twentieth-century present. "It would be strange," Williams writes, "if the study of the previous upheaval did not at least leave us with certain ideas and principles for the examination of what is going on around us" (209–10).[94]

The substantive labor of the conclusion unfolds over five historiographical "principles" that inform, and are articulated in, the historical argument of *Capitalism and Slavery*. They constitute something like a *schema* for a philosophy of history inasmuch as all of them are internally—one might say, *dialectically*—interconnected, and all, broadly speaking, turn on the problem of historical *determination*, on the relation between ideas and their material conditions. Together they perhaps suggest not only a profound philosophic reflection on the problem of history but also Williams's proximity to Marxist debates in the 1930s and 1940s (debates by which he is partly formed and against which he is partly reacting) and more specifically the proximity of Williams and James in the elaboration of their respective anticolonial histories.

The first principle has to do with the decisive role of economic factors generally in shaping the course of history. These economic forces develop not rapidly or visibly but slowly and imperceptibly, such that human agents are rarely aware of the implications of their own actions. Thus, in a paradoxical way, the economic factors driven by monopoly and slavery propelled the development of eighteenth-century commercial capitalism that, gradually and beyond the register of human awareness, generated the European wealth that stimulated the engine of nineteenth-century industrial capitalism, which then contributed to the destruction of slavery and monopoly. This, formally, is history as irony—history as a process of self-subversion. The second principle develops the idea of the relation between knowledge and action, the extent to which human agents understand—or not—what they do. In a phrasing that again reminds one of James, Williams suggests that, contending groups of actors (merchants, say, or industrialists or politicians), although more or less aware of the immediate interests and stakes in what they do, are, "and for that very reason," unable to see

292   PART III

the overall and long-range implications and consequences of their actions—they can see the trees in their vicinity but not the wider forest. The instance Williams cites is instructive for the way he is, in fact, thinking the past through and *for* his own present. In the late eighteenth century, the loss of the American colonies seemed a catastrophe for Britain as the events unfolded before the eyes of contemporary actors. But as it turned out, in retrospect, it was the beginning of a period of unprecedented wealth and political power for Britain. And here, with his focus on the implication of his colonial past for his anticolonial present, is the reflection Williams offers:

> From this point of view, the problem of the freedom of Africa and the Far East from imperialism will be finally decided by the necessities of production. As the new productive power of 1833 destroyed the relations of mother country and colonies which had existed sixty years before, so the incomparably greater productive power of today will ultimately destroy any relations which stand in its way. This does not invalidate the urgency and validity of arguments for democracy, for freedom now or for freedom after the war. But mutatis mutandis, the arguments have a familiar ring. It is helpful to approach them with some experience of similar arguments and the privilege (apparently denied to active contemporaries) of a dispassionate investigation into what they represented. (210)

This, as I have suggested, is clearly part of the deep story of *Capitalism and Slavery*—namely, the relation between the American anticolonialism of the late eighteenth century and the Caribbean anticolonialism of the mid-twentieth century.

The third principle in the interconnected series again extends and supplements the materialist view that the political and moral ideas of any age should be understood in "the very closest relation" to economic forces. Whereas positions are always, and understandably, defended "on the high moral and political plane," he argues, the "thing defended is always something that you can touch and see," something tangible, determinate. This, Williams holds, is a simple truth, even if one that is only recognized *retrospectively*—after the fact, so to speak, belatedly. Consequently, the fourth principle suggests that there is often a *misalignment* between material conditions and the dominant ideas of an age. Ideas can *lag behind* conditions and act as a brake on historical development and change.

And the fact that this is not discerned by contemporary actors is not surprising and has to do with "the powerful service" these ideas have "previously rendered and the enrichment previously gained" that shields from view the truth of what is taking place. How else, Williams maintains, can one explain the defense put up by West Indian planters and their interests when it was clear (or *should* have been) that their historical time was up, that they had already outlived their shelf life. Finally, the fifth connected principle is that old ideas built on old interests often "continue long after the interests have been destroyed and work their old mischief, which is all the more mischievous because the interests to which they correspond no longer exist" (211). Such is the case, Williams maintains, with the racist idea of the inferiority of Blacks. This is a prejudice that, having come into being under specific circumstances, nevertheless lingers on long after these circumstances have been swept away (212).

And here, Williams formally brings *Capitalism and Slavery* to a close with the following reflection:

> The points made above are not offered as solutions of present-day problems. They are noted as guide-posts that emerge from charting another sea which was in its time as stormy as our own. The historians neither make nor guide history. Their share in such is usually so small as to be almost negligible. But if they do not learn something from history, their activities would then be cultural decoration, or a pleasant pastime, equally useless in these troubled times. (212)

This passage strikes a prophetic note. Williams, of course, was himself to not only write but to also *make* and *guide* history as the political leader he was shortly to become, charting a course in a very stormy sea. His reading of the history of the colonial slave past was by no means merely decorative; it was also to inform his demand for the end of the colonial relation: "Massa day done," as he famously declared in his public lecture in Woodford Square in 1961.[95]

Capitalism and Slavery is offered formally and explicitly as a substantive economic treatise; it certainly is that but is a treatise cast in the story-form of an ironic anticolonial narrative, a moral tale used to illustrate not only a history of gross wrongdoing enacted over centuries, and the phenomenal private and public enrichment derived from that wrongdoing, but also the cynical efforts made to cover over that wrongdoing (or to forget it, disown it, disavow it) with

294   PART III

the palliative of a pleasing, self-congratulatory humanitarianism. Once upon a time not all that long ago, so that satirical parable might go, Englishmen crossed the Atlantic and found in the islands misnamed as the West Indies an exploitable resource. They fought wars over their possessions. In the mercantilist idiom that defined their age, they discovered that large-scale monocrop export-oriented agriculture was the key to their commercial fortunes, and their Elizabethan state keenly supported them in their endeavors. Having decided upon large-scale agriculture, they saw that they needed a ready supply of cheap, pliable labor. They initially tried the Native people, but this was unsuccessful. They turned next to their own countrymen, but this proved too expensive and too complicated. Gradually, and then rapidly, they discovered that on the recently explored continent of Africa they could secure (for mere trinkets and old muskets) labor as chattel, and they happily resolved the problem. Thus for three hundred years or so they carried on a lucrative trade in African men, women, and children to feed the hungry maw of their plantations, which in turn provided a soon-to-be indispensable commodity for their daily consumption: sugar. By and large, the plantation owners were not interested in founding new societies, properly speaking, in these islands, and as soon as their fortunes permitted they repaired to their island-home where they translated their wealth in a variety of status-enhancing economic, cultural, and social ways in cities made with the blood and sweat of the enslaved. But in the curious—or ironic—way that history has, these very fortunes stimulated an economic transformation in which the old sources of wealth—that is, the slavery business—became not simply less and less important but in fact a hindrance and a brake on their further accumulation of wealth. And in this context, conveniently, there emerged a profound consciousness of the moral wrong involved in the old system that made them rich, and this consciousness animated a new language of humanitarian sentiment that helped to quicken and legitimize the righteous destruction of that system. Williams was a public moralist, in Stefan Collini's uses of the term, and *Capitalism and Slavery* was meant to puncture this fairytale, to undermine any serious appreciation of what to Williams was a kind of conceit, and *deceit*.[96]

The upshot of Williams's parable about the slave past in the colonial relation is sovereignty. The argument that West Indian slaves made gigantic contributions to British wealth, and that this contribution is obscured by the hegemonic story that British humanitarianism abolished slavery, is folded principally into an anticolonial *political* project. Williams recognizes a historical relation of debt, but what he thinks is owed in consequence of this structure of asymmetrical enrichment based on the labor of people kidnapped and forced into enslavement is not the material equivalent of what was taken from the enslaved and their descendants. Like other anticolonial intellectual elites, Williams wants political sovereignty not reparation, let alone sovereignty formulated *as* a moral-political reparation. The problem for Williams is formulated as a problem about the colonial *relation*, and therefore the response to the problem will have to come in the form of a demand to *break* that relation. For anticolonial intellectuals like Williams (and James), the structure of colonial domination, including colonial enslavement, does not give rise to a claim for repair but a claim for self-determination as a demand for political equality in international society.

REPARATION AS NEOLIBERAL LEGALISM

In closing, I want to briefly consider one attempt to write an explicitly postcolonial reparatory history of the Caribbean past—namely, Hilary Beckles's *Britain's Black Debt: Reparations for Caribbean Slavery and Native Genocide*, published in 2013.[97] Beckles is an economic historian of the Caribbean slave past, in particular that of Barbados, "the first fully matured slave society in the seventeenth century Americas," as he appropriately reminds us.[98] A British colony since the 1620s, Barbados is the fatal beginning of the whole slave plantation experiment, and Beckles's scholarship (not least his work on enslaved women and the relation between White servitude and Black slavery) has been instrumental in shaping a generation of scholarship on Caribbean history.[99] But Beckles has also become, in the last decade and a half or so, a prominent voice (perhaps the most public voice) in what is sometimes referred to as the Caribbean "reparations movement," a civic-political movement seeking to mobilize pan-Caribbean state and popular support in favor of legal redress for the slave past.[100] On Beckles's account, significantly enough, this movement emerged in the wake of the impasse arrived at during the historic United Nations–sponsored World Conference Against Racism organized in Durban, South Africa, in August–September 2001.[101] This was a clearly catalytic moment, one of enormous expectation and, it would turn out, grave disappointment. As Beckles tells it, the mission of the Caribbean delegation, of which he was a leading member, was to establish the legal framework for a global reparations agenda. This ambition was frustrated and eventually defeated, however, by a convergence of hegemonic powers (led, not surprisingly, by the United States and European states, especially Britain) whose representatives argued, in effect, that appalling and regrettable as slave-trading and slavery may have been, they were not *crimes* when they were practiced and therefore are not strictly eligible for a formal *contemporary* legal claim of reparatory justice.[102] It is easy to understand that for Beckles and his colleagues this was nothing more than a shamefully cynical replay of the familiar strategy deployed by global powers to evade historical obligations—namely, *disavowal* couched in complacent, casuistic terms. *Britain's Black Debt* is a direct and indignant response to this disingenuous evasion of responsibility for an indisputable historical wrong. Staged as a blend of public history, personal narrative, and civic advocacy, it seeks to show that slave-trading and slavery were, in fact, *known* to be not only wrongs (i.e., transgressions of morality) but also, and most importantly, *crimes* (i.e., transgressions of law) at the time they were practiced, and *therefore* to warrant a *legal* claim of reparatory justice.

Given this agenda, it is not surprising that *Britain's Black Debt* does not aim necessarily to bring fresh historical evidence to the old historiographical debates about Caribbean slavery. It is an account, Beckles says, "of the known features of British colonialism; its terrorism of adults and ruthless exploitation of children; its maddening material poverty; and the racial brutality it bred within the prison known as the plantation."[103] What it does aim to do, however, as a matter of establishing the point of a reparatory history, is to develop a *connection* between the slave past's harm and the legitimacy of the postslave present's demand for justice. No one seriously disputes the efficacy of this connection: the plantation-dominated world of the postindependence Caribbean remains, in many respects, a continuation of the "dictatorship of white supremacy" established by British colonial slavery. So that when, for example, Barbados became independent in 1966, "Its people, like all those in the region, were still living in the racially oppressive world of white supremacy built by British minds. Millions of impoverished, illiterate, economically disenfranchised descendants of the enslaved were still gridlocked in the plantation world perfected by British hands."[104] Importantly, then, part of what Beckles aims to establish in assembling the historical picture needed for the work of his reparatory history is a clear and direct relationship between the inaugural colonial world of plantation slavery and the contemporary postcolonial Caribbean worlds of material impoverishment, dependence, and crippling racial order.

Like many thinking about Black reparations today, Beckles is inspired by Randall Robinson's powerful, impassioned polemic *The Debt: What America Owes to Blacks*, published in the same year as the Durban conference, that high-water mark of reparations consciousness.[105] Robinson was an African American lawyer and, as the founder of TransAfrica, a Washington, D.C.–based lobby organization that has sought since the late 1970s to influence U.S. foreign policy in Africa and the Caribbean, he was a man of unusual and admirable commitment to the global Black world. Notably, he was a leading member of a team of Harvard lawyers, the Reparations Coordinating Committee, which included the distinguished Charles Ogletree, who were engaged from the 1990s in legal action against U.S. institutions and corporations known to have links to the slave past.[106] *The Debt*, then, was in many ways symptomatic of the larger human rights shift from politics to law as the terrain of advocacy for change with regard to the condition of Blacks in the United States. It was an effect of the ethical turn, as I am thinking of it. *The Debt* has often and rightly been invoked as one of the texts that set the U.S. slavery reparations discussion in motion. Robinson's critique of the past in the present was as incisive as it was fluid. True, a good deal of the content of *The Debt* was not exactly novel, but what made it uncannily irresistible as a polemic against anti-Black racism was its *reframing* of the African American discussion of the past in the present in terms of a relationship of *responsibility* for past wrong and the *obligation* to redress it. As its title so resolutely insists, the relation between the slave past and the postslave present is a relationship of moral *debt*. Something is morally *owed* by the United States to African Americans. This reframing is, I think, of singular importance to both the conceptual and polemical shape of Beckles's intervention.

Importantly, too, Beckles sees the argument of *Britain's Black Debt* as building on and in conversation within a Caribbean intellectual tradition—the dimension of it, anyway, that as almost a *founding* theme has been concerned with the ways in which the enslavement of Africans and their descendants on sugar plantations for hundreds of years systematically enriched the lives and worlds of the colonial powers in the metropole at the expense of the lives and worlds of the disempowered and dispossessed colonized—within but also beyond the period of slavery. Understandably, then, first among these intellectual sources is Eric Williams's *Capitalism and Slavery*. This book, Beckles argues, "constructed the framework for the reparations case," even though Williams "stopped short" of articulating an explicitly reparatory argument. It was Williams who showed that

298   PART III

"Britain's magnificent, enviable, industrial civilization emerged from the foul waters of colonial slavery."[107] Williams helped to found a certain way of thinking about the relation between the colonial slave plantation and colonial Europe that has informed generations of Caribbean scholars who would see in the plantation complex a deep story not only of the formal asymmetrical relation between metropole and colony but of an enduringly distorted mode of colonial and postcolonial life. In this sense, for example, in their idea of a "plantation society," the revisionary New World political economists of a generation later—Lloyd Best and George Beckford, principal among them—were inheritors of the larger (anticolonial) point of Williams's intervention.[108]

But if Williams is emblematically central to the whole political-historiographic orientation staged in *Britain's Black Debt*, Beckles's argument is also in part dependent upon the scholarly *return* to Williams's seminal work undertaken by Nicholas Draper in *The Price of Emancipation*.[109] Draper's book is itself part of a larger collective project intervening in a normative British (imperial) historiography that has, by and large, evaded the constitutive relation between Caribbean racial slavery and the making of modern capitalist Britain.[110] Rereading the archive of the slave compensation records—that is, the official records pertaining to the unprecedented payout of twenty million pounds by the British government in 1834 to slaveowners to compensate them for their loss of property in enslaved people—Draper's work (along with that of his colleagues) begins to track the material and ideological legacies of British slave ownership in very concrete terms.

Before turning to the substance and character of Beckles's argument, it is useful to consider the conjuncture of questions to which it might be read as responding. I have already mapped (in chapter 1) something of the wider, global conjuncture, shaped by the post–Cold War rise of a new normative ethical-juridical idiom for thinking about the relation between historical wrongdoing and contemporary justice. How, though, might the regional Caribbean conjuncture be thought of? What is the contemporary problem-space in which reparations appears increasingly to be a compelling language of historical redescription, cultural criticism, and political mobilization? How might we more adequately situate the rise of a politics and poetics of reparation to better clarify what is at stake in it (at least in its current form)—what story of the past is being linked to what demand in the present and what imagination of the future? How does the reparations claim connect or not connect to earlier radical arguments for social and political change? After all, it might well be wondered why it has taken more than half a century of postcolonial politics (and more since the publication of Williams's book) to arrive at these arguments and demands. The point, of course, is not to diminish the legitimacy of a politics of reparations but only to seek to situate it in order to better think it through. Imagined as moral-politics, reparations is important not merely because it is right as a matter of principle (whatever that might be) but also because it is timely as a mode of response, in a particular conjuncture, to a historical wrong.

Arguably, there is across the regional anglophone Caribbean a sense that the development model of the postcolonial nation-states—whether enacted through 1960s liberal-nationalist or 1970s socialist-nationalist ideologies—has arrived, exhausted, at a dead-end after four or five decades of postcolonial experience. Inaugurated inside the nationalist movements in the years following the Second World War (precisely by anticolonial statesmen like Eric Williams), this was a heroic model of anticolonial political sovereignty that depended on the idea that the new nation-states could progressively transcend the distorted structures of the colonial past on their way to a liberated, independent future. In view of the widespread poverty, it was fully recognized that some form of economic support would need to be forthcoming from the North Atlantic economies (in the form of bilateral government agreements, World Bank loans, International Monetary Fund stopgap fiscal interventions, and so on) to finance this development program, but this was conceived by the anticolonial elites now in postcolonial power on the basis of the principle of equality among sovereigns in international society. One of the powerful and poignant lessons of the socialist and anti-imperialist 1970s, however, was a recognition of the fundamental structural hierarchy within international society and the consequent "persistent poverty" (as George Beckford was to call it) that resulted from the historically entrenched regime of export-oriented, monocrop plantation economies inherited from the slave past. As a result, there is now a widespread consensus in the region (especially among the generation that came of age in the 1960s, 1970s, and 1980s) that this model has only further crippled the economies of Caribbean nation-states, driven them deeper into the proverbial debt trap, and hobbled their prospects for a meaningful sovereignty.[111] At the same time, as the radical

300   PART III

1970s regimes were structurally adjusted out of power in the 1980s and the non-aligned idea of an anti-imperialist socialist project fell into disrepute, another transformation (at once generational and color-class based) was underway in which the leadership of a new Black elite was emerging, largely indifferent to the old ideologies of the Left but with a far keener sense of racial injury, Black identity, and the legacies of slavery.

This is the problem-space of the new discourse on reparation. In this context, a significant part of what a reparations argument potentially does is to redescribe the past's relation to the present in such a way as to foreground the sense in which Caribbean debt is the other side of European theft—the theft and the debt being internally not accidentally connected. In this sense, what a Caribbean politics of reparations seeks is not economic aid (with all the disciplining technologies and moral hubris that have been our experience), not help in the subservient manner of a mendicant seeking assistance, but simply what is owed to the Caribbean by the former slave-trading and slave-owning European powers as a matter of the justice of redress. What is far from clear, however, is whether or to what extent this new development funding strategy, as it might be called, is meant to do anything more than underwrite the chronic political impoverishment of the neoliberal regimes that now command the nation-states in the Caribbean. The question is whether the reparations politics represented by books such as Beckles's *Britain's Black Debt* consist of anything more robust than the elitist blather and posturing of the liberal legalism that shapes and drives so much of the human rights debates about Black repair.

Beckles sets his concerns explicitly within a vocabulary of reparatory justice for past atrocities. He argues that the human rights discourse of atonement and reconciliation "provides an opportunity for European nations to reflect on and express remorse for [their] crimes." Britain, needless to say, has not availed itself of this opportunity. Beckles writes: "While it took the lion's share of the profits from selling enchained Africans and continued to build fortunes and power from the sweat and blood of millions of the enslaved on Caribbean plantations, [Britain] has persistently refused to apologize for its crimes and has generally ignored any call to engage officially in a formal discussion about reparations."[112]

Whereas in 1995 Queen Elizabeth II issued a measured apology to the Maori in New Zealand for the atrocities committed against them (stemming from the British failure to observe the 1840 Treaty of Waitangi, itself a dubious document of colonial conquest and land appropriation), it is a significant fact that nothing remotely similar has been offered in respect of the transatlantic slave trade and Caribbean slavery.[113] This is despite the fact that the British queen's immediate family—not unlike other prominent members of the British aristocracy and nobility—is itself directly implicated in the historical extraction of fabulous wealth from the atrocity of the trade and labor of Black slaves.[114] In a notable chapter of *Britain's Black Debt*, an extension of an earlier one on the wider economics of colonial enrichment, Beckles recounts the story of the rise of the Lascelles family from very modest beginnings in seventeenth-century Leeds to the very center of the British aristocracy (as Earls of Harewood) by the late eighteenth century and even into royal marriage by the early twentieth century, all on the basis of slave-trading, slave-connected commerce, and slave plantations primarily in Barbados and Jamaica.[115] In an astonishing photograph that forms the front cover of Beckles's book, we see the young Queen Elizabeth II, with her signature impassive smile and complacent wave, being hosted in Barbados in 1966 (the year of Barbados independence) by her first cousin, the seventh Earl of Harewood, at the Belle, a sugar plantation that had come into his family in 1780. As Beckles writes, the story of the Earls of Harewood, from 1648 to 1975 (when they divested themselves of their Barbados holdings) represents a "startling journey of slave-derived enrichment that gave the Lascelles access to the British economic elite and earned them a place in the line of succession to the British throne."[116]

Yet, Beckles argues, despite the history of denial and obfuscation, the case for reparations for New World slavery is really a straightforward and self-evident one in international law. Here is where the stakes are for his argument. It has been shown, he maintains, that international law sets out a clear path linking past crime with the legal claim for reparations. Drawing on the work of the critical legal scholar Mari Matsuda, who offers a typology for determining what constitutes a warrantable claim for reparations, Beckles suggests that in each instance the conditions are met in the case of Caribbean slavery: the injustice is voluminously documented, the historical victims constitute an identifiable group, and current members of this group continue to experience harm that can be connected to that past.[117]

302   PART III

At the center of Beckles's argument is his claim about the racist bad faith of the British state and its apologist scholars who have falsified the historical record. These scholars (who are not named and whose claims are not specified) have by and large supported the position of the state to the effect that slavery was "legal at the time, since it was provided for by the imperial government which was acting within the context of acceptable European norms." Slavery, they have argued, was part of an international standard and therefore not illegal. But this, Beckles asserts, is a spurious argument. Many influential people, he maintains, including, apparently, luminaries such as John Locke, "recognized the criminal nature of the English undertaking."[118] But again, as elsewhere, we are offered no evidence of the claim that Locke was aware of the "illegality" of the enterprise in which he became so intimately involved. It is difficult to say exactly (because, unfortunately, *Britain's Black Debt* is in places not as clearly argued as one might have hoped), but the suggestion seems to be that the British imperial posture rested on a kind of sleight-of-hand concerning the borders of the English homeland and those of the overseas British Empire. Slavery, Beckles insists, was indeed viewed as a crime but one that could be tolerated *elsewhere* than within England and for the explicit sake of the "national interest." That is, "the crime of slavery" could be committed in the outstations of the empire, Beckles writes, but "English soil should produce no fruit other than that nurtured in the free air of the nation."[119] Not that there weren't instances of enslaved persons in England, but the point, so it seems, is that slavery as an institution was not sanctioned in *positive law*. By contrast, of course, a framework of positive "slave law" and ordinances and enacted regulations underwrote the arrangements in commerce and government that made slavery viable in the Caribbean and did so because it was in the national interest of the British people. It seems to be this discrepancy, in effect between metropole and colony, that Beckles seeks to fasten our attention to in making his case that slavery was not only a crime but indeed *recognized* as a crime—namely, a crime if practiced in England but not a crime if practiced on Africans in the Caribbean. Of course, this double standard of a rule of freedom in the metropole and a rule of unfreedom in the colonies—what Partha Chatterjee once referred to, in another context, as a "rule of colonial difference"—would be articulated in terms of race: the racial humanity of the English and the racial subhumanity of Africans and their Caribbean descendants.[120]

Now, it is a curious fact about Beckles's book, its expressly polemical character notwithstanding, that although so much stands or falls on the question of the status of slavery in English law, little or no substantive attention is actually paid to its relevant history: it is simply asserted as a fact of the matter that slavery was "illegal" in English law and known to be so by jurists and others. As though, now, by declaring the supposed self-evidence of the illegality of the past, the contemporary reparations case against the British state should be open-and-shut. For this is Beckles's wager: if slavery was illegal and known to be illegal by those who perpetrated the injustice, then there can be no question but that there is liability, and that consequently reparation is owed in contemporary international law. But oddly, Beckles makes no mention, for example, of William Blackstone, the leading eighteenth-century legal interpreter of the grounds and scope of legal personality, and whose volumes of the *Commentaries on the Laws of England* were treated as authoritative reference works, not least where slavery, as a matter of property, was concerned. Nor, more surprising still, does Beckles offer more than a passing mention of the much-debated judgment handed down by Lord Chief Justice Mansfield in June 1772, in the famous case involving James Somerset that supposedly was so central to the cause of the abolitionists.[121] Surely, though, these would be among the jurists whose thinking about the *standing* of slavery in English law would matter. In the event, arguably, neither Blackstone nor Mansfield enable us to draw so unambiguous a picture of the juridical position of slavery as Beckles would have us imagine we can.

This, assuredly, is not the place to reconstruct anything resembling a comprehensive account of English legal history where slavery is concerned, nor even a full account of the complications involved in the *Somerset* case.[122] For my purposes here, it is necessary only to note that, if anything, the field of English law with respect to slavery was notoriously inconclusive—some might say, deliberately so. As Ruth Paley has suggested, for example, the failure of a bill governing the relations between masters and servants introduced into the House of Lords in 1674 "is perhaps the earliest known example of the reluctance of the English to make a clear decision about the status of slaves in their country."[123] Moreover, the conundrum did not seem to stem simply from English racial attitudes regarding Blacks, widespread though anti-Black racism might have been by the eighteenth century. Rather, as Teresa Michals has exactingly shown, it was in part a consequence of a tension between competing conceptions of the alienability of property embedded, on the one hand, in the old common law tradition (with its diversity of unfree statuses and heterogenous practices) and, on the other, in the emerging codifications regulating the increasing hegemony of commercial society.[124] The Black slave, in a sense, precisely embodied this tension—at once a member of a class of subordinate persons intelligible within a feudal order made up of varying degrees of alienability and the quintessence of the moveable and alienable property at the center of the rapidly liberalizing commercial order. Blackstone's thinking about slavery, Michals maintains, reflects this complexity and undecidability. For him, liberty was so foundationally bound to real property (emblematically *land*) that it was conceptually impossible for an enslaved person to gain freedom in their persons without simultaneously undermining the liberty their masters assumed through their property (and, of course, this would be the conundrum resolved by the extraordinary twenty million pounds sterling paid to slaveowners by the British Parliament at the time of the abolition of slavery). Thus the seeming contradiction in Blackstone's conceptualization of slavery's standing in the law. On the one hand, he holds that the "law of England abhors, and will not endure the existence of, slavery within this nation," and that therefore "a slave or negro, the instant he lands in England, becomes a freeman." But on the other hand, he immediately continues as though there was no paradox: "Yet, with regard to any right which the master may have lawfully acquired to the perpetual service of John or Thomas, this will remain exactly in the same state as before."[125]

Therefore, the predicament facing metropolitan courts when enslaved persons were brought to England with their masters was "whether a land-based hierarchy that involved certain well-defined property rights in persons could or could not incorporate the wider commercial rights of slaveowners."[126] This, in effect, was the vexed question that confronted Lord Chief Justice Mansfield in the summer of 1772. Mansfield may not have been an antislavery advocate, but he was a consummate navigator of the rival traditions of English law. It is well known that although he was popularly thought to have freed all the slaves in England, he himself adamantly maintained that, technically, the *Somerset* case went no further than curtailing a master's power to send his slave out of the country for purposes of sale. As Michals writes:

> The debate that was started by the forcible movement of slaves to England was decided, in a sense, by the common law's refusal to allow them to

be forcibly moved out. The demand to deny formally freedom of movement, not any other form of personal liberty, was the one point that Lord Mansfield was at last unable to concede in favor of the rights of property. In the case of James Somerset, he ruled that "so high an act of dominion [as forcibly detaining a slave in order to sell him abroad] must be recognized by the law of the country where it is used," and concluded that it was not recognized by the law of England.[127]

My point here, again, is not to offer anything resembling a conclusive set of historical arguments regarding the standing of slavery in English law but simply to suggest that this clearly important question is far more complicated than appears in Beckles's largely simplistic and instrumental account of the supposed widespread agreement on the illegality of slavery while it was practiced.

Even so, whatever the reliability of Beckles's account of English law on slavery, there remains the question of why the law should be made the principal modality of the search for contemporary reparations. In a sympathetic discussion of *Britain's Black Debt*, Alfred Brophy, a U.S. legal scholar and the author of an important book on reparations, draws out the limits of its underlying assumption regarding the illegality of slavery and the legal dimension of the reparations project.[128] The British state, Beckles argues, knowingly engaged not only in a moral outrage but also in a culpably "criminal" one, and it is *this* formulation of the problem of slavery that principally drives the direction of his idea of Britain's Black debt and his claim for Caribbean reparations. But, asks Brophy pointedly, "Who judges legality?" Beckles, he says, "uses the term 'legal' as something that is judged from some seemingly universal moral standard, rather than as a positive term of whatever judges or political bodies decide is (or was) 'legal.'" Thus, in appealing to a standard of what counts as law outside of the historical institutions of courts or parliaments (or other legislating bodies), Beckles assumes a "natural law" as opposed to a "positive law" conception of the legitimacy and efficacy of the law. Brophy goes on to argue insightfully, moreover, that focusing on the dimension of law reduces a moral issue to a "technical" one, where the technique of law, he maintains, is not going to "provide a definitive answer" to the problem about slavery. Reparations, in his view, are properly a *moral* and *political* question and will ultimately depend on "wide-spread action aimed toward a transformative social welfare program designed to lift all descendants of enslaved Africans in the Caribbean vocationally and economically."[129] Now,

306 PART III

it is true that Brophy doesn't quite say it this way, but part of what is at stake here in his description of *Britain's Black Debt* is the clearly *neoliberal* context of the prevailing *legalistic* approach to slavery reparations, a legalism that attaches to the wider rights (including human rights) paradigms and therefore constrains the conceptualization of the problem of slavery and repair understood as *moral-political* demands. This is the real nub of the matter. If Brophy is right (as I believe he is), the question to ask is what kind of "social welfare program" this might be, exactly, that aims to "lift all descendants of enslaved Africans in the Caribbean vocationally and economically" out of the state of want and dependence in which the history of New World slavery and its aftermaths has left them.

Surely, no such program is, or indeed, *can* be, contemplated within the context of the contemporary rationalities and imperatives of neoliberalism, certainly not in the Caribbean. The radical Caribbean intellectual tradition, to which Beckles sometimes appeals as the discursive context of his intervention, oriented itself by and large around a critique of colonial and neocolonial liberalism and around the critical contemplation of an agenda of anticapitalist social and political transformation often imagined in the name of some idea of socialism. In contrast, Beckles's book shares no such radical agenda. Although perhaps not openly neoliberal in its moral-political sympathies, *Britain's Black Debt* does, nevertheless, promote demands that do not touch the fundamentally asymmetrical social, economic, and political structures of Caribbean states. They do not envisage, for example, as an elementary condition for reparation, the reorganization of the social and political orders of these states in such a way as to promote a more just and more participatory polities. So that, in the end, alas, Beckles's politics remain as elitist and conformist as those of Eric Williams.

To sum up: For Caribbean critics writing within a Caribbean intellectual tradition, C. L. R. James's *The Black Jacobins* and Eric Williams's *Capitalism and Slavery* established the agenda of an anticolonial historiography. In retrospect, it is not surprising that through their respective books James and Williams established this agenda in relation to the story of slavery because, with the genocide of the Indigenous populations, it is the transplantation of Africans into plantation slavery that stands at the origin of the *modern* Caribbean—modern in terms of its internal structure of domination and modern in terms of its constitutive insertion into an emerging global capitalist order. Nor is it surprising that they established this agenda in relation not simply to the story of slavery but specifically to the received *authoritative* colonial story of the making and unmaking of that institution. In other words, the anticolonial retelling of the story of the Caribbean past required a labor of radically *resituating* the problem about colonial slavery for the agenda of their anticolonial present and the postcolonial future they anticipated. My point in this chapter has been to suggest that this anticolonial agenda was established within a problem-space in which the fundamental horizon was that of the political demand for nation-state sovereignty. The search for the political kingdom, after all, was the paradigm for anticolonialism. Or to put it another, perhaps less charitable, way: for the Black Creole elites (including intellectual elites like Williams) seeking to come to power in the period of constitutional decolonization, the problem about slavery legitimized and rationalized a demand for political independence, not, for example, a demand to compensate generations of the descendants of the enslaved for the value appropriated from their racialized bodies. Or again, and less charitably still, the remedy (if that is what it can be called) that was sought by anticolonial nationalists, whether Marxists or liberals, was one that vindicated the right of these elites to the spoils of office and the presumption of sovereign equality with their former masters, not the right to a form of socialization of wealth, redistribution of resources, and substantive political participation, which might have ensured the descendants of freed people the possibility of a decent collective existence—let alone the prospect of collective flourishing.

The British colonial story of the Caribbean slave past naturalized the relationship between the slave plantations in the colonies and the European slaving states in such a way as to obscure or misrepresent or disavow (or all these together) its true nature. For colonial historiography, that relationship constituted a structure of dependence in which the *direction* of value and relevance flowed from metropole to colony. Europe was the sui generis source of civilization and progress and freedom, and, in its munificence, it had sought, so far as possible, to bestow these glorious gifts upon the backward and benighted enslaved Blacks. Central of course to this self-serving colonial narrative about slavery was the episode of abolition, the story of how the institution of slavery was ended and the enslaved freed after two hundred years of British slavery. Until the 1930s or thereabouts, the hegemonic version of that story held that slavery had been destroyed by the heroic efforts of the humanitarian Saints led by William Wilberforce who, with immense self-sacrifice and strategic ingenuity, aroused in Britain a moral outrage against the foul history in which it had, willy-nilly, become entangled, and in turn forced its great Parliament to pass the legislative act that wiped away the blot. The remarkable contribution of James and Williams to the Caribbean intellectual tradition was to overturn this colonial conceit and to inaugurate a counternarrative of the relation between the slave past and their postslave present. Though neither would have used these terms, both James and Williams recognized that colonialism rested on a blatant structure of *evil* enrichment. In *The Black Jacobins*, James sets his story of slave insurrection and slave revolution in motion precisely by subverting the colonial canard concerning the relation between colony and metropole and about the sources of slave emancipation. The undisputed greatness of eighteenth-century France, James wrote, was not a miracle of European self-invention but the result of the gross and brutish exploitation of the labor of half a million enslaved people in Saint-Domingue. It was not Europe, therefore, that conferred value and relevance on the slave colonies but the reverse; it was the enslaved whose blood and sweat made Europe what it was. The elaboration of this thesis was of course the labor undertaken by Eric Williams in *Capitalism and Slavery*. As is well known, *Capitalism and Slavery* is not just the story about the (industrial) capitalism that helped to abolish slavery (and thus a critique of the presumption of colonial humanitarianism); it is also the story of the earlier (commercial) capitalism that helped to establish it in the first place and on the basis of which it flourished. *Capitalism and Slavery* is the story of a *paradoxical* process in which historical capitalism at first drew breath from the system of slavery and then, when it no longer needed it, stifled its existence.

It should again be noted that what has interested me in thinking about *Capitalism and Slavery* is not the "Williams debate" that has so consumed the North Atlantic academy, the debate concerning whether or to what extent the details of the "Williams theses" are factually correct or based on methodologically sound calculations or drawn from adequate data. Rather, what has interested me is, on the one hand, the problem-space of *Capitalism and Slavery*, the moral-political problem about colonialism that Williams was at intellectual war with; and on the other, the rhetorical poetics through which he engaged this anticolonial war of position. Williams, I argue, was, consummately, an ironist, and *Capitalism and Slavery* is a fundamentally ironic text. Unlike its anticolonial kin, *The Black Jacobins*, that works through the Romantic narrative of revolutionary overcoming, *Capitalism and Slavery* functions through an insouciant poetics of ironic *exposure*, a wry and sometimes mordant unmasking of colonial deceit and imposture. It is the *fraudulence* of imperial historiography that motivates Williams. What he aims to demonstrate is that the nature of the colonial relation between Britain and its colonial possessions was not only one of brutality and inequality but also one of *debt* based on a structure of negative reciprocity: the glory of the British Empire (or at least the so-called First Empire up to the American Revolution) was made possible only at the cost of the misery of millions of enslaved people. For Williams, colonial slavery was foul; but it was also shielded by perversity—namely, the perversity of shallow British imperial historians who sought to occlude the moral-economic reality of this relation of extraction and in so doing to exonerate Britain, congratulate its humanity, and safeguard it from moral blame and the obligations of repair. In Williams's view, Britain certainly owed a debt, but what was owed was the release of the colony into the hands of those to whom it properly belonged and into the charge of those with a more legitimate right to exercise rule.

But alas, as everyone knows, decolonization has turned out not to be what it might have been. To say that it has been a disaster is of course to court controversy. But that it has not been an unmitigated success, at least for the descendants of the enslaved, is indisputable. The slave past is not entirely in the past. The postcolonial story of the Caribbean has remained one of continued debt and prolonged dependence in a relation of entrenched asymmetry with the former slaving powers and their global allies and successors. In this context of persistent poverty and Black misery, there has been a *return* of the question of the problem of debt, now more directly a debt thought of as what is owed in the present for what was coercively and materially extracted from the bodies of the enslaved in the past. As we have seen, in his forceful book *Britain's Black Debt*, Hilary Beckles is one prominent advocate for this direction of thinking. The inestimable value of his book is to have initiated a *reparatory* history within the genealogy of a Caribbean intellectual tradition, and therefore to have opened up the prospect of *rereading* the intellectual inheritance (from C. L. R. James and Eric Williams through George Beckford and Lloyd Best and Walter Rodney) in direct relation to the conjuncture of the postcolonial Caribbean present. Its failure, however, as

I have argued, quite apart from the quibble about the status of slavery in English law, is to have reread the implications of the historical problem of Europe's evil enrichment from slavery into the normalizing paradigm of liberal legalism. Rather than facing up to the fundamental radical social, political, and economic transformation that reparation should entail if it is indeed to repair the structures that reproduce Black misery, Beckles's book remains ensnared by a human rights framework that can do little more than trifle with the pallid shibboleths of international law.

EPILOGUE

On Irreparability

It should be evident from the foregoing chapters that I am both a critic and an admirer of Hannah Arendt. She provokes, if nothing else, often enough to outrage. Although I do not belong to the relatively closed circle of her best and most devoted disciples and interpreters, and so do not share their intimate sources of influence and anxiety, I too am compelled by much in her thinking. I have engaged Richard Bernstein critically, but he is not wrong to insist that we read Arendt *now*. Not simply because she was prescient, however, though she undoubtedly was, but also because significant dimensions of her insight are of such force and complexity as to provoke us, long after her passing, to read her out of her presents into ours. As C. L. R. James and Stuart Hall variously reminded us, the challenge involved in taking up any thinker in any given conjuncture is to always learn to read the contours of the *contrast* between what they were doing in their presents and what we need them to do in ours. Thus, reading Arendt now should entail a sense, minimally, that the concepts she put to work may well have been embedded in problem-spaces that cannot possibly be ours, and that, consequently, part of reading her adequately requires an approach attuned to the ways our conjuncture differs from hers. The subject-position of White normativity that she so easily assumed in reference to Black people and Black history as she became an American in a context of U.S. White supremacy is not excusable; but it need not cancel her insight into the structures of certain kinds of domination that are pertinent to the ways we should think of the pasts in the present of New World slavery. Again, Bernstein is right that Arendt's idea that the practice of making human beings *as* human beings superfluous is a fundamental dimension of absolute evil. But, as Arendt herself recognized, this practice is not straightforwardly equivalent to extermination—although it can,

312 EPILOGUE

and has, paved the way for mass murder. The Holocaust and New World slavery, as Laurence Mordekhai Thomas enables us to see, offer contrasting institutions of radical evil inasmuch as they perpetrated contrasting modes of making people superfluous, through contrasting ideologies and technologies of evil and toward contrasting pernicious ends.

The insight of Arendt's with which I close this book concerns how we confront such atrocities of the past as present matters of *repair*. In a key paragraph in "Concluding Remarks" in the first edition of *The Origins of Totalitarianism*, Arendt proposes an inflection on her theme of total domination having to do with crime and its punishment—or rather, with precisely the *limits* of punishment in the face of certain kinds of crime, those irreconcilable moral crimes involved in making people superfluous. The central feature of total domination, Arendt held (a conception that runs all the way through part 3, "Totalitarianism"), is the pervasive conceit that "everything is possible." Total power over the lives of the dominated encourages totalitarians to believe that nothing is beyond their reach, there is nothing they cannot accomplish, nothing they cannot inflict on those within their power. This conceit, Arendt argues, has implications for how we should think about the *aftermath* of these atrocities, as we try to place them in a context of justice and repair:

> Until now the totalitarian belief that everything is possible seems to have proved only that everything can be destroyed. Yet, in their effort to prove that everything is possible, totalitarian regimes have discovered without knowing it that there are crimes which men can neither punish nor forgive. When the impossible was made possible it became the unpunishable, unforgivable absolute evil which could no longer be understood and explained by the evil motives of self-interest, greed, covetousness, resentfulness, lust for power, and cowardice; and which therefore anger could not revenge, love could not endure, friendship could not forgive. Just as the victims in the death factories or the holes of oblivion are no longer "human" in the eyes of their executioners, so the newest species of criminals is beyond the pale even of solidarity in human sinfulness.[1]

Notice how the practice of evil, in spite of its absolute repugnance and horror or perhaps *because* of it, teaches us something about our humanity, about the limits of what can and cannot be supported, borne, tolerated—even within the community of "human sinfulness." Indeed, it is the totalitarians themselves who have made a moral "discovery" about the necessary implications of their infamy. As Arendt says in the preface to the first edition of *The Origins of Totalitarianism*, without the perpetration of these deeds, we might not have known what human beings are capable of, but we might also not have known what the limits are of the wrongs we can respond to within the conventions of moral and legal recourse. There are evils, it turns out, that lie *beyond* the pale not only of comprehension but of redress as well—or, rather, of the latter because of the former.

It is of some interest to me that this elaboration of the moral-legal implications of the perpetration of the absolute evil embodied in total domination—the conceit that everything is possible—is subsequently relocated in the revised second edition published in 1958, so that it forms a sort of preamble to the now famous paragraph on Kant and evil that closes the chapter "Totalitarianism in Power." For in the same year, Arendt published *The Human Condition*, a book with a complex genealogical relation to *The Origins of Totalitarianism* and in which she develops the theme of the moral implications of evildoing, allusively, not surprisingly, but significantly and powerfully nonetheless.[2] As readers of the book well know, *The Human Condition* is impossible to quite characterize or easily summarize. Like others of her books, if perhaps more emphatically so, this is also one that, as Margaret Canovan describes, does not conform to any known genre of scholarly writing, certainly neither political philosophy nor social history.[3] And indeed, it is precisely this defiant nonconformity that makes *The Human Condition* so challenging a provocation, but nevertheless so insistently necessary to think with. It was meant, Canovan reminds us, to be a ground-clearing exercise, preparatory to a major work that was never written in its imagined form: "a kind of prolegomena," Arendt said, for a work to come.[4] Memorably, in its prologue, Arendt describes it as an intervention into her present, offered from the "vantage point of our newest experiences and our most recent fears." What she proposes, she says, "is very simple: it is nothing more than to think what we are doing."[5] The locution may be awkward, but its sense is both concise and precise.

It is well known that at the center of *The Human Condition* is an argument about *action*. In Arendt's view, human action has been deeply misunderstood by the entire tradition of Western thought that culminated, disastrously, so far as she was concerned, in the Marxism embodied in the Soviet Union's "totalitarianism" (a story that figured unevenly in *The Origins of Totalitarianism*). Action was one of

314 EPILOGUE

the principal activities structuring the human condition, the others being labor and work. Famously, as Arendt described them, *action* corresponded to the fact of our plurality, *labor* corresponded to our biological life and its indestructible needs, and *work* corresponded to our being makers and fabricators of an artificial but durable world. On her account, our capacity to act derives essentially from the ordinary fact that as humans we are beings who are forever starting activities, initiating processes—in a word, *beginning*. This ontological capacity to begin, given at birth (and therefore making birth itself a founding beginning), is in many ways the defining characteristic of our humanity. In her description of it, human action is pervasively subject to contingency, and therefore is immanently unpredictable and often enough irreversible. This sense of the fundamental fragility and vulnerability of human action (which we have already seen taken up in Martha Nussbaum's sense of tragedy) is a potential source at once of great novelty and beauty as well as of disaster and catastrophe, a source of our excellences but also of our doom. Because the world consists of a plurality of individuals all variously setting activities in motion, action is necessarily constitutive of a field of potential conflict—indeed, of potentially *tragic* collision.[6]

For this simple and unavoidable reason, human action needs the means of undoing the damage that is inevitably done in such conditions, the means, as Arendt puts it, of "redeeming" itself from the hazards and perils of unpredictability and irreversibility. One might say that in order to sustain the possibility of human futurity, action needs some resource for redressing past harms and wrongs. These means, she holds, arise from within the potentialities of action itself:

> The possible redemption from the predicament of irreversibility—of being unable to undo what one has done though one did not, and could not, have known what he was doing—is the faculty of forgiving. The remedy for unpredictability, for the chaotic uncertainty of the future, is contained in the faculty to make and keep promises. The two faculties belong together in so far as one of them, forgiving, serves to undo the deeds of the past, whose "sins" hang like Damocles' sword over every new generation; and the other, binding oneself through promises, serves to set in the ocean of uncertainty, which the future is by definition, islands of security without which not even continuity, let alone durability of any kind, would be possible in the relationships between men.[7]

Now, I am principally concerned here with forgiving as the faculty able to redress harmful or wrongful deeds of the past. As I described earlier, though in a different conceptual language, Thomas also urges the vital necessity of a commitment to forgiving. Thomas would undoubtedly agree with Arendt that "without being released from the consequences of what we have done, our capacity to act would . . . be confined to one single deed from which we could never recover; we would remain the victims of its consequences forever, not unlike the sorcerer's apprentice who lacked the magic formula to break the spell."[8] Like Thomas, Arendt sees a Christian provenance for the virtue of forgiveness. He specifically commends that self-implicating posture of humility embodied in the Christian dictum: There but for the Grace of God go I. For her part, Arendt attributes the origin of the role of forgiveness to Jesus of Nazareth. It is Jesus's radical formulation, she argues, that God forgives only if and when human beings exercise their own duty to pardon those who trespass against them. And this duty is imposed upon us, she says, because human beings do not always act with reflective knowledge about what they do.

However, on Arendt's account there is a category of wrongful actions that *cannot* admit of forgiveness—actions in the face of which no pardon is conceivable or possible. These are not merely trespasses or even very bad deeds. They are "willed evils," when human beings act with at least some understanding of what they are doing, such that, as Claudia Card says, they cause "foreseeable, intolerable harm." They are actions to which it is impossible to *reconcile* oneself, as Arendt would put it, to bring about any refurbishing measure of restoration or closure. They involve wrongful harms of an *ultimate* sort. In a passage I feel obliged to quote at some length, Arendt writes,

> The alternative to forgiveness, but by no means its opposite, is punishment, and both have in common that they attempt to put an end to something that without interference could go on endlessly. It is therefore quite significant, a structural element in the realm of human affairs, that men are unable to forgive what they cannot punish and that they are unable to punish what has turned out to be unforgivable. This is the true hallmark of those offenses which, since Kant, we call "radical evil" and about whose nature so little is

316   EPILOGUE

known, even to us who have been exposed to one of their rare outbursts on the public scene. All we know is that we can neither punish nor forgive such offenses and that they therefore transcend the realm of human affairs and the potentialities of human power, both of which they radically destroy wherever they make their appearance. Here, where the deed itself dispossesses us of all power, we can indeed only repeat with Jesus: "It were better for him that a millstone were hanged about his neck, and he cast into the sea."[9]

Alas, Arendt then says nothing more on the subject. Shifting the focus, she simply goes on to talk for two paragraphs about the reasons forgiving and acting have the relationship they have, before turning to an elaboration of the faculty of promising (in which evil scarcely figures). Given the finality of the passage, perhaps there is simply *nothing* else to say. There is, analytically, *nowhere* further to go.

Arendt was shortsighted in a now recognizable way in presuming that it is only the totalitarianisms of Hitler's Germany and Stalin's Soviet Union that warrant discussion in terms of total domination and the conceit that everything is possible. However novel Nazi and Stalinist totalitarianisms may have been, total power, power that presumes and acquires the technologies and ideologies of total domination, did not get its start in the early twentieth century. As I have described, New World slavery produced regimes of total power—total *racial* power, to be more precise—exercised through the racist ideology that there was nothing White people could not inflict with impunity on the Black people they enslaved. The sugar plantation was an institutionalized structure of total power, a "total institution," in the phrase Erving Goffman made famous in the late 1950s.[10] Indeed, in the early 1930s Edgar Thompson had already sketched the contours of the plantation as a type of institutional power, but work on the social-psychological nature of totalitarianism in the 1950s, beginning with Arendt's *The Origins of Totalitarianism*, encouraged scholars of American slavery to think of the plantation in terms of the idea of a relatively closed system of institutionalized power that produced distinctive effects on the personality of the enslaved.[11] Stanley Elkins (whom Arendt evidently admired) was one such scholar. But more important to my purpose here is the work of Orlando Patterson, whose ideas of natal alienation and social death are ways of conceptualizing the dynamic of the all-encompassing domination that constituted New World slavery, one in which power presumed that everything was possible.

Yet Arendt's insight into the limits of redress is acutely relevant to thinking the present of the past of slavery's evil. Quite clearly, though an absolute or (as Thomas would say) ultimate evil, New World slavery was an evil differently organized and differently justified than that of the Holocaust. If it generally did not have as its formal objective the extermination of the enslaved on the grounds of their human unsuitability, it did nevertheless depend, fundamentally, on its capacity to inflict death at will and with impunity. Vulnerability to violence, including violent death, defined the existence of the enslaved. But more significantly, as an intergenerational structure of systemic domination aimed at docile, dependent labor, New World slavery relied as much if not more on the permanent coercive alienation of its captives from their former contexts of cultural life and the systematic imposition on them of a dishonored and degraded lifeworld. Moreover, this entire structure of endless brutality and suffering in the slave colony produced, at the metropolitan end of the colonial chain, an incalculable, misbegotten enrichment—not simply in terms of the accumulation of personal or even social wealth but also in terms of the dynamic structure for the generation and reproduction and transformation of capitalist modernity as a whole. Here is an atrocity of such scale and duration, an enormity so long cynically disavowed, as to lie beyond the pale of redemption. There is no punishment that can be imagined for what was perpetrated for so long, and consequently no forgiveness that could conceivably redeem the evil actions and the evil enrichment it greedily enabled. Evil such as this lies beyond repair. It is irreparable. And yet, something is owed for what was perpetrated, and that debt awaits a reparatory response.

ACKNOWLEDGMENTS

This book was written under the peculiar pressures of being chair of my department at Columbia University for six years. I would therefore first like to thank my inimitable colleagues for providing a stimulating intellectual environment in which to think and write and a challenging—indeed, sometimes trying—community to strive to lead. I learned a great deal in this unforgettable time.

I have been tentatively exploring the theme of reparation for more than a decade, trying to find a path. In 2010, I presented a paper titled "On the Moral Justification of Reparation for New World Slavery" at a conference in honor of the distinguished political theorist James Tully, which was subsequently published under the same title in *Freedom and Democracy in an Imperial Context: Dialogues with James Tully*, edited by Robert Nichols and Jakeet Singh (2014). Here my concern was primarily to inquire critically into the ways in which the issue of reparations for New World slavery was hedged about by questions of practicability and feasibility such that its *moral* justification was obscured. In 2015 I sought to engage the crucial problem of time in reparatory thinking (that is, as a critique of liberal progressivism in conventional reparatory thinking) in an essay titled "Black Futurities Past and Present: Thinking Reparations Through," presented as a lecture in the Humanities Institute, University of Texas, Austin, and again a few years later as a plenary lecture presented at the 2018 conference "Planetary Utopias: Hopes, Desires, Imaginaries in a Postcolonial World," in the Akademie der Künste, Berlin. This essay is now published in the 2019 catalog *The Other Side of Now* that accompanied the exhibition of the same name at the Pérez Art Museum, Miami. Between these two, I had been at work on an adjacent theme of reparatory justice in the context of researching and writing *Omens* of *Adversity: Tragedy, Time, Memory, Justice* (2014), which also is concerned with a postrevolutionary time of response to wrong and injustice. Here my immediate interest was the 1983 collapse of the Grenada Revolution and the U.S. invasion that followed, and the neoliberal human rights framework of transitional and restorative justice that came to envelope its understanding. So the question of reparation has been on my mind for a while.

But it is thinking about and thinking through the (or at any rate, *an*) idea of *evil* that enabled me to move beyond some of the impasses by which I felt constrained. Evil seemed to me to offer a conceptual language for a richer idea of harms and wrongs, a deeper complication of character and context, and a more profound attunement to the tragic paradoxes of human action in time. This is, perhaps, especially true where atrocities are concerned. In the summer of 2017, I was invited by Paul Preciado to give a talk as part of "The Parliament of Bodies" public programs in *documenta 14*, Kassel, Germany, in the context of the exhibition there of an original copy of the 1685 *Code Noir*, Louis XIV's decree defining the legal conditions of slavery in the French colonies. I used the opportunity to write and present a short paper titled "Irreparable Evil," a version of which was then published as "Preface: Evil Beyond Repair" in *Small Axe* 55 (March 2018). This little essay turned out to be the impetus for *Irreparable Evil*.

Very little of the content of this book has previously circulated in the public domain. An earlier version of what is now chapter 1 was presented in September 2019 to a workshop for the Legacies of British Slave-Ownership project at University College, London. I am grateful to Catherine Hall for that invitation, and I take this opportunity to thank her too for the many conversations we've had over the years on New World slavery and its long and perverse aftermaths. Her own stimulating work on the topic has, of course, also been an inspiration. Revised versions of that chapter were later presented as lectures in February 2020 at both the Pembroke Center at Brown University and the University of Illinois, Champaign–Urbana. I am grateful to Suzanne Stewart-Steinberg for the invitation to the former, and to Susan Koshy for the invitation to the latter.

Books, alas, are what they literally are: words in motion, sometimes scarcely predictable motion. Where one starts out on the journey is not always—perhaps rarely ever is—where one ends up. Therefore, however exacting and determined one's plans might be, one is never entirely in command of the text. There is never not, in addition to what one wills, an ineradicably accidental quality—which, I assume, only underlines the unfinished character of thinking, the fact that there

ACKNOWLEDGMENTS 321

is always more to be said, elsewhere, on some other occasion. To me this is simply par for the course, a lesson I have learned from two of the finest thinkers I have been privileged to know, Stuart Hall and Talal Asad. Thinking and writing, I have come to see, are really dimensions of a single intellectual process—which is only to say that writing is itself an uneven and unending form of working it out. It is not surprising, then, that for me there is no writing without the constant work of revision, not only in substantive matters but in formal ones as well. In this respect, I would expressly like to thank my copyeditor Kelly Martin, whose scrutiny of my sentences is always at once didactic and forbearing. She does not know how much I have learned from her modest but persistent wisdom over the years. I also thank my editor at Columbia University Press, Eric Schwartz, for his generous reception of the manuscript and for shepherding it through the various stages of production. Thanks, too, to the readers for the press for their perceptive insights and instructive doubts. I hope they will forgive me where I have ignored their sage advice. Finally, to Vanessa Pérez-Rosario I owe a complex and unsayable debt, which I hope in time to honor.

—Berlin, May 2023

NOTES

PROLOGUE: ON THE DEVASTATION OF LIFEWORLDS AND FORMS OF LIFE

1. Think of the contrasting perspectives embodied in Sylvia Wynter, "Jonkunnu," *Jamaica Journal* 4, no. 2 (1970): 34–48, and Edward Kamau Brathwaite, *Contradictory Omens: Cultural Diversity and Integration in the Caribbean* (Mona, Jamaica: Savacou, 1974). See, too, in the language of historical anthropology, Sidney Mintz and Richard Price, *The Birth of African-American Culture: An Anthropological Perspective* (Boston: Beacon, 1992).

2. Orlando Patterson's *The Sociology of Slavery* is taken to be the locus classicus of the idea of Caribbean slavery as destructive. We shall see in a later chapter that this, while true, is too simple a way of thinking about Patterson's work. Similarly, Kamau Brathwaite's *The Development of Creole Society in Jamaica* is taken to be the locus classicus for the idea of slavery as opening possibilities for creative self-fashioning. In *Mastery, Tyranny, and Desire* and other work, Trevor Burnard agrees (with some qualification) with Patterson. I return to Patterson and Brathwaite in chapter 4. See Orlando Patterson, *The Sociology of Slavery: An Analysis of the Origins, Development, and Structure of Negro Slave Society in Jamaica* (London: MacGibbon and Kee, 1967); Edward [Kamau] Brathwaite, *The Development of Creole Society in Jamaica, 1770–1820* (Oxford: Oxford University Press, 1971); and Trevor Burnard, *Mastery, Tyranny, and Desire: Thomas Thistlewood and His Slaves in the Anglo-Jamaican World* (Chapel Hill: University of North Carolina Press, 2004).

3. For the idea of the lifeworld, see Alfred Schutz, *The Phenomenology of the Social World*, trans. George Walsh and Frederick Lehnert (Evanston, IL: Northwestern University Press, 1967); and Alfred Schutz and Thomas Luckmann, *The Structures of the Life-World*, vol. 1, trans. Richard M. Zaner and H. Tristram Engelhardt Jr. (Evanston, IL: Northwestern University Press, 1973). On forms of life, see Ludwig Wittgenstein, *Philosophical Investigations*, trans. G. E. M. Anscombe (New York: Macmillan, 1953). The phrase is found throughout: "And to imagine a language means to imagine a form of life" (§19); "Here the term 'language-game' is meant to bring into prominence the fact that the *speaking* of language is part of an activity, or of a form of life" (§23); "It is what human beings *say* that is true and false; and they agree in the *language* they use. That is not an agreement in opinions but in form of life" (§241); "Can only those hope who can talk? Only those who

324 PROLOGUE

have mastered the use of a language. That is to say, the phenomena of hope are modes of this complicated form of life" (174); and "What has to be accepted, the given, is—so one could say—*forms of life*" (226). (Wittgenstein's remarks are cited by § number in part 1, and by page number in part 2; all italics in original.)

4. Jonathan Lear, *Radical Hope: Ethics in the Face of Cultural Devastation* (Cambridge, MA: Harvard University Press, 2006).

5. See especially Jonathan Lear, *Aristotle: The Desire to Understand* (Cambridge: Cambridge University Press, 1988); Jonathan Lear, *Freud* (New York: Routledge, 2005); and Jonathan Lear, *A Case for Irony* (Cambridge, MA: Harvard University Press, 2011). Agree with them in every detail, or not, these books offer abundant food for critical thought.

6. In a constructive way, Lear's work is remarkably in tune with a direction of philosophical thinking recently associated with Pierre Hadot and Michel Foucault, in which the boundary between thinking and life is helpfully, provocatively, blurred. See Pierre Hadot, *Philosophy as a Way of Life: Spiritual Exercises from Socrates to Foucault*, trans. Michael Chase (Oxford, UK: Blackwell, 1995).

7. Lear, *Radical Hope*, 7.

8. Lear, *Radical Hope*, 7.

9. Lear, *Radical Hope*, 2.

10. Lear is a University of Chicago–based philosopher, so it may not be entirely surprising that the principal anthropologist he draws on for conceptual remarks about anthropology is Marshall Sahlins, in particular his influential book *Islands of History* (Chicago: University of Chicago Press, 1985). In this book, Sahlins's thesis turns on the constitutive role of culture in the construction of the experience of historical time.

11. Lear, *Radical Hope*, 50.

12. Lear, *Radical Hope*, 7–8.

13. In an instructive review, the anthropologist Adam Kuper raises some doubts around Lear's assumptions about the historical and anthropological Crow. See Adam Kuper, "A Philosopher Among the Crow," *Journal of the Royal Anthropological Institute* 14, no. 2 (June 2008): 426–30.

14. I am thinking here of Michel Foucault, *The Archaeology of Knowledge*, trans. A. M. Sheridan Smith (London: Tavistock, 1972).

15. Lear, *Radical Hope*, 6.

16. One is reminded here of Stuart Hall's critique of the "expressive culture" of Raymond Williams. See Stuart Hall, "Lecture 2: Culturalism," in *Cultural Studies 1983: A Theoretical History*, ed. Jennifer Daryl Slack and Lawrence Grossberg (Durham, NC: Duke University Press, 2016), 25–53.

17. See Jonathan Lear, "Leaving the World Alone," *Journal of Philosophy* 79, no. 7 (July 1982): 382–403. See also Stanley Cavell, "The Availability of Wittgenstein's Later Philosophy," *Philosophical Review* 71, no. 1 (January 1962): 67–93, which in some ways sets some of the terms—and tone—of the debate.

18. For a sympathetic account of the "transcendental" position, including Lear's, see Lynne Rudder Baker, "On the Very Idea of a Form of Life," *Inquiry* 27, nos. 1–4 (1984): 277–89. For the "anthropological" position, see Kathleen Emmett, "Forms of Life," *Philosophical Investigations* 13, no. 3 (July 1990): 213–31.

PROLOGUE 325

19. Lear, *Radical Hope*, 162n40. See the posthumously compiled work John Haugeland, *Dasein Disclosed: John Haugeland's Heidegger* (Cambridge, MA: Harvard University Press, 2013). For an absorbing reading of Wittgenstein's idea of "form of life" through the frame of Giorgio Agamben's idea of "potentialities of life," see David Kishik, *Wittgenstein's Form of Life* (London: Continuum, 2008). The pertinent inspiration for Kishik is the essay by Giorgio Agamben, "Form-of-Life," in *Means Without End: Notes on Politics*, trans. Vincenzo Binetti and Cesare Casarino (Minneapolis: University of Minnesota Press, 2000), 3–12.

20. Lear, *Radical Hope*, 6.

21. Lear, *Radical Hope*, 8 (italics in original).

22. Lear, *Radical Hope*, 24.

23. In a very perceptive discussion of *Radical Hope*, one that picks up Lear's latent—or not so latent—Heideggerian concerns, Hubert Dreyfus raises a question about the ambiguity, and perhaps slippage, between what Lear thinks is a culture's way of life becoming "impossible" and that way of life becoming "unintelligible." See Hubert Dreyfus, "Comments on Jonathan Lear's *Radical Hope*," *Philosophical Studies* 144, no. 1 (May 2009): 63–70. Notably, Haugeland was a student of Dreyfus's.

24. Lear, *Radical Hope*, 32 (emphases in original).

25. Lear, *Radical Hope*, 34.

26. Lear, *Radical Hope*, 162n39.

27. Cora Diamond, "Losing Your Concepts," *Ethics* 98, no. 2 (January 1988): 255–77. This is in many ways a remarkable essay that is as much about *reading* in general as it is about *concept loss* in particular. Diamond is a philosopher intellectually shaped by Wittgenstein and Anscombe. See Cora Diamond, *Reading Wittgenstein with Anscombe, Going On to Ethics* (Cambridge, MA: Harvard University Press, 2019). For a wide-ranging discussion of Diamond's work, see Alice Crary, ed., *Wittgenstein and the Moral Life: Essays in Honor of Cora Diamond* (Cambridge, MA: MIT Press, 2007). For further discussion of concepts and concept loss, with special reference to Iris Murdoch, that fully demonstrates the profound importance of taking this aspect of ordinary and theoretical language seriously, see Niklas Forsberg, *Language Lost and Found: On Iris Murdoch and the Limits of Philosophical Discourse* (London: Bloomsbury, 2013).

28. Diamond, "Losing Your Concepts," 267.

29. Alasdair MacIntyre, *After Virtue: A Study in Moral Theory*, 2nd ed. (Notre Dame, IN: University of Notre Dame Press, 1984), 2.

30. See Elizabeth Anscombe, "Modern Moral Philosophy," *Philosophy* 33, no. 124 (January 1958): 1–19. It would be difficult to overstate the huge and widespread influence of this essay for reshaping the very idea of moral thinking.

31. Anscombe, "Modern Moral Philosophy," 5.

32. Diamond, "Losing Your Concepts," 256–57.

33. Diamond, "Losing Your Concepts," 257.

34. Anscombe, "Modern Moral Philosophy," 6. In a wonderful analogy that precisely captures the misalignment that she and MacIntyre are getting at, Anscombe writes, "If someone professes to be expounding Aristotle and talks in a modern fashion about 'moral' such-and-such, he must be very imperceptive if he does not constantly feel like

326 PROLOGUE

someone whose jaws have somehow got out of alignment: the teeth don't come together in a proper bite" (2).

35. Diamond, "Losing Your Concepts," 266. She goes on: "To be able to use the concept 'human being' is to be able to think about human life and what happens in it; it is not to be able to pick human beings out from other things or recommend that certain things be done to them or by them. The criticism I am making could be put this way: linguistic philosophers have brought to their study of language an impoverished view of what can be involved in conceptual life" (266).

36. See Lear, *Radical Hope*, 37–38.

37. On Lear's sympathetic though critical views on MacIntyre, see his review of MacIntyre's two volumes of selected essays: Jonathan Lear, "Can the Virtuous Person Exist in the Modern World?," *London Review of Books* 28, no. 21 (November 2006), https://www.lrb .co.uk/the-paper/v28/n21/jonathan-lear/can-the-virtuous-person-exist-in-the-modern -world. See also the exchange between them on the concept of irony and its value, in Jonathan Lear, "Irony and Humanity: A Dialogue Between Jonathan Lear and Alasdair MacIntyre," Harvard University Press, April 2012, https://www.hup.harvard.edu/features /irony-and-humanity. The idea of irony figures in Lear's idea of concept loss—it is a way of responding to the collapse of one's conceptual world.

38. Lear, *Radical Hope*, 42–43.

39. Lear, *Radical Hope*, 37.

40. Speaking about the process of "acculturation," Stanley Diamond writes: "In fact, acculturation has always been a matter of conquest. Either civilization directly shatters a primitive culture that happens to stand in its historical right of way; or a primitive social economy, in the grip of a civilized market, becomes so attenuated and weakened that it can no longer contain the primitive culture. In both cases, refugees from the foundering groups may adopt the standards of the more potent society in order to survive as individuals. But these are conscripts of civilization, not volunteers." See Stanley Diamond, *In Search of the Primitive: A Critique of Civilization* (New Brunswick, NJ: Transaction, 1974), 204. Memorably, Talal Asad took up this idea and refracted it in his own way; see Talal Asad, "Conscripts of Western Civilization," in *Dialectical Anthropology: Essays in Honor of Stanley Diamond*, vol. 1, *Civilization in Crisis*, ed. Christine Gailey (Gainesville: University Press of Florida, 1992), 333–51. See also Talal Asad, "Are There Histories of Peoples Without Europe? A Review Article," *Comparative Studies in Society and History* 29, no. 3 (July 1987): 594–607. Needless to add, this was one inspiration for my own book: David Scott, *Conscripts of Modernity: The Tragedy of Colonial Enlightenment* (Durham, NC: Duke University Press, 2004).

41. For a recently crafted picture of eighteenth-century Jamaica, see Jack P. Greene, *Settler Jamaica in the 1750s: A Social Portrait* (Charlottesville: University of Virginia Press, 2016). Greene has also edited the enormously valuable early eighteenth-century history by the planter, merchant, and legislator James Knight; see Jack P. Greene, ed., *The Natural, Moral, and Political History of Jamaica*, by James Knight (Charlottesville: University of Virginia Press, 2021). See Greene's important introductory essay, "James Knight and His History" (xv–lxxvii), and Trevor Burnard's closing historiographic essay, "Those Other English Colonies: The Historiography of Jamaica in the Time of James Knight" (643–54).

PROLOGUE 327

42. Christer Petley, *White Fury: A Jamaican Slaveholder and the Age of Revolution* (Oxford: Oxford University Press, 2018), 46.

43. See Carla Gardina Pestana, "English Character and the Fiasco of the Western Design," *Early American Studies* 3, no. 1 (2005): 1–31; and the superb Carla Gardina Pestana, *The English Conquest of Jamaica: Oliver Cromwell's Bid for Empire* (Cambridge, MA: Belknap, 2017). For a description of Jamaica in the years prior to the earthquake, see David Buisseret, ed., *Jamaica in 1687: The Taylor Manuscript at the National Library of Jamaica* (Kingston, Jamaica: University of the West Indies Press, 2010). On Port Royal, see Michael Pawson and David Buisseret, *Port Royal, Jamaica* (Kingston, Jamaica: University of the West Indies Press, 2000).

44. See Richard Dunn, *Sugar and Slaves: The Rise of the Planter Class in the English West Indies, 1624–1713* (Chapel Hill: University of North Carolina Press, 1972); and Trevor Burnard, *Planters, Merchants, and Slaves: Plantation Societies in British America, 1650–1820* (Chicago: University of Chicago Press, 2015).

45. For enslavement in the Gold Coast forts, see Simon Newman, *A New World of Labor: The Development of Plantation Slavery in the British Atlantic* (Philadelphia: University of Pennsylvania Press, 2013), chaps. 6 and 7. On the slave ship, see Marcus Rediker, *The Slave Ship: A Human History* (New York: Penguin, 2008).

46. Moses Finley introduced the distinction between "societies with slaves" and "genuine slave societies" in his classic work; see Moses Finley, *Ancient Slavery and Modern Ideology* (New York: Viking, 1980). For more on the debate, see Noel Lenski and Catherine Cameron, eds., *What Is a Slave Society? The Practice of Slavery in Global Perspective* (Cambridge: Cambridge University Press, 2020). In *Mastery, Tyranny, and Desire*, Burnard writes: "By 1750, Jamaica had been a slave society for at least three-quarters of a century. It was one of the most complete slave societies in history, with over 90 percent of the population racially distinctive chattel slaves and with a system of laws predicated on the nearly total obedience of slaves to white authority" (244).

47. See C. L. R. James, *The Black Jacobins: Toussaint L'Ouverture and the San Domingo Revolution* (1938; repr. New York: Vintage, 1963); Sidney Mintz, *Sweetness and Power: The Place of Sugar in Modern History* (New York: Viking, 1985); and Justin Roberts, *Slavery and Enlightenment in the British Atlantic, 1750–1807* (Cambridge: Cambridge University Press, 2013).

48. On the evolution of colonial government in the British West Indies, see D. J. Murray, *The West Indies and the Development of Colonial Government* (Oxford: Oxford University Press, 1965).

49. Burnard, *Mastery, Tyranny, and Desire*, 20.

50. With publication of the 1932 dissertation by Edgar Tristram Thompson, we now have wider access to this early analytical profile of the plantation as a regime of power. See Edgar Tristram Thompson, *The Plantation*, ed. Sidney Mintz and George Baca (Columbia: University of South Carolina Press, 2010).

51. B. H. Higman, *Plantation Jamaica, 1750–1850: Capital and Control in Colonial Economy* (Kingston, Jamaica: University of the West Indies Press, 2005).

52. Petley, *White Fury*, 24. Petley reminds us that during this period more than six hundred thousand Africans had been imported into Jamaica, giving some indication of the "deadly nature of slavery" (24). For some contrasts between Jamaica and mainland North

328 PROLOGUE

America, see Richard Dunn, *A Tale of Two Plantations: Slave Life and Labor in Jamaica and Virginia* (Cambridge, MA: Harvard University Press, 2014).

53. Trevor Burnard, "A Failed Settler Society: Marriage and Demographic Failure in Early Jamaica," *Journal of Social History* 28, no. 1 (1994): 63–82. Burnard writes, "Creole settlers were unable to create a consensus about what Jamaican identity should be. Instead, the dominant tone of the place was largely set by expatriate English and Scottish immigrants who had no intention of making Jamaica their home and by the large majority of brutalized Africans who gave clear evidence in several large-scale rebellions that they had an entirely different idea from white creoles about what life in Jamaica should be like" (63–64).

54. See Burnard, *Mastery, Tyranny, and Desire*, 138. Vincent Brown speaks eloquently of an "ecology of fear" around the time of the revolts of 1760; see Vincent Brown, *Tacky's Revolt: The Story of the Atlantic Slave War* (Cambridge, MA: Belknap, 2020), 131.

55. In Brown, *Tacky's Revolt*, he describes the systemic violence on the plantations as exemplifying the brutality internal to the whole dynamic of the Atlantic slavery system (54). He writes, "The violence of enslavement continued on the plantations, just as it did along the slaving routes that brought these workers to the Americas. As conflict between African polities produced captives for the slave trade, violence on the plantations produced for export, and the everyday antagonisms inherent in plantation production connected slavery to imperial war" (72). Slavery not only profited from war but was itself a kind of war.

56. Burnard, *Mastery, Tyranny, and Desire*, 98.

57. See Burnard, *Mastery, Tyranny, and Desire*, 260–61.

58. Scott, *Conscripts of Modernity*.

59. See Scott, *Conscripts of Modernity*; David Scott, *Omens of Adversity: Tragedy, Time, Memory, Justice* (Durham, NC: Duke University Press, 2014); and David Scott, *Stuart Hall's Voice: Intimations of an Ethics of Receptive Generosity* (Durham, NC: Duke University Press, 2017).

60. Hannah Arendt, *The Origins of Totalitarianism* (New York: Harcourt, 1951); and Hannah Arendt, *Eichmann in Jerusalem: A Report on the Banality of Evil* (New York: Viking, 1963).

61. Laurence Mordekhai Thomas, *Vessels of Evil: American Slavery and the Holocaust* (Philadelphia: Temple University Press, 1993).

62. Orlando Patterson, *Slavery and Social Death: A Comparative Study* (Cambridge, MA: Harvard University Press, 1982).

63. I do not exempt myself from this misreading. See David Scott, "The Government of Freedom," in *Refashioning Futures: Criticism After Postcoloniality* (Princeton, NJ: Princeton University Press, 1999), 73–77.

64. Patterson, *Slavery and Social Death*; Orlando Patterson, *Freedom in the Making of Western Culture* (New York: Basic Books, 1991); and Patterson, *The Sociology of Slavery*.

65. Orlando Patterson, *Die the Long Day* (New York: Morrow, 1972).

66. James, *The Black Jacobins*.

67. Eric Williams, *Capitalism and Slavery* (Chapel Hill: University of North Carolina Press, 1944).

68. Hilary Beckles, *Britain's Black Debt: Reparations for Caribbean Slavery and Native Genocide* (Kingston, Jamaica: University of the West Indies Press, 2013).

69. Hannah Arendt, *The Human Condition* (Chicago: Chicago University Press, 1958).

1. THE IDEA OF A MORAL AND REPARATORY HISTORY

1. Another way of framing the question is: What is the demand of criticism of New World Slavery? This is an old question for me. See David Scott, "A Note on the Demand of Criticism," *Public Culture* 8, no. 1 (1995): 41–50.

2. See, variously, Michel Foucault, "History of Systems of Thought," in *Language, Counter-Memory, Practice: Selected Essays and Interviews by Michel Foucault*, ed. Donald F. Bouchard (Ithaca, NY: Cornell University Press, 1977), 199–204. Michel Foucault, "Polemics, Politics, and Problematizations," in *Michel Foucault: Ethics, Subjectivity, and Truth*, ed. Paul Rabinow, trans. Robert Hurley (New York: New Press, 1997), 111–19; and Michel Foucault, *The Use of Pleasure*, trans. Robert Hurley (New York: Viking, 1985), 11. More generally on "problematizations," see Colin Koopman, *Genealogy as Critique: Foucault and the Problems of Modernity* (Bloomington: Indiana University Press, 2013). On Foucault's turn to ethics, see Timothy O'Leary, *Foucault and the Art of Ethics* (New York: Continuum, 2002); and John Rajchman, *Truth and Eros: Foucault and Lacan and the Question of Ethics* (New York: Routledge, 1991).

3. See R. G. Collingwood, *An Autobiography* (Oxford: Oxford University Press, 1939).

4. On intellectual traditions, see David Scott, "The Temporality of Generations: Dialogue, Tradition, Criticism," in "Interpretation and Its Rivals," special issue, *New Literary History* 45, no. 2 (Spring 2014): 157–81. Notably, in their respective historiographies of the anglophone Caribbean, neither Elsa Goveia nor Barry Higman offers a story of quite this cast of preoccupation, but each of their reconstructions can be productively *reread* in this genealogical direction. See Elsa Goveia, *A Study of the Historiography of the British West Indies to the End of the Nineteenth Century* (1956; repr., Washington, DC: Howard University Press, 1980); and Barry W. Higman, *Writing West Indian Histories* (London: Macmillan, 1999).

5. I am thinking here of Stuart Hall's whole intellectual style from the 1950s onward, but specifically of the intellectual innovation that constitutes Stuart Hall, Chas Critcher, Tony Jefferson, John Clarke, and Brian Roberts, *Policing the Crisis: Mugging, the State, and Law and Order* (London: Macmillan, 1978).

6. The kind of ontology I mean to evoke is best represented in Ian Hacking, *Historical Ontology* (Cambridge, MA: Harvard University Press, 2004). In respect of the idea of a founding rupture, I note here work on the role of "cultural trauma" in shaping the narrative of social identity. See, generally, Jeffrey Alexander, Ron Eyerman, Bernhard Giesen, Neil Smelser, and Piotr Sztompka, *Cultural Trauma and Collective Identity* (Berkeley: University of California Press, 2004); and more relevantly Ron Eyerman, *Cultural Trauma: Slavery and the Formation of African American Identity* (New York: Cambridge University Press, 2001).

7. See Robin D. G. Kelley, *Freedom Dreams: The Black Radical Imagination* (Boston: Beacon, 2002); and Anthony Bogues, *Black Heretics, Black Prophets: Radical Political Intellectuals* (New York: Routledge, 2003). Indeed, one of the great attempts to formulate a coherent and comprehensive and progressive conceptual-historical account of the framework for understanding the totality of New World Black experience can be found in Cedric Robinson, *Black Marxism: The Making of the Black Radical Tradition*, updated third edition (Chapel Hill: University of North Carolina Press, 2021).

330   1. THE IDEA OF A MORAL AND REPARATORY HISTORY

8. David Scott, *Refashioning Futures: Criticism After Postcoloniality* (Princeton, NJ: Princeton University Press, 1999).

9. See Ernesto Laclau, *Emancipation(s)* (London: Verso, 1996).

10. I am thinking here of the formulation in Reinhart Koselleck, *Futures Past: On the Semantics of Historical Time*, trans. Keith Tribe (Cambridge, MA: MIT Press, 1985).

11. See Cora Diamond, "Losing Your Concepts, *Ethics* 98, no. 2 (January 1988): 266–67. See also the prologue to this book.

12. See David Scott, *Conscripts of Modernity: The Tragedy of Colonial Enlightenment* (Durham, NC: Duke University Press, 2004); and C. L. R. James, *The Black Jacobins: Toussaint L'Ouverture and the San Domingo Revolution* (1938; repr., New York: Vintage Books, 1963). James's book is now the subject of a good deal of critical engagement. See Rachel Douglas, *Making "The Black Jacobins": C. L. R. James and the Drama of History* (Durham, NC: Duke University Press, 2019); and Charles Forsdick and Christian Høgsbjerg, eds., *"The Black Jacobins" Reader* (Durham, NC: Duke University Press, 2017).

13. On vindicationism, see Robert A. Hill, "C. L. R. James: The Myth of Western Civilization," in *Enterprise of the Indies*, ed. George Lamming (Port of Spain: Trinidad and Tobago Institute of the West Indies, 1999), 255–59. Needless to say, another singular text in this vein would be W. E. B. Du Bois, *Black Reconstruction* (1935; repr., New York: Athenium, 1969). Indeed, James saw this connection later in life in his lectures at the Institute of the Black World in 1971. See C. L. R. James, *"The Black Jacobins* and *Black Reconstruction:* A Comparative Analysis" (1971), in "Lectures on *The Black Jacobins*," special section, *Small Axe*, no. 8 (September 2000): 65–112, at 83–98.

14. See Albert Camus, "The Future of Tragedy" (1955), in *Lyrical and Critical Essays*, ed. Philip Thody, trans. Ellen Conroy Kennedy (New York: Vintage, 1970), 295–310; Sidney Hook, "Pragmatism and the Tragic Sense of Life" (1959), in *Pragmatism and the Tragic Sense of Life* (New York: Basic Books, 1974); Hannah Arendt, *The Human Condition*, 2nd ed. (Chicago: University of Chicago Press, 1958); George Steiner, *The Death of Tragedy* (New York: Knopf, 1961); and Raymond Williams, *Modern Tragedy* (London: Chatto and Windus, 1966).

15. See David Scott, "C. L. R. James, Totalitarianism, and the Sense of the Tragic," introduction to *"Preface to Criticism," and Other Writings*, by C. L. R. James, ed. Robert A. Hill (Durham, NC: Duke University Press, forthcoming).

16. See David Scott, "The Tragic Vision in Postcolonial Time," *PMLA* 129, no. 4 (2014): 799–808, from which I have borrowed some language here. And more generally on the tragic, see Martha Nussbaum, *The Fragility of Goodness: Luck and Ethics in Greek Tragedy and Philosophy* (New York: Cambridge University Press, 1986).

17. For an insightful reading of James in moral terms, see Alasdair MacIntyre, *Ethics in the Conflicts of Modernity: An Essay on Desire, Practical Reasoning, and Narrative* (Cambridge: Cambridge University Press, 2016), 273–96.

18. C. L. R. James, *Mariners, Renegades, and Castaways: Herman Melville and the World We Live In* (New York: James, 1953), 106.

19. I am using "morality" and "ethics" to cover roughly the same domain. The technical philosophical quarrel about their differences does not concern me. The sort of history that seems important to me is found in, for example, Alasdair MacIntyre, *A Short History of Ethics* (New York: Collier, 1966).

. THE IDEA OF A MORAL AND REPARATORY HISTORY   331

20. There is much that could be cited here. But briefly, in philosophy, see Thomas Kuhn, *The Structure of Scientific Revolutions* (Chicago: University of Chicago Press, 1962); Richard Rorty, *Philosophy and the Mirror of Nature* (Princeton, NJ: Princeton University Press, 1979); and Michel Foucault, *The Archaeology of Knowledge* (New York: Pantheon, 1971). In anthropology, see Clifford Geertz, *The Interpretation of Cultures* (New York: Basic Books, 1973); and George Marcus and James Clifford, eds., *Writing Culture: The Poetics and Politics of Ethnography* (Berkeley: University of California Press, 1986).

21. In history, see George Cotkin, "History's Moral Turn," *Journal of the History of Ideas* 69, no. 2 (2008): 293–315. In anthropology, see Didier Fassin, "Introduction: Toward a Critical Moral Anthropology," in *A Companion to Moral Anthropology*, ed. Didier Fassin (New York: Wiley, 2012), 1–17; and Michael Lambek, Veena Das, Didier Fassin, and Webb Keane, *Four Lectures on Ethics: Anthropological Perspectives* (Chicago: HAU, 2015). And in literature, see Todd Davis and Kenneth Womack, eds., *Mapping the Ethical Turn: A Reader in Ethics, Culture, and Literary Theory* (Charlottesville: University of Virginia Press, 2001).

22. In this vein, see Jonathan Glover, *Humanity: A Moral History of the Twentieth Century* (London: Jonathan Cape, 1999).

23. For some thinking through of this, see Domenico Losurdo, *War and Revolution: Rethinking the Twentieth Century*, trans. Gregory Elliott (New York: Verso, 2015).

24. I am setting aside the doubtlessly valid distinction, in certain contexts, between humanitarianism and human rights as institutional and discursive forms. See Michael Barnett, *Empire of Humanity: A History of Humanitarianism* (Ithaca, NY: Cornell University Press, 2011), 16–17.

25. I am alluding here to the well-known Samuel Moyn, *The Last Utopia: Human Rights in History* (Cambridge, MA: Harvard University Press, 2010). There is much to be said, pro and con, about this book and its contribution to the contemporary debate. The "self-image of the age" idea comes from Alasdair MacIntyre, *Against the Self-Images of the Age: Essays on Ideology and Philosophy* (Notre Dame, IN: University of Notre Dame Press, 1978).

26. On how the emergence of new concepts can alter the way we think about particular matters, see Bernard Yack, *The Longing for Total Revolution: Philosophic Sources of Discontent from Rousseau to Marx and Nietzsche* (Berkeley: University of California Press, 1992).

27. Didier Fassin, *Humanitarian Reason: A Moral History of the Present* (Berkeley: University of California Press, 2012). More recently Fassin has extended these considerations in Didier Fassin, *Life: A Critical User's Manual* (Cambridge: Polity, 2017); and Didier Fassin, *The Will to Punish* (Berkeley: University of California Press, 2018).

28. In this sense, Fassin would disagree with Elazar Barkan, who writes in an early and poignant book as though a new international morality rather than a new international regime of morality has emerged. See Elazar Barkan, *The Guilt of Nations: Restitutions and Negotiating Historical Injustices* (New York: Norton, 2000).

29. Fassin, *Humanitarian Reason*, 243.

30. Fassin, *Humanitarian Reason*, 245–46.

31. Fassin, *Humanitarian Reason*, 246. For a contrasting view of the practice of criticism, see Michael Walzer, *The Company of Critics: Social Criticism and Political Commitment in the Twentieth Century* (New York: Basic Books, 1988); and its companion, Michael Walzer, *Interpretation and Social Criticism* (Cambridge, MA: Harvard University Press, 1993).

332   1. THE IDEA OF A MORAL AND REPARATORY HISTORY

32. On this, see, usefully, Alexander Broadie, *The Scottish Enlightenment* (Edinburgh, Scotland: Birlinn, 2007).

33. Fassin, *Humanitarian Reason*, 4–5.

34. On concepts and their histories, see, in one direction, Reinhart Koselleck, *The Practice of Conceptual History: Timing History, Spacing Concepts* (Stanford, CA: Stanford University Press, 2002); and, in another, Quentin Skinner, *Visions of Politics*. Vol. 1, *Regarding Method* (New York: Cambridge University Press, 2002).

35. Fassin, *Humanitarian Reason*, 6.

36. Fassin, *Humanitarian Reason*, 252.

37. Fassin, *Humanitarian Reason*, 254. One is reminded here of Richard Rorty's (somewhat ironic) response to Clifford Geertz's Tanner lecture; Rorty casts the anthropologist as an "agent of love" (as opposed to the philosopher, an "agent of justice") whose great contribution is that of rendering empathetically intelligible to "us" the otherness of others. See Clifford Geertz, "The Uses of Diversity," *Michigan Quarterly Review* 25, no. 1 (1986): 105–23; and Richard Rorty, "On Ethnocentrism: A Reply to Clifford Geertz," *Michigan Quarterly Review* 25, no. 3 (1986): 525–34. For a critique of this entire structure of benevolent giving, see Romand Coles, *Rethinking Generosity: Critical Theory and the Politics of Caritas* (Ithaca, NY: Cornell University Press, 1997). I have been powerfully influenced by Coles's idea of a "receptive generosity." See David Scott, *Stuart Hall's Voice: Intimations of an Ethics of Receptive Generosity* (Durham, NC: Duke University Press, 2017).

38. Fassin, *Humanitarian Reason*, 256.

39. Regarding evil as wrong, see John Kekes, *Facing Evil* (Ithaca, NY: Cornell University Press, 1994); John Kekes, *The Roots of Evil* (Ithaca, NY: Cornell University Press, 2005); Claudia Card, *The Atrocity Paradigm: A Theory of Evil* (Oxford: Oxford University Press, 2002); Claudia Card, *Confronting Evils: Terrorism, Torture, Genocide* (Cambridge: Cambridge University Press, 2010); Laurence Mordekhai Thomas, *Vessels of Evil: American Slavery and the Holocaust* (Philadelphia: Temple University Press, 1993); Todd Calder, "Is Evil Just Very Wrong?," *Philosophical Studies* 163, no. 1 (2013): 177–96; Paul Formosa, "A Conception of Evil," *Journal of Value Inquiry* 42, no. 2 (2008): 217–39; Luke Russell, "Evil Revivalism Versus Evil-Skepticism," *Journal of Value Inquiry* 40, no. 1 (2006): 89–105; Luke Russell, "Is Evil Action Qualitatively Distinct from Ordinary Wrongdoing?," *Journal of Australasian Philosophy* 85, no. 4 (2007): 659–77; Marcus Singer, "The Concept of Evil," *Philosophy* 79, no. 308 (2004): 185–214; Mary Midgely, *Wickedness* (New York: Routledge, 1984); Raimond Gaita, *Good and Evil: An Absolute Conception* (New York: Routledge, 1991); and Raimond Gaita, "Evil Beyond Vice," in *A Common Humanity* (New York: Routledge, 1998), 29–56. Regarding a philosophical concept of evil, see Richard Bernstein, *Radical Evil: A Philosophical Interrogation* (Cambridge: Polity, 2002); Susan Neiman, *Evil in Modern Thought: An Alternative History of Philosophy* (Princeton, NJ: Princeton University Press, 2002); and Peter Dews, *The Idea of Evil* (Oxford: Blackwell, 2008). Needless to say, the literature is much vaster than is indicated by this list.

40. On the political abuse of evil, see Richard Bernstein, *The Abuse of Evil: The Corruption of Politics and Religion since 9/11* (Cambridge: Polity, 2006). Bernstein laments the absolutism and thoughtless dogma that has come to characterize the public conversation about evil in the United States since 9/11. He speaks of a "clash of mentalities" (as opposed to a "clash of civilizations") that confronts us in the post-9/11 present (preface, viii).

1. THE IDEA OF A MORAL AND REPARATORY HISTORY   333

Following Arendt's idea that *thinking* is the best security against evil, Bernstein calls for a robust and flexible fallibilism in both theoretical and public discourse. There are, of course, those who significantly doubt the conceptual usefulness of the idea of evil in contemporary critical thinking. See, for example, Phillip Cole, *The Myth of Evil: Demonizing the Enemy* (Edinburgh, Scotland: University of Edinburgh Press, 2006). For Cole, in the end evil is merely an ideological concept: "I conclude that the idea of evil is not a philosophical concept, certainly not a psychological one, and not even a religious one. It is a mythological concept that has no role in the grand narratives of world history. To describe someone as evil is not to say anything about *them*, but is to place them as victims of a narrative force, as characters in a story in which they play a specific and prescribed role" (23; italics in original). It is to be wondered whether all concepts worth the name aren't "contested" in this way. I return to this in the following chapter.

41.   See, for example, Calder, "Is Evil Just Very Wrong?," and Gaita, "Evil Beyond Vice."

42.   See Singer, "The Concept of Evil," 185.

43.   See Kekes, *The Roots of Evil*; Card, *The Atrocity Paradigm*; and Formosa, "A Conception of Evil."

44.   Formosa, "A Conception of Evil," 229.

45.   David Cooper, *The Measure of Things: Humanism, Humility, and Mystery* (New York: Oxford University Press, 2002).

46.   It is hardly surprising that "life" has become a renewed topic of concern in the contemporary human sciences. See, for example, Nikolas Rose, *The Politics of Life Itself* (Princeton, NJ: Princeton University Press, 2007); and, more recently, Fassin, *Life: A Critical User's Manual*.

47.   For a cognate view, see Dews, introduction to *The Idea of Evil*, 1–16.

48.   See the fascinating account in Margaret Abruzzo, *Polemical Pain: Slavery, Cruelty, and the Rise of Humanitarianism* (Baltimore, MD: Johns Hopkins University Press, 2011). See also Lynn Hunt, *Inventing Human Rights: A History* (New York: Norton, 2007).

49.   See Barnett, *Empire of Humanity*, 57. As with Fassin's account, so in Barnett's, it remains unclear how to connect these eighteenth-century ideas and sensibilities to those that emerged in the post–Cold War world.

50.   The phrase "pioneers of humanitarian action" is Barnett's. See Barnett, *Empire of Humanity*, 57. See also Abruzzo, *Polemical Pain*, chaps. 1 and 2.

51.   On Equiano and *The Interesting Narrative of the Life of Olaudah Equiano*, see Vincent Carretta, *Equiano the African: Biography of a Self-Made Man* (Athens: University of Georgia Press, 2005). I borrow the term "Black cosmopolitans" from the fascinating Ifeoma Nwankwo, *Black Cosmopolitanism: Racial Consciousness and Transnational Identity in the Nineteenth-Century Americas* (Philadelphia: University of Pennsylvania Press, 2005).

52.   The ruling in the *James Somerset* case was ambiguous because Lord Chief Justice Mansfield, ambivalent as he was on the question of slavery, made it clear that he was not ruling on the *general* question of the legality of the slave trade; he acknowledged that in Virginia and Jamaica, for example, slaves were "goods and chattels" by law. Thus, in his narrow judgment he declared in part, "The state of slavery is of such a nature, that it is incapable of being introduced on any reasons, moral or political; but only positive law. . . . It is so odious, that nothing can be suffered to support it, but positive law. Whatever inconveniences, therefore, may follow from a decision, I cannot say this

334 1. THE IDEA OF A MORAL AND REPARATORY HISTORY

case is allowed or approved by law of England; and therefore the black must be discharged." Quoted in Norman Poser, *Lord Mansfield: Justice in the Age of Reason* (Montreal, Canada: McGill–Queens University Press, 2013), 296. For an illuminating discussion of Mansfield's situation and the competing interests he sought to accommodate, see James Oldham, "New Light on Mansfield and Slavery," *Journal of British Studies* 27, no. 1 (1988): 45–68. See also Steven Wise, *Though the Heavens May Fall: The Landmark Trial That Led to the End of Human Slavery* (Cambridge, MA: Da Capo, 2005).

53. Quobna Ottobah Cugoano, *Thoughts and Sentiments on the Evil of Slavery*, ed. Vincent Carretta, with introduction and notes by Carretta (1787; repr., New York: Penguin, 1999).

54. For an instructive discussion of Cugoano in this respect, see Anthony Bogues, "The Political Thought of Quobna Cugoano: Racialized Natural Liberty," chap. 1 in *Black Heretics, Black Prophets*, 25–46.

55. On the poetics of Cugoano's polemic, see Helena Woodard, "Ukawsaw Gronniosaw and Ottobah Cugoano: Perspectives on a Theological Chain," in *African-British Writings in the Eighteenth Century: The Politics of Race and Reason* (Westport, CT: Greenwood, 1999), 31–65; and Brycchan Carey, *British Abolitionism and the Rhetoric of Sensibility: Writing, Sentiment, and Slavery, 1760–1807* (New York: Palgrave, 2005). See also Julie Ward, "The Master's Tools: Abolitionist Arguments of Equiano and Cugoano," in *Subjection and Bondage: Critical Essays on Slavery and Social Philosophy*, ed. Tommy L. Lott (Lanham, MD: Rowman and Littlefield, 1998), 79–98. And for a broad discussion, see Christopher Brown, *Moral Capital: Foundations of British Abolitionism* (Chapel Hill: University of North Carolina Press, 2006).

56. Cugoano, *Thoughts and Sentiments*, 10.

57. Steven Mintz, introduction to *The Problem of Evil: Slavery, Freedom, and the Ambiguities of American Reform*, ed. Steven Mintz and John Stauffer (Amherst: University of Massachusetts Press, 2007), 3.

58. Mintz, introduction, 5.

59. Mintz, introduction, 7. In terms of David Brion Davis's moral-historical orientation, see, in particular, David Brion Davis, *The Problem of Slavery in Western Culture* (Ithaca, NY: Cornell University Press, 1966), the first volume in the trilogy that continued with David Brion Davis, *The Problem of Slavery in the Age of Revolution, 1770–1823* (Ithaca, NY: Cornell University Press, 1975), and finally, if less successfully, David Brion Davis, *The Problem of Slavery in the Age of Emancipation* (New York: Vintage, 2015). Perhaps, though, Davis's vision for a moral history, indeed his progressivist vision of a moral history, is most explicitly embodied in David Brion Davis, *Slavery and Human Progress* (New York: Oxford University Press, 1984).

60. Think of Randall Robinson, *The Debt: What America Owes to Blacks* (New York: Plume, 2001).

61. The allusion here, obviously, is to Karl Marx, *The Eighteenth Brumaire of Louis Bonaparte* (1852). On "afterness" as a quality of contemporary sensibility, see Gerhard Richter, *Afterness: Figures of Following in Modern Thought and Aesthetics* (New York: Columbia University Press, 2011).

62. Here I depart in some measure from Avery Gordon's more capacious, more wide-ranging use of the idea of "haunting" as marking the limit of a positivist imagination. See Avery

Gordon, *Ghostly Matters: Haunting and the Sociological Imagination* (Minneapolis: University of Minnesota Press,1997).

63. I acknowledge here the enormous importance of Catherine Hall's work and our many conversations around the question of "disavowal" and "denial" in the history of New World slavery. See especially the recent essay Catherine Hall, "Doing Reparatory History: Bringing 'Race' and Slavery Back Home," *Race and Class* 60, no. 1 (2018): 3–21; and Catherine Hall and Daniel Pick, "Thinking About Denial," *History Workshop Journal*, no. 84 (Autumn 2017): 1–23. More generally, see Stanley Cohen, *States of Denial: Knowing About Atrocity and Suffering* (Cambridge: Polity, 2001).

64. George Steiner, *The Death of Tragedy* (1961; repr., New Haven, CT: Yale University Press, 1996), 8.

65. I completely agree here with John Kekes, who aims to resist the Pollyannaish temptation to naïve optimism; for him, as for me, the "shattering lessons of history" are all too compellingly present. See Kekes, *The Roots of Evil*, xii.

66. See Jeremy Waldron, "Redressing Historic Injustice," *University of Toronto Law Journal* 52, no. 1 (Winter 2002): 135–60; and Jeremy Waldron, "Superseding Historic Injustice," *Ethics* 103, no. 1 (1992): 4–25.

67. Waldron, "Redressing Historic Injustice," 159.

68. Waldron, "Redressing Historic Injustice," 160.

69. See Robinson, *The Debt*; and Bernard Boxill, "The Morality of Reparations," *Social Theory and Practice* 2, no. 1 (1972): 113–23.

70. Janna Thompson, *Taking Responsibility for the Past: Reparation and Historical Injustice* (Cambridge: Polity, 2002). Thompson reprises her argument more recently in Janna Thompson, *Should Current Generations Make Reparations for Slavery?* (Cambridge: Polity, 2018). I discuss aspects of Thompson's work in David Scott, "On the Moral Justification of Reparations for New World Slavery," in *Freedom and Democracy in an Imperial Context: Dialogues with James Tully*, ed. Robert Nichols and Jakeet Singh (New York: Routledge, 2014), 100–120.

71. See Boxill, "The Morality of Reparations."

72. In this Thompson agrees with Rodney Roberts, "The Morality of a Moral Statute of Limitations on Injustice," *Journal of Ethics* 7, no. 1 (2003): 115–38.

73. Margaret Urban Walker, *Moral Repair: Reconstructing Moral Relations After Wrongdoing* (Cambridge: Cambridge University Press, 2006), 34, 205; and J. Angelo Corlett, *Heirs of Oppression: Racism and Reparations* (Lanham, MD: Rowman and Littlefield, 2010), xii.

74. For the classic instance of the argument regarding historical title, see Robert Nozick, *Anarchy, State, and Utopia* (New York: Basic Books, 1974).

75. Thompson, *Taking Responsibility for the Past*, xix.

76. Thompson, *Taking Responsibility for the Past*, xviii.

77. Thompson, *Taking Responsibility for the Past*, xviii–xix.

78. Thompson, *Taking Responsibility for the Past*, xix. Thompson has further developed the idea of intergenerational communities in Janna Thompson, *Intergenerational Justice: Rights and Responsibilities in an Intergenerational Polity* (New York: Routledge, 2009).

79. Thompson, *Taking Responsibility for the Past*, xi.

80. Thompson, *Taking Responsibility for the Past*, xix.

81. Charles W. Mills, *The Racial Contract* (Ithaca, NY: Cornell University Press, 1997).

336   1. THE IDEA OF A MORAL AND REPARATORY HISTORY

82. Mills died in September 2021, still developing his ideas about race and philosophy. In addition to *The Racial Contract*, he is the author of the following books: Charles W. Mills, *Blackness Visible: Essays on Philosophy and Race* (Ithaca, NY: Cornell University Press, 1998); Charles W. Mills, *From Class to Race: Essays on White Marxism and Black Radicalism* (Lanham, MD: Rowman and Littlefield, 2003); Charles W. Mills, *Radical Theory, Caribbean Reality: Race, Class, and Social Domination* (Kingston, Jamaica: University of the West Indies Press, 2010); and Charles W. Mills, *Black Rights/White Wrongs: The Critique of Racial Liberalism* (New York: Oxford University Press, 2017).

83. See John Gray, *Post-liberalism: Studies in Political Thought* (New York: Routledge, 1993). Gray's challenging work, since his own shift away from a classically liberal position, has been to offer a critique of liberalism's self-image but from a politically conservative perspective. On post-Marxism, see Ernesto Laclau and Chantal Mouffe, *Hegemony and Socialist Strategy: Towards a Radical Democratic Politics* (London: Verso, 1985).

84. See, in this regard, Raymond Geuss, "Liberalism and Its Discontents," *Political Theory* 30, no. 3 (2002): 320–38.

85. John Rawls, *A Theory of Justice* (Cambridge, MA: Harvard University Press, 1971).

86. On the contract tradition, see David Boucher and Paul Kelly, eds., *The Social Contract from Hobbes to Rawls* (New York: Routledge, 1994).

87. There are notable convergences between Mills's work and that of David Theo Goldberg. See David Theo Goldberg, *Racist Culture: Philosophy and the Politics of Meaning* (Oxford: Blackwell, 1993); and David Theo Goldberg, *The Racial State* (Oxford: Blackwell, 2002).

88. Domenico Losurdo, *Liberalism: A Counter-History*, trans. Gregory Elliott (New York: Verso, 2011).

89. Losurdo, *Liberalism*, 344.

90. Losurdo, *Liberalism*, 37.

91. John Kekes offers a critique of liberalism that worries about its inability to seriously conceptualize and critically accommodate an account of evil. See John Kekes, *Against Liberalism* (Ithaca, NY: Cornell University Press, 1997); and Kekes, *Facing Evil*. I discuss Kekes's important work in chapter 3 of this book.

92. Losurdo, *Liberalism*, 340–41.

93. Losurdo, *Liberalism*, 343.

94. Charles W. Mills, "Racial Liberalism," *PMLA*, 123, no. 5 (October 2008): 1380–97, at 1384. This essay was later incorporated into Charles W. Mills, *Black Rights/White Wrongs* (New York: Oxford University Press, 2017), 28–48. See also Charles W. Mills, "'Ideal Theory' as Ideology," in *Black Rights/White Wrongs* (New York: Oxford University Press, 2017), 72–90.

95. Rawls, *A Theory of Justice*, esp. chap. 3, "The Original Position."

96. Mills, "Racial Liberalism," 1381.

97. Mills, "Racial Liberalism," 1385.

98. Mills, "Racial Liberalism," 1386.

99. Among Mills's various reflections on "white supremacy" as a paradigm for thinking about historical liberalism, see Charles W. Mills, "Revisionist Ontologies: Theorizing White Supremacy," in *Blackness Visible* (Ithaca, NY: Cornell University Press, 2018), 97–118; and Charles W. Mills, "Racial Exploitation," in *Black Rights/White Wrongs* (New York: Oxford University Press, 2017), 113–35.

100. Mills, "Racial Liberalism," 1391.

2. INCOMPARABLE EVIL

1. See María Pía Lara, "Introduction: Contemporary Perspectives," in *Rethinking Evil: Contemporary Perspectives*, ed. María Pía Lara (Berkeley: University of California Press, 2001), 1–14; hereafter cited as "Contemporary Perspectives." In addition to Lara, contributors include Jeffrey Alexander, Henry Allison, Carol Bernstein, Richard Bernstein, Isabel Cabrera, Maeve Cook, Manuel Cruz, Peter Dews, Alessandro Ferrara, Robert Fine, Gustavo Leyva, Susan Neiman, Carlos Pereda, and Sergio Pérez. I do not suggest that Lara's assumptions are held by all of her contributors. Lara is also the author of a notable book on evil; see María Pía Lara, *Narrating Evil: A Postmetaphysical Theory of Reflective Judgement* (New York: Columbia University Press, 2007).

2. See, for example, Joan Copjec, ed., *Radical Evil* (New York: Verso, 1996); Alan Schrift, ed., *Modernity and the Problem of Evil* (Bloomington: Indiana University Press, 2005); and Ruth Grant, ed., *Naming Evil, Judging Evil* (Chicago: University of Chicago Press, 2006).

3. Lara, "Contemporary Perspectives," 1.

4. See Richard Shorten, "Hannah Arendt on Totalitarianism: Moral Equivalence and Degrees of Evil in Modern Political Violence," in *Hannah Arendt and the Uses of History: Imperialism, Nation, Race, and Genocide*, ed. Richard King and Dan Stone (New York: Berghahn, 2007), 173–74.

5. Lara, "Contemporary Perspectives," 2.

6. Bernstein demurs, but even as he disavows a theory drive, he too can't help thinking in terms of a progressive rhythm of conceptualization in his understanding of the earlier and later ideas about evil in Arendt. See Bernstein, *Radical Evil*, 6, 98.

7. See St. Augustine, *Divine Providence and the Problem of Evil: A Translation of St. Augustine's "De Ordine,"* trans. Robert Russell (Whitefish, MT: Kessinger, 2010). For an illuminating discussion, see G. R. Evans, *Augustine on Evil* (Cambridge: Cambridge University Press, 1982). For more context, see the splendid Peter Brown, *Augustine of Hippo: A Biography* (Berkeley: University of California Press, 1967).

8. John Milbank, "Darkness and Silence: Evil and the Western Legacy," in *The Religious*, ed., John Caputo (Oxford: Blackwell, 2002), 277–300. Here Milbank expresses some doubts about the views of those he dubs "postmodern Kantians." For many recent philosophers, Milbank writes (and he has in mind contributors to Copjec's edited volume *Radical Evil*), the old privation view of evil is "inadequate in the face of what they consider to be the unprecedented evil of the twentieth century." "Such evil, they argue, cannot be regarded as privative, because this view claims that evil arises only from the deliberate pursuit of a lesser good. Power directed towards extermination suggests, rather, destruction and annihilation pursued perversely for its own sake, as an alternative end in itself. Such a motive towards the pure negation of being, as towards the cold infliction of suffering— that may not even be enjoyed by its perpetrators—suggests that the will to destroy is a positive and surd attribute of being itself and no mere inhibition of being in its plenitude" (277).

9. Immanuel Kant, *Religion Within the Boundaries of Mere Reason*, ed. Allen Wood and George de Giovani (1793; repr., New York: Cambridge University Press, 1998). For a very helpful variety of essays specifically discussing Kant's views on evil, see Sharon Anderson-Gold

338   2. INCOMPARABLE EVIL

and Pablo Muchnik, eds., *Kant's Anatomy of Evil* (Cambridge: Cambridge University Press, 2010).

10. For the decision on whether his *Religion Within the Boundaries of Mere Reason* was to be judged a work of theology or philosophy, Kant submitted the completed manuscript not to the Berlin censors but to the faculty of theology at the University of Halle, who determined that it was a work of philosophy. For a fascinating discussion of the making and reception of Kant's book, see Manfred Kuehn, *Kant: A Biography* (Cambridge: Cambridge University Press, 2001); on the matter of the work's standing as philosophy, see 364–65.

11. See Todd Calder, "The Concept of Evil," in *Stanford Encyclopedia of Philosophy*, ed. Edward Zalta and Uri Nodelman (Winter 2022), https://plato.stanford.edu/entries/concept-evil.

12. See Bernstein, *Radical Evil*, 32–33.

13. Lara, "Contemporary Perspectives," 3. Lara cites Susan Neiman, "What's the Problem of Evil?," in *Rethinking Evil: Contemporary Perspectives*, ed. María Pía Lara (Berkeley: University of California Press, 2001), 29.

14. See also Susan Neiman, *Evil in Modern Thought: An Alternative History of Philosophy*, rev. ed. (Princeton, NJ: Princeton University Press, 2015), 3; all citations here are to the revised edition. Bernstein also replays this script. Early in his book *Radical Evil*, he says this position agrees with Arendt and Hans Jonas and Emmanuel Levinas and Adorno and others, "that Auschwitz signifies a rupture and break with tradition, and that 'after Auschwitz' we must rethink both the meaning of evil and human responsibility" (4). He feels no need to elaborate, to clarify what tradition it is that has been broken, and who specifically are implicated in the rupture. And again, in an all too familiar way, the script of the twentieth century is only unsettled (and here only partially) by the more recent institution of "9/11" as the "very epitome of evil in our time" (x).

15. Lara, "Contemporary Perspectives," 8.

16. Lara, "Contemporary Perspectives," 10.

17. Lara, "Contemporary Perspectives," 12.

18. In a 1971 lecture, significantly dedicated to W. H. Auden, Arendt writes: "Some years ago, reporting the trial of Eichmann in Jerusalem, I spoke of 'the banality of evil' and meant by this no theory or doctrine but something quite factual, the phenomenon of evil deeds, committed on a gigantic scale, which could not be traced to any particularity of wickedness, pathology, or ideological conviction in the doer, whose only personal distinction was a perhaps extraordinary shallowness." See Hannah Arendt, "Thinking and Moral Considerations: A Lecture," *Social Research* 38, no. 3 (Autumn 1971): 417. Auden and Arendt were acquaintances. Famously, in an apparently chaotic moment Auden proposed marriage to her. See Elisabeth Young-Bruehl, *Hannah Arendt: For Love of the World* (New Haven, CT: Yale University Press, 1982), 436. Arendt wrote a moving remembrance of Auden when he died: see Hannah Arendt, "Remembering W. H. Auden," *New Yorker*, January 20, 1975; https://www.newyorker.com/magazine/1975/01/20/remembering-wystan-h-auden-who-died-in-the-night-of-the-twenty-eighth-of-september-1973. But as importantly, Auden was the author a poem on evil titled "Herman Melville," first published in 1939. According to Richard King, it is very likely that Arendt knew it, although there seems little evidence that they talked about it. See Richard King, *Arendt and America* (Chicago: University of Chicago Press, 2015), 195.

2. INCOMPARABLE EVIL   339

19. I am alluding here to a whole practice of reading the conceptual-political past in the present that has been enormously influential for me, reading for the conjuncture or the problem-space, that I have derived from the work of Quentin Skinner and R. G. Collingwood, Stuart Hall, and C. L. R. James. See my discussion in chapter 1 of this book.

20. Even the intellectual historian Richard King, in his otherwise very valuable book *Arendt and America*, seems uninterested in these sorts of questions. See King, *Arendt and America*.

21. In particular, I am thinking about Bernstein's work from early books, such as Richard Bernstein, *Beyond Objectivism and Relativism: Science, Hermeneutics and Praxis* (Philadelphia: University of Pennsylvania Press, 1983); Richard Bernstein, *Philosophical Profiles: Essays in a Pragmatic Mode* (Philadelphia: University of Pennsylvania Press, 1986); and Richard Bernstein, *The New Constellation: The Ethical-Political Horizons of Modernity/Postmodernity* (Cambridge: Polity, 1991); to more recent work, such as Richard Bernstein, *Ironic Life* (Cambridge: Polity, 2016). Richard Bernstein, *The Abuse of Evil: The Corruption of Politics and Religion Since 9/11* (Cambridge: Polity, 2005), follows up on his earlier books on Arendt and evil and is a fine demonstration of the worldly character of his philosophical orientation. For part of the story of Bernstein's relation to Arendt (and more generally for part of the story of his life), see Judith Friedlander, "A Philosopher from New York," in *Pragmatism, Critique, Judgment: Essays for Richard J. Bernstein*, ed. Seyla Benhabib and Nancy Fraser (Cambridge, MA: MIT Press, 2004), 329–51.

22. See also Neiman's book on Kant, Susan Neiman, *The Unity of Reason: Rereading Kant* (New York: Oxford University Press, 1994); and, more recently, Susan Neiman, *Moral Clarity: A Guide for Grown-Up Idealists* (Princeton, NJ: Princeton University Press, 2009).

23. "Eighteenth- and nineteenth-century philosophy was guided by the problem of evil. Like most short statements, this one is too simple. Nevertheless, I intend to show that as an organizing principle for understanding the history of philosophy the problem of evil is better than alternatives." Neiman, *Evil in Modern Thought*, 7.

24. Neiman, *Evil in Modern Thought*, 1 (italics in original). See also Neiman, "What's the Problem of Evil?" (in Lara, *Rethinking Evil*), which opens in the same way. Neiman is well aware of the Port Royal earthquake of 1692 that virtually drowned the notorious colonial port in Jamaica, but in the essay it doesn't detain her more than parenthetically, as though the colonial was merely external or incidental to the structure and discourse of the emerging modern world. Speaking of the 1755 earthquake in Portugal that destroyed Lisbon, she writes: "Let us note that the earthquake that destroyed Port Royal, Jamaica, fifty years earlier, had produced no intellectual shockwaves; less, I think, because Jamaica was even farther from the center of European discourse than Lisbon, but because even its own inhabitants viewed it to be full of half-bred buccaneers and women of easy virtue, who must have had it coming" ("What's the Problem of Evil?," 27). This is, at best, a rather simple explanation. Note that the Port Royal earthquake was sixty-three not fifty years before the Lisbon earthquake.

25. *Evil in Modern Thought* ends with the events in New York on September 11, 2001. But there is no real integration of 9/11 into the larger story. In part, this may well be a matter of timing. In any case, 9/11 is merely an appendix that confirms Neiman's overall thesis.

26. See Neiman, *Evil in Modern Thought*, 281–88.

340 2. INCOMPARABLE EVIL

27. More recently, and notably in a familiar move, Neiman is the author of a book about what postslave America might learn from Germany. See Susan Neiman, *Learning from the Germans: Race and the Memory of Evil* (New York: Farrar, Straus and Giroux, 2019). Part of what is odd is that Germans don't seem to have something to learn from Black America.

28. See Neiman, "Afterword to the Princeton Classics Edition," in Neiman, *Evil in Modern Thought*, 330. The critic was Franklin Perkins, *Heaven and Earth Are Not Humane: The Problem of Evil in Classical Chinese Philosophy* (Bloomington: Indiana University Press, 2014).

29. Neiman, "Afterword to the Princeton Classics Edition," 330. Neiman cites Perkins, *Heaven and Earth Are Not Humane*, 10.

30. See Jeffrey Alexander, "On the Social Construction of Moral Universals: The 'Holocaust' from War Crime to Trauma Drama," in *The Meanings of Social Life: A Cultural Sociology* (New York: Oxford University Press, 2003), 27–84. The essay first appeared in the *European Journal of Social Theory* 5, no. 1 (2002): 5–86, and it has been anthologized elsewhere since. It also has been much discussed, including in Jeffery Alexander, Martin Jay, Bernhard Giesen, Michael Rothberg, Robert Manne, Nathan Glazer, and Elihu Katz, *Remembering the Holocaust: A Debate* (New York: Oxford University Press, 2009).

31. Alexander, "On the Social Construction of Moral Universals," 28.

32. Alexander, "On the Social Construction of Moral Universals," 31.

33. See, in this respect, the work on the idea of "cultural trauma" that Alexander and his colleagues have been doing, collected in Jeffrey Alexander, Ron Eyerman, Bernhard Giesen, Neil Smelser, and Piotr Sztompka, eds., *Cultural Trauma and Collective Identity* (Berkeley: University of California Press, 2004). Alexander's "On the Social Construction of Moral Universals" is also republished here (196–263).

34. Readers may remember that this basic argument was set out in Peter Novick, *The Holocaust in American Life* (New York: Houghton Mifflin, 2001), 19–20.

35. Alexander, "On the Social Construction of Moral Universals," 38.

36. Alexander, "On the Social Construction of Moral Universals," 49.

37. Alexander, "On the Social Construction of Moral Universals," 50.

38. Alexander, "On the Social Construction of Moral Universals," 51.

39. See United Nations Office of the High Commissioner for Human Rights, "Convention on the Prevention and Punishment of the Crime of Genocide," adopted December 9, 1948, by General Assembly resolution 260 A (III); https://www.ohchr.org/en/professional interest/pages/crimeofgenocide.aspx. Its principal article (Article 2) defines genocide as any of a number of acts "committed with intent to destroy, in whole or in part, a national, ethnical, racial, or religious group." The first act it names is that of "killing members of the group," but it does go on to name other genocidal acts, among them "causing serious bodily or mental harm," and "deliberately inflicting on the group conditions of life calculated to bring about its physical destruction in whole or in part." But undoubtedly, it is the image of mass killing that has come to define genocide. For reflections on Lemkin and Arendt, see Seyla Benhabib, "International Law and Human Plurality in the Shadow of Totalitarianism: Hannah Arendt and Raphael Lemkin," *Constellations* 16, no. 2 (June 2009): 331–50.

40. Alexander, "On the Social Construction of Moral Universals," 235n31. See also Novick, *The Holocaust in American Life*, 100–101.

2. INCOMPARABLE EVIL   341

41. Alexander, "On the Social Construction of Moral Universals," 54, 57.

42. Alexander, "On the Social Construction of Moral Universals," 28.

43. Alexander, "On the Social Construction of Moral Universals," 55.

44. See, in particular, Jeffrey Alexander, "A Cultural Sociology of Evil," chap. 4 in *The Meanings of Social Life: A Cultural Sociology* (New York: Oxford University Press, 2003), 109–19.

45. An "engorged evil," he writes, is one that "overflows with badness. Evil becomes labile and liquid; it drips and seeps, ruining everything it touches. Under the sign of the tragic narrative, the Holocaust became engorged, and its seepage polluted everything with which it came into contact." Alexander, "On the Social Construction of Moral Universals," 68.

46. In the introduction to his edited volume *Hannah Arendt in Jerusalem*, Steven Aschheim offers that Arendt played a "crucial role in the formulation and creation of the ubiquitous postwar 'discourse on evil,' one in which Nazism and Auschwitz have become emblematic of Western culture's conceptions of absolute inhumanity." This seems to me not quite right. I would say that this "discourse on evil" is not postwar so much as post–Cold War. Steven Aschheim, "Introduction: Hannah Arendt in Jerusalem," in *Hannah Arendt in Jerusalem*, ed. Steven Aschheim (Berkeley: University of California Press, 2001) 20.

47. Richard King is one of the few scholars to note how thin and unspecified Arendt's "analysis" of evil is in her *The Origins of Totalitarianism*. See King, *Arendt and America*, 63.

48. C. L. R. James, *Mariners, Renegades, and Castaways: The Story of Herman Melville and the World We Live In* (New York: C. L. R. James, 1953), 106. Significantly, the remark is made at the beginning of the chapter "Neurosis and the Intellectuals." Arendt writes of *Billy Budd* in *On Revolution* (New York: Viking, 1963), 73–74. On Arendt and *Billy Budd*, see King, *Arendt and America*, 139.

49. See Ian Hacking, *The Social Construction of What?* (Cambridge, MA: Harvard University Press, 1999). 5. This is also an orientation associated with Quentin Skinner. For a discussion, see James Tully, ed., *Meaning and Context: Quentin Skinner and His Critics* (Princeton, NJ: Princeton University Press, 1988), especially Tully's introductory essay, "The Pen Is a Mighty Sword: Quentin Skinner's Analysis of Politics" (7–25). It is to me a notable fact that Arendt's thought has not been made the object of a systematic conceptual history in the manner of Quentin Skinner. It would seem that, especially given her very oblique relation to both liberalism and Marxism, and the possibility of routing her through a political history of republicanism, this would make for a potentially illuminating enterprise.

50. Richard Bernstein, *Hannah Arendt and the Jewish Question* (Cambridge, MA: MIT Press, 1996), 137. Bernstein cites Hannah Arendt, "Nightmare and Flight" (1945), in *Essays in Understanding, 1930–1954: Formation, Exile, and Totalitarianism*, ed. Jerome Kohn (New York: Schocken, 1994), 134. The essay was originally published in the *Partisan Review*.

51. There are a number of reviews of Arendt's *The Origins of Totalitarianism* from the early 1950s worth mentioning here: H. Stuart Hughes, "Historical Sources of Totalitarianism," *Nation*, March 24, 1951; David Reisman, "The Path to Total Terror," *Commentary* 11, no. 4 (April 1951): 392–97; Dwight Macdonald, *The New Leader* (review), August 15, 1951; and Philip Rieff, "The Theology of Politics: Reflections on Totalitarianism as the Burden of Our Time (A Review Article)," *Journal of Religion* 32, no. 2 (April 1952): 119–26.

342   2. INCOMPARABLE EVIL

52. See, in particular, Joanna Vecciarelli Scott and Judith Chelius Stark, "Rediscovering Hannah Arendt," in *Love and Saint Augustine*, by Hannah Arendt, ed. Joanna Vecciarelli Scott and Judith Chelius Stark (Chicago: University of Chicago Press, 1996). They write critically of "mainstream Arendt scholars": "For those interested in maintaining the orthodox Arendt cannon [*sic*], defending Arendt's virtue is the primary agenda. For them a clear break between Arendt's pre-Holocaust and post-Holocaust writings is fundamental and necessary. Central to this plan, however, is the marginalization of Arendt's dissertation and a renewed interest in her study of Rahel Varnhagen" (127). As they say, for example, of Arendt's biographer Elisabeth Young-Bruehl, in her definitive study *Hannah Arendt for Love of the World*, Young-Bruehl "confines the dissertation to an appendix and Arendt's interest in Augustine to an early, romantic enthusiasm long since put aside for a focus on the public world" (128). King, in *Arendt and America*, scarcely mentions the dissertation (2, 4); Bernstein, in both *Hannah Arendt and the Jewish Question* and *Radical Evil*, basically overlooks it.

53. See Scott and Stark, "Rediscovering Hannah Arendt," but also Charles Mathewes, *Evil and the Augustinian Tradition* (Cambridge: Cambridge University Press, 2001).

54. Arendt, *Love and Saint Augustine*, 17.

55. Denis de Rougemont, *The Devil's Share: An Essay on the Diabolic in Modern Society*, trans. Haakon Chevalier (New York: Pantheon, 1944). Originally published in 1942 as *La part du diable*.

56. Denis de Rougemont, *Love in the Western World* (Princeton, NJ: Princeton University Press, 1940).

57. Rougemont, *The Devil's Share*, 14.

58. Arendt, "Nightmare and Flight," 133.

59. Arendt, "Nightmare and Flight," 133–34. In Lara, "Contemporary Perspectives," María Pía Lara engages "Nightmare and Flight," taking the view that Arendt's attitude toward Rougemont's book is one of "disdain" (9–10). I do not agree. Granted, disdain is perhaps an attitude Arendt perfected, but I think the case with Rougemont is more complicated than that.

60. Arendt, "Nightmare and Flight," 134. To take just one example, see Hannah Arendt, "Organized Guilt and Universal Responsibility" (1945), in *Essays in Understanding, 1930–1954: Formation, Exile, and Totalitarianism*, ed. Jerome Kohn (New York: Schocken, 1994), 132. See also Hannah Arendt, *The Origins of Totalitarianism* (New York: Harcourt, Brace, 1951); 2nd enl. ed. (Cleveland, OH: Meridian, 1958). All citations here are to these editions and are identified by the year published.

61. Arendt, "Nightmare and Flight," 134.

62. Arendt, "Nightmare and Flight," 134.

63. See Hannah Arendt, "What Is Existential Philosophy?," in *Essays in Understanding, 1930–1954: Formation, Exile, and Totalitarianism*, ed. Jerome Kohn (New York: Schocken, 1994), 163–87. For a useful reflection on this essay in relation to Arendt's later reflections on Heidegger, see Seyla Benhabib, *The Reluctant Modernism of Hannah Arendt* (Lanham, MD: Rowman and Littlefield, 2000), chap. 2.

64. Arendt, "Nightmare and Flight," 135. On the gnostic elements in Heidegger's philosophy, see Susan Anima Taubes, "The Gnostic Foundations of Heidegger's Nihilism," *Journal*

2. INCOMPARABLE EVIL   343

of Religion 34, no. 3 (1954): 155–72. Theology, as she says, haunted German idealism, and Heidegger's "covert theology" can be understood within the frame of reference of the gnostic tradition. According to Taubes, the source of the "deeper currents of thought" are to be found "not in the academic tradition but in the theological tradition and, specifically, in the tradition of gnostic heresy" (156). Regarding Arendt, given this polemical connection to Gnosticism, it is interesting that in her more deliberate treatment of existentialism, "What Is Existential Philosophy," which appeared shortly after "Nightmare and Flight," she does not discuss the impact of this gnostic tradition, especially in Kierkegaard, Heidegger, and Jaspers.

65. Arendt, "Nightmare and Flight," 135.

66. The essay is clearly connected to a cluster of others from this period, including "Organized Guilt and Universal Responsibility" (1945), "What Is Existential Philosophy?" (1948), and "The Concentration Camps" (1948), in which evil (sometimes barely rising to the level an idea much less a concept) makes an appearance. These essays are now collected in Arendt, *Essays in Understanding*.

67. Rieff, "The Theology of Politics," 120.

68. In a roundtable discussion held during the conference "On the Work of Hannah Arendt," York University, Toronto, November 1972, Arendt refers to people's "banisters," their "safe guiding lines." The discussion included Christian Bay, George Beard, F. M. Bernard, Richard Bernstein, Michael Gerstein, Melvyn Hill, Hans Jonas, C. B. Macpherson, Mary McCarthy, Hans Morganthau, Albrecht Wellmer, and Ed Weissman. For the transcript, see Hannah Arendt, "On Hannah Arendt" (1972), in *Hannah Arendt. The Recovery of the Public World*, ed. Melvyn Hill (New York: St Martin's, 1979), 301–39 (see 336); and Hannah Arendt, "Hannah Arendt on Hannah Arendt," in *Thinking Without a Banister: Essays in Understanding, 1953–1975*, ed. Jerome Kohn (New York: Schocken, 2018), 443–75 (see 472).

69. For a helpful discussion of *The Origins of Totalitarianism*, see Roy Tsao, "The Three Phases of Arendt's Theory of Totalitarianism," *Social Research* 69, no. 2 (Summer 2002): 579–619.

70. Arendt offers the following idea of the war's causes: "In this sense, it must be possible to face and understand the outrageous fact that so small (and, in world politics, so unimportant) a phenomenon as the Jewish question and antisemitism could become the catalytic agent for, first, the Nazi movement, then a world war, and finally the establishment of death factories." Arendt, *The Origins of Totalitarianism* (1951), viii.

71. Arendt, *The Origins of Totalitarianism* (1951), viii.

72. Arendt, *The Origins of Totalitarianism* (1951), ix.

73. Arendt, *The Origins of Totalitarianism* (1951), 433.

74. In the preface, Arendt makes it clear that the "additions and enlargements" in the new edition are not *revisions*, per se: "The changes are technical additions and replacements which do not alter either the analysis or argument of the original text." Arendt, "Preface to the Second Enlarged Edition," in *The Origins of Totalitarianism* (1958), xi–xii.

75. Arendt, *The Origins of Totalitarianism* (1958), 459.

76. Arendt, *The Origins of Totalitarianism* (1958), 459. In the second enlarged edition, the preface, dated April 1958, contains no mention of evil (xi–xii).

77. Richard Bernstein, *Why Read Hannah Arendt Now* (Cambridge: Polity, 2018).

78. On the productive idea of "mentalities," see Bernstein, *The Abuse of Evil*, chap. 1.

344   2. INCOMPARABLE EVIL

79. Richard King's judgment is different. He thinks that by the late 1960s Arendt had become a "prominent figure in the intellectual landscape of the country." See King, *Arendt and America*, 272. But I think here Bernstein is right, that although Arendt was certainly known by the late 1960s, it is much later that she became as indispensable a thinker as she has now become.

80. Bernstein, *Why Read Hannah Arendt Now*, 1.

81. See Elisabeth Young-Bruehl, *Why Arendt Matters* (New Haven, CT: Yale University Press, 2006). With great nuance, Young-Bruehl uses the admittedly now much trivialized idea of "the banality of evil" as a means of illuminating wider regions of Arendt's way of thinking. This idea has a very specific provenance (in her reading of Eichmann's behavior at his trial) and points to a specific contrast (with Kant's idea of radical evil), but for Young-Bruehl it captures something profound about both the substance and the orientation of Arendt as an intellectual. Removed from its "soundbite circuit," she says, and used as an analytical lens into Arendt's oeuvre, the trope of the banality of evil "will take you right to the core of her thinking, right to her abiding preoccupations, to the small cluster of hugely significant thoughts that she thought and rethought for all her adult life." For Young-Bruehl, it is this "poetic" capacity for a constant clarifying rethinking that gives Arendt's ideas their resonant character. "And it is because of these ideas, and the example of how she used them that Arendt matters for us, now, as thinking and acting people, as citizens" (5). One of these "hugely significant thoughts" that formed a recurring and generative motif in Arendt's work, Young-Bruehl argues, is that of "dark times." As she suggests, it is not the occurrence of evil deeds or evil events that makes for dark times so much as the collapse or destruction of the conditions of the public realm that might secure their repair, the conditions in which people, in their essential humanity, their essential difference, can appear to each other and account for their actions. The darkness, Young-Bruehl writes, is "what comes when the open, light spaces between people, the public spaces where people can reveal themselves, are shunned or avoided; the darkness is a hateful attitude toward the public realm, toward politics" (6–7). Lamentably, there have been many such historical periods, when evil is combined with or sheltered by a regime of power that obliterates what Arendt believed to be vital for human flourishing. As "our world has grown darker," Young-Bruehl says, she found herself asking: "What would Arendt have said? What would she think of this world we live in, three decades after her death? What would she consider importantly *new* about it?" (14; italics in original). These are, indeed, crucial questions. Young-Bruehl does not quite answer them.

82. Bernstein, *Why Read Hannah Arendt Now*, 2–3.

83. Bernstein, *Why Read Hannah Arendt Now*, 120–21.

84. Jerome Kohn also speaks of how important the question of experience is for thinking about Arendt. See, for example, Jerome Kohn, introduction to *Essays in Understanding, 1930–1954: Formation, Exile, and Totalitarianism*, by Hannah Arendt, ed. Jerome Kohn (New York: Schocken, 1994), xv. See also the 1972 conference roundtable transcript published in *Thinking Without a Banister*.

85. To be fair, in her biography Young-Bruehl addresses at least the question of Arendt's essay "Reflections on Little Rock" quite extensively. See Young-Bruehl, *Hannah Arendt: For Love of the World*, 308–18, 418–19.

86. Bernstein, *Why Read Hannah Arendt Now*, 48.

2. INCOMPARABLE EVIL 345

87. See King, *Arendt and America*, 16–17.

88. Hannah Arendt, "Reflections on Little Rock," *Dissent* 6, no. 1 (Winter 1959): 45–55; and collected in Hannah Arendt, *Responsibility and Judgment*, ed. Jerome Kohn (New York: Schocken, 2003), 193–213.

89. Bernstein, *Why Read Hannah Arendt Now*, 48–51.

90. See Ralph Ellison, "The World and the Jug," in *Shadow and Act* (New York: Vintage, 1964), 108. In conversation with Robert Penn Warren, Ellison elaborates on his critique. See Penn Warren, *Who Speaks for the Negro?* (New York: Random House, 1965), 342–44. Arendt replied to Ellison in a letter dated July 29, 1965. For more discussion on this, see Young-Bruehl, *Hannah Arendt: For Love of the World*, 315–18. See also King, *Arendt and America*, chap. 8, in which King, acknowledging the ignorance that pervades Arendt's understanding of the real issues involved, offers the view that among New York intellectuals there were "relatively few experts on American race and ethnic relations" and therefore, he concludes, "there were few people in Arendt's circle who might have set her straight on matters having to do with the South or with race" (166). But is this a sufficient excuse? What does it say about "Arendt's circle"?

91. Bernstein, *Why Read Hannah Arendt Now*, 52. His reference is to Danielle Allen, *Talking to Strangers: Anxieties of Citizenship Since Brown v. Board of Education* (Chicago: University of Chicago Press, 2004); and Kathryn Gines, *Hannah Arendt and the Negro Question* (Bloomington: Indiana University Press, 2014).

92. Gines, *Hannah Arendt and the Negro Question*, 13.

93. The story of the United States in the early twentieth century is the story of the making, unmaking, and remaking of racial identity—in particular, White identity. "Racially, Jews had become 'white' " by the early twentieth century, King suggests in *Arendt and America*, 46. See also Eric Goldstein, *The Price of Whiteness: Jews, Race, and American Identity* (Princeton, NJ: Princeton University Press, 2006). More generally, see Noel Ignatiev, *How the Irish Become White* (New York: Routledge, 1995); and Matthew Frye Jacobson, *Whiteness of a Different Color: European Immigrants and the Alchemy of Race* (Cambridge, MA: Harvard University Press, 1998).

94. See Bernstein, *Why Read Hannah Arendt Now*, 54–55.

95. In *Arendt and America*, King devotes many pages to thinking about Arendt's attitude to race and Black people. Like Bernstein he is adamant that Arendt was not a "racist" in the sense that she "advanced no biological explanation for group differences" (154), although he does allow that an "endemic sense of cultural superiority" (163) was a feature of her attitude toward Blacks. It is not clear how to parse the difference between racism and this sense that peoples of African descent are inferior to Europeans, even if on balance. "circa 1950, . . . when placed beside her European, German, and American contemporaries, Arendt looks better than most" (154).

96. Bernstein, *Why Read Hannah Arendt Now*, 52.

97. In Gines, *Hannah Arendt and the Negro Question*, Gines writes this with respect to Arendt's discussion of imperialism: "Despite the fact that Arendt seeks to take a position against racism, there are still traces of racism in her analysis. This is marked in part by her frequent use of the word 'savage' and by the way that she naturalizes Africans, asserting that they are pure nature and suggesting that they are somehow not capable of culture and the formation of (or participation in) the political" (78).

346 2. INCOMPARABLE EVIL

98. Gines, *Hannah Arendt and the Negro Question*, chap. 5. See also Arendt, *The Origins of Totalitarianism* (1951; 1958), esp. chaps. 6 and 7 of part 2, "Imperialism." These chapters are expanded (but not revised) in the second edition.

99. Gines, *Hannah Arendt and the Negro Question*, 79.

100. See Hannah Arendt, "What Remains? The Language Remains: A Conversation with Günter Gaus," in Hannah Arendt, *Essays in Understanding, 1930–1954: Formation, Exile, and Totalitarianism*, ed. Jerome Kohn (New York: Schocken, 1994), 1–2.

101. Indeed, I believe Bernstein is aware of this. See Bernstein, *Hannah Arendt and the Jewish Question*, 3–4.

102. It is not surprising that a number of authors have explicitly taken up the theme of the specificity of Arendt's ethics. See, for example, Deidre Lauren Mahony, *Hannah Arendt's Ethics* (London: Bloomsbury, 2018).

103. Bernstein, *Hannah Arendt and the Jewish Question*, 137.

104. Arguably this is not the only genealogy possible. In Peter Dews, *The Idea of Evil* (Oxford: Blackwell, 2013), Dews offers an arc from Kant through Fichte, Hegel, Schopenhauer, Nietzsche, Levinas, that ends with Adorno. Arendt does not frame his more critical theory concerns.

105. In point of fact, Bernstein's chapter 8 on Arendt in *Radical Evil* draws significantly, almost entirely, in somewhat rearranged form, from chapter 7 of *Hannah Arendt and the Jewish Question*.

106. Bernstein, *Radical Evil*, ix. Bernstein also references Andrew Delbanco, *The Death of Satan* (New York: Farrar, Straus, Giroux, 1995), 1, in this regard. This connecting of the sense of evil to what one finds one cannot reconcile oneself to is articulated by Arendt in the well-known conversation in Arendt, "What Remains? The Language Remains." Arendt is trying to give an account of what was for her (and for her husband) the pivotal recognition of the Nazi atrocity: "What was decisive," she says, "was the day we learned about Auschwitz." She goes on: "That was in 1943. And at first we didn't believe it. . . . And then half a year later we believed it after all, because we had the proof. That was the real shock. Before that we said: Well, one has enemies. That is entirely natural. Why shouldn't a people have enemies? But this was different. It was really as if an abyss had opened. Because we had the idea that amends could somehow be made for everything else, as amends can be made for just about everything at some point in politics. But not for this. This ought not to have happened. And I don't mean just the number of victims. I mean the method, the fabrication of corpses and so on—I don't need to go into that. This should not have happened. Something happened there to which we cannot reconcile ourselves. None of us ever can" (13–14). This sense of the impossibility of *reconciling* oneself to what has been done is central to the experience of evil.

107. Bernstein, *Radical Evil*, 3. This theme is further developed by Bernstein in *The Abuse of Evil*.

108. Bernstein, *Radical Evil*, 3.

109. Bernstein, *Radical Evil*, 6–7.

110. Bernstein, *Radical Evil*, ix.

111. Bernstein, *Radical Evil*, x.

112. See also Bernstein's introduction to *Abuse of Evil* for another instance of the exorbitant, exceptionalizing language used to talk about "Auschwitz" and "9/11" as defining events

2. INCOMPARAELE EVIL   347

of evil. See Richard Bernstein, *The Abuse of Evil: The Corruption of Politics and Religion Since 9/11* (Cambridge: Polity, 2006).

113. Bernstein, *Radical Evil*, 210–11. Bernstein then spends some paragraphs talking about the relation between individuality and spontaneity in *The Origins of Totalitarianism* and between natality and plurality in *The Human Condition* (see 211–13).

114. With terrifying poignancy, Arendt writes: "Nothing then remains but ghastly marionettes with human faces, which all behave like the dog in Pavlov's experiments, which all react with perfect reliability even when going to their own death, and which do nothing but react." Arendt, *The Origins of Totalitarianism* (1951), 426–27.

115. Bernstein, *Radical Evil*, 214.

116. Bernstein, *Radical Evil*, 214; Bernstein quotes from *Hannah Arendt/Karl Jaspers: Correspondence, 1926–1969*, ed. Lotte Kohler and Hans Saner (New York: Harcourt Brace Jovanovich, 1992), 54.

117. Bernstein, *Radical Evil*, 214–15; Bernstein, quoting from *Hannah Arendt/Karl Jasper*, 62.

118. Bernstein, *Radical Evil*, 215.

119. Hannah Arendt, *Eichmann in Jerusalem: A Report on the Banality of Evil* (New York: Viking, 1963), 247.

120. Arendt, *Eichmann in Jerusalem*, 246, 248.

121. Arendt, *Eichmann in Jerusalem*, 287. Arendt returns to this theme of Eichmann's fundamental thoughtlessness in the opening to her last, posthumously, published book, Hannah Arendt, *The Life of the Mind* (New York: Harcourt, 1978), 3–6. Of the idea of "the banality of evil" Arendt says: "Behind that phrase, I held no thesis or doctrine, although I was dimly aware of the fact that it went counter to our tradition of thought—literary, theological, or philosophic—about the phenomenon of evil. Evil, we have learned, is something demonic" (3). This is not what she found in the courtroom watching and listening to Eichmann: "However, what I was confronted with was utterly different and still undeniably factual. I was struck by a manifest shallowness in the doer that made it impossible to trace the uncontestable evil of his deeds to any deeper level of roots or motives. The deeds were monstrous, but the doer—at least the very effective one now on trial—was quite ordinary, commonplace, and neither demonic nor monstrous" (4).

122. Arendt, *Eichmann in Jerusalem*, 276.

123. Bernstein, *Radical Evil*, 218; Bernstein quotes "Eichmann in Jerusalem: An Exchange of Letters Between Gershom Scholem and Hannah Arendt," in *Hannah Arendt, the Jew as Pariah: Jewish Identity and Politics in the Modern Age*, ed. Ron Feldman (New York: Grove, 1978), 251.

124. Bernstein, *Radical Evil*, 218 (italics in original).

125. Bernstein, *Radical Evil*, 218.

126. Arguably, this idea that there was something missing in Arendt's earlier account that was made good in the later one is more sharply and explicitly articulated in *Radical Evil* than in *Hannah Arendt and the Jewish Question*.

127. As anyone who is familiar with Elizabeth Anscombe's unbendingly complex interrogation of intention, and the debates around it within the philosophy of action, can appreciate, intention is an enormously fraught and multifaceted problem. Memorably in this respect, her concern with intention is set in motion precisely by her astute reflections on the "intention" in Harry Truman's action to use the bomb against the Japanese.

348   2. INCOMPARABLE EVIL

See the pamphlet in G. E. M. Anscombe, *Mr. Truman's Degree* (Oxford: Anscombe, 1957), reprinted in *Collected Philosophical Papers*, vol. 3, *Ethics, Religion, and Politics* (Oxford: Blackwell, 1981), 62–71. The reflections in this pamphlet were central to the impetus in her *Intention* (1957; repr., Cambridge, MA: Harvard University Press, 2000). For a helpful discussion, see Rachael Wiseman, *Anscombe's "Intention"* (New York: Routledge, 2016).

128.   Bernstein, *Hannah Arendt and the Jewish Question*, 152–53.

129.   See David Rousset, *Les Jours de Notre Mort* (Paris: Le Pavois, 1947); Eugen Kogon, *Der SS-Staat* (Berlin: Bermann-Fischer, 1947); and Bruno Bettelheim, "On Dachau and Buchenwald," in *Nazi Conspiracy and Aggression*, vol. 7 (Washington, DC: U.S. Government Printing Office, 1946).

130.   Arendt, *The Origins of Totalitarianism* (1951), 414.

131.   Arendt, *The Origins of Totalitarianism* (1951), 415 (italics in original).

132.   In a memorable and perhaps controversial passage in *Discourse on Colonialism*, Aimé Césaire writes: "Yes, it would be worthwhile to study clinically, in detail, the steps taken by Hitler and Hitlerism and to reveal to the very distinguished, very humanistic, very Christian bourgeois of the twentieth century that without his being aware of it, he has a Hitler inside of him, that Hitler *inhabits* him, that Hitler is his *demon*, that if he rails against him, he is being inconsistent and that, at bottom, what he cannot forgive Hitler for is not the *crime* in itself, *the crime against man*, it is not *the humiliation of man as such*, it is the crime against the white man, the humiliation of the white man, and the fact that he applied to Europe colonialist procedures which until then had been reserved exclusively for the Arabs of Algeria, the coolies of India, and the blacks of Africa." Aimé Césaire, *Discourse on Colonialism*, trans. Joan Pinkham (New York: Monthly Review, 1972), 14 (italics in original). See Karuna Mantena, "Genealogies of Catastrophe: Arendt on the Logic and Legacy of Imperialism," in *Politics in Dark Times: Encounters with Hannah Arendt*, ed. Seyla Benhabib (Cambridge: Cambridge University Press, 2010), 83–112.

133.   Arendt, *The Origins of Totalitarianism* (1951), 416.

134.   Arendt, *The Origins of Totalitarianism* (1951), 416–17.

135.   Arendt, *The Origins of Totalitarianism* (1951), 417.

136.   Kenneth Stampp, *The Peculiar Institution: Slavery in the Ante-Bellum South* (New York: Knopf, 1956); Ulrich B. Phillips, *American Negro Slavery* (New York: Appleton, 1918); and Ulrich B. Phillips, *Life and Labor in the Old South* (1929; Boston: Little, Brown, 1946). For a discussion of the Phillips tradition and the attempts to break away from it, see Robert Fogel, *The Slavery Debates, 1952–1990: A Retrospective* (Baton Rouge: Louisiana State University Press, 2003), 4–23.

137.   Carter B. Woodson, *The Mis-education of the Negro* (1933; repr., Trenton: Africa World, 1990); W. E. B. Du Bois, *Black Reconstruction in America, 1860–1880* (1935; repr., New York: Free Press, 1998); and C. L. R. James, *The Black Jacobins: Toussaint L'Ouverture and the San Domingo Revolution* (1938; repr., New York: Vintage, 1963).

138.   See King, *Arendt and America*, 192. Arendt refers to Elkins's book in favorable terms in Hannah Arendt, "Civil Disobedience" (1970), in *Crises of the Republic* (New York: Harcourt Brace Jovanovich, 1972), 81n50. A version of the essay was first published in the *New Yorker*, September 12, 1970.

3. INCOMMENSURABLE EVILS

1. The story of the *Zong* slave ship is recounted in various ways in a number of scholarly works. See, for example, James Walvin, *The "Zong": A Massacre, the Law, and the End of Slavery* (New Haven, CT: Yale University Press, 2011); and Michelle Faubert, *Granville Sharp's Uncovered Letter and the "Zong" Massacre* (New York: Palgrave Pivot, 2018). On Lord Mansfield, see Norman Poser, *Lord Mansfield: Justice in the Age of Reason* (Montreal, Canada: McGill-Queen's University Press, 2013). "Long after deciding the Somerset case," Poser writes, "Mansfield continued to regard black slaves not as human beings having inalienable rights but as chattels—personal property that their owners could dispose of as they wished. He exhibited this view most chillingly in the infamous case of the slave ship *Zong*, decided in May 1783, eleven years after his *Somerset* ruling" (297). Poser goes on: "It was implicit in Mansfield's decision, that if the ship owner could prove that sufficient water was lacking it would have been legal—and within the terms of the insurance policy as one of the normal perils of the sea—to throw the slaves overboard. Nowhere in his short opinion was there any suggestion that the captain and crew of the *Zong* were murderers" (298).

2. Famously, James Kelsall, the ship's first mate, later claimed to have objected when he first heard of the proposal. See Walvin, *The "Zong,"* 97.

3. I am thinking, of course, of William Turner's well-known 1840 painting *The Slave Ship*; the novel by Fred D'Aguiar, *Feeding the Ghosts* (Hopewell, NJ: Ecco, 1997) and the long poem by M. NourbeSe Phillip, *Zong!* (Middletown, CT: Wesleyan University Press, 2008).

4. Walvin, *The "Zong,"* 10.

5. Laurence Mordekhai Thomas, *Vessels of Evil: American Slavery and the Holocaust* (Philadelphia, PA: Temple University Press, 1993). For reviews and discussions, see Martin Goldman, "Review of *Vessels of Evil: American Slavery and the Holocaust*," *Shofar* 14, no. 3 (Spring 1996): 202–4; James Sterba, "Understanding Evil: American Slavery, the Holocaust, and the Conquest of the American Indians," *Ethics* 106, no. 2 (January 1996): 424–48; and Howard Harriott, "Review of *Vessels of Evil: American Slavery and the Holocaust*," *African American Review* 30, no. 2 (1996): 283–85. The following year Harriott published the review article, Howard Harriott, "The Evils of Chattel Slavery and the Holocaust: An Examination of Laurence Thomas's *Vessels of Evil*," *International Philosophical Quarterly* 37, no 3 (September 1997): 329–47. See also Todd Calder, "Toward a Theory of Evil Acts: A Critique of Laurence Thomas's Theory of Evil Acts," in *Earth's Abominations: Philosophical Studies of Evil*, ed. Daniel M. Haybron (Leiden, Netherlands: Brill, 2002), 51–61.

6. See Laurence Mordekhai Thomas, "The Morally Obnoxious Comparisons of Evil: American Slavery and the Holocaust" (2002), cogprints.org/4634/1/Suffering_AS&H. pdf, 25. Translated from the German, *Grazenlose Vorurteile: Antisemitismus, Nationalismus, und Ethnik Konflikte*, 2002 Yearbook of the Fritz Bauer Institut, Frankfurt on the Main, Germany.

7. Thomas is a philosopher of both Black and Jewish heritages and has spoken sensitively about their intersection in his life and work: "With respect to my identity," he said, in response to a question put to him by George Yancy, "Blackness is there and Jewishness is there. I think that those two things come together nicely and they've not been the major

350 3. INCOMMENSURABLE EVILS

tension that the world makes them out to be. On the other hand, they're not overarching in my life and I don't want them to be because I think that in the end I have this stupid view that we are human beings first and I think that's the way it should be." See George Yancy, ed., *African-American Philosophers: Seventeen Conversations* (New York: Routledge, 1998), 303.

8. See Michelle Moody-Adams, *Morality, Culture, and Philosophy: Fieldwork in Familiar Places* (Cambridge, MA: Harvard University Press, 1997); Bernard Boxill, *Blacks and Social Justice*, rev. ed. (Lanham, MD: Rowman and Littlefield, 1992); Tommy Lott, ed., *Subjugation and Bondage: Critical Essays on Slavery and Social Philosophy* (Lanham, MD: Rowman and Littlefield, 1998); Howard McGary and Bill Lawson, *Between Slavery and Freedom: Philosophy and American Slavery* (Bloomington: Indiana University Press, 1992); and Charles W. Mills, *Black Rights/White Wrongs: A Critique of Racial Liberalism* (New York: Oxford University Press, 2017).

9. Laurence Thomas, *Living Morally: A Psychology of Moral Character* (Philadelphia, PA: Temple University Press, 1989). See also the more recent Laurence Thomas, *The Family and the Political Self* (Cambridge: Cambridge University Press, 2006).

10. Thomas, *Living Morally*, x.

11. Thomas, *Vessels of Evil*, x.

12. Thomas, *Vessels of Evil*, 7.

13. For a different approach to the matter of comparison, see Michael Rothberg, *Multidirectional Memory: Remembering the Holocaust in an Age of Decolonization* (Stanford, CA: Stanford University Press, 2009).

14. Thomas, *Vessels of Evil*, x.

15. Thomas, *Vessels of Evil*, 11, 8.

16. Thomas, *Vessels of Evil*, x.

17. Compare this with Richard Bernstein's evasion of a theory of evil mentioned in chapter 2. See Richard Bernstein, *Radical Evil: A Philosophical Interrogation* (Cambridge: Polity, 2002),

18. Martha Nussbaum, *The Fragility of Goodness: Luck and Ethics in Greek Tragedy and Philosophy* (New York: Cambridge University Press, 1986).

19. See Orlando Patterson, *Slavery and Social Death* (Cambridge, MA: Harvard University Press, 1982).

20. See Laurence Thomas, "Evil and Forgiveness: The Possibility of Moral Redemption," in *Evil, Political Violence, and Forgiveness: Essays in Honor of Claudia Card*, ed. Andrea Veltman and Kathryn Norlock (Lanham, MD: Lexington, 2009), 115–33.

21. This list of questions is not novel. I have drawn it largely from Claudia Card, *The Atrocity Paradigm: A Theory of Evil* (New York: Oxford University Press, 2002), 3; and Todd Calder, "The Concept of Evil," in *Stanford Encyclopedia of Philosophy*, ed. Edward Zalta and Uri Nodelman (Winter 2022); plato.stanford.edu/entries/concept-evil.

22. See John Kekes, *Facing Evil* (Princeton, NJ: Princeton University Press, 1990), and Card, *The Atrocity Paradigm*.

23. Thomas, *Vessels of Evil*, 73–74n2.

24. John Kekes, *The Roots of Evil* (Ithaca, NY: Cornell University Press, 2005). In what follows, I focus on his first book on evil because there he develops his argument in more detail. See John Kekes, *Facing Evil* (Ithaca, NY: Cornell University Press, 1994).

3. INCOMMENSURABLE EVILS   351

25. See John Kekes, *Against Liberalism* (Ithaca, NY: Cornell University Press, 1997); John Kekes, *A Case for Conservatism* (Ithaca, NY: Cornell University Press, 1998); and John Kekes, *The Human Condition* (New York: Oxford University Press, 2010).

26. I am thinking of the work of Alasdair MacIntyre, *After Virtue: A Study in Moral Theory* (Notre Dame, IN: University of Notre Dame Press, 1981); and Alasdair MacIntyre, *Three Rival Versions of Moral Inquiry: Encyclopaedia, Genealogy, and Tradition* (Notre Dame, IN: University of Notre Dame Press, 1990); see also John Gray, *In Enlightenment's Wake: Politics and Culture at the Close of the Modern Age* (New York: Routledge, 1995); John Gray, *Two Faces of Liberalism* (New York: New Press, 2000); and Nussbaum, *The Fragility of Goodness*.

27. For some suggestive doubts about Truman and the response to him and his decision, see G. E. M. Anscombe, *Mr. Truman's Degree*, originally published as a pamphlet in 1957 in order to try to persuade Oxford University against awarding Truman an honorary degree. The essay appears in G. E. M. Anscombe, *Collected Philosophical Papers*. Vol. 3, *Ethics, Religion, and Politics* (Hoboken, NJ: Blackwell, 1981), 62–71. On the significance of this essay for Anscombe's later work, see Rachael Wiseman, *Anscombe's "Intention"* (New York: Routledge, 2016).

28. Kekes, *Facing Evil*, 4.

29. Kekes, *Facing Evil*, 5.

30. Kekes, *Facing Evil*, 5.

31. Kekes, *Facing Evil*, 6.

32. In her brief notice of Kekes's book, Mary Midgely expresses some doubt about the contrast he draws between choice- and character-morality. It is odd, she says, that given the focus on character, Kekes isn't more interested in the moral psychology of motivation. In the end she suggests that choice and character are matters of emphasis: "Choice and character are not alternative explanations of evil nor alternative types of morality." Mary Midgely, "Review of *Facing Evil*, by John Kekes," *Pailosophy* 66, no. 258 (October 1991): 538.

33. Kekes, *Facing Evil*, 7.

34. Kekes, *Facing Evil*, 44.

35. Kekes, *Facing Evil*, 183.

36. Kekes, *Facing Evil*, 182.

37. Kekes, *Facing Evil*, 185.

38. Kekes, *Facing Evil*, 189.

39. Kekes, *Facing Evil*, 196.

40. Kekes, *Facing Evil*, 197.

41. Kekes, *Facing Evil*, 198.

42. See, for example, Kekes, *Facing Evil*, 33.

43. Nussbaum, *The Fragility of Goodness*, 398.

44. Nussbaum, *The Fragility of Goodness*, 405.

45. Kekes, *Facing Evil*, 199.

46. Kekes, *Facing Evil*, 199–200.

47. Card, *The Atrocity Paradigm*, 3.

48. Card, *The Atrocity Paradigm*, 64–68.

49. Claudia Card, ed., *Feminist Ethics* (Lawrence: University Press of Kansas, 1991).

50. Claudia Card, *Lesbian Choices* (New York: Columbia University Press, 1995).

352   3. INCOMMENSURABLE EVILS

51. Claudia Card, *The Unnatural Lottery: Character and Moral Luck* (Philadelphia, PA: Temple University Press, 1996). For the contributions of Bernard Williams and Thomas Nagel, and the wider discussion prompted by their respective essays, see Daniel Statman, ed., *Moral Luck* (Albany: State University of New York Press, 1993).

52. For wonderfully insightful discussions of the arc of Card's work in moral philosophy, see Veltman and Norlock, *Evil, Political Violence, and Forgiveness*; and Robin Dillon and Armen Marsoobian, eds., *Criticism and Compassion: The Ethics and Politics of Claudia Card* (New York: Wiley, 2018).

53. By defining evil as intolerable harm caused by culpable wrongdoing, Card means to negotiate a path between utilitarian and Kantian ethics. Utilitarians aim at an ethical theory focused on reducing harms and therefore giving some precedence to the sufferer of harms. By contrast, for Kant, radical evil emanates from a choice made by a moral agent to subordinate moral principles to self-interest. Evil, for Kantians, is wrongful willing, and therefore the suffering of victims is not part of what makes evil evil. (Interestingly, as critical as Kekes is of Kant's choice-morality, both he and Kant share a focus on the agents of evil rather than the sufferers of evil.) Card, by contrast, holds that the harm suffered by the victim is a defining feature of evil. However, she does not want to simply abandon Kant; she too sees evildoing in reference to intention and will. See the discussion in Card, *The Atrocity Paradigm*, chaps. 3 and 4.

54. Card, *The Atrocity Paradigm*, 28.

55. For another version of this critique of Nietzsche and Foucault, see MacIntyre, *Three Rival Versions of Moral Enquiry*.

56. Card, *The Atrocity Paradigm*, 29.

57. Card, *The Atrocity Paradigm*, 8.

58. Card, *The Atrocity Paradigm*, 9.

59. Card, *The Atrocity Paradigm*, 3.

60. Card, *The Atrocity Paradigm*, 5.

61. Card, *The Atrocity Paradigm*, 24. See also Claudia Card, "Inequalities Versus Evils," in *Controversies in Feminism*, ed. James Sterba (Lanham, MD: Rowman and Littlefield, 2001), 83–98.

62. Card, *The Atrocity Paradigm*, 4. For a helpful engagement with Card, see Todd Calder, "The Prevalence of Evil," in *Evil, Political Violence, and Forgiveness: Essays in Honor of Claudia Card*, ed. Andrea Veltman and Kathryn Norlock (Lanham, MD: Lexington, 2009), 13–34.

63. Card, *The Atrocity Paradigm*, 13.

64. Card, *The Atrocity Paradigm*, 15.

65. Claudia Card, *Confronting Evils: Terrorism, Torture, Genocide* (New York: Cambridge University Press, 2010), 16.

66. Claudia Card, afterword in *Evil, Political Violence, and Forgiveness: Essays in Honor of Claudia Card*, ed. Andrea Veltman and Kathryn Norlock (Lanham, MD: Lexington, 2009), 214.

67. Card, afterword, 214–15.

68. Patterson, *Slavery and Social Death*.

69. Claudia Card, "Genocide and Social Death," *Hypatia* 18, no. 1 (Winter 2003): 63–79; "Genocide Is Social Death," chap. 9 in *Confronting Evils: Terrorism, Torture, Genocide* (New York: Cambridge University Press, 2010), 237–66.

3. INCOMMENSURABLE EVILS 353

70. Card, *Confronting Evils*, 237.

71. Card, *Confronting Evils*, 239.

72. It is most interesting that Card makes no mention of Arendt in "Genocide Is Social Death," chap. 9 of *Confronting Evils*, but she talks about radical evil involved in the destruction of the humanity of those still living and the production of living corpses in *Confronting Evils* (38), and she discusses torture and the production of "gestating corpses" in *Confronting Evils* (285). Whereas Card thinks about Arendt primarily in relation to the question of "forgiveness" in *The Atrocity Paradigm* (174–79), she makes much wider use of Arendt, both in relation to the earlier work on radical evil and the later work on the relation between evil and thinking morally, in *Confronting Evils* (20).

73. Card, *Confronting Evils*, 263.

74. Thomas, *Vessels of Evil*, 13.

75. See, in this connection, Laurence Thomas, "Liberalism and the Holocaust: An Essay on Trust and the Black-Jewish Relationship," in *Echoes from the Holocaust: Philosophical Reflections on a Dark Time*, ed. Alan Rosenberg and Gerald Myers (Philadelphia, PA: Temple University Press, 1988), 105–17.

76. Thomas, *Vessels of Evil*, 15.

77. Thomas, *Vessels of Evil*, 43n8.

78. Stanley Milgram, *Obedience to Authority: An Experimental View* (New York: Harper, 1974); and Philip Zimbardo, *The Lucifer Effect: Understanding How Good People Turn Evil* (New York: Random House, 2008).

79. Thomas, *Vessels of Evil*, 55.

80. Thomas, *Vessels of Evil*, 64–65. See also the explicit argument in Laurence Thomas, "Becoming an Evil Society: The Self and Strangers," *Political Theory* 24, no. 2 (May 1996): 271–94.

81. See Kekes, *Against Liberalism*. In Thomas, "Liberalism and the Holocaust," Thomas writes more explicitly about liberalism's complicity in a denuded moral-civic lifeworld, a lifeworld that does not foster the virtues of moral courage important to civic social trust: "Liberalism does not insist or even invite the members of society to identify with an objective good; indeed, it often denies that a satisfactory case can be made for such a good. Moreover, it denies that there is an objective reason why individuals should identify with the good of others. Accordingly, individuals are encouraged to pursue their good as they conceive of it, provided that they do not harm others. Consider the dearth of good Samaritan laws, at least in the United States. Liberalism thus conceived does not inspire moral courage. For courage is born of the conviction that there is something out there worth risking one's life or well-being for, that there are objective reasons for taking seriously the good of others. Courage is at odds with the view that all goods in life are anchored in the self-interest of persons" (107–8). On the United States as a procedural republic, see Michael Sandel, *Democracy's Discontent: America in Search of a Public Philosophy* (Cambridge, MA: Belknap, 1996).

82. Thomas, *Vessels of Evil*, 73.

83. Thomas, *Vessels of Evil*, 74.

84. Thomas, *Vessels of Evil*, 82. See Kekes, *Facing Evil*, chap. 3.

85. Thomas, *Vessels of Evil*, 82.

86. Thomas, "Liberalism and the Holocaust," 109.

354   3. INCOMMENSURABLE EVILS

87. On Thomas Thistlewood, see Douglas Hall, *In Miserable Slavery: Thomas Thistlewood in Jamaica, 1750–86* (London: Macmillan, 1989); and Trevor Burnard, *Mastery, Tyranny, and Desire: Thomas Thistlewood and His Slaves in the Anglo-Jamaican World* (Kingston, Jamaica: University of the West Indies Press, 2004).

88. Thomas, *Vessels of Evil*, 89.

89. Thomas, *Vessels of Evil*, 90. One is reminded of the remark Jean-Paul Sartre makes in his introduction to Albert Memmi, *The Colonizer and the Colonized*, trans. Howard Greenfield (New York: Orion, 1965): "No one can treat a man like a dog without first regarding him as a man" (xxvii).

90. Thomas, *Vessels of Evil*, 90.

91. Thomas, *Vessels of Evil*, 91.

92. See Laurence Thomas, "The Psychology of Doubling," chap. 5 in *Vessels of Evil: American Slavery and the Holocaust* (Philadelphia, PA: Temple University Press, 1993), 92–113.

93. It is a curious fact that in his discussion of and disagreement with Thomas's conception of evil action, Todd Calder does not once mention the larger project with which Thomas is engaged. See Calder, "Toward a Theory of Evil Acts."

94. Card, *The Atrocity Paradigm*, 24. This insight is also at the center of the shift we've seen Card make in *Confronting Evils*, from thinking about "culpable" evils (largely individual) to "inexcusable" evils (largely institutional).

95. Thomas, *Vessels of Evil*, 117.

96. Thomas, *Vessels of Evil*, 118.

97. Thomas, *Vessels of Evil*, 119.

98. Eugene Genovese, *Roll, Jordan, Roll: The World the Slaves Made* (New York: Vintage, 1976); see also Howard McGary, "Paternalism and Slavery," in Howard McGary and Bill Lawson, *Between Slavery and Freedom: Philosophy and American Slavery* (Bloomington: Indiana University Press, 1992), 16–34. Stanley Elkins, *Slavery: A Problem in American Institutional and Intellectual Life* (Chicago: University of Chicago Press, 1959).

99. Thomas, *Vessels of Evil*, 122.

100. Thomas, *Vessels of Evil*, 123.

101. Thomas, *Vessels of Evil*, 124.

102. Thomas, *Vessels of Evil*, 124.

103. Thomas, *Vessels of Evil*, 125.

104. Thomas, *Vessels of Evil*, 125. See also the discussion of the 1982 film *Sophie's Choice* in Thomas, "The Morally Obnoxious Comparisons of Evil." Whereas it is undeniably true that death "forecloses all options forever," he argues, the choice presented to Sophie (to decide which of her two children the Nazis would murder) "reveals a most poignant truth, namely that there are some acts of cruelty that the Nazis performed that we regard as worse than the acts of murder that they routinely performed" (14).

105. Thomas, *Vessels of Evil*, 125.

106. Thomas, *Vessels of Evil*, 126.

107. John Blassingame, *The Slave Community: Plantation Life in the Antebellum South* (New York: Oxford University Press, 1972).

108. Thomas, *Vessels of Evil*, 127.

109. Thomas, *Vessels of Evil*, 132. Where the Caribbean is concerned, there is an important debate around how to think about the often-ambiguous relation between *accommodation*

3. INCOMMENSURABLE EVILS   355

and *resistance*, the ways in which one sometimes worked through the other, the fact that an enslaved person who at one point appeared to have accommodated might at another time be the leader of a revolt. See Sylvia Wynter, "Jonkonnu in Jamaica," *Jamaica Journal* 4, no. 2 (June 1970): 34–48; and Kamau Brathwaite, *Contradictory Omens: Cultural Diversity and Integration in the Caribbean* (Mona, Jamaica: Savacou, 1974).

110. Thomas, *Vessels of Evil*, 133.

111. Thomas, *Vessels of Evil*, 137. Thomas is referring to Douglass's description in Frederick Douglass, *Narrative of the Life of Frederick Douglass, An American Slave* (1845; repr., New York: Penguin Classics, 1986), 91–92. It is interesting that Thomas does not focus on that earlier scene in Douglass's *Narrative* in which he describes the outrages inflicted on his Aunt Hester (51–52). See also Thomas, "The Morally Obnoxious Comparisons of Evil," in which he emphasizes that commentators often miss the poignant incongruousness between the "demand of utter loyalty and on-going complete insubordination to the will of another" (11). "Minimally," Thomas continues, elaborating on the nature of this perverse incongruity, "loyalty is a human virtue because it is an expression of the desire to act on behalf of another in the realization of her or his goals. Loyalty is to be contrasted with deliberate betrayal and deception. Complete subordination is thus incompatible with loyalty. Slavery is never just about the subjugation of subordination. It is necessarily about inculcating utter loyalty on the part of the slaves" (10–11).

112. Thomas, *Vessels of Evil*, 138.

113. Thomas, *Vessels of Evil*, 139. Or, as Thomas puts the contrast in "The Morally Obnoxious Comparisons of Evil": "The Nazis showed a methodicalness about killing people that humanity had never before witnessed. Yet, what the Nazis did not demand is loyalty from the very people they sought to kill. By contrast, slavery aimed to deliver the good of utter loyalty, on the one hand, combined with the ease of complete subordination, on the other. What is more, just as it would have made no sense for the Nazis to have demanded loyalty of the very people whom they overtly sought to kill, it would have made no sense for those involved in slavery to have had as their aim the death of the very people from whom they wanted utter loyalty and subordination. The aims of American Slavery could not have included the ends of the Holocaust; and conversely, the aims of the Holocaust could not have included the ends of American Slavery" (11–12).

114. Thomas, *Vessels of Evil*, 148.

115. Thomas, *Vessels of Evil*, 149. See also Thomas, "The Morally Obnoxious Comparisons of Evil," 10.

116. See the discussion in John Bodel and Walter Scheidel, eds., *On Human Bondage: After "Slavery and Social Death"* (Chichester, UK: Wiley, 2017).

117. Patterson, *Slavery and Social Death*, 5.

118. Thomas, *Vessels of Evil*, 150–51.

119. Thomas, *Vessels of Evil*, 154.

120. Thomas, *Vessels of Evil*, 156.

121. Thomas *Vessels of Evil*, 153.

122. Card, *Confronting Evils*, 264.

123. Thomas, "The Morally Obnoxious Comparisons of Evil," 9.

124. Thomas, *Vessels of Evil*, 161.

125. Thomas, *Vessels of Evil*, 163.

356   3. INCOMMENSURABLE EVILS

126. Thomas, "Evil and Forgiveness: The Possibility of Moral Redemption," 115–33. Although this essay is more handily in dialogue with Card, it incorporates several directions from an earlier, more wide-ranging essay on forgiveness. See Laurence Thomas, "Forgiving the Unforgivable," in *Moral Philosophy and the Holocaust*, ed. Eva Gerrard and Geoffrey Scarre (Burlington, UK: Ashgate, 2003), 201–30.

127. Thomas, "The Morally Obnoxious Comparisons of Evil," 22.

128. See Card, *The Atrocity Paradigm*, 168, and more broadly the whole of chapter 8, "The Moral Powers of Victims," 166–87.

129. See Thomas, "Forgiving the Unforgivable," 204. On the virtuous reluctance to forgive, see Thomas Brudholm, *Resentment's Virtue: Jean Améry and the Refusal to Forgive* (Philadelphia, PA: Temple University Press, 2008). On forgiveness as foreswearing resentment, see Jeffrie Murphy, "Forgiveness and Resentment," in *Forgiveness and Mercy*, by Jeffrie Murphy and Jean Hampton (New York: Cambridge University Press, 1988), 14–34. Murphy wrote the foreword to Brudholm's *Resentment's Virtue*.

130. Thomas, "Evil and Forgiveness," 115–16.

131. Thomas, "Forgiving the Unforgivable," 203.

132. In "Forgiving the Unforgivable," Thomas explores the idea of a Nazi in Hitler's army through the fictive figure of "Adolph Paul-Damascus," obviously a compound of Hitler and the biblical Paul, who underwent a conversion experience on the road to Damascus. In Thomas's plausible account, Adolph Paul-Damascus was responsible for deporting hundreds of Jews to what he knew was certain death in the camps. After the war he escaped to South America and then, with a new identity, emigrated to America where he amassed a fortune, which he gave away to Jewish charities. He subsequently turned himself in to the Israeli state.

133. See Geoffrey Scarre, "Evil Collectives," *Midwest Studies in Philosophy* 36 (2012): 74–92.

134. Famously, Wallace was visited in hospital by one of his rivals for the 1972 Democratic nomination, the African American congresswoman Shirley Chisholm, and it is her act of courage and her openness to forgiveness that is said to have set in motion the moral journey that led to Wallace's expression of regret seven years later.

135. As is well known, Mansfield's great-niece Dido Elizabeth Belle, daughter of Sir John Lindsay (Mansfield's nephew), and Maria Belle, an African enslaved woman in the Caribbean, remained formally a slave in Mansfield's household at Kenwood House until his death in 1793, when his will freed her and provided her with an inheritance. See Poser, *Lord Mansfield*, 392.

136. On the extraordinary life of Olaudah Equiano, see Vincent Carretta, *Equiano the African: Biography of a Self-Made Man* (Athens: University of Georgia Press, 2005).

4. SLAVERY'S EVIL LIFEWORLD

1. Orlando Patterson, *Die the Long Day* (New York: William Morrow, 1972).

2. Think of the advertisement for a runaway slave that appeared in the Spanish Town workhouse in January 1791: "Quasheba, a creole, to Williken's estate, marked W, HD on left shoulder, 5 feet 6½ inches high. 14 [January 1791]." Quoted in Diana Paton, *No Bond but the Law: Punishment, Race, and Gender in Jamaican State Formation, 1780–1870* (Durham, NC: Duke University Press, 2004), 11. Paton uses this instance to reflect on the strategies of sovereign and disciplining power by which the late eighteenth-century Jamaican state

sought to police the refractory slave population. Although likely to have been branded, and undoubtedly defiant, Patterson's Quasheba does not appear to have been a perennial runaway.

3. See Douglas Hall, *In Miserable Slavery: Thomas Thistlewood in Jamaica, 1750–1786* (Kingston, Jamaica: University of the West Indies Press, 1998); and Trevor Burnard, *Mastery, Tyranny, and Desire: Thomas Thistlewood and His Slaves in the Anglo-Jamaican World* (Kingston, Jamaica: University of the West Indies Press, 2004).

4. Patterson, *Die the Long Day*, 30.

5. For an excellent discussion on the ontology of Black selfhood embodied in the Jamaican Creole noun *smaddy* and the process of *smadditization*, see Charles W. Mills, "Smadditizin'," in *Radical Theory, Caribbean Reality: Race, Class, and Social Domination* (Kingston, Jamaica: University of the West Indies Press, 2010), 164–84. Mills owes this idea, of course, to Rex Nettleford.

6. On some of the complexities of this history, see Kenneth Bilby, *True-Born Maroons* (Gainesville: University Press of Florida, 2005).

7. For some reflections on his sociological practice (with respect to slavery studies most particularly), see Orlando Patterson, "The Denial of Slavery in Contemporary American Sociology," *Theory and Society* 48, no. 6 (December 2019): 903–14. See also George Steinmetz, "Sociology and Sisyphus: Postcolonialism, Anti-positivism, and Modernist Narrative in Patterson's Oeuvre," *Theory and Society* 48, no. 6 (December 2019): 799–822.

8. See Orlando Patterson, "Recent Studies on Caribbean Slavery and the Atlantic Slave Trade," *Latin American Research Review* 17, no. 3 (1982): 251. This idea is borrowed from Gordon Wright, "History as a Moral Science," *American Historical Review* 81, no. 1 (February 1976): 1–11. See also George Cotkin, "History's Moral Turn," *Journal of the History of Ideas* 69, no. 2 (2008): 298–315.

9. On David Riesman, see Orlando Patterson's remembrance of him: Orlando Patterson, "The Last Sociologist," *New York Times*, May 19, 2002.

10. Orlando Patterson, *The Sociology of Slavery: An Analysis of the Origins, Development, and Structure of Negro Slave Society in Jamaica* (London: MacGibbon and Kee, 1967); Orlando Patterson, *Slavery and Social Death: A Comparative Study* (Cambridge. MA: Harvard University Press, 1982); and Orlando Patterson, *Freedom*. Vol. 1, *Freedom in the Making of Western Culture* (London: Tauris, 1991).

11. Indeed, the policy work beginning in the 1970s displaced the 1960s work on fiction. On the turn to policy, see David Scott, "The Paradox of Freedom: An Interview with Orlando Patterson," *Small Axe*, no. 40 (March 2013): 206–15. This interview has now been republished in an updated and expanded form and with a fresh introduction in David Scott and Orlando Patterson, *The Paradox of Freedom: A Biographical Dialogue* (Cambridge: Polity, 2023). However, all citations here are to the *Small Axe* version. On Patterson's literary contribution, see Bridget Jones, "Orlando Patterson," in *Fifty Caribbean Writers: A Bio-Bibliographical Critical Sourcebook*, ed. Daryl Cumber Dance (New York: Greenwood, 1986), 368–76. Like other West Indian intellectuals whom he admired (the novelist C. L. R. James, the poet M. G. Smith), Patterson has been a practicing artist—as though there was something in the nature of the historical reality of Caribbean postslave societies that resisted or anyway evaded intelligibility in any single genre that seemed to call for fictive as well as nonfictive forms of engagement.

4. SLAVERY'S EVIL LIFEWORLD

12. Orlando Patterson, *The Children of Sisyphus* (London: New Authors, 1964); and Orlando Patterson, *An Absence of Ruins* (London: New Authors, 1967). He also published short fiction during this time: Orlando Patterson, "The Very Funny Man: A Tale in Two Moods," and Orlando Patterson, "One for a Penny" are anthologized in Andrew Salkey, ed., *Island Voices: Stories from the West Indies* (London: Elek, 1965), 133–38, 139–45, respectively; see also Orlando Patterson, "The Alien," *New Left Review*, no. 33 (September–October 1965): 82–92; and Orlando Patterson, "Into the Dark," *Jamaica Journal* 2, no. 1 (March 1968): 62–68.

13. See Orlando Patterson, *Ethnic Chauvinism: The Reactionary Impulse* (New York: Stein and Day, 1977).

14. On May 1, 2023, Patterson gave a presentation in the Townsend Center for the Humanities at the University of California, Berkeley; see Orlando Patterson, "Slavery and Genocide: The U.S., Jamaica, and the Historical Sociology of Evil," https://townsendcenter .berkeley.edu/events/orlando-patterson. I did not hear, nor have I read, the lecture, but its title does suggest that Patterson may well be moving in the direction of considering evil.

15. Orlando Patterson, "Introduction: Life and Scholarship in the Shadow of Slavery," in *The Sociology of Slavery: Black Society in Jamaica, 1655–1838*, 2nd ed. (Cambridge: Polity, 2022), xxxviii; hereafter cited as "Life and Scholarship in the Shadow of Slavery."

16. Patterson, "Life and Scholarship in the Shadow of Slavery," liv.

17. Patterson, "Life and Scholarship in the Shadow of Slavery," xlviii.

18. Patterson, "Life and Scholarship in the Shadow of Slavery," li.

19. Patterson, "Life and Scholarship in the Shadow of Slavery," lix.

20. Claudia Card, "Genocide and Social Death," *Hypatia* 18, no. 1 (Winter 2003): 63. See Patterson, "Life and Scholarship in the Shadow of Slavery," lviii. On Kaplan and Goldhagen, see Patterson, "Life and Scholarship in the Shadow of Slavery," lvii–lviii.

21. Patterson, "Life and Scholarship in the Shadow of Slavery," xxxiii.

22. On Patterson's relation to Parsons and Parsonian sociology, see Scott, "The Paradox of Freedom," 136, 187–92; and on Patterson's argument regarding the inadequacy of Parsons's approach, see Patterson, "Life and Scholarship in the Shadow of Slavery," xxxviii–xlii.

23. Patterson has acknowledged this. See Patterson, "Life and Scholarship in the Shadow of Slavery," vii.

24. See the essays collected in M. G. Smith, *The Plural Society in the British West Indies* (Berkeley: University of California Press, 1965).

25. Stanley Elkins, *Slavery: A Problem in American Institutional and Intellectual Life* (Chicago: University of Chicago Press, 1959).

26. On Patterson and culture, see Orlando Patterson, "Taking Culture Seriously: A Framework and an Afro-American Illustration," in *Culture Matters: How Values Shape Human Progress*, ed. Lawrence Harrison and Samuel Huntington (New York: Basic Books, 2000): 202–18; and, more recently, Orlando Patterson, "Making Sense of Culture," *Annual Review of Sociology* 40, no. 1 (2014): 1–30. But the matter is more complicated than this. As early as 1969, Patterson was theorizing cultural symbols. See, for example, Orlando Patterson, "The Ritual of Cricket," *Jamaica Journal* 3 (1969): 22–25. Of course, *Slavery and Social Death* is deeply indebted to an "anthropological" approach to symbolic analysis.

27. Patterson, it seems, had earlier started a piece of fiction, tentatively titled "Jane and Louisa," but discarded it. One part of it was subsequently published as "Into the Dark" (see note 12 above). But given what he was trying to do in *The Sociology of Slavery*, it is unsurprising that the historical novel would be the challenge he would take up. See Scott, "The Paradox of Freedom," 180.

28. See Colin McGinn, *Ethics, Evil, and Fiction* (Oxford: Clarendon, 1997), vi. But see also Georges Bataille, *Literature and Evil* (London: Penguin, 2012).

29. The story I tell here is informed by and intersects with but is not identical to the one offered by Patterson either in his recent "Life and Scholarship in the Shadow of Slavery" or my 2013 discussion with him, "The Paradox of Freedom."

30. On the history of the university, see Phillip Sherlock and Rex Nettleford, *The University of the West Indies: A Caribbean Response to the Challenge of Change* (Kingston, Jamaica: Macmillan, 1990).

31. See Barbara Bush, "Colonial Research and the Social Sciences at the End of Empire: The West Indian Social Survey, 1944–57," *Journal of Imperial and Commonwealth History* 41, no. 3 (2013): 451–74.

32. Madeline Kerr, *Personality and Conflict in Jamaica* (London: Collins, 1952); and Edith Clarke, *My Mother Who Fathered Me: A Study of the Family in Three Selected Communities in Jamaica* (London: Allen and Unwin, 1957). Clarke directed the survey project. For a review of Kerr's *Personality and Conflict in Jamaica*, see Manet Fowler, "Jamaican Personality and Cultural Dynamics," *Phylon* 14, no. 2 (1953): 217–19. *Phylon* was the journal on race and culture founded by W. E. B. DuBois in 1940 at Atlanta University. The 1953 issue in which the review of Kerr appears also contains other Jamaica materials.

33. Kerr, *Personality and Conflict in Jamaica*, ix. This is the idea that would be central to M. G. Smith's theory of pluralism.

34. Certainly Kerr was very much influenced by the psychoanalyst Abram Kardiner, the author of such hugely influential books as Abram Kardiner, *The Individual and His Society: The Psychodynamics of Primitive Social Organization* (New York: Columbia University Press, 1947); and Abram Kardiner and Lionel Ovesey, *The Mark of Oppression: Explorations in the Personality of the American Negro* (New York: Meridian, 1951).

35. Prior to Patterson's *The Sociology of Slavery*, there were three landmark books on Jamaican slavery, of which one was by a Jamaican: Philip Curtain, *Two Jamaicas: The Role of Ideas in a Tropical Colony* (Cambridge, MA: Harvard University Press, 1955); Douglas Hall, *Free Jamaica: 1838–1865* (New Haven, CT: Yale University Press, 1959); and Gisela Eisner, *Jamaica, 1830–1930: A Study in Economic Growth* (Manchester, UK: Manchester University Press, 1961). Hall, the Jamaican, is also the author of the important essay Douglas Hall, "Slaves and Slavery in the British Caribbean," *Social and Economic Studies* 11, no. 4 (1962): 305–18. On Worthy Park, see Michael Craton and James Walvin, *A Jamaican Plantation: A History of Worthy Park, 1670–1970* (Toronto, Canada: University of Toronto Press, 1970); and Michael Craton, *Searching for the Invisible Man: Slaves and Plantation Life in Jamaica* (Cambridge, MA: Harvard University Press, 1978). Patterson offers a telling account of trying to gain access to the Worthy Park archives. See Patterson, "Life and Scholarship in the Shadow of Slavery," xx.

36. Part of what interested Patterson about *The Black Jacobins* was the simple but important fact that it was, in part, a *social* history of slave life. See Scott, "The Paradox of Freedom," 151.

360   4. SLAVERY'S EVIL LIFEWORLD

C. L. R. James, *The Black Jacobins: Toussaint L'Ouverture and the San Domingo Revolution*, rev. ed. (1938; repr., New York: Vintage, 1963). Citations are to the Vintage edition.

37. It would appear that Patterson had a very complicated relation with Smith. See Scott, "The Paradox of Freedom," 128. Patterson repeated some of this and a good deal more it seems in his controversial keynote address at a conference on Smith's work at the University of the West Indies, Mona—the Sixth Caribbean Reasonings Conference. See Orlando Patterson, "M. G. Smith: Social Theory and Anthropology in the Caribbean and Beyond," Centre for Caribbean Thought, June 14, 2008. See Brian Meeks, ed., *M. G. Smith: Social Theory and Anthropology in the Caribbean and Beyond* (Kingston, Jamaica: Ian Randle, 2011).

38. On Smith, see Douglas Hall, *A Man Divided: Michael Garfield Smith, Jamaican Poet and Anthropologist, 1921–1993* (Kingston, Jamaica: The Press, University of the West Indies, 1997). Hall was a contemporary of Smith's.

39. J. S. Furnivall, *Colonial Policy and Practice: A Comparative Study of Burma and Netherlands India* (Cambridge: Cambridge University Press, 1948).

40. For an account of this moment in the evolution of the nationalist movement, see Trevor Munroe, *The Politics of Constitutional Decolonization: Jamaica, 1944–62* (Kingston, Jamaica: Institute of Social and Economic Research, 1972).

41. Smith's essays across this period are collected in Smith, *The Plural Society in the British West Indies*. For a remarkably insightful discussion of the arc of Smith's essays on pluralism in relation to the story of Jamaican nationalism, see Don Robotham, "Pluralism as an Ideology," *Social and Economic Studies* 29, no. 1 (March 1980): 69–89. See also David Scott, "The Permanence of Pluralism," in *Without Guarantees: In Honour of Stuart Hall*, ed. Paul Gilroy, Lawrence Grossberg, and Angela McRobbie (London: Verso, 2000), 282–301.

42. I pose this question in relation to Patterson's 1964 novel, *The Children of Sisyphus*, in David Scott, "The Tragic Vision in Postcolonial Time," *PMLA* 129, no. 4 (2014): 799–808.

43. See H. Orlando Patterson, "Outside History: Jamaica Today," *New Left Review*, no. 31 (May–June 1965): 35–43.

44. Patterson, *The Sociology of Slavery*, 9.

45. See Trevor Burnard, "A Failed Settler Society: Marriage and Demographic Failure in Early Jamaica," *Journal of Social History* 28, no. 1 (1994): 63–82; and Burnard, *Mastery, Tyranny, and Desire*, 18. Patterson has underlined in recent years his sense that Burnard shares his conception of eighteenth-century Jamaica, especially with respect to the relevance of Hobbes. See Patterson, "Life and Scholarship in the Shadow of Slavery," xln2.

46. Of course, one of the great exceptions to this was Simon Taylor, the most formidable and wealthy of the eighteenth-century slaveowners, who steadfastly refused to leave Jamaica, even as the abolitionists were making inroads into the hegemonic justification for the world he had long taken for granted. See Christer Petley, *White Fury: A Jamaican Slaveholder and the Age of Revolution* (Oxford: Oxford University Press, 2018).

47. Arguably, among British West Indian colonies only Barbados could have counted as a "settler" colony. I thank Richard Drayton for pointing this out to me. Note also the contrast drawn by Richard Dunn between the plantations, Mesopotamia, Jamaica, and Mount Airy, Virginia, in Richard Dunn, *A Tale of Two Plantations: Slave Life and Labor in Jamaica and Virginia* (Cambridge, MA: Harvard University Press, 2014).

48. Patterson, *The Sociology of Slavery*, 9. This point is underscored in Patterson's more recent book, Orlando Patterson, *The Confounding Island: Jamaica and the Postcolonial Predicament* (Cambridge, MA: Belknap, 2019).

49. Patterson, *The Sociology of Slavery*, 9.

50. Patterson, *The Sociology of Slavery*, 10. Patterson develops this more incisively in "Life and Scholarship in the Shadow of Slavery," xxxviii–xlii.

51. Patterson, *The Sociology of Slavery*, 11. Jamaica was anything but a harmoniously multicultural society, as incisively portrayed in his first novel, Patterson, *The Children of Sisyphus*.

52. Patterson, *The Sociology of Slavery*, 11. Patterson has underlined that this had not been done before in studies of Jamaican slavery. See Patterson, "Life and Scholarship in the Shadow of Slavery," xii–xv.

53. Elkins, *Slavery*. See Orlando Patterson, "The Socialization and Personality Structure of the Slave," chap. 6 in *The Sociology of Slavery: An Analysis of the Origins, Development, and Structure of Negro Slave Society in Jamaica* (London: MacGibbon and Kee, 1967), 145–81.

54. Elkins, *Slavery*, 128.

55. Frank Tannenbaum, *Slave and Citizen: The Negro in the Americas* (New York: Vintage, 1946)—another largely forgotten book. However, see instructively, Alejandro de la Fuente, "From Slaves to Citizens? Tannenbaum and the Debates on Slavery, Emancipation, and Race Relations in Latin America," *International Labor and Working-Class History* 77 (Spring 2010): 154–73.

56. The idea of a contrast between "open" and "closed" social systems, although initially developed in 1932 (see Henri Bergson, *The Two Sources of Morality and Religion* [New York: Macmillan, 1935]), began a pronounced and influential career with Karl Popper, *The Open Society and Its Enemies*, 2 vols. (London: Routledge and Kegan Paul, 1945). Remember, too, that this whole problematic of the individual and society, the individual and totalizing or totalitarian society, was crucial to C. L. R. James in his American years and is at the heart of C. L. R. James, *Mariners, Renegades, and Castaways: Herman Melville and the World We Live In* (New York: C. L. R. James, 1953).

57. Against Elkins, in *Slavery and Social Death* Patterson would argue that the Sambo-like figure was "an imperative of all systems of slavery, from the most primitive to the most advanced" (96). See also Patterson, "Life and Scholarship in the Shadow of Slavery," xiv.

58. Bruno Bettelheim, "Individual and Mass Behavior in Extreme Situations," *Journal of Abnormal and Social Psychology* 38, no. 4 (October 1943): 417–52. In this famous essay, Bettelheim reports on his observations in two concentration camps, Dachau and Buchenwald, between 1938 and 1939. Bettelheim's work would become controversial in later years.

59. By the end of the 1960s, the debate had become so significant (or so bitter) that it was necessary to organize it more formally. See the discussion in Ann Lane, ed., *The Debate Over Slavery: Stanley Elkins and His Critics* (Urbana: University of Illinois Press, 1971), in particular Elkins's response to the debate, Elkins, "Slavery and Ideology" (325–78). For helpful discussions of Elkins that aim to locate the debate, see Peter Ling, "The Incomparable Elkins," *Rethinking History* 1, no. 1 (1997): 67–74; and Richard King, "Domination and Fabrication: Re-thinking Stanley Elkins' *Slavery*," *Slavery and Abolition* 22, no. 2 (2001): 1–28. This latter essay, retitled "Culture, Accommodation, and Resistance I: Rethinking Elkins' *Slavery*," was included as a chapter in King's important intellectual

362   4. SLAVERY'S EVIL LIFEWORLD

history of race and culture in the postwar United States. See Richard King, *Race, Culture, and the Intellectuals, 1940–1970* (Baltimore, MD: Johns Hopkins University Press, 2004), chap. 6.

60. For a not very sympathetic account in an otherwise instructive book on the persistence of the Black damage imagery, see Daryl Michael Scott, *Contempt and Pity: Social Policy and the Image of the Damaged Black Psyche, 1880–1996* (Chapel Hill: University of North Carolina Press, 1997), 89–91, 114–18. Scott's opening sentence on Elkins sets the overall tone: "The image of the African American as damaged by oppression reached its apogee in 1959 with the publication of the historian Stanley Elkins's *Slavery*" (89).

61. See Patterson, *The Sociology of Slavery*, 174–81, and Scott, "The Paradox of Freedom," 153–57. Patterson also engages Elkins in *Slavery and Social Death*, 96–97, pointing to the connection between the stereotype of Sambo and dishonor (see note 57 above).

62. Patterson, *The Sociology of Slavery*, 173.

63. Patterson, *The Sociology of Slavery*, 174.

64. Patterson, *The Sociology of Slavery*, 174.

65. Patterson, *The Sociology of Slavery*, 178.

66. Patterson, *The Sociology of Slavery*, 178.

67. Patterson, *The Sociology of Slavery*, 179.

68. Patterson, *The Sociology of Slavery*, 179.

69. Patterson, *The Sociology of Slavery*, 180.

70. Patterson, *The Sociology of Slavery*, 260.

71. Patterson, *The Sociology of Slavery*, 260. See James, *The Black Jacobins*, 5.

72. Patterson, *The Sociology of Slavery*, 260.

73. Patterson, *The Sociology of Slavery*, 283; Patterson quotes Albert Camus, *The Rebel*, 14. As Patterson tells it, he had to cut a significant amount of material from "The Mechanisms of Resistance to Slavery," content that subsequently became Orlando Patterson, "Slavery and Slave Revolts," *Social and Economic Studies* 19, no. 3 (1970): 289–325.

74. For valuable discussions of Camus's work, in particular the relation between *The Myth of Sisyphus* and *The Rebel*, see John Foley, *Albert Camus: From the Absurd to Revolt* (Stocksfield, UK: Acumen, 2008); and David Carroll, "Rethinking the Absurd: *Le Mythe de Sisyphe*," in *The Cambridge Companion to Camus*, ed. Edward J. Hughes (Cambridge: Cambridge University Press, 2007), 53–66. For a remarkable discussion of Camus's idea of rebellion alongside that of Hannah Arendt's, see Jeffrey Isaac, *Arendt, Camus, and Modern Rebellion* (New Haven, CT: Yale University Press, 1992).

75. Camus, *The Rebel*, 144.

76. Camus, *The Myth of Sisyphus*, 123.

77. Maurice Merleau-Ponty, *Humanism and Terror: The Communist Problem* (Boston: Beacon, 1969). Camus's 1946 essays brought together in *Neither Victims nor Executioners* (Philadelphia: New Society, 1986) were in part a response to the wider context of debate in which Merleau-Ponty's book appears.

78. Thus the footnote James adds to the 1963 revised edition, asserting that he stands by the view that even if the insurgent Blacks in Saint-Domingue "destroyed tirelessly," still their violence was "surprisingly moderate." James, *The Black Jacobins*, 88, 88n1.

79. See Foley, *Albert Camus*, esp. chap. 6.

4. SLAVERY'S EVIL LIFEWORLD   363

80. See Patterson, "Outside History: Jamaica Today."

81. I am alluding to Elsa Goveia, *Slave Society in the British Leeward Islands at the End of the Eighteenth Century* (New Haven, CT: Yale University Press, 1965). From the 1950s onward, Goveia was a profoundly important humanistic voice in the study of Caribbean slavery, not least in seeking to connect that story to the colonial and postcolonial periods. See, especially, her landmark work, Elsa Goveia, *A Study on the Historiography of the British West Indies to the End of the Nineteenth Century* (1956; repr. Washington, DC: Howard University Press, 1980). Not surprising, perhaps, she disagreed with Patterson's view on the character of Caribbean slavery. Significantly, in the introduction to the first issue of *Savacou* she repeats the claim from her book that a "slave society" is "held together by principles of racial subordination and inequality," and explicitly contrasts this with Patterson's view. See Elsa Goveia, "Introduction," *Savacou* 1, no. 1 (June 1970): 3. In Patterson, "Life and Scholarship in the Shadow of Slavery," xxv, Patterson responds to Goveia, suggesting that in fact their views are not as far apart as she suggested. There is far too little written on Goveia, but see Mary Chamberlain, "Elsa Goveia: History and Nation," *History Workshop Journal* 58, no. 1 (Autumn 2004): 167–90. Since 1984 lectures have been held in her honor at the University of the West Indies, Mona. A selection of these have been collected in Hilary Beckles, ed., *Inside Slavery: Process and Legacy in the Caribbean Experience* (Kingston, Jamaica: University of the West Indies Press, 2002).

82. Edward [Kamau] Brathwaite, "Jamaican Slave Society: A Review Essay," *Race* 9, no. 3 (1968): 331–42. The idea of a "Creole society" was introduced by Goveia in *Slave Society in the British Leeward Islands at the End of the Eighteenth Century*, where she describes her undertaking as using her analysis of the British Leeward islands to shed "light on the characteristics of plantation slavery and of the 'Creole' society of the eighteenth century throughout the islands" (viii). Notably, *Creole* is capped and in scare quotes. The term was not then in common use in Caribbean historiography. Later, more analytically, Goveia writes of the Whites having a "European-based Creolised culture," and the Blacks as having an "African-based Creolised culture," and concludes: "In spite of its segmentation, the culture of the Leeward Islands formed a coherent whole, faithfully reflecting the social structure of the Creole society of the islands" (249). Brathwaite was profoundly indebted to this book, and to Goveia's sensibility in general. Patterson discusses this in "Life and Scholarship in the Shadow of Slavery," xxvi–xxvii. Part of the enormous significance of this moment is that Brathwaite was one of the initiators (along with John La Rose and Andrew Salkey) in London in December 1966 of an organization of Caribbean artists and intellectuals, the Caribbean Artists Movement, and Patterson was an inaugural participant. See Edward Brathwaite, "The Caribbean Artists Movement," *Caribbean Quarterly*, 14, nos. 1–2 (March–June 1968): 57–59; and Ann Walmsley's study, *The Caribbean Artists Movement, 1966–1972: A Literary and Cultural History* (London: New Beacon, 1992).

83. Brathwaite, "Jamaican Slave Society," 332.

84. Brathwaite, "Jamaican Slave Society," 333.

85. See Edward Kamau Brathwaite, "Caribbean Man in Space and Time," *Savacou*, nos. 11–12 (September 1975): 5–6. Goveia and Brathwaite were quite close. In the second issue of *Savacou*, she offers her disagreement with M. G. Smith's pluralism in much the same

364   4. SLAVERY'S EVIL LIFEWORLD

terms as she criticized Patterson. See Elsa Goveia, "The Social Framework," *Savacou*, no. 2 (September 1970): 7–15. For her, the value that held slave and postslave Caribbean society together was less the coercive apparatus of the state than the hegemony of racial ideology, perpetrated on one side (racial superiority) and accepted on the other (racial inferiority).

86. Brathwaite, "Jamaican Slave Society," 334, 336.

87. Brathwaite, "Jamaican Slave Society," 338–40.

88. See Walter Jackson, "Melville Herskovits and the Search for Afro-American Culture," in *History of Anthropology*. Vol. 4, *Malinowski, Rivers, Benedict, and Others: Essays on Culture and Personality*, ed. George W. Stocking Jr. (Madison: University of Wisconsin Press, 1986), 95–126; and Sidney Mintz, introduction to *The Myth of the Negro Past*, by Melville Herskovits (Boston: Beacon, 1990), ix–xxi. On the Carnegie project, see Walter Jackson, "The Making of a Social Science Classic: Gunnar Myrdal's *An American Dilemma*," *Perspectives in American History* 2 (1985): 269–95; and Walter Jackson, *Gunnar Myrdal and America's Conscience: Social Engineering and Racial Liberalism, 1938–1987* (Chapel Hill: University of North Carolina Press, 1990).

89. Edward [Kamau] Brathwaite, introduction to *Life in a Haitian Valley*, by Melville Herskovits (1937; repr., New York: Anchor, 1971), vii.

90. Brathwaite, "Jamaican Slave Society," 342. Subsequently, in his reflections on Caribbean imaginative writing (literary and scholarly), in Edward [Kamau] Brathwaite, "Timehri," *Savacou*, no. 2 (September 1970): 35–44, Brathwaite writes polemically: "Most of us, coming from islands, where there was no evident lost civilization—where, in fact, there was an 'absence of ruins'—faced a real artistic difficulty in our search for origins. The seed and root of our concern had little material soil to nourish them. Patterson's view was that we should accept this shallow soil (we begin from an existential absurdity of nothing) and grow our ferns in a kind of moon dust. Fertility would come later; if not, not" (42). This clearly contrasted with Brathwaite's own sense that although there was fragmentation there was a "healing" or "transcending" need to see the fragments whole. Patterson did not, so far as I am aware, respond to these criticisms. However, in a certain sense, his essays of the early 1970s can be read as a kind of rejoinder to Brathwaite's assessment. See, for example, Orlando Patterson, "Rethinking Black History," *Harvard Educational Review* 41, no. 3 (1971): 229–304; and Orlando Patterson, "Toward a Future That Has No Past: Reflections on the Fate of Blacks in the Americas," *Public Interest*, no. 27 (Spring 1972): 25–62. Patterson has felt that he was intellectually ill-treated by Brathwaite, that indeed, Brathwaite's whole project owes more to him than Brathwaite allows or reveals. See Scott, "The Paradox of Freedom," 151–52.

91. Patterson, *The Children of Sisyphus*; Edward [Kamau] Brathwaite, "Wings of a Dove," in *Rights of Passage* (London: Oxford University Press, 1967), 41–44.

92. See John Blassingame, *The Slave Community: Plantation Life in the Antebellum South* (New York: Oxford University Press, 1972), revised and enlarged in 1979; and Al-Tony Gilmore, *Revisiting Blassingame's "The Slave Community": The Scholars Respond* (New York: Praeger, 1978). See also the later Sterling Stuckey, *Slave Culture: Nationalist Theory and the Foundations of Black America* (New York: Oxford University Press, 1987). In the same year as his monograph, Brathwaite published the pamphlet Edward [Kamau] Brathwaite, *Folk Culture of the Slaves in Jamaica* (London: New Beacon, 1971). The anthropologists of

the African Americas, Sidney Mintz and Richard Price, would pick up on this in their important essay, also published first during this period. See Sidney Mintz and Richard Price, *An Anthropological Approach to the Afro-American Past: A Caribbean Perspective* (New York: Institute for the Study of Human Issues, 1976), republished as Sidney Mintz and Richard Price, *The Birth of African-American Culture: An Anthropological Perspective* (Boston: Beacon, 1992).

93. Patterson would see himself as working precisely on the "culture" of the enslaved in *The Sociology of Slavery*. This interest, of course, becomes explicit in *Slavery and Social Death*, where the language of symbolic anthropology is pervasive. Perhaps the way to draw the contrast is to say that for Patterson culture was part of a social structure, whereas for Brathwaite it was the sign of an agential resistance to slavery, an area of Black (African) authenticity.

94. See Scott, 'The Permanence of Pluralism."

95. *Die the Long Day* was not the first Jamaican novel to tarry with the problem of representing slavery. Herbert G. de Lisser's novels were the earliest, so far as I am aware. See Herbert G. de Lisser, *Revenge* (London: Ernest Benn, 1919); Herbert G. de Lisser, *The White Witch of Rosehall* (London: Ernest Benn, 1929); and Herbert G. de Lisser, *Psyche* (London: Ernest Benn, 1952). Since de Lisser's novels, there have been a few, although not many—among them, James Carnegie, *Wages Paid* (Havana, Cuba: Casa de las Americas, 1976); Marlon James, *The Book of Night Women* (New York: Riverhead, 2009); Andrea Levy, *The Long Song* (New York: Farrar, Straus, and Giroux, 2010); Martin Mordecai, *Free* (Kingston, Jamaica: University of the West Indies Press, 2018); and Curdella Forbes, *A Tall History of Sugar* (Brooklyn, NY: Akashic, 2019).

96. Patterson refers to it as one of the "sequels" to *The Sociology of Slavery*. See Patterson, "Life and Scholarship in the Shadow of Slavery," lxi. Patterson has talked about wanting to write a slave novel when he returned to Jamaica in the late 1960s. See Scott, "The Paradox of Freedom," 180.

97. This is what Patterson was famously accused of by the novelist John Hearne in his painfully gratuitous review of *Die the Long Day*. See John Hearne, "The Novel as Sociology as Bore," *Caribbean Quarterly* 18, no. 4 (December 1972): 78–81. Hearne believed Patterson to be an "intruder" in the world of fiction (78) and the novel "a piece of false fiction" (81).

98. See Stathis Gourgouris, *Does Literature Think? Literature as Theory for an Antimythical Era* (Stanford, CA: Stanford University Press, 2003).

99. I am thinking here with and through the phenomenological work of Alfred Schutz, in particular; see Alfred Schutz, *The Phenomenology of the Social World*, trans. George Walsh and Frederick Lehnert (Evanston, IL: Northwestern University Press, 1967).

100. I have in mind here the way in which Alasdair MacIntyre talks about moral life and moral inquiry: see Alasdair MacIntyre, *Ethics in the Conflicts of Modernity: An Essay on Desire, Practical Reasoning, and Narrative* (Cambridge: Cambridge University Press, 2016).

101. For other treatments of the novel from which I have benefited, see Donette Francis, " 'Transcendental Cosmopolitanism': Orlando Patterson and the Novel Jamaican 1960s," *Journal of Transnational American Studies* 5, no. 1 (2013): 1–14; and Janelle Rodrigues, " 'It's Enough to Survive This Hell to Make Ourselves Immortal in the Eyes of Our Descendants': Myal, Death, and Mourning in Orlando Patterson's *Die the Long Day*," *Cultural Dynamics* 34, nos. 1–2 (June 2021): 1–17.

366   4. SLAVERY'S EVIL LIFEWORLD

102.   See, usefully, Richard Sheridan, "The Wealth of Jamaica in the Eighteenth Century," *Economic History Review* 18, no. 2 (1965): 292–311; and Trevor Burnard, " 'Prodigious Riches': The Wealth of Jamaica Before the American Revolution," *Economic History Review* 54, no. 3 (2001): 506–24.

103.   See Patterson, *The Sociology of Slavery*, 195–98. On death in eighteenth-century Jamaica, see Vincent Brown, *The Reaper's Garden: Death and Power in the World of Atlantic Slavery* (Cambridge, MA: Harvard University Press, 2010). Patterson has disagreed with this book. See Patterson, "Life and Scholarship in the Shadow of Slavery," xxix–xxx.

104.   The other is a passage from Matthew "Monk" Lewis, *Journal of a West India Proprietor: Kept During a Residence in the Island of Jamaica* (London: John Murray, 1834).

105.   Indeed, James Scott cites Patterson from *Slavery and Social Death* approvingly in James Scott, *Domination and the Arts of Resistance: Hidden Transcripts* (New Haven, CT: Yale University Press, 1990), 24, in which the Jamaican proverb "Play fool to catch wise" frames the synopsis of the book found on the inside front flap. Patterson has cited this appreciatively against those—like Michael Craton—who he thinks have distorted his argument. See Patterson, "Life and Scholarship in the Shadow of Slavery," xx–xxii.

106.   I mean this in the sense used by Pierre Bourdieu in Pierre Bourdieu, *Outline of a Theory of Practice*, trans. Richard Nice (Cambridge: Cambridge University Press, 1977).

107.   I mean "ordinary ethics" in the rough sense suggested by the anthropologists (several inspired by Stanley Cavell) collected in Michael Lambek, ed., *Ordinary Ethics: Anthropology, Language, and Action* (New York: Fordham University Press, 2010).

108.   Vincent Brown, *Tacky's Revolt: The Story of an Atlantic Slave War* (Cambridge, MA: Belknap, 2020). This is an intriguing book, arguing both for the military singularity of the 1760 revolt associated with Tacky's name and for its connection to knowledge about war brought to Jamaica by "Coromantee" Gold Coast slaves. See Patterson's disagreement in "Life and Scholarship in the Shadow of Slavery," xlii–xlvi.

109.   Arguably, this is the question posed by Toni Morrison, *Beloved* (New York: Knopf, 1987). The connection between his book and Morrison's was not lost on Patterson. See Scott, "The Paradox of Freedom," 181–82.

110.   For his later, more deliberate reflections on Camus in relation to the problem of Black history, see Patterson, "Toward a Future That Has No Past."

111.   Patterson's *Die the Long Day* is hereafter cited in the text.

112.   See Scott, "The Paradox of Freedom," 181. Very early, Patterson took the lives of enslaved women seriously. See Patterson, "Life and Scholarship in the Shadow of Slavery," xviii–xx. Needless to say, since *Die the Long Day* the study of the lives of Caribbean slave women has been a special focus in the historiography of Caribbean plantation slavery. In thinking about Quasheba's context, I have benefited from the inaugural work Lucille Mathurin-Mair, *A Historical Study of Women in Jamaica, 1655–1844* (Kingston, Jamaica: University of the West Indies Press, 2006), especially "The Black Woman: Demographic Profile, Occupation, and Violent Abuse" (chap. 6) and "The Black Woman: Agency, Identity, and Voice" (chap. 7). This work was originally Mathurin-Mair's PhD dissertation written under Elsa Goveia and defended in 1974. Also helpful is Barbara Bush, *Slave Women in Caribbean Society, 1650–1838* (Kingston, Jamaica: Ian Randle, 1990), especially chapter 1 on the invisibility of Black women in Caribbean slave history, but the book as a whole is

of enormous value. For an acutely insightful inquiry into the ramifying issues concerning the reconstruction of lives of enslaved Black women in the Americas, see Marisa Fuentes, *Dispossessed Lives: Enslaved Women, Violence, and the Archive* (Philadelphia: University of Pennsylvania Press, 2018).

113. See Martha Nussbaum, *The Fragility of Goodness: Luck and Ethics in Greek Tragedy and Philosophy* (New York: Cambridge University Press, 1986).

114. On humiliation, see, usefully, Ute Frevert, *The Politics of Humiliation: A Modern History* (New York: Oxford University Press, 2020); and on dignity, see Michael Rosen, *Dignity: Its History and Meaning* (Cambridge, MA: Harvard University Press, 2012). I am grateful to Saphe Shamoun for bringing Rosen's book to my attention.

115. See Laurence Mordekhai Thomas, *Vessels of Evil: American Slavery and the Holocaust* (Philadelphia, PA: Temple University Press, 1993), 119.

116. See Alfred Schutz and Thomas Luckmann, *The Structures of the Life-World*, Vol. 1, trans. Richard Zaner and H. Tristram Engelhardt Jr. (Evanston, IL: Northwestern University Press, 1973).

117. I am thinking, of course, of Michel Foucault's late work on ethics. See, in particular, Michel Foucault, "The Ethics of Concern for the Self as a Practice of Freedom," in *Essential Works of Michel Foucault: 1954–1984*. Vol. 1, *Ethics*, ed. Paul Rabinow, trans. Robert Hurley and others (New York: New Press, 1997), 281–301.

118. See Michel Foucault, "The Subject and Power," in *Essential Works of Foucault*. Vol. 3, *Power*, ed. James Faubion, trans. Robert Hurley (New York: New Press, 2000), 342. Part of the problem here is that for Foucault slavery is a physical relationship of constraint, not a power relationship; it is merely a theoretical foil deployed to illuminate other states of power.

119. Earlier that morning, Cicero had an encounter with the bookkeeper David, which Patterson describes as follows: "The Irishman stared suspiciously at Cicero, knowing that something was up. Cicero, almost compulsively, egged on the Irishman's suspicions by fidgeting defensively, covering his mouth with his cupped right hand. The bookkeeper sensed the challenge to a battle of wits and he knew that there was more than a trace of insolence in the challenge. But there was nothing he could do, for it was a challenge cloaked in utter submissiveness. Besides, it was a battle of wits he could never win and to give in to the urge he presently felt to hit him would only mean a further loss of face since the black was behaving like a perfect slave" (35). Note again the subtlety of the interpersonal encounter. Cicero's actions, under Patterson's description, are "almost" compulsively brought into play. They are not thoughtless, but they are not premeditated either. They are defensive not aggressive, and yet they constitute a "challenge," a "battle of wits," a habituated mode of navigating an overwhelming structure of negating violence while holding on to a modicum of self-respect, shielding a space of personhood.

120. Recall the description in "De la violence," the opening chapter of Frantz Fanon, *Les damrés de la terre* (Paris: Presence African, 1963). Patterson has acknowledged his appreciation of Fanon in Orlando Patterson, "Frantz Fanon: My Hope and Hero," in "Guyana Independence Issue," ed. George Lamming and Martin Carter, New World Quarterly 2, nos. 3–4 (1966): 93–95.

368   4. SLAVERY'S EVIL LIFEWORLD

121.   McKenzie is a not unfamiliar figure in the Caribbean literary history, the newcomer to slave-plantation Jamaica, fresh with his ideals of fairness and enlightenment intact but who, within the space of a short stay, begins to sink to the level of the other Whites.

122.   Laurence Thomas, "Self-Deception as the Handmaiden of Evil," *Midwest Studies in Philosophy* 36, no. 1 (2012): 53–61.

123.   On the Scots in the story of Caribbean slavery, see Richard Sheridan, "The Role of the Scots in the Economy and Society of the West Indies," in *Comparative Perspectives on Slavery in New World Plantation Societies*, ed. Vera Rubin and Arthur Tuden (New York: New York Academy of Sciences, 1977), 94–106; and T. M. Devine, ed., *Recovering Scotland's Slavery Past: The Caribbean Connection* (Edinburgh, Scotland: Edinburgh University Press, 2015), esp. T. M. Devine, "Lost to History" (21–40); Eric Graham, "The Scots Penetration of the Jamaican Plantation Business" (82–98); and Nicholas Draper, "Scotland and Colonial Slave Ownership: The Evidence of the Slave Compensation Records" (166–86).

124.   David Hume's "Of National Characters" was originally published in 1748 in his *Essays Moral, Political, and Literary*. In the 1753 edition of the collection, he added to the essay a note that reads: "I am apt to suspect the negroes, and other species of men (for there are four or five different kinds) to be naturally inferior to the whites. There never was a civilized nation of any other complexion than white, nor even any individual eminent either in action or speculation. No ingenious manufactures amongst them, no arts, no sciences. On the other hand, the most rude and barbarous of the whites, such as the ancient GERMAN the present TARTARS have still something eminent about them, in their valour, form of government, or some other particular. Such a uniform and constant difference could not happen, in so many countries and ages, if nature had not made an original distinction between these breeds of men. Not to mention our colonies, there are NEGROE slaves dispersed all over EUROPE, of which none ever discovered any symptom of ingenuity; tho' low people, without education will start up amongst us, and distinguish themselves in every profession. In JAMAICA, indeed, they talk of one negroe as a man of parts and learning; but 'tis likely he's admired for very slender accomplishments, like a parrot, who speaks a few words plainly" (capitalization in original); see https://davidhume.org/texts/empl1/nc. For some discussion of the Scottish Enlightenment in this regard, see Silvia Sebastiani, *The Scottish Enlightenment: Race, Gender, and the Limits of Progress*, trans. Jeremy Carden (New York: Palgrave, 2013), esp. chap. 1, "Hume Versus Montesquieu: Race Against Climate," 23–44. On Hume and racism, see Emmanuel Eze, "Hume, Race, and Human Nature," *Journal of the History of Ideas* 61, no. 4 (October 2000): 691–98.

125.   See, helpfully, Vincent Carretta, "Who Was Francis Williams?," *Early American Literature* 38, no. 2 (2003): 213–37.

5. EVIL ENRICHMENT

1.   C. L. R. James, "Preface to the First Edition," in *The Black Jacobins: Toussaint L'Ouverture and the San Domingo Revolution* (1938; repr., New York: Vintage, 1963), ix.

2.   Eric Williams, *Capitalism and Slavery* (Chapel Hill: University of North Carolina Press, 1944). Throughout this chapter I cite the first British edition: Eric Williams, *Capitalism and Slavery* (London: Andre Deutsch, 1964).

5. EVIL ENRICHMENT 369

3. On John Jacob Thomas, see Faith Smith, *Creole Recitations: John Jacob Thomas and Colonial Formation in the Late Nineteenth-Century Caribbean* (Charlottesville: University of Virginia Press, 2002). *Froudacity* was written in response to Froude's *The English in the West Indies, or The Bow of Ulysses*, published in 1888. Froude was a distinguished English historian, novelist, biographer, and friend of the notorious Thomas Carlyle.

4. For a useful account of the relationship between James and Williams, see the well-regarded but unpublished essay Humberto Garcia-Muñiz, "Eric Williams and C. L. R. James: Intellectual Symbiosis and Political Counterpoint" (available at Academia.edu).

5. On James's rapid transformation during this period, see Robert A. Hill, "In England, 1932–1938," in *C. L. R. James: His Life and Work*, ed. Paul Buhle (London: Allison and Busby, 1986), 61–80.

6. For more detail, see Garcia-Muñiz, "Eric Williams and C. L. R. James," 34; Colin Palmer, *Eric Williams and the Making of the Modern Caribbean* (Chapel Hill: University of North Carolina Press, 2006), 134; Jerome Teelucksingh, "The Good, the Bad, and the Ugly: Eric Williams and the Labor Movement in Trinidad and Tobago, 1955–1981," in *The Legacy of Eric Williams Into the Postcolonial Moment*, ed. Tanya Shields (Jackson: University of Mississippi Press, 2015), 130–32; and Maurice St. Pierre, *Eric Williams and the Anticolonial Tradition: The Making of a Diasporan Intellectual* (Charlottesville: University of Virginia Press, 2015), 84–87.

7. "Interview with C. L. R. James," in *Kas-Kas: Interviews with Three Caribbean Writers in Texas: George Lamming, C. L. R. James, and Wilson Harris*, ed. Ian Munro and Reinhard Sander (Austin, TX: African and Afro-American Research Institute, 1972), 23–42. In letters to Constance Webb in the 1940s, James would refer to Williams (speaking of him typically as "Bill") with affection and enthusiasm as his "pupil" and "friend" from whom he expected a great deal. See C. L. R. James, *Special Delivery: The Letters of C. L. R. James to Constance Webb, 1939–1948* (Oxford: Blackwell, 1996), 50–51, 88, 124, 162, 203, 209.

8. James, in "Interview with C. L. R. James," 36–37.

9. Eric Williams, "Education of a Young Colonial," chap. 3 in *Inward Hunger: The Education of a Prime Minister* (1969; repr., Chicago: University of Chicago Press, 1971), 30–39.

10. Eric Williams, *Inward Hunger: The Education of a Prime Minister* (1969; repr., Chicago: University of Chicago Press, 1971), 77.

11. Eric Williams, *British Historians and the West Indies* (1964; repr., New York: Scribner's, 1966), 209, 209–10. Perhaps the best-known and most important review of this work is Elsa Goveia, "New Shibboleths for Old," *Caribbean Quarterly* 10, no. 2 (June 1964): 48–54 (Goveia reviewed the 1964 edition from PNM, Port of Spain). Goveia found Williams's book, famously written within the space of two weeks, at once "disappointing" and "irresponsible" (48). The whole book, she says, "gives the impression of being basically misconceived" because the "relation between its title and actual content is loose to the point of arbitrariness" (49). Defending the neglected work of her colleagues in the 1950s and castigating Williams for his desire to cast himself as the "only voice crying out in the wilderness of an alien and hostile historical tradition" (52), Goveia closes with a terse reminder about the challenge of critical historical work: "No one is ever educated or liberated from the past by being taught how easy it is to substitute new shibboleths for old" (54). Goveia was the author of a historiographical survey: see Elsa Goveia, *A Study on the Historiography of the British West Indies to the End of the Nineteenth Century* (1956; repr., Washington, DC: Howard University Press, 1980).

370 5. EVIL ENRICHMENT

12. Leonard Woolf published C. L. R. James, *The Case for West Indian Self-Government* (London: Hogarth, 1933). For some sense of James in these years, see C. L. R. James, *Letters from London*, ed. Nicholas Laughlin (Port of Spain: Prospect, 2003).

13. Williams, *British Historians and the West Indies*, 210.

14. Williams, *British Historians and the West Indies*, 211. See also the later account in Williams, *Inward Hunger*: "Britain's most revolutionary publisher, Warburg, who would publish all of Stalin and Trotsky, told me: 'Mr. Williams, are you trying to tell me that the slave trade and slavery were abolished for economic and not humanitarian reasons? I would never publish such a book, for it would be contrary to the British tradition'" (53).

15. William Darity Jr., "Eric Williams and Slavery: A West Indian Viewpoint?," *Callaloo* 20, no. 4 (Autumn 1997): 801.

16. Darity, "Eric Williams and Slavery," 813. In some closing comments, Darity reminds us that not only anticolonialists but also Black scholars warmed to *Capitalism and Slavery*. The first of these scholars was, of course, Carter G. Woodson, whose favorable "Review of Eric Williams' *Capitalism and Slavery*" appeared in the journal he founded: see Carter G. Woodson, "Review of Eric Williams' *Capitalism and Slavery*," *Journal of Negro History* 30 (1945): 93–95. In Darity, "Eric Williams and Slavery," the author writes: "Black scholars generally have been enthusiastic about *Capitalism and Slavery*. To this day there is a persistent racial gulf in scholarly attitudes towards Williams' work. While not all of Williams' intellectual supporters have been black—e.g. Michael Craton, Barbara Solow, and the late Michael Minchenton—virtually all of his critics have been nonblacks—e.g. Stanley Engerman, David Richardson, David Eltis, Seymour Drescher, Howard Temperley, David Brion Davis, the late Roger Anstey, the late Frank Tannenbaum, etc." (814).

17. Darity, "Eric Williams and Slavery," 807–12. See also William Darity Jr., "The Williams Abolition Thesis Before Williams," *Slavery and Abolition* 9, no. 1 (1988): 29–41, in which Darity aims to show that there was scholarship in Britain that would have supported his case concerning the economic self-interest that motivated abolition.

18. See Eric Williams, *The Economic Aspects of the Abolition of the West Indian Slave Trade and Slavery*, ed. Dale Tomich (Lanham, MD: Rowman and Littlefield, 2014).

19. Gordon K. Lewis, *The Growth of Modern West Indies* (New York: Monthly Review, 1968), 198.

20. C. L. R. James, *The Life of Captain Cipriani: An Account of British Government in the West Indies* (Nelson, UK: Coulton, 1932).

21. See Lewis, *The Growth of the Modern West Indies*, 206.

22. See St. Pierre, *Eric Williams and the Anticolonial Tradition*, 22–24; and Palmer, *Eric Williams and the Making of the Modern Caribbean*, 7. These scholars get this information from an early draft of *Inward Hunger*. For reasons that are unclear, Williams leaves mention of Marryshow out of the published version. See Garcia-Muñiz, "Eric Williams and C. L. R. James," 40n3.

23. See Reinhard Sander, *The Trinidad Awakening: West Indian Literature of the Nineteen-Thirties* (New York: Greenwood, 1988). See also C. L. R. James, "Discovering Literature in Trinidad: The Nineteen-Thirties" (1969), in *Spheres of Existence: Selected Writings* (London: Allison and Busby, 1980), 237–44; and Albert Gomes, *Through a Maze of Colour* (Port of Spain: Key Caribbean, 1974).

5. EVIL ENRICHMENT 371

24. Eric Williams, "Life with Father," chap. 2 in *Inward Hunger: The Education of a Prime Minister* (1969; repr., Chicago: University of Chicago Press, 1971), 26–29.

25. See Eric Williams, "Education of a Young Colonial," chap. 3 in *Inward Hunger: The Education of a Prime Minister* (1969; repr., Chicago: University of Chicago Press, 1971), 30–39. For an instructive history of colonial education in Trinidad and Tobago and its impact on young colonials like Williams, see Carl Campbell, *The Young Colonials: A Social History of Education in Trinidad and Tobago, 1834–1939* (Kingston, Jamaica: The Press, University of the West Indies, 1996), especially chaps. 2 and 3.

26. Williams, *British Historians and the West Indies*, 197.

27. J. D. Fage, introduction to *The British Anti-Slavery Movement*, by Reginald Coupland (1933; repr., New York: Barnes and Noble, 1964), ix, x.

28. Wm. Roger Lewis, introduction to *Oxford History of the British Empire. Vol. 5, Historiography*, ed. Wm. Roger Lewis (Oxford: Oxford University Press, 1999), 23.

29. See Kelvin Jarvis, "The Historical Society of Trinidad and Tobago, 1932–1954," *Caribbean Quarterly* 44, nos. 3–4 (September–December 1998): 94.

30. Lewis, introduction, 24.

31. Fage, introduction, xiii.

32. Frederick Madden, "The Commonwealth, Commonwealth History, and Oxford," in *Oxford and the Idea of Commonwealth: Essays Presented to Sir Edgar Williams*, ed. Frederick Madden and D. K. Fieldhouse (London: Routledge, Kegan, and Paul, 1983), 13.

33. Reginald Coupland, *Wilberforce* (London: Collins, 1923).

34. See Jessica Moody, "Remembering the Imperial Context of Emancipation Commemoration in the Former British Slave-Port Cities of Bristol and Liverpool, 1933–1934," *Slavery and Abolition*, 39, no. 1 (2018): 169–89.

35. Reginald Coupland, *The British Anti-Slavery Movement* (1933; repr., New York: Barnes and Noble, 1964), 11.

36. Coupland, *The British Anti-Slavery Movement*, 11–12.

37. Coupland, *The British Anti-Slavery Movement*, 12.

38. Coupland, *The British Anti-Slavery Movement*, 35.

39. Coupland, *The British Anti-Slavery Movement*, 36.

40. Coupland, *The British Anti-Slavery Movement*, 58.

41. Of course, the story of Wilberforce's life and work is told as one of calling and crusade, and persistence and commitment, in Coupland, *Wilberforce*.

42. Coupland, *The British Anti-Slavery Movement*, 141.

43. Coupland, *The British Anti-Slavery Movement*, 142.

44. On Whig interpretations of history, see John Burrow, *A Liberal Descent: Victorian Historians and the English Past* (Cambridge: Cambridge University Press, 1981).

45. Fage, introduction, xvii.

46. Fage, introduction, xx–xxi.

47. See Williams, *British Historians and the West Indies*, 199.

48. See Williams, *British Historians and the West Indies*, 194–213, 233–34.

49. See Pepijn Brandon, "From Williams's Thesis to Williams Thesis: An Anti-colonial Trajectory," *International Review of Social History* 62, no. 2 (August 2017): 305–27.

50. See Williams, *Inward Hunger*, 51. See also Garcia-Muñiz, "Eric Williams and C. L. R. James," 9.

372   5. EVIL ENRICHMENT

51. See C. L. R. James, *The Black Jacobins: Toussaint L'Ouverture and the San Domingo Revolution* (1938; repr., New York: Vintage, 1963), 24.

52. Williams, *The Economic Aspects*, 5.

53. Howard Temperley's essay, initially presented at the famous symposium on Williams held at the Rockefeller Study and Conference Center at Belagio, Italy, May 21–25, 1984, was later published as Howard Temperley, "Eric Williams and Abolition: The Birth of a New Orthodoxy," in *British Capitalism and Caribbean Slavery: The Legacy of Eric Williams*, ed. Barbara Solow and Stanley Engerman (New York: Cambridge University Press, 1987), 229–57.

54. Temperley, of course, is invoking Goveia, "New Shibboleths for Old." See notes 11 and 62.

55. Temperley, "Eric Williams and Abolition," 38–39.

56. In a roughly contemporary essay, essentially on intellectual dishonesty among some historians of the African Americas, not least some of those involved in the "Williams debate," Darity offers a more detailed and more unsparing critique of what he calls Temperley's "canard" regarding the supposed contrast between Williams's dissertation and his *Capitalism and Slavery*. For Darity, there was simply no foundation whatsoever for this spurious view. "I was stunned," he writes, "at how misleading I found Temperley's interpretation to be. In my reading, there is no substantive difference between the presentation of the abolition thesis in *The Economic Aspect* and *Capitalism and Slavery*." See William Darity Jr., "Disposal of an Old Orthodoxy: Reading Eric Williams' Dissertation," *Review* 35, no. 2 (2012): 171. Underlining the issue of plain intellectual dishonesty, Darity refers shockingly to an incident involving Seymour Drescher, "the modern doyen of the humanitarian school on British abolition of the slave trade" (172). At a 2011 Oxford University conference on Williams where Darity presented the content of Williams's thesis, Drescher, his discussant, "repeated Temperley's canard about the dissertation being more 'balanced.' Again, the claim was made that the dissertation gave greater weight to humanitarian motives for abolition than *Capitalism and Slavery*. When challenged on his persistence with this claim in spite of textual evidence to the contrary, Drescher finally admitted he never had read Williams' dissertation!" (174).

57. William Darity Jr., "From the Dissertation to *Capitalism and Slavery*: Did Williams's Abolition Thesis Change?," introduction to Eric Williams, *The Economic Aspects of the Abolition of the West Indian Slave Trade and Slavery*, ed. Dale Tomich (Lanham, MD: Rowman and Littlefield, 2014), xviii (italics in original).

58. Darity, "From the Dissertation to *Capitalism and Slavery*," xxiii.

59. Dale Tomich, preface to Eric Williams, *The Economic Aspects of the Abolition of the West Indian Slave Trade and Slavery*, ed. Dale Tomich (Lanham, MD: Rowman and Littlefield, 2014), ix (my italics).

60. Temperley, "Eric Williams and Abolition," 246. In an interesting and again clever move, and drawing some of the unimpeachable Caribbean scholars to his cause, Temperley recruits Arthur Lewis in his attempt to demonstrate that Williams violates the "strict requirements of scholarship" (253).

61. Temperley, "Eric Williams and Abolition," 248.

62. In Goveia, "New Shibboleths for Old," reflecting on the way in which Williams, in *British Historians and the West Indies*, affects to be concerned with reviewing the work of British

historians but in fact is concerned with a quite other topic, Goveia writes, with a shade of indignation: "For the one theme which does give his book real internal coherence is the obvious relevance of the books discussed, not to his ostensible subject, but to the spiritual autobiography of Dr. Williams' own intellectual development into 'a rebel against the British historical tradition which Oxford has done so much to develop.' This brief description of himself may serve to emphasise more sharply that the real subject of the book, obscured by its title, is Dr. Williams' own reaction against the racialism and moral self-righteousness which he has found to be integral parts of the traditional interpretation of British and imperial history. In my opinion, it is this hidden theme which will give its lasting value to the work. . . . It would have been much more relevant and genuinely enlightening for us all if Dr. Williams had abandoned the scholarly mask and given us an honest account of his own struggle to liberate himself from 'the inferior status to which these writings sought to condemn' him and his fellow countrymen" (50). Here, I think, is a profound, if clearly reproving, recognition of the ironic stance that Williams was fond of adopting.

63. I am thinking of Hayden White, *Metahistory: The Historical Imagination in Nineteenth-Century Europe* (Baltimore, MD: Johns Hopkins University Press, 1973). Readers of my *Conscripts of Modernity* will no doubt remember that *Metahistory* is of enormous importance to my thinking about the textuality of historical works. Here, as there, I am perhaps more faithful to the spirit of his conceptual intervention than I am to the formalist letter of his vast and intricate typology of historiographical styles. See David Scott, *Conscripts of Modernity: The Tragedy of Colonial Enlightenment* (Durham, NC: Duke University Press, 2004).

64. See Eric Williams, *Inward Hunger*, chaps. 5–11. See also St. Pierre, "Life Abroad," chap. 2 in *Eric Williams and the Anticolonial Tradition*; and Palmer, "Intellectual Decolonization," chap. 1 in *Eric Williams and the Making of the Modern Caribbean*," 15–39.

65. For a sensitive survey, see O. Nigel Bolland, *On the March: Labour Rebellions in the British Caribbean, 1934–39* (London: James Currey, 1995).

66. Williams, *Inward Hunger*, 61. See John Hope Franklyn, "Eric Williams and Howard University," in *"Capitalism and Slavery" Fifty Years Later: Eric Eustace Williams—A Reassessment of the Man and His Work*, ed. Heather Cateau and Selwyn Carrington (New York: Lang, 2000), 24–28.

67. See Lowell Ragatz, *The Fall of the Planter Class in the British Caribbean, 1763–1833* (New York: Century, 1928); and Frank Pitman, *The Development of the British West Indies, 1700–1763* (New Haven, CT: Yale University Press, 1917).

68. Williams tells the story in *Inward Hunger*, chap. 9.

69. Eric Williams, *The Negro in the Caribbean* (1942; repr., Brooklyn, NY: A&B, 1994). *The Negro in the Caribbean* was the last of Locke's Bronze Booklet series. See Jeffrey C. Stewart, *The New Negro: The Life of Alain Locke* (New York: Oxford University Press, 2018), 826. According to Stewart, in this splendid biography, Locke was searching for a more generative Black diasporic perspective, and Williams's book was crucial to this attempt to widen the understanding of the New World Black racial experience.

70. Williams actually received two grants, one on April 17, 1940, and the other on April 18, 1942. See Williams, *Inward Hunger*, 63.

374   5. EVIL ENRICHMENT

71. Williams would boast that this travel had made him more knowledgeable about the Caribbean than any other West Indian in 1940. See Williams, *Inward Hunger*, 68.

72. Williams, *The Negro in the Caribbean*, 11.

73. Williams, *The Negro in the Caribbean*, 12–13.

74. Williams, *The Negro in the Caribbean*, 14.

75. Williams, *The Negro in the Caribbean*, 14 (ellipses in original).

76. Williams, *The Negro in the Caribbean*, 99.

77. Williams, *The Negro in the Caribbean*, 100. For Williams, popular internal democracy was linked to the prospect of both political and economic federation. But Williams also linked this to the strategic suggestion that the United States might take a greater interest in the Caribbean as part of its natural sphere of interest.

78. Denis W. Brogan, introduction to Williams, *Capitalism and Slavery* (London: Andre Deutsch, 1964), ix. Brogan, a Scottish scholar and an authority on the United States, was a fellow of Corpus Christi College, Oxford, between 1934 and 1939. In *Inward Hunger*, Williams writes warmly of Brogan's influence on him in those years when he was trying to establish a bridgehead on an intellectual direction: "By contrast with the futility of philosophy and the inadequacy of economics, I found politics very digestible, and I established contact with one of Oxford's leading thinkers and scholars, D. W. Brogan, who was later annexed by Cambridge. Here it was not only the course that was interesting, but also the tutor" (48). And he goes on a moment later: "I owe a great deal to Brogan, not only for the amount of knowledge he put my way, but also for the intellectual attitude he helped me to cultivate and develop" (49). Clearly, there remained a resonance of sorts between the former tutor and pupil.

79. Williams, *Inward Hunger*, 71.

80. White, *Metahistory*, xii.

81. White, *Metahistory*, 37.

82. Michael Roth, *The Ironist's Cage: Memory, Trauma, and the Construction of History* (New York: Columbia University Press, 1995).

83. A certain conception of intention and choice inflect White's critical intervention. See, in this respect, Martin Jay, "Intention and Irony: The Missed Encounter Between Hayden White and Quentin Skinner," *History and Theory* 52, no. 1 (February 2013): 32–48.

84. See Ewa Domańska, "Hayden White: Beyond Irony," *History and Theory* 37, no. 2 (May 1998): 173–81. For a wide-ranging assessment of White's achievement, see Frank Ankersmit, Ewa Domańska, and Hans Kellner, eds., *Re-figuring Hayden White* (Stanford, CA: Stanford University Press, 2009).

85. See, usefully, Claire Colebrook, *Irony in the Work of Philosophy* (Lincoln: University of Nebraska Press, 2002); and in a clear and handy format, Claire Colebrook, *Irony* (New York: Routledge, 2004). It is interesting that Colebrook does not engage White in either of these books.

86. See, for example, Ken Boodoo, *The Elusive Eric Williams* (Kingston, Jamaica: Ian Randle, 2002). Boodoo aims to reflect on Williams's complex personality, the private man behind the public mask, with his standard equipment of dark glasses and suit and hearing aid.

87. Williams, *Capitalism and Slavery*, v.

88. David Brion Davis, *The Problem of Slavery in Western Culture* (Ithaca, NY: Cornell University Press, 1966).

89. Williams, *Capitalism and Slavery*, v–vi.

90. Williams, *Capitalism and Slavery*, 20. Hereafter page numbers are cited in text.

91. Memorably, in Washington Irving's 1819 story, Rip Van Winkle is a character of Dutch descent in North America who, having imbibed the liquor of some Dutchmen he happens to meet on his wanderings, falls asleep for twenty years. When he awakens, he finds himself in a scarcely recognizable world, having completely missed the great event of the American Revolution.

92. Williams had already invoked it at the end of chapter 5 in Williams, *Capitalism and Slavery* (107). On Swift as an ironist or satirist, see Colebrook, *Irony*, chap. 4.

93. Indeed, perhaps James not merely inspired but *urged* the revision. See Selwyn Ryan, *Eric Williams: The Myth and the Man* (Kingston, Jamaica: University of the West Indies Press, 2009), 43; and Garcia-Muñiz, "Eric Williams and C. L. R. James," 22.

94. Of course, Williams's *The Negro in the Caribbean* was a response to this moment as well.

95. Eric Williams, "Massa Day Done," lecture, Woodford Square, Port of Spain, March 22, 1961; reprinted as Eric Williams, "Massa Day Done," *Callaloo* 20, no. 4 (Autumn 1997): 724–30.

96. Stefan Collini, *Public Moralists: Political Thought and Intellectual Life in Britain, 1850–1939* (Oxford: Oxford University Press, 1991).

97. Hilary Beckles, *Britain's Black Debt: Reparations for Caribbean Slavery and Native Genocide* (Kingston, Jamaica: University of the West Indies Press, 2013). See also Hilary Beckles, "Reparations," in *The Oxford Companion to Black British History*, ed. David Dabydeen, John Gilmore, and Cecily Jones (Oxford: Oxford University Press, 2007).

98. Beckles, *Britain's Black Debt*, 3, 60.

99. Think of the following works by Beckles: Hilary Beckles, *Natural Rebels: A Social History of Enslaved Women in Barbados* (New Brunswick, NJ: Rutgers University of Press, 1989); Hilary Beckles, *Centering Woman: Gender Discourses in Caribbean Slave Society* (Kingston, Jamaica: Ian Randle, 1998); Hilary Beckles, *White Servitude and Black Slavery, 1627–1715* (Knoxville: University of Tennessee Press, 1989); and most recently, Hilary Beckles, *The First Black Slave Society: Britain's 'Barbarity Time' in Barbados, 1636–1876* (Mona, Jamaica: University of the West Indies Press, 2016).

100. Beckles is chairman of the regional CARICOM Reparations Commission. For more information including the CARICOM 10–Point Reparation Plan, go to https://caricom reparations.org. The Centre for Reparation Research has also been established at the University of the West Indies, Mona, directed by the historian Verene Shepherd. Notably, it is really Black slavery and not Native genocide that is the central focus of *Britain's Black Debt*.

101. The story of this contentious conference is instructive. On the conference, see Eric Mann, *Dispatches from Durban* (Los Angeles: Frontlines, 2002); and Suhas Chakma, "The Issue of Compensation for Colonialism and Slavery at the World Conference Against Racism: A Fine Balance Between Rhetoric and Legality," in *Human Rights in Development Yearbook 2001: Reparations: Redressing Past Wrongs*, ed. George Ulrich and Louise Crabbe Boserup (The Hague: Kluwer, 2003), 57–71. The events of September 11, 2001, and the

376   5. EVIL ENRICHMENT

shifting alignments that followed around the war on terror had the effect of completely eclipsing the momentum for reparations.

102. I am relying of Beckles's account. I have not found in any of the literature on Durban (which is scant) a confirming or contradicting account of what took place.

103. Beckles, *Britain's Black Debt*, 2.

104. Beckles, *Britain's Black Debt*, 3.

105. Randall Robinson, *The Debt: What America Owes to Blacks* (New York: Plume, 2001).

106. On the reparations committee, see Emily Newburger, "Breaking the Chain," *Harvard Law Bulletin*, July 1, 2001. See also Charles Ogletree, "Repairing the Past: New Efforts in the Reparations Debate in America," *Harvard Civil Rights-Civil Liberties Law Review* 38 (2003): 279–320.

107. Beckles, *Britain's Black Debt*, 4.

108. I am thinking of Lloyd Best, "Outlines of a Model of Pure Plantation Economy," *Social and Economic Studies* 17, no. 3 (September 1968): 283–326; and George Beckford, *Persistent Poverty: Underdevelopment in Plantation Economies in the Third World* (New York: Oxford University Press, 1972)—but more broadly I am thinking of the theoretical ethos of the New World movement in general.

109. Nicholas Draper, *The Price of Emancipation: Slave-Ownership, Compensation, and British Society at the End of Slavery* (Cambridge: Cambridge University Press, 2010). For some remarks, see David Scott, "Preface: Who Were the Subjects of Slave Emancipation?," *Small Axe*, no. 37 (March 2012): vii–x.

110. Draper's book is part of a larger project, the Legacies of British Slave Ownership project, housed at University College London. For details, go to https://www.ucl.ac.uk/lbs. See Catherine Hall, Nicholas Draper, Keith McClelland, Katie Donington, and Rachel Lang, *Legacies of British Slave Ownership: Colonial Slavery and the Formation of Victorian Britain* (Cambridge: Cambridge University Press, 2014); and Catherine Hall, "Doing Reparatory History: Bringing 'Race' and Slavery Home," *Race and Class* 60, no. 1 (2018): 3–21. See also S. D. Smith, *Slavery, Family, and Gentry Capitalism in the British Atlantic: The World of the Lascelles, 1648–1834* (Cambridge: Cambridge University Press, 2006). Beckles acknowledges Draper profusely, but somewhat shoddily it has to be admitted, and he neglects to acknowledge the larger project and its principals, in particular Catherine Hall. For other work on capitalism and slavery, see Edward Baptist, *The Half Has Never Been Told: Slavery and the Making of American Capitalism* (New York: Basic Books, 2016); and Sven Beckert, *Empire of Cotton: A Global History* (New York; Vintage, 2015).

111. The classic work here is Cheryl Payer, *The Debt Trap: The International Monetary Fund and the Third World* (New York: Monthly Review, 1975).

112. Beckles, *Britain's Black Debt*, 12.

113. The queen's apology to the Maori was not uncontroversial. See "Queen's Apology Will Not Appease Majority of Maoris," *Inter Press Service*, November 2, 1995. In 2006, in the context of the bicentenary of the abolition of the transatlantic slave trade and the vaguely multiculturalist politics of New Labour, then British prime minister Tony Blair offered a statement of "sorrow and regret" for the slave trade, blaming merchants for the atrocity and commending the British government for being the first country to abolish the trade. See "Text of Tony Blair's Statement on Slavery," *History News Network*, November 27, 2006; https://historynewsnetwork.org/article/32322. For comment, see

David Scott. "Preface: Soul Captives Are Free," *Small Axe*, no. 23 (June 2007): v–x; and Hall, "Doing Reparatory History," 5.

114. The Royal African Company (previously known as the Company of Royal Adventurers of England Trading with Africa) was established in 1660 by the House of Stuart, led by James Stuart, the future King James II.

115. See Beckles, "Earls of Harewood: Slave Route to Buckingham Palace," chap. 9 in *Britain's Black Debt*, 121–30: see also Beckles, "Criminal Enrichment: Building Britain with Slavery," chap. 7 in *Britain's Black Debt*, 82–108. In chapter 9, Beckles draws largely on the research of Smith, *Slavery, Family, and Gentry Capitalism*.

116. Beckles, *Britain's Black Debt*, 122.

117. See Mari Matsuda, "Looking to the Bottom: Critical Legal Studies and Reparations," *Harvard Civil Rights-Civil Liberties Law Review* 22, no. 323 (1987): 362–97.

118. Beckles, *Britain's Black Debt*, 18, 19.

119. Beckles, *Britain's Black Debt*, 20.

120. See Partha Chatterjee, "The Colonial State," chap. 2 in *The Nation and Its Fragments: Colonial and Postcolonial Histories* (Princeton, NJ: Princeton University Press, 1993), 14–34.

121. Beckles, *Britain's Black Debt*, 70–71.

122. For useful reference, see the instructive "Forum: *Somerset's Case* Revisited," in *Law and History Review* 26, no. 3 (Fall 2006): 601–71. The centerpiece of the forum is the essay by George Van Cleve, " 'Somerset's Case' and Its Antecedents in Imperial Perspective," *Law and History Review* 26, no. 3 (Fall 2006): 601–45; with comments by Daniel Hulsebosch and Ruth Paley, and a concluding response from Van Cleve. Hulsebosch, "Nothing but Liberty: *Somerset's Case* and the British Empire" (647–58); Paley, "Imperial Politics and English Law: The Many Contexts of 'Somerset,' " (659–64); Van Cleve, "Mansfield's Decision: Toward Human Freedom" (65–71). For information on Charles Steuart, see Mark Weiner, "New Biographical Evidence on Somerset's Case," *Slavery and Abolition* 23, no. 1 (2002): 121–36. And for a wider context, see Steven Wise, *Though the Heavens May Fall: The Landmark Trial That Led to the End of Human Slavery* (Cambridge, MA: Da Capo, 2005).

123. Paley, "Imperial Politics and English Law," 660. See also Ruth Paley, "After *Somerset*: Mansfield, Slavery, and the Law in England, 1772–1830," in *Law, Crime, and English Society 1660–1830*, ed. Norma Landau (Cambridge: Cambridge University Press, 2002), 165–84.

124. Teresa Michals, " 'That Sole and Despotic Dominion': Slaves, Wives, and Game in Blackstone's Commentaries," *Eighteenth-Century Studies* 27, no. 2 (Winter 1993–94): 196. Michals writes that "however they behaved elsewhere, in court, metropolitan Englishmen did not defend legal inequality through open assertions of racial inferiority" (197).

125. Blackstone. quoted in Michals, " 'That Sole and Despotic Dominion,' " 198. On the history of the changes to this passage, see Wilfrid Prest, *William Blackstone: Law and Letters in the Eighteenth Century* (Oxford: Oxford University Press, 2008), 250–51.

126. Michals, " 'That Sole and Despotic Dominion,' " 201.

127. Michals, " 'That Sole and Despotic Dominion,' " 210.

128. Alfred Brophy, "The Case for Reparations for Slavery in the Caribbean," *Slavery and Abolition* 35, no. 1 (2014): 165–69; and Alfred Brophy, *Reparations: Pro and Con* (New York: Oxford University Press, 2008).

129. Brophy, "The Case for Reparations," 168.

EPILOGUE: ON IRREPARABILITY

1. Hannah Arendt, "Concluding Remarks," in *The Origins of Totalitarianism* (New York: Harcourt, Brace, 1951), 433; Arendt, "Totalitarianism in Power," in *The Origins of Totalitarianism*, 2nd ed. (Cleveland, OH: Meridian, 1958), 459.
2. Hannah Arendt, *The Human Condition* (Chicago: University of Chicago Press, 1958). On the relation between this book and *The Origins of Totalitarianism*, see Margaret Canovan, introduction to Arendt, *The Human Condition*, 2nd ed. (Chicago: University of Chicago Press, 1998), xi; and more generally, Margaret Canovan, *Hannah Arendt: A Reinterpretation of Her Political Thought* (Cambridge: Cambridge University Press, 1994), esp. chaps. 2, 3, and 4.
3. Canovan, introduction, viii.
4. See Canovan, introduction, ix.
5. Arendt, *The Human Condition*, 5.
6. I have argued that in *The Human Condition* Arendt offers an essentially tragic perspective even though the idea of the tragic does not formally appear. See David Scott, *Omens of Adversity: Tragedy, Time, Memory, Justice* (Durham, NC: Duke University Press, 2014).
7. Arendt, *The Human Condition*, 237.
8. Arendt, *The Human Condition*, 237.
9. Arendt, *The Human Condition*, 241.
10. See Erving Goffman, "On the Social Characteristics of Total Institutions," in *Asylums: Essays on the Situation of Mental Patients and Other Inmates* (New York: Penguin, 1961), 13–115.
11. See Edgar Thompson, *The Plantation*, ed. Sidney Mintz and George Baca (1932; repr., Columbia: University of South Carolina Press, 2010).

INDEX

abolitionism: anticolonialism and, 278–79; culture of, 289–90; in England, 265–66, 370n17, 372n56; humanitarianism and, 271–73; idealism and, 280–81; Middle Passage and, 375n113; philosophy of, 38–41; politics of, 267–68, 306–10; Slavery Abolition Act, 265–68; to E. Williams, 269–74

Absence of Ruins, An (Patterson), 198

absolute evil, 106–7

accommodation, 174

acculturation, 3, 17, 326n40

Africa: Black people and, 284–85; culture of, 39; England and, 20, 300–301; New World slavery and, 260; violence in, 128; West, 137; to White people, 348n132

Africans: in Caribbean, 297–98, 302, 305–6; descendants of, 37, 39; Jews and, 164; in Middle Passage, 1–2, 56; Native Americans and, 24–25, 149; in New World slavery, 55–56; reparations for, 41, 74, 300–306; slavery of, 113–14; in society, 306–10; in U.S., 199, 276–77, 372n56; in White supremacy, 265–66

After Virtue (MacIntyre), 12–13

Alexander, Jeffrey, 89, 94–97, 143

Allen, Danielle, 112

American Civilization (James), 42–43

American Dilemma, An (Myrdal), 219

American Negro Slavery (Phillips), 131–32

American slavery. *See* New World slavery; slavery

Anglo-Spanish War, 19–20

Anscombe, Elizabeth, 12–13, 86, 149, 325n27, 326n34, 347n127

anthropology, 8–9, 17–18, 44–45

anti-Black racism, 297

anticolonialism, 31–32, 254–55, 259–61, 278–79, 370n16

anti-imperialism, 299–300

anti-Semitism, 113, 114, 172

Arendt, Hannah: Bernstein and, 99–101, 109–10, 114, 117–26, 132, 311–12, 332n40, 337n6, 344n79, 345n95; Black life and, 112–13; Card and, 315–16, 353n72; death camps and, 210; Europe and, 128–29; evil and, 98–104; Heidegger and, 342n64; history and, 89–90; on imperialism, 345n97; intellectualism of, 110–11; on intentionality, 347n121; interpretations of, 126–27; Jaspers and, 121–23; on Jews, 130–31, 163; Kant and, 101, 147, 313; on language, 346n106; Lara and, 87–89, 108; on Nazis, 338n18, 341n43; Neiman and, 118; philosophy of, 104–5, 114–15, 311–17; politics of, 108–14; radical evil and, 98, 162–63; reputation of, 95, 126–33, 143, 311, 339n21, 344n81; Rougemont and, 342n59; scholarship from, 27–28, 32, 104–8, 115–17, 134–35; Skinner and, 341n49; slavery and, 130–32; on tragedy, 378n6; undeserved harm and, 149–50; virtue of, 342n52; on World War II, 343n70

Aristotle, 5

380 INDEX

Aschheim, Steven, 341n46
atrocity. *See specific topics*
Atrocity Paradigm, The (Card), 155–63, 181
Augustine, 84–85, 342n52
Australia, 113–14
autonomy, 147
Axis Rule in Occupied Europe (Lemkin), 96

background morality, 151–52
banality of evil. *See* Arendt
Barbados, 200, 262, 301, 360n47
barbarism, 23
Barkan, Elazar, 331n28
Beckford, George, 299, 309
Beckles, Hilary, 32, 261, 295–303, 305–6, 309–10, 375n100, 376n110
Being and Time (Heidegger), 103
Belle, Dido Elizabeth, 356n135
Bernstein, Richard: Arendt and, 99–101, 109–10, 114, 117–26, 132, 311–12, 332n40, 337n6, 344n79, 345n95; Black people to, 111–12; on critical fallibility, 90–91; on Holocaust, 338n14; Lara and, 84, 119–20; philosophy of, 339n21; on race relations, 112–13
Best, Lloyd, 309
Bettelheim, Bruno, 127, 210–11
Beyond a Boundary (James), 42–43
Beyond Good and Evil (Nietzsche), 157
Billy Budd (Melville), 99
Black culture, 211–12, 219–20, 235–36, 238–41, 275
Blackfeet Nation, 10
Black Jacobins, The (James): *Capitalism and Slavery* and, 306–10; scholarship on, 131–32, 205, 219, 283, 359n36; themes of, 31, 41–43, 252–58, 260–61
Black life: Arendt and, 112–13; Black critique of, 58–59; Black futurity, 40–41, 59; Black Marxism, 39; Black power, 41–42; embodied traditions of, 39; New World slavery and, 25, 111–12, 186, 221, 224, 329n7; on plantations, 231–33; after slavery, 38; social death and, 30; in U.S., 311–12; in White supremacy, 27

Blackness, 112–13, 237
Black people: Africa and, 284–85; to Bernstein, 111–12; Black emancipationism, 40–41; Black redemption, 40; cosmopolitanism and, 333n51; Crow Nation and, 24–25; group autonomy to, 180; human rights for, 275; identity of, 173–74; intellectual traditions of, 37; Jews and, 140–44, 171; King on, 345n95; in New World, 82–83; property of, 23; race relations for, 76–77; religion to, 185–86; reparations for, 74; after slavery, 307–8; sovereignty of, 73; in Tacky Revolt, 21–22; in U.S., 69–70, 297; voting by, 183–84; in Western culture, 171–72; White people and, 171, 187–88; White supremacy to, 135. *See also specific topics*
Black Reconstruction (Du Bois), 131–32
Black Rights/White Wrongs (Mills), 69
Blackstone, William, 303–4
Blassingame, John, 173–74
Bloomsbury set, 257–58
Boissière, Ralph de, 263
Boodoo, Ken, 374n86
Boxill, Bernard, 141
Bradford, John, 183–85
Brathwaite, Edward Kamau, 203, 218–21, 285, 363n85, 364n90, 364n92
Britain. *See* England
Britain's Black Debt (Beckles), 32, 261, 295–303, 305–6, 309–10
British Anti-Slavery Movement, The (Coupland), 265–70
British Caribbean slavery. *See specific topics*
British Historians and the West Indies (Williams, E.), 257
Brogan, Denis, 279–80, 282–83
Brophy, Alfred, 305–6
Bunche, Ralph, 275
Burnard, Trevor, 328n53, 360n45
Butler, Uriah, 263, 274

Calder, Todd, 85–86, 354n93
Camus, Albert, 153, 203, 214–17, 362n73, 362n77

Canovan, Margaret, 313
capitalism: commercial, 20; liberal, 61–62; New World slavery and, 27, 251–58; philosophy of, 286–87; scholarship on, 268–74, 279–85; slavery and, 31–32, 57–58, 262–68, 274–79, 285–95
Capitalism and Slavery (Williams, E.): *The Black Jacobins* and, 306–10; intellectualism in, 254–58; problem-space of, 262–68, 274–79, 285–95; reception of, 269–74, 280–85; themes in, 31–32, 57–58; West Indies and, 258–61
Card, Claudia: Arendt and, 315–16, 353n72; Kekes and, 145–47, 158, 166–67, 186, 223–24; Patterson and, 162–63; philosophy of, 252; on rape, 170; scholarship from, 18, 28–29, 52, 165; on secular morality, 155–63; on social death, 200; Thomas and, 155, 160, 176, 180–81
Caribbean: Africans in, 297–98, 302, 305–6; anticolonialism in, 254–55; Beckles on, 261; Caribbean cultural theory, 2–3, 19–23, 31–32, 221–22; after colonialism, 285; England and, 274–75, 298–300, 307–8; history of, 221–22; intellectualism in, 329n4; Scottish enlightenment in, 368n121; slavery in, 19–22, 323n2, 354n109, 363n81, 363n82; U.S. and, 39, 275–76, 288–89, 374n77
CARICOM Reparations Commission, 375n100
Cavell, Stanley, 12
Césaire, Aimé, 128
character-morality, 153
Chatterjee Partha, 302
Cheyenne Nation, 10
children, 111–12, 154–55, 158, 164
Children of Sisyphus, The (Patterson), 198, 215, 220–21
China, 93, 286
Chisholm, Shirley, 356n134
choice-moralists, 151–52
Christianity: Christian Enlightenment, 85; evangelical, 55; Hitler and, 348n132; humanity in, 56–57; Kant and, 101, 108;

liberalism and, 57; philosophy of, 84–85; psychology in, 128; in U.S., 183–84
Churchill, Winston, 275, 277–78
Cipriani, Andrew A., 262–63, 274
Clarke, Edith, 204–5
Clarkson, Thomas, 56, 289
classic liberalism, 336n83
Codrington, Christopher, 269–70
Cold War, 45, 114–15, 117, 214, 256, 298–99
Cole, Phillip, 51
Collingwood, Luke, 137
Collingwood, R. G., 36
Collini, Stefan, 294
colonialism: Anglo-Spanish War and, 19–20; in Australia, 113–14; in Barbados, 360n47; Caribbean after, 285; colonial debt, 31–32; culture and, 262–68; education in, 371n25; England in, 194–95, 207; Europe in, 251–58, 339n24, 348n132; gender after, 49–50; history of, 295–300; neocolonialism, 32, 77; in New Zealand, 62–63; politics of, 69–70; settler colonial power, 15–16; slavery and, 56–57, 93. *See also specific topics*
Colonial Policy and Practice (Furnivall), 206
Commentaries on the Laws of England (Blackstone), 303
commercial capitalism, 20
common-sense morality, 165–66
communal atrocities, 182–83
compassion, 47–48
concentration camps. *See* Holocaust
conceptual attention, 44
conceptual language, 105–6, 119
conceptual-political ideology, 158
conflict, Kekes on, 150–55
Confronting Evils (Card), 160–63, 353n72
conjuncture, 37–38
Conscripts of Modernity (Scott), 41
conservatism, 148
contrition, 183
Convention on the Prevention and Punishment of the Crime of Genocide, 96
Cooper, David, 54
Corlett, J. Angelo, 65

382 INDEX

cosmopolitanism, 64, 67, 333n51
Coupland, Reginald, 264–72
Craton, Michael, 366n105
Creole culture, 193–94, 218–22, 363n82
critical fallibility, 90–91
Cromwell, Oliver, 19–20
Crow Nation, 6–8, 10–11, 14–18, 24–25
Crown Colony, 262
Cugoano, Quobna Ottobah, 56–57
culture: of abolitionism, 289–90; of Africa,
39; Alexander on, 95–96; assumptions
in, 63–64; Black, 211–12, 219–20, 235–36,
238–41; after Cold War, 114–15, 117;
colonialism and, 262–68; cultural
devastation, 14–18; cultural hegemony,
46; cultural reproduction, 177; in death
camps, 338n14; despair in, 105–6; of
England, 255–57; of Europe, 49–50;
expressive, 324n16; forms of life in, 2; after
Holocaust, 179–80; humanitarianism
in, 294; humanity and, 8–9; of Jews, 104;
justifications in, 39; liberalism and, 73–75;
of Native Americans, 6–8, 10–11; of New
World slavery, 60–61, 87, 89, 185–86;
patriarchy in, 73; Patterson on, 365n93;
philosophy and, 3–4; on plantations,
194–95; postmetaphysical perspectives
in, 132–33; race relations and, 361n59;
reform in, 183; religion in, 55–56; "Sambo"
in, 171–72; of slavery, 30–31, 131–32;
systematic wrongs in, 52–53; tragedy in,
154–55; of U.S., 171–72, 255–56; violence
in, 2; Waldron on, 66–67; Western, 46, 93,
171–72. *See also specific topics*

Darity, William, Jr., 259–60, 270–73,
370nn16–17, 372n56
Davis, David Brion, 58, 285, 334n59
death camps. *See* Holocaust
Debt, The (Robinson), 297
deficiency laws, 21–22
dehumanization, 227
deracination, 3
despair, 105–6
destructive-constructive power, 200–201

devastation: of Crow Nation, 14; cultural,
14–18; historical atrocity and, 18–25,
29–30; of lifeworlds, 1–5; of Middle
Passage, 25; philosophy and, 11–14; power
of, 19; psychology of, 5–11; scholarship
on, 28–30
Development of Creole Society in Jamaica, The
(Brathwaite), 203, 218, 220–22, 285
Devil's Share, The (Rougemont), 101–2
Diamond, Cora, 12–14, 41, 325n27, 326n35
Diamond, Stanley, 17, 326n40
Die Schuldfrage (Jaspers), 122–23
Die the Long Day (Patterson): characters in,
228–33, 238–41; lifeworlds in, 212–14;
scholarship on, 201–4, 222–24, 241–50;
themes in, 30–31, 191–96, 198, 224–28,
233–38
Discourse on the Origins of Inequality
(Rousseau), 72
distorted life, 29
Douglass, Frederick, 174–75
Draper, Nicholas, 298, 376n110
Dreyfus, Hubert, 325n23
Du Bois, W. E. B., 131–32

*Economic Aspect of the Abolition of the West
Indian Slave Trade and Slavery, The*
(Williams, E.), 260, 270–72
education, 5–6, 255–58, 264, 275, 371n25
Egerton, Hugh, 264
Eichmann, Adolf, 123, 126
Eichmann in Jerusalem (Arendt), 28, 90–91,
104–5, 117–18, 122–23, 126, 134–35
Elizabeth II (queen), 301
Elkins, Stanley, 132, 171, 202–3, 209–12, 218,
316
Ellison, Ralph, 112
empiricism, 12
England: abolitionism in, 265–66, 370n17,
372n56; Africa and, 20, 300–301;
Caribbean and, 274–75, 298–300, 307–8;
in colonialism, 194–95, 207; Coupland
on, 266–68; culture of, 255–57; education
in, 257–58; France and, 287, 308; history
from, 372n62; Industrial Revolution in,

284; law in, 303–6; Middle Passage and, 267; Nazis to, 284–85; New Zealand and, 301; racism in, 302–6; religion in, 263–64; slavery to, 376n113; society of, 185, 287–88; U.S. and, 290–91; West Indies and, 275–79, 288–89; White supremacy in, 296; *Zong* from, 136–37. *See also* Europe

engorged evil, 341n45

Enlightenment, 24–25, 85, 271

epistemology, 114–15

Equiano, Olaudah, 56, 185–86

ethics. *See* morality

ethos, 44

Euripides, 154–55

Europe: Arendt and, 128–29; in colonialism, 251–58, 339n24, 348n132; culture of, 49–50; Enlightenment in, 271; Eurocentrism, 111; history of, 163–64, 274–79; intellectualism in, 102–3; James on, 252–53; Jews in, 27–28, 94–95, 97–98, 116; Middle Passage and, 20; neoliberalism in, 300–306; New World slavery and, 92–93, 168; philosophy in, 295–300; slavery and, 258–61, 306–10; society in, 262–68; U.S. and, 100, 295–96; West Indies and, 260–61; Whiteness in, 128; after World War II, 103–4

evangelical Christianity, 55

evil. *See specific topics*

"Evil and Forgiveness" (Thomas), 180–86

Evil in Modern Thought (Neiman), 91–92, 118

exceptionalism, 120, 135, 186

exploitation, 35–36

expressive culture, 324n16

Facing Evil (Kekes), 147–55

Fage, J. D., 264–65, 268–69

fallibility, 120

Fanon, Frantz, 216, 367n120

fascism, 99

Fassin, Didier, 46–50, 331n28

fatalism, 216–17

feminism, 72–73, 156, 159

Feminist Ethics (Card), 156

fiction: lifeworlds in, 224–28; from Patterson, 222–28, 367n119; philosophy and, 30–31;

plantations in, 230–31, 241; realism in, 223; slavery in, 191–96; violence in, 231. *See also specific novels*

Finley, Moses, 327n46

flexibility, 71

forced labor, 128–30

Forde, Daryl, 206

forgiveness, 180–88, 356n129

Formosa, Paul, 52

forms of life: concept of, 3–4, 12–14; in culture, 2; etymology of, 323n3; genocide and, 144–45; *habitus* as, 39; humanity and, 1; Lear on, 24–25; morality and, 5–11, 17–18; natal alienation and, 177; recognizable, 15; totality of, 179; to Wittgenstein, 325n19

Forster, E. M., 258

Foucault, Michel, 8, 36, 47, 157, 234–35, 324n6, 367n118

fragility, 164–66, 185

Fragility of Goodness, The (Nussbaum), 145, 150, 153–54, 164, 229–30

France, 214, 287, 308

Frazier, E. Franklin, 275

freedom, 174–75

Freedom in the Making of Western Culture (Patterson), 197–98, 235, 249

French Revolution, 41

Freud, Sigmund, 5

Froude, James Anthony, 255

Furnivall, J. S., 206

Geertz, Clifford, 332n37

gender, 49–50, 72–73

gendered power, 22

genealogical critique: reparations and, 76–77; reparatory history as, 53–67; scholarship on, 67–75

genocide: forms of life and, 144–45; history of, 149, 200; against Native Americans, 77, 113–14; by Nazis, 27–28, 96–97, 116–17, 162–63; philosophy of, 75–80; slavery and, 20–21, 306–7; as social death, 161–62; violence in, 83

"Genocide and Social Death" (Card), 161–62

384 INDEX

Genovese, Eugene, 171
Germany, 130, 170–71, 175, 316, 340n27
Gines, Kathryn, 112–13
Girvan, Norman, 205
Gnosticism, 103
God, 183–86, 215
Goffman, Erving, 316
Goldhagen, Daniel, 200
Gomes, Albert, 263
good, concepts of, 167–68
Gordon, Avery, 334n62
Goveia, Elsa, 217–19, 272–73, 329n4, 363n81, 363n85, 369n11, 372n62
Gray, John, 68, 148
Gregson, William, 137
Groundwork for a Metaphysics of Morals (Kant), 85
group autonomy, 180

habitus, 39
Hacking, Ian, 329n6
Hadot, Pierre, 324n6
Haiti, 41–42
Hall, Catherine, 335n63
Hall, Stuart, 37–38, 311, 324n16, 329n5
Hannah Arendt and the Jewish Question (Bernstein), 99–100, 101, 117, 120–21, 126
Hannah Arendt and the Negro Question (Gines), 112
Harris, Abram, 260
Haugeland, John, 9
Hegel, Georg, 118–19, 217, 245
Heidegger, Martin, 9, 11, 101–3, 342n64
Hemings, Sally, 169
Herskovits, Melville, 219–20
Higman, Barry, 329n4
historical blindness, 128
historical crimes, 70–71
historicity, 27–28, 35–43, 135. *See also specific topics*
historiographic anticolonialism, 259
historiography, 60–61
history. *See specific topics*

History of Jamaica (Long), 212
Hitler, Adolf, 102, 123, 151, 316, 348n132
Holocaust: authority in, 104–8; Bernstein on, 338n14; culture after, 179–80; engorged evil in, 341n45; history of, 133–35; identity in, 96; legacy of, 181; liberalism and, 353n81; as meta-evil, 89, 91–98; moral history of, 93–94; Nazis and, 175; New World slavery and, 28–29, 91, 94, 116–17, 133–35, 139–46, 165, 312, 316–17; slavery and, 27–28, 160, 170–75; violence of, 27–28, 87
Hook, Sidney, 154
hope, 152–53
human achievement, 154–55
Human Condition, The (Arendt), 32, 104–5, 313–14
human flourishing, 148, 178
Humanism and Terror (Merleau-Ponty), 216
humanitarianism: abolitionism and, 271–73; in culture, 294; human rights and, 331n24; international, 46–47; New World slavery and, 288–89; philosophy of, 55–56, 76, 185, 271, 294
Humanitarian Reason (Fassin), 46–50
humanity: barbarism and, 23; in Christianity, 56–57; culture and, 8–9; C. Diamond on, 326n35; discourse in, 44; evil and, 51–52; forms of life and, 1; human universality, 7; inhumanity, 174–75; integrity of, 247–48; morality and, 54–55; narratives in, 36; Nazis to, 355n113; Nussbaum on, 229–30; psychology of, 29–30; revolutions in, 42–43; scholarship on, 32, 163–70, 187; in slavery, 169–70; social action and, 4–5; of White people, 241–47
human rights: for Black people, 275; humanitarianism and, 331n24; philosophy of, 84; scholarship on, 81–84; slavery and, 137–38; to United Nations, 340n39; in Western culture, 93
Hume, David, 47–48, 243, 246, 368n124
Husserl, Edmund, 4
Hutcheson, Francis, 47–48

idealism, 264–65, 280–81

identity: Blackness and, 237; of Black people, 173–74; in Holocaust, 96; in Jamaica, 328n53; of Jews, 179–80; of Patterson, 196–201; in radical evil, 123–24; in social death, 162; of Thomas, 349n7; in U.S., 345n93

ideology: of change, 61–62; conceptual-political, 158; of exceptionalism, 120, 135, 186; of freedom, 174–75; ideological self-image, 26, 28; to Kekes, 148–49; morality and, 53, 151, 285; of Nazis, 116; perspectives from, 45; racist, 114; religion and, 107–8; since Cold War, 134; social, 165; of socialism, 299; of White supremacy, 187–88

imagination, 40

imperialism, 105–6, 113–14, 264, 299–300, 345n97

indisputable evil, 58–59

individualism, 142

individuality, 166

Industrial Revolution, 284

ingratitude, 174–75

inhumanity, 174–75

institutions, 36, 53, 146–47, 161, 170–80, 249–50

integrity, 168, 247–48

intellectualism: anti-Semitism in, 172; of Arendt, 110–11; in Black culture, 275; in Caribbean, 329n4; in Europe, 102–3; Nazis and, 128; psychology and, 140; after World War II, 99–100

intellectual-political traditions, 42–43

intellectual traditions, 37

intentionality, 124, 149–50, 159–60, 163–70, 245–46, 347n121

Interesting Narrative of the Life of Olaudah Equiano, The (Equiano), 56

international humanitarianism, 46–47

international law, 301

International Monetary Fund, 299

intolerable harm, 352n53

Inward Hunger (Williams, E.), 257, 274, 279–80

irony, 31–32, 282–83

irrecoverable wrongs, 181

irreparable loss, 14

Irving, Washington, 375n9

Jamaica: Barbados and, 200, 262; in Caribbean cultural theory, 19–23; history of, 242–43, 250, 361nn51–52; identity in, 328n53; Neiman on, 339n24; Patterson on, 204–9; plantations in, 224–28; slavery in, 30–31, 327n46, 356n2, 366n108; West Africa and, 137. *See also specific topics*

James, C. L. R.: Cipriani to, 262–63; on Europe, 252–54; Marx to, 286; philosophy of, 31, 41–43, 98–99, 131–32; on reading, 110; reputation of, 202–3, 205, 311; on slave revolts, 280; Webb and, 369n7; E. Williams and, 254–58, 283, 289–90, 306–10

James Somerset case, 56, 303, 333n52

Japan, 149, 347n127

Jaspers, Karl, 87, 121–23

Jefferson, Thomas, 125, 168–69

Jews: Africans and, 164; anti-Semitism against, 113; Arendt on, 130–31, 163; Black people and, 140–44, 171; culture of, 104; in death camps, 356n132; in Europe, 27–28, 94–95, 97–98, 116; in Germany, 175; history of, 116–17; identity of, 179–80; moral history of, 122, 175–76; Nazis and, 29, 95–96, 133–34, 172

Julius Rosenwald Fund, 275

justice, 48, 63–64, 67–69, 72–73

justifications, 39, 74–75

Kant, Immanuel: Arendt and, 101, 147, 313; autonomy to, 147; Christianity and, 101, 108; to Eichmann, 123; Hegel and, 118–19; individualism and, 142; to Kekes, 352n53; to Neiman, 91–92; philosophy of, 51, 64, 67–68; postmetaphysical perspectives of, 86–87; on radical evil, 87–88, 107–8, 122, 124; on religion, 85; theology of, 338n10; violence to, 85–86

Kaplan, Marion, 200

386 INDEX

Kardiner, Abram, 205
Kekes, John: Card and, 145–47, 158, 166–67, 186, 223–24; on conflict, 150–55; on evil, 146–55; on habitual evil, 242; ideology to, 148–49; on individuality, 166; on intentionality, 149–50, 245–46; Kant to, 352n53; on liberalism, 336n91; to Midgely, 351n32; Nussbaum and, 150, 153–54; on optimism, 335n65; reputation of, 28–29, 52, 70, 155–56; Thomas and, 147–48, 163; on vices, 164
Kelley, Robin D. G., 39
Kerr, Madeline, 204–5
Keynes, Maynard, 258
Kierkegaard, Søren, 5
King, Richard, 132, 338n18, 344n79, 345n95
Knight, James, 21
Kogon, Eugen, 127
Kojève, Alexandre, 217
Kristallnacht, 95
Kuper, Adam, 324n13

labor, 75–76, 128–30
Laclau, Ernesto, 68
language: Arendt on, 346n106; in Black culture, 235–36; conceptual, 105–6, 119; language-games, 11; linguistic philosophy, 13–14, 44; of morality, 12–13; political, 88; to readers, 171; Rougemont on, 102–3; social-political, 48; speculative, 122; Wittgenstein on, 9
Lara, María Pía, 81–84, 87–89, 96, 108, 119–20, 125
Lawson, Bill, 141
Lear, Jonathan: on cultural devastation, 15–18; Dreyfus and, 325n23; on forms of life, 24–25; Kuper and, 324n13; language to, 14; MacIntyre and, 15, 326n37; philosophy of, 5–12, 187, 324n6; Sahlins and, 324n10
Leeward islands, 363n82
legal violence, 121
Lemkin, Raphaël, 96
Lesbian Choices (Card), 156
Lévi-Strauss, Claude, 6

Lewis, Arthur, 372n60
Lewis, Gordon K., 262–63
Lewis, Wm. Roger, 264–65
liberal capitalism, 61–62
liberalism: Christianity and, 57; classic, 336n83; conservatism and, 148; culture and, 73–75; Holocaust and, 353n81; Kekes on, 336n91; Marxism and, 115, 307; ontology of, 71–72; politics of, 54, 69–70; post-Marxist, 68; racial, 69; rationalizations in, 128
Liberalism (Losurdo), 69–71
Life and Labor in the Old South (Phillips), 131–32
Life in a Haitian Valley (Herskovits), 220
Life of the Mind, The (Arendt), 104–5, 117–18
lifeworlds: concept of, 14–18; devastation of, 1–5; in fiction, 224–28; morality in, 11–14; Patterson and, 212–14; scholarship on, 5–11, 222–24; Thomas on, 353n81
Linderman, Frank, 7
Lindsay, John, 356n135
linguistic philosophy, 13–14, 44
Living Morally (Thomas), 141–42
Locke, Alain, 275, 373n69
Locke, John, 68, 302
Long, Edward, 21, 212
"Losing Your Concepts" (Diamond, C.), 12
loss. *See specific topics*
Losurdo, Domenico, 69–71, 75
Lott, Tommy, 141
Louverture, Toussaint, 41–42, 257
Love and Saint Augustine (Arendt), 101
Love in the Western World (Rougemont), 102
Lowie, Robert, 7
loyalty, 355n111
Lucifer Effect, The (Zimbardo), 164–65

MacIntyre, Alasdair, 12–14, 15, 45, 86, 148, 326n34, 326n37
Madden, Frederick, 265
Magna Carta, 278–79
malignity, 84–85
Manley, Michael, 220
Manley, Norman Washington, 206

INDEX   387

Mansfield, Lord Chief Justice, 56, 137, 185–86, 303–5, 333n52, 356n135

Maori people, 62–63

Mariners, Renegades, and Castaways (James), 43

Maroon War, 21–22

Marryshow, T. A., 263, 274

Marx, Karl, 198–99, 286

Marxism, 54, 67–69, 115, 198–99, 291, 307, 313–14

mass extermination. *See* genocide

McGary, Howard, 141

meaning-in-use, 99

Measure of Things, The (Cooper), 54

Melville, Herman, 42–43, 99

memory, 58, 62–63, 178–79

Mendes, Alfred, 263

mercantilism. *See Capitalism and Slavery*

Merleau-Ponty, Maurice, 216, 362n77

Merton, Robert, 213

meta-evil, 89, 91–98

Metahistory (White), 281–82

Michals, Teresa, 303–5

Michelet, Jules, 41

Middle Passage: abolitionism and, 376n113; Africans in, 1–2, 56; devastation of, 25; England and, 267; Europe and, 20; forms of life and, 10; historiography of, 60–61; narratives of, 136–37; plantations after, 29, 249–50; psychology of, 1–2, 24, 136, 138–39; violence of, 39

Midgely, Mary, 351n32

Milbank, John, 84–85, 337n8

Milgram, Stanley, 164–65

Mills, Charles, 67–75, 77, 141, 336n82

Mintz, Steven, 57–58

Mis-education of the Negro (Woodson), 131–32

"Modern Moral Philosophy" (Anscombe), 13

modern society, 82

Moody-Adams, Michelle, 141

moral bivalence, 167–70

moral debt, 58

moral disapprobation, 168

moral fragility, 185

moral history: Davis on, 334n59; evil and, 50–58; of Holocaust, 93–94; of Jews, 122, 175–76; Nazis in, 10–11; of radical evil, 132–33; reparatory history and, 44–50

morality: Anscombe on, 149; authority for, 88–91; background, 151–52; in Black culture, 238–41; character-morality, 153; common-sense, 165–66; Coupland on, 265–70; forms of life and, 5–11, 17–18; to Foucault, 234–35; humanity and, 54–55; ideology and, 53, 151, 285; of institutions, 146–47, 161; judgment of, 157; justifications in, 74–75; language of, 12–13; in lifeworlds, 11–14; New World slavery and, 26–27; ordinary ethics, 366n107; philosophy and, 115, 141–42, 146–55, 243–45, 330n19; politics and, 26, 61, 68, 76–77, 81–84, 89–90; privilege and, 88–89; psychology of, 123–24, 164, 166; of punishment, 128–30; race relations and, 21–22; reparatory history and, 35–43, 50–58, 67–77; scholarsh p on, 17–18, 25–27, 265–66; secular, 155–63; slavery and, 370n14; social action and, 94–95; of society, 182–83, 249–50; suffering and, 159; in U.S., 16–17

morally invidious comparisons, 136–40

moral pain, 144–45

moral philosophy, 13, 44–45

moral priorities, 125

moral psychology, 72

moral simpletons, 171–75

moral-sociological philosophy, 65–66

moral sociology, 187, 196–97, 247

moral vocabulary, 119–20

Mouffe, Chantal, 68

Mounier, Emmanuel, 102

Moyn, Samuel, 45, 331n25

murderous extermination. *See* genocide

Murdoch, Iris, 12, 325n27

Murphy, Jeffrie, 181–82

My Mother Who Fathered Me (Clarke), 204–5

Myrdal, Gunnar, 219

Myth of Sisyphus, The (Camus), 203, 214–16, 227–28

Myth of the Negro Past (Herskovits), 219–20

388 INDEX

Nagel, Thomas, 154
narratives: Alexander on, 94–95; from Brathwaite, 203, 364n90; of emancipationism, 38–39; of evil, 53–54; history from, 177–78; in humanity, 36; of Middle Passage, 136–37; of New World slavery, 30–31, 55–57; from plantations, 301; of slavery, 11, 279–85
natal alienation, 170–80, 186–87, 201
Native Americans, 6–11, 20–21, 24–25, 77, 113–14, 149, 375n100
Nazis: Arendt on, 338n18, 341n46; authority of, 27–28, 101–2; death camps of, 104, 116, 346n106; to England, 284–85; in France, 214; genocide by, 27–28, 96–97, 116–17, 162–63; Hitler and, 123; Holocaust and, 175; to humanity, 355n113; ideology of, 116; intellectualism and, 128; Jews and, 29, 95–96, 133–34, 172; Kristallnacht in, 95; in moral history, 110–11; policy of, 122–23; psychology of, 169; reputation of, 128; society of, 131; technology of, 121–22; Thomas on, 354n104; totalitarianism and, 316; after World War II, 96
Negro in the Caribbean, The (Williams E.), 276–78
Neiman, Susan, 91–93, 118, 120, 125, 339n24
neocolonialism, 32, 77
neoliberalism, 50; in Europe, 300–306; reparations in, 295–300, 306–10
New World slavery: Africa and, 260; Africans in, 55–56; Beckles on, 300–306; Black life and, 25, 111–12, 186, 221, 224, 329n7; Black reparation for, 74; capitalism and, 27, 251–58; conditions of, 178–79; Crow Nation and, 17–18, 24; culture of, 60–61, 87, 89, 185–86; death camps and, 130–31; domination in, 213–14; Europe and, 92–93, 168; evil in, 76–77; historicity of, 27–28, 35–43, 135; history of, 1–2, 26, 116; Holocaust and, 28–29, 91, 94, 116–17, 133–35, 139–46, 165, 312, 316–17; humanitarianism and, 288–89; imperialism and, 113–14; institutionalization of, 53; international law and, 301; legacy of, 75; morality and, 26–27; narratives of, 30–31, 55–57; Native Americans and, 375n100;

Patterson and, 176–77, 217–22; philosophy of, 195–96; politics of, 18–25; race relations after, 59–60; self-deception in, 169–70; violence of, 32, 82–83, 248–49; White supremacy and, 311–12
New Zealand, 62–63, 301
Nietzsche, Friedrich, 157–58
"Nightmare and Flight" (Arendt), 103–4
nuclear weapons, 149
Nuremberg Laws, 95
Nussbaum, Martha: on humanity, 229–30; Kekes and, 150, 153–54; philosophy of, 145, 148, 164, 314; romanticism of, 154–55; on Stoicism, 156

Obedience to Authority (Milgram), 164–65
obligations, 65–66
On Revolution (Arendt), 104–5
On the Genealogy of Morality (Nietzsche), 157
"On the Social Construction of Moral Universals" (Alexander), 94–95
ontological priorities, 142
ontological vulnerability, 11, 183
ontology, 7–8, 24–25, 71–72, 193–94, 329n6
optimism, 105–6
ordinary ethics, 366n107
Origins of Totalitarianism, The (Arendt): death camps in, 122; philosophy of, 312–13; publication of, 28, 105, 107, 122–23, 316; radical evil in, 117–18, 121; reception of, 103–4, 113, 116–17, 126–27, 131, 134–35; rhetorical construction of, 129; themes of, 90–91, 163
Ovesey, Lionel, 205

Padmore, George, 257–58
Paley, Ruth, 303
paradigms of evil, 158–59
parents, 164
parody, 31–32
Pateman, Carole, 72
patriarchy, 73
Patterson, Orlando: art and, 357n11, 359n27; Brathwaite and, 285; Burnard and, 360n45; Camus and, 214–17, 362n73;

Card and, 162–63; on Caribbean slavery, 323n2; on culture, 365n93; Elkins and, 209–12; fiction from, 222–28, 367n119; identity of, 196–201; on Jamaica, 204–9; New World slavery and, 176–77, 217–22; philosophy of, 178; reputation of, 29–31, 241–47; scholarship on, 201–4, 224–28, 247–50; Scott and, 366n105; on slavery, 212–14, 238–41; M. G. Smith and, 360n37; on social death, 116–17, 161–62; on social history, 359n36; on sociology, 145–46, 357n7; Thomas and, 186–87; on violence, 233–38; on women, 228–33, 366n112. *See also specific works*

Paul-Damascus, Adolph, 356n132

Penn, William, 19–20

People's National Party, 206

Personality and Conflict in Jamaica (Kerr), 204–5

phenomenology, 3–4, 30–31, 247

Phenomenology of Spirit (Hegel), 217

Phillips, Ulrich B., 131–32

Philosophical Investigations (Wittgenstein), 99

philosophy: of abolitionism, 38–41; of absolute evil, 106–7; of agency, 16–17; of Anscombe, 347n127; anthropology and, 8–9, 17–18; approaches in, 7–8; of Arendt, 104–5, 114–15, 311–17; of Bernstein, 339n21; of capitalism, 286–87; of Card, 252; of Christianity, 84–85; conceptual language and, 105–6; culture and, 3–4; devastation and, 11–14; of education, 5–6; of Enlightenment, 24–25; in Europe, 295–300; of fatalism, 216–17; fiction and, 30–31; flexibility in, 71; of genocide, 175–80; of Goveia, 273; of Heidegger, 101–2; history of, 339n23; of humanitarianism, 55–56, 76, 185, 271, 294; of human rights, 84; imagination and, 40; of intellectual-political traditions, 42–43; of James, 31, 41–43, 98–99, 131–32; of justice, 48, 67; of Kant, 51, 64, 67–68; language in, 12; of Lear, 5–12, 187, 324n6; linguistic, 13–14, 44; moral, 13, 44–45; morality and, 115, 141–42, 146–55, 243–45, 330n19; moral-sociological, 65–66; of New

World slavery, 195–96; of Nussbaum, 145, 148, 164, 314; of obligations, 65–66; of Patterson, 178; politics and, 100, 117, 188; of race relations, 67–75; of racism, 246, 368n124; from reading, 100–101; of reconciliation, 62–63; of reparations, 41; scholarship on, 84–91, 139–46; of Scottish Enlightenment, 47–48; secular, 51, 146, 152–53; of society, 90–91; of suffering, 160–61; theology and, 342n64; of Thomas, 28–30, 139–48, 186–88, 223–24, 315; of J. Thompson, 64–65; of undeserved harm, 147–48; Western, 118–19; of E. Williams, 31–32, 57–58; of Wittgenstein, 3–4

Pitman, Frank, 275

Pitt, William, 288

plantations: acculturation on, 3; Black life on, 231–33; Creole, 221–22; culture on, 194–95; in fiction, 230–31, 241; in Jamaica, 224–28; after Middle Passage, 29, 249–50; narratives from, 301; racism on, 22–23; violence on, 236–38. *See also specific topics*

Plenty Coups (chief), 7–8, 14, 17–18

Polanyi, Karl, 284

politics: of abolitionism, 267–68, 306–10; of anticolonialism, 261, 370n16; of anti-Semitism, 114; of Arendt, 108–14; of Beckles, 295–303, 305–6, 309–10; of Caribbean slavery, 21–22; of colonialism, 69–70; of communal atrocities, 182–83; idealism in, 264–65; intellectual-political traditions, 42–43; of liberalism, 54, 69–70; of Marxism, 198–99, 291; morality and, 26, 61, 68, 76–77, 81–84, 89–90; of New World slavery, 18–25; philosophy and, 100, 117, 188; political abuse, 332n40; political destinies, 110; political freedom, 32; political knowledge, 157–58; political language, 88; political progress, 54; power in, 20–21, 50; radical, 76; of reconciliation, 66; of reconstruction, 68–69; social-political language, 48; of violence, 227–28; Wallace in, 183–84; of E. Williams, 274–79, 285–90, 374n77

postcolonialism, 49–50, 295–306

390 INDEX

post-Marxist liberalism, 68
postmetaphysical perspectives, 83–88, 132–33
pragmatism, 154
precarity, 46–47, 50
Price of Emancipation, The (Draper), 298
privilege, 88–89
problematization, 36–38, 44–50
Problem of Evil, The (Mintz), 57–58
Problem of Slavery in Western Culture, The (Davis), 285
problem-spaces, 262–68, 274–79, 285–95
psychology: of accommodation, 174; anthropology and, 44–45; of Black futurity, 40–41; in Christianity, 128; of coercion, 21; of conjecture, 37–38; critical thinking and, 4; of dehumanization, 227; of devastation, 5–11; of emancipationism, 38–39; of forgiveness, 187–88; of human achievement, 154–55; of human flourishing, 178; of humanity, 29–30; intellectualism and, 140; memory and, 58, 62–63; of Middle Passage, 1–2, 24, 136, 138–39; moral, 72; of morality, 123–24, 164, 166; of Nazis, 169; of optimism, 105–6; psychological legacies, 59; of race relations, 6–7; of racism, 2; of readers, 98–99; retemporalization in, 75–76; of slavery, 241–47; of subjectivity, 234–35; in tragedy, 150, 153–54; of victims, 8–9
punishment, 128–30

race relations: Bernstein on, 112–13; for Black people, 76–77; culture and, 361n59; morality and, 21–22; after New World slavery, 59–60; philosophy of, 67–75; psychology of, 6–7; racial injustice in, 72–73; racial justice in, 72; racial solidarity, 185–86; religion and, 166; in U.S., 345n90
Racial Contract, The (Mills), 67–75, 77, 141
racism: accusations of, 345n95; anti-Black, 297; of deficiency laws, 21–22; in England, 302–6; hubris of, 283; philosophy of, 246, 368n124; on plantations, 22–23;

psychology of, 2; racial domination, 75; racial liberalism, 69; racist ideology, 114; United Nations World Conference Against Racism, 295–96; White supremacy and, 74
radical evil: Arendt and, 98, 162–63; concepts of, 51, 107–8, 121; contrition after, 183; identity in, 123–24; Kant on, 87–88, 107–8, 122, 124; moral history of, 132–33; in rhetorical economy, 125–26; violence and, 115–16; writing about, 117–18. *See also specific topics*
Radical Evil (Bernstein), 117–19, 120–21
Radical Hope (Lear), 5–12, 17–18, 325n23
radical politics, 76
Ragatz, Lowell, 275
Ramsey, James, 56
rape, 170
Rawls, John, 68–69, 71
readers/reading, 98–99, 100–101, 110, 171
realism, 223
Rebel, The (Camus), 214, 216–17, 227–28
reconciliation, 62–63, 66–67
Reconstruction, 68–69, 184
"Redressing Historic Injustice" (Waldron), 62–64
"Reflections on Little Rock" (Arendt), 111–12
reflective tempers, 153
reflexive hesitation, 120
reform, in culture, 183
religion: to Black people, 185–86; conceptual language and, 119; in culture, 55–56; in England, 263–64; God in, 183–86; ideology and, 107–8; Kant on, 85; race relations and, 166; slavery and, 183–84. *See also specific religions*
Religion Within the Boundaries of Mere Reason (Kant), 85, 107–8, 338n10
reparations: for Africans, 41, 74, 300–306; genealogical critique and, 76–77; in neoliberalism, 295–300, 306–10
reparatory history: as genealogical critique, 58–67; moral history and, 44–50; morality

and, 35–43, 50–58, 67–77; scholarship on, 26–27
resentment, 181–82, 356n129
reservations, 16
restitution, 65
retemporalization, 75–76
Rethinking Evil (Lara), 81–91
rhetorical economy, 102–3, 125–26
rhetorical labor, 31–32
Rieff, Philip, 104
Riesman, David, 197
Roberts, Rodney, 64–65
Robinson, Randall, 297
Rodney, Walter, 205, 309
Roll, Jordan, Roll (Genovese), 171
romanticism, 154–55
Roosevelt, Franklin, 275
Roots of Evil, The (Kekes), 148. *See also Facing Evil*
Rorty, Richard, 332n37
Rougemont, Denis de, 101–3, 342n59
Rousseau, Jean-Jacques, 68, 72
Rousset, David, 127
Royal African Company, 20
Russia, 130, 214, 313–14, 316
Russian Revolution, 41–42

Sahlins, Marshall, 324n10
"Sambo," 171–72, 210, 212
Scholem, Gershom, 124–26
Schutz, Alfred, 3–4
Scott, James, 226, 366n105
Scottish Enlightenment, 47–48, 368n121
secular morality, 155–63
secular philosophy, 51, 146, 152–53
self-deception, 169–70
self-determination, 43, 74, 220–21
self-image, 45–46, 59
self-love, 85
settler colonial power, 15–16
sexism, 156
Sexual Contract, The (Pateman), 72
Sharp, Granville, 56
Siege of Santo Domingo, 19–20

Singer, Marcus, 52
Sioux Nation, 10–11, 16
Skinner, Quentin, 341n49, 374n83
Slave and Citizen (Tannenbaum), 209–10
Slave Community, The (Blassingame), 173–74
slavery: of Africans, 113–14; Arendt and, 130–32; Black life after, 38; Black people after, 307–8; capitalism and, 31–32, 57–58, 262–68, 274–79, 285–95; in Caribbean, 19–22, 323n2, 354n109, 363n81, 363n82; colonialism and, 56–57, 93; critiques of, 56–57 culture of, 30–31, 131–32; death camps and, 127; descendants in, 2–3; emancipationism, 38–39; to England, 376n113; Europe and, 258–61, 306–10; exploitation in, 35–36; in fiction, 191–96; forced labor and, 129–30; to Foucault, 367n118; genocide and, 20–21, 306–7; Goveia on, 217–19; as historical atrocity, 18–25, 29–30; history of, 36–37, 131, 251–58; Holocaust and, 27–28, 160, 170–75; humanity in, 169–70; human rights and, 137–38; illegality of, 32; institutionalized, 36, 53; in Jamaica, 30–31, 327n46, 356n2, 366n108; to Jefferson, 125; labor and, 75–76; legacy of, 64–65, 181; memory of, 178–79; morality and, 370n14; narratives of, 11, 279–85; natal alienation in, 186–87; Patterson on, 212–14, 238–41; psychology of, 241–47 religion and, 183–84; scholarship on, 27–28, 268–74; slaveholders, 55–56, 168–75; slave revolts, 226–27, 280; *telos* of, 144; violence in, 138–39, 328n55; White people and, 192, 212, 224, 236–37; White supremacy and, 70, 168, 187–88; women in, 228–33, 238–41. *See also specific topics*
Slavery (Elkins), 132, 171, 202, 209–12, 218
Slavery Abolition Act, 265–68
Slavery and Social Death (Patterson), 29–30, 176–77, 197–98, 201, 231, 249
Slave Society in the British Leeward Islands (Goveia), 219

392 INDEX

Smith, Adam, 47–48, 285, 286–87
Smith, M. G., 205–6, 218, 360n37
social action, 4–5, 94–95
social death, 30, 116–17, 161–62, 200
social evil, 97
social-historical lifeworld, 13
social history, 359n36
social ideology, 165
socialism, 42, 299
social phenomenology, 3–4
social-political language, 48
society: Africans in, 306–10; authority
    in, 127–28; children in, 111–12;
    choice-moralists in, 151–52; Creole,
    218–21, 363n82; domination in, 187;
    of England, 185, 287–88; in Europe,
    262–68; influences in, 117–18; modern,
    82; morality of, 182–83, 249–50; moral
    simpletons in, 172–73; moral vocabulary
    in, 119–20; of Nazis, 131; paradigms of evil
    in, 158–59; philosophy of, 90–91; with
    totalitarianism, 102, 210, 361n56; White
    supremacy in, 168
sociology, 66–67, 145–46, 187, 196–97, 207–8,
    247, 357n7
Sociology of Slavery, The (Patterson):
    reputation of, 197–204, 217–22,
    249–50; scholarship from, 205–9,
    211–12, 225–26; themes in, 30, 204–9,
    285, 323n2
Socrates, 282
sovereignty, 73–74
Soviet Union, 214, 313–14, 316
Spain, 19–20
speculative language, 122
Stalin, Joseph, 151, 316
Stanley, Edward, 267–68
Steiner, George, 60
Stephen, James, 267–68
Stewart, James, 56
Stoicism, 156
Stratchey, Lytton, 258
subjectivity, 234–35
suffering, 50–51, 159–61

Sullivan, Harry Stack, 211
Swift, Jonathan, 288
sympathy, 47–48
systematic wrongs, 52–53

Tacky Revolt, 21–22
Taking Responsibility for the Past (Thompson,
    J.), 64–65
Talking to Strangers (Allen), 112
Tannenbaum, Frank, 209–10
technology, 121–22
teleologies, 42–43
telos, 15, 144
Temperley, Howard, 272–73, 372n53, 372n60
terrorism, 375n101
theology, 104, 338n10, 342n64
Theory of Justice, The (Rawls), 68–69, 71
theory-space, 82
Thistlewood, Thomas, 23, 168–69, 192, 228,
    243–44
Thomas, Laurence Mordekhai: on
    authority, 125; Card and, 155, 160,
    176, 180–81; on forgiveness, 180–86;
    identity of, 349n7; on intentionality,
    163–70; Kekes and, 147–48, 163; legacy of,
    146–47; on lifeworlds, 353n81; loyalty to,
    355n111; on natal alienation, 170–80; on
    Nazis, 354n104; Patterson and, 186–87;
    philosophy of, 28–30, 139–48, 186–88,
    223–24, 315; scholarship from, 139–45
Thompson, Edgar Tristram, 327n50
Thompson, Janna, 62, 64–67, 76
Thoughts and Sentiments (Cugoano), 56–57
tolerance, 52
total domination, 162–63
totalitarianism, 102, 107–10, 127, 210, 313–16,
    361n56. See also specific topics
tragedy, 150, 153–55, 378n6
TransAfrica, 297
transgenerational atrocities, 24
transgenerational institutional evil,
    249–50
Treaty of Waitangi, 301
Trinidad. See West Indies

Truman, Harry S., 125, 149, 347n127, 351n27
typology, 373n63

undeserved harm, 147–50
United Nations, 295–96, 340n39
United States (U.S.): Africans in, 199, 276–77, 372n56; Black culture in, 219–20; Black life in, 311–12; Black people in, 69–70, 297; Caribbean and, 39, 275–76, 288–89, 374n77; Christianity in, 183–84; Crow Nation in, 6–8, 10–11, 14–18, 24–25; culture of, 171–72, 255–56; education in, 255–56, 275; England and, 290–91; Europe and, 100, 295–96; Germany and, 340n27; history of, 316–17; identity in, 345n93; international humanitarianism to, 46; Japan and, 149, 347n127; race relations in, 345n90; terrorism in, 375n101
Unnatural Lottery, The (Card), 156
U.S. *See* United States

Venables, Robert, 19–20
Vessels of Evil (Thomas): forgiveness in, 181–83; humanity in, 163–70, 187; institutions in, 170–80; philosophy in, 139–48; themes of, 28–30
vices, 152, 164, 167
victims, 8–9, 52–53, 133–34, 149, 184–85
violence: in Africa, 128; authority for, 125; in culture, 2; domination of, 156; in fiction, 231; in genocide, 83; in Haiti, 41–42; of Holocaust, 27–28, 87; to Kant, 85–86; legal, 121; of Middle Passage, 39; of New World slavery, 32, 82–83, 248–49; Patterson on, 253–38; on plantations, 236–38; politics of, 227–28; power and, 22–23; radical evil and, 115–16; ranking, 143–44, rape, 170; relationships and, 162; by slaveholders, 55–56; in slavery, 138–39, 328n55; suffering and, 50–51; in totalitarianism, 107, 109–10; transgenerational atrocities from, 24; vulnerability to, 131–32; of White

supremacy, 22–23; against women, 193–94
vulnerability, 11, 131–32, 183

Waldron, Jeremy, 62–64, 65–67, 76
Walker, Margaret, 65
Wallace, George, 183–84
Wealth of Nations, The (Smith, A.), 286–87
Webb, Constance, 369n7
West Africa, 137
Western culture, 46, 93, 171–72
Western philosophy, 118–19
West Indies, 258–61, 275–79, 288–89. *See also* Caribbean
White, Hayden, 281–82, 373n63, 374n83
Whiteness, 112–13, 128, 170–71
White people: Africa to, 348n132; Black people and, 171, 187–88 humanity of, 241–47; slavery and, 192, 212, 224, 236–37
White supremacy: Africans in, 265–66; Black life in, 27; to Black people, 135; in England, 296; Hume on, 368n124; ideology of, 187–88; justice after, 72–73; New World slavery and, 311–12; racial domination in, 75; racism and, 74; after Reconstruction, 184; self-determination in, 220–21; slavery and, 70, 168, 187–88; violence of, 22–23
Why Read Hannah Arendt Now (Bernstein), 109
Wilberforce (Coupland), 265, 371n41
Wilberforce, William, 265–68, 270, 288–89, 308, 371n41
William (slave ship), 137
Williams, Eric: abolitionism to, 269–74; Beckles and, 297–99; Boodoo on, 374n86; Coupland and, 268–70; Darity and, 259–60, 271–72; Goveia and, 369n11, 372n62; James and, 254–58, 283, 289–90, 306–10; philosophy of, 31–32, 57–58; politics of, 274–79, 285–90, 374n77; reputation of, 279–85, 290–95, 369n7, 372n56; Temperley on, 372n53. *See also specific works*
Williams, Francis, 246

394 INDEX

Williams, Wilson, 260
"Wings of a Dove" (Brathwaite), 220–21
Wittgenstein, Ludwig, 3–5, 9, 11, 99, 325n19, 325n27
women, 154–55, 193–94, 228–33, 238–41, 366n112
Woodson, Carter B., 131–32
Woolf, Leonard, 258
Woolf, Virginia, 258
World Bank, 299

World War II, 89, 95–96, 99–100, 103–4, 299, 343n70
Wretched of the Earth, The (Fanon), 216
writing, 81–82, 98–99, 102–3, 117–18, 364n92

Yancy, George, 349n7
Young-Bruehl, Elisabeth, 125, 344n81

Zimbardo, Philip, 164–65
Zong (slave ship), 136–38, 176–77, 185, 349n1